National Geographic Guide to the

National
Parks

of the United States

NATIONAL GEOGRAPHIC
Washington, D.C.

National Geographic Guide to the

National
Parks
of the United States

Published by
The National
Geographic Society

John M. Fahey, Jr.
*President and Chief
Executive Officer*

Gilbert M. Grosvenor
Chairman of the Board

Nina D. Hoffman
Executive Vice President

Kevin Mulroy
*Vice President and
Editor-in-Chief*

Prepared by
the Book Division

Guidebook Staff

Elizabeth L. Newhouse
*Editor and Director of Travel
Books*

Linda B. Meyerriecks
Illustrations Editor

David M. Seager
Art Director

Carl Mehler
Director of Maps

Melanie Ann Patt-Corner
Research Editor

Thomas B. Allen
Carole Douglis
Writer-Editors

John L. Culliney
Kim Heacox
Catherine Herbert Howell
Gary Krist
Mark Miller
Jeremy Schmidt
Gene S. Stuart
John M. Thompson
Scott Thybony
Mel White
Writers

Paulette L. Claus
Mary Grady
Mary Jennings
Keith R. Moore
Lise Swinson Sajewski
Anne E. Withers
Editorial Researchers

Mary Grady
Map Editor

Lise Swinson Sajewski
Style

T. Destry Jarvis
Chief Consultant

Staff for 2003 Edition

Caroline Hickey
Project Manager

Barbara A. Noe
Jane Sunderland
Editors

Cinda Rose
Art Director

Meredith Wilcox
Illustrations Editor

Mapping Specialists, Ltd.
*Map Edit, Research, and
Production*

Melissa Crawford
Lawrence Porges
Nicholas P. Rosenbach
Theodore Tucker
Rebecca Tunstall
Gregory Ugiansky
Contributors

Connie Binder
Indexer

R. Gary Colbert
Production Director

Richard S. Wain
Production Project Manager

Cover: Rio Grande and Chisos Mountains at dusk, Big Bend NP
Preceding pages: Hikers surveying falling water and granite cliffs,
two of Yosemite's main attractions

Contents

Green River canyon in Canyonlands National Park

The Gift of the Parks

One of the things that distinguishes this guidebook is its conscience— its attention to the welfare of the parks it describes. As you read, you will find the travel information interspersed with news of some threat to a park, or the history of a threat that lost out. National parks have been battlegrounds of the conservation movement, and the battles continue.

But even the battles can offer inspiration and instruction, and both the parks and the ideals by which we manage them evolve continually. Indeed, it has been said that the establishment of a park is only the beginning; that if we do it right, we never stop establishing that park, because we never stop learning about it, and about ourselves.

There was a time when Congress set up national parks to protect a few specific things: the wildlife here, the geysers there, the scenery over there. Other parts of the park got less attention, or were even mistreated. Well into the 1930s managers killed predators in some parks to protect the "good" animals. In the early days of Yosemite National Park, woodpeckers were shot if their tapping disturbed the sleep of hotel guests. Yellowstone allowed commercial fishing until well after 1900.

Only as the science of ecology matured, and we began to realize that everything in the park was interrelated, did our view change. Slowly, we realized that what we had was not best measured in acres of meadow and that a park is not a zoo.

Instead, we seek to save the whole thing, the whole creeping, flying, grazing, preying, photosynthesizing, eroding, raining, erupting, evolving

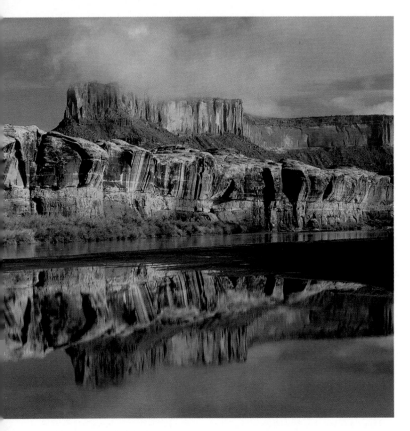

scene. Call it wildness, or naturalness, or an ecosystem, or whatever you like, it is this entangled collection of processes that we must save.

That means many things, some of which haven't been easy to hear. It means that people like me, who love to fish, have to leave enough trout in the streams to feed the otters, pelicans, bears, and other wild fishermen. It means we don't pick flowers, or collect rocks, removing them from their place in the natural system. It means we stop feeding wildlife, and let the animals find their own way, in balance with their environment.

In short, it means a revolution in the way we appreciate nature. We as a nation have decided that here, in these precious, rare places, we shall give nature a little more room to make its choices. If that means we must be prepared to watch a bear half a mile away through binoculars rather than watch it eating aluminum foil right outside the car window, so be it; everybody knew all along which was best for the bear. If that means we must respect the role naturally caused fire has played in regenerating forests for thousands of years, so be it.

Anyone who reads the papers knows that this doesn't always work smoothly. Nature isn't much for respecting our rules. Bears have a way of reminding us we're not always in charge. And, as Yellowstone showed us in 1988, fires can get a lot bigger than anybody expected. Nobody said this was going to be easy. But the more we try, the more we learn.

And so these great parks, which enchant us with their beauty and restore us with their peace, have yet another gift to give. They are laboratories of ideas, offering profound lessons in the natural way of things, and in what that way can mean to the human soul. The lessons don't always come easily, but they're always worth the trip.

Paul Schullery
Yellowstone National Park

Sightseers at Geyser Hill, Yellowstone

Using the Guide

Each of the 57 scenic parks offers you fun, adventure, and—usually—enthralling splendor. What you experience will depend on where you go and what you do. But exploring an unknown land is best done with a guide, a companion who has tested the trail and learned the lore.

Our coverage of each park begins with a portrait of its natural wonders, ecological setting, history, and, often, its struggles against pollution, erosion, development, and other environmental threats. You'll see why a single step off a trail can harm fragile plants, and why visitors are detoured from certain areas that shelter wildlife. The parks are not just for people; they conserve ecosystems that sustain plants and animals. Thirteen parks have been designated United Nations World Heritage sites for their outstanding scenic and cultural wonders; twenty have international biosphere

reserve status, signaling the distinctive qualities of their natural environments.

Before starting off on your park exploration, use the *Guide* to preview the parks you may want to visit. You'll notice that each park introduction is followed by the following three how-and-when sections:

How to Get There

You may be able to include more than one park in your trip. The maps at the beginning of each regional section show the connecting highways. Base your itinerary not so much on mileage as on time, remembering that parks do not lie alongside interstates; park roads are usually rugged—and, in summer, crowded.

When to Go

Instead of going to a popular park in midsummer, avoid peak crowds by scheduling the trip for June or late August and timing your arrival early on a weekday. In many parks, fall is glorious, and autumn vistas coincide with a relative scarcity of visitors. Spring brings wildflowers to many parks and with winter comes snow-swept beauty, summoning cross-country skiers, snowshoe hikers, and ice skaters. Although parks are generally open year-round, off-season visitor facilities may be limited. Consult this heading in each park chapter.

How to Visit

Don't rush through a park. Give yourself time to savor the beauty. Incredibly, the average time the typical visitor spends in a park is half a day. Often, that blur of time flashes past a windshield. No matter how long you decide to stay, spend at least part of that time in the park, not in your car. Each park's **How to Visit** section recommends a plan for visits of one-half, one, two, or more days. *Guide* writers devised the plans and trekked every tour, but don't be afraid to explore on your own. And don't neglect the **Excursions** at the end of many park entries; they take you to other natural areas nearby.

Other features of the *Guide:*

Maps

The park maps and regional maps were prepared as an aid in planning your trip. For more detail on hiking trails and other facilities inside a park, contact the Park Service or phone the park itself. Always use a road map when traveling.

The maps note specially designated areas within park borders: *Wilderness Areas* are managed to retain their primeval quality. Roads, buildings, and vehicles are not allowed in them. *National Preserves* may allow hunting.

The following abbreviations are used for federal lands:

NP   *National Park*
NRA   *National Recreation Area*
NF   *National Forest*
NM   *National Monument*
NWR   *National Wildlife Refuge*

Information & Activities

This section, which follows each park entry, offers detailed visitor information. Call or write the park, or visit the park's website for further details. Brochures are usually available free of charge from the parks. For a small fee you can buy a copy of the "National Park System Map and Guide" by writing to the Consumer Information Cen-

Exploring Big Bend's backcountry

ter, P.O. Box 100, Pueblo, CO 81002; or phoning (719) 948-3334. Visit the Park Service website at: http://www.nps.gov. **Entrance Fees.** The entrance fees listed in this book reflect fees at press time. In addition to daily or weekly fees, most parks also offer a yearly fee, with unlimited entries.

For $50 you can buy a National Parks Pass, which is good for a year and admits all occupants of a private vehicle to all national parks with a vehicle entrance fee. The pass does not cover parking fees where applicable. For an additional $15 you can purchase a Golden Eagle hologram to affix to the pass for unlimited admission to U.S. Fish and Wildlife Service, U.S. forest service, and Bureau of Land Management sites.

People over 62 can obtain a lifetime Golden Age Passport for $10, and blind and disabled people are entitled to a lifetime Golden Access Passport for free, both of which admit all occupants of a private vehicle to all national parks and other federal sites and a discount on usage fees. These documents are available at any Park Service facility that charges entrance fees.

For further information on purchasing park passes, call (888) 467-2757 or visit www.national parks.org.
Pets. Generally they're not allowed on trails, in buildings, or in the backcountry. Elsewhere, they must be leashed. Specific rules are noted.
Facilities for Disabled. This section

of the *Guide* explains which parts of each park, including visitor centers and trails, are accessible to visitors with disabilities.

Special Advisories. • Do not take chances. People are killed or badly injured every year in national parks. Most casualties are caused by recklessness or inattention to clearly posted warnings.

• Stay away from wild animals. Do not feed them. Do not try to touch them, not even raccoons or chipmunks (which can transmit diseases). Try not to surprise a bear and do not let one approach you. If one does, scare it off by yelling, clapping your hands, or banging pots. Store all your food in bear-proof containers (often available at parks); keep it out of sight in your vehicle, with windows closed and doors locked. Or suspend it at least 15 feet above ground, and 10 feet out from a post or tree trunk.

• Guard your health. If you are not fit, don't overtax your body. Boil water that doesn't come from a park's drinking-water tap. Chemical treatment of water will not kill *Giardia,* a protozoan that causes severe diarrhea and lurks even in crystal clear streams. Heed park warnings about hypothermia and Lyme disease, which is carried by ticks. In western parks, take precautions to prevent Hantavirus pulmonary syndrome, a potentially fatal airborne virus transmitted by deer mice.

● Expect RV detours. Check road regulations as you enter a park. Along some stretches of many roads you will not be able to maneuver a large vehicle, especially a trailer.

Campgrounds. The National Parks Reservation System (NPRS) handles advance reservations for campgrounds at the following parks: Acadia, Channel Islands, Death Valley, Everglades, Grand Canyon, Great Smoky Mountains, Joshua Tree, Katmai, Mammoth Cave, Mount Rainier, Rocky Mountain, Sequoia & Kings Canyon, Shenandoah, Waterton-Glacier, and Zion.

For a single campsite, reserve up to five months in advance by calling (800) 365-CAMP (365-2267), or visit-ing the NPRS website at http://reserva tions.nps.gov. Pay by credit card over the phone or Internet, or by check or money order within 21 days. Or, write to NPRS, 3 Commerce Dr., Cumberland, MD 21502.

Hotels, Motels, & Inns. The *Guide* lists accommodations as a service to its readers. The lists are by no means comprehensive, and listing does not imply endorsement by the National Geographic Society. The information can change without notice. Many parks keep full lists of accommodations in their areas, which they will send you on request. You can also contact local chambers of commerce and tourist offices for accommodations suggestions.

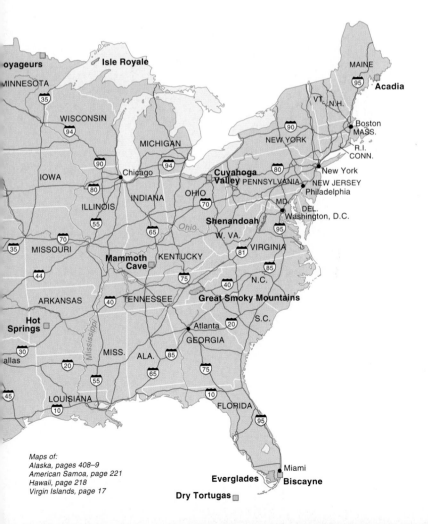

Maps of:
Alaska, pages 408–9
American Samoa, page 221
Hawaii, page 218
Virgin Islands, page 17

The East

Not until well into the 20th century, long after the idea of preserving the West's grand vistas had taken hold, did park planners turn their attention to the more subtle beauties of eastern scenery. The threats to nature from expanding cities and, after World War I, the surge in automobile travel and highway building boosted the movement to create eastern parks. Between 1919 and 1926, Congress authorized the first three in the crumpled belt of the Appalachian Mountains. Today these parks— Acadia, Great Smoky Mountains,

Preceding pages: Deer grazing in a Cades Cove meadow, Great Smoky Mountains NP

This map plots all the U.S. national parks, plus the Excursions sites featured in this book.

and Shenandoah—rank among the most visited in the nation.

Acadia protects the plants and animals that inhabit the mountains, islands, sea, and tide pools along a stretch of wild New England coast. The hardwood forests and flowering meadows of Shenandoah, on land that had been logged, farmed, and grazed for 250 years, are studies in nature's power of recuperation. Great Smoky preserves large stands of virgin forest on 6,000-foot slopes and shelters more than a hundred species of trees.

Since the 1920s, Congress has moved to safeguard other distinctive eastern biomes. Inside Mammoth Cave lies the world's longest known

cave network, with more than 350 miles of mapped passages. Isle Royale on the U.S.-Canada border

Americans' love for the automobile led to the demand for highways to drive and helped spur the creation of national parks in the East. In 1935 the Blue Ridge Parkway was begun as a public works project. It became part of the Park Service the following year. The parkway receiving the most recreational use, the Blue Ridge links Shenandoah's Skyline Drive to Great Smoky Mountains National Park. Together, the drives create a spectacular 574-mile stretch of ridgetop road punctuated by wayside exhibits and trails.

encompasses an entire island ecosystem. In and around its lakes, thick forest, and fjordlike coast live wolves and moose, their prey.

Not far away, scores of lakes and streams lace the forests of Voyageurs National Park, named for the French-Canadian fur traders who for 100 years paddled these waters.

Other kinds of waters inspired the creation of diminutive Hot Springs National Park. Most of the 47 hot springs lead into the plumbing of this former resort town's bathhouses.

Underwater wilderness awaits visitors to Florida's Biscayne National Park, home of the northernmost living coral reef in the continental United States. West of Biscayne lies Everglades National Park, established in 1947 less to preserve scenery than to safeguard the unique ecosystem created by a slow-moving river, inches deep and 50 miles wide. Itself endangered by the diversion of water to the

W. VA.

BREAKS
INTERSTATE
PARK ■

DANIEL
BOONE
NF

■ CUMBERLAND
GAP NHP

Knoxville

PISGAH
NF

Asheville

Great Smoky Mountains NP

NANTAHALA NF

CHATTAHOOCHEE
NF

Atlanta

Columbia

GEORGIA

Richmond

VIRGINIA

NORTH
CAROLINA

Charlotte

SOUTH
CAROLINA

ATLANTIC
OCEAN

Blue Ridge Parkway

Jacksonville

FLORIDA

Lake
Okeechobee

J.N. "DING" DARLING
NWR

Naples

BIG CYPRESS
NAT. PRESERVE

GREAT WHITE HERON
NWR

CORKSCREW SWAMP
SANCTUARY

Miami

Biscayne NP

Everglades
NP

JOHN PENNEKAMP CORAL REEF
STATE PARK

Dry Tortugas
NP

KEY
WEST
NWR

NATIONAL KEY DEER REFUGE

Key West

ATLANTIC OCEAN

Charlotte
Amalie

St. Thomas

U.K.
U.S.

Virgin
Islands
NP

Cruz
Bay

St.
John

CARIBBEAN SEA

BUCK ISLAND
REEF NM ■

St. Croix

0   5 km

0   5 mi

0 5 10 km

0   5   10 mi

0   100   200 km

0   100   200 mi

This map plots all the U.S. national parks,
plus the Excursions sites featured in this
book.

towns and agribusinesses of South
Florida, Everglades provides habitat
for an enormous variety of wildlife.

About 70 miles west of Key West,
on a 7-mile-long archipelago rich
with birds and marine creatures,
Dry Tortugas National Park maintains
an abandoned 19th-century brick
fortress, the largest from that century
in America. And far to the southeast,
Virgin Islands National Park protects
much of St. John, where hillsides thick
with bay, mango, and trumpet trees
slope to crescent beaches rimmed by
coral reefs.

*In the 1960s the National Park
Service set a goal to create a park
as a "vignette of primitive America"
in every major natural community in
the country. The newer parks of the
East—Cuyahoga Valley, Biscayne,
Voyageurs, and Dry Tortugas—have
expanded the already considerable
diversity of the region's parks.*

Otter Cliffs, one of the highest coastal headlands north of Rio de Janiero

Acadia

Maine

Established February 26, 1919

47,633 acres

Sea and mountain meet at Acadia, where, as one presumably ambidextrous visitor wrote, "you can fish with one hand and sample blueberries from a wind-stunted bush with the other."

Most of Acadia is on Mount Desert Island, a patchwork of parkland, private property, and seaside villages that seasonally fill with what residents call "the summer people." Other bits of the park are scattered on smaller islands and a peninsula.

Mount Desert Island once was continental mainland, a mountainous granite ridge on the edge of the ocean. Some 20,000 years ago, towering glacial ice sheets—sometimes a mile thick—flowed over the mountains, rounding their tops, cutting passes, gouging out

lake beds, and widening valleys. As the glaciers melted, the sea rose, flooding valleys and drowning the coast. The pre-glacier ridge was transformed into today's lake-studded, mountainous island, which thrusts from the Atlantic like a lobster's claw.

Samuel de Champlain, who explored the coast in 1604, named the island L'Isle des Monts Déserts, sometimes translated as "the island of barren mountains." From his ship he probably could not see the mountains' forested slopes. The summer people rediscovered Mount Desert in the mid-19th century, built mansions they called "cottages," anchored their yachts in rock-girt harbors, and cherished the wild. To preserve it, they donated the nucleus land for the park, the first east of the Mississippi. The original name, Lafayette National Park, was changed in 1929.

Dependent on donated land since its inception, the park took what it could get, skirting around private property and growing piece by piece. Acadia's real estate was so patchy that not until 1986 did Congress set its official boundaries.

The sixth smallest national park, Acadia is one of the ten most visited—by almost three million people a year. Heavy traffic can produce a phenomenon unknown to Mount Desert's first summer people: gridlock. The Island Explorer shuttle bus has helped alleviate the problem.

How to Get There

From Ellsworth, 28 miles southeast of Bangor, follow Me. 3 south for 18 miles to Mount Desert Island, where most of the park is located; the visitor center is 3 miles north of Bar Harbor. Another section lies southeast of Ellsworth, on the Schoodic Peninsula, a 1-hour drive from Bar Harbor. To get to the park's islands, see **The Islands** p. 24. Airports: Bangor and Bar Harbor.

When to Go

All-year park, but main visitor center is open from mid-April through October. Expect heavy traffic in July and August. Spectacular foliage also attracts crowds around the end of September. Snow and ice close most park roads from December through April, but parts of the park are open for cross-country skiing.

How to Visit

Allow at least a day for **Mount Desert Island,** with a drive on the 20-mile **Park Loop Road** and the road to the summit of **Cadillac Mountain.** If fog comes, enjoy its gift: a softening of sights and sounds. On a second day, enjoy an uncrowded view of the rocky coast of Maine by visiting the **Schoodic Peninsula.** If you have more time, take your pick of one of the trails or smaller islands.

Mount Desert Island
60 miles; at least a full day

To get the most from a tour of Mount Desert Island on the Park Loop Road in summer, get up very early. (On clear days, traffic is heaviest between 10 a.m. and 3 p.m.) The day before, check the time of sunrise in a local newspaper or at the visitor center. About 30 minutes before dawn, take coffee and a blanket and drive from the visitor center to 1,530-foot **Cadillac Mountain.** The 3.5-mile mountain road switchbacks up to a parking area.

Autumn on Cadillac Mountain

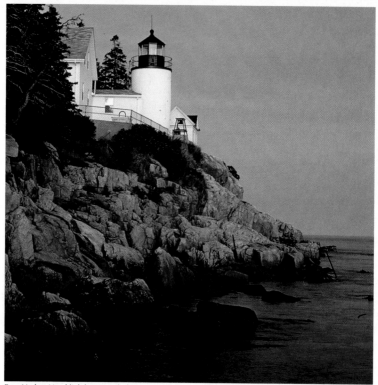

Bass Harbor Head lighthouse at dusk

From there walk to the **Summit Trail,** find an east-facing niche in the rocks, and settle in on the highest east coast mountain north of Brazil. Here is one of the places where dawn first touches the continental United States. After enjoying the sunrise, hunt for blueberries along the trails radiating from the summit. The blueberry season runs from late July through August.

On the way down, stop at one of the eastern overlooks for a view of **Frenchman Bay,** a vast, island-dotted seascape; its name takes note of the area's early French settlers. (Another way to see the bay is on a 2-hour sea cruise; check schedules at the Municipal Pier in Bar Harbor or in the park's publication, "Beaver Log.")

Return to the loop road and turn right. Less than a half mile farther, bear right again (here the road becomes one-way), and continue south toward the ocean. Two worthwhile stops you'll soon approach are the **Sieur de Monts Spring Nature Center** and the **Wild Gardens of Acadia,** both of which showcase the habitats of Mount Desert Island.

Farther along the road, pass up **Sand Beach** for now. You may want to return to the beach later for sunbathing or a very brisk swim (the summer water temperature remains between 50°F and 55°F).

Not quite a mile farther, a sign marks **Thunder Hole.** Park on the right and walk down the concrete steps to the cleft in the rocks, named for the roars produced when air, trapped and squeezed by incoming surf, explodes out of a cavern. A stop here may disappoint you, for you'll probably hear the thunder only at half tide with a rising sea, or during a storm. Other times, you may hear only gurgles and sloshes.

Continue to the 110-foot **Otter Cliffs.** Park, cross the road, and walk the shore path to **Otter Point.** Numerous brightly colored lobster buoys bob offshore. Linger here to savor the essence of the Maine coast: rocks, gulls, the tang of salt air. At **Hunters Head** the loop road turns away from the sea and soon becomes two-way as you head back to where you started. You'll pass **Jordan Pond,** one of many glacier-

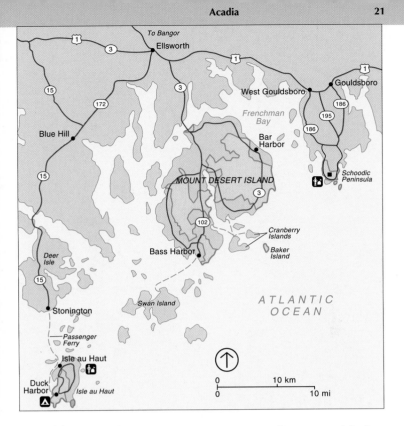

carved ponds on the island.

Your drive has taken you around the eastern side of the island. To explore the western side, you must drive out of park property and back in again. Continue north on the loop road, cross the bridge, and bear right to get on Me. 233. Head west to Me. 198, then head south on Me. 102 toward Southwest Harbor. Continue south. On your left though obscured is **Somes Sound**, the only fjord on the U.S. Atlantic coast. On your right is **Echo Lake**, a swimming spot with a small beach.

Me. 102 passes through Southwest Harbor. Beyond, near Manset, bear left on Me. 102A, which leads into a large patch of park property. You can picnic at **Seawall**, then stretch your legs on the nearby 1.25-mile **Ship Harbor Nature Trail**, which gives a lesson in how a forest shore is knit to the tidal sea.

A short detour off Me. 102A takes you to **Bass Harbor Head**, site of a 19th-century lighthouse. Take Me. 102A through **Bass Harbor** and bear left on Me. 102 toward Tremont. Continue north for 7 miles to a tract of park called **Pretty Marsh**, a beautiful

picnic spot. A short worn path leads to the rock-strewn shore. Continue on Me. 102 and retrace your route from Somesville to the visitor center.

Carriage Roads & Hikes

In 1917 John D. Rockefeller, Jr., a summer resident of Mount Desert Island, launched the building of a 57-mile network of broken stone roads for horse-drawn carriages. Convinced that the newfangled automobile would destroy the tranquillity of the island, he banned it from the carriage roads. The roads were graced by 17 hand-built granite bridges, each a unique work of art. Rockefeller later donated most of the road network, along with 11,000 acres of his land, to the park. The carriage roads, still not open to cars, are a treasure prized by hikers, bikers, horseback riders, cross-country skiers, and anyone seeking a respite from the incessant hum of the internal combustion engine.

To introduce yourself to the carriage roads, try the 4-mile **Had-**

Ranger Station
Campground
Lighthouse
Carriage Roads
Hiking Trail
Unpaved Road

Parker Point

Hulls Cove

Hulls Cove Visitor Center

Ferry to Yarmouth, Nova Scotia

Long Porcupine Island

Witch Hole Pond

Bar Island

Sheep Porcupine Island

Bald Porcupine Island

BAR HARBOR

Cadillac Mountain Entrance
(begin one-way)

233

Kebo Mountain 407 ft.

Dorr Mountain 1,270 ft.

Sieur de Monts Entrance

Cadillac Mountain 1,530 ft

Park Loop Road

Schooner Head

bles

ubble Rock

Jordan Pond

Gorham Mountain 525 ft.

Great Head

Sand Beach
Thunder Hole

Otter Creek

Park Loop Road

(end one-way)

Blackwoods

Otter Cliffs

SEAL HARBOR

Otter Point

Otter Cove

Stanley Brook Entrance

Little Hunters Beach

Seal Harbor

Ingraham Point

Eastern Way

ATLANTIC OCEAN

ton Island

sleford storical useum

Islesford

Little Cranberry Island

Baker Island

0   1   2   3 km
0   1   2 mi

lock Brook Loop. Park at the Me. 198 (Parkman Mountain) parking area just north of **Upper Hadlock Pond** and walk to the trailhead. Take the left fork east toward **Hemlock Bridge,** a gem of hand-hewn stone. Follow the rising road to another handsome span, **Waterfall Bridge,** site of a 40-foot cascade. (You can turn around here, cutting your hike to about 2 miles round-trip.) Cross the bridge and walk south for a mile to one of the network's well-marked intersections. Turn right at intersection 19 and right again at intersection 18 and continue along the pond. Watch for loons—and listen for their haunting call. The road crosses **Hadlock Brook Bridge** and loops back to the trailhead.

The park has more than 120 miles of hiking trails, which range from easy strolls along the ocean or around ponds to steep climbs up Cadillac and other mountains. For a jaunt into history try the **Gorge Path,** which, like several other trails, has stone steps to ease your way up slopes. The steps, flat stones imbedded in rising ground, were built by turn-of-the-20th-century summer people who wanted to rough it, but not too much. The path begins at a parking spot on the Park Loop Road, near 407-foot **Kebo Mountain,** and leads to a wood trail. Cairns mark the trail when it follows a rocky, brook-washed ravine. About a mile into the woods is an intersection. Depending upon your time and stamina, you can turn and retrace your steps or push on to Cadillac or **Dorr Mountain,** each a steep hike of more than 1.5 miles.

Blue mussels and a dog whelk with eggs

Grove of white birch, sunrise

Schoodic Peninsula

100 miles; a half day

The 45-mile drive around French-man Bay to the park's only mainland portion, the Schoodic Peninsula, provides several scenic views of Mount Desert Island. Beginning from Bar Harbor, take Me. 3 to US 1, south of Ellsworth, and head east to West Gouldsboro. Go south via Me. 186 to Winter Harbor, then follow signs to the park entrance. From there, drive or bike the 6-mile one-way road to **Schoodic Point.** The massive granite rocks here are laced by black diabase dikes, the product of magma that welled up into cracks. Schoodic's displays of thundering surf usually top those of Mount Desert Island. And the audiences are much smaller; the peninsula does not draw crowds the way Mount Desert does.

A trail system explores the western section of the point, running through wetland and forest with spurs to the ocean. The longest is the **Anvil Trail,** which begins at the Blueberry Hill parking lot and climbs about 440 for views of Little Moose Island and Frenchman Bay. In this wilderness, keep a lookout for moose, white-tailed deer, rabbits, porcupines, and raccoons.

The Islands

a full day each

Fragments of Acadia are on islands. Two worth visiting are Isle au Haut, about half of which is park property, and Little Cranberry Island, home to the Islesford Historical Museum. Both islands are served all year by mail boats and by seasonal tour boats. Get boat schedules from the visitor center or from the boat operators.

The trip to **Isle au Haut,** or "high island," named by Samuel de Champlain, begins at Stonington, at the tip of Deer Isle, about 40 miles from Ellsworth. To make the boat on time from Mount Desert Island, allot at least 2 hours for the drive and for finding a rare legal parking place near the harbor. Bring lunch. The mail boat takes passengers on a first-come, first-served basis. The 45-minute voyage ends at the Town Landing. In summer, the boat also stops at **Duck Harbor,** a park campsite and trailhead.

For a fine hike, get off at the Town Landing and turn right. A short distance down the road is a ranger station. Here begins the 4-mile **Duck Harbor Trail,** which takes you through upland forest, along the shore, and past blueberry brambles (picking and

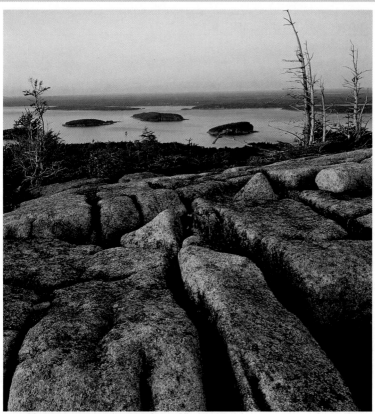
View of the Porcupines in Frenchman Bay, from Cadillac Mountain

Herring gull in Schoodic fog

eating allowed) to Duck Harbor. Spend the day here wandering the area's trails, enjoying woods-and-water scenery, and watching for ospreys and bald eagles. Catch the late afternoon boat back.

The 2.5-mile boat ride from North-east Harbor to **Little Cranberry Island** takes about 20 minutes in good weather; you can also catch a boat at Southwest Harbor, on the opposite side of Somes Sound.

The tiny island, with rocky shores, spruce trees, and quiet country lanes,

boasts 75 year-round residents, most of whom can trace their ancestry back to the 18th century. As your boat nears the picturesque village of **Isleford,** winding among bobbing lobster boats in the protected harbor, you'll spot two buildings of note: the gabled, wooden **Blue Duck Ships's Store** and, directly behind, the **Islesford Historical Museum,** housed in a brick Georgian Revival building. Both structures are part of Acadia National Park. They contain turn-of-the-20th-century ship models, navigation aids, dolls and toys, photographs, tools, and other relics that tell the story of the Cranberry Isles—a cluster of five islands—and their seafaring people.

Another option for getting out on the water is to take an **Islesford Historical Cruise** (207-276-5352. Fee, reservations required), a ranger-led boat tour focusing on island history and making stops at Sutton Island, Big Cranberry Island, and Little Cran-berry Island. Meet at the municipal pier in Northeast Harbor.

Information & Activities

Headquarters
P.O. Box 177, Bar Harbor, ME 04609.
Phone (207) 288-3338.
www.nps.gov/acad

Seasons & Accessibility
Park open all year. In winter visitor
facilities close and much of the Park
Loop Road is unplowed. For recorded
weather information call (207) 667-
8910. For boats to Isle au Haut call
(207) 367-5193; for Islesford on Little
Cranberry Island call (207) 276-5352.

Visitor & Information Centers
Visitor center on Me. 3 just south
of Hulls Cove, open daily mid-April
through October. **Thompson Island
Information Center** on Me. 3, just
before crossing onto Mount Desert
Island. Open May to mid-Sept. Off season, information at **headquarters** 2.5
miles west of Bar Harbor on Me. 233.

Entrance Fee
May through October only: $10 per
vehicle for 7-day pass.

Pets
Permitted on leashes except on swimming beaches, in public buildings,
on a few hiking trails, and at Isle au
Haut campsite.

Facilities for Disabled
Visitor center, some rest rooms, and
carriage roads are wheelchair accessible. Wildwood Stables has two carriages designed to hold wheelchairs.
Free guidebook available.

Things to Do
Free ranger-led activities: nature
walks, photography workshops,
stargazing, films, slide shows. Also
available, bus tours—call (207) 288-
3327) for National Park tours or (207)
288-9899 for Oli's Trolley—bay and
island cruises, carriage rides, auto tape
tour, hiking, bicycling, swimming,
fishing, cross-country skiing, snowshoeing, ice-skating and ice fishing,
and snowmobiling.

Special Advisories
● Be careful on ledges and rocks along
shore; algae are slippery.
● In spring and fall, watch out for
strong storm waves.

Overnight Backpacking
Not allowed.

Campgrounds
Two campgrounds, 14-day limits.
Blackwoods open all year. Reserve
through National Parks Reservation
Service (see p. 11)—recommended
May through October; other times first
come, first served. Fee $20 per night.
Seawall open late May through Sep-
tember; first come, first served. Fees
$14-$20 per night. Showers outside
park. Tent and RV sites; no hookups.
Food services in park.

Hotels, Motels, & Inns
*(unless otherwise noted, rates are for 2
persons in a double room, high season)*
In Bar Harbor, ME 04609:
Bar Harbor Inn Newport Dr. (800)
248-3351 or (207) 288-3351. 153
units. $189-$525. Pool, restaurant. **Bar
Harbor Regency Holiday Inn** 123
Eden St. (800) 234-6835 or (207) 288-
9723. 221 units. $145-$345. AC, pool,
restaurant. Mid-May to late Oct.
Bayview 111 Eden St. (800) 356-3585
or (207) 288-5861. 33 units. $135-
$260. Pool. Mid-May to mid-Oct. **Best
Western Inn** 452 Me. 3. (800) 528-
1234 or (207) 288-5823. 94 units.
$105-$125. AC, pool, restaurant. May
to late Oct. **Cleftstone Manor** 92 Eden
St. (207) 288-4951. 16 units. $100-
$200. Mid-April to late Oct. **Cromwell
Harbor Motel** 359 Main St. (207) 288-
3201. 26 units. $85-$125. **Wonder
View Inn & Suites** 5 Eden St. (888)
439-8439 or (207) 288-3358. 79 units.
$103-$180. Pool, restaurant. May to Oct.
In Northeast Harbor, ME 04662:
Asticou Inn Me. 3/198. (800) 258-3373
or (207) 276-3344. 47 units. $225-$325,
2 meals. Pool, restaurant. Mid-May to
mid-Oct. **Kimball Terrace Inn** 10
Huntington Rd. (800) 454-6225 or (207)
276-3383. 72 units. $150-$163. Pool, rest.
In Southwest Harbor, ME 04679:
Moorings Inn Shore Rd., Manset. (800)
596-5523 or (207) 244-5523. 22 units,
some kitchens; 4 cottages. $85-$110.
Restaurant. May to Oct. Boat rental.

*For additional accommodations,
call the Chambers of Commerce of
Bar Harbor (207) 288-5103, Northeast Harbor (207) 276-5040, or
Southwest Harbor (207) 244-9264.*

Excursions

Moosehorn
National Wildlife Refuge
Calais, Maine

At dawn and dusk in spring, the male woodcock soars into the air to begin his mating ritual. The refuge's two units protect the essential habitat of the American woodcock as well as other waterfowl and forest wildlife species. Contains two wilderness areas. 24,409 acres. Hiking, boating, bicycling, fishing, hunting, winter sports. Open all year, dawn to dusk. Headquarters at the Baring Unit, off US 1, about 75 miles from Acadia NP. (207) 454-7161.

Petit Manan
National Wildlife Refuge
Steuben, Maine

Migrating waterfowl and shorebirds take rest on Petit Manan Peninsula and more than 25 offshore islands here. The peninsula's two hiking trails lead visitors through spruce-fir forests, blueberry barrens, and along the rugged rocky coastline. Petit Manan Island features one of the largest seabird nesting colonies in Maine and a 123-foot lighthouse; closed to public access April through Aug. 7,000 acres. Hiking trails. Peninsula open all year, dawn to dusk. Accessible from US 1 in Steuben, about 35 miles from Schoodic Unit of Acadia NP. (207) 546-2124.

Rachel Carson
National Wildlife Refuge
Wells, Maine

Stretching along Maine's southern coast from Kittery to Cape Elizabeth, this refuge's ten units protect the fragile and dynamic world of the tidal estuary. The unit at Wells contains the 1-mile-long self-guided Carson Trail. Breeding and migrating shorebirds, wading birds, waterfowl, and raptors also featured. 5,000 acres. Hiking, canoeing, hunting, scenic drives, cross-country skiing. Picnic areas, handicapped access. Open all year, dawn to dusk. Headquarters at Wells, on Me. 9, off US 1, about 160 miles from Acadia NP. (207) 646-9226.

School of blue-striped grunts in the underwater splendor of Biscayne Bay

Biscayne

Florida

Established June 28, 1980

172,924 acres

Biscayne, a seascape in watercolor, offers vistas ashore and beneath the sea. Standing on the park's narrow shore, you look out upon a bay that is tranquil on the surface and teeming with life below. Aboard a glass-bottom boat, you look down and see some of that life—dazzlingly colored fish, fantastically shaped corals, gently waving fronds of sea grass.

Biscayne is an underwater wilderness. Only five percent of the park is land—about 40 small barrier islands and a mangrove shoreline, the longest such undeveloped shore on the East Coast. Park wildlife musters under water in the form of minuscule, unusual, or rarely seen animals. The most extensive life-form is a community known as the coral reef—colonies of tiny polyps that secrete limestone and live within ever growing rocky crannies. The coral reefs at Biscayne are part of the only living ones in the continental United States.

The park reprieved a living system condemned to die under the pressure of progress. The threat came in the 1960s, when developers were making plans to build resorts and subdivisions on Florida's northern keys, from Key Biscayne to Key Largo. Conservationists campaigned to preserve Biscayne Bay; it became a national monument in 1968. When Biscayne National Park was established, boundaries were expanded to encompass several more of the bay's keys and reefs.

Biscayne embraces a complex ecosystem that extends from the

When to Go

All-year park. The best time to visit the park's islands is from mid-December to mid-April, subtropical Florida's dry season. In summer, you face the perils of mosquitoes and fast-moving thunderstorms, but seas are generally the calmest—making it ideal for snorkeling and diving. Hurricanes are occasional.

How to Visit

Unless you have your own boat, plan to see Biscayne on a concessioner-run cruise. You can look underwater on a **reef cruise** aboard a glass-bottom boat or swim the shallow waters on a snorkeling cruise. There are also scuba cruises to the outer reef for qualified divers. You should make reservations in advance. Cruises may be canceled if there are too few passengers or the weather is inclement. Although this is a water park, a walk around the mangrove shore will give you a chance to examine the coastal edges of the bay's ecosystem. The Dante Fascell Visitor Center offers a museum, audiovisual programs, and ranger talks.

Reef Cruise

a half day

Sign up for a cruise well ahead (see **Information & Activities** p. 34 for details). Schedules vary by season. At **Convoy Point,** the glass-bottom boat's home port and site of **Dante Fascell Visitor Center,** you can get an orientation to the bay's unique flora

mangrove shoreline to the Gulf Stream. Besides the mangrove coast and living reef, the ecosystem includes two other biological realms found on the small islands and the shallow bay's marine nursery. The realms are interwoven, and each sustains still other webs of life.

Guarding all this are the northernmost Florida Keys, barrier islands that keep ocean waves from battering the bay. Thus shielded, the bay offers sanctuary to the life within it and beauty to those who come to look beneath the surface.

How to Get There

From Miami, take Florida's Turnpike (Fla. 821) south to Speedway Boulevard, and turn left (south). Continue 4 miles on Speedway Boulevard to North Canal Drive and turn left (east). Follow Canal Drive to the park entrance. From Homestead (about 9 miles), take S.W. 328th Street (N. Canal Dr.) to the park entrance at Convoy Point. Airport: Miami.

Diver and sea fans near Elliott Key

826
Kendall

To Miami

MATHESON
HAMMOCK PARK
(Dade County)

KEY BISCAYNE

BILL BAGGS
CAPE FLORIDA STATE PARK

SW 67th Avenue

Old Cutler Road

Shoal Point

1

Cutler Ridge

NATIONAL PARK BOUNDARY

Old Cutler Road

Safety Valve

SOLDIER KEY

BLACK POINT
PARK AND MARINA
(Dade County)

Black Point

Coconut Palm Drive
(SW 248th Street)

Fender Point

Feathered Bank

Spoil Area

RAGGED
KEYS
(private)

harbor
Boca Chita Key

Bowles
Bank

B I S C A Y N E   B A Y

SANDS KEY

Sands Cut

Bache
Shoal

North Canal Drive
(SW 328th Street)

Dante Fascell Visitor Center
Park Headquarters (Convoy Point)

University Dock

Sea Grape
Point

To
Florida
City

1

HOMESTEAD BAYFRONT
PARK AND MARINA
(Dade County)

Palm Drive
(SW 344th Street)

Pelican Bank

Turkey Point

Intracoastal Waterway

Elliott Key
Ranger Station
Elliott Key Harbor

Ott Point

ELLIOTT KEY

Hawk Channel

Billys Point

Spoil
Area

Sandwich
Cove

Adams
Key

Spoil Area

Christmas Point

Caesar Creek

Schooner
Wreck

Mangrove Point

TOTTEN
KEY

Jones
Lagoon

OLD RHODES
KEY

Elkhorn
Coral
Reef

Spoil Area

Ranger Station

Primitive Campground

Nature Trail

Public Launching Ramp

Lighthouse

Wreck

Coral Reef

Hiking Trail

KEY LARGO

JOHN PENNEKAMP
CORAL REEF
STATE PARK

PARK BOUNDARY

KEY LARGO
NATIONAL MARINE
SANCTUARY

905

0   1   2   3 km

0   1   2 mi

Tropical hardwood edging Elliott Key's shoreline

and fauna before setting out. A cruise takes about 3 hours. Cruises for snorkelers and scuba divers last longer and cost more.

The center of the boat's deck is a rectangular viewing chamber. Rows of broad, angled windows make up its floor. Passengers line rails around the chamber and peer down at the constantly changing, green-tinted scene.

As the boat crosses the bay, a park ranger prepares the audience by passing out pieces of hard coral and previewing the sights that will be seen in the reefs. A ruffled seabed and waving strands of turtle grass pass under the windows. Vast beds of turtle grass and water only 4 to 10 feet deep make Biscayne Bay a nursery for a host of young marine animals, including shrimp, spiny lobsters, sponges, and crabs. You can see some of these animals through the windows. More than 325 types of fish swim in park waters. You may also see large, graceful sea turtles.

If you walk to the outer edge of the deck, you can watch boats skimming the bay and brown pelicans flapping by. When they spot fish, they dive headfirst into the sea to scoop them

Florida manatee

up in their huge bills. Among the many other birds you will see are cormorants and herons; together, their calls can be deafening.

Through the bay runs the Intracoastal Waterway, marked by posts whose signs bear numbers keyed to navigational charts. In one short, shallow stretch near the waterway are natural grass beds rising near the surface and visible at low tide. Bonefish, prized by sportfishermen for their speed and strength, inhabit the grass beds.

The boat slips through the keys

Spiny lobsters in the sea grass of Biscayne Bay

toward the reefs beyond. Once it arrives at its destination, the boat lingers for the floor show: the multi-colored flash of a passing parrotfish, the sinuous glide of an angelfish, the little jungles of coral. Slowly the boat moves to another vantage point, and a new seabed show begins to roll by. Giant brain coral and mountainous star coral dominate the reefs, many so high that the glass bottom of the boat seems close enough to graze them. Sea fans and other soft corals ripple in the calm, clear water. The ranger helps viewers identify the vibrantly colored fish flitting around the massive coral formations. Before reaching the outer reefs the boat turns for home.

The cruise passes through **Caesar Creek,** named for Black Caesar, a legendary pirate said to have lurked here in the 1700s. More than 50 shipwrecks have been cataloged within park boundaries. Federal law protects them from salvagers or souvenir collectors. Visitors who have made the trip in their own boats can also dock at Adams Key for a picnic and walk on a nature trail.

Elliott Key has primitive campsites, rest rooms, a nature trail, a swimming area, a ranger station, and what conservationists label a "road scar"—a bulldozer's legacy and a reminder of how close devastation came to these keys. To the north is **Boca Chita Key,** which has a boat dock, primitive campsites, and rest rooms, but no drinking water. The lighthouse is only ornamental.

Mangrove Shore
0.25 mile; at least an hour

If you have little time, no boat, and some curiosity, walk the shore around **Convoy Point,** a fine place for a picnic. If you have more time, inquire about renting a canoe or kayak to explore mangrove tidal creeks.

The mangroves are critical to this marine environment. They stabilize the shore, trapping their own fallen leaves and other organic material in the tangles of their stiltlike roots. The trees attract many birds—including, on rare occasions, the peregrine falcon and bald eagle, 2 of the 13 endangered animal species monitored by park scientists. Barnacles, fish, and other sea creatures cluster at the trees' half-submerged roots. The decaying mangrove leaves, rich in protein, provide food to the tiny animals at the bottom of a food chain that ends with the fisherman who eats the gray snapper he caught in the bay.

The mangroves also filter damaging pollutants from the freshwater runoff into the bay. Whether you walk or paddle a boat, watch carefully for the bay animals that find food and refuge in the mangrove waterways. On a winter's day the creatures may include a huge, grass-chewing "cow of the sea"; they can reach 10 to 12 feet long and weigh up to 1,800 pounds. The scene keeps changing as each outgoing tide carries its bounty of nutrients out to sea and each incoming tide brings in new inhabitants for the sheltering mangroves.

Life on the Coral Reef

A diver inspecting a coral reef at Biscayne NP

Queen angelfish

Filefish on soft coral

Porcupine fish

Nassau grouper

Information & Activities

Headquarters
9700 S.W. 328th St., Homestead, FL 33033. Phone (305) 230-1144. www.nps.gov/bisc

Seasons & Accessibility
Open year-round. Keys (islands) can be reached by boat only. Private concessioners operate daily, though underbooked cruises may be canceled in the off-season. Private boats allowed; boat docks available on Elliott, Adams, and Boca Chita Keys ($15 overnight docking fee at Elliot and Boca Chita).

Visitor & Boat Information
Dante Fascell Visitor Center open daily all year. For park information, call (305) 230-7275.

For information and reservations for concessioner-run glass-bottom boat, snorkeling, scuba diving, island and canoe trips, call (305) 230-1100. Rentals available. Tours leave from Convoy Point.

Entrance Fees
None. $15 overnight docking fee for private boats at Elliott and Boca Chita Keys. Fees charged by concessioner for boat trips.

Pets
Allowed on leashes (6-ft. maximum length) in the developed areas of Convoy Point and Elliott Key. Not permitted on boat tours.

Facilities for Disabled
Dante Fascell Visitor Center is fully accessible, as are rest rooms at Elliott Key and Boca Chita Key. Concessioner boat tours accessible with assistance.

Things to Do
Ranger-led activities: glass-bottom boat tours, canoe trips, island nature tours, interpretive exhibits. Also available: swimming, snorkeling, scuba diving, water skiing, boating, canoe rentals, fishing, lobstering, hiking, birding. Special events: Family Fun Fests, Saturday classes, lecture series. Offered seasonally; call for details.

Special Advisories
● Do not touch coral or other living things on the reef. They are easily damaged; they can also inflict deep cuts and cause serious infections.

● Mosquitoes and other insects can be a problem on the islands, particularly from April to December; carry plenty of repellent.

Campgrounds
Two boat-in campgrounds, both with 14-day limit. **Elliott Key** and **Boca Chita Key** open all year, first come, first served. Water at Elliott Key only. Tent sites only. $10 fee per site per night; one campsite is free with overnight docking. Group campground at Elliott Key. Fees $25 per site per night.

Hotels, Motels, & Inns
(unless otherwise noted, rates are for 2 persons in a double room, high season)
In Florida City, FL 33034:
Comfort Inn 333 S.E. First Ave./US 1. (305) 248-4009. 123 units. $59-$169. AC, pool.
Coral Roc Motel 1100 N. Krome Ave. (305) 247-4010. 16 units, 4 with kitchenettes. $36-$89. AC, pool.
Knights Inn 1223 N.E. 1st Ave./US 1. (305) 247-6621. 49 units, 6 with kitchenettes. $79-$169. AC, pool.
In Homestead, FL 33030:
Days Inn 51 S. Homestead Blvd. (305) 245-1260. 100 units. $109. AC, pool, restaurant.
Everglades Motel 605 S. Krome Ave. (305) 247-4117. 14 units. $68. AC, pool.

For additional accommodations, write or call the Homestead/Florida City Chamber of Commerce, 43 N. Krome Ave., Homestead, FL 33030. (305) 247-2332.

Excursions

John Pennekamp Coral Reef State Park
Key Largo, Florida

In the world's first undersea park, a living coral reef may be viewed through a diver's mask or a glass-bottom boat. 63,085 acres. Visitor center, 47 campsites, trails, boating, boat ramps, fishing, picnic areas, water sports, handicapped access. Open all year during daylight. Off US 1 in Key Largo, about 40 miles from Biscayne NP and 35 from Everglades NP. (305) 451-1202.

National Key Deer Refuge
Big Pine Key, Florida

The Key deer—a diminutive subspecies of the white-tailed deer—struggle to survive in this mangrove and pine-palm habitat. It's illegal to feed them. 8,932 acres. Hiking and wildlife observation. Open year-round, dawn to dusk. Off US 1 on Big Pine Key, about 150 miles south of Biscayne NP. (305) 872-0774.

Great White Heron National Wildlife Refuge
Big Pine Key, Florida

Dedicated to the protection of the great white heron, this site partly overlaps the National Key Deer Refuge. These mangrove islands also shelter ibis, white-crowned pigeon, and the roseate spoonbill. 192,584 acres. No facilities. Access by boat only. Open all year, dawn to dusk. Information at National Key Deer Refuge; see above.

Key West National Wildlife Refuge
Big Pine Key, Florida

Encompassing nearly all the islands west of Key West, this refuge offers protection to terns, frigate birds, ospreys, herons, and pelicans. 208,308 acres. No camping or other facilities. Access by boat only. No pets allowed. Open year-round, dawn to dusk. Information at National Key Deer Refuge; see above.

White-tailed deer grazing under a giant red oak

Cuyahoga Valley

Ohio

Established October 11, 2000

33,000 acres

If there is one word that typifies Cuyahoga Valley, it might well be *surprise*. To begin, many people are surprised by the simple fact that a national park exists in northeastern Ohio, between the sprawling cities of Cleveland and Akron. In fact, it hasn't existed for long: Cuyahoga Valley was given national park status only in 2000.

Those who explore find more surprises: Belying its setting in a heavily industrialized, densely populated region, the park offers secluded trails through rugged gorges that seem far removed from civilization; vistas of tree-covered hills where the urban world is out of sight; marshes where beaver, herons, and wood ducks thrive.

Crisscrossed by roads and freeways, encompassing towns, private attractions, and city parks, Cuyahoga Valley is hardly comparable to the vast western wilderness parks—a circumstance that leads to even more surprises. Here, visitors can ride a scenic railroad, hear a symphony concert, attend an art exhibit, play golf, or, in winter, zoom down snowy ski slopes, all within the national park boundaries.

The park's history is unique as its potpourri of natural and man-made attractions. In the 1960s, local citizens and public officials became concerned that commercial and residential development was threatening the scenic Cuyahoga River Valley, with its villages, quiet byways, and forests. In 1974, Congress passed a bill creating a hoga Valley may not fit everyone's idea of a national park, but that doesn't tarnish the appeal of its many rewards.

How To Get There
From Cleveland, 10 miles south on I-77; from Akron, 5 miles north on I-77 or Ohio 8; from the east or west, I-80 (the Ohio Turnpike) bisects the park, as does I-271. Airports: Cleveland or Akron.

When to Go
Year-round park. Weekends can be crowded along the Towpath Trail from spring through fall, and especially in summer. Many activities are curtailed in winter, but downhill skiing, cross-country skiing, snowshoeing, and sledding are popular. Spring wildflowers and fall foliage make these especially colorful and appealing seasons.

How To Visit
Stop at the **Canal Visitor Center** for an overview of canal and valley history and information on park activities; be sure to ask about ranger-led tours and special events. Walk or bicycle a portion of the **Towpath Trail** before driving east to take in the beauty of **Tinkers Creek Gorge.** Then head south to see **Brandywine Falls,** continuing to the towns of **Boston** and **Peninsula** for museums and exhibits. Walk some of the scenic trails south of the Happy Days Visitor Center, especially in the area called **The Ledges.**

National Recreation Area, administered by the National Park Service. Park staff began acquiring private land within the designated 33,000 acres, as well as working out cooperative agreements with developments already in place, such as Cleveland and Summit County metropolitan park districts and Blossom Music Center, the summer home of the Cleveland Orchestra. Over time, confusion about the meaning of "recreation area" led supporters to call for full national park status, which was granted in 2000.

Today, Cuyahoga Valley NP serves the metropolitan area in a multitude of ways. Nearby residents find it a convenient place to jog, ride bicycles, or picnic; local children ride sleds down its hills in winter; nature-lovers find refuge in its pockets of wild greenery, home to dozens of species of birds and wildflowers; fans of the arts watch Shakespeare and musicals at Kent State University's Porthouse Theatre. Cuya-

A 19th-century barn

Fall hiking on the Ohio & Erie Canal Towpath Trail

Canal Towpath Trail

2 hours to a half-day or more

A few decades ago, the notoriously polluted **Cuyahoga River** seemed an odd choice to be at the heart of a national park. The Cuyahoga (an American Indian word meaning "crooked") is far cleaner today, after extensive rehabilitation efforts. Though park personnel still don't recommend swimming or boating, the river corridor serves as a thread of life running 22 miles through the center of the park, home to a surprising diversity of wildlife.

During the 1820s, a canal constructed parallel to the river opened up commercial boat traffic between Lake Erie and the Ohio River, fostering economic growth in the Cuyahoga Valley. Made obsolete by railroads, the Ohio & Erie Canal has long been abandoned—but the adjacent towpath, where mules once trudged towing boats, has been converted into one of the area's most popular hiking and bicycling trails. Running nearly 20 miles through the park (and extending both north into Cleveland and south into Akron), the **Ohio & Erie Canal Towpath Trail** is in many ways the heart of recreational activity in Cuyahoga Valley. Passing through forests, meadows, and wetlands, the fully accessible trail invites casual walking and serious fitness running or biking.

At the **Canal Visitor Center,** an 1820s canal house off Canal Road in the northern part of the park, you can watch a video and inspect historical displays. Just outside is **Lock 38,** the canal's last operational lock within the park, one of a series that allowed boats to negotiate 395 feet of elevation change as they traveled inland from Lake Erie to Akron, and vice versa. Costumed rangers and volunteers demonstrate the lock's function on summer weekends.

As you explore the Towpath Trail (and the rest of the Cuyahoga Valley), consider taking advantage of one of the park's partners: The **Cuyahoga Valley Scenic Railroad** parallels the river on its route from Akron to Independence, making seven stops within the park. Some trips allow hikers and bikers to follow the Towpath Trail as far as they wish, then board the train and return to their starting point. Themed rail trips are offered throughout the year.

Drive east along Tinkers Creek Road and Gorge Parkway into beautiful **Tinkers Creek Gorge,** a national natural landmark within the Cleveland Metroparks System. An overlook along the parkway presents a fine view of the wooded valley and the creek, 200 feet below. Farther east is the parking lot for **Bridal Veil Falls,** where a short walk into a steep-sided valley brings you to a pretty spot where a tributary of **Tinkers Creek** drops over a series of sandstone ledges—one of nearby 70 waterfalls in the gorge. Here, as at scattered other spots in the park, the shaded ravine is home to hemlocks, beeches, maples, oaks, and birches, creating an environment reminiscent of more northerly hardwood forests. The paths that meander through the gorge comprise part of 186 miles of trails in the Cuyahoga Valley, allowing short strolls just off paved roads and day-long loop hikes that can take in a variety of habitats and landscapes.

Brandywine Falls & the Ledges

a full day or more

Perhaps the park's most-visited natural feature, **Brandywine Falls** cascades over a staircase-like series of sandstone-covered shelves in the eastern part of the park, reached by a walkway to viewing platforms, one high and another lower, at streamside. The falls' winter aspect can be just as striking as that of spring's high water, with flows and icicles creating a white curtain of columns and swirls. Not quite so grand, but also exquisite and always less crowded, **Blue Hen Falls** is just minutes away on the west side of the Cuyahoga River, in an intimate valley forested in maple and beech.

Be sure to stop at the 1836 **Boston Store,** in the nearby village of Boston. Here you'll enjoy a fascinating national park exhibit on the design and building of the boats that plied the Ohio & Erie Canal during its heyday as a thriving commercial corridor. Just south, the town of **Peninsula** produced boats in its workshops that were widely regarded as the best on the canal. Today, Peninsula is a charming village of shops, cafés, and art galleries, as well as a bike-rental facility for those who'd like to take a spin on the adjacent Towpath Trail.

One of the park's must-see sites can be found southeast of Peninsula, on Kendall Park Road. The main trail at the **Ledges** arcs around a small plateau, following a path beneath dramatically eroded bluffs of 320-million-year-old sandstone conglomerate. The evocative setting of tall trees, ferns, and mosses makes this a hike to be taken slowly, enjoying the chattering of red squirrels, the scolding calls of chickadees, and the infinite variety of rock shapes. On the east side of the Ledges, venture into the tight passageways of **Ice Box Cave**; on the west, the **Ledges Overlook** is a fine spot for sunset views over wooded ridges rolling away to the horizon.

Check the park schedule during your visit for activities at the **Happy Days Visitor Center**, on Ohio 303. A hub for park arts activities, the center hosts concerts, dances, lectures, and children's activities. Thanks to the park's artist-in-residence program and to active local groups, you may run across a painter or folksinger as you walk the Towpath Trail or visit other sites in the park at any time during the warm months.

Ask nearby residents about favorite stretches of the Towpath Trail and you'll get a different answer from nearly everyone. For nature-lovers, though, the section just north of the **Ira Road Trailhead** ranks at the top. Here you'll find an extensive marsh created by beaver, which returned to the Cuyahoga Valley in the late 1970s after an absence of 140 years. Great blue herons, rose-breasted grosbeaks, and prothonotary warblers are just a few of the many birds found in this wetland, along with muskrat and white-tailed deer (best seen at dawn or dusk, as are beaver). Belted kingfishers dive for prey among white water lilies, and red-winged blackbirds nest in the extensive reed beds.

Moving from natural to human history: **Hale Farm & Village,** on Oak Hill Road in the southwestern part of the park, near Bath, is a living-history museum operated by a local historical society and open May through October. Re-creating life in a typical mid-19th-century Cuyahoga Valley community, the village centerpiece is the 1826 farm of the pioneer Hale family. Other historic buildings have been

Brandywine Falls

relocated here to reproduce an early village, where costumed interpreters spin thread, weave cloth, make baskets and candles, blow glass, shape iron in a blacksmith shop, and tell stories. A short drive north, the **Everett Road covered bridge** is a re-creation of an 1870s structure that was destroyed in a 1975 flood.

Civilization, in the form of highways, suburbs, and commercial development, is never far away in Cuyahoga Valley NP. But perhaps that, in a way, is the point: that such a variety of natural beauty and attractions can endure in an urban setting, and can so reward those who take time to explore.

Spring snow along Akron-Peninsula Road

Information & Activities

Headquarters
Cuyahoga Valley NP, 15610 Vaughn Rd., Brecksville, OH 44141. (216) 524-1497. www.nps.gov/cuva

Seasons & Accessibility
Park open year-round for individual activities and scheduled events.

Visitor & Information Centers
Canal Visitor Center, Canal and Hillside Roads, Valley View, open year-round. (216) 524-1497. **Happy Days Visitor Center,** 500 W. Streetsboro, Peninsula, offers information on concerts and special events. Open seasonally. (330) 650-4636. **Hunt Farm Visitor Information Center,** along Towpath Trail, open seasonally. **Peninsula Depot Visitor Center** serves as a welcome center for the park; hours coincide with train schedule.

Entrance Fee
Free to enter park. Some concerts, events, and programs charge fees.

Pets
Permitted on leashes.

Facilities for Disabled
Many trails, visitor centers, historic properties, and activities accessible. The crushed limestone of the 20-mile Canal Towpath Trail is fully accessible. Contact park for detailed information on sites and events.

Things to Do
Park personnel and volunteers lead tours and nature walks, while cultural events abound spring through fall at venues such as the Blossom Music Center, (330) 920-8040; and the Porthouse Theatre, (330) 929-4416.

Summer activities: picnicking, golfing, walking, fishing, bicycling, horseback riding (no horse rentals inside the park); winter activities: sledding tobogganing, cross-country skiing, snowshoeing. For an easy way to explore the park take the **Cuyahoga Valley Scenic Railroad,** (800) 468-4070.

Campgrounds
No campgrounds exist within park and backcountry camping is not permitted. Contact the visitor bureaus listed below for a list of private campgrounds in the area.

Hotels, Motels, & Inns
(unless otherwise noted, rates for 2 persons, double room, high season)
INSIDE THE PARK:
Inn at Brandywine Falls 8230 Brandywine Rd., Sagamore Hills, OH 44067. (330) 467-1812. 3 rooms, 3 suites. $108-$295, includes breakfast. AC.
Stanford Hostel 6093 Stanford Rd., Peninsula, OH 44264. (330) 467-8711. 30 beds in historic structure. Separate dorms for men, women. $15 per night for Hosteling International members. $2 bedding rental fee.

For accommodations contact Akron/Summit Convention & Visitors Bureau, (800) 245-4254 or (330) 374-7560, www.visitakron-summit.org; or Convention & Visitors Bureau of Greater Cleveland, (800) 321-1001 or (216) 621-4110, www.travelcleveland.com.

Bird's-eye view of Fort Jefferson

Dry Tortugas

Florida

Established October 26, 1992

64,701 acres

In the Gulf of Mexico, about 70 nauti-cal miles west of Key West, Florida, a 7-mile-long archipelago of seven low-lying islands forms the centerpiece of Dry Tortugas National Park. A bird and marine life sanctuary, it harbors some of the healthiest coral reefs remaining off North American shores. Towering incongruously in the midst of this subtropical Eden is Fort Jeffer-son, a relic of 19th-century military strategy. The largest American coastal fort built in that century, it sprawls over 16-acre Garden Key.

Barely 85 acres of the park's 100 square miles are above water. Three easterly keys are little more than spits of white coral sand. A stone's throw from park headquarters in Fort Jeffer-son, Bush Key is home to a tangle of bay cedar, sea grape, mangrove, sea oats, and prickly pear cactus that reflect the original "desert island" character of the islands. The chain ends about 3 miles west with 30-acre Loggerhead Key, where a lighthouse completed in 1858 still flashes a beacon to mariners.

Spanish explorer Juan Ponce de León, the first European to describe the Florida peninsula, dropped anchor here in 1513, found pellucid waters teeming with green, hawksbill, leatherback, and loggerhead turtles, and so named the islands Las Tortugas. For the next three centuries, pirates relied on the turtles for meat and eggs; they also raided the sandy nests of roosting sooty and noddy terns, over 100,000 of which descend on Bush Key every year between March and September. By 1825, when the islands' first lighthouse began to of Mexico. As a result, they decided to build a 450-gun, 2,000-man fort on Garden Key. The intimidating bulk of the 50-foot-high, three-level hexagon, whose 2,000 arches run half a mile around, spared it from ever having to fire a shot in anger. A Union prison for Civil War deserters, it also held physician Samuel Mudd, who was convicted of conspiracy in Abraham Lincoln's murder after he (unknowingly, he claimed) set the broken leg of fugitive assassin John Wilkes Booth. He served four years before being released.

Unfinished after nearly 30 years of intermittent construction, the "Gibraltar of the Gulf" succumbed in 1874 to several factors: yellow fever, hurricane damage, and the new rifled cannon, which rendered its 8-foot-thick walls obsolete. Revived in 1898 as a Navy coaling station—the battleship *Maine* steamed from here to its infamous destiny in Havana's harbor 90 miles south—the fort was permanently abandoned in 1907. In 1935 President Franklin D. Roosevelt signed the papers naming the site a national monument.

How to Get There

Access to Dry Tortugas is by boat or seaplane. Yankee Fleet and Sunny Days run regular boat service. For Yankee Fleet, call (800) 634-0939 or (305) 294-7009; for Sunny Days, call (800) 236-7937 or (305) 292-6100. For names of authorized air taxis and charter boats, call park headquarters. Boat passage from Key West takes about 3 hours; by air, 40 minutes. Private boaters should refer to NOAA

alert sailors of surrounding reefs and shoals—a grave for more than 200 ships wrecked here since the 1600s—nautical charts warned that the Tortugas were "dry."

In 1846, U.S. Army strategists were concerned that hostile nations could disrupt shipping lanes in the Gulf

Divers surveying the rich marine life off Garden Key

Chart #11434 ("Sombrero Key To Dry Tortugas") and Chart #11438 ("Dry Tortugas").

When to Go
All-year park. Temperatures range from the mid-80s to the low 50s. Moderate weather prevails in April and May, when visitation is at its peak. Winter is often windy with rough seas. The tropical storm or "hurricane" season lasts from June through November, when temperatures and humidity are highest.

How to Visit
A day trip by boat or floatplane permits an unhurried visit to **Garden Key** including a self-guided walking tour of **Fort Jefferson,** a stroll around the fort's marine life-rich seawall, swimming, and snorkeling. If **Bush Key** is open to visitors and you can spare an hour, consider swimming the narrow channel to experience a true "desert island" environment.

Garden Key and Fort Jefferson

70 miles from Key West; a full day

When you arrive, check dockside announcement boards for ranger-led activities. The **visitor center** is just inside the fort entrance. A Florida National Parks and Monuments Association bookstore has hours posted on its door. View the self-operated video orientation program, then take a self-guided tour of **Fort Jefferson's** massive architecture and parklike parade ground. Granite spiral staircases lead to open-air gun emplacements atop the fort, where visitors will find splendid 360-degree views—excellent vantage points for binocular-aided bird-watching. (Early on, the Tortugas' population of terns, cormorants, gulls, boobies, plovers, pelicans, peregrine falcons, and twin-tailed frigate birds caught the attention of naturalists like John James Audubon, who sailed here from Key West in 1832 to study them.) Visit the **Garden Key harbor light,** and stroll the grassy parapet, where huge coastal guns are on display.

Stroll along the fort's 0.6-mile-long **seawall** and moat, a sheltered habitat favored by queen conch, yellow stingray, gray snapper, sea stars, and other creatures. Outside the wall, a superb snorkeling area—chest deep and decorated with sea fans, brain coral, and turtle grass—teems with many of the 442 species of fish identified in this protected marine sanctuary. (The visitor center has a limited number of goggles, snorkels, and flippers available for loan.)

If you can enlist a companion for mutual safety, consider swimming from the campground's bathing beach

Sunlit archways of Fort Jefferson

along the wall, where fish tend to congregate. Watch for barracuda, which though seldom aggressive are territorial and should be given wide berth.

Information & Activities

Headquarters
Dry Tortugas NP headquarters is located at Everglades NP, 40001 State Rd. 9336, Homestead, FL 33034. Phone (305) 242-7700. www.nps.gov/drto

Seasons & Accessibility
Park open year-round. Visitation peaks in spring, when advance boat or plane reservations are advised. Only Garden Key offers overnight stays (in campgrounds). Loggerhead and Bush Keys available for day use only. Bush Key is closed from March to September during nesting season.

Visitor & Information Centers
Visitor center open daily all year.

Entrance Fee
None for day visit.

Pets
Permitted only in the campground and must be leashed at all times.

Facilities for Disabled
Dock, visitor center, ground level of fort, and Fort Jefferson campground are accessible.

Things to Do
Occasional ranger-led activities. Self-guided walking tours of Fort Jefferson. Also, swimming, snorkeling, wreck diving, underwater photography, birdwatching, sportfishing, camping, stargazing.

Special Advisories
● Plan to bring all water, food, fuel,

and supplies. There is no fresh water available for campers, and no showers for rinsing after swimming.
● Private boats must anchor offshore in designated areas. There are no public boat moorings or slips.
● No public telephone service to the Tortugas.

Campgrounds
Camping is permitted only on Garden Key, which has 10 primitive sites available. First come, first served. 14-day limit. Fees are $3 per person per night. Groups of ten or more must obtain a special permit in advance from park headquarters. Write for reservations at P.O. Box 6208, Key West, FL 33041; allow 30 days for processing.

Hotels, Motels, & Inns
(unless otherwise noted, rates are for 2 persons in a double room, high season)
In Key West, FL 33040:
Best Western Key Ambassador Resort Inn 3755 S. Roosevelt Blvd. (800) 432-4315 or (305) 296-3500. 101 units. $139-$219. AC, pool. **Duval House** 815 Duval St. (305) 294-1666. 28 units, 3 kitchenettes. $175-$245. AC, pool. **The Marquesa Hotel** 600 Fleming St. (305) 292-1919. 27 units. $260-$395. AC, pool, restaurant. **Westwinds** 914 Eaton St. (800) 788-4150 or (305) 296-4440. 22 units, 4 kitchenettes. $110-$170. AC.

For other area accommodations, contact the Key West Chamber of Commerce, 402 Wall St., Key West, FL 33040. (800) 527-8539 or (305) 294-2587.

Sunrise over mangroves in Florida Bay

Everglades

Florida

Established December 6, 1947

1,508,570 acres

A short parade of visitors follows a ranger on an Everglades nature walk. For more than an hour she has shown them the living wonders around them—butterflies and snails, alligators and fish, and bird after bird. Near the end of the walk, she gathers the visitors around her. She points to a string of nine white ibis coursing a cloudless sky.

"Imagine seeing ibis in the 1930s," she says. "That would have been a flight of about 90 birds. We are seeing only about 10 percent of the wading birds that were here then. When you get home, write your congressmen and tell them we have to save Everglades." In this threatened national park, lobbying happens on nature walks and appears in official literature.

The park is at the southern tip of the Everglades, a hundred-mile-long subtropical wilderness of saw-grass prairie, junglelike hammock, and mangrove swamp, running from Lake Okeechobee to Florida Bay. Water, essential to the survival of this ecosystem, once flowed south from the lake unhindered. But as the buildup of southern Florida has intensified, canals, levees, and dikes have increasingly diverted the water to land developments and agribusinesses. Vast irrigated farmlands have spread to the park's gates. The waning of the ibis carries a warning: Watery habitats in the park are shrinking because not enough water is getting to Everglades.

The park's special mission inspires the crusade to save it. Unlike early parks established to protect scenery,

When humans change it, they put Everglades life at risk.

How to Get There

South from Miami, take US 1 or the Florida Turnpike to Florida City, then go west on Fla. 9336 (Palm Dr.) to the Ernest F. Coe Visitor Center, about 50 miles from Miami. West from Miami, take US 41 (the Tamiami Trail) to Shark Valley Visitor Center. From Naples, head east on US 41 to Fla. 29, then south to Everglades City. Airports: Miami and Naples.

When to Go

Everglades has two seasons: dry (mid-December through mid-April) and wet (the rest of the year). The park schedules most of its activities in the dry season; hot, humid weather and clouds of mosquitoes make park visitors extremely uncomfortable during the wet season.

How to Visit

If you can stay only a day for a drive-in visit, get out of your car and learn about Everglades ecology by taking self-guided walks at road turnoffs on the drive from the **Ernest F. Coe Visitor Center** to Flamingo. For a longer stay, pick either **Flamingo** or **Everglades City** as your base and time your travels to the schedules of concession boat tours. In wet or dry season, only a boat or canoe gives you access to the backcountry. Because of mosquitoes, the dry season is best for canoeing. (Near park entrances you'll see signs advertising airboat rides; airboats, which disturb wildlife and tear up saw grass, are banned in the park.)

Everglades was created to preserve a portion of this vast ecosystem as a wildlife habitat. The park's unique mix of tropical and temperate plants and animals—including more than 700 plant and 300 bird species, as well as the endangered manatee, crocodile, and Florida panther—has earned it international biosphere reserve and United Nations World Heritage site designations.

Everglades crusaders urge the purchase of privately owned wetlands east and north of the park. This would further protect the ecosystem and give the park a larger claim to the water that Everglades shares with its thirsty neighbors.

The diverse life of Everglades National Park, from algae to alligators, depends upon a rhythm of abundance and drought. In the wet season, a river inches deep and miles wide flows, almost invisibly, to the Gulf of Mexico. In the dry season, the park rests, awaiting the water's return. The plants and animals are a part of this rhythm.

Royal Palm to Flamingo

76 miles round-trip; a full day

The main park road connects the main entrance, southwest of Florida City, with Flamingo on Florida Bay. Make the drive an exploration, not a 55-mph dash. Stops at the sites suggested can be made on the way to or from Flamingo, depending upon when you want to board a concession tour boat there. Check on that day's cruises by calling the concessioner (see **Information & Activities** p. 54).

At the **Ernest F. Coe Visitor Center**, get oriented to this complex park. A short film stresses environmental

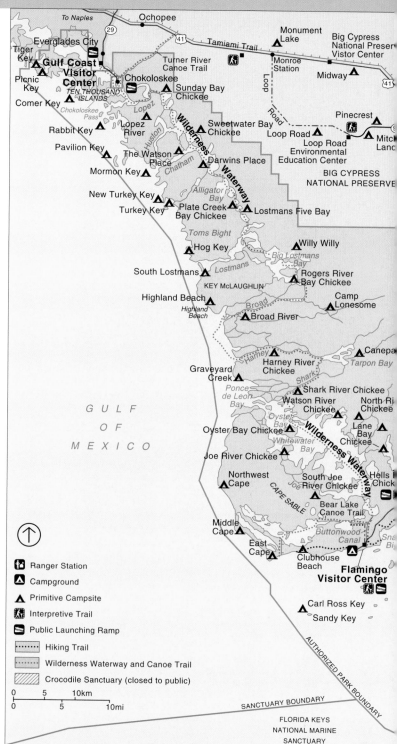

To Naples
Ochopee

Everglades City

Tiger Key

Gulf Coast Visitor Center

Picnic Key

TEN THOUSAND ISLANDS

Comer Key

Chokoloskee Pass

Rabbit Key

Pavilion Key

Mormon Key

New Turkey Key

Turkey Key

South Lostmans

Highland Beach

Graveyard Creek

Middle Cape

East Cape

Monument Lake

Tamiami Trail

Monroe Station

Midway

Big Cypress National Preserve Visitor Center

Turner River Canoe Trail

Chokoloskee

Sunday Bay Chickee

Lopez River

Lopez

Huston

Sweetwater Bay Chickee

Loop Road

Pinecrest

Mitchell Landing

The Watson Place

Chatham

Darwins Place

Loop Road Environmental Education Center

BIG CYPRESS NATIONAL PRESERVE

Alligator Bay

Plate Creek Bay Chickee

Lostmans Five Bay

Toms Bight

Hog Key

Big Lostmans Bay

Willy Willy

Lostmans

KEY McLAUGHLIN

Rogers River Bay Chickee

Camp Lonesome

Highland Beach

Broad

Broad River

Canepatch

Harney

Harney River Chickee

Tarpon Bay

Shark

Ponce de Leon Bay

Shark River Chickee

Watson River Chickee

North River Chickee

Oyster Bay

Oyster Bay Chickee

Whitewater Bay

Lane Bay Chickee

Joe River Chickee

G U L F

O F

M E X I C O

Northwest Cape

CAPE SABLE

South Joe River Chickee

Hells Bay Chickee

Bear Lake Canoe Trail

Buttonwood Canal

Snake Bight

Clubhouse Beach

Flamingo Visitor Center

Carl Ross Key

Sandy Key

Ranger Station

Campground

Primitive Campsite

Interpretive Trail

Public Launching Ramp

Hiking Trail

Wilderness Waterway and Canoe Trail

Crocodile Sanctuary (closed to public)

0   5   10km
0   5   10mi

AUTHORIZED PARK BOUNDARY

SANCTUARY BOUNDARY

FLORIDA KEYS
NATIONAL MARINE
SANCTUARY

Miccosukee
Cultural Center

Tamiami
Ranger
Station

**Shark Valley
Visitor Center**

Tram Tour

Observation
Tower

SHARK RIVER SLOUGH

Tamiami Trail

821

826

27 Hialeah

997

Miami
International
Airport

MIAMI

95

112

41

1

Chekika
Richmond Dr
SW 168th St

Biscayne
Bay

1

Homestead
Airport

BISCAYNE
NATIONAL
PARK

Pa-hay-okee
Overlook

Pinelands

Long Pine
Key

Daniel
Beard
Center

Hidden Lake
Environmental
Education Center

**Ernest F.
Coe
Visitor
Center**

Homestead

9336 Florida City

North Canal Dr
SW 328th St.

Turkey Point

**Royal Palm
Visitor Center**
Gumbo Limbo Trail
Anhinga Trail

Card Sound Road (Toll)

Mahogany
Hammock

Hells Bay
Canoe
Trail

Old
Ingraham

Ernest Coe

Nine Mile
Pond

Canoe Trail

Noble Hammock
Canoe Trail

TAYLOR SLOUGH

Seven
Palm
Lake

West Lake
Canoe Trail

Madeira
Bay

Little
Madeira
Bay

Joe Bay

North
Nest
Key

1

Card
Sound

Toll Bridge

Barnes
Sound

Blackwater
Sound

Key Largo

Hawk Channel

JOHN PENNEKAMP
CORAL REEF
STATE PARK

Key Largo
Ranger Station

STATE PARK BOUNDARY

Little Rabbit Key

F L O R I D A   B A Y

1

Hawk Channel

FLORIDA KEYS NATIONAL
MARINE SANCTUARY

A T L A N T I C   O C E A N

To Key West

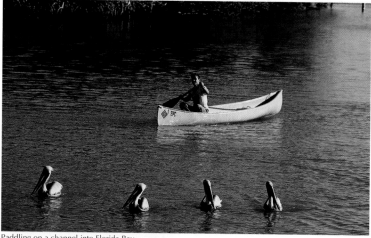
Paddling on a channel into Florida Bay

Snail kite in search of food

American alligator

threats to the park and alerts you to the subtle, imperiled beauty you will be seeing. Check the center's daily posted schedule for ranger-led walks and talks at the Royal Palm Visitor Center, just ahead, and for that day's cruises at Flamingo, 38 miles away. Time your road travel each way by adjusting to the day's schedules.

Egrets, herons, and other species dot the saw grass and roadside trees. On the road, use a passenger as a bird spotter; simultaneous driving and bird-watching can be dangerous. At 4 miles, turn off to the **Royal Palm Visitor Center.** There are two trails here to stroll.

You can walk the half-mile **Anhinga Trail** on your own, but if you join a ranger-led group you'll have a better chance of spotting wildlife. The boardwalk trail skirts a shallow, freshwater slough (pronounced slew). You almost certainly will see alligators and some fascinating birds, including the long-necked, long-beaked fish-spearer for which the trail is named.

The ranger adds lore to what you see: That beautiful zebra butterfly tastes terrible; a predatory bird never tries for second helpings. Those white egg sacs on that branch will hatch apple snails, the prime food of the endangered snail kite. That slim, long-snouted fish gliding through the clear water is a gar; in the dry season it can survive in a mudhole because a primitive lung allows it to breathe air. That alligator loosens the muck in water-filled solution holes and sweeps it away with its

Watching the alligators at Shark Valley

tail; in the dry season the gator-made oasis keeps fish, frogs, snails, and birds alive—as long as they are wary of the major resident. In Everglades, unusual adaptations and delicate balances sustain the park's astonishing variety of animals and plants.

The other trail here is the half-mile **Gumbo Limbo Trail**, named for a tree whose peeling red bark gives it another name: tourist tree. The trail takes you to a hammock, an elevated island of tropical hardwood—including gumbo limbos and some magnificent examples of strangler figs—in a sea of saw grass. The slight elevation keeps the ground drier, permitting the hardwoods to flourish and creating a shaded habitat for many creatures, from snakes to deer, foxes, and raccoon.

Watch for "solution holes," limestone depressions that hold moisture and become miniature ecosystems in the dry season. Filled with organic material and seeded by winds or bird droppings, some solution holes evolve into hammocks.

Back on the road, visit the roadside exhibits. Stop-and-walk lessons begin on the 0.75-mile **Pineland Trail,** 7 miles along the road. Slash pines grow on high ground, so pinelands were wiped out to develop Miami and other towns. What you see here are remnants of the pines that once covered southeastern Florida.

Driving toward Flamingo, you can stop and take a short boardwalk stroll that leads you to **Pinnacle Rock,** a sample of the porous limestone that is

South Florida's bedrock. At 12 miles, stop again to see dwarf cypress, trees stunted by shallow soil.

Half a mile farther is an overlook called **Pa-hay-okee,** or "grassy waters," the Indian name for the Everglades. A boardwalk takes you to a shaded observation stage where you can look out on a seemingly endless prairie of grassy waters. At 19.5 miles is **Mahogany Hammock,** where a boardwalk leads to the largest living mahogany tree in the United States.

If you want to picnic, there are fine spots at **Paurotis Pond** (at 24.5 miles), **Nine Mile Pond** (at 26.5 miles), and **West Lake** (at 30.5 miles).

At **Flamingo,** which offers the only in-park accommodations, sign up for a boat tour in the marina ticket office near the visitor center. While you are waiting, take the self-guided, half-mile walk around the waterfront to see **Florida Bay,** a marine nursery protected by the park. Roseate spoonbills, raccoon, black bear, and manatees are just some of the out-of-water critters often spotted here.

The 2-hour backcountry cruise begins in the marina and enters **Buttonwood Canal,** built in 1957. Among the spidery roots of the three species of mangrove you will see along the waterway, watch for shy crocodiles, which sometimes sun on the banks of the canal. The cruise crosses **Coot Bay** and enters **Whitewater Bay,** where backcountry canoeists camp on chickees, tent-size platforms raised on poles. Don't expect to see flamingos; they rarely appear at their namesake town.

White ibis, herons, pelicans, and spoonbills on mangrove islands

Raccoon hiding in mangrove roots

Shark Valley to Everglades City

49 miles one way; a full day

The **Tamiami Trail** (US 41) forms part of the park's northeastern border. Near the eastern park entrance, stop at the **Shark Valley Visitor Center.** Here is a 15-mile loop road accessible only on foot, on bike, or, year-round, on a 2-hour, narrated tour aboard an open-sided concessioner tram.

You will not see sharks. The valley gets its name from the **Shark River;** sharks gather at its mouth in the Gulf of Mexico. But you will see alligator trails leading to hammocks in the saw grass—and you will almost certainly see alligators and wading birds. A pathway leads to a 65-foot tower looking down on the vista that became a name: glades that seem to go on forever. It's a marvelous place to spot turtles, alligators, and wading birds. Look for red-shouldered hawks, snail kites, northern harriers, and occasional rare short-tailed hawks over the marsh.

Return to US 41, which veers northward into the 2,400-square-mile **Big Cypress National Preserve,** part of the

Slash pines and saw-palmettos, remnants of Florida's flatwoods

Bull thistle in Shark Valley

Everglades ecosystem. Most of the water flowing into the park comes through four floodgates that you can see north of the highway along the park boundary.

At Fla. 29, turn south for Everglades City. Follow the highway through the town to the waterfront. Sign up for one of the regularly scheduled, round-trip, narrated concessioner boat tours (or you can explore by boat or kayak on your own).

The **Ten Thousand Island** trip ex-

plores mangrove islands in the Gulf of Mexico. On the way to and from the islands, protected sea mammals—sleek bottlenose dolphins and lumbering manatees—often pop up to look at the boat. You can usually see ospreys, pelicans, and cormorants. From a distance, the islands look like a solid stretch of low-lying green land. Close up, you see a labyrinth of thousands of waterways.

There are far fewer than 10,000 islands, but the number is unknown and ever changing. Islands form from the buildup of leaves and other organic material among the stilt-rooted mangroves. As an island grows, storms and tidal forces may break it into fragments, which continue to grow and spread. The islands, ranging in size from a couple of trees to several hundred acres, provide shelter and food for many creatures in the gulf web of life.

The boat crosses **Chokoloskee Bay,** which shares its name with an island of shells, 15 feet high and 147 acres, built by Native Americans long before the first white men appeared here. The bay is the northern end of the 99-mile Everglades City-to-Flamingo **Wilderness Waterway,** a system of backcountry canoe trails through the estuarine fringes of the park.

Information & Activities

Headquarters
40001 State Rd. 9446, Homestead, FL 33034. Phone (305) 242-7700. www.nps.gov/ever

Seasons & Accessibility
Park open daily, year-round; some facilities and services limited or unavailable during off-season, May to mid-December.

Visitor & Information Centers
Ernest F. Coe Visitor Center on Fla. 9336 at park entrance. **Royal Palm Visitor Center** off main park road a few miles inside park entrance. **Flamingo Visitor Center** on main park road at Florida Bay; may close temporarily off-season. **Shark Valley Visitor Center** at north end of park on US 41. **Gulf Coast Visitor Center** at Everglades City on Fla. 29 at northwest entrance.

Entrance Fees
$10 per car per week at main entrance; $8 at Shark Valley. $5 per person biking or walking in.

Pets
Pets must be on leashes and are allowed in the campgrounds only.

Facilities for Disabled
All visitor centers, campgrounds, rest rooms, and tram tours are accessible. Several trails are at least partly accessible. In the backcountry, Pear Bay Chickee is accessible.

Things to Do
Free naturalist-led activities: nature walks and talks, hikes, exhibits, seasonal evening programs. Also, tram tours; sight-seeing boats; canoe, kayak, houseboat, motorboat, and bicycle rentals; fishing (need license); crabbing; shrimping (ask about regulations). In winter and on holidays, call to reserve space on guided activities. Rentals and boat tours in Flamingo: (239) 695-3101 ext. 355. Tram tour at Shark Valley: (305) 221-8455. Boat tours and rentals at Everglades City: (239) 695-2591, or (800) 445-7724 in Florida.

Special Advisories
• You'll need insect repellent year-round, but especially April to December.
• Swimming not advised; alligators, crocodiles, and snakes live in ponds, sharks and barracuda in saltwater areas.

Wilderness Camping
Permits required; they are obtainable in person, no more than 24 hours before trip, at Flamingo and Everglades City. Fees collected mid-November through April only. No reservations; first come, first served; limits on number of people and length of stay.

Campgrounds
Three campgrounds, 14-day limit November to May; otherwise 30-day limit. $14 a night per site collected November through May only. **Flamingo** and **Long Pine Key** open all year. Reservations available mid-December to April; reserve through National Parks Reservation Service (see p. 11); rest of year, first come, first served. Cold showers at Flamingo. Tent and RV sites; no hookups. Three group campgrounds; reservations suggested in-season. Food services in park; limited April through November.

Hotels, Motels, & Inns
(unless otherwise noted, rates are for 2 persons in a double room, high season)
INSIDE THE PARK:
Flamingo Lodge (end of main park road) 1 Flamingo Lodge Hwy. (800) 600-3813 or (239) 695-3101. 127 units. Lodge rooms $95; cottages with kitchens $135. AC, pool, restaurant.
OUTSIDE THE PARK:
In Florida City, FL 33034:
Comfort Inn 333 S.E. 1st Ave./US 1. (305) 248-4009. 123 units. $59-$169. AC, pool. **Coral Roc Motel** 1100 N. Krome Ave. (305) 247-4010. 16 units, 4 kitchenettes. $36-$89. AC, pool. **Knights Inn** 1223 N.E. 1st Ave./US 1. (305) 247-6621. 49 units, 6 kitchenettes. $79-$169. AC, pool.
In Homestead, FL 33030:
Days Inn 51 S. Homestead Blvd. (305) 245-1260. 100 units. $109. AC, pool, restaurant. **Everglades Motel** 605 S. Krome Ave. (305) 247-4117. 14 units. $68. AC, pool.

For other lodgings, contact the Homestead/Florida City Chamber of Commerce, 43 N. Krome Ave., Homestead, FL 33030. (305) 247-2332.

Excursions

Big Cypress National Preserve

Ochopee, Florida

Dispensing life-giving fresh water to the Everglades and coastal estuaries, this preserve contains marshes, wet and dry prairies, hardwood hammocks, pinelands, and mangrove forests, along with wading birds and alligators. The endangered Florida panther roams the area. 729,000 acres. Hiking, fishing, hunting, canoeing, off-road vehicles, scenic drives. Five primitive camp-grounds, picnic areas. On US 41 (Tami-ami Trail); adjoins Everglades NP. (239) 695-4111.

Corkscrew Swamp Sanctuary

Naples, Florida

A 2.25-mile-long boardwalk takes visi-tors on a self-guided tour through this Audubon Society site featuring the country's largest stand of virgin bald cypress forest and varied wildlife, in-cluding alligators. 11,000 acres. Hiking and picnic areas. Open year-round. Off Fla. 846, about 50 miles northwest of Everglades NP. (239) 348-9151.

J. N. "Ding" Darling National Wildlife Refuge

Sanibel, Florida

Migratory songbirds and a large popu-lation of roseate spoonbills feature among the 276 bird species on this island refuge named for Pulitzer Prize-winning political cartoonist and refuge system pioneer Jay Norwood Darling. 6,300 acres. Hiking, canoeing, bicycling, fishing, scenic drive. Open all year, dawn to dusk (closed on Fri-days). Visitor center off US 41, about 75 miles northwest of Everglades NP. (239) 472-1100.

Mist-shrouded autumn view from Clingmans Dome

Great Smoky Mountains

North Carolina and Tennessee

Established June 15, 1934

521,490 acres

The fact invariably stated about Great Smoky is this: It is the nation's busiest park, drawing some ten million visitors a year, more than twice the number of any other national park. Most of the millions see the park from a mountain-skimming scenic highway that, on a typical weekend day during the summer, draws 60,000 people, bumper-to-bumper.

Luckily, there is plenty of park, thinly laced by 384 miles of mountain roads. And you can pull off the road, park the car, and stroll one of Great Smoky's many Quiet Walkways, quarter-mile paths into what the signs call a "little bit of the world as it once was." Eight hundred miles of hiking trails, from a half mile to 70 miles long, also

give you that world. Relatively few visitors walk the trails, for most people prefer to stay in their cars.

The park, which covers 800 square miles of mountainous terrain, preserves the world's best examples of deciduous forest and a matchless variety of plants and animals. Because it contains so many types of eastern forest vegetation— much of it old growth—the park has been designated an international biosphere reserve.

The Smoky Mountains are among the oldest on earth. Ice Age glaciers stopped their southward journey just short of these mountains, which became a junction of southern and northern flora. Rhododendron and mountain laurel thrust from the weathered rocks. Amid the woodland and craggy peaks bloom more than 1,500 species of flowering plants, some

How to Get There

From Knoxville, Tenn. (about 25 miles away), take I-40 to Tenn. 66, then US 441 to Gatlinburg entrance. From Asheville, N.C. (about 40 miles away), take I-40 west to US 19, then US 441, to park's southern entrance near Cherokee, N.C. For a scenic, low-speed approach, take the 469-mile Blue Ridge Parkway that connects Virginia's Shenandoah National Park with Great Smoky. Airports: Knoxville and Asheville.

When to Go

All-year park. In summer and in fall (when spectacular foliage draws huge crowds), time your visit to midweek, and arrive early. Visitor centers open year-round.

How to Visit

On a 1-day visit, take the **Newfound Gap Road** to **Clingmans Dome** and get the best overview of the park by seeing it from the highest point. The best second-day activity is the **Cades Cove loop road,** a chance to drive or cycle through pioneer history. For a longer stay, focus on the self-guided nature trails and drives, which get you away from the crowds and show you the flora and fauna.

found only here. Shrubs take over in places, creating tree-free zones called heath balds, laurel slicks (because of the shiny leaves), or just plain hells (because they are so hard to get through).

The tangle of brush and trees forms a close-packed array of air-breathing leaves. The water and hydrocarbons exuded by the leaves produce the filmy "smoke" that gives the mountains their name. Air pollution in recent years has added microscopic sulfate particles to the haze, cutting visibility back about 60 percent since the 1950s. The pollution has also affected the park's red spruce stand—the southern Appalachians' largest. And insects are destroying the Fraser fir, the spruce's high-altitude companion.

The park also preserves the humble churches, cabins, farmhouses, and barns of the mountain people who began settling here in the late 1700s. When the park was founded, most people left. But some chose to stay and live out their lives here.

Newfound Gap Road to Clingmans Dome

40 to 45 miles; a half to full day

Newfound Gap Road, which begins at 2,000 feet and ascends to 5,048 feet, connects the park's major visitor centers, **Sugarlands** and **Oconaluftee.** The road, passing from lowland hardwood timber to high-altitude spruce-fir forests, gives you a vertical trip that is ecologically equivalent to a journey from Georgia to Canada. Be prepared for rain on almost any day. A clear day below can be a day of mist and fog on high. From Sugarlands (for an Oconaluftee start, reverse the order below), stop after 5 miles at **Chimneys,** a fine picnic spot. Stretch your legs on the 0.75-mile self-guided

To Knoxville · 129
To Knoxville · 441
Pigeon Forge

Ranger Station
Developed Campground
Self-guiding Nature Trail
Observation Tower
--- **Unpaved Road**
······ **Hiking Trail**

411
321
Little

Maryville
411
129

National Park Information Center
Cove Mountain

321

Townsend

Sugarlands Visitor Center

Little River Road

Look Rock
Foothills Parkway

Great Smoky Mountains Institute at Tremont

Elkmont

Abrams Creek
Rich Mtn. Road (one-way)
Cades Cove

Cades Cove Visitor Center

Spence Field

Appalachian Trail

Chilhowee
Parson Branch Road (one-way)

TENNESSEE
NORTH CAROLINA

Thunderhead Mountain 5,527 ft

Silers Bald

Calderwood Lake
129

CHEROKEE NATIONAL FOREST

Twentymile

Fontana Dam

Fontana Lake

Lake Cheoah

Fontana Village
129

28

Santeetlah Lake

Cheoah Mountains

NANTAHALA

NATIONAL

JOYCE KILMER MEMORIAL FOREST

Appalachian Trail

FOREST

19 74

To Atlanta
143

To Atlanta

Wesser

Cove Hardwood Nature Trail. Then return to the car for a short drive to the **Chimney Tops Overlooks,** which offer views of the double summits the Cherokee called Duniskwal-guni ("forked antlers").

Here you can extend your stop with a hike on the steep, 4-mile round-trip **Chimney Tops Trail** through an old-growth forest and up 1,335 feet to the sheer cliffs named the Chimneys. Depending on your time and stamina, you can also get out of the car and hike at the next overlook, where a trail-head leads to a steep climb to **Alum Cave Bluffs,** site of a 19th-century commercial alum mine and reputedly a source of saltpeter for Civil War gunpowder. The trail begins with an easy 1.3-mile trail along a tree-bordered

creek to **Arch Rock,** a tunnel made by eons of erosion. The trees include towering 200-year-old eastern hemlocks. This is a magnificent spot for a spring wildflower hike serenaded by the songs of nesting warblers. You can return to your car or continue on a steep 0.9-mile ascent to the bluffs.

Back in the car, continue on to **Newfound Gap** (5,048 feet), through which runs the Tennessee-North Carolina state line and a long leg of the Appalachian Trail. From the overlook here, on a clear day, you can see **Mount LeConte** (6,593 feet) and your next stop, **Clingmans Dome.** The 7-mile Clingmans Dome Road veers sharply off here and winds through a spruce-fir forest to a parking lot.

There begins a steep half-mile trail

Little Pigeon

321
Cosby

CHEROKEE
NATIONAL FOREST

32

Pigeon

40

321

Cosby
TENN.
N.C.

Big Creek

Gatlinburg

Greenbrier

PISGAH
NAT.
FOREST

Roaring Fork
Motor Nature Trail
(one-way)

Mt. Guyot
6,621 ft

Mount
Sterling +
5,842 ft

Cherokee Orchard

Appalachian Trail

Waterville
Lake

Mt. LeConte
+ 6,593 ft

Alum Cave
Bluffs

+ Charlies Bunion
5,565 ft

Cataloochee

Tops
Trail

Newfound Gap

Oconaluftee

Balsam Mountain
Road (one-way)

Heintooga
Overlook

Clingmans Dome
6,643 ft

NEWFOUND
GAP ROAD

Smokemont

Balsam
Mountain

Blue Ridge
Parkway

Maggie
Valley

19

To
Asheville

Oconaluftee
Visitor Center

Mountain Farm
Museum

CHEROKEE INDIAN
RESERVATION

Cherokee

Blue Ridge
Parkway

Deep Creek

19

441

23
74

Bryson
City

74

CHEROKEE INDIAN
RESERVATION

441

Plott Balsams

Blue Ridge
Parkway

0   4   8 km
0   4   8 mi

Sylva

To Atlanta

23
441

Carter Shields Cabin in Cades Cove

Mountain laurel along the Pigeon River

ending at a spiral ramp. It leads to a lookout tower at the top of the 6,643-foot dome, the highest point in the park, where you get either a panoramic view or a sense of floating on a sea of churning clouds. From here retrace the route to Sugarlands or, depending on time and destination, continue on to Oconaluftee Visitor Center. The **Mountain Farm Museum,** a cluster of farm buildings gathered from their original locations within the park, stands adjacent to the visitor center. Pioneer-costumed park employees, playing farmstead roles, give demonstrations spring through October. (Between May and October, at **Mingus Mill,** a miller explains how cornmeal and flour would have been produced on an ingenious water-run turbine.)

Cades Cove Loop Road

11 miles; at least a half day

Follow Little River and Laurel Creek Roads for 25 miles from Sugarlands

Visitor Center to the Cades Cove loop road. **Cades Cove** traces its history to 1819, when, under a treaty with the Cherokee Indians, settlers cleared the broad, high valley. By 1850 more than 680 people were living there. They left behind structures that evolved into an open-air museum whose galleries are sites along the paved, 11-mile one-way loop road. Official sites are well marked. But you may find yourself making unofficial stops to admire the quietude, to watch white-tailed deer bounding across the valley, or to see black bears feed on acorns or wild grapes.

The first stop is **John Oliver Place,** site 3. The small cabin was built with split-wood shingles and hand-hewn logs. Stand on the porch and look down the long, green-carpeted valley that drew the family to this place, the edge of the American world in 1826. **Primitive Baptist Church,** site 4, is skipped by some visitors because it lies on a two-way dirt road off the loop road. Don't miss it. The plain white-frame church, organized in 1827, guards a small graveyard. Time has made many stones nameless, but the past still can be read on them. The church shut down during the Civil War because, a letter says, "we was Union people and the Rebels was too strong here in Cades Cove." **Methodist Church,** site 5, had a door for men and another for women and children. During services, the separation was enforced in the pews by a barrier.

Just past the church is **Hyatt Lane,** an old road out of Cades Cove and today a shortcut that slices off a big piece of the tour. Stay on the loop road and continue to **Missionary Baptist Church,** site 7, formed in 1839 by expelled members of the Primitive Baptist Church. Because the congregation split between Union and Confederacy sympathizers, this church also closed during the Civil War.

Continue on the road, past **Rich Mountain Road,** site 8. Save this for another day. The gravel road, laid over an Indian trail, goes up **Rich Mountain** and provides a spectacular backward glance at Cades Cove before exiting the park. Also requiring more time is the **Cooper Road Trail,** site 9, a onetime wagon road that is now a 13-mile hiking trail ending outside the park.

Ahead on the right is a short, two-way road to the next stops, **Abrams Falls,** site 10, and **Elijah Oliver Place,** site 11. If you take this offshoot, you come to a parking lot and a choice: a 2-hour, 2.5-mile hike up to stunning Abrams Falls, or a half-mile hike to another rustic farmstead owned by early settler Elijah Oliver. The latter features a smokehouse, springhouse, and corn crib.

Continue your drive along the loop road to the next offshoot, which leads to **John Cable Mill,** site 12, where corn was ground into meal. Here, the **Cades Cove Visitor Center** displays artifacts and pictures depicting life in Cades Cove that help visitors connect intellectually and emotionally with the people who called this serene valley their home. Now leave the center and wander about, reliving the life that centered on the old mill.

Other buildings—a blacksmith shop, a large cantilever barn, a smokehouse—were imported from elsewhere in the park. Check at the visitor center for schedules of farm-life demonstrations; they include the making of sorghum molasses: a horse-powered mill squeezes juice from the stalks, which is then boiled down in an open-air vat.

Just beyond the Cable Mill area is

Rhododendron along Clingmans Dome

Raccoon in a yellow poplar

Parson Branch Road, which can take you out of the park—and the 21st century. The narrow winding one-way dirt road (sometimes closed by weather) was carved out of wilderness about 1838. The 8-mile trip to US 129 can take an hour. If prudence keeps you on the loop road, your next stop will be **Tipton Place,** site 17. Built by Hamp Tipton shortly after the Civil War, it later became the home of a blacksmith, who put up his shop nearby.

Drive on to the last stop, **Carter Shields Cabin,** site 18. Log cabins like this would be succeeded by board houses, which arrived with lumbering in the early 1900s.

Hikes & Drives

Self-guided nature trails begin with an honor system document rack. You drop in 50 cents and pluck out a leaflet keyed to numbered stops. **Balsam Mountain Trail** is the easiest climbing trail in the park, a 1.5-mile loop from Balsam Mountain Campground. The trail gives you a short lesson in the identification of trees, and especially in spring, wildflowers. **Laurel Falls Trail** is paved. The 2.5-mile round-trip trail, which starts on Little River Road near

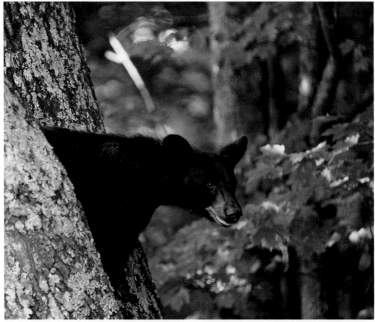

Black bear climbing down from a cherry tree after an all-night gorge

White-tailed buck, often seen at dawn and dusk

Slimy salamander, one of the park's 23 kinds

Elkmont, winds through thickets of mountain-laurel and rhododendron to one of the park's many waterfalls.

For a longer stay in the park, try some of the more rugged trails. The most rewarding hike is to **Mount LeConte,** at 6,593 feet the park's third highest peak. The shortest (though steepest) way up is via the **Alum Cave Trail,** which starts at Newfound Gap Road (see Newfound Gap Road tour). Here begins a steep 5-mile climb to the summit of LeConte. At one point the trail skirts a cliff face so sheer that hikers must grasp a cable to make their way up.

For the motorist, there are also self-guided nature trails using roads. The **Roaring Fork Motor Nature Trail,** 4 miles from Gatlinburg off

Cherokee Orchard Road, is a 5-mile curvy, one-way road with a well-warranted 10 mph speed limit. About a mile before the trail begins, you will see the **Noah "Bud" Ogle Place** on your right. A 0.75-mile path takes you around the remains of a farm—a mill, a barn, and the historic Ogle family house.

At the Roaring Fork trail, avail yourself of the self-guiding booklet that suggests scenic stops. The road climbs a hill that provides, on clear days, a splendid view of **Sugarland** and **Cove Mountains.** Along the roadside is an old-growth hemlock forest. Here and there, moldering chestnut logs are poignant reminders of the blight that struck down the one-time forest king.

Information & Activities

Headquarters
107 Park Headquarters Rd., Gatlinburg, TN 37738. Phone (865) 436-1200. www.nps.gov/grsm

Seasons & Accessibility
Park open year-round. The road to Clingmans Dome and some unpaved roads closed in winter.

Visitor & Information Centers
Open daily all year: **Sugarlands,** on US 441 south of Gatlinburg, Tenn., entrance; **Oconaluftee,** on US 441 north of Cherokee, N.C., entrance; **Cades Cove Visitor Center,** near Townsend, Tenn., entrance; enter off US 321, east of Townsend. Call park headquarters for information.

Facilities for Disabled
Visitor centers and rest rooms are wheelchair accessible. The Sugarlands Valley Nature Trail (a quarter mile south of the Sugarlands Visitor Center) was custom built for visitors with visual or mobility impairments. Clingmans Dome and Laurel Falls Trails are paved but steep; negotiable with assistance only. Free brochure.

Things to Do
Free naturalist-led activities: nature walks (day and evening), children's and campfire programs, pioneer exhibits and demonstrations, slide talks. Also, annual festivals, auto tape tour, hiking, bicycling, fishing (permit needed), horseback riding (several stables in park).

Overnight Backpacking
Permit required; available free from visitor centers and ranger stations. You can reserve rationed sites and shelters up to 30 days in advance; call (865) 436-1231.

Campgrounds
Ten campgrounds, most with a 7-day limit mid-May through October; other times 14-day limit. **Cades Cove** and **Smokemont** open all year; **Elkmont** open April through October. Reservations required mid-May through October; available through National Parks Reservation Service (see p. 11). Other campgrounds open mid-March through October, first come, first served. Fees $12-$17 per night. No showers. Tent and RV sites; nohookups. Seven group campgrounds; reservations recommended; contact park headquarters.

Hotels, Motels, & Inns
(unless otherwise noted, rates are for 2 persons in a double room, high season)
INSIDE THE PARK:
LeConte Lodge (atop Mount LeConte; access by hiking trail) 250 Apple Valley Rd., Sevierville, TN 37862. (865) 429-5704. 10 cabins, no electricity, shared bathrooms. $163, includes 2 meals. Open late March to late Nov.
OUTSIDE THE PARK:
In Bryson City, NC 28713:
Hemlock Inn (on Galbraith Creek Rd., off US 19) P.O. Box 2350. (828) 488-2885. 25 units, $144-$195, includes 2 meals. Restaurant. Open mid-April through Oct.
In Cherokee, NC 28719:
Best Western Great Smokies Inn US 441 and Acquoni Rd., P.O. Box 1809. (800) 528-1234 or (828) 497-2020. 152 units. $89. AC, pool, restaurant.
Holiday Inn Cherokee US 19 S., P.O. Box 1929. (828) 497-9181. 154 units. $99-$130. AC, 2 pools, restaurant.
In Fontana Dam, NC 28733:
Historic Fontana Village Resort N.C. 28, P.O. Box 68. (800) 849-2258 or (828) 498-2211. 90 rooms, $79; 120 cottages with kitchens, $89-$229. AC, 3 pools, 2 restaurants.
In Gatlinburg, TN 37738:
Buckhorn Inn 2140 Tudor Mountain Rd. (865) 436-4668. 9 rooms, 7 cottages, 2 guest houses. $115-$250. AC, restaurant.
Gillette Motel 235 Historic Nature Trail, P.O. Box 231. (800) 437-0815 or (865) 436-5601. 80 units. $75-$95. AC, pool.
Holiday Inn of Gatlinburg 520 Historic Nature Trail, P.O. Box 1130. (800) 435-9201 in Tenn. or (865) 436-9201. 400 units. $119-$129. AC, 3 pools, restaurant.
Park Vista Hotel 705 Cherokee Orchard Rd., P.O. Box 30. (800) 421-7275 or (865) 436-9211. 312 units. $109-$149. AC, pool, restaurant.

For other accommodations in Gatlinburg, call the Chamber of Commerce at (800) 822-1998 or (865) 436-4178.

Excursions

Pisgah National Forest
Asheville, North Carolina

The Blue Ridge Parkway traverses this mountainous forest with slopes of mixed hardwoods, azaleas, and rhododendrons, rocky gorges, and delicate waterfalls. Outstanding in spring and fall. Contains three wilderness areas and Mount Mitchell, the highest peak east of the Mississippi. 506,296 acres. 447 campsites, picnic areas. Hiking, fishing, horseback riding, hunting, scenic drives, swimming. Open all year; most campsites open spring to late fall. Visitor center on US 276, about 50 miles from Great Smoky Mountains NP. (828) 257-4200.

Nantahala National Forest
Asheville, North Carolina

The hardwood-covered mountains here contain deep, narrow valleys, canyons, and waterfalls. Noted for azaleas, rhododendrons. Contains three wilderness areas. 530,899 acres. Hiking, boating, fishing, horseback riding, hunting, scenic drives. 395 campsites, boat ramps, picnic areas, handicapped access. Open all year; most campsites open spring to late fall. Adjoins Great Smoky Mountains NP on the south. (828) 257-4200.

Breaks Interstate Park
Breaks, Virginia

Russell Fork cuts through the Pine Mountains here, creating Breaks Canyon, the "Grand Canyon of the South." Features class VI white water. Two rhododendron species provide long blooming season, mid-May through June; fall leaves peak mid-Oct. Gospel music festival Labor Day weekend. 4,600 acres. Hiking, boating, fishing, scenic drives, swimming. 138 campsites, cottages and motel units, visitor center, food service, boat ramp, picnic areas, handicapped access. Open all year; most facilities available April to mid-Dec. On Va. 80, about 190 miles from Great Smoky Mountains NP. (276) 865-4413.

Big South Fork National River & Recreation Area
Oneida, Tennessee

The Big South Fork of the Cumberland River bisects the Cumberland Plateau, yielding white water as well as calm stretches, sandstone cliffs, waterfalls, and natural arches. 120,000 acres, part in Kentucky. Hiking, horseback riding, boating, fishing, swimming, hunting. 235 campsites, boat ramp, picnic areas. Open all year. Off US 27, about 100 miles northwest of Great Smoky Mountains NP. (423) 286-7275.

Cherokee National Forest
Cleveland, Tennessee

This rugged mountain backcountry is densely wooded with mixed pines and hardwoods, azaleas, mountain laurels. 640,000 acres. Hiking, boating, fishing, hunting, scenic drives, swimming. 29 campgrounds, boat ramp, 30 picnic sites. Open all year; most campgrounds open May through October. Adjoins Great Smoky Mountains NP on northeast and southwest. (423) 476-9700.

Chattahoochee National Forest
Gainesville, Georgia

This hardwood forest encompasses a mix of terrain—lakes, streams, valleys, mountains, and piedmont plateau. Contains ten wilderness areas and a stretch of the Chattooga Wild and Scenic River with Tallullah Gorge. Also, Brasstown Bald, the state's highest mountain at 4,784 feet. 750,000 acres. Hiking, sailing, fishing, hunting, scenic drives, swimming. More than 25 campgrounds, boat ramp, picnic areas, handicapped access. Open year-round; campsites open May through Sept. On US 129, about 95 miles from Great Smoky Mountains NP. (770) 297-3000.

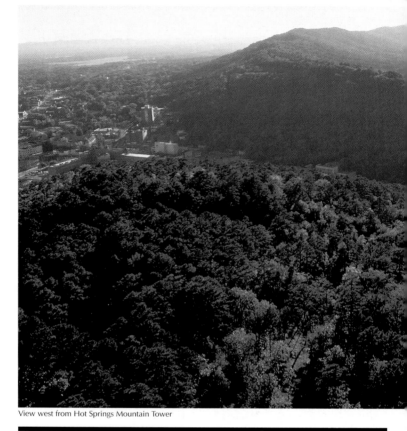

View west from Hot Springs Mountain Tower

Hot Springs

Arkansas

Established March 4, 1921

5,549 acres

Most national parks cover hundreds of thousands of acres, are far from city streets, and keep natural resources away from commercial users … but not Hot Springs. This smallest of national parks is centered in a city that has made an industry out of tapping and dispensing the park's major resource: mineral-rich waters of hot springs.

The heart of this peculiar park is Central Avenue, the main street of Hot Springs, Arkansas. Rising above Central Avenue is Hot Springs Mountain, from which the waters flow. The mountain's lower western side once was coated with tufa, a milky-colored, porous rock formed of minerals deposited from the hot springs' constant cascade.

When Hot Springs prospered as a health spa in the mid-19th century, promoters covered, piped, and diverted the springs into Central Avenue bathhouses. They also prettified the slope by covering it with tons of dirt and planting grass and shrubs. "Ever since then," a longtime Hot Springs resident says, "it's been afflicted by eastern landscape architects who can't stand the sight of rocks."

The park calls itself the "oldest area in the national park system" because in 1832, 40 years before Yellowstone became the first national park, President Andrew Jackson set aside the hot springs as a special reservation. The federal land became a national park in 1921. By then Hot Springs had long been famous as a spa where people "took the duce spectacular foliage. Winter is usually short and mild; four-petaled bluets, the first of many wildflowers, appear in February.

How to Visit

Walk **Central Avenue's Bathhouse Row,** then continue north to explore Hot Springs on the genteel trails of an urban hillside. To see a more rugged side of the park, hike the woodland trails of **Gulpha Gorge.**

Bathhouse Row

4 city blocks; 2 hours

In the early years of this century, elegant buildings lined a stretch of **Central Avenue** dubbed Bathhouse Row. In later years, as medical science's faith in hot springs faded, so did the bathhouses. But you can still enjoy the mystique of taking the waters. First visit the **Hot Springs National Park Visitor Center** (in the former Fordyce Bathhouse), a restored "temple of health and beauty" adorned with stained-glass windows and statuary. In rooms full of gleaming plumbing and luxurious tubs, you walk through a **museum** of the ritual, which in its full form involved three weeks of daily baths and massage. The **Buckstaff** is the Row's only bathhouse still offering a traditional bath. (Some hotels also have baths; ask for information at the visitor center.)

waters," seeking relief from bunions, rheumatism, and other afflictions.

The park preserves the springs' "recharge zone," slopes where rain and snow soak into the ground, and the "discharge zone," which contains 47 springs belonging to the park. Each day about 850,000 gallons of water—at 143°F—flow from the springs into a complex piping and reservoir system. This supplies water to commercial baths and to park-maintained "jug fountains," where people flock daily to fill containers with the odorless, fresh-tasting, chemical-free water.

How to Get There

From Little Rock, about 55 miles west on I-30, US 70, and Ark. 7; from the south, Ark. 7; from the west, US 70 or US 270. Airport: Little Rock.

When to Go

All-year park. Summers are hot and July is crowded. Try the late fall, when mountains around Hot Springs pro-

Springs flowing over Tufa Terrace

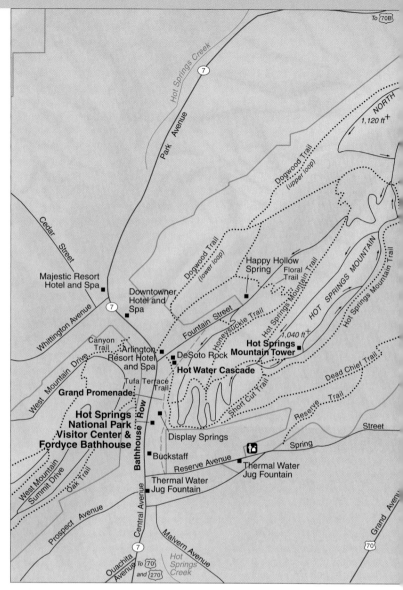

Hot Springs

a half mile; 2 hours

At the foot of the mountain (the corner of Central Avenue and Fountain Street) look for **DeSoto Rock,** a huge boulder that commemorates both the Indians who named this "place of the hot waters" and the explorer Hernando De Soto. He and his party are supposed to have bathed in the waters in 1541, beginning a tourist tradition. Visit the hot spring pool next to DeSoto Rock. Here you can see and touch the water. It is hot! Next head up the trail adjacent to the **Hot Water Cascade,** created in 1982. The water flowing here began its journey as long as 4,000 years ago when it fell as rain and seeped through fractures. Heated deep in the Earth, the water returns through the faults in the rock of the mountain in a year or two, hardly enough time to cool off.

Tiled tub in Fordyce Bathhouse

a landscaped brick walkway that runs behind the bathhouses.

The springs are sealed off—and thus kept sterile—by locked green bunkers that jut out of the lawns carpeting the slope. When some of the hillside springs were open, men and women discreetly took turns soaking their feet at one of them; at another, people cooked eggs. To see more of the famous hot water bubbling out of the earth, follow the trail to **Open Springs** behind the Maurice Bathhouse. The two springs flow into a collecting pool, where you can safely touch the water.

Go up the stairs and finish your trek on the **Grand Promenade**. The walkway, which took 30 years to build and landscape, serves as a pleasant transition between the formal architecture of the bathhouses and the trails of the wooded hillside.

Gulpha Gorge

1.6 miles round-trip; 2 hours

To find the more traditional terrain of a national park, leave **Hot Springs** on Ark. 7 heading north and turn right onto US 70B for Gulpha Gorge Campground, about 3 miles from downtown Hot Springs. Near the amphitheater pick up the **Gulpha Gorge Trail**, which crosses **Gulpha Creek** on stepping-stones and courses a woodland rich in dogwood and redbud; in spring and early summer wildflowers flank the trail. In less than a mile the trail intersects with another up to **Goat Rock**, a fine overlook for viewing the mountains around the city. In nearby quarries, Indians once mined novaculite for making arrowheads and spearpoints; under the name Arkansas Stone it is used today as a whetstone.

Map legend

↑

🛈 Ranger Station

⛺ Campground

········· Hiking Trail

– – – Walkway (Grand Promenade)

0   .25 km
0   .25 mi

The tufa created by the cascade's splashing waters is building up at the rate of an eighth of an inch a year. The brilliant blue-green algae is the only plant species that can survive in the hot waters. So can ostracods, a crustacean about the size of a sand grain found in some of the other springs.

Near the Hot Water Cascade is the **Tufa Terrace Trail**, which takes you by many concealed springs. To get there, cross the **Grand Promenade**,

Information & Activities

Headquarters
P.O. Box 1860, Hot Springs, AR 71902.
Phone (501) 624-3383 ext. 620.
www.nps.gov/hosp

Seasons & Accessibility
Park open year-round. Bathing facilities open generally Monday through Saturday all year.

Visitor & Information Centers
Hot Springs National Park Visitor Center, in the middle of Bathhouse Row. Open daily. For information call (501) 624-3383 ext. 640.

Entrance Fee
None, but fees charged for the concessioner-operated thermal baths.

Pets
Not allowed in buildings; otherwise permitted on leashes.

Facilities for Disabled
Visitor center is fully accessible to wheelchairs; the Thermal Feature and the Bathhouse Row Tours are partially accessible.

Things to Do
Free naturalist-led activities: hikes and bathhouse tours. Also available: audiovisual and interpretive exhibits, hiking, horseback riding; six bathing facilities offering thermal baths, whirlpools, steam cabinets, hot packs, massages.

Special Advisory
● Bathing in thermal waters not recommended for people with certain ailments; consult your doctor if in doubt.

Camping
One campground, **Gulpha Gorge**, with 14-day limit. Open all year on first-come, first-served basis. Fees $10 per night. No showers. Tent and RV sites; no hookups.

Hotels, Motels, & Inns
(unless otherwise noted, rates are for 2 persons in a double room, high season)
In Hot Springs, AR:
Arlington Resort Hotel & Spa 239 Central Ave., 71901. (800) 643-1502 or (501) 623-7771. 481 units. $58-$295. AC, 2 pools, 3 restaurants.
Austin Hotel 305 Malvern Ave., 71901. (800) 445-8667 or (501) 623-6600. 200 units. $89-$99. AC, pool, restaurant.
Bay Point Resort 2803 Albert Pike, 71914. (501) 767-8606. 69 units. $84-$94. AC, pool, restaurant.
Buena Vista Resort 201 Aberina St., 71913. (800) 255-9030 or (501) 525-1321. 50 units with kitchenettes. $115. AC, pool.
Knights Inn 1871 E. Grand Ave., 71901. (800) 238-4891 or (501) 624-4436. 50 units. $55-$89. AC, pool, restaurant.
SunBay Resort 4810 Central Ave., 71913. (800) 468-0055 or (501) 525-4691. 109 condos. $99-$199. AC, 3 pools, restaurant.
Williams House Bed & Breakfast Inn 420 Quapaw Ave., 71901. (800) 756-4635 or (501) 624-4275. 6 units. $99-$165, includes breakfast. AC.

For additional accommodations, write or call the Hot Springs Convention & Visitors Bureau, Box 6000, Hot Springs, AR 71902. (800) 543-2284 or (501) 321-2277.

Excursions

Ouachita National Forest
Hot Springs, Arkansas

Pine-hardwood forest blankets the Ouachita Mountains, and water abounds in lakes, springs, waterfalls, and the Ouachita River. Contains six wilderness areas. 1.8 million acres, part in Oklahoma. Hiking, boating, boat ramp, fishing, horseback riding, hunting, water sports. 24 campgrounds, picnic areas, handicapped access. Open all year. Entrance on US 270, about 5 miles west of Hot Springs NP. (501) 321-5202.

Holla Bend National Wildlife Refuge
Dardanelle, Arkansas

Wintering bald eagles and immense flocks of migratory waterfowl share this site along the Arkansas River. 7,055 acres. Hiking, boating, fishing, hunting, scenic drives. Boat ramp. Open year-round, dawn to dusk. Off Ark. 154, about 60 miles from Hot Springs NP. (479) 229-4300.

Ozark National Forest
Russellville, Arkansas

Oak, hickory, and pine cover the high Ozark mountain bluffs. Many streams and lakes offer excellent fishing. Features Blanchard Springs Caverns and five wilderness areas. 1.2 million acres. Hiking, boating, fishing, hunting, horseback riding, scenic drives, water sports. 359 campsites, 9 cabins, boat ramp, picnic areas, handicapped access. Open year-round, including some of the campsites. Information in Russellville on US 64, 80 miles north of Hot Springs NP. (479) 968-2354.

Buffalo National River
Harrison, Arkansas

This park preserves 135 miles of the Buffalo River and adjacent lands. White water on upper river, calmer stretches on lower. 95,700 acres. Boating, fishing, hunting, swimming. 14 campgrounds, food services, picnic areas. Open all year, including most campsites. Headquarters at Harrison off Ark. 7, about 170 miles from Hot Springs NP. (870) 741-5443.

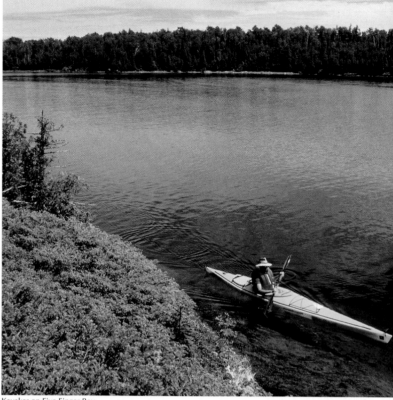

Kayaker on Five Finger Bay

Isle Royale

Michigan

Established April 3, 1940

571,790 acres

Out of the vastness of Lake Superior rises an island known more for its immigrant wolves and moose than for its splendors as a park. But the people who discover Isle Royale treat this isolated realm like no other park: Isle Royale visitors typically stay there 3.5 days, while the average visit to a national park is about 4 hours.

Most people get to the 45-mile-long island aboard a commercial or Park Service boat. As soon as they touch land in this wilderness park, they are on their own. They must pack in what they need and carry out their refuse.

This is rough, untamed country. Waterways may be fogbound and trails muddy. Blackflies and mosquitoes may descend upon hikers in swarms. And, because campsites cannot be reserved, a backpacker is never certain where the day's trek may end.

"It's not like deciding to drive into Yellowstone, see Old Faithful, and drive out," a ranger says. In an entire year Isle Royale gets fewer people than Yellowstone sees in a day.

Everyone who lands on Isle Royale—even day-trippers—must stop near dockside to hear a ranger talk about low-impact hiking and camping. For example, water must be boiled for 2 minutes or filtered; chemical purifiers will not wipe out tapeworm cysts.

Human hikers share trails with wolves and moose, the island's most famous inhabitants. They are descendants of the mainlanders that made Isle Royale an unexpected ark—moose presumably by swimming to it in the

Information & Activities p. 77. Isle Royale is 56 miles from the Michigan mainland, 18 miles from Minnesota's shore, 2 hours or 22 miles from Grand Portage. Airports: Houghton, Michigan; Duluth, Minnesota.

When to Go

Late June to September; park closes from November to mid-April. Mosquitoes, blackflies, gnats are most pesky in June and July. Summer can be cool (40°F at night). Blueberries and thimbleberries ripen in late July and August.

How to Visit

Although 1-day visits are feasible at **Rock Harbor** or **Windigo,** you need a longer stay to appreciate the wild beauty of Isle Royale. A 1-day visitor must sandwich a couple of hours of sight-seeing between boat arrival and departure. Voyages take 2 to 6.5 hours, depending on the starting point. The best way to see the park is to backpack to campsites strung along the park's 165 miles of trails. Noncampers who plan well ahead can reserve lodgings at Rock Harbor and explore on tour boats and on foot.

Windigo
a full day

Take the *Wenonah,* a concessioner passenger boat that makes the trip from Grand Portage, Minnesota, in 3 hours, the shortest from any port serving Isle Royale. On the way into fjordlike **Washington Harbor,** watch for the buoy marking the resting place

early 1900s; wolves likely by walking across the ice between 1945 and 1950. Scientists have been studying the interplay of predator and prey since 1958.

On the trails, all you can expect to see are the animals' tracks and droppings, although quietly grazing moose do surprise hikers, particularly in swamps or dense forest. On beaver ponds you may spot the rippling Vs of the ponds' creators. At campsites watch for fox looking for a hand-out. Remember: Feeding the animals is illegal. It is not healthy for them and increases the likelihood that they will scavenge for people's food and equipment.

How to Get There

Make reservations well in advance for passenger boats from Houghton or Copper Harbor, Michigan, or Grand Portage, Minnesota. The port you pick will determine the length of your visit. Interpretive programs are held aboard the *Ranger III* between Houghton and Isle Royale. For information about boats and charter seaplane service, see

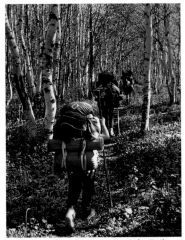

Backpacking along the Greenstone Ridge Trail

of the *America,* a 183-foot lake steamer that went down in 1928; the wreck rests at a sharp angle, its ghostly bow about 2 feet below the surface. Scuba divers, with permits, frequently prowl this and the other nine major wrecks around Isle Royale.

As soon as you land, check at the ranger station for the the next **Windigo Nature Walk,** a 1-hour ramble around this western entrance to the park that explores many of the area's natural and cultural resources.

If you miss the ranger-guided walk, try the **Windigo Nature Trail,** a 1.25-mile loop that shows the power that Lake Superior exerts on an island molded by fire and ice. You'll learn how the island was born: As glacial ice retreated some 10,000 years ago, Isle Royale rose above what would become Lake Superior. Gouges in the barren rocks became lakes. Early migrants—lichens, mosses, birdborne seeds—drifted into cracks and crannies, beginning the long work of building soil. Animals also found their way onto Isle Royale, and an ecosystem emerged. It still evolves, with some animals appearing, as did the wolves and moose, and some animals disappearing, as did caribou and coyotes. Be sure to take the short

side trip to the fenced-in **Moose Exclosure,** which shows how differently a forest grows when moose don't munch on it. Your stay—about 2.5 hours—will depend on your boat's schedule. So you may have time to stroll westward a while along the **Feldtmann Lake Trail.** This shoreline stretch gives you a view of **Beaver Island** and the harbor's forested northern shore.

Rock Harbor

1 or more days

A 1-day visit to Rock Harbor, the park's eastern gateway, can be tight. The voyage aboard *Isle Royale Queen III* from Copper Harbor takes about 4.5 hours. You have 2.5 hours to explore the Rock Harbor area.

If you can stay longer and aren't a backpacker, Rock Harbor offers many relatively easy sojourns. But make advance reservations at the Rock Harbor Lodge (see **Information & Activities** p. 77). From there you can set out for a choice of adventures.

Begin with a walk along **Stoll Trail,** a 4-mile loop that starts at Rock Harbor Lodge and winds through forest and plank-pathed bog. After about half a mile, you'll come to an area where

Bull moose feeding on water plants

Indians once chipped away, stone on stone, at shallow mining pits to extract outcrops of copper. Unmarked, these pits are hard to detect. Mining here began around 2500 B.C. and continued for at least 1,500 years. The copper, traded along the upper Mississippi Valley, was formed into fishhooks, knives, and awls. More than a thousand mining pits have been found on Isle Royale.

Continue another 1.5 miles, mostly along a rocky shore, to craggy **Scoville**

Point, a fine spot for viewing some of the roughly 200 rocky islets that form the Isle Royale archipelago. On the way back you can switch to a branch trail that clings to the forested shore of **Tobin Harbor.** As the trail nears the lodge, you can see traces of **Smithwick Mine,** one of many relics of 19th-century mining ventures.

For a small round-trip fee you can take a shuttle boat from Rock Harbor across a half mile of usually calm water to **Raspberry Island,** where a 1-mile trail introduces you to a boreal forest—white spruce, balsam fir, paper birch, aspen—and a bog. You'll also see a pit dug in 1848 in a vain search for copper. Bring a picnic.

For another fee a boat takes you on a half-day, guided tour into history. The first stop is **Edisen Fishery,** which belonged to the late Pete Edisen, one of the last commercial fishermen on the island. The Park Service has restored his jumble of moss-chinked log cabins and shacks made of odds and ends. Here park employees demonstrate mid-20th-century fishing techniques for visitors, and their catch makes it to Rock Harbor Lodge. A short trail leads to the **Rock Harbor Lighthouse,** which contains a maritime exhibit. Erected in 1855 to guide ore ships, the lighthouse closed in 1859 when the mines shut down and reopened between 1874 and 1879 during a second mining venture.

Into the Backcountry

3 to 5 days

To savor Isle Royale's isolated grandeur you must venture into the island's great beyond. Plan your 3- or 5-day stay around passenger boat arrivals and departures.

A sample 5-day itinerary: Arrive at Rock Harbor on Monday aboard the *Isle Royale Queen III* and hike southwest along the **Rock Harbor Trail** that courses forest, bog, and slanted rocks and roots. At not quite 2 miles, look for a sign to **Suzy's Cave,** about 80 yards up a side trail. The cave is an unusual, water-carved arch. At 3 miles is Three Mile Campground. Stay here and head out next morning on the 4.5-mile shore trail to **Daisy Farm;** in this spot daisies have flourished where vegetables never would.

You can camp here for 3 days and start back early Friday to meet the returning *Queen.* Or you can split the hike into 2 days by spending Thursday night at Three Mile Campground.

While at Daisy Farm, climb **Mount Ojibway Trail,** a moderate 1.75-mile ascent up the 1,136-foot mountain, which is topped by a lookout tower. You're welcome to climb as far as the cabin, which houses a solar-powered, air-monitoring station. The Park Service runs a network of such monitors to check on air quality in 65 national park areas. From the tower take the **Greenstone Ridge Trail,** which runs about 40 miles along the backbone of the island. About 1.5 miles west of the tower look for the wooden post marking the **Daisy Farm Trail,** which winds back to the campground.

The Wolves of Isle Royale

Visitors to Isle Royale probably will never see a gray wolf. Wolves live in packs as social animals, but avoid people. Only the dominant male and female—the alpha pair—mate and produce young. Others help protect and feed the pups born each spring.

Hundreds of thousands of wolves once roamed North America. But early settlers killed or drove away most of them. Today North America has only about 60,000 gray wolves, principally in Canada and Alaska.

When the first wolves arrived on Isle Royale, between 1945 and 1950, presumably by crossing frozen Lake Superior, they found a growing moose herd with no natural predators. The wolves hunted the old, the young, and the sickly. Both species prospered, the wolves increasing to 50 in 4 packs.

By 1980 a smaller moose herd provided few easy targets, and the wolf population began to fall. As moose numbers

Gray wolf

rose, the wolves' decline mysteriously continued. Recently, the relationship has become more in sync, with both moose and wolf populations declining, due largely in part to a trend of dry summers and mild winters.

Information & Activities

Headquarters
800 East Lakeshore Dr., Houghton, MI 49931. Phone (906) 482-0984. www.nps.gov/isro

Seasons & Accessibility
Park open mid-April through October; can be reached by boat or seaplane only; full services available mid-June through August. $4 per day fee. Weather and rough waters may delay departures; allow extra time. Mainland headquarters open year-round.

Boat & Seaplane Information
Reservations required (one to two months in advance suggested).

Write or call headquarters for boat schedule from Houghton to Rock Harbor. (The Park Service's boat, *Ranger III*, will transport boats 20 feet and under between those points.)

For boats from Copper Harbor to Rock Harbor, write to the Royale Line, Box 24, Copper Harbor, MI 49918, or call (906) 289-4437. For boats from Grand Portage to Windigo and Rock Harbor write to GPIR Transport Lines, 1507 N. 1st St., Superior, WI 54880, or call (715) 392-2100.

Visitor & Information Centers
Windigo Visitor Center at west end of island, **Rock Harbor Visitor Center** at east end. Both open daily all season. Phone park headquarters for information.

Pets
Not allowed on boats or within park boundaries, which extend 4.5 miles into Lake Superior.

Facilities for Disabled
Park headquarters at Houghton, Rock Harbor Lodge, both visitor centers, and a campsite at Daisy Farm are wheelchair accessible. Boats to island require assistance.

Things to Do
Free naturalist-led nature walks and evening programs. Canoe tour; lighthouse, copper mine, and Edisen Fishery tours; and films. Also, boating (motorized crafts permitted on Lake Superior only), canoeing (rentals at Windigo and Rock Harbor; permit required), hiking, scuba diving, fishing (license required for Lake Superior only), boat cruises to the outer islands.

Special Advisories
● Expect sudden squalls and rough seas on Lake Superior. Do not attempt to take boats under 20 feet across it. Have the park service transport small boats; see above.

● No public phone service in the park.

Camping
Thirty-six backcountry camping areas; 1-day to 5-day limit. Camping allowed from mid-April through October. First come, first served. No fees. Permit required; available at ranger stations. Seventeen of the areas permit group camping; contact park headquarters for information.

Hotels, Motels, & Inns
(unless otherwise noted, rates are for 2 persons in a double room, high season)
INSIDE THE PARK:
Rock Harbor Lodge P.O. Box 605, Houghton, MI 49931. (906) 337-4993. From Oct. to April write c/o Mammoth Cave, KY 42259. (270) 773-2191. 60 lodge rooms. $203 with meals. 20 cabins with kitchenettes $130. Restaurant. Open mid-June to mid-Sept.
OUTSIDE THE PARK:
In Copper Harbor, MI 49918:
Bella Vista Motel P.O. Box 26. (906) 289-4213. 30 units. $42-$60. Open May through Oct.
Keweenaw Mountain Lodge US 41. (906) 289-4403. 42 units. $67. Cottages $87. Rest. Open May to mid-Oct.
Lake Fanny Hooe Resort & Campground 505 2nd St. (off US 41) (800) 426-4451. 17 units. $65-$80. 64 campsites. $20-$30. Open mid-May to mid-Oct.
In Grand Portage, MN 55605:
Grand Portage Lodge & Casino US 61 and Marina Rd. (800) 543-1384 or (218) 475-2401. 100 units. $66.50. Pool, rest.
In Houghton, MI 49931:
Best Western-Franklin Square Inn 820 Shelden Ave. (888) 487-1700 or (906) 487-1700. 104 units. $104. AC, pool, restaurant.
Best Western King's Inn 215 Shelden Ave. (800) 528-1234 or (906) 482-5000. 69 units. $75. AC, pool.

Excursions

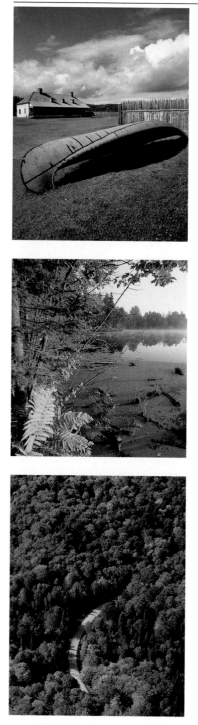

Grand Portage National Monument
Grand Portage, Minnesota

In the 18th and 19th centuries, fur traders called voyageurs converged at this central supply depot of the North West Company. Visitors can tour the reconstructed stockade, great hall, kitchen, and canoe warehouse. Open late May to early Oct. The Grand Portage Trail, open all year, follows the route used by voyageurs who portaged their furs almost 9 miles to avoid the rapids and falls of the Pigeon River. 710 acres. Hiking, historic exhibits, cross-country skiing, snowshoeing. Handi-capped access. Off US 61, about 22 miles from Isle Royale NP by boat to Grand Portage. (218) 387-2788.

Chequamegon-Nicolet National Forest
Park Falls, Wisconsin

Wisconsin's largest national forest, Chequamegon (Sho-WAH-ma-gon) means "place of shallow water." Laced with many lakes, streams, and a river, the forest is a lush medley of spruce, maple, aspen, and pine. 1.5 million acres. Bird-watching, boating, hunting, scenic drives, nature study, photography, cross-country skiing, snowshoeing. Campgrounds, picnic areas. Chequamegon headquarters on Wisc. 13, 220 miles from Isle Royale NP. Open year-round. (715) 762-2461.

Hiawatha National Forest
Escanaba, Michigan

In two units, this mixed evergreen-and-hardwood forest dotted with lakes descends to the shores of Lake Superior, Lake Michigan, and Lake Huron. Con-tains six wilderness areas and a section of the North Country National Scenic Trail. 860,000 acres. Boating, fishing, horseback riding, hunting, scenic dri-ves, winter sports, water sports. 25 campgrounds, handicapped access. Open all year; most campsites open mid-May to mid-Sept. Information at Rapid River, Manistique, Munising, and other locations. More than 300 miles from Isle Royale NP (via Michigan-side ferry). (906) 786-4062.

Apostle Islands National Lakeshore

Bayfield, Wisconsin

This national lakeshore encompasses 21 of the 22 remote, densely forested Apostle Islands and 12 miles of Lake Superior shoreline. Access to islands by boat; commercial and charter boats, charter fishing trips available. 42,160 acres. Hiking, boating, fishing, winter sports, water sports, sea kayaking. 65 campsites (permits required), picnic areas, handicapped access. Open year-round, including campsites. Visitor center in Bayfield near Wisc. 13, about 250 miles from Isle Royale NP (Michigan-side ferry). (715) 779-3397.

Pictured Rocks National Lakeshore

Munising, Michigan

Sandstone cliffs sculptured by nature into formations resembling castles and palisades give this first national lakeshore (1966) its name. The site also features extensive dunes and banks, sand beaches, forests, inland lakes, streams, and waterfalls. 71,400 acres. Hiking, boating, backpacking, fishing, hunting, winter sports, water sports. 66 campsites, picnic areas, handicapped access. Open year-round; campsites open mid-May to Oct. Visitor center at Munising on Mich. 28, about 335 miles from Isle Royale NP (via Michigan-side ferry). (906) 387-3700 or 2607.

Ottawa National Forest

Ironwood, Michigan

Lakes, streams, rivers, and waterfalls abound in this isolated ski-country forest. Also features three wilderness areas, Black River Harbor Recreation Area, and the North Country National Scenic Trail. Nearly one million acres. Hiking, canoeing, kayaking, mountain biking, fishing, hunting, winter sports. 26 campgrounds, boat ramp, picnic areas, handicapped access. Open all year, campsites May through Nov. Visitor center in Watersmeet on US 2, about 140 miles from Isle Royale NP (via Michigan-side ferry). (906) 932-1330.

Torch tossing—no longer done—to demonstrate 19th-century way of lighting caves

Mammoth Cave

Kentucky

Established July 1, 1941

52,830 acres

Under a swath of Kentucky hills and hollows is a limestone labyrinth that became the heartland of a national park. The surface of Mammoth Cave National Park encompasses about 80 square miles. No one knows how big the underside is. More than 350 miles of the five-level cave system have been mapped, and new caves are continually being discovered. Two layers of stone underlie Mammoth's hilly woodlands. A sandstone and shale cap, as thick as 50 feet in places, acts as an umbrella over limestone ridges. The umbrella leaks at places called sinkholes, from which surface water makes its way underground, eroding the limestone into a honeycomb of caverns.

Mammoth, the world's longest known cave system, a United Nations World Heritage site and the core area of an international biosphere reserve, still is as "grand, gloomy, and peculiar" as it was when Stephen Bishop, a young slave and early guide, described it. By a flickering lard-oil lamp he found and mapped some of Mammoth's passages. Bishop died in 1857. His grave, like his life, is part of Mammoth; it lies in the Old Guide's Cemetery near the entrance.

Most visitors see the eerie beauty of the caverns on some of the 10 miles of passages available for tours. Rangers dispense geological lore and tell tales about real and imagined happenings 200 or 300 feet down. The tours are hikes inside the Earth; uphill stretches can be hard going for some visitors. Few seem frightened; people terrified

70 to the park. Don't be misled by signs proclaiming commercial "mammoth" caves. Airports: Nashville and Louisville.

When to Go

All-year park. Underground, all days are about the same; temperatures in interior passages fluctuate from the mid-50s to the low 60s. Summer brings the most people, and frequent tours are offered. Though there are fewer tours the rest of the year, they are less crowded.

How to Visit

The tours vary greatly; pick ones to fit your time and stamina. All require you to buy a ticket. Reservations are strongly advised in summer, on holidays, and on spring and fall weekends. For a half-day visit, you might take the **Historic Tour,** which combines geology with Mammoth's rich history, or the **Introduction to Caving Tour.** If you plan to stay longer, consider the fairly strenuous **Grand Avenue Tour** (there are three steep hills, each nearly 90 feet high). To enjoy the caves safely and comfortably, wear shoes with nonskid soles and take a jacket. Top off your underground trips with a river trip or a walk on the **River Styx Spring Trail.**

The least arduous cave tour (0.25 mile, 75 minutes) is the **Travertine Tour.** A modified version of the **Frozen Niagara Tour,** it has only 18 steps each way (plus an optional 49) and is designed for visitors who want a short and easy trip. The toughest challenge is the 5-mile, 6-hour, belly-crawling **Wild Cave Tour,** offered daily in summer and weekends year-round. By reservation.

by darkness or tight spots naturally avoid caves. Rangers say they rarely have problems guiding the 500,000 men, women, and children who venture below yearly.

Mammoth does not glamorize the underworld with garish lighting. You never forget that you are deep in the Earth. And nowhere else can you get a better lesson in the totality of darkness and the miracle of light. Usually on a tour a ranger gathers everyone and, after a warning, switches off the lights. The darkness is sudden, absolute. Then the ranger lights a match and the tiny dot of light magically spreads, illuminating a circle of astonished faces.

How to Get There

Mammoth Cave, 9 miles northwest of I-65, is nearly equidistant (about 85 miles) between Louisville, Kentucky, and Nashville, Tennessee. From the south, take the exit at Park City and head northwest on Ky. 255 to the park; from the north, take the exit at Cave City and head northwest on Ky.

Historic Tour

2 miles; 2 hours

You leave daylight and walk into dimly lit gloom at the **Historic Entrance,** discovered by pioneers in the 1790s and by Indians thousands of years before. Near the entrance, at the **Rotunda,** 140 feet down, are relics of the cave's use as a nitrate mine. Slaves hauled in logs, built leaching vats, and filled them with cave dirt. Water, poured into the vats, trickled into a trough as brine. Two pipelines of hollowed-out logs carried water in and brine out. The residue, nitrate crystals, was used to make gunpowder, some of which found its way into the War of 1812.

Broadway, an underground avenue, leads to a spot called **Methodist Church,** where services may have been conducted in the 1800s. Farther on, **Booth's Amphitheater** recalls the visit of actor Edwin Booth. Here, Edwin, brother of assassin John Wilkes Booth, recited Hamlet's famous Soliloquy.

The **Bottomless Pit** looked that way to early visitors; it's 105 feet deep; looking up, you see its dome 38 feet above. (The top of a shaft is a dome, the bottom a pit.) On your way back toward the entrance you pass through **Fat Man's Misery,** a passage polished smooth by generations of squirming spelunkers. You emerge into **Great Relief Hall,** a large chamber where you are able to stand upright. Then back on the trail for the final spectacles: **Mammoth Dome**—192 feet from floor to ceiling—carved by water dripping through a sinkhole, and the **Ruins of Karnak,** a cluster of gleaming

limestone pillars that look like an Egyptian temple.

Introduction to Caving Tour

1 mile; about 3 hours

Cave exploring, otherwise known as "spelunking," can be fun and challenging. Led by park rangers, the Introduction to Caving Tour gives visitors 10 and up some first-hand experience in underground exploration. Offered daily in summer and on weekends in spring and fall, this trip involves hand-and-knees crawling, climbing, stooping, and even canyon-walking, with feet on different ledges and nothing but air in between. Straying from traditional walking paths, you will visit the twisting, convoluted canyons and crawls of **Fox Avenue,** emerging at **Frozen Niagara.** Along the way rangers will explain the geologic processes that result in the varied subterranean spaces. You will also learn the basic rules of safe caving, including what to do if you get lost.

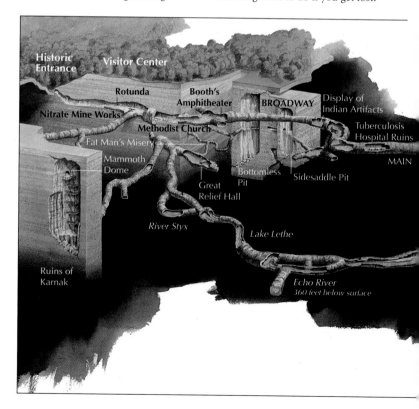

Historic Entrance · Visitor Center · Rotunda · Booth's Amphitheater · BROADWAY · Display of Indian Artifacts · Nitrate Mine Works · Methodist Church · Tuberculosis Hospital Ruins · Fat Man's Misery · Mammoth Dome · MAIN · Bottomless Pit · Sidesaddle Pit · Great Relief Hall · River Styx · Lake Lethe · Ruins of Karnak · Echo River 360 feet below surface

Crawling through a stretch of the Wild Cave Tour

Eyeless, colorless cave amphipod

Cave cricket on a Mammoth ceiling

Cave formations in the Frozen Niagara area

Helmets and lights are provided. Participants should bring knee pads (no Rollerblade type or hard plastic knee pads allowed). Long pants and boots required and gloves recommended. Rest rooms not available. Youths 10 to 15 must be accompanied by an adult.

Grand Avenue Tour
4 miles; 4.5 hours

The tour (likely to be very crowded in summer) begins with a 5- to 10-minute bus ride from the visitor center to the **Carmichael Entrance,** a concrete bunker and stairway that leads down to **Cleaveland Avenue,** a long tubular chamber tunneled out by a river. Its walls sparkle with flowery patches of gypsum. The white mineral crystallizes below the surface of the limestone from seeping moisture, then bursts out in blossomlike designs (it takes a thousand years for one cubic inch of gypsum to form).

About a mile beyond is the **Snowball Room,** where the tour stops for lunch. Food service here is limited to sandwiches, candy, and drinks. The snowball-like features on the roof, once a dull gray, have been cleaned of much of the black fungus that grows on cave formations, which is caused by the residue of phosphates found in the lint from visitors' clothing. Environmentalists have long been lobbying for the restaurant's removal.

Another river canyon, **Boone Avenue,** takes you 300 feet into the Earth along a passage so narrow you can touch both walls. The tour ends at **Frozen Niagara,** a massive cascade of flowstone—the legacy of mineral-laden water that seeped here, vanished, and left behind the shimmering stalactites and stalagmites. Such for-

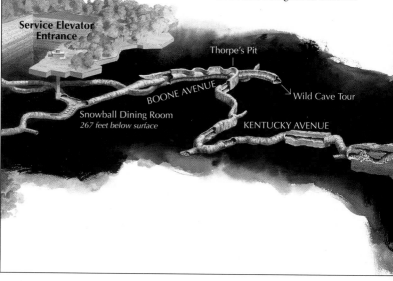

Service Elevator Entrance

Thorpe's Pit

BOONE AVENUE

Wild Cave Tour

Snowball Dining Room
267 feet below surface

KENTUCKY AVENUE

Scenic boat cruise on Green River

mations build up at the rate of about a cubic inch every 200 years.

Boat Trips & Hikes

To explore the **Green River,** which winds through the park, you can buy tickets at the visitor center for a sedate, 1-hour scenic boat cruise aboard the *Miss Green River II.* Or you can walk the **River Styx Spring Trail,** which leads to the river. The trail, which begins near the Historic Entrance to Mammoth, shows you the interplay between surface features and the cave's underworld. At **River Styx Spring** you can see water emerging from the cave and flowing into the Green River. Farther along the shore, you see **Cave Island,**

formed of waterborne logs, silt, and other materials.

Most of the park's 70 miles of trails are in the backcountry across the Green River. Within the park, there are no bridges over the river. You can drive onto the Green River Ferry at a crossing southwest of the visitor center, or Houchins Ferry at the western edge of the park; ferries have carried people and their vehicles across the river since the 1800s. Head north on **Green River Ferry Road** to Maple Spring Group Campground. A gravel road there leads to **Good Spring Church,** founded in 1842. From here you can walk 10 miles on a trail that winds through forests slowly reclaiming land once cleared by farming and logging.

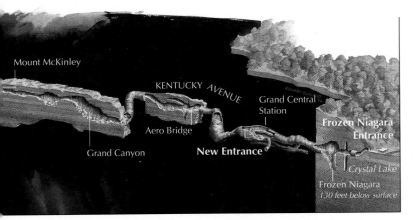

Mount McKinley

KENTUCKY AVENUE

Grand Central Station

Aero Bridge

Grand Canyon

New Entrance

Frozen Niagara Entrance

Crystal Lake

Frozen Niagara
130 feet below surface

Information & Activities

Headquarters
P.O. Box 7, Mammoth Cave, KY 42259.
Phone (270) 758-2328.
www.nps.gov/maca

Seasons & Accessibility
Park open year-round. Visitors must
join a tour to view the caves; tours
offered daily.

Visitor & Information Centers
Visitor center open daily. If space is
available, you can buy tickets there on
the day for all tours except Wild Cave,
for which advance reservations are
essential. But tours sell out quickly—
especially in summer, on holidays, and
on spring and fall weekends—so if at
all possible, buy tickets in advance
through the National Parks Reservation Service (see p. 11) or online at
www.nps.gov/maca.
  For more information on ranger-
led activities, call (270) 758-2328.

Entrance Fees
None. Fees required for tours, $4-$22
for adults and youths; free for children
under 6. Higher fees for special tours;
the Wild Cave Tour is $45 per person.

Pets
Permitted on leashes except in caves
and visitor center. Kennel facilities
through the Mammoth Cave Hotel
(see below).

Facilities for Disabled
Visitor center, some sites at Headquarters Campground, and rest rooms are
accessible. The 0.5-mile Pond Walk,
0.25-mile Heritage Trail, and 0.1-mile
Sand Cave Trail are fully accessible.

Things to Do
Naturalist-led activities: cave tours,
(12 in summer, 5 the rest of the year),
children's exploration program, nature
walks, evening programs. Nature trails,
fishing (no license required), horseback riding, Green River boat trip,
bicycling, occasional special events.

Special Advisory
• Cave tours are strenuous; talk with a
ranger before selecting one if you have
difficulty walking or trouble with your
heart or lungs. Wear sturdy shoes and
bring a jacket.

Overnight Backpacking
Permits required. They are free and
available at the visitor center.

Campgrounds
Three campgrounds, all with a 14-
day limit. Fees: $11-$25 per night.
Tent and RV sites at **Headquarters;** no
hookups; showers nearby for a fee;
open March through November. Tents
only at **Maple Spring Group Campgrounds,** open March through November; and at **Houchins Ferry,** open all
year, first come, first served. Use the
National Parks Reservation Service (see
p. 11) to reserve at Headquarters and
Maple Spring. Food services in park.

Hotels, Motels, & Inns
*(unless otherwise noted, rates are for 2
persons in a double room, high season)*
INSIDE THE PARK:
Mammoth Cave Hotel Mammoth
Cave, KY 42259. (270) 758-2225. 92
units. Hotel $68; motor lodge $75;
cottages $59. AC, restaurant.
OUTSIDE THE PARK:
In Cave City, KY 42127:
Best Western Kentucky Inn 1009 Doyle
Ave. (800) 528-1234 or (270) 773-3161.
51 units. $69-$79. AC, pool.
Days Inn Cave City 822 Mammoth
Cave St. (800) 329-7466 or (270) 773-
2151. 110 units. $66. AC, pool.
Howard Johnson 1006A Doyle Rd.
(800) 321-4245 or (270) 773-2181.
100 units. $80. AC, pool, restaurant,
playground.
Quality Inn 102 Gardner Ln. (800) 228-
5151 or (270) 773-3101. 105 units.
$69. AC, pool.
In Park City, KY 42160:
Park Mammoth Resort (I-65 and
US 31W) P.O. Box 307. (270) 749-4101.
92 units. $66. AC, pool, restaurant, and
2 golf courses.
In Bowling Green, KY 42104:
Bowling Green Bed & Breakfast 3313
Savannah Dr. (270) 781-3861. 3 rooms.
$60, includes breakfast. AC.
New's Inn 3160 Scottsville Rd. (270)
781-3460. 48 units. $44-$65. AC, pool.

*For additional accommodations, call
the Chambers of Commerce of Cave
City (270) 773-5159 and Bowling
Green (270) 781-3200.*

Excursions

Daniel Boone National Forest
Winchester, Kentucky

Impressed with eastern Kentucky's vegetative bounty, Daniel Boone called this land Eden. The region's geologic wonders also attracted the 18th-century pioneer: 150 natural sandstone arches in the Red River Gorge Geological Area, left by 70 million years of wind and water. One of these arches, Sky Bridge, offers a panoramic view of the gorge. The Sheltowee Trace National Recreation Trail, linking many of the forest's recreation sites, memorializes Boone's Indian name, Sheltowee, or "Big Turtle." Also contains two wilderness areas. 697,902 acres. Hiking, boating, fishing, hunting, off-road vehicle routes, scenic drives, water sports, horseback riding. Approximately 1,000 campsites, boat ramps, marinas, picnic areas, handicapped access. Open all year; most campsites open April through Nov. Information at London off I-75, about 125 miles from Mammoth Cave NP. (859) 745-3100.

Cumberland Gap National Historical Park
Middlesboro, Kentucky

Following the path trod by bison and deer, Indian hunters breached the great wall of the Appalachians long before westering pioneers "discovered" the gap in the mid-18th century. In 1775 Daniel Boone and his band of axmen forged the Wilderness Trail into Kentucky, opening the West to its first wave of expansion. More than 60 miles of hiking trails lead visitors to the Pinnacle Overlook, White Rocks, Sand Cave, and to the Hensley Settlement atop Brush Mountain—an early 20th-century effort at self-sufficient living. 20,281 acres, part in Virginia and Tennessee. Hiking, scenic drives, cave tours. 160 campsites, picnic areas, handicapped access. Open all year, including campsites. Visitor center at Middlesboro on US 25E, about 190 miles from Mammoth Cave NP. (606) 248-2817.

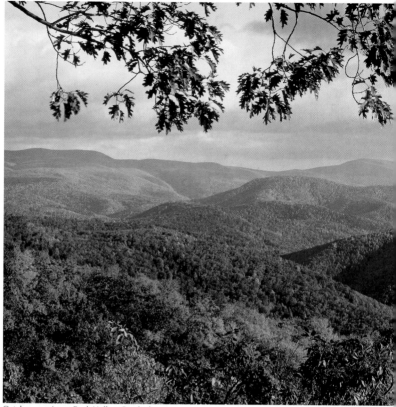

October morning at Buck Hollow Overlook

Shenandoah

Virginia

Established December 26, 1935

196,295 acres

Skyline Drive, which runs for 105 miles along the crest of the Blue Ridge mountains, is flanked by a rumpled panorama of forests and mountains. To many who travel the drive, the highway itself is a park, complete with numerous deer-sitings along the way. But the cars are passing the real Shenandoah. Nearly 500 miles of trails can be reached from Skyline Drive, and the Appalachian Trail roughly parallels it for nearly its entire length.

The long, narrow park flows outward, upward, and downward from the highway that splits it. The drive, following ridge trails walked by Indians and early settlers, transports visitors to a park built on a frontier that lingered into modern times.

Unlike most national parks, Shenandoah is a place where settlers lived for over a century. To create the park, Virginia state officials acquired 1,088 privately owned tracts and donated the land to the nation. Never before had a large, populated expanse of private land been converted into a national park. And never before had planners made a park of land so used by humans.

In the decade before the park opened, some 465 families moved or were moved from their cabins and resettled outside the proposed park boundaries. A few mountaineers, though, lived out their lives in the park and were buried in the secluded graveyards of Shenandoah's vanished settlements.

Much of Shenandoah consisted of farmland and second- or third-growth forests logged since the early 1700s.

Today the marks of lumbering, grazing, and farming have mostly disappeared, as forests have slowly come back.

Spring arrives first in the park valleys and then moves upward. Walking up a valley trail, a visitor can follow spring's path and see, in a single day, a variety of flowers that bloom elsewhere over a span of weeks.

How to Get There

From Washington, D.C. (about 70 miles away), take I-66 west to US 340, then head south to the park's Front Royal (North) Entrance. From Charlottesville, take I-64 to the Rockfish Gap (South) Entrance. From the west, take US 211 through Luray to the Thornton Gap (Middle) Entrance or head east on US 33 to the Swift Run Gap Entrance. Airports: Dulles International, near Washington, and Charlottesville.

When to Go

Of the nearly 2,000,000 people who visit the park each year, 400,000 go

in October to see the foliage. To avoid fall traffic jams, arrive early (preferably on a weekday), park at an overlook, and walk a trail. Snowstorms sometimes close Skyline Drive, the park's north-south highway. Facilities close in winter. Campgrounds fill on summer weekends, but day-trippers still have plenty of park. Wildflowers bloom from early spring to late fall.

How to Visit

On a day's drive-in visit, whatever entrance you use, get out and walk a trail. Even if you venture only a few hundred feet from an overlook, you will see a different Shenandoah beyond the scenic drive. For a longer stay, make a base at one place, such as **Big Meadows** or **Skyland,** and explore from there.

Skyline Drive from Front Royal to Big Meadows
51 miles; a full day

Not quite 5 miles south of the **Front Royal Entrance Station** is the **Dickey Ridge Visitor Center,** where exhibits introduce you to the park and its facilities along Skyline Drive. To walk a path of mountain life, cross the drive at the visitor center and start the self-guided, 1.3-mile **Fox Hollow Trail,** named for the family that first settled this hollow, as tenant farmers, in 1837. Their houses have disappeared, but you can see relics of their toil: large, well-stacked piles of rock cleared from farmland. Other stones—rough and dimly lettered—jut from the family graveyard.

Along the drive, stop at overlooks for views of the **Shenandoah Valley** and the peaks looming above it. The views are magnificent (except when pollution levels or fog mar visibility). At many overlooks there are signposts for well-marked trails. Daubs of paint on trees identify the trails: white, the **Appalachian Trail;** blue, a park hiking trail; yellow, a horse trail (hiking also allowed).

At Mathews Arm Campground, 22 miles from Front Royal, the easily accessible 1.75-mile **Traces Trail** takes you through an oak forest back to the time of the earliest white settlers. The traces are faint: an old road,

Ranger Station
Campground
Self-guiding Trail
Hiking Trail

0   5 km
0   5 mi

GEORGE
WASHINGTON
NATIONAL
FOREST

To 66 340
Front Royal
55
To 66
Front Royal (North)
Entrance Station
Appalachian Trail

649
604
522

Dickey Ridge
Visitor Center

Skyline
Drive
Hogwallow Flats
Overlook
630

Bentonville
613
Mt. Marshall
3,368 ft
Gravel Springs Gap
2,655 ft
Hogback Mt.
3,474 ft
Mathews
Arm
622
Piney River
Elkwallow
622
Pignut Mt.
2,530 ft
340
Jeremys Run
Overlook
654
Beahms Gap
2,485 ft
Three Sisters
2,085 ft
Pass Mt.
Sperryville
Pass Run
211
Panorama
Park Headquarters
Tunnel
Thornton Gap
Entrance Station
522
231
Luray
Appalachian
Trail
Hazel
Mountain
211
340
Corbin
Cabin
Pinnacles
Nicholson Hollow
Stony Man
4,011 ft
Pinnacle Peak
3,401 ft
600
707
601
Skyland
Highest Point on Drive
3,680 ft
Old Rag
3,268 ft
Crescent Rock Overlook
Hawksbill
4,051 ft
643
340 BUS 340
689
611
Stanley
Upper Hawksbill
Parking
600
231
Big Meadows
Byrd Visitor Center
Dark Hollow
Falls Parking
Rapidan Camp
(formerly Camp Hoover)
670
643
670
649
Banco
Skyline
Drive
Hazeltop
3,812 ft
Grindstone
Mountain
2,850 ft
Bearfence
Mountain

South Fork Shenandoah
Hawksbill Creek
Whiteoak Canyon
Rose
Hughes
Rapidan

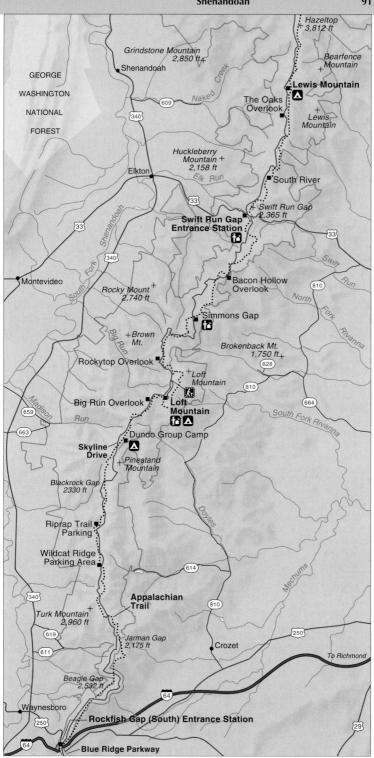

Hazeltop
3,812 ft

Grindstone Mountain
2,850 ft

Shenandoah

Bearfence
Mountain

Lewis Mountain

GEORGE

WASHINGTON

NATIONAL

The Oaks
Overlook

FOREST

Lewis
Mountain

Naked Creek

609

340

Huckleberry
Mountain
2,158 ft

South River

Elkton

Elk Run

33

Swift Run Gap
2,365 ft

**Swift Run Gap
Entrance Station**

33

33

810

Shenandoah

340

Montevideo

Rocky Mount
2,740 ft

Bacon Hollow
Overlook

North Fork Rivanna

South Fork

Brown
Mt.

Simmons Gap

Big Run

Brokenback Mt.
1,750 ft

Rockytop Overlook

628

Loft
Mountain

810

Big Run Overlook

**Loft
Mountain**

664

659

Madison Run

South Fork Rivanna

663

Dundo Group Camp

**Skyline
Drive**

Pinestand
Mountain

Blackrock Gap
2330 ft

Doyles

Riprap Trail
Parking

Wildcat Ridge
Parking Area

614

340

**Appalachian
Trail**

810

Turk Mountain
2,960 ft

619

Jarman Gap
2,175 ft

Crozet

250

Mechums

To Richmond

611

Beagle Gap
2,532 ft

64

Waynesboro

250

Rockfish Gap (South) Entrance Station

29

64

Blue Ridge Parkway

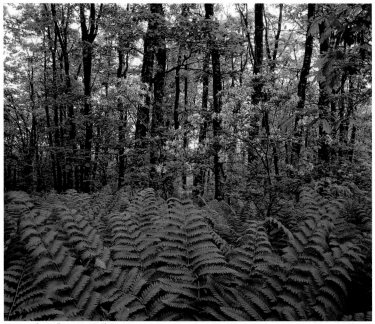

Ferns on forest floor near Swift Run Gap

trees, tumbling stone walls.

For a more rugged hike into the past, stop at the parking area past milepost 37 and take the **Corbin Cabin Cutoff Trail.** The steep trip (1.5 miles each way) ends at **Corbin Cabin,** a typical mountain residence. In 1909 George Corbin cut and hewed logs and, with the help of neighbors, built this cabin. The Corbin family, like many others, lived on what they grew or made, including brandy from peaches and apples. The Potomac Appalachian Trail Club maintains the cabin for rent to members and the public, one of six rustic cabins scattered through the park's backcountry.

Skyland (near milepost 42) dates from the 1890s. The resort, which includes guest rooms, dining room, and cabins, is open from April through November. The 1.5-mile **Stony Man Nature Trail** begins near the parking area and, climbing about 340 feet, reaches the cliffs of **Stony Man's** summit (4,011 feet, second highest point in the park). From an outcrop on the cliffs you get a sweeping view. The trail loops back around to the start.

The **Limberlost Trail** (near milepost 43), a gently winding walkway of crushed green stone, passes through old-growth hemlocks before crossing over Whiteoak Canyon Run on a wooden bridge. The 1.3-mile trail is wheelchair accessible with numerous benches located at intervals for hikers to rest and contemplate their surroundings.

Stop at **Crescent Rock Overlook** (near milepost 44) for a look at **Hawksbill Mountain,** at 4,051 feet the highest point in park. Then, 6 miles farther, stop at the parking area for the **Dark Hollow Falls Trail,** a 1.5-mile round-trip to a waterfall, the shortest route to any falls in the park. The steep trail takes you past clusters of ferns, mosses, and liverworts. Split-log benches offer a rest en route.

Big Meadows (milepost 51) has trails, a campground, a lodge, facilities for visitors, and the **Byrd Visitor Center,** where changing exhibits tell the stories of the park.

Today the defoliated trees you see attest to the presence of a natural phenomenon—the gypsy moth—among other pests and diseases. But, unlike the chestnut blight early in the 20th century, the gypsy moths will not wipe out an entire species. Healthy trees will renew the forest in future decades.

You can end your day at Big Meadows with a wildflower walk through the gently undulating meadowlands that give the area its name. On the way, you may startle a deer or two (or even a black bear!).

Corbin Cabin, relic of a mountaineer past

Scarlet tanager in summer plumage

Rapidan Camp to Rockfish Gap

54 miles; a full day

Park at the west side of Skyline Drive at **Milam Gap** (mile 52.8). Cross the drive to a trail marker to begin the 4-mile round-trip to Rapidan Camp (formerly Camp Hoover). You walk a short distance on the Appalachian Trail, then turn left onto the **Mill Prong Trail,** which passes through a wooded tract, descends to a small waterfall, crosses three streams, and meets a road. Turn right and continue toward the cabins of **Rapidan Camp,** a national historic landmark. The camp satisfied President Herbert Hoover's three requirements for a hideaway: It had to be within 100 miles of Washington, have a trout stream, and be high enough to discourage mosquitoes. The President and First Lady used the camp as a summer White House in 1931. You can walk around and look at the out-side of the cabins (the exteriors have recently been restored to their 1931 appearance, and interior work is scheduled for completion by fall 2003). President Hoover's cabin can be visited during the summer and fall on tours from the Byrd Visitor Center.

An 0.8-mile, 1.5-hour hike to **Bearfence Mountain** starts at mile 56.4 before the Lewis Mountain Campground. It demands some scrambling over rocks but finally rewards with a spectacular 360-degree view. The easy 2-mile round-trip to the **Pocosin Mission,** which starts past milepost 59, takes you to the ruins of a missionary church and graveyard.

The **Swift Run Gap Entrance** (near milepost 65) is an old Blue Ridge crossing now paved by US 33. In May, wildflower seekers climb the nearby **Hightop Summit Trail** (3 miles round-trip) to see wildflowers.

Loft Mountain (near milepost 79), with campground and information center, is a southern base for exploring the park. Near a service complex along Skyline Drive, look for the trailhead to the **Frazier Discovery Trail,** a 1.5-mile loop that demonstrates how pasture is evolving back into forest. After the demise of the chestnut trees, other trees and shrubs began repopulating the land. You can see it happening here, and from a rocky vantage point on the trail you can also see it happening on a grand scale throughout the park. Two summit viewpoints offer views to the west, over the Shenandoah Valley to undulating peaks beyond.

At **Rockfish Gap,** near the **Rockfish Entrance Station,** a bison path evolved into a colonial road, and later a modern highway. Here, at the park's southern end, begins the **Blue Ridge Parkway,** a National Park Service highway that connects Shenandoah and Great Smoky Mountains NPs.

Information & Activities

Headquarters
3655 US 211E, Luray, VA 22835. Phone (540) 999-3500. www.nps.gov/shen

Seasons & Accessibility
Park open year-round. For recorded information call (540) 999-3500. Skyline Drive may close temporarily during heavy snow or hazardous ice conditions. For weather and road information, call (540) 999-3500.

Visitor & Information Centers
Dickey Ridge Visitor Center, near North Entrance, open daily late March through November. **Byrd Visitor Center** at Big Meadows, near center of park, open daily late March through November. Opening and closing dates vary each year.

Entrance Fee
$10 per car allows 7-day access.

Pets
Must be kept on leash; not allowed on posted trails or in park buildings.

Facilities for Disabled
Visitor centers, amphitheaters, picnic areas, and campgrounds are accessible to wheelchairs. Rest rooms, lodges, and restaurants are also accessible. The Limberlost Trail is handicapped accessible.

Things to Do
Free ranger-led activities: interpretive walks, talks, evening programs (summer through fall only). Also available, fishing, horseback riding, hiking on some 500 miles of trails.

Special Advisories
● Rocks around waterfalls are very slippery and dangerous.
● Pull off the road completely when stopping for a view.
● Do not feed or chase wildlife.

Overnight Backpacking
Permits required and available free of charge from headquarters, visitor centers, and entrance stations.

Campgrounds
Five campgrounds, all with 14-day limit. **Mathews Arm, Lewis Mountain,** and **Loft Mountain** open mid-May through October, first come, first served. **Big Meadows** open late March through November. Reservations recommended from Memorial Day weekend through October, available through the National Parks Reservation Service (see p. 11); other times, first come, first served. Fees $14-$17 per night. Tent and RV sites; no hookups. Camp stores and restaurants near the campground. **Dundo Group Campground,** open April through November. $30 a night, reservations required. Call the National Parks Reservation Service (see p. 11), or write Shenandoah National Park, Swift Run Entrance Station, Rte. 3, Box 311, Elkton, VA 22827. Showers and laundry facilities (except at Mathews Arm and Dundo).

Hotels, Motels, & Inns
(unless otherwise noted, rates are for 2 persons in a double room, high season)
INSIDE THE PARK:
P.O. Box 727, Luray, VA 22835. (800) 999-4714 or (540) 743-5108.
Big Meadows Lodge (mile 51.3) Lodge rooms $68-$129; cabins $75-$87; suites $105-$142. Restaurant. Late April through October.
Lewis Mountain Cabin (mile 57.6) Ten cabins with outdoor grills. $62-$94. Mid-May through October.
Skyland Lodge (miles 41.7 and 42.5) 177 units. Lodge units $79-$122; suites $116-$170; cabins $53-$103. Restaurant. Early April through November.
OUTSIDE THE PARK:
In Front Royal, VA 22630:
Quality Inn 10 Commerce Ave. (800) 821-4488 or (540) 635-3161. 107 units. $75-$85. AC, pool, restaurant.
Woodward House on Manor Grade 413 S. Royal Ave. (800) 635-7011 or (540) 635-7010. 8 units. $95-$135, includes breakfast. AC.
In Sperryville, VA 22740:
Conyers House Inn and Stable 3131 Slate Mills Rd. (540) 987-8025. 7 units. $150-$300, includes breakfast. AC, restaurant.
In Stanley, VA 22851:
Jordan Hollow Farm Inn 326 Hawksbill Park Rd. (888) 418-7000 or (540) 778-2285. 15 rooms. $133-$190. AC, rest.
In Waynesboro, VA 22980:
The Inn at Afton I-64 at US 250. (800) 860-8559 or (540) 942-5201. 118 units. $83-$91. AC, pool, restaurant.

Excursions

George Washington & Jefferson National Forests
Harrisonburg and Roanoke, Virginia

These two national forests were administratively combined in 1995, together containing nearly 1.8 million acres of public land. **George Washington National Forest** flanks the Shenandoah Valley, rich in Civil War history. Excellent fishing and fall color. Contains six wilderness areas and 57 miles of Appalachian Trail. 1,065,232 acres in three sections, part in West Virginia. Boating, fishing, hiking, horseback riding, hunting, water sports. 807 campsites, food services, boat ramp, picnic areas, handicapped access. Open all year, including many campsites. Visitor center at Massanutten on US 211, about 8 miles from Shenandoah NP. (540) 265-5100.

In **Jefferson National Forest,** some 300 miles of the Appalachian Trail traverse mountains blanketed in hardwood, pine, and rhododendron. Streams and waterfalls abound. Contains 11 wilderness areas and Mount Rogers National Recreation Area. 720,431 acres, part in West Virginia and Kentucky. Hiking, boating, fishing, horseback riding, hunting, water sports. 670 campsites, picnic areas, boat ramp, handicapped access. Open all year, including some campsites. Information at USFS Roanoke headquarters, about 120 miles south of Shenandoah NP. (540) 265-5100.

Mason Neck National Wildlife Refuge
Lorton, Virginia

The nation's first refuge dedicated to the protection of the bald eagle lies on a peninsula in the Potomac River, near Washington, D.C. Hardwood forest and marsh combine to form ideal habitat or the eagles and for numerous other wildlife species such as great blue herons, wood ducks, bluebirds, beavers, and deer. 2,277 acres. Hiking, birdwatching. Open year-round during daylight hours. On Va. 242, about 75 miles from Shenandoah NP. (703) 490-4979.

Trunk Bay, renowned for its beauty

Virgin Islands

United States Virgin Islands

Established August 2, 1956

12,909 acres

High green hills dropping down to enchanting turquoise bays, white powdery beaches, coral reefs, and ruins that evoke an era of sugar and a tragic period of slavery all find protection on St. John, one of about a hundred specks of Caribbean land known as the Virgin Islands.

Despite its small size—19 square miles—St. John's wide range of rainfall and exposure give it surprising variety. More than 800 subtropical plant species grow in areas from moist, high-elevation forests to desertlike terrain to mangrove swamps, among them mangoes, soursops, turpentine trees, wild tamarind, century plants, and sea grapes. Around the island live the fringing coral reefs—beautiful,

complex, and exceedingly fragile communities of plants and animals, which St. John's famous beaches depend upon.

In 1493 Columbus sighted the large assemblage of islands and cays and named it after St. Ursula's legendary 11,000 virgins. Since then, Spain, France, Holland, England, Denmark, and the United States have controlled various islands at different times. The Danes began colonization in the 17th century, and in 1717 planters arrived on St. John. By mid-century 88 plantations had been established there; slaves stripped the steep hillsides of virgin growth and cultivated the cane. By the time the Danes abolished slavery in 1848, the sugar industry was doomed. A fallow, century-long period known as the "subsistence era" followed.

Fearful that the Germans might capture the islands during World War I, the United States bought St. John, St. Croix, St. Thomas, and about 50 smaller islands from Denmark for $25,000,000. In 1956 conservationist Laurance S. Rockefeller donated more than 5,000 acres for a national park on St. John; in 1962 the park acquired 5,650 undersea acres off the northern and southern coasts. Today, though its boundary includes three-quarters of St. John, the park owns only slightly more than half the island. Of increasing concern is the escalating pace of development on private inholdings inside its borders. It also feels pressure from the many cruise ships that disgorge large numbers of visitors at once, badly straining park resources. Some of the park's trails may be closed for maintenance work; ask at the visitor center.

When to Go
All-year park. High season is mid-December to mid-April.

How to Get There
By plane to Charlotte Amalie, St. Thomas, then taxi or bus to Red Hook, then ferry across Pillsbury Sound to Cruz Bay, a 20-minute ride. Or, try to catch one of the less frequently scheduled ferries from Charlotte Amalie—the boat takes 45 minutes, but the dock is much nearer the airport.

How to Visit
If you have only 1 day, drive the **North Shore Road** as far as the **Annaberg Sugar Mill Ruins,** taking time to stretch your legs along some seaside trails—and perhaps do a little snorkeling. Return via **Centerline Road,** stopping at the ruins of **Catherineberg Sugar Mill.** On a second day, consider hiking the **Reef Bay Trail,** explore the island's **East End,** visit **Saltpond Bay,** and walk to **Ram Head.** With more time, sign up for some of the excellent ranger-led tours and activities.

If you're driving yourself, be prepared for steep, often potholed roads with blind curves, and *stay on the left.* The speed limit is 20 mph. An alternative is to hire a taxi and guide.

North Shore Road-Centerline Road Loop
15 miles; 3 hours to a full day

Begin your visit with a stop at the park visitor center in **Cruz Bay** to pick up a map and a trail brochure, and to find out what ranger-led activities are scheduled. Head north out of town along the **North Shore Road** (Route 20). This road is in good condition but very steep in places. Near the top of the hill, pull off at the overlook for a bird's-eye view of the picturesque town and harbor, the many small adjacent islands, and the big island of **St. Thomas** across the sound. For an even better view of **St. John's West End,** climb **Caneel Hill**; the 0.8-mile, moderately strenuous trail begins a short distance ahead on the right, across the road from the Park Service sign. (Or save this hike for sunset, when it's cooler and the view from the hilltop spectacular.)

Stop at the next overlook a half mile farther along the road for a view of **Caneel Bay** and, to the northeast, the big island of **Jost van Dyke,** one of the British Virgins. Since the 1930s the site

ATLANTIC OCEAN

Lovango Cay

Ferries to Tortola, B.V.I.

Durloe Cays

Whistling Cay

Mary Point

Francis Bay

Maho Bay

Ma Cre

Hawksnest Point

Underwater Trail

Cinnamon Bay

Maho Bay

20

Peace Hill

Trunk Bay

Cinnamon Bay

20

Hawksnest Bay

Trunk Bay
North Shore Road

Ruins

Mamey Peak
1,147 ft

1

Hawksnest Bay

Caneel Bay

Biosphere Reserve Center

Lind Point

20

Caneel Hill
+719 ft

Catherineberg Sugar Mill (ruins)

10

Centerline Road

Camelberg Peak
+1,193 ft

108

Reef Bay

Cruz Bay

Cruz Bay

Visitor Center

Gift Hill Road

S T.   J O H N

Petroglyphs

Ferries to St. Thomas

104

104

+Gift Hill
827 ft

Reef Bay Sugar Mill (ruins)

Trail

Lamest Bay T

Great Cruz Bay

Reef Bay

PARK BOUNDARY

Rendezvous Bay

WHI CLIFF

Bovocoap Point

Dittlif Point

Ranger Station

Campground

Interpretive Trail

Primitive Road

Trail

CARIBBEAN   SEA

of a famous resort, Caneel Bay was a sugar plantation for most of the 18th and 19th centuries. Its name, both Dutch and Danish for "cinnamon," comes from the cinnamony leaves of the bay tree, a member of the myrtle family. (From the 1860s to the 1930s, oil from the leaves was used to make St. John Bay Rum cologne.)

The entrance to the Caneel Bay resort is down the hill on the left, past road marker 1.5. The land belongs to the park but is leased to the resort, owned until recently by the Rockefellers. To get a look at its lovely beaches and bays—and palm-studded grounds flowered with bougainvillea and pink oleander—walk the mostly level **Turtle Point Trail** around **Hawksnest Point,** which takes about an hour.

The resort management asks only that you register as a day guest at the front desk; ask there for directions to the trailhead.

From Caneel Bay the road climbs steeply and descends to **Hawksnest Beach,** where you can swim, snorkel, and picnic. Visitors tend to bypass this beach, but locals flock here on weekends. Exhibits describe the damage being done to the island's fragile reefs by pollutants, swimmers, snorkelers, and the anchors of careless boaters— and strongly urge you not to touch, stand, or sit on the coral.

One of the Caribbean's premier vistas awaits you a mile farther up the road. From the overlook, **Trunk Bay** with its lush palm-fringed crescent beach and dozens of bobbing

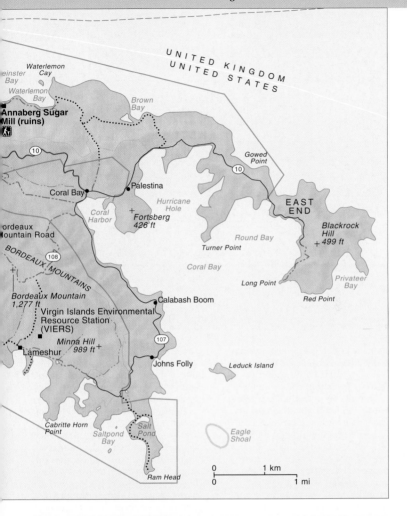

United Kingdom
United States

Waterlemon Cay

einster Bay

Waterlemon Bay

Annaberg Sugar Mill (ruins)

Brown Bay

10

Gowed Point

10

Coral Bay   Palestina

Hurricane Hole

EAST END

Coral Harbor   + Fortsberg 426 ft

Blackrock Hill + 499 ft

ordeaux ountain Road

Round Bay

Turner Point

BORDEAUX MOUNTAINS

108

Coral Bay

Long Point

Privateer Bay

Red Point

Bordeaux Mountain 1,277 ft

Calabash Boom

Virgin Islands Environmental Resource Station (VIERS)

107

Minna Hill 989 ft +

Lameshur

Johns Folly

Leduck Island

Cabritte Horn Point   Salt Pond

Saltpond Bay

Eagle Shoal

Ram Head

0   1 km
0   1 mi

Partly restored Annaberg Sugar Mill, built in the 18th century

Snorkelers bobbing toward a coral reef off Caneel Bay resort

sailboats lies before you. Off a point in the middle distance is **Whistling Cay,** where in the 19th century a customs shed stopped boats plying the passage between the Danish and British Virgins. Trunk Bay's beauty draws many visitors, especially on days when cruise ships are in. The park has set up an underwater nature trail for snorkelers here; some 16 plaques identify the reef's plants and animals. If you're a serious snorkeler, however, you might want to skip this reef for a less traveled one farther along.

Beyond Trunk Bay's entrance be prepared for the road to sharply steepen. Near the top of the hill is the multimillion-dollar development at **Peter Bay,** a private inholding that has been a model for preventing the sediment runoff that other developments have allowed. Park officials and environmentalists say that runoff damages the reefs and sea grass beds.

At **Cinnamon Bay** (road marker 4.5) are a campground and, across the road, the ruins of the Danish (first Dutch) Cinnamon Bay sugar factory, one of the island's oldest. Plaques along the 1-mile trail tell you its history and point out native trees such as bay, lime, teyer palm, and calabash, which produces a gourdlike fruit that's

carved into bowls. If you're lucky enough to be there for a tour led by one of the Virgin Islanders on the park staff, you'll learn some colorful local lore as well.

Continue down the road a half mile to yet another stunning, sweeping view—**Maho Bay, Francis Bay,** where sea turtles come to feed, and **Mary Point.** You'll see diving pelicans and frigate birds, which, to avoid waterlogging their own enormous wings, harass other seabirds for food. The red roofs visible in the trees belong to a house built in 1952 by an American eccentric named Ethel McCully, who swam ashore from a boat and stayed. Since no paved roads or automobiles existed on St. John then, donkeys hauled the materials from Cruz Bay— a 4-hour trip.

Down the hill, the road flattens, passing a stretch of beach on the left. Continue on for a mile to the road's end and then turn right toward **Annaberg.** On the right, you'll see a thick mangrove swamp, one of many on the island. Its large, tangled roots help protect the shoreline and provide a breeding ground for fish.

On the left, about 100 yards from the turnoff, look for the marker identifying one of the toxic manchineel trees common to the

Sea horse, a seldom seen Caribbean creature

Caribbean; Columbus called their green fruit "death apples." Do not stand under this tree in the rain: Runoff can raise painful blisters on your skin.

Just ahead is **Mary Creek** with a view of Mary Point. An important marine community inhabits the shallow reefs and sea grass beds of the creek, site of a weekly naturalist-led seashore walk. If you wade out (be sure to wear something on your feet), you can find brilliantly colored conchs, spiny black sea urchins, and brittle stars that regenerate their tentacles. Coral rocks host many tiny animals. Pick up and examine the rocks, but put them back as you found them.

From here consider an easy walk along the 0.8-mile **Leinster Bay Trail,** which follows the seashore east to **Waterlemon Bay** and some of the best snorkeling in the park. You can swim and snorkel off the sandy beach at the trail's end. Better yet if you have the stamina, walk out to the point and swim across the narrow channel to snorkel around little **Waterlemon Cay.**

Back at the Leinster Bay trailhead, park in the small lot and walk up the hill to the partially restored ruins of the **Annaberg Sugar Mill.** A quarter-mile self-guided walk introduces you to the slaves quarters, windmill, horse mill, oven, cistern, and factory that for much of two centuries produced raw sugar, molasses, and rum for Denmark. Native stone, ballast brick, and coral went into building the thick walls.

From the overlook you can see a number of other Virgin Islands across the narrows, including **Tortola,** largest of the British Virgins, and the dinosaur shape of Britain's **Great Thatch** on the left. In winter, humpback whales sometimes cruise by. Annaberg slaves reportedly tried to swim to Great Thatch after the British freed their slaves in 1833, 15 years ahead of the Danes. Before leaving the overlook, treat yourself to the scent of a frangipani blossom from the nearby tree.

To return to Cruz Bay, drive the more level **Centerline Road** (Route 10), watching out for blind curves. Slow speeds should pose no hardship, however: The views of the island's **East End** are truly spectacular. If you have time, look for the **Catherineberg Road** on the right after driving about 3 miles. A short way up this road are the ruins of the area's 18th-century **Catherineberg Sugar Mill.** The outer shell of the windmill has been restored, and there are 4-foot stone walls, handsome archways, a massive stone pillar, and some original beams to see.

East End: Coral Bay & Saltpond Bay

26 miles round-trip; at least a half day

Take Centerline Road (Route 10) out of Cruz Bay, stopping after nearly 3 miles at the Catherineberg Sugar Mill (see above), if you haven't already been there. About a half mile farther is the **Konge Vey Overlook,** where a wayside exhibit points out Jost van Dyke, Great Thatch, and other islands and bays to the north.

The popular **Reef Bay Trail** begins after another 1.25 miles. It descends into a steep V-shaped valley through moist, subtropical forest to dry forest to acacia scrub near the coast. Ruins of sugar estates can be seen along its 2.5 miles and nearby are some mysterious petroglyphs. Walk this trail at least partway to experience the lush forest, or even better, save it for the ranger-led trip ($15), when a boat meets you at the coast and spares you the hike back up.

Back in your car, continue on to the overlook near **Mamey Peak** for a lovely view of Coral Bay and the island's East End. The name of the bay comes not from the island's abundant coral but from an 18th-century Dutch corral *(kraal)* here. The Danes established their first plantations at this end of the island, among them the vast Estate Carolina, once the property of the king. They built a fort—called **Fort Frederik**—on **Fortsberg Hill** on the bay's eastern shore. In 1733 a bloody slave uprising began here, reputedly the first in the New

World. It would have succeeded—1,087 of the island's 1,295 inhabitants were slaves—had the French not sailed in to quell it.

Continue on Route 10 as it winds eastward outside the park to the village of **Coral Bay,** about 2 miles away. You may well see a mongoose scuttering across the road. Introduced a century ago to kill rats, the mongoose has multiplied explosively, to the detriment of some native island fauna. At Coral Bay, stop to see the handsome pink-roofed **Emmaus Church,** built by Moravian missionaries in the 1780s. If you continued on, you'd be rewarded with magnificent views of **Hurricane Hole, Round Bay,** and the British Virgins. But for now backtrack a short distance and turn left at the intersection of Route 108. Drive 4 miles along the coast to the trailhead for **Saltpond Bay** and a wilder part of the island.

About a fifth of a mile beyond the parking area, the horseshoe bay is fringed by a wide, sandy beach, gently lapped by transparent waters. Continue around the beach and onto the rocky 0.9-mile **Ram Head Trail** that winds up a promontory and down the other side. There a blue pebbly beach and an arid environment await you. Plants include several kinds of cactuses and the century plant, which takes 15 to 20 years to bloom, then dies.

Continue to the crest of the hill for a grand Caribbean view. Watch your footing and hold onto any children you've brought on this windswept point 200 feet above the sea. Here at **Ram Head** you'll be standing on rock that emerged some 108 million years ago, the oldest land on St. John.

Information & Activities

Headquarters
1300 Cruz Bay Creek, St. John, USVI 00830. Phone (340) 776-6201. www.nps.gov/viis

Seasons & Accessibility
Park open year-round. Access by boat. Climate does not vary much during the year, though summers can be hot. Hurricane season here runs typically from June through November.

Visitor Center
Cruz Bay Visitor Center, at west end of St. John, open daily all year. Call (340) 776-6201.

Entrance Fee
There is no entrance fee for the park. However, there is a user fee to enter Trunk Bay and Annaberg Mill ruins: $4 for adults; children 16 and under admitted free. $10 annual fee.

Pets
Not allowed on public beaches, in picnic areas, or in campgrounds. Permitted elsewhere on leashes.

Facilities for Disabled
Some ferries to St. John are accessible to wheelchairs, with assistance. The visitor center, several Cinnamon Bay campsites, and rest rooms there and at Trunk Bay and Hawksnest Bay are also accessible.

Things to Do
Free naturalist-led activities: interpretive talks and exhibits, nature and history walks, hikes, snorkel tours, cultural demonstrations, evening programs. Also available, self-guided nature and underwater trails, swimming, snorkeling, boating, fishing (no license needed), windsurfing, birdwatching, photography workshops, archaeology digs, occasional historic bus tours.

Overnight Backpacking
Not allowed in park.

Campgrounds
One park campground, **Cinnamon Bay;** 14-day limit December to mid-May; other times 21-day limit. Open all year. Reservations recom-mended; contact Cinnamon Bay Campground, P.O. Box 720, Cruz Bay, St. John, USVI 00831. (800) 539-9998 or (340) 776-6330. Nightly for 2 persons: $27 for bare sites; $80 for tents; $110-$140 for cottages. Cold showers. Food services.

Also, **Maho Bay;** reservations, Maho Bay Camp, 17-A E. 73rd St., New York, NY 10021. (800) 392-9004 or (212) 472-9453. 114 equipped tent-cottages, central baths. $110 per night December through April; $75 per night May through November. Reserve early for December to May.

Hotels, Motels, & Inns
(unless otherwise noted, rates are for 2 persons in a double room, high season)
On St. John, USVI 00831:
Caneel Bay P.O. Box 720, Cruz Bay. (800) 928-8889 or (340) 776-6111. 166 units. $450-$1,100. Pool, 4 restaurants.
Gallows Point Suite Resort P.O. Box 58. (800) 323-7229 or (340) 776-6434. 52 units, kitchens. $365-$465. Pool, restaurant.
St. John Inn P.O. Box 37. (800) 666-7688 or (340) 693-8688. 13 units, some kitchens. $120-$175.
Westin Resort St. John P.O. Box 8310. (340) 693-8000. 349 units. $539-$709. AC, 3 pools, 4 restaurants.

Excursion

Buck Island Reef National Monument
St. Croix, U.S. Virgin Islands

A coral reef nearly encircles this small island, 1 mile north of St. Croix. A marked underwater trail guides snorkelers or passengers of glass-bottom boats through the exquisite reef ecosystem. Breathtaking views of St. Croix and the reef can be had from the top of Buck Island's hiking trail. 176 land acres; 18,839 undersea acres. Trail, picnic areas, water sports. Open year-round. Access by charter boat from Christiansted, St. Croix (charter operators supply snorkeling equipment). (340) 773-1460.

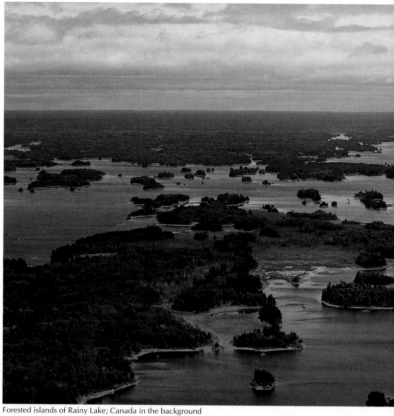

Forested islands of Rainy Lake; Canada in the background

Voyageurs

Minnesota

Established April 8, 1975

218,054 acres

From the air, the forest areas of
Voyageurs look like green pieces of
a jigsaw puzzle scattered on a huge
mirror. A North Woods realm of more
than 30 lakes and more than 900
islands, Voyageurs spans a watery
stretch of the U.S.-Canada border.

A third of the park's area is water,
most of it in four large lakes—Rainy,
Kabetogama, Namakan, and Sand
Point—linked by narrow waterways.
Smaller lakes gleam in the forests
and bogs of Voyageurs' terra firma,
which consists of small islands, a
strip of mainland shore, and the
Kabetogama Peninsula, a long, bay-
fringed landmass.

The splendors of this 55-mile-long
park can be reached primarily by
water. Motorboats (banned in the
adjacent Boundary Waters Canoe Area
Wilderness) churn the lakes. Canoes
and kayaks glide the narrow waterways. Fishermen sit at the rails of
houseboats, hoping to hook walleye,
smallmouth bass, and northern pike.
Nearly every lake is haunted by the cry
of the loon. And probably in no other
national park in the lower 48 states is
there a better chance to see bald eagles
on the nest and on the wing or hear
wolves howl at night.

The park is named for the voyageurs, French Canadians who paddled
birchbark canoes for fur trading companies in the late 18th and early 19th
centuries. The voyageurs were famous
for stamina—paddling up to 16 hours
a day—and roisterous songs. Their
canoe route between Canada's northwest and Montreal is cited as part of
the U.S.-Canada border in the treaty

River, stay on US 53 for 25 more miles, turn right at the Ash River Trail sign, and continue for 10 miles. For Kabetogama Lake Visitor Center, stay on US 53 for 3 more miles, turn right onto County Road 122, and drive to the lakeshore. For Rainy Lake, stay on US 53 to International Falls, then head east for 12 miles on Minn. 11 to the park's entrance road, following highway information signs; turn right to go to the visitor center. Airports: Duluth and International Falls, Minnesota; and Fort Frances, Ontario.

When to Go

All-year park, but most accessible from spring through early fall. Water travel is curtailed by freeze-up in late fall and ice break-up in early spring. Winter opens the park to cross-country skiing, snowshoeing, snowmobiling, and ice fishing. And the 7-mile ice road at Rainy Lake provides a unique entry into the park: You drive your car on the ice to places that in other seasons you can reach only by boat or floatplane.

How to Visit

The only way to the heart of this park is by water. **Kabetogama Lake, International Falls, Crane Lake, and Ash River** are resort communities that, though not within the park, serve as entrances. Begin your trip planning by choosing an entrance; each of them is widely spaced and offers a different experience. You can make motel or lodge reservations at one of the area's resorts or motels listed in the park's newspaper, the *Rendezvous*, or in the **Information & Activities** section on p. 110. You can also stay in a car campground and use the resort as a base for park activities, including fishing and wildlife watching, or rent a houseboat or camp out

that ended the American Revolution.

In a boat in the labyrinth of waterways and islands, you can unwittingly cross this border. Be sure to take along a high-quality map that includes navigational markers to tell you where you are.

How to Get There

From Duluth, drive north about 110 miles on US 53. For Crane Lake, turn east at Orr and drive 28 miles on County Roads 23 and 24. For Ash

Modern voyageurs on Kabetogama Lake

Map legend:
- Ranger Station
- Campground
- Primitive Campsite
- Public Launching Ramp
- Unpaved Road
- Hiking Trail
- Portage
- Park Maintained Ice Road

0   5 km
0   5 mi

by boat. Guides, canoes, houseboats, and motorboats are for hire. If you are sufficiently experienced, you can also tow in your own craft.

Tour boats, with park naturalists aboard, also operate out of visitor centers. Even if you have your own boat, you may want to take a commercial cruise and rely on experienced navigators; the lakes are broad with submerged rocks in shallow areas, and they're sometimes brushed by stiff winds.

If your time is limited, Kabetogama Lake is a good place for exploring and understanding the park.

Kabetogama Lake

at least a full day

At the **Kabetogama Lake Visitor Center,** reserve a naturalist-led Sunset Wildlife Cruise, Kettle Falls Cruise, guided canoe trip, or children's program. Or, borrow one of the park's cached canoes at Locator Lake by reserving it and picking up the key at the visitor center. If you do this, you must get to the Locator Lake trailhead on your own, with a guide, or in a rented boat. You leave the boat at the

ONTARIO

RAINY LAKE

Cormorant Bay

Rat River Bay

Pound Net Bay

Mackenzie Point

Stokes Bay

Falls

CANADA
UNITED STATES

Brown Lake

Beast Lake

Cruiser Lake

Mica Bay

Weir Lake

Oakpoint Island

Kettle Falls

Dam

Voyageur Narrows

Moose Island

Blackstone Island

NAMAKAN LAKE

Namakan

Namakan Island

Moose Bay

Sullivan Bay

Hoist Bay

Sheen Point

Randolph Bay

Tooth Lake

Namakan Narrows

Sand Point Lake

Ash River

Moose

Gannon

Little Johnson Lake

Johnson Lake

Harrison Narrows

Mukooda Lake

SUPERIOR

Creek

NATIONAL

FOREST

King Williams Narrows

CRANE LAKE

Canada Customs

Crane Lake

U.S. Customs

To Orr and 53

Dovre Lake

Vermilion

Autumn forest and cattails on Rainy Lake

Showy lady's slipper

American white pelican

trailhead for a 2-mile hike along a spruce bog and past a beaver pond, dam, and lodge. The trail climbs to a ridge and drops to the lakeshore. There you launch your reserved cached canoe and paddle around the lake, watching for muskrat, bald eagles, loons, and blue-winged teal. Another exciting way to explore the park is on an all-day guided cruise to **Kettle Falls.** For details see **Crane Lake & Ash River,** below. The 21-mile **Kabetogama to Ash River Trail** travels through the park and state forest lands; three trailheads, all car-accessible, offer a variety of opportunities.

Rainy Lake
at least a full day

Although this lake is large—60 miles long, 12 miles wide—you can safely explore it in your own or a rented motorboat, houseboat, or canoe. At the **Rainy Lake Visitor Center** get weather and navigation information and take a self-guided waterborne excursion. About 1.5 miles northwest is **Little American Island,** where the discovery of gold set off a short-lived gold rush a hundred years ago. A short interpretive trail on the island gives a view to the past. About 2 miles east is **Bushyhead Island,** where a mine shaft is carved into the rock.

Lacking your own boat, you can still explore. The park offers naturalist-led tour boat trips from the visitor center, as well as free trips aboard a 26-foot reproduction of a voyageurs canoe, guided trips aboard contemporary canoes, and programs for children.

Trails near Rainy Lake Visitor Center: The 2-mile **Oberholtzer Trail** travels through a variety of habitats. The short, water-accessible **Black Bay Beaver Pond Trail** takes visitors to an active beaver pond habitat.

Crane Lake & Ash River
at least 1 to 2 days each

Near the Ash River resort area is a visitor center where you can launch your boat, get information about camping, set off on hikes (see below), and obtain charts for navigating the lakes. If you're new to the lakes, *don't fail to use charts.*

For a good exploratory voyage, go to **Kettle Falls,** a waterways hub used

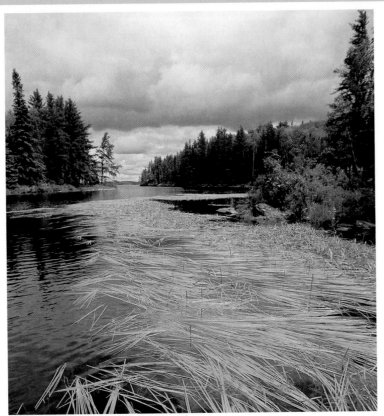

A skein of bur reed edging Browns Bay, on Rainy Lake

by Native Americans, voyageurs, loggers, fishermen, and, during Prohibition, bootleggers smuggling liquor from Canada.

From Crane Lake you travel north through **King Williams Narrows,** across **Sand Point Lake,** and through **Namakan Narrows,** then west across **Namakan Lake** along the U.S.-Canada border, which veers northward here.

From Ash River you go the length of **Sullivan Bay** to the river mouth, then weave through a string of islands into **Moose Bay.** For a scenic trip, pass through the channel on the south side of **Williams Island** (site of a primitive campsite) into **Hoist Bay,** named for the hoisting of logs that were loaded onto a train. You can see pilings that supported a train track, which ran from the middle of the bay to a white-pine sawmill on the mainland. Head north toward **Namakan Island,** site of other campsites, and go around the island's western side.

Both courses take you to the southern end of **Voyageur Narrows.** Pass through the narrows, then head east along the border through **Squirrel Narrows** to Kettle Falls. Near the dock, a dam serves a regional system regulating water flow for electric power. At the dock is a gravel road, a portage trail. Walk the road for about a quarter mile to a white clapboard building with a long front porch—the **Kettle Falls Hotel.** Built in 1910, the hotel welcomed lumberjacks and their money; it still hosts guests—those who make their reservations well ahead.

Another way to get to Kettle Falls is to take a cruise boat. Trips are run several times a week out of the visitor center at Kabetogama Lake. The all-day trip is timed for you to eat lunch or dinner at the hotel before the return voyage.

Trails near Ash River Visitor Center: Three short trails—the **Voyageurs Forest, Beaver Pond,** and **Kabetogama Lake Overlook**—leave from pull-offs on the road to the visitor center. The 2-mile **Blind Ash Bay Trail,** from the visitor center to the mouth of Blind Ash Bay, wends along rock cliffs through pine forest.

Information & Activities

Headquarters
3131 Hwy. 53, International Falls, MN 56649. Phone (218) 283-9821. www.nps.gov/voya

Seasons & Accessibility
Park open year-round. Travel within it is by boat, floatplane, and foot in summer; snowmobile, snowshoes, cross-country skis, and ski-plane in winter. Limited access during lake freeze-up (mid-Nov. to mid-Dec.) and break up (April). In winter, weather permitting, an ice road on Rainy Lake connects the visitor center to Cranberry Bay, 7 miles into the park.

Visitor & Information Centers
Rainy Lake, on Minn. 11 at northwest edge of park, open daily; call (218) 286-5258. **Kabetogama Lake,** on County Road 123 at southwest edge of lake, open daily mid-May through September; call (218) 875-2111. **Ash River,** on southeast edge of Kabetogama Lake, open mid-May through September. Call (218) 374-3221.

Entrance Fee
None.

Pets
Permitted on leashes in developed areas and at tent, houseboat, and day-use sites on major lakes. Not allowed on park trails, in backcountry, or on interior lakes.

Facilities for Disabled
Kabetogama Lake, Rainy Lake, and Ash River Visitor Centers are wheelchair accessible, as is the Kettle Falls Hotel, guided boat trips, and a campsite; call Kabetogama Lake for reservations. Fact sheet available.

Things to Do
Free naturalist-led activities: nature walks, canoe trips (reserve at visitor centers), children's and campfire programs, films, exhibits, winter programs. Also, hiking, canoes and rowboats (boats on Interior Lakes Program $10 a day), boat tours, rental boats, fishing and ice fishing (guides available, ask park for list; license required), swimming, waterskiing, snowmobiling, cross-country skiing, snowshoeing.

Special Advisory
● Practice safe boating: Use navigational maps; be aware of weather conditions; make sure your boat is well equipped; do not overload it.

Camping & Houseboating
All park sites reached by water. 214 backcountry boat-in campsites, 14-day limit. Open all year (mostly inaccessible during fall freeze-up and spring thaw); first come, first served. Free permit required for overnight stays, available at visitor centers and boat launches. No showers. Sites designated for tent camping or houseboats. Also, two small campgrounds. In winter, access mainly by snowmobile, cross-country skis, or snowshoes. Private campgrounds with tent and RV sites near park. Request "Camping, Houseboating, and Day-Use" brochure for planning.

Hotels, Motels, & Inns
(unless otherwise noted, rates are for 2 persons in a double room, high season)
INSIDE THE PARK:
Kettle Falls Hotel (15 miles by water from the Ash River Trail) 10502 Gamma Road, Ray, MN 56669. (888) 534-6835. 12 hotel rooms. $70 double; lodge and suites nearby, some with kitchens, $140-$170.
OUTSIDE THE PARK:
In International Falls, MN 56649:
Holiday Inn 1500 US 71. (800) 331-4443 or (218) 283-8000. 126 units. $80-$130. AC, pool, restaurant. **Island View Lodge** (on Rainy Lake) 1817 Hwy. 11E. (800) 777-7856 or (218) 286-3511. 9 rooms $77-$95; 12 cabins with kitchens, $150-$360. AC, restaurant.
In Kabetogama, MN 56669:
Rocky Point Resort 12953 Ness Rd. (218) 875-2411. 8 cabins with kitchens, $300-$1,000 per week; 2 lodge rooms, $25 per person. Rest. **Voyageur Park Lodge** 10436 Waltz Rd. (800) 331-5694 or (218) 875-2131). 11 cabins with kitchens (summer only), $588-$1,200 per week.

For a listing of accommodations, call Kabetogama Tourism Bureau (800) 524-9085; Crane Lake Visitor and Tourism Bureau (800) 362-7405; International Falls Area Convention & Visitors Bureau (800) 325-5766; Ash River Commercial Club (800) 950-2061.

Excursions

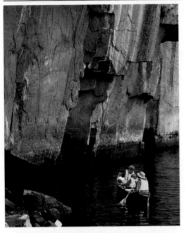

Superior National Forest
Duluth, Minnesota

Here the northern lights preside over stands of pine, spruce, fir, alder, and birch, and loons bob on the more than 1,000 portage-linked lakes of the Boundary Waters Canoe Area Wilderness (permit required). Reservations essential for this popular site. 2.2 million acres. Hiking, boating, fishing, hunting, winter sports, water sports, scenic drives. Campsites, food services, boat ramp, picnic areas. Open all year. La Croix Visitor Center west of Cook on US 53 about 15 miles from Orr, Minn., the southern gateway to Voyageurs NP. (218) 666-5251.

Chippewa National Forest
Cass Lake, Minnesota

This lake-country forest boasts one of the largest breeding bald eagle populations outside Alaska and offers a variety of water-based recreation, including the chance to explore the Mississippi's headwaters by canoe. More than 660,000 acres. Hiking, boating, fishing, scenic drives, historic sites with summer interpretive programs, winter sports, hunting. 23 campgrounds, picnic areas, boat ramps, handicapped access. Open all year; campsites generally open mid-May to mid-Sept. Information at Cass Lake on US 2, about 85 miles from Voyageurs NP. (218) 335-8600.

Agassiz National Wildlife Refuge
Middle River, Minnesota

More than 285 species of migratory and upland game birds utilize the resources of this wetlands refuge on the Mississippi flyway. They share the site with 75 moose and a resident pack of eastern gray wolves—one of the few such packs in any national refuge outside Alaska. 61,500 acres. Hiking, hunting, scenic drives, bird-watching. Handicapped access. Open all year (Lost Bay Habitat Dr. and Maakstad Hiking Trail open May-Oct.). Headquarters on Marshall County Rd. 7, 11 miles east of Holt, 185 miles from Voyageurs NP. (218) 449-4115.

This map plots all the U.S. national parks, plus the Excursions sites featured in this book.

Preceding pages: Dunes, Guadalupe Mountains

The Southwest

The national parks of the Southwest, all set in the Chihuahuan Desert, offer scenery ranging from underground caves to high and rugged mountain peaks. Sparse vegetation opens the spectacular vistas up to visitors without their having to go above tree line.

Water sculptured these landscapes. A reef from an ancient sea forms the 50-mile-long Guadalupe mountain chain. The seeping of water over millions of years created the cool, dark world of Carlsbad Caverns. Rivers etched out the dramatic canyons of Big Bend, and flash floods still tumble boulders from the steep Chisos mountaintops, continuing to rearrange the scenery.

The vagaries of yearly precipitation also determine whether the visitor beholds a land of blossoms—Texas bluebonnets, brilliant red and orange cactus flowers, heavy stalks of white yucca blooms—or, more often, a parched terrain dominated by creosote bush, prickly pear, and dagger-sharp lechuguilla. Where water flows year-round, oases produce gardens that resonate with birdsong.

Visitors to the Southwest parks have a chance to view wildlife as diverse as multicolored lizards and snakes, the elusive mountain lion, deer, hundreds of species of birds, and, in Big Bend, pig look-alikes called javelinas. Paleontologists have found fossils of many other creatures, including giant crocodiles and the Big Bend pterosaur, the largest animal ever to fly.

Hikers may take their own trip back in time by climbing up to the pine-fir forests that cloak the cooler, moister mountaintops in the Guadalupes and Big Bend. This type of forest probably covered the region at the end of the last Ice Age, when early peoples hunted camels, mammoths, and four-horned antelope.

Carlsbad Caverns and Guadalupe Mountains National Parks are linked by the Lincoln National Forest; proposals have been made to unite the three areas into one large park encompassing the Guadalupe range. Base yourself at Carlsbad or, even closer, in Whites City to visit these areas. Allow a day to drive the 250 miles from Guadalupe to Big Bend.

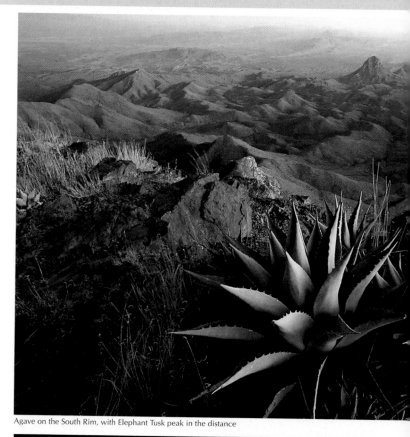

Agave on the South Rim, with Elephant Tusk peak in the distance

Big Bend

Texas

Established June 12, 1944

801,163 acres

As the Rio Grande winds south along the Texas-Mexico border, it suddenly veers northward in a great horseshoe curve before continuing its journey. Inside the horseshoe lies the region of Texas known as the Big Bend; Big Bend National Park flanks the river at the southerly tip of the curve. A wild and surprising land, the park remains remote enough that only the dedicated reach it.

Chihuahuan Desert vegetation—bunchgrasses, creosote bushes, cactuses, lechuguillas, yuccas, and sotols—covers most of the terrain. But the Rio Grande and its lush floodplains and steep, narrow canyons almost form a park of their own. So do the Chisos Mountains; up to 20

degrees cooler than the desert floor, they harbor pine, juniper, and oak, as well as deer, mountain lions, bears, and other wildlife. A heavy rain transforms the desert: Normally dry creek beds roar with water, and seeds long dormant burst into fields of wildflowers.

The rocks of Big Bend are a complex lot. Two seas, one after another, flowed and subsided in the region hundreds of millions of years ago, leaving thick deposits of limestone and shale. The present mountains, except the Chisos, uplifted along with the Rockies, roughly 75 million years ago. Around the same time, a 40-mile-wide trough—most of the present-day park—sank along fault lines, leaving the cliffs of Santa Elena Canyon to the west and the Sierra del Carmen to the east rising 1,500 feet above the desert floor. In the center, volcanic activity

Ranch Road 170, from Presidio, joins Tex. 118 shortly before the west entrance. Nearest airports: El Paso (325 miles) and Midland-Odessa (230 miles).

When to Go

All-year park, though fall and winter may be the best seasons. Deciduous leaves turn color in the mountains in autumn; winters are mild. Summer temperatures in the desert can exceed 110°F; the Chisos Mountains remain cooler. If enough rain falls, the desert blooms stunningly in early spring, and again in late summer. Bird-watching is good all year, but especially in March, April, and May.

How to Visit

Allow several days, especially if you plan to hike. Explore the **Chisos Mountains Basin** and the **Ross Maxwell Scenic Drive,** engineered to take you past many of the park's geological and scenic highlights. Ideally, devote the better part of a day to each area. With extra time on the second afternoon, or on a third day, drive out to **Rio Grande Village** and the **Boquillas Canyon Overlook** to experience the river environment and enjoy views of the Sierra del Carmen, particularly spectacular at sunset. On your way in or out, view the landscape and exhibits along US 385 between **Panther Junction** and **Persimmon Gap.** For an extended visit, try more of the many rewarding hikes, drive some dirt roads, and consider a leisurely float trip along the Rio Grande through one of the park's three major canyons.

spewed layer upon layer of ash into the air and squeezed molten rock up through the ground to form the Chisos Mountains some 35 million years ago. Molten rock also cooled and hardened underground later to be exposed by erosion.

Big Bend's topographic variety supports a remarkable diversity of life, including 1,200 plant species—some found nowhere else in the world. More species of birds—more than 400— have been counted here than in any other U.S. national park.

People have passed through this terrain for at least 10,000 years. The human pageant in historical times has included Apache, Spanish conquistadores, Comanche, U.S. soldiers, miners, ranchers and farmers, Mexican revolutionaries, and international outlaws and bandits.

How to Get There

US 385 leads from Marathon to the north entrance to the park; Tex. 118 from Alpine leads to the west entrance;

Rocks at entrance to Santa Elena Canyon

↑

🏠 Ranger Station
▲ Campground
▲ Primitive Campsite
🚶 Interpretive Trail
–·–·– Unpaved (2-wheel-drive road)
–·–·– Unpaved (4-wheel-drive road)
········· Trail

0   5   10 km
0   5   10 mi

To Alpine

118

+ Graytop
   5,502 ft

+ Camels Hump

+ Agua Fria Mountain

Corazones Peaks +
   5,319 ft

Hen Egg Mountain +
   4,963 ft

CHRISTMAS
MOUNTAINS

■ Terlingua
  Ranch

Croton
Peak +

BLACK MESA

Terlingua
(Ghost Town)

Slickrock +
Mountain

Dogie Mountain

▲ 10 m

170

Study Butte/
Terlingua

13 mi

118

Santa Elena
Junction

Entrance

**Ross Maxwell
Scenic Drive**

▲

Maverick
Junction

BURRO
MESA

The Window +
4,600 ft

🏠

To Presidio
Lajitas

Tule +
Mountain

**Chisos Basin
Visitor Center**

· Homer Wilson
  Ranch

MESA DE ANGUILA

Javelina Wash

SANTA ELENA

▲

Peña
Mountain

Sotol
Vista
Overlook

22 mi

CHISOS

CANYON

▲ **Santa Elena Canyon
Overlook**

🚶

TUFF
CANYON

8 mi

Mule Ears Viewpoint

SIERRA

+ Cerro Castellan
  3,293 ft

Cottonwood
▲ Castolon
Santa
Elena
🏠

+ Mule Ears
  Peaks
  3,881 ft

Triangulation Station
Mountain
+ 3,143 ft

PONCE

▲

▲

Rio Grande

▲ ▲

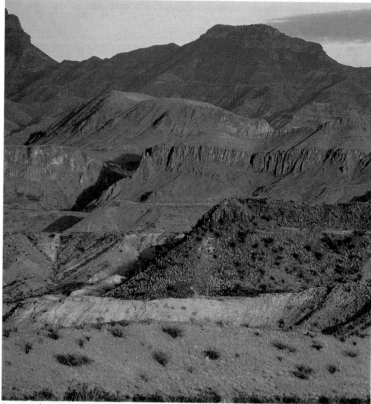

Sunset on the Maverick Badlands

Panther Junction to the Chisos Basin

10 miles one way; at least a half day

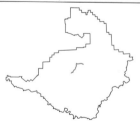

Start your tour at the visitor center at Panther Junction. Collect maps, information on hiking, and safety tips on avoiding encounters with rattlesnakes, mountain lions, and flash floods. Don't miss **Panther Path**—the 50-yard nature trail near the visitor center entrance whose self-guiding pamphlet provides an excellent introduction to the plants you'll see on much of your trip. Behind the visitor center lie the **Chisos Mountains,** the

southernmost range in the continental United States, and your destination. When ready, return to your car and turn left out of the visitor center, then left at **Basin Junction** in 3 miles. Ahead on the right looms **Pulliam Bluff.** Look closely and you might see in the mountain the profile of a man's face, reclining. Legend relates that the man is Alsate, an important Apache chief whose ghost lives on in the high Chisos Mountains, and whose campfire can occasionally be seen at night. At 2.5 miles, the jagged summit to your left is **Lost Mine Peak.** Spanish explorers, it is told, discovered a rich silver mine near the summit and enslaved Indians to work it. The miners rebelled, killed their overlords, and sealed the entrance to the mine so that it might remain lost forever. As you drive on, the castlelike summit of **Casa Grande**—"big house"—will be straight ahead, a landmark for much of the park.

The road climbs higher into the mountains through a canyon called

Eroded, soft rock "plugs" created by volcanic eruptions

Green Gulch: Watch the vegetation change from desert shrub to sotol grasslands, then to pinyon pine, juniper, and oak woodland. The Chisos form a cooler, moister island in the surrounding desert. Some 10,000 years ago, pinyon-juniper forests extended down to the desert floor, but the trees withdrew to higher altitudes as the climate gradually warmed at the end of the Ice Age. In about 5 miles the road hits its highest point at **Panther Pass** (5,770 feet), named for the mountain lions that still roam these hills. Only the lucky few ever see one. If you have time, park at the nearby trailhead for the **Lost Mine Trail,** a self-guided nature trail with an informative booklet. The panorama from the top, one of the grandest in the park, makes the moderately strenuous 4.8-mile round-trip well worth the trek. But if you're short of time, just hike the 2-mile round-trip to the **Juniper Canyon Overlook,** for good vistas of wooded **Juniper Canyon** to the south and Pulliam Bluff to the northwest.

After Panther Pass, the road descends in hairpin curves to the basin, a 3-mile-wide depression in the mountains, chiseled by wind and water. Many of the park's choice hikes start from the basin trailhead, west of the ranger station. At the least, make sure you stroll the easy 0.3-mile round-trip **Window View Trail.** Particularly photogenic at sunset, the **Window** is a V-shaped opening, or pour off, in the mountains, through which all rain and meltwater from the

Claret cup cactus abloom in the high Chisos

basin drains. A more challenging trail descends through desert and shady canyon to the Window itself, offering classic afternoon views of Casa Grande framed by oaks and pines. In summer, take this and other lower elevation hikes in early morning or late afternoon.

The literal high point of many visitors' trips to the park is a hike to the **South Rim** (7,400 feet), a moderately steep 13-mile round-trip that provides unforgettable vistas of much of the park. At **Boot Canyon,** 4.5 miles up the trail to the South Rim, lives an oasis of bigtooth maple, Douglas-fir, and Arizona pine. The gray-and-yellow Colima warbler nests on the canyon floor, its only home in the United States.

Before you hike, check at the **Chisos Basin Visitor Center** for maps and hiking tips, and make sure you carry plenty of water. At the visitor center, ask also about the presence of peregrine falcons. Several of these endangered birds nest in the Chisos.

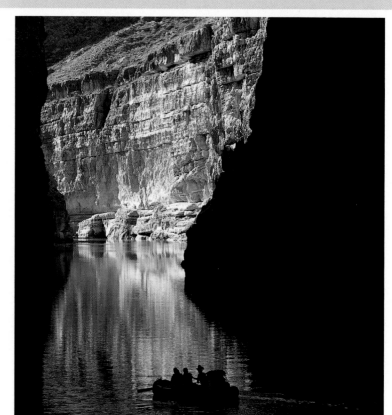

Rafting the Rio Grande through Santa Elena Canyon

Ross Maxwell Scenic Drive: Santa Elena Junction to Santa Elena Canyon

30 miles one way; a half to full day

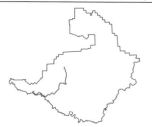

Heading south from Santa Elena Junction, **Burro Mesa**—named for the burros that once grazed the top—will be to your right, and the Chisos to your left. After 2 miles, stop at the exhibit on the left for a fine view of the Window framing Casa Grande. Drive on a little over a mile, then park at the old **Sam Nail Ranch** and stroll

the short path to the remains of windmills and a ranch house. The shade of the pecan and willow trees the Nails planted makes a fine resting and birdwatching spot. Walk back to your car and motor on. In about a mile, long walls of rock traverse the landscape. They are dikes, created by molten rock that squeezed up into underground cracks before hardening. The softer rock layers above them eventually eroded away, leaving the erosion-resistant dikes.

Stop next at the **Blue Creek Ranch** (Homer Wilson Ranch) **Overlook.** A century ago most of Big Bend was cloaked in grasses. But ranchers grazed thousands of cattle, sheep, and goats, destroying the grass and exposing the topsoil to erosion. Creosote, mesquite, allthorn, and other spiny shrubs moved into the damaged areas. Here, and elsewhere in the park, grasses are slowly returning.

Go back to the road and take a quick left onto the **Sotol Vista** spur road, named for the ridge's rich growth of sotol, the bright green plant with sawlike teeth on the edges of the leaves. Indians roasted and ate the heart of the sotol and fermented it to yield an alcoholic drink. The parking lot at the top provides vistas of the surrounding mountains, and a plaque at the end of the loop identifies what's what.

Return to the main road; an exhibit on the left in about 6.5 miles describes how volcanism shaped this striking landscape. Take the next spur road on the left, for an excellent view of the peaks known as **Mule Ears,** a name explained at a glance. During the 1930s, Army Air Corps pilots drilled by flying planes between the twin peaks. Stop again after 4.5 miles to see **Tuff Canyon,** carved by **Blue Creek** through layers of lava flows, boulders, and compressed volcanic ash called tuff. Stroll the short trail to the right to view the canyon. The trail at the left of the parking lot provides a moderately steep hike down into the canyon, a 0.75-mile round-trip.

Back in your car, you will be approaching **Cerro Castellan,** another important landmark, rising 1,000 feet above its surroundings. Turn left into **Castolon** to stroll around the old Army post that protected residents from bandits during the 1914-18 border troubles with Mexico. The main building, originally the barracks, was converted to a frontier trading post around 1920. Today you can buy cold drinks and picnic there.

After leaving Castolon, the road parallels the **Rio Grande,** passing the scattered remains of adobe houses dating back to the turn of the 20th century. The occupants once grew food crops and cotton in the Rio Grande's fertile floodplain.

Be sure to stop about 8 miles from Castolon, at the parking area for the **Santa Elena Canyon Overlook.** Laden with abrasive silt and gravel, the Rio Grande sculptured the canyon 1,500 feet deep, through the cliffs that tower above the geological trough that forms the bulk of the park.

Drive on to the end of the road, put on some old shoes, and, if the water is low, wade across **Terlingua Creek** to reach the **Santa Elena Canyon Trail.** The moderate 1.7-mile round-trip trail leads into the canyon mouth, amply rewarding the hiker with striking views.

Mule Ears Peaks and prickly pear cactus

Cerro Castellan looming over an old Army post

Panther Junction to Rio Grande Village & Boquillas Canyon Overlook

24 miles one way; a half to full day

Before starting this tour, check at the visitor center for the condition of the Hot Springs road. The main road, heading southeast, descends nearly 2,000 feet through desert shrub, terminating near the willows and cottonwoods on the banks of the Rio Grande.

After about 6.5 miles, turn left onto the unpaved road to see the spring at **Dugout Wells,** formerly the site of a ranch and schoolhouse, and now a fine place to picnic and look for wildlife. Return to the main road. As you continue, the peak aptly named **Elephant Tusk** will be on your right in the distance, and **Chilicotal Mountain** closer to the road. Far ahead looms the **Sierra del Carmen** in Mexico. Its striated rock formations are the same

124

Greater roadrunner speeding across the desert

limestone and shale as in the cliffs at
Santa Elena Canyon.

If you're up to a somewhat rough
ride, be sure to take the turnoff to **Hot
Springs,** whose mineral waters were valued for centuries. Look for Indian pictographs on the cliffs along the trail to
the springs, just beyond the old motel.

After returning to the main road,
pull over at the **Rio Grande Overlook**
just past the tunnel on the right and
stroll a 50-yard trail for superb views
of the Sierra del Carmen, the river
floodplain, and part of **Boquillas del
Carmen** village in Mexico. Big Bend
bluebonnets bloom profusely here
during a well-watered springtime.

Back on the road, continue straight
for half a mile, then turn left and continue another 3 miles to the paved
spur road to **Boquillas Canyon Overlook.** Turn left onto the main road,
then left again to visit **Rio Grande Village,** an excellent place to watch birds.
Don't miss the nature trail starting
across from site No. 18 in the campground. This easy 0.75-mile loop leads
through junglelike floodplain vegetation before climbing onto a ridge that
provides terrific views of the river and
the Sierra del Carmen.

Panther Junction to
Persimmon Gap

26 miles one way; 2 hours

This drive from park headquarters at
Panther Junction to Persimmon Gap,
the park's northern entrance, follows
an ancient trail used by the Comanche

Javelina, a cactus-loving omnivore

on their annual raiding forays into
Mexico, and by Army expeditions, settlers, and miners of silver and lead. The
road descends gently to Tornillo Creek
and **Tornillo Flat,** one of the park's
most overgrazed and poorly recovered
areas. The mountains forming the
ridge to the east are the **Dead Horse
Mountains,** the Sierra del Carmen's
northernmost reach.

Highlights along the way include a
view of **Dog Canyon,** through which
camels once lumbered in a 19th-century
U.S. Army experiment, and, near the
north end of the Tornillo Creek bridge,
an exhibit of fossil mammal bones; the
fossils were found in the park in sandstone dating from 50 million years ago.

For an excellent self-guided auto
tour, pick up a pamphlet at either
end of the road and, if it's springtime,
ask whether the giant dagger yuccas
are in bloom. (If so, be sure to take the
unpaved **Dagger Flat Auto Trail** to see
stalkfuls of white blooms weighing up
to 70 pounds; if not, skip the detour.)

Information & Activities

Headquarters
1 Panther Junction, Big Bend NP, TX 79834. Phone (915) 477-2251. www.nps.gov/bibe

Seasons & Accessibility
Open all year. Check current conditions before driving dirt roads.

Visitor & Information Centers
Panther Junction and **Chisos Basin Visitor Centers** open daily all year. Call headquarters for visitor information.

Entrance Fee
$10 per car per week.

Facilities for Disabled
Visitor center and two nature trails are wheelchair accessible. Free brochure.

Things to Do
Free naturalist-led activities: nature walks, workshops, evening programs. Also, hiking, fishing, river-running (permit required), cycling, nature seminars.

Overnight Backpacking
Free permits required. Obtain in person at visitor centers or ranger stations within 24 hours of trip.

Campgrounds
Three campgrounds with 14-day limit. Open all year, first come, first served. Fees $8 per night. Tent and RV sites. At **Rio Grande Village Trailer Park,** full hookups only available. Three group campgrounds; reservations through headquarters for groups of 10 or more.

Hotels, Motels, & Inns
(unless otherwise noted, rates are for 2 persons in a double room, high season)
Big Bend Motor Inn (Tex. 118 and Rte. 170) P.O. Box 336, Terlingua, TX 79852. (800) 848-2363 or (915) 371-2218. 86 rooms, 10 with kitchenettes, $69-$79; 4 duplexes with kitchens, $105-$124. AC, pool, restaurant.
Chisos Mountains Lodge National Park Concessions, Inc., Basin Rural Station, Big Bend NP, TX 79834. (915) 477-2291. 72 rooms, including 4 cottages, $83-$88. AC, restaurant.
Gage Hotel (US 90 and US 385) P.O. Box 46, Marathon, TX 79842. (800) 884-4243 or (915) 386-4205. 37 units. $69-$155. AC, restaurant.
Lajitas Resort (on Tex. 170) Star Rte. 70, Box 400, Terlingua, TX 79852. (877) 525-4827 or (915) 424-3471. 218 rooms; 12 condos, kitchenettes. $125. AC, pool, restaurant.

For a full list of accommodations contact the Alpine Chamber of Commerce. (915) 837-2326.

Excursion

Rio Grande Wild and Scenic River
Big Bend National Park, Texas

Floating the Rio Grande is an experience not to be missed. Big Bend NP administers both the section along its border and the Wild and Scenic stretches downstream. Easy floats include the Mariscal and Boquillas Canyons; Santa Elena and the Lower Canyons are more difficult. Boating permits required. Main access point to Lower Canyons in Mexico; most take-out points fall on private land in Texas (permission required). 196 Wild and Scenic miles. Primitive camping, hiking, fishing; inner-tubing and swimming not recommended. Information about outfitters offering half-day to 1-week trips at Panther Junction. (915) 477-2251.

Hall of Giants in the Big Room

Carlsbad Caverns

New Mexico

Established May 14, 1930

46,766 acres

The Chihuahuan Desert, studded with spiky plants and lizards, offers little hint that what Will Rogers called the "Grand Canyon with a roof on it" waits underground. Yet, at the northern reaches of this great desert, underneath a mountain range called the Guadalupes, lies one of the deepest, largest, and most ornate caverns ever found.

Water molded this underworld 4 to 6 million years ago. Some 250 million years ago, the region lay underneath the inland arm of an ancient sea. Near the shore grew a limestone reef. By the time the sea withdrew, the reef stood hundreds of feet high, later to be buried under thousands of feet of soil. Some 15 to 20 million years ago, the

ground uplifted. Slightly acidic groundwater seeped into cracks in the limestone, gradually enlarging them to form a honeycomb of chambers. Millions of more years passed before the cave decoration began. Then, drop by drop, limestone-laden moisture built an extraordinary variety of glistening formations. Some of these are six stories tall; others tiny, delicate confections.

Cave scientists have explored more than 30 miles of passageways of the main cavern of Carlsbad, and investigation continues. Visitors may tour 3 of these miles on a paved trail. The Slaughter Canyon Cave provides the hardy an opportunity to play spelunker, albeit with a guide. The park has more than 100 other caves open primarily to specialists.

Some visitors think the park's most spectacular sight is the one seen at the

When to Go

All-year park. The weather underground remains a constant 56°F. The main cavern gets crowded, especially in summer and on major holiday weekends. Either spring or fall, when the desert's in bloom, is an excellent time to go. You'll see the bats fly from April or early May through October, sometimes later.

How to Visit

One full day allows you time to tour the main cavern and take a nature walk or a drive before watching the bats fly at sunset. For a second day's activity, reserve space on a tour of "unimproved" **Slaughter Canyon Cave,** if you're ready for a more rugged caving experience.

At the visitor center, select either the **Natural Entrance Tour** or the Big Room Tour (both are 1-mile walks). Try the first unless you have walking, breathing, or heart problems. It starts at the natural entrance and is mostly downhill, except for one stretch where you climb 83 feet; an elevator whisks you back to ground level. The Natural Entrance Tour is more intimate and may be less crowded than the Big Room.

The **Big Room Tour** begins with an elevator ride directly to the Big Room, in which you can see most of the types of formations visible in the other sections. If after this tour you want to see more caves, take the elevator back up to ground level and proceed with the first half of the Natural Entrance Tour.

Another option, the **Kings Palace Tour** (see **Other Trails & Sights** p. 131) visits the stunning formations in the scenic rooms.

cave's mouth. More than a half million Mexican free-tailed bats summer in a section of the cave, and around sunset they spiral up from the entrance to hunt for insects. The nightly exodus led to the discovery of the cave in modern times. Around the turn of the 20th century, miners began to excavate bat guano—a potent fertilizer—for shipment to the citrus groves of southern California. One of the guano miners, James Larkin White, became the first to explore and publicize the caverns beyond the Bat Cave.

How to Get There

The park is off US 62/180, 20 miles southwest of Carlsbad and 164 miles east of El Paso, Texas. For the visitor center, turn west at Whites City and drive 7 miles. For Slaughter Canyon, turn west on County Road 418, 5 miles south of Whites City; drive another 11 miles, some unpaved, to the parking lot. Airports: Carlsbad, New Mexico, and El Paso, Texas.

Natural Entrance Tour

1 mile; about 1 hour

The visitor center rents an audio guide, if you wish. Exit to the right, following the path to the cavern's natural entrance. The opening formed when part of the cave's ceiling collapsed thousands of years ago. Once in the mouth of the cave, glance right to spot 1,000-year-old red and black pictographs high on the wall. Indians knew of the cavern and used the entrance for shelter. But without dependable lighting they could not have gone very far past the small sunlit area. You are descending the **Main**

Desert
Nature Trail

Bat Flight
Amphitheater

Bat Cave

Natural Entrance

Devils Spring

Visitor Center

Natural Bridge

THE MAIN CORRIDOR

*Passage to the Underground
Lunchroom and elevators*

*Iceberg
Rock*

Boneyard

Veiled Statue

*Kings
Palace*

*Green Lake
Room*

*Queens
Chamber*

SCENIC ROOMS

Feet below Visitor Center

100
200
300
400
500
600
700
800
900

800

900

Corridor, which, if you keep looking around and up, conveys some of the cavern's enormity: The ceiling at times rises more than 200 feet above the path.

The trail soon passes **Devils Spring.** Here cave decoration continues. As water from rain and snow percolates through the ancient reef, it picks up calcite crystals from the limestone. The water then releases the crystals with each drop, splattering them onto the floor as the water drips—producing a stalagmite—or leaving them on the ceiling as the water discharges carbon dioxide into the cave air—creating a stalactite. (Park rangers like to repeat the mnemonic that stalactites "hang tight" to the ceiling, while stalagmites "might grow off your head.") You would have heard a lot more dripping 10,000 years ago,

Guadalupe Escarpment

Feet below Visitor Center

200
300
400
500
600
700
750

Tunnel to Painted Grotto
Crystal Spring Dome
The Big Room

Bottomless Pit

750
800
900

Twin Domes
Hall of Giants
Temple of the Sun

Mirror Lake

Top of the Cross

Lower Cave

LINCOLN
NATIONAL
FOREST

To
Carlsbad

Walnut Canyon
Desert Drive

GUADALUPE RIDGE

Rattlesnake
Canyon Trail

**Visitor
Center**

7

Whites
City

North Slaughter
Canyon Trail

62
180

**Slaughter
Canyon Cave**

**Rattlesnake
Springs**

418

Yucca Canyon Trail

🏚 Ranger Station   - - - Unpaved Road

🏚 Interpretive Trail   ⋯⋯ Hiking Trail

0   2   4 km
0   2   4 mi

To Guadalupe
Mts. NP and
El Paso, Tex.

Twin Domes in the Hall of Giants

when the climate was wetter. Now the Guadalupes receive only about 14 to 19 inches of precipitation a year, and most of the formations are no longer growing.

The trail soon skirts **Iceberg Rock,** a 200,000-ton boulder that crashed down from the ceiling thousands of years ago. After climbing **Appetite Hill,** stroll on past the **Boneyard,** which probably resembles the cavern of 4–6 million years ago, when water filled the chambers. Follow the signs to the **Underground Lunchroom** to have a meal, if you like. To reach ground level, take the nearby elevator up to the visitor center.

Big Room Tour

1 mile; 1 hour

After a minute's elevator ride, you'll be 755 feet, or about 75 stories, underground. (Compare your entrance to that of visitors of the early 1920s: They entered by "bucket elevator," as a pulley lowered them into the Bat Cave in a guano bucket.) Follow the signs for the Big Room: For the next hour or so, you'll be circling one gigantic chamber.

The **Big Room** is the largest single room most visitors will ever see

(unless they go to Borneo, where there is a cave with a larger, undecorated chamber), 1,800 feet long at its longest point, and 1,100 feet at its widest. It encompasses 8.2 acres.

To best enjoy the tour, linger, look, listen, and above all let loose your imagination. What do the various formations look like to you? Layer cakes? Chinese friezes? Fossilized bonsai? In recent years the Park Service removed labels from many of the formations, so now you can name the fantasyscape yourself.

Near the beginning of the walk, the **Hall of Giants** sports some of the largest formations in the cave, many of them about six stories tall. Look for **Giant Dome,** a 62-foot-high stalagmite, flanked by two 42-foot-high deputies. Appearances are deceptive here because of the immensity of the chamber.

The trail continues along the periphery of the room (resist the call of the shortcut) and leads past a view of the **Lower Cave,** accessible by reserved tour. Farther along, at **Top of the Cross,** rangers sometimes give talks at an amphitheater. Glance up: The ceiling here soars to 255 feet, its highest point above the trail.

The footpath continues through a less ornate area that was once a bat roost. The so-called **Bottomless Pit** has been measured at about 140 feet in depth; it does not lead to other passages. As you proceed, take a good look at sparkling **Crystal Spring Dome,** the cave's largest active stalagmite: Each drop of water adds crystals that make it infinitesimally bigger. Iron carried in the water delicately stains the formations of the Painted Grotto. Just a few minutes past the grotto, you will reach the elevator and ascend to daylight.

In the visitor center, don't miss the exhibits on cave restoration. There are also historical photographs here depicting the days of guano mining and early tourism. Then climb the stairs to the **Observation Tower.** Standing high above the ancient reef, you see a striking vista of the reef's seaward side (the slope past the parking lot) and the ancient seabed, called the Delaware Basin. If it's a clear day, the panorama before you will extend 100 miles or more into Texas.

Mexican free-tailed bats emerging from their cave

Other Trails & Sights

Desert Nature Trail: This easy half-mile loop makes an interesting diversion before the evening bat flight program. The trail's interpretive plaques describe how Indians made use of virtually every plant in sight. The trail starts to the right of the cave's natural entrance.

Walnut Canyon Desert Drive: An alternative introduction to the area's natural history. A booklet available at the start guides you along this 9.5-mile gravel loop off the main park road, just before the visitor center.

Kings Palace Tour: Led by park rangers, this 1.5-hour tour visits four highly decorative rooms, including the Kings Palace, which may be one of the world's most ornate cave rooms. Tour participants descend 830 feet to the deepest part of the cave open to the public. Look for the giant draperies, formed when water trickles down a slanted ceiling. Visitors will also find soda-straw stalactites, columns, and other interesting speleothems. Tours are offered several times a day throughout the year. Make reservations at the visitor center or by calling the park reservation number, (800) 967-2283.

Bat Flight: Don't miss the evening cyclone of bats; at its peak, more than

Immature bats in Bat Cave

5,000 bats per minute speed out of the cave on their way to consume some three tons of insects. From the visitor center, walk to the amphitheater, at the natural entrance, or drive there by turning right onto the main road, then right again.

Slaughter Canyon Cave: Be prepared to slip and slide as you explore an "unimproved" cave for 2 hours by flashlight. Accompanied by rangers, you'll see several types of formations not found in the main cave, after a steep half-mile climb up to the cave's entrance from the parking lot in Slaughter Canyon. The cave is open daily in summer; weekends only in winter. Make reservations at the visitor center or by calling the park reservation number, (800) 967-2283.

Information & Activities

Headquarters
3225 National Parks Hwy., Carlsbad, NM 88220. Phone (505) 785-2232. Off-trail trip reservations (800) 967-2283. www.nps.gov/cave

Seasons & Accessibility
Park open year-round.

Visitor & Information Centers
The visitor center is 7 miles from Whites City; open daily all year. Call headquarters for information.

Entrance Fees
No entrance fee for park. Fees to enter cavern and tour Natural Entrance route and Big Room: adults $6; children ages 6-15, $3; children under 6 free. To tour Kings Palace, additional $8 for adults, children under age 16, $4, children under 6 free, under 4 not permitted. To tour Slaughter Canyon Cave, additional $15 for adults, $7.50 for children under age 16; children under 6 not permitted. For off-trail caving tour, additional $12 for adults, $6 for children under age 16; children under 6 not permitted. No charge for bat flight program.

Pets
Not allowed in caves or backcountry. Kennel at the visitor center.

Facilities for Disabled
The visitor center and Bat Flight Amphitheater are wheelchair accessible, as is a portion of the Big Room Tour. Picnic area and rest rooms accessible at Rattlesnake Springs.

Things to Do
Ranger-led activities: tours of the main cavern (call park for details), cavern talks, dusk bat flight programs, flashlight trip into Slaughter Canyon Cave (see p. 131; reservations required). Also available, self-guided Desert Nature Trail, self-guided Walnut Canyon Desert Drive, backcountry trails.

Special Advisories
● Wear low-heeled, nonskid shoes in the caverns, and bring a jacket.
● Intense summer thunderstorms may cause floods in low-lying areas, lightning strikes in higher areas.
● Watch out for rattlesnakes when hiking the backcountry trails.
● Cactuses and other spiny desert plants can inflict painful injuries.
● Baby strollers are not permitted on cave trails.

Overnight Backpacking
Permits required. Available free at the visitor center.

Campgrounds
None; backcountry camping only. Food services in park. Note that campfires are not permitted in park.

Hotels, Motels, & Inns
(unless otherwise noted, rates are for 2 persons in a double room, high season)
In Whites City, NM 88268:
Best Western Cavern Inn 17 Carlsbad Cavern Hwy., P.O. Box 128. (800) 228-3767 or (505) 785-2291. 42 units. $89. AC, pool, restaurant.
In Carlsbad, NM 88220:
Best Western Stevens Inn 1829 S. Canal St., P.O. Box 580. (800) 730-2851 or (505) 887-2851. 220 units, 28 with kitchenettes. $69. AC, pool, restaurant.
Carlsbad Super 8 3817 National Parks Hwy. (800) 800-8000 or (505) 887-8888. 60 units. $60, includes breakfast. AC, pool.
Continental Inn 3820 National Parks Hwy. (505) 887-0341. 60 units. $45-$50. AC, pool.
Great Western Inn & Suites 3804 National Parks Hwy. (800) 987-5535 or (505) 887-5535. 87 units, 25 with kitchenettes. $69-$90. AC, pool.
Quality Inn 3706 National Parks Hwy. (800) 321-2861 or (505) 887-2861. 123 units. $60. AC, pool, restaurant.

Contact the Carlsbad Chamber of Commerce for a full list of accommodations: P.O. Box 910, Carlsbad, NM 88221. (505) 887-6516.

Excursions

Lincoln National Forest
Alamogordo, New Mexico

In 1950, a game warden here rescued a black bear cub from a forest fire and named him Smokey Bear—he became a famous symbol of fire prevention. Lincoln contains life zones from desert to subalpine forest and limestone caves. 1,103,441 acres. 370 campsites. Hiking, fishing, horseback riding, hunting, picnicking, winter sports. Open all year; most campsites open seasonally. Adjoins Carlsbad Caverns NP on west. Information at Carlsbad on US 285, about 20 miles from park. (505) 434-7200.

White Sands National Monument
Alamogordo, New Mexico

Waves of gypsum sand, some 50 feet high, offer an ever changing vista here in the Tularosa Basin. Weathered rock from surrounding highlands settles in Lake Lucero and adjacent alkali flats; scouring southwest winds create the dunes. Features 16-mile-long Dunes Drive. 144,420 acres. Primitive camping, food services, picnic areas. Hiking. Open daily except Christmas. Visitor center on US 70, about 190 miles from Carlsbad Caverns NP. (505) 479-6124.

Bosque del Apache National Wildlife Refuge
Socorro, New Mexico

The Rio Grande bisects this refuge, where carefully maintained ponds and marshes shelter wintering snow geese and other waterfowl, as well as sandhill cranes, bald eagles, and peregrine falcons. 57,191 acres. Hiking, fishing (in summer), biking, hunting, scenic drives. Open year-round, from 1 hour before sunrise to 1 hour after sunset. Visitor center on N. Mex. 1, off I-25, about 270 miles from Carlsbad Caverns NP. (505) 835-1828.

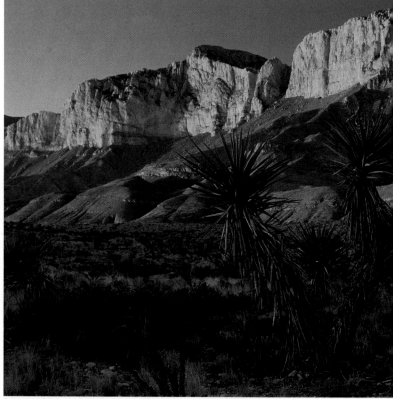

Sunset on El Capitan, beacon of the Guadalupes

Guadalupe Mountains

Texas

Established September 30, 1972

86,416 acres

In West Texas, only about 40 miles southwest of Carlsbad Caverns, lies a gem of a park that few people outside the state have ever heard of, let alone visited. Guadalupe Mountains National Park contains the southernmost, highest part of the 50-mile-long Guadalupe range. From the highway, the mountains resemble a nearly monolithic wall through the desert. But drive into one of the park entrances, take even a short stroll, and surprises crop up: dramatically contoured canyons, shady glades surrounded by desert scrub, a profusion of wildlife and birds.

Some 80 miles of trails can lead the more energetic hiker to Guadalupe Peak, the highest point in Texas (8,749 feet), and to mountaintops with scattered but thick conifer forests typical of the Rockies hundreds of miles to the north. The range's origins may be surprising too: The Guadalupe Mountains were once a reef growing beneath the waters of an ancient inland sea. That same vanished sea spawned the honeycomb of the Carlsbad Caverns.

Pottery, baskets, and spear tips found in the mountains suggest that people first visited the Guadalupes about 12,000 years ago, hunting the camels, mammoths, and other animals that flourished in the wetter climate of the waning Ice Age. When the Spaniards arrived in the Southwest in the mid-16th century, Mescalero Apache were periodically camping near the springs at the base of the mountains and climbing to the highlands to hunt and forage.

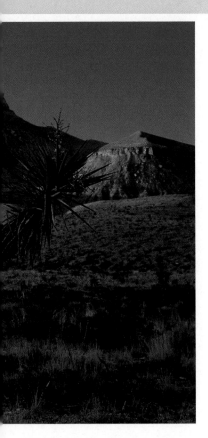

main visitor center, then continue 4 miles to the parking lot. For Dog Canyon, either hike 12 miles from Pine Springs Campground or drive north on US 62/180, then west on Cty. Rd. 408, and south on N. Mex. 137, about 105 miles total from Pine Springs. Airports: Carlsbad, New Mexico, and El Paso, Texas.

When to Go
All-year park, but spring and fall are best. In spring, the foliage is fresh and, with enough rain, the blossoms abundant. In late October to mid-November, changing leaves provide splashes of red, yellow, and burgundy.

How to Visit
On a day trip, head to the visitor center and **Pine Springs;** take at least a short hike. On a second day, visit **McKittrick Canyon** for a stroll through a hidden oasis. To visit a wilder, more isolated area, where trails take you quickly into the high country, drive about 3 hours to reenter the park at **Dog Canyon** in the north.

Pine Springs-Frijole Area
a half to full day

Pick up maps and trail information at the **Headquarters Visitor Center,** where you can also enjoy audiovisual programs on the park's ecology, geology, and history. Fill your water bottles before leaving. Then stroll to **The Pinery** or drive back to the highway, turn left in about a tenth of a mile, and park. The stone walls remain from the 1858 Pinery Station of the Butterfield Overland Mail Line—forerunner of the Pony Express. Buy a self-guiding leaflet, if you wish, to learn about the colorful local history. Return to your car, and go back to the highway and turn left. Go left again in about a mile onto a dirt road. Park at the end near the **Frijole Ranch,** the 1870s ranch house that now preserves artifacts and exhibits the park's cultural history.

Be sure to walk the easy 2.3-mile loop trail to **Smith** and **Manzanita Springs,** an excellent introduction to the striking contrasts the Chihuahuan Desert presents. Bear right at the trailhead. The thorny plants may seem forbidding, but the Mescalero Apache

Both the Apache and Europeans spun legends of fabulous caches of gold in these mountains.

As American prospectors, settlers, and cavalry pushed west, the Apache made the mountainous areas their bases and fought to ward off encroachers. By the late 1880s, however, virtually all the Indians had been killed or forced onto a reservation.

Donations of ranchlands eventually gave impetus to the park. In 1998 the park acquired 10,000 acres adjacent to its then western boundary, including some 2,000 acres of white gypsum sand dunes and dunes of brick red quartzose, both deposits left by the ancient sea.

How to Get There
The main visitor center and most visitor activities are located in the Pine Springs-Frijole area, off US 62/180, 55 miles southwest of Carlsbad and 110 miles east of El Paso. For McKittrick Canyon, turn off US 62/180 about 7 miles northeast of the

To El Paso Gap 137
LINCOLN NATIONAL FOREST

Dog Canyon

UPPER DOG CANYON

Tejas Trail

Wilderness Ridge

Permian Reef Geology Trail

Pratt Cabin

McKittrick Ridge
7,716 ft

McKittrick Canyon

Lost Peak
7,830 ft

McKittrick Canyon Trail

Grotto Picnic Area

MC KITTRICK CANYON

SOUTH

Mescalero

Gate
To Outer Gate

Tejas

M O U N T A I N S

THE BOWL

To Carlsbad, NM

Pine Top

62 180

Smith Springs

SPRING CANYON

Tejas Trail

Bear Canyon Trail

Manzanita Spring

Frijole Ranch

Guadalupe Peak

The Pinery

Pine Springs

Headquarters Visitor Center

Guadalupe Peak
8,749 ft

El Capitan
8,085 ft

El Capitan Trail

GLOVER CANYON

Salt Basin Overlook

GUADALUPE CANYON

62 180

DELAWARE MOUNTAINS

↑

🏠 Ranger Station
🔺 Campground
▲ Primitive Campsite
– · – Unpaved Road
········ Hiking Trail

Gate

0   1   2 km
0   1   2 mi

To El Paso Gate

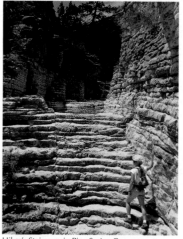

Hiker's Staircase, in Pine Spring Canyon

used a great majority of the plants in sight for food or fiber. Their diet consisted largely of mescal—the heart of the agave plant, one of the succulents with spikes at the tips of the leaves— hence the culture's name. You'll soon approach **Manzanita Spring,** a place to spot wildlife.

Continue on to **Smith Spring,** a veritable garden of maidenhair ferns, Texas madrone trees (the ones shedding layers of paper-thin bark), alligator juniper (named for its distinctively textured bark), oak, and maple. As you loop back to your car, bear left at the fork.

Return to the highway and drive west-southwest about 2 miles, or at least as far as the first pullover, for a superb view of **El Capitan** (8,085 feet), the southernmost bluff of the Guadalupes. Late afternoon light shows off this imposing symbol of the region, once the beacon for conquistador, stagecoach driver, and homesteader.

McKittrick Canyon

a half to full day

The walls of McKittrick Canyon shelter the only year-round stream in the park; the water creates a 3-mile-long oasis of oak and juniper, madrone and maple. The canyon itself is nearly 5 miles long. Pick up a self-guiding booklet on the area's human and natural history at the **McKittrick Canyon Contact Station** near the trailheads. For an easy hike (although the trail is

rocky and best negotiated in hiking boots), walk the 2.3 miles to the **Pratt Lodge.** If you have time, continue another mile through the woods that border the intermittent stream to the **Grotto** picnic area. Because the canyon plants are fragile, be sure to stay on the trail.

McKittrick Canyon exposes millions of years of geological events. During the Permian era, about 250 million years ago, an inland sea covered parts of West Texas and southeast New Mexico. Along the shore of the sea grew a reef of lime-secreting algae, sponges, other marine organisms, and calcium carbonate precipitated from the water. After millions of years, the climate changed and the ocean dried up; the Capitan Reef loomed hundreds of feet high in a horseshoe 400 miles long. Sediments and mineral salts buried both basin and reef over the next eons. Later, the region began to rise, and erosion slowly reexposed the seabed with part of the fossil reef—today's Guadalupe range— towering above.

As you walk into McKittrick Canyon, you are entering the Capitan Reef from the seaward side. To best observe the reef's varied formation and fossils, try the **Permian Reef Geology Trail.** You'll see layers of the ancient reef exposed by centuries of cutting by McKittrick Creek. The trail—4.5 miles one way—climbs the 2,000-foot ridge to a ponderosa forest on the top.

Dog Canyon

a half to full day

Accessibility to the forested high country and its spectacular scenery make Dog Canyon well worth the drive. Ask a ranger to point out Apache mescal-roasting pits, still visible among the hip-high grasses, creosote bushes, and succulents. Then picnic and hike; the trails begin past the stables. Popular hikes include the **Bush Mountain Trail,** which, in about 3 miles, leads through open pinyon-juniper woodland to splendid views of the Guadalupes and the **Cornudas Mountains,** 55 miles to the west. The **Tejas Trail** offers similar views and in about 4 miles climbs into a temperate woodland of Gambel oak, Douglas-fir, and limber and ponderosa pine. This forest is a relict of the plant communities that cloaked the region in the last Ice Age. It still survives because of the particular, unusual combination of temperature and humidity at this high-altitude site.

Other Hikes

Hikers may find the following three treks rewarding. They all begin from Pine Springs Campground; ask a ranger for information:

Guadalupe Peak, 8.3 miles round-trip. Because lightning storms can quickly gather on hot summer afternoons, it's best to begin your ascent by 8 a.m. and your descent by 1 p.m. *Watch the weather. If you see a storm coming, start down immediately.*
The Bowl, a lush area of relict ice age conifer forest. The 9.5-mile loop comprises the Tejas, **Bowl,** and **Bear Canyon Trails.**
Devils Hall, a steep, narrow canyon; 4.5 miles round-trip, mostly level.

Information & Activities

Headquarters
HC 60, Box 400, Salt Flat, TX 79847. Phone (915) 828-3251.
www.nps.gov/gumo

Seasons & Accessibility
Open year-round but may be inaccessible for brief periods in winter due to snowstorms. Best to phone park.

Visitor & Information Centers
Headquarters Visitor Center, a tenth of a mile off US 62/180 at Guadalupe Pass, open all year except Christmas. **McKittrick Canyon Visitor Center,** off US 62/180 on eastern edge of park and **Dog Canyon Ranger Station** in the north open intermittently. Call park for details.

Entrance Fee
None.

Pets
Not permitted on trails or in buildings; elsewhere must be leashed.

Facilities for Disabled
The visitor centers, rest rooms, and Pine Springs Campground and amphitheater are wheelchair accessible.

Things to Do
Hikes, horseback trail rides (no rentals), evening and children's programs.

Special Advisories
● Rattlesnakes and other potentially harmful desert animals live here; watch out!
● Bring maps with you if planning to hike; park is managed as wilderness, so trail signs are minimal.

Overnight Backpacking
Allowed at designated sites only; permits required; they are free and may be obtained at visitor centers. Backcountry use permits required to bring a horse into the park, available from main visitor center or Dog Canyon. Horses are not allowed in the backcountry overnight; they can be stabled in Frijole Ranch and Dog Canyon corrals; reserve space by calling (915) 828-3251.

Campgrounds
Two campgrounds, both with 14-day limit. Open all year, first come, first served. $8 per night at **Dog Canyon** and **Pine Springs.** No showers. Tent and RV sites; no hookups. Two group campgrounds; reservations required through headquarters.

Hotels, Motels, & Inns
(unless otherwise noted, rates are for 2 persons in a double room, high season)
In Whites City, NM 88268:
Best Western Cavern Inn, 12 Carlsbad Cavern Hwy., P.O. Box 128. (800) 228-3767 or (505) 785-2291. 132 units. $89. AC, pool, restaurant.
In Van Horn, TX 79855:
Best Western American Inn 1309 W. Broadway, Box 626. (800) 621-2478 or (915) 283-2030. 33 units. $55. AC, pool.
Ramada, Ltd., 200 Golf Course Dr., P.O. Box 1568. (915) 283-2780. 60 units. $68. AC, pool.

See also Carlsbad Caverns NP listings, p. 132

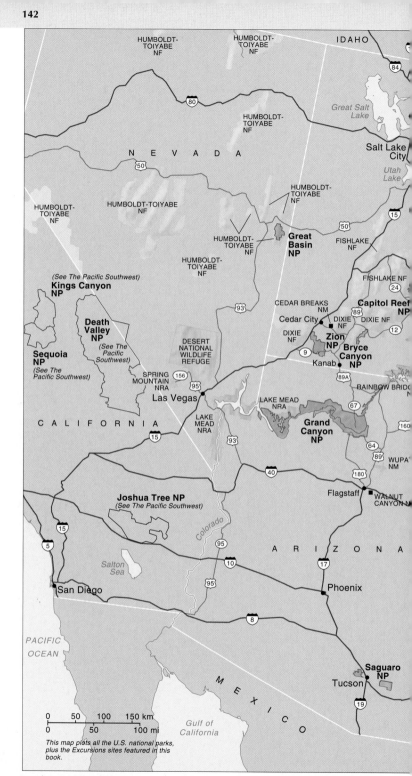

This map plots all the U.S. national parks, plus the Excursions sites featured in this book.

Preceding pages: Grand Canyon

The Colorado Plateau

Theodore Roosevelt called the Grand Canyon "the one great sight ... every American should see." Although the Grand Canyon remains the most famous sight on the Colorado Plateau, this high desert drained by the Colorado River and its tributaries teems with scenic treasures. Numerous gorges slice the colorfully layered rock; stairstep terraces, buttes, and spires embellish it. The region contains the nation's largest concentration of national parks.

The striated cliffs of the canyon parks collectively encompass nearly two billion years of Earth's history, divulging tales of ancient seas and volcanoes, deserts and dinosaurs. The rush of rivers sculptured the colossal gorges and side canyons of Grand Canyon, Zion, and Canyonlands. Grit-bearing winds and the freeze and thaw of water droplets chiseled multihued rock into the hoodoos, arches, and pinnacles visible in Arches and Bryce Canyon.

Although one of the most sparsely populated regions of the United States today, the plateau features some of the country's richest remains of early Indian civilizations. Archaeological highlights range from petroglyphs in Canyonlands, Capitol Reef, and Saguaro to pueblos and solstice markers in Petrified Forest to spectacular cliff dwellings in Mesa Verde.

Thanks to abrupt changes in elevation, the canyon parks shelter a wide diversity of plants and animals. Desert or semidesert at canyon bottom gives way to pinyon-juniper woodland and then ponderosa pine and spruce-fir forests. Lizards and deer, cottontails and bighorn sheep can coexist in the same park. The desert park, Saguaro, protects North America's largest cactus, as well as the many other plants and animals of the vast Sonoran Desert.

Flagstaff, Arizona, makes a convenient base for the South Rim of the Grand Canyon and for Petrified Forest. From Kanab, Utah, you can visit Grand Canyon's North Rim, Bryce, Capitol Reef, and Zion. Just west of the plateau, a 5-hour drive from Kanab, lies Great Basin. For Arches and Canyonlands, Moab, Utah, is the place to stop, and to visit Saguaro, head for Tucson, Arizona.

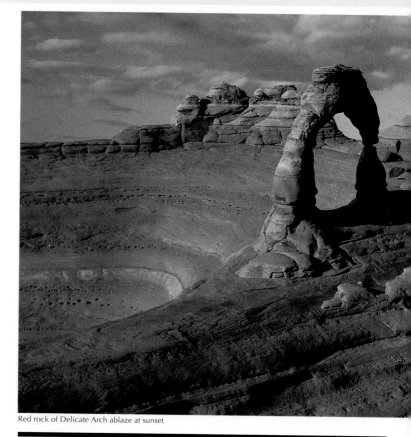

Red rock of Delicate Arch ablaze at sunset

Arches

Utah

Established November 12, 1971

76,359 acres

This park contains more than 2,000 natural arches—the greatest concentration in the world. But numbers have no significance beside the grandeur of the landscape—the arches, the giant balanced rocks, spires, pinnacles, and slickrock domes against the enormous sky.

Perched high above the Colorado River, the park is part of southern Utah's extended area of canyon country, carved and shaped by eons of weathering and erosion. Most of the formations at Arches are made of soft red sandstone deposited 150 million years ago in a vast desert. As underlying salt deposits dissolved, the sandstone collapsed and weathered into a maze of vertical rock slabs called

"fins." Sections of these slender walls eventually wore through, creating the spectacular rock sculptures you see today.

The land has a timeless, indestructible look that is misleading. Almost a million visitors each year threaten the fragile high desert ecosystem. One concern is a dark crust called cryptobiotic soil composed of algae, fungi, and lichens that grow in sandy areas in the park. Footprints tracked across this living community may remain visible for years. In fact, the aridity helps preserve traces of past activity for centuries. Visitors are asked to walk only on designated trails or stay on slickrock or wash bottoms.

Well-preserved petroglyphs carved into a low cliff near a pioneer cabin offer evidence that Indians roamed this land. Pictures of riders on horseback date the carvings to historic times, after the Spaniards introduced horses to the Southwest.

How to Get There

From Moab, take US 191 north 5 miles to the park entrance. From I-70, exit at Crescent Junction and follow US 191 south for 25 miles to the entrance. Airport: 15 miles north of Moab and at Grand Junction, Colorado, about 120 miles away.

When to Go

All-year park, but spring and fall are best; moderate temperatures are ideal for hiking in the high desert. Summers are hot and winters mild. Wildflowers peak in April and May.

How to Visit

Take the **Arches Scenic Drive** at least as far as **The Windows Section.** Allow time for hiking one of the park's spectacular trails. If it's spring, summer, or fall (and you're not bothered by heights), consider joining a naturalist-led 3-hour hike through **Fiery Furnace** (fee). It's

strenuous, but you'll appreciate the shade in summer's heat. Contact the visitor center for reservations and tickets.

Arches Scenic Drive

18 miles one way; a half to full day

The scenic drive climbs from the floor of **Moab Canyon** to **Devils Garden,** passing through the heart of the park with spur roads leading to **The Windows Section, Wolfe Ranch,** and **Delicate Arch** area. Numerous pull-offs allow leisurely viewing of the park's major features.

From the visitor center the road winds up the canyon wall. Pull off after 2 miles at the **Park Avenue Viewpoint and Trailhead** for a view down an open canyon flanked by sandstone skyscrapers. If you have a willing driver (or don't mind the 320-foot return climb), walk the easy 1-mile path to the **Courthouse Towers** parking area, where you can be picked up. Here signs describe nearby rock formations that show the birth and death of an arch.

Continue your drive to the beautiful slickrock expanse known as the **Petrified Dunes.** Here you skirt knolls—ancient dunes turned to stone—as the **La Sal Mountains** rise nearly 13,000 feet in the far distance. Farther along, stop at the **Balanced Rock** pull-off where a 0.4-mile trail loops past this classic hoodoo, a strangely eroded rock spire 128 feet high. Edward Abbey wrote his classic *Desert Solitaire* after living in a trailer here as a park ranger. Just beyond, turn onto the paved road leading to The Windows.

The road to the right passes a cluster of pinnacles and monoliths called **Garden of Eden** and ends at a parking area fronted by a sandstone wall perforated by several arches. Short trails lead to closeup views of these colossal gateways. The 0.3-mile walk to **South Window,** 105 feet wide, also gives you good views of **North Window** and **Turret Arch.** If time allows walk the half-mile trail for a dramatic closeup look at **Double Arch.**

Retrace your route back to the main road. A road leaves the scenic drive and leads 1.5 miles to historic **Wolfe Ranch,** where a Civil War veteran raised cattle around the turn of the 20th century, and the **Delicate Arch Viewpoint,** 1 mile farther. The

Campground

Interpretive Trail

Unpaved (2-wheel-drive road)

Unpaved (4-wheel-drive road)

Hiking Trail

| 0 | 1 | 2 | 3 km |

| 0 | 1 | 2 | 3 mi |

WINTER CAMP RIDGE

Salt Wash

Delicate Arch

Wolfe Ranch

Delicate Arch Viewpoint

CACHE VALLEY

Panorama Point

DRY MESA

Garden of Eden

Double Arch

North Window

Turret Arch South Window

THE WINDOWS SECTION

Colorado

To Castle Valley To Cisco and 70

128

Colorado

NEGRO BILL CANYON

distant view of **Delicate Arch** is disappointing, so if you have the stamina and at least 2 extra hours return to Wolfe Ranch and hike to the foot of the arch. The magnificent views make this one of the most rewarding hikes in canyon country, but you're better off saving it for a second day if you plan to take the full drive and other walks.

The trail to Delicate Arch gains 500 feet in elevation as it traverses 1.5 miles across slickrock as smooth and cambered as the back of a whale. Near the trail, juniper trees grow from cracks so small the trunks seem to emerge from solid rock. Keep your eye out for the rock cairns that mark the trail; they're easy to miss. The arch perches on the edge of a bowl, framing white-capped mountains in winter; the suddenness of your encounter with it at trail's end adds to its drama.

Return to the main road. Skip the **Salt Valley Overlook** but pull off at **Fiery Furnace**, a dense array of red fins that appear to ignite when the sun is low in the west. Here you see a world standing on end—hoodoos, spires, and slabs 200 feet high. It's easy to get lost in the maze of deeply grooved slots and dead-end passageways. Note that visitors who are not part of a guided walk will need a permit to explore Fiery Furnace.

Continue your drive. Take the 0.2-mile walk to the cool shade of **Sand Dune Arch,** tucked between two fins, but save **Broken Arch** for another time. Farther down the road **Skyline Arch** comes into view. In 1940 a great rock mass broke from the arch, doubling the size of the opening to 45 by 69 feet.

The road ends at the Devils Garden campground and trailhead beyond. The **Devils Garden Trail** meanders 7.2 miles to seven major arches, each with its own character. Be sure to save enough time to walk at least as far as **Landscape Arch,** eight-tenths of a mile down the

Landscape Arch in winter

trail. Here a narrow ribbon of stone 306 feet long appears to defy gravity as it floats in a graceful span above a steep dune. It's one of the world's longest freestanding natural arches. From here, take the curving, primitive trail that leads toward Double O Arch.

If you walk the trail in early morning, watch for the white evening primrose. As the sunlight grows stronger, the flowers wilt, turning the petals pink. Though also primitive beyond Landscape Arch, the trail continues on another mile to **Double O Arch**, a 160-foot-wide circular arch that hangs above a smaller bore. From here you can walk about half a mile to the rock spire known as the **Dark Angel**.

Information & Activities

Headquarters
P.O. Box 907, Moab, UT 84532. Phone (435) 719-2299. ww.nps.gov/arch

Seasons & Accessibility
Park open year-round. Some unpaved roads may become temporarily impassable after heavy rains. Call headquarters for current weather and road information.

Visitor & Information Centers
Visitor center, on US 191 at park entrance, open daily all year. Call headquarters number for visitor information.

Entrance Fees
$10 per car per week allows multiple entries. Yearly fee of $25 is also good at Canyonlands NP, and Natural Bridges and Hovenweep NMs.

Pets
Prohibited on all hiking trails and in the backcountry.

Facilities for Disabled
Visitor center and one of its rest rooms are wheelchair accessible. Rest room and one campsite accessible in Devils Garden Campground. Park Avenue and Delicate Arch Viewpoints are accessible to wheelchairs.

Things to Do
Naturalist-led activities: nature hikes and talks, evening programs. Also available, geological and historical exhibits, self-guided auto tour, hiking, jeep tours, sight-seeing flights. Contact park headquarters for list of concessioners offering rental and guide services.

Special Advisories
● Always carry water on hikes—at least a gallon a day per person is recommended in summer.

● Stay on trails to protect fragile desert soils and plant life.

● Sandstone slickrock crumbles easily and can make climbing dangerous. Consult a ranger before going out.

Overnight Backpacking
Permits required (free from visitor center).

Campgrounds
One campground, **Devils Garden**, with a 7-day limit. Open all year. Winter, first come, first served; March through Oct., preregister at the visitor center, which opens at 7:30 a.m. Fees $10 per night. No showers. Tent and RV sites; no hookups. Reservations required for **Devils Garden Group Campgrounds**; tent sites only. Call (435) 719-2299.

Hotels, Motels, & Inns
(unless otherwise noted, rates for 2 persons, double room, high season)
In Moab, UT 84532:
Best Western Green Well Motel 105 S. Main St. (800) 528-1234 or (435) 259-6151. 72 units. $79-$130. AC, pool, rest. **Big Horn Travelodge** 550 S. Main St. (800) 325-6171 or (435) 259-6171. 58 units. $70. AC, pool, restaurant. **Cedar Breaks Condos** Center and 4th E. (800) 505-5343. Six 2-bedroom units with full kitchens. $75-$130. AC. **Pack Creek Ranch** (15 miles southeast of Moab, off LaSal Mountain Loop Rd.) P.O. Box 1270. (435) 259-5505. Cabins, houses, bunkhouses. $135-$300, includes breakfast. Trail rides and massages for a fee. AC, pool. **Ramada Inn—Moab** 182 S. Main St. (435) 259-7141. 82 units. $85-$109. AC, pool, restaurant.

For other accommodations in the area, contact Utah's Canyonlands Region, 805 N. Main St., Moab, UT 84532. (800) 233-8824 or (435) 259-7814.

Excursions

Manti-LaSal National Forest
Moab, Utah

Mountains, densely wooded with
aspen, pine, fir, and spruce and rugged
grassland-covered plateaus, provide
cool contrast here in red-rock country.
Contains Dark Canyon Wilderness.
1,265,254 acres, part in Colorado.
Hiking, climbing, bicycling, fishing,
horseback riding, hunting, winter
sports. 136 campsites, picnic areas.
Open year-round; campsites open late
May through October. Information at
Moab on US 191, about 5 miles southeast of Arches NP. (435) 259-7155 or
(435) 637-2817.

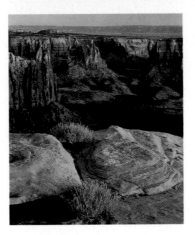

Colorado
National Monument
Fruita, Colorado

The 23-mile-long Rim Rock Drive
and well-maintained trails with gentle
switchbacks provide easy access to
this monument's small, sheer-walled
canyons and sandstone monoliths.
Shelters mule deer, bighorn sheep, and
mountain lions. 20,533 acres. Hiking,
climbing, bicycling, horseback riding,
scenic drives, winter sports. 80 campsites, picnic areas, handicapped access.
Open year-round. Located on Colo.
340, about 100 miles from Arches NP.
(970) 858-3617.

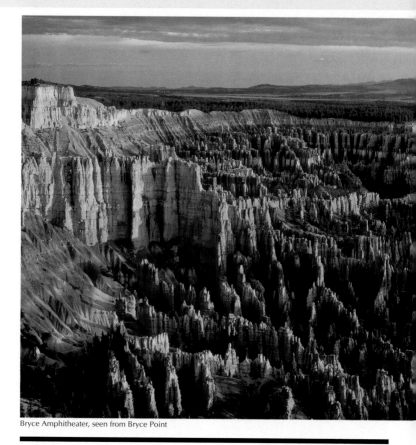

Bryce Amphitheater, seen from Bryce Point

Bryce Canyon

Utah

Established September 15, 1928

35,835 acres

Perhaps nowhere are the forces of natural erosion more tangible than at Bryce Canyon. Its wilderness of phantom-like rock spires, or hoodoos, attracts more than 1.7 million visitors a year. Many descend on trails that give hikers and horseback riders a close look at the fluted walls and sculptured pinnacles.

The park follows the edge of the Paunsaugunt Plateau. On the west are heavily forested tablelands more than 9,000 feet high; on the east are the intricately carved breaks where the country drops 2,000 feet to the Paria Valley. Many ephemeral streams have eaten into the plateau, forming horseshoe-shaped amphitheaters. The largest and most striking is Bryce Amphitheater. Encompassing 6 square miles, it is the scenic heart of the park.

Water has been helping carve Bryce's rugged landscape for millions of years and is still at work. Water may split rock as it freezes and expands in cracks—a cyclic process that occurs some 200 times a year. In summer, runoff from violent cloudbursts etches into the softer limestones and sluices through the deep runnels. In about half a century the present rim will be cut back into the plateau another foot. But there is more here than spectacular erosion.

In the early morning you can stand for long moments on the rim, held by the amphitheater's mysterious blend of rock and color. Warm yellows and oranges radiate from the deeply pigmented walls as scatterings of light illuminate the pale rock spires.

October. Winter lasts from November through March; snow highlights the brilliantly colored cliffs and provides fine cross-country skiing.

How to Visit

On a 1-day visit, tour the **Bryce Amphitheater,** beginning, if possible, with sunrise at **Bryce Point.** If limited time requires choosing between the scenic drive or a walk beneath the rim, take the walk. On a longer stay, drive to **Rainbow Point;** consider a moonlight stroll among the hoodoos.

Bryce Amphitheater
8 miles; 2 hours to a full day

Watch sunrise from **Bryce Point,** one of the highest overlooks along the rim of the amphitheater. Drive about 4 miles south of the visitor center, then walk a short distance from the parking lot to the viewpoint.

Colors begin to glow even before the sun breaks over the **Aquarius Plateau,** at over 10,000 feet the highest plateau in North America. First light catches the rim of the amphitheater, then drops into the basin, igniting the crowded pillars of rock. From this vantage point you see shallow caves along the rim called the **Grottoes.** Look for the **Alligator,** a sharply incised butte that appears reptilian from above, and the **Sinking Ship,** which resembles a vanishing prow.

Drive back to **Inspiration Point,** bypassing the **Paria View** turnoff. From the parking lot walk up a short but steep trail to upper Inspiration Point. If the trail looks too ambitious, stay below at the lower viewpoint. Both look over the head of the amphitheater and place you close to the rock formations. No matter what time of day, they provide excellent all-around views.

In the valley below is the small town of **Tropic.** Scottish emigrant Ebenezer Bryce and his wife, Mary, homesteaded nearby in 1875. They grazed cattle in Bryce Canyon but moved away 5 years later, leaving behind little more than their name.

Continue on to **Sunset Point.** The name is misleading since the viewpoint faces east, limiting sundown views. But the mix of shadows and deep-hued colors makes this an excellent vantage point in the low-angled light of later

There is a sense of place here that goes beyond rocks. Some local Paiute Indians explained it with a legend. Once there lived animal-like creatures that changed themselves into people. But they were bad, so Coyote turned them into rocks of various configurations. The spellbound creatures still huddle together here with faces painted just as they were before being turned to stone.

How to Get There

From Zion National Park (83 miles west), follow Utah 9 east, turn north onto Utah 89, then continue east on Utah 12 to Utah 63, which is the park entrance road. From Capitol Reef National Park (about 120 miles away), follow Utah 12 southward to Utah 63. Airport: Salt Lake City.

When to Go

All-year park. Wildflowers are at their peak in spring and early summer; the greatest variety of the park's 170 bird species appears between May and

Thor's Hammer at sunrise

afternoon. To the left is **Thor's Hammer;** to the right is the **Silent City**—a gridwork of deep ravines that divide turreted walls suggesting the ruins of an ancient metropolis.

Those with time and stamina can follow the **Navajo Loop Trail,** a fairly strenuous 1.5-mile loop into the canyon. The trail drops steeply in a series of tight switchbacks before entering a narrow, steep-walled gorge called **Wall Street.** Several Douglas-firs, two of them 700 years old, grow

between the towering cliffs.

Continue down the trail to the junction with **Queen's Garden Trail,** the least strenuous trail below the rim. It winds along the bottom of the amphitheater to Queen's Garden, then climbs to the rim at Sunrise Point, passing weird rock formations and occasional bristlecone pines. From Sunrise Point follow the **Rim Trail** a half mile back to your car at Sunset Point.

The Drive to Rainbow Point

17 miles; 3 hours to a half day

Following the edge of the gently tilted plateau, a scenic drive ascends over a thousand feet to Rainbow Point, the plateau's southernmost reach. Before beginning the drive, be sure to see **Fairyland Point.**

Just after you enter the park boundaries, but before the entrance station, a mile-long spur road leads to the Fairyland overlook. The temptation is to leave this for later, but here you see one of the finest vistas in the park. In colorful array, spires and monoliths rise close at hand. Some stand isolated like chess pieces; others group together like a Greek chorus. A

Exploring Bryce Canyon on horseback

short hike down the trail takes you right among them—a quick immersion course in the effects of erosion.

When you return to your car, drive past the Sunset Point turnoff (trailers are not allowed beyond here) and on past the Bryce Point turnoff. You leave the ponderosa pine forest behind and quickly find yourself among the high-elevation Douglas-fir and blue spruce.

Pull in at **Farview Point** for a panoramic view of **Table Cliffs** and a series of broad platforms stairstepping southeast to the **Kaibab Plateau** at the North Rim of the **Grand Canyon.**

Continue south to **Natural Bridge** pull-off. Here you have a closeup view of a natural arch 85 feet long and 125 feet high. Its bright rusty red contrasts with the deep green of the trees below and the deep blue of the sky above.

The next pull-off is **Agua Canyon,** one of the finest vistas in the park. Massive hoodoos stand close to the rim; farther off are the vividly colored

Pink Cliffs; and on the far horizon is the domed profile of **Navajo Mountain,** over 10,000 feet high.

Continue to the end of the road at **Rainbow Point.** Stop here for a picnic among the thick stands of fir on the park's highest elevation, 9,115 feet. A pleasant mile walk follows the **Bristlecone Loop Trail** to expansive views. A spur trail leads to more views at **Yovimpa Point;** the cliffs that descend from there in stairsteps are named for their rock colors—

pink, gray, white, vermilion, and chocolate. A stand of ancient bristlecone pines grows on the exposed edge of the plateau; the oldest bristlecone pine in the park has been alive for more than 1,500 years.

Acoustic studies have found that the natural silence in the park equals the quality of a sound studio. The park boasts some of the nation's best air quality as well. But rangers worry that this purity will be threatened by possible development on adjacent lands.

Information & Activities

Headquarters
Bryce Canyon, UT 84717. Phone (435) 834-5322. www.nps.gov/brca

Seasons & Accessibility
Park open year-round. Roads may be closed for short periods due to snowstorms. Some spur roads closed in winter for cross-country skiing. Phone headquarters for information.

Visitor & Information Centers
Visitor center on main road, 1 mile inside park boundary. Open all year. Call headquarters for visitor information.

Entrance Fees
$20 per car per week. From mid-May through September, visitors leave their cars near the entrance. From there, a new shuttle system will transport visitors to points throughout the park.

Facilities for Disabled
Visitor center partially accessible to wheelchairs; all viewpoints and a half-mile stretch of trail between Sunset and Sunrise Points also accessible.

Things to Do
Free naturalist-led activities (summer): prairie dog and other nature walks, history and geology talks, evening programs, night sky programs, moonlight walks. Also, hiking, guided trail rides (inquire at Bryce Lodge or call 435-679-8665), cross-country skiing, snowshoeing.

Overnight Backpacking
Allowed only on the **Under-the-Rim Trail** near Bryce Point. Purchase permits for $5 at visitor center or, in summer, at nature center.

Campgrounds
Two campgrounds; 14-day limit. Part of **North** open all year. **Sunset** open May through September. Both first come, first served. Fees $10 per night. Showers nearby. Tent and RV sites; no hookups. **Sunset Group Campground;** reservations required; contact park. Food services in park.

Hotels, Motels, & Inns
(unless otherwise noted, rates for 2 persons, double room, high season)
INSIDE THE PARK:
Bryce Canyon Lodge (south of Utah 12 on Utah 63) Xanterra Parks & Resorts, Bryce Canyon NP, UT 84717. (888) 297-2757 or (435) 834-5361. Cabins, rooms, suites. $99-$122. Restaurant. Open April through Oct.
OUTSIDE THE PARK:
In Bryce, UT 84764:
Best Western Ruby's Inn (on Utah 63). (800) 528-1234 or (435) 834-5341. 368 units. $90-$150. AC, pool, rest.
Bryce Canyon Pines Motel (on Utah 12) P.O. Box 43. (435) 834-5441. 45 rooms; 7 cabins, 2 kitchenettes. $75. Pool, restaurant.
Bryce Canyon Resorts (on Utah 12) P.O. Box 6. (435) 834-5303. 6 cabins, 3 cottages, 58 rooms. $85-$95. AC, pool, rest.
In Panguitch, UT 84759:
Adobe Sands Motel 390 N. Main St., P.O. Box 593. (435) 676-8874. 33 units. $59. AC. Open May through Oct.
Best Western New Western Motel 180 E. Center St., P.O. Box 73. (800) 528-1234 or (435) 676-8876. 55 units. $65-$75. AC, pool, rest.
Color Country Motel 526 N. Main St., P.O. Box 163. (435) 676-2386. 26 units. $39-$77. AC, pool. All year.

Excursions

Dixie National Forest
Cedar City, Utah

Four sections of this canyon-country forest fan out across southwestern Utah, featuring unusual rock formations, "stands" of petrified forest, and sections of the historic Spanish Trail. 1,967,129 acres. Hiking, boating, fishing, horseback riding, hunting, scenic drives, winter sports, water sports. 27 campgrounds, boat ramp, picnic areas. Open year-round; most campsites open May through Oct. Information at Cedar City on I-15, about 70 miles from Bryce Canyon NP. (435) 865-3700.

Cedar Breaks National Monument
Cedar City, Utah

Erosion carved an immense amphitheater in a 10,000-foot southern Utah plateau; in it are extraordinary rock shapes colored by iron and manganese. 6,155 acres. Hiking, scenic drives, winter sports, daily ranger-led activities. 29 campsites, picnic areas, handicapped access. Services and roads closed late fall and winter. Visitor center on Utah 148, about 60 miles from Bryce Canyon NP. (435) 586-9451.

Fishlake National Forest
Richfield, Utah

Fish Lake, hopping with splake and trout (including 35-pound Mackinaw), is only one attraction of this region of dense forests, mountains, and plateaus. The Skyline Trail winds through its 12,000-foot peaks and the largest known village of the prehistoric Fremont people lies within its boundaries. 1.5 million acres. Hiking, boating, bicycling, fishing, horseback riding, hunting, scenic drives, winter sports. 40 campsites, boat ramp, handicapped access. Open year-round; most campsites open May through October. Information at Richfield, off US 89, about 80 miles from Bryce Canyon NP. (435) 896-9233.

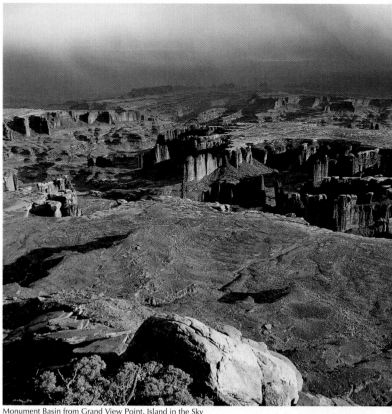

Monument Basin from Grand View Point, Island in the Sky

Canyonlands

Utah

Established September 12, 1964

337,598 acres

From the rim you glimpse only segments of the Green River and the Colorado River, which flow together at the heart of Canyonlands. But everywhere you see the water's work: canyon mazes, unbroken scarps, sandstone pillars.

The paths of the merging rivers divide the park into three districts. The high mesa known as the Island in the Sky rises as a headland 2,000 feet above the confluence. South of the Island and east of the confluence is The Needles, where red and white banded pinnacles tower 400 feet over grassy parks and sheer-walled valleys. A fine confusion of clefts and spires across the river to the west marks The Maze, a remote region of pristine soli-

tude. On every side the ground drops in great stairsteps. Flat benchlands end abruptly in rock walls on one side and sheer drops on the other. It is a right-angled country of standing rock, and only a few paved roads probe the edges of the park's 527 square miles.

Sandstone layers of varying hardness comprise Canyonland's visible rock. But the character of the land is largely shaped by underlying salt deposits, which, under tremendous pressure from the rock above, push upward, forming domes that fracture the surface.

Yearly rainfall averages 8 inches but varies greatly from year to year. Trees that grow here have to be tough and resilient. In drought years, junipers survive by limiting growth to a few branches, letting the others die. Gnarled juniper and pinyon pine take root in the rimlands wherever soil collects, including slickrock cracks and potholes.

How to Get There

Island in the Sky District: From Moab (35 miles away), take US 191 north to Utah 313 to The Neck entrance road.

Needles District: From Moab (75 miles away), follow US 191 south to Utah 211 and then west for 34 miles to park entrance.

Maze District: From Green River, take I-70 west to Utah 24, then south to a well-marked dirt road leading 46 miles to Hans Flat Ranger Station.

Ground shuttles are available from Salt Lake City and Grand Junction, Colo. Air shuttles fly between Canyonlands Airport and Salt Lake City. The airport at Grand Junction is about 115 miles from The Neck.

When to Go

Spring and fall are ideal for exploring by foot or vehicle. Summer is hot, but humidity low. Snow and cold can make it hard to get around in winter.

How to Visit

The park's isolation and preponderance of backcountry make visiting a spectacular experience, but not for everyone; there are few visitor facilities and paved roads. A four-wheel-drive vehicle will let you explore. If you have only 1 day, visit the **Island in the Sky** for an overview. On another day, go to **The Needles** for a chance to explore classic canyon country. With more time, focus on the hiking trails and four-wheel-drive routes to **The Maze** and other remote areas.

Island in the Sky

40 miles; a half to full day

The road enters the park just before you cross **The Neck,** a rock span not much wider than the road that connects the mesa to the rimlands.

For a sweeping view of the park's narrow, interlocked canyons and its wide skies, drive right to the end of the road at **Grand View Point Overlook** (6,080 feet). Directly below in **Monument Basin,** stone columns rise more than 300 feet from the canyon floor.

Hidden in deep gorges to the south,

Snakeweed tussocks along the Colorado

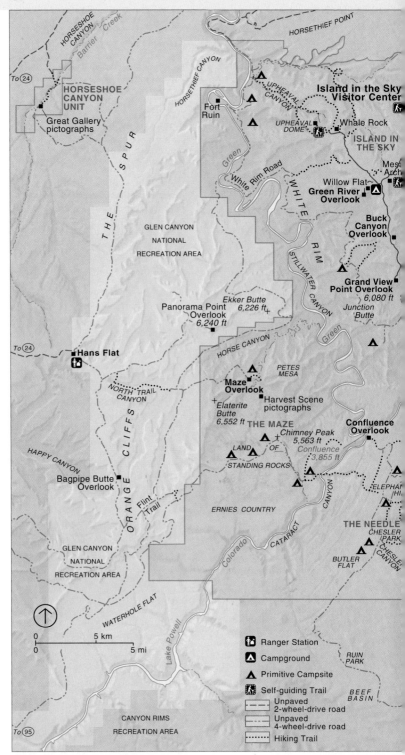

HORSESHOE CANYON

Barrier Creek

HORSETHIEF POINT

To 24

HORSESHOE CANYON UNIT

Great Gallery pictographs

THE SPUR

HORSETHIEF CANYON

Fort Ruin

UPHEAVAL CANYON

Island in the Sky Visitor Center

UPHEAVAL DOME

Whale Rock

ISLAND IN THE SKY

Green

White Rim Road

WHITE

Mesa Arch

Willow Flat
Green River Overlook

Buck Canyon Overlook

GLEN CANYON NATIONAL RECREATION AREA

RIM

STILLWATER CANYON

Grand View Point Overlook
6,080 ft

Junction Butte

Ekker Butte
6,226 ft +

Panorama Point Overlook
6,240 ft

Green

To 24

Hans Flat

HORSE CANYON

PETES MESA

NORTH TRAIL CANYON

Maze Overlook

Harvest Scene pictographs

+ Elaterite Butte
6,552 ft

THE MAZE

Confluence Overlook

HAPPY CANYON

ORANGE CLIFFS

Chimney Peak
5,563 ft +

LAND OF

Confluence
3,855 ft

Bagpipe Butte Overlook

STANDING ROCKS

ELEPHANT HI

Flint Trail

ERNIES COUNTRY

THE NEEDLE

CHESLER PARK

CATARACT

BUTLER FLAT

CHESLER CANYON

GLEN CANYON NATIONAL RECREATION AREA

Colorado

WATERHOLE FLAT

RUIN PARK

0   5 km
0   5 mi

Lake Powell

BEEF BASIN

🏠 Ranger Station

◾ Campground

▲ Primitive Campsite

🚶 Self-guiding Trail

--- Unpaved 2-wheel-drive road

-·- Unpaved 4-wheel-drive road

···· Hiking Trail

CANYON RIMS RECREATION AREA

To 95

the **Green River** joins the **Colorado River.** During his exploration of the Colorado in 1869, John Wesley Powell scaled the canyon walls at the confluence and discovered a strangely carved landscape. "Wherever we looked," he wrote, "there was a wilderness of rocks."

Drive back the way you came, bypassing **Buck Canyon** and **Murphy Point Overlooks.** Turn left onto the road leading to **Upheaval Dome,** then follow the paved spur road past Willow Flat Campground to **Green River Overlook.** Here you view a wide expanse of canyon country: Below, a quiet stretch of the Green River runs through **Stillwater Canyon,** with **The Maze** beyond and the **Henry Mountains** topping the distant horizon.

Continue on to Upheaval Dome, where the road ends at a good picnic spot shaded by junipers and pinyon pines. Stretch your legs on the half-mile trail to the lip of this unusual geological feature. Here the surface drops into a mile-wide crater enclosed by rock strata upturned in concentric circles, with a rock spire at the center. Some geologists believe that a meteorite collided with Earth here. Return to the main road.

Be sure to pull off at the **Mesa Arch Trailhead.** An easy half-mile loop takes you through a pinyon-juniper woodland to a small natural arch carved from the rim. The curve of the arch frames a magnificent view of the **Washer Woman Arch** and the **La Sal Mountains,** snowy in winter.

Just before leaving the park, stop at the **Shafer Canyon Overlook.** The short trail leads along a promontory above canyons gouged from miles of layered stone. In late afternoon, the rocks seem to ignite in the low angle of the setting sun.

La Sal Mountains through Mesa Arch

The Needles, weathered spires of sandstone

The Needles

18 miles; most of a day

Unless you have decided to camp, you'll probably be driving from Moab, 1.5 hours away, or Monticello, an hour away. The Needles area covers a lattice of canyons, flat-bottomed valleys called grabens, arches, and spectacular sandstone walls notched by rocky spires and columns. To the north, **Island in the Sky** and **Junction Butte** stand silhouetted against the horizon.

Utah 211 will take you directly to the Needles Visitor Center, where a dirt road heads north to the **Colorado River Overlook.** This road makes for rough going; don't take it unless you have a four-wheel-drive vehicle.

Continue on the paved road to the **Roadside Ruin** pull-off. Stretch your legs on a quarter-mile self-guided nature trail that leads to a small but well-preserved granary used by Indians to store corn more than 700 years ago. These ancient farmers were related to the ancestral Puebloans of Mesa Verde and Chaco Canyon. Pick up an interpretive booklet at the trailhead to learn how they used the native plants.

Your next stop will be **Pothole Point,** where a half-mile trail leads past

Unusual pictograph called the All-American Man

Pothole Point, in The Needles

depressions in the sandstone that fill
with water after a rain. Although the
water looks as still as the rock, the
depressions often teem with life. Snails,
fairy shrimp, and horsehair worms lay
eggs that survive the heat of summer
encased in dried mud. When the rains
come, they hatch in days.

The road ends at **Big Spring Canyon
Overlook,** where squat columns of
sandstone rise from barren bedrock.
Here the 5.5-mile **Confluence Overlook Trail** climbs the far side of the
canyon by a ladder and ends at a
point 930 feet above the junction
of the rivers. This is a popular trail
with most park visitors. More scenic
is the 2.5-mile **Slickrock Trail,** which
begins just before the road ends at the
overlook. If time allows, stop here
on your return drive for a moderate
hike across slickrock balds of Cedar
Mesa sandstone.

The Needles' Molar Rock and Angel Arch

Turn on the **Elephant Hill** spur, a
graded dirt road that leads to the base
of a notorious climb for four-wheel
drivers. Along the road are great views
of **The Needles.** You see tall fingers of
rock arrayed along the skyline, their
red and white bands created by the
interlayering of ancient river deposits
with sand dunes. A shaded area at the
end of the graded road makes a good
place to picnic.

The Chocolate Drops, shale and sandstone formations in The Maze

Hikes & Four-Wheel-Drive Routes

To really explore Canyonlands—85 percent of which is backcountry—you must leave your car and proceed on foot, mountain bike, or four-wheel-drive vehicle.

In The Needles, **Chesler Park Trail** leads 2.9 miles to a grassland sunk in a wide rock pocket rimmed by colorful spires. **Druid Arch Trail** branches off at **Elephant Canyon** and leads another 2.4 miles with a short ladder climb to the great arch that resembles a megalithic ceremonial site.

Elephant Hill Trail, a route only for rugged four-wheel-drive vehicles, runs 9 miles to the **Confluence Overlook.** It begins by climbing Elephant Hill's jaw-clenching switchbacks and 40 percent grade and ends with a half-mile walk to the overlook.

White Rim Road in Island in the Sky is one of the park's most popular jeep roads. Near the entrance, the **Shafer Trail** will take you to it. It follows a broad bench, lunar white along the edge where the red talus has been stripped to bedrock. For more than 80 miles it stays above the inner gorge, 1,200 feet below the Island, as it meanders through prime desert

bighorn sheep country.

Northwest of The Maze lies a detached section of the park, the **Horseshoe Canyon Unit,** entered by way of a 3.5-mile trail. You follow an old road into the canyon, then walk up **Barrier Creek** past some of the continent's finest prehistoric rock art. At the **Great Gallery,** ghostly figures painted in red ocher stare through eerie hollow eyes as the centuries pass. Archaeologists believe these life-size pictographs may be more than 3,000, perhaps as much as 6,000, years old.

The **Maze Overlook** can be reached by a 14-mile hike beginning at **North Trail Canyon,** 3.5 rough miles past **Hans Flat Ranger Station.** Reaching the trailhead can be an adventure, but the views from the rim of this isolated wedge of canyon country make it worth the effort. And the quiet is as expansive as the vistas. The trail passes north of **Elaterite Butte** for a tantalizing view into the twists and blind alleys of The Maze.

With a high-clearance four-wheel-drive vehicle you can drive the 34 miles from **Hans Flat** to the overlook. This is one of the park's classic jeep routes. Negotiating steep switchbacks allows the driver little chance to sightsee, and with winter snows the route becomes impassable.

Information & Activities

Headquarters
2282 S.W. Resource Blvd., Moab, UT 84532. Phone (435) 719-2313. www.nps.gov/cany

Seasons & Accessibility
Park open year-round. Flash floods from July through September can temporarily close dirt and gravel roads.

Visitor & Information Centers
Moab boasts a large multiagency visitor center. Visitor centers by entrances to **Island in the Sky** and **The Needles,** and at **Hans Flat Ranger Station,** just outside park near The Maze, open all year. **Headquarters** is 3 miles south of Moab.

Entrance Fees
$10 per vehicle good for 7 days, multiple entries. Annual permit $25, also good at Arches National Park, and Natural Bridges and Hovenweep National Monuments.

Pets
Must be leashed at all times. Not allowed on hiking trails, in river corridors, or on backcountry roads.

Facilities for Disabled
The visitor centers and Moab headquarters are wheelchair accessible.

Things to Do
Free naturalist-led activities: nature walks, interpretive exhibits. Hiking, boating, rafting (permit needed), bicycling. Contact park for list of concessioners offering four-wheel-drive (some areas require permit), mountain biking, hiking, and river-running trips.

Special Advisories
● Always carry water when hiking—at least a gallon per person per day. Water available near Squaw Flat Campground and at visitor centers.
● Use care near cliff edges and on slickrock surfaces; falls often fatal.
● Do not walk on cryptobiotic crust; it is a fragile, crunchy, black soil that is composed of living plants.

Overnight Backpacking
Permits and reservations fee required for backpacking and four-wheel-drive trips. May be obtained at visitor centers, ranger stations, and park headquarters. For information on reservations, call (435) 259-4351. Campsites along the **White Rim Trail,** in Island in the Sky, are available to mountain bikers and campers in four-wheel-drive high-clearance vehicles.

Campgrounds
Two campgrounds, **Squaw Flat** and **Willow Flat,** both with 14-day limit. Open all year, first come, first served; March to October filled by midmorning. Fees $5-$10 per night. No showers. Tent and RV sites; no hookups. Three group campsites in **The Needles;** reservations required; contact park headquarters. No food services inside park.

Hotels, Motels, & Inns
(unless otherwise noted, rates are for 2 persons in a double room, high season)
In Moab, UT 84532:
Best Western Green Well Motel 105 S. Main St. (800) 528-1234 or (435) 259-6151. 72 units. $79-$130. AC, pool, rest.
Big Horn Travelodge 550 S. Main St. (800) 325-6171 or (435) 259-6171. 58 units. $70-$85. AC, pool, restaurant.
Cedar Breaks Condos Center and 4th E. (435) 259-7830. 62 units, all with full kitchens. $65. AC.
Pack Creek Ranch (15 miles southeast of Moab, off La Sal Mountain Loop Rd.) P.O. Box 1270. (435) 259-5505. Cabins, houses, bunkhouses. $135-$300. Includes breakfast. Trail rides for fee. AC, pool.
Ramada Inn—Moab 182 S. Main St. (435) 259-7141. 82 units. $85-$109. AC, pool, restaurant.
In Monticello, UT 84535:
Best Western Wayside Inn 197 E. Central Hwy. 666. (800) 633-9700 or (435) 587-2261. 35 units. $64-$69. AC, pool.
Triangle H Motel 164 E. Central Hwy. 666. (800) 657-6622 or (435) 587-2274. 26 units. $42-$59. AC.

For other area accommodations, contact Utah's Canyonlands Region, P.O. Box 550-R9, Moab, UT 84532. (800) 635-MOAB or (435) 259-8825.

Excursions

Westwater Canyon
Moab, Utah

The names of the rapids on this 17-mile section of the Colorado River tell all: Skull, Sock-it-to-Me, Last Chance. Only experienced boaters (18 and over) should attempt them; permits and reservations required. Sights: natural arches, mining ruins, a desperadoes' hideout, and many bird species. Hiking, boating, fishing, picnic areas, swimming. Primitive camping (limited to 1 night), boat ramp, picnic areas. Open all year. Information (April-Oct.) at Westwater, about 80 miles NE of Canyonlands NP. (435) 259-7012.

Henry Mountains Buffalo Herd
Hanksville, Utah

This herd's 360 bison roam to 11,000 feet in summer. 150,000 acres. Hiking, climbing, rockhounding, hunting, picnicking, horseback riding, scenic drives (high-clearance 4x4s only). 3 campgrounds, primitive camping. Open all year. Information Mon. through Fri. at Hanksville BLM, Utah 24 and 95, 110 miles west of Canyonlands NP. (435) 542-3461.

Natural Bridges National Monument
Lake Powell, Utah

Three natural bridges here represent different states of development: youth, maturity, and old age. First discovered by white men in 1883, the three bridges bear Hopi names: Sipapu, Kachina, and Owachomo. Site also features ancestral Puebloan ruins and what was once the world's largest photovoltaic power system. 7,779 acres. 1 campground, primitive campsites, picnic area, scenic drive. Trails closed in winter; campsites open all year. Visitor center on Utah 275, 4 miles off US 95, about 95 miles from Canyonlands NP. (435) 692-1234.

Excursions

Glen Canyon National Recreation Area
Page, Arizona

The centerpiece of Glen Canyon NRA is Lake Powell, 186 miles of the Colorado River backed up behind one of the world's highest dams. The lake and the desert and canyons around it offer memorable experiences for boaters, anglers, hikers, and campers. Fishing for bass, black crappie, catfish, walleye available; trout thrive below the dam. Free dam tours. 1,217,403 acres, most in Utah. Fishing, hunting (in season with permit), boating (rentals available), water sports. Tent and RV campsites, 5 marinas, lodging, food services, picnic areas, boat ramp, handicapped access. Area and campsites open all year. Adjoins Canyonlands NP to the north. (928) 608-6404.

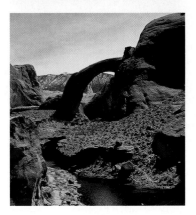

Rainbow Bridge National Monument
Page, Arizona

To the Navajo this 290-foot-high pink sandstone bridge is a sacred "rainbow of stone." Rough foot- or horse trails lead to it through the Navajo reservation (permits required)—a vigorous trip for the fit only. Most visitors to the world's largest natural bridge boat in from Lake Powell in Glen Canyon NRA (see above), via Halls Crossing, Bullfrog, or Wahweap Marinas. 160 acres. Boat dock, rest rooms. About 135 miles from Canyonlands NP. (928) 608-6404.

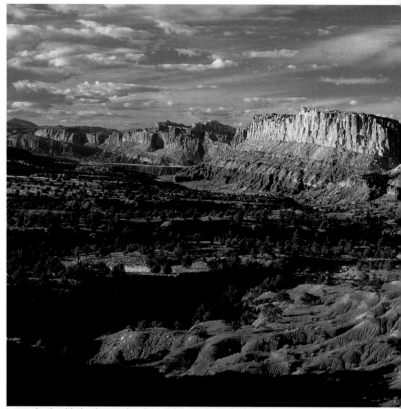

Layers of rock uplifted and exposed on the west face of Waterpocket Fold

Capitol Reef

Utah

Established December 18, 1971

241,904 acres

The unifying geographic feature of Capitol Reef is the Waterpocket Fold. For a hundred miles its parallel ridges rise from the desert like the swell of giant waves rolling toward shore. Exposed edges of the uplift have eroded into a slickrock wilderness of massive domes, cliffs, and a maze of twisting canyons.

Geologists know the fold as one of the largest and best exposed monoclines on the North American continent. Travelers know it as a place of dramatic beauty and serenity so remote that the nearest traffic light is 78 miles away. And even though its 378 square miles are off the beaten track, the park still attracts nearly 750,000 visitors each year.

Capitol Reef is named for a particularly colorful section of the fold near the Fremont River where sheer cliffs formed a barrier to travel for early pioneers. It reminded them of an ocean reef. Although a highway now crosses the "reef," travel is still challenging for those wishing to see the park's more remote regions.

The southern end of the fold offers fine wilderness backpacking in Lower Muley Twist Canyon and Halls Creek Narrows. Along the park's northern border lies Cathedral Valley, a repository of quiet solitude where jagged monoliths rise hundreds of feet.

The middle region is best known. Here the raw beauty of the towering cliffs contrasts with the green oasis that 19th-century Mormon pioneers created along the Fremont River, establishing the village of Fruita. Their irrigation ditches still water fruit trees

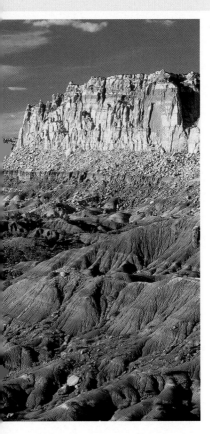

in fields abandoned by Fremont Indians 700 years ago. Mule deer now graze on orchard grasses and alfalfa, and park visitors harvest the apples, peaches, and apricots.

The most striking reminder of the Fremont culture is the fine rock art it produced. Figures resembling bighorn sheep crowd many petroglyph panels. The last sighting in the park of a native desert bighorn, a subspecies, occurred in 1948. Their disappearance is attributed to overhunting and various diseases caught from domestic sheep. The Park Service reintroduced desert bighorn sheep in 1984, 1996, and 1997. These herds have survived.

How to Get There

From Green River (about 85 miles away), take I-70 to Utah 24, which leads to the east entrance. For a scenic approach, start at Bryce Canyon National Park. Follow Utah 12 over Boulder Mountain to Utah 24, just outside the park's west entrance. Airport: Salt Lake City.

When to Go

All-year park. Spring and fall are mild and ideal for hiking. Winter is cold but brief. Back roads can become impassable during spring thaw, summer rains, and winter snows at higher elevations.

How to Visit

On a 1-day visit, take Utah 24 along the **Fremont River** and then the **Scenic Drive** through the heart of the park. This section offers fine hiking on nearly 40 miles of developed trails. The best second-day activity is a drive along portions of the **Burr Trail Loop** with a walk to **Strike Valley Overlook.** For a longer stay, drive the **Cathedral Valley Loop** or hike in one of the more remote canyons of the **Waterpocket Fold.**

Fremont River & Scenic Drive

35 miles; a half to full day

Drive east on Utah 24 as you enter the park from the west. Ahead of you rises the eroded west face of the **Waterpocket Fold,** a massive line of cliffs running north and south. After the first few miles, the highway follows the course cut through the rock wilderness by the swift Fremont River, named for frontier explorer John C. Frémont.

Take the unpaved spur road to the **Goosenecks Overlook.** From the parking area an easy 0.1-mile trail ends above the deeply entrenched meanders

Imposing Chimney Rock

To Fremont and (72)

To (70)

+ Black Mountain 6,938 ft

CATHEDRAL VALLEY

△ Upper Cathedral Valley Overlook

Road closed during winter

■ Elkhorn
△

Monoliths

0   5   10 km
0   5   10 mi

FISHLAKE

Factory Butte +
6,358 ft

NATIONAL

THE HARTNET

North Caineville Mesa

To Green River and (70)

FOREST

SOUTH DESERT WATERPOCKET FOLD

SPRING CANYON

Sulphur Creek

Bentonite Hills

To Bicknell

Chimney Rock
Goosenecks ■
(24)

Chimney Petroglyphs
Hickman Bridge 🚹

Fremont

(24)

Caineville

South Caineville Mesa

Upper Blue Hills

Visitor Center 🚹

Fruita △
(24)

Behunin Cabin

Notom ●

Sandy Creek

● Grover

Miners Mountain

CAPITOL

Notom-Bullfrog Road

HENRY

(12)

△

CAPITOL GORGE

REEF

DIXIE

Pleasant Creek

NATIONAL

△

FOREST

△

Oak Creek

Dry Bench

+ Boulder Mountain 10,908 ft

Road may be closed briefly during winter

WATERPOCKET FOLD

Cedar Mesa
△

△

MOUNTAINS

Tarantula Mesa

Steep Creek

CIRCLE CLIFFS

MULEY

Swap Mesa

Boulder ● ANASAZI STATE PARK
■

Burr Trail Road

CIRCLE

Strike Valley Overlook ■

Muley Creek

(12)

Deer Creek

CLIFFS

TWIST CANYON

Wagon Box Mesa

△
Calf Creek
■ Recreation Area

The Gulch

GRAND STAIRCASE-ESCALANTE
NATIONAL MONUMENT

Halls Creek

To Bryce Canyon National Park

Escalante

To Starr Spring and (276)

Big Thompson Mesa

Halls Creek Overlook
■

🚹 Ranger Station

🚹 Self-guiding Nature Trail

△ Campground

▲ Primitive Campsite

━ ━ ━ Unpaved (2-wheel-drive road)

┅┅┅┅ Unpaved (4-wheel-drive road)

GLEN CANYON

NATIONAL RECREATION AREA

To Glen Canyon National Recreation Area

HALLS CREEK NARROWS

of **Sulphur Creek.** Another short walk takes you to **Sunset Point** for a sweeping view of the **Capitol Reef** section of the Waterpocket Fold.

Bypass the **Chimney Rock** turnoff unless you plan to walk the 3.5-mile Chimney Rock loop trail or the more ambitious 9-mile **Spring Canyon** route. This follows a deep gorge cutting through fine exposures of Wingate and Navajo sandstones and ends with a ford at the Fremont River to rejoin Utah 24. (Check on river levels and trail conditions before setting out.)

Stop at the visitor center on the edge of **Fruita,** the remnants of the Mormon frontier community settled in the 1880s and now part of the national park. Be sure to see the 10-minute slide show—the view of the red sandstone cliffs from the theater window is itself worth the stop.

Take the 25-mile round-trip **Scenic Drive** along the rugged face of Capitol Reef. This paved road follows a century-old wagonway known as the Blue Dugway. The old road was used by Indians, outlaws, gypsies, and once even the devil himself, according to an early pioneer who chased him off by brandishing the *Book of Mormon.* Take the short spur road into **Grand Wash.** Look high on the cliff rim for **Cassidy Arch** named for outlaw Butch Cassidy, who reportedly used the canyon as a hideout. A 2.25-mile trail from the parking area leads down Grand Wash through spectacular narrows to the Fremont River. Another trail climbs 1.75 miles to Cassidy Arch. The Scenic Drive ends with a winding 2-mile spur road into **Capitol Gorge.** This was the main road through the reef before 1962. It now ends at a parking area where an easy 1-mile trail continues down into the canyon to historic inscriptions and a series of natural waterpockets, popular among desert denizens.

Return by the same road to Fruita, then go east on Utah 24, passing well-maintained orchards. Turn in at the **Petroglyphs** pull-off. Here Fremont Indians pecked into the cliff large human figures in headdresses. Since you can view this cliff art only at a distance, binoculars come in handy; spotting scopes are mounted on the main panel boardwalk.

The origin of these Indian farmers about A.D. 600 and their disappearance

Fruita orchards along the Fremont River

Desert bighorn sheep

six centuries later are still mysteries. Early settlers found what appeared to be remnants of their irrigation ditches, granaries, and pit-houses. One unusual discovery was a brick of tule sugar, grass seeds, and pulverized grasshoppers—thought to have been emergency food.

Continue down the highway a short distance to the **Hickman Bridge** parking area. Stretch your legs with a 1-mile hike up a self-guided nature trail that leads under the natural bridge, 125 feet above. For a longer and more arduous hike, take the 2.25-mile **Rim Overlook Trail** along the cliff tops. It ends at a 1,000-foot drop to the Fremont River, providing a good vantage point to view the green pocket of Fruita enclosed in a landscape of tilted rock.

Farther along the road, pull off at the **Behunin Cabin.** This one-room stone cabin was once home to a family of ten. The parents and two youngest children slept inside, the girls in a wagon box outside, and the boys in a nearby rock alcove.

Temple of the Sun, a butte

Claret cup cactus

Burr Trail Loop
125 miles; at least a full day

The drive begins at the visitor center. Go east on Utah 24 to the **Notom-Bull-frog Road.** Paved for the first several miles of its southbound route, the road becomes dirt, skirting the uplift where rock has pushed skyward at 70-degree angles. It crosses several washes that turn into slot canyons where they cut into the east flank of the Waterpocket Fold.

At the junction with the **Burr Trail Road,** you must decide whether to return to the visitor center (half-day trip) or take a full day to complete the loop. If you decide to continue, turn west and climb a series of spectacular switchbacks to the high rim of the fold. Views of the **Henry Mountains** to the east, and **Burr Canyon** straight below, are dramatic.

One of the finest vistas in the park

is the **Strike Valley Overlook** in **Upper Muley Twist Canyon.** Many visitors walk the 2.5 miles from the hikers' parking area to the overlook trailhead through a beautiful canyon with double arches and a large rock window on the rim. High-clearance, four-wheel-drive vehicles can follow the canyon floor to a parking area near the overlook. From the parking area the trail continues up canyon another 6.5 miles, passing several large arches.

Those looking for solitude can backpack into **Lower Muley Twist Canyon** and its miles of fine slickrock wilderness (free backcountry permits required; available at visitor center). Bends in the canyon are so tight, early teamsters said, a mule had to twist itself to get through.

Burr Trail Road becomes paved as it leaves Capitol Reef and continues west to the town of Boulder. Turn north on paved Utah 12, which winds up and over **Boulder Mountain** through a high alpine forest. Here you join Utah 24 about 10 miles west of the visitor center.

Cathedral Valley Loop
70 miles; a half to full day

A high-clearance, two- or four-wheel-drive vehicle is recommended for this scenic trip; check unpaved road conditions before setting out. Follow Utah 24 for 11 miles east of the visitor center. At a marked crossing, turn off Utah 24 and ford the Fremont River. If the river is too high for your vehicle, use the Caineville access to reach Cathedral Valley.

As the road heads north, it passes through the colorful badlands of the **Bentonite Hills** and follows a mesa called **The Hartnet** to the edge of a 400-foot escarpment overlooking **South Desert.** On the mesa's opposite side is a spectacular view into **Upper Cathedral Valley.** In this vast open space, keep a lookout for soaring golden eagles.

Eroded spires and monoliths of Entrada sandstone jut 500 feet from the valley floor like enormous weathered teeth. The road loops to the south and drops among the unusual formations, following the valley past such landmarks as the **Walls of Jericho,** the **Gypsum Sinkhole,** and the **Temples of the Sun** and **Moon.** The drive ends at Utah 24, near Caineville.

Information & Activities

Headquarters
HC 70 Box 15, Torrey, UT 84775. Phone (435) 425-3791. www.nps.gov/care

Seasons & Accessibility
Park open year-round. Many roads are unpaved. The Scenic Drive may close briefly during rainy weather and in winter. Driving dirt roads, including Cathedral Valley Loop, may require high-clearance or four-wheel-drive vehicles. Call headquarters or ask at visitor center for latest weather and road conditions.

Visitor & Information Centers
The visitor center on Utah 24 at the north end of park is open all year. Phone headquarters for information.

Entrance Fee
$5 per car per week.

Pets
Permitted on leashes, except on trails and in backcountry.

Facilities for Disabled
The visitor center, rest rooms, and the Petroglyphs Trail are accessible to wheelchairs.

Things to Do
Free ranger-led activities: evening programs. Also available, interpretive exhibits, auto tour, hiking, fruit picking, bird-watching. For information on horseback trips, jeep tours, and other recreational activities, contact the Wayne County Travel Council at (800) 858-7951.

Special Advisories
● Always carry water, even on short hikes. Except for tap water, most water in park is not drinkable.
● Watch out for flash floods between July and September.
● Let someone know your itinerary.

Overnight Backpacking
Permits required. They are free and can be obtained at the visitor center or from any park ranger.

Campgrounds
Three campgrounds, all with 14-day limit. Open year-round on a first-come, first-served basis. Fees $10 per night. No showers. Tent sites at **Cathedral Valley** and **Cedar Mesa.** Tent and RV sites at **Fruita;** no hookups.

Hotels, Motels, & Inns
(unless otherwise noted, rates are for 2 persons in a double room, high season)
In Bicknell, UT 84715:
Aquarius Inn 240 W. Main St. (435) 425-3835. 28 units, 6 with kitchenettes. $40. AC, RV park, restaurant.
Sunglow Motel 63 E. Main St., P.O. Box 68. (435) 425-3821. 15 units, most with AC. $35. Restaurant.
In Torrey, UT 84775:
Capitol Reef Inn 360 W. Main St., P.O. Box 100. (435) 425-3271. 10 units. $44. Restaurant. Open Easter through October.
Wonderland Inn Utah 12 at Utah 24. (800) 458-0216 or (435) 425-3775. 50 units. $54-$76. AC, pool, restaurant.

For a more complete list of accommodations near the park, write or call park headquarters.

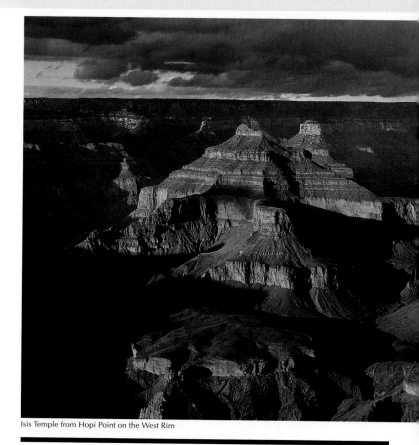

Isis Temple from Hopi Point on the West Rim

Grand Canyon

Arizona

Established February 26, 1919

1,217,403 acres

The road to the Grand Canyon from the south crosses a gently rising plateau that gives no hint at what is about to unfold. You wonder if you have made a wrong turn. All at once an immense gorge a mile deep and up to 18 miles wide opens up. The scale so vast that even from the best vantage point only a fraction of the canyon's 277 miles can be seen.

Nearly five million people travel here each year; 90 percent first see the canyon from the South Rim with its dramatic views into the deep inner gorge of the Colorado River. So many feet have stepped cautiously to the edge of major overlooks that in places the rock has been polished smooth. But most of the park's 1,904 square miles

are maintained as wilderness. You can avoid crowds by hiking the park's many trails or driving to the cool evergreen forests of the North Rim where people are fewer and viewing more leisurely.

The Grand Canyon boasts some of the nation's cleanest air, with visibility averaging 90 to 110 miles. Increasingly, though, air pollution blurs vistas that once were sharp and rich hued. Hazy days have become more common, with visibility dropping as low as 20 miles. Haze from forest fires and pollen has always been present, but the recent increase is traced to sources outside the park, like copper smelters and urban areas in Arizona, southern California, and even Mexico.

It's hard to look at the canyon and not be curious about geology. Some of the oldest exposed rock in the world, dating back 1.8 billion years, ber to mid-May. Hikers and mule riders to the inner canyon, where temperatures reach 118°F, prefer spring and fall; the prime river season is April through October. During summer on the South Rim, time your visit to midweek, arriving early to avoid the crowds.

How to Visit

On a 1-day visit to the South Rim take the **Hermit Road** west of the village for classic views of the main canyon. The drive is closed to automobiles, but, March through November, free buses take you to the overlooks. The best second-day activity is the **Desert View Drive** tour east of Mather Point for great views of the Colorado River and eastern canyon.

On a longer stay, take the North Rim's **Cape Royal Road** for broad panoramic vistas. You may also enjoy a hike on a backcountry trail; a mule ride down the **Bright Angel Trail;** a week-long raft trip through the canyon on the **Colorado River;** and a scenic flight for a bird's-eye view of the canyon. The mule and raft trips and backcountry hikes require reservations far in advance.

South Rim: Hermit Road

8 miles; at least a half day; closed to vehicles March through November

Begin at the **Canyon View Information Center** near Mather Point for a classic panoramic view into the heart of the Grand Canyon. Great solitary buttes rise from narrow ridges reaching out from the distant North Rim. Far below, a green cluster of Fremont cottonwood trees marks **Phantom Ranch,** a lodge and campground reached only by mule or foot. The observation station at nearby **Yavapai Point** explores the canyon's geological history and identifies major landmarks (closed for renovation until spring 2004). If bad weather threatens, duck into its glass-enclosed observation room and watch as storm clouds roll in.

Board the free Hermits Rest Route bus, which travels along Hermit Road between the information center and Hermits Rest from March through November. Skirting the rim of the canyon for 8 miles, it offers superb views of the **Colorado River** and the labyrinth of side canyons and broad platforms below the rim. The buses

lies at the bottom. Exactly how the river formed the canyon is still unclear, but geologists generally agree that most of the cutting occurred within the last five million years.

How to Get There

South Rim: From Flagstaff, Arizona (about 90 miles away), take US 180 skirting the San Francisco Peaks to South Rim entrance, or take US 89 to Cameron, then Ariz. 64 with views of the Little Colorado River Gorge to Desert View entrance.

North Rim: Take Ariz. 67 from Jacob Lake through the Kaibab National Forest to North Rim entrance. The two rims are 10 air miles apart but 215 miles by car, a 5-hour drive. Airports: Grand Canyon near South Rim; Flagstaff; Las Vegas; Phoenix.

When to Go

South Rim is open all year; North Rim facilities are closed from mid-October to mid-May. Ariz. 67 usually closes due to deep snows late Novem-

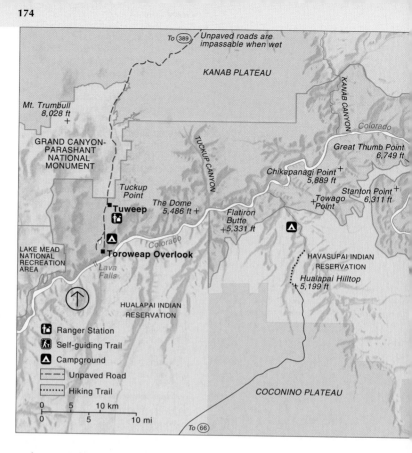

To (389)

Unpaved roads are
impassable when wet

KANAB PLATEAU

Mt. Trumbull
8,028 ft
+

GRAND CANYON-
PARASHANT
NATIONAL
MONUMENT

Tuckup
Point

Tuweep

The Dome
5,486 ft +

LAKE MEAD
NATIONAL
RECREATION
AREA

Toroweap Overlook

Lava
Falls

KANAB CANYON

Colorado

Great Thumb Point
6,749 ft

Chikapanagi Point +
5,889 ft

Stanton Point +
6,311 ft

Towago +
Point

Flatiron
Butte
+5,331 ft

Colorado

HAVASUPAI INDIAN
RESERVATION

Hualapai Hilltop
+ 5,199 ft

HUALAPAI INDIAN
RESERVATION

TUCKUP CANYON

COCONINO PLATEAU

Ranger Station

Self-guiding Trail

Campground

Unpaved Road

Hiking Trail

0   5   10 km
0   5   10 mi

To (66)

can be crowded at peak times of day.

The first stop is the **Trailview Overlook**. Here you get a hint of the canyon's size. To the south, the historic **El Tovar Hotel** and **Bright Angel Lodge** look small and insignificant perched on the brink of the great precipice. Mule strings and hikers file along the **Bright Angel Trail** as it zigzags 8 miles and 4,460 feet down to the river.

Don't miss **Hopi Point,** a promontory jutting deep into the gorge. Magnificent views 45 miles both eastward and westward make this an ideal spot for watching sunset or sunrise. To avoid crowds, leave the main overlook and walk along the **Rim Trail** (see below) to find your own observation point. Across the river rise the intricately carved walls of **Isis Temple** and tree-topped **Shiva Temple,** described as "the grandest of all buttes."

The bus route continues west, passing **Mohave Point** and skirting breathtakingly close to **The Abyss,** where a sheer cliff plunges 3,000 feet to a plateau below. From here the road follows the sweep of the rim out to **Pima Point,** where you see the Colorado River threading through the deep gorge. On a still day you can hear the distant rumble of **Granite Rapids** almost a mile below. What looks like a stream from above is a river 300 feet wide that, with its tributaries, drains eight percent of the continental U.S.

The road ends at **Hermits Rest,** a limestone building that looks as if Hobbits built it on the canyon's rim; it serves as a curio shop. Those with time and stamina can hike partway down the steep **Hermit Trail** to **Dripping Springs,** 7 miles and 6 to 9 hours round-trip. Here the hermit Louis Boucher raised goldfish in a watering trough at the turn of the 20th century. It's a good place to see some of the canyon's 315 species of birds. Permits are not needed for day hikes, but first ask a park ranger for conditions and advisories. On the return, buses stop only at Mohave and Hopi Points.

For the adventurous, the **Rim Trail** hugs the canyon's edge for nearly 11

To Jacob Lake
and 89A

KAIBAB NATIONAL FOREST

KAIBAB PLATEAU

Road closed
in winter

67

MARBLE CANYON

+Steamboat
Mountain
7,422 ft

OWELL PLATEAU

North Rim
Entrance Station

NAVAJO
INDIAN
RESERVATION

+ Holy Grail
Temple

Point Imperial
8,803 ft

Colorado

Vista
Encantada

GRANITE GORGE

Point Sublime
7,459 ft

Grand Canyon
Lodge

Bright Angel Point

Cape Royal Road

Cape Solitude
6,144 ft

+
Havasupai
Point
6,635 ft

Shiva+
Temple
Isis +
Temple

Zoroaster
Temple

+Cape Royal

PAINTED DESERT

Phantom Ranch

Hermit Road

Vishnu Temple +
7,829 ft

GRANITE

Watchtower
7,438 ft

KAIBAB N.F.

Hermits
Rest

Yavapai Point
Mather Point

GORGE

Grand Canyon Village

Yaki
Point HORSESHOE
MESA

Lipan
Point

Desert
View

Canyon View
Information Plaza

Grandview
Point

64

Desert View Drive

Tusayan

Grand Canyon
Airport

180

64

To Williams
and Flagstaff

KAIBAB NATIONAL
FOREST

Tusayan Ruins
and Museum

To Cameron and 89

White-water rafting down the Colorado River

Tassel-eared squirrel, also known as Abert's squirrel

miles from Mather Point to Hermits Rest, roughly paralleling Hermit Road. The path is paved to **Maricopa Point;** the rest is dirt. The trail is generally level except for a steep stretch between the village and Trailview. Short hikes can be combined with rides by catching the shuttle bus at any of the main overlooks. You can also pick up the bus at the the trail's end for an easy return.

South Rim: Desert View Drive

23 miles; a half to full day

Desert View Drive (Ariz. 64) begins just south of Mather Point. The drive skirts the rim eastward for 23 miles to **Desert View,** providing numerous pull-offs for long views of the main canyon. In summer, parking at the major overlooks can be a problem, so between March and November only the park shuttle is allowed on the Yaki Point/South Kaibab Trailhead road. (Board at the Canyon View Information Center.) Along the roadside are shaggy-barked Utah juniper and low clumps of Gambel oak.

Yaki Point provides a fine view of the darkly shining **Granite Gorge,** the innermost canyon. The imposing pyramid-shaped profile of **Vishnu Temple,** 7,533 feet high, dominates the eastern skyline. The practice of naming major park landforms after world deities began with Clarence Dutton, who published a classic report on the geology of the Grand Canyon in 1882.

On the way back to the main road

you can leave the shuttle and hike the **South Kaibab Trail,** which switchbacks down the west side of Yaki Point. Allot a third of your time for going down and two-thirds for hiking back up. The trail eventually reaches the Colorado River at the bottom of the canyon, but a strenuous 3-mile, 2.5-hour round-trip takes you only partway down to **Cedar Ridge.** Even though you drop 1,140 vertical feet, none of the major landforms of the canyon look any closer. Fossil ferns lie exposed in the bedrock on the west side of Cedar Ridge.

Return to your car and follow the main road as it climbs into a tall ponderosa forest. Take the turnoff to **Grandview Point,** one of the finest vistas on the South Rim. From the overlook, **Grandview Trail** drops a rugged 3 miles to **Horseshoe Mesa,** where miners once worked copper ore from the Last Chance Mine. John Hance, a prospector known for his tall tales and quick wit, led the first sightseeing parties into the canyon near here in the 1880s. On one trip a woman with a knowledge of botany described to him how trees breathe. "You know," Hance said, "that explains something that has puzzled me a long time; I used to make camp under a big mesquite tree, and night after night that thing would keep me awake with its snoring."

Drive farther east to **Moran Point** for the best view of one of the Colorado's major rapids. Here you look directly down on **Hance Rapids;** its rocky 30-foot drop is considered by river guides to be among the most difficult to run. Continue on down the road, and if you need a change of pace, stop at the small **Tusayan Museum.** It displays well-designed exhibits of Indian cultures, and the nearby ruins offer a self-guided tour of an excavated ancestral Puebloan village from A.D. 1185.

Take your time when you reach **Lipan Point,** the finest view of the eastern canyon. Here the Colorado River makes a great bend to the west, where it has carved through the **Kaibab Plateau** to form the deepest portion of the Grand Canyon. Below, the river makes an S-curve around **Unkar Delta,** which prehistoric people extensively farmed.

Bypass **Navajo Point** and continue on to **Desert View,** where you might stop at the snack bar and curio shop. While here, climb the stairs to the top of the 70-foot **Watchtower,** built in

North Rim aspen in fall foliage

1932. On the tower's walls Indian artist Fred Kabotie painted murals depicting Hopi legends.

North Rim: Cape Royal Road

23 miles; a half to full day

Averaging a thousand feet higher than the South Rim, the North Rim's alpine vegetation and more varied vistas appeal to many travelers. Still, you won't find the South Rim crowds here. The focus is the historic **Grand Canyon Lodge,** built in the 1920s on the lip of the canyon and rebuilt after a disastrous fire in 1932. From its Sun Room you'll get an excellent view of **Bright Angel Canyon** incised 11 miles into the plateau and overshadowed by **Deva, Brahma,** and **Zoroaster Temples.**

Pick up a self-guiding pamphlet from the box by the log shelter near the parking lot. Follow one of the paved trails to **Bright Angel Point,** which divides a side canyon called **The Transept** from **Roaring Springs Canyon.** Listen for the sound of the springs cascading from a cave 3,000 feet below the rim. This is a fine spot for watching sunrise or sunset. Those needing to stretch their legs can take the **Transept Trail,** 1.5 miles along the nearly level canyon rim, or a short hike on the **North Kaibab Trail** (1 mile down takes you 650 feet beneath the rim—and that mile back up feels like 3).

From the lodge, drive north 3 miles to the **Cape Royal Road,** one of the most scenic drives in the park.

It passes through forests of spruce, fir, locust, and ponderosa pine mixed with stands of quaking aspen, and through lovely meadows of blue lupine and scarlet bugler. Long-eared mule deer often bound across the road, and you might glimpse the reclusive white-tailed Kaibab squirrel found only in the North Rim forests on the Kaibab Plateau.

Those looking for a dramatic sunrise perch can turn off onto the 3-mile road to **Point Imperial,** at 8,803 feet the highest viewpoint on either rim. Here amid tall evergreens you look across the canyon to the high plateau of the Navajo Indian Reservation. Evidence of a 2000 fire is evident in this vicinity (you probably spotted more evidence along the first portion of Cape Royal Road). Return to the main road and continue on, passing through the forested **Walhalla Plateau.** Stop at **Vista Encantada** for superb views of the northeastern canyon and the carved pinnacles of **Brady** and **Tritle Peaks.**

The road ends at a parking lot on **Cape Royal.** A paved half-mile nature trail leads along a narrow peninsula past **Angels Window,** an opening eroded through the rock spur that frames the river below. Watch your children. From the overlook **Wotans Throne** and Vishnu Temple dominate the foreground. Across the canyon rise the **Palisades of the Desert.** The unusually broad vista here provides a fine vantage point to watch the sun set and to absorb what naturalist John Burroughs described as Grand Canyon's "strange new beauty."

Hikers on bridge along the North Kaibab Trail

Mule, River, & Air Trips

If the extremely challenging hike to the canyon floor (8 miles down the Bright Angel Trail and 6.5 miles on the steeper South Kaibab Trail) is not for you, consider going by muleback. (Though mule trips are not for everyone either—acrophobes especially!) Mules leave the South Rim for day trips and overnights at **Phantom Ranch,** which accommodates guests in rustic cabins and dormitories. The ranch lies in a deep gorge of the inner canyon near the confluence of Bright Angel Creek and the Colorado River. The creek's clear waters are known for their excellent trout fishing (license required). The lodge is the only place within the canyon where you can spend the night without camping, and it serves as a good base for hikes up Bright Angel Canyon. Advance reser-

vations—as much as 6 months ahead for mule trips—are necessary.

Many regard a raft trip through the Grand Canyon as the experience of a lifetime. Long, quiet stretches through the scenic heart of the canyon are broken by more than 150 major rapids, two of which are consistently rated 10 on a scale of 10. Most trips stop for day hikes at waterfalls, Indian ruins, and interesting side canyons. A number of river companies offer the raft trips, which generally take 1 to 2 weeks; some companies offer partial trips. Write the park or check the park website for a list of the companies; reserve well in advance.

Companies giving helicopter and airplane tours are based at Grand Canyon Airport. Flights are no longer allowed below the rim, and because of safety and noise concerns, use of the canyon's airspace is being regulated.

Carving the Grand Canyon

What looks timeless is constantly changing: The Grand Canyon's variegated layers encode two billion years of Earth's history.

Some of Earth's oldest rock lies at the canyon's bottom. Thousands of feet thick, the rock formed from sediments. About 1.8 billion years ago, cataclysmic geological forces crumpled and uplifted this rock to create a range of mountains that towered probably 5 to 6 miles high. (**1**)

The tremendous heat and pressure recrystallized the rock to schist; molten material from deep inside Earth oozed up, forcing itself into the rock and hardening into veins of pink granite. Over eons, wind and water gnawed the mountain range into a plain, and a primordial sea submerged it. Again, sediments wafted to the sea bottom, solidifying into rock; magma continued to well up from inside the Earth. (**2**)

About a billion years ago, Earth shuddered again, cracking its crust into giant fault blocks that tilted upward to form a second range of mountains. (**3**) The rains, frosts, and winds of millions of years wore away these mountains also.

Much of the Grand Canyon rock visible today (blue layers, **4**) accumulated over the schist in the last 600 million years. During some ages the region sank beneath advancing seas; primitive shellfish fossilized in sea bottoms that hardened to shale. During other periods the restless region rose. Topping the Grand Canyon today—some 8,000 feet above sea level—is a 300-foot layer of cream-colored limestone, formed from the remains of countless corals, sponges, and other marine animals.

In recent geological time (about six million years ago) the young, southward-flowing Colorado River—perhaps later captured by the ancestral Hualapai River encroaching from the west—began to slice into the upper layers of the canyon. Gouging inch by inch over the centuries, the river eventually reached the schist 4,000 feet below the rim and continued to cut. (**5**) Wind and water still wear away at the massive gorge, ever widening and ever deepening the canyon's floor and walls.

Information & Activities

Headquarters

P.O. Box 129, Grand Canyon, AZ 86023. Phone (928) 638-7888. www.nps.gov/grca

Seasons & Accessibility

South Rim open all year. North Rim roads often close due to snow mid-November to mid-May. For weather and road information, call (928) 638-7888.

Visitor & Information Centers

Canyon View Information Plaza near Grand Canyon Village open all year. Call (928) 638-7888. **North Rim Visitor Station** open mid-May to mid-November. Call (928) 638-7864.

Entrance Fee

$20 per car for 7 days; $10 per person arriving on foot, bike, or motorcycle.

Pets

Allowed, leashed, on rim trails, but not below rim. Kennels available; call (928) 638-0534.

Facilities for Disabled

Visitor center and some shuttle buses are wheelchair accessible. Free brochures available. Hermit Road open to vehicles carrying disabled persons, with permit. Call ahead to make arrangements, (928) 638-0591.

Things to Do

Free ranger-led activities: day and evening nature walks, slide shows, talks, cultural demonstrations, and campfire programs. Also, mule trips into canyon, hiking, bicycling, fishing, river rafting, air tours, cross-country skiing. For activities, call (928) 638-7888. Write headquarters for list of concessioners offering wide variety of tours.

An Imax Theater featuring *Grand Canyon—The Hidden Secrets* is located a mile south of the South Rim Entrance, on Ariz. 64. (928) 638-2468.

Special Advisory

● Be very careful near the rim; protective barriers are intermittent.

Overnight Backpacking

Permits required; $10 fee plus $5 per person per night. Backcountry Information Center, P.O. Box 129, Grand Canyon, AZ 86023. (928) 638-7875.

Campgrounds

Four campgrounds, 7-day limit, 3 on South Rim, 1 on North Rim. **Mather** open all year; reservations recommended March to December; reserve through the National Parks Reservation Service (see p. 11); other times, first come, first served. **Desert View** (first come, first served) and **North Rim** (recommend reservations through National Parks Reservation Service) mid-May to mid-Oct. **Trailer Village** open all year; reservations recommended; contact Xanterra Parks & Resorts (303) 297-2757. Fee $24 per night. Showers at North Rim and near Mather campground. Tent and RV sites at all campgrounds; hookups only at Trailer Village. Two group campgrounds; must reserve. Food services in park.

Hotels, Motels, & Inns

(unless otherwise noted, rates are for 2 persons in a double room, high season) The properties inside the park are operated by Xanterra Parks & Resorts (888) 297-2757. www.xanterra.com. Reservations recommended 6 to 9 months in advance. For same-day reservations, try (928) 638-2631.
INSIDE THE PARK (On South Rim): **Bright Angel Lodge & Cabins** 89 units, some share baths. Cabins $84-$234; rooms $59-$71. Rest. **El Tovar Hotel** 78 units. $127-$289. AC, rest. **Kachina Lodge** 49 units. $119-$129. AC. **Maswik Lodge** 278 units. Cabins $66 (June-Aug.); rooms $79-$121. Rest. **Thunderbird Lodge** 55 units. $119-$129. AC. **Yavapai Lodge** 358 rooms. $93-$105. Rest. Open March through Oct. *(On North Rim):* **Grand Canyon Lodge** (303) 297-2757. 201 units. $87-$151. Rest. Open mid-May to mid-Oct. *(In the canyon):* **Phantom Ranch** (reached by hiking, mule, or raft trips) Dorm $28 per night. Cabin $75 per night. Mule trip $343, includes cabins and meals. AC, rest., shared showers. Reserve up to 23 months ahead. *OUTSIDE THE PARK: In Grand Canyon, AZ 86023:* **Quality Inn** (on Ariz. 64) P.O. Box 520. (800) 999-2521 or (928) 638-2673. 232 units. $103-$168. AC, pool, rest. **Seven Mile Lodge** (on Ariz. 64) P.O. Box 56. (928) 638-2291. 20 units. $75-$82. No reservations; first come, first served. AC. Closed Jan.

Excursions

Lake Mead National Recreation Area
Boulder City, Nevada

Lake Mead, water impounded from the Colorado River by Hoover Dam, is the center of this NRA, the nation's first (established in 1936). More than 2,000 bighorn sheep roam the desert canyons and plateaus surrounding the reservoir. 1,501,216 acres, part in Arizona. Boating, fishing, naturalist programs, water sports. 1,021 campsites, 191 rooms, picnic areas, food services, handicapped access. Open all year. Adjoins Grand Canyon NP on west. Visitor center at US 93 and Nev. 166, about 280 miles from Grand Canyon's South Rim entrance. (702) 293-8906.

Wupatki National Monument
Flagstaff, Arizona

Eight hundred years ago, people moved to the Wupatki area to farm the volcanic soil. Little more than a century later they left behind extensive accomplishments, including a 100-room pueblo, amphitheater, ball court, and pottery. 35,253 acres. Hiking, picnicking, scenic drives. Open all year. Off US 89, about 65 miles southeast of Grand Canyon NP. (928) 679-2365.

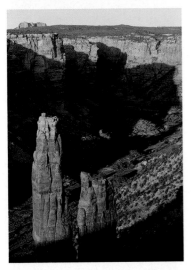

Canyon de Chelly National Monument
Chinle, Arizona

These spectacular red-rock canyons, spires, and mesas rival any natural site in the Southwest. The same is true of their cultural legacy: ancient Basketmaker pithouses, the remains of ancestral Puebloan dwellings on 1,000-foot cliffs, and the many reminders of the Navajo past and present. Navajo guides offer tours into the canyons; only the White House ruin may be visited without a guide. North and South Rim drives have many scenic overlooks. 83,840 acres. Hiking, horseback riding, jeep tour, scenic drives. 95 campsites, food services, handicapped access. Open all year. Off US 191, about 230 miles east of Grand Canyon NP. (928) 674-5500.

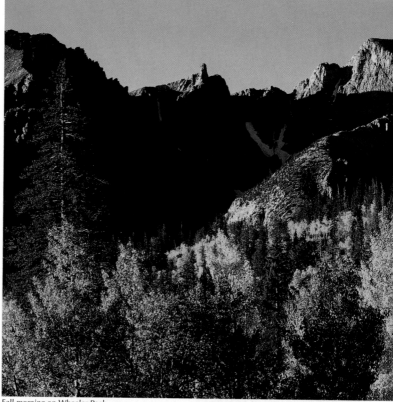

Fall morning on Wheeler Peak

Great Basin

Nevada

Established October 27, 1986

77,180 acres

An Ice Age landscape of glacier-carved peaks rises more than a mile from the desert floor. The park takes its name from the vast region that extends east from California's Sierra Nevada to Utah's Wasatch Range, and from southern Oregon to southern Nevada, encompassing most of Nevada and western Utah. Called Great Basin by explorer John C. Frémont in the mid-1800s, the region actually comprises not one but at least 90 basins, or valleys, and its rivers all flow inland—not to any ocean.

The park road winds up Wheeler Peak, the second highest mountain in the state of Nevada. When the road ends at 10,000 feet, trails lead to the 13,063-foot summit and to the region's only glacier, near a stand of bristlecone pines. Great Basin is a young park compared to the likes of a Yellowstone or Yosemite, yet within its confines are some of the world's oldest trees.

The bristlecones form the rear guard of a Pleistocene forest that once covered much of the region. Now surviving in scattered stands, some trees are 3,000 years old—alive when Tutankhamun ruled Egypt.

In the flank of the mountain, at an altitude of 6,800 feet, lies Lehman Caves with 1.5 miles of underground passages. These formed when higher water tables during the Ice Age made pockets in the limestone. Park rangers guide visitors past flowstone, stalactites, and delicate white crystals that grow in darkness.

The number of visitors has reached more than 80,000 yearly since 1986, when the cave and neighboring moun-

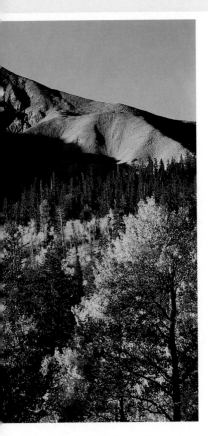

weather and fewer crowds. Hikers must beware of sudden thunderstorms that can catch them on exposed ridges anytime of year.

The best time to view Wheeler Peak is in early morning. In winter, visitors enjoy excellent cross-country skiing.

How to Visit

On a 1-day visit, take the **Wheeler Peak Scenic Drive** for dramatic views of high alpine landscapes. On your way back, stop at **Lehman Caves** for a chance to walk underground through intriguing passages.

Wheeler Peak Scenic Drive

12 miles; 1.5 hours to most of a day

A paved road climbs steeply from the visitor center to the Wheeler Peak Campground at 10,000 feet (vehicles longer than 24 feet not recommended). Those not used to mountain driving may find both the view and the drive breathtaking. The road passes from the tough, drought-resistant pinyon-juniper woodland into the high-elevation forest of Engelmann spruce, limber pine, and aspen.

Begin the scenic drive near the visitor center. A short trail at the first pull-off takes you to the historic **Osceola Ditch,** built in the late 1880s to carry water for hydraulic gold mining. Save this for your next trip, if pressed for time.

Skip the **Mather Overlook,** but notice the old stand of mountain

tains became a national park. But the park has 65 miles of trails, offering access to the hills and a chance to see glacial moraines, alpine lakes, and spectacular sweeping views of the surrounding basin and range country.

How to Get There

From Las Vegas (about 300 miles away), take I-15 to US 93, then US 50 to Nev. 487. At Baker, take Nev. 488 to the park entrance. From Salt Lake City, Utah (about 250 miles away), take I-15 to US 50, then Nev. 487 to Baker and Nev. 488 to the park entrance. Airport: Ely (about 67 miles away).

When to Go

Great Basin is open year-round, but the upper 8 miles of Wheeler Peak Scenic Drive (beyond Upper Lehman Campground) are closed from November to May, or as long as heavy snows makes it impassable. In summer, the most popular season for people to visit, temperatures are generally mild. September and October bring cool

Ancient bristlecone pine on Mount Washington

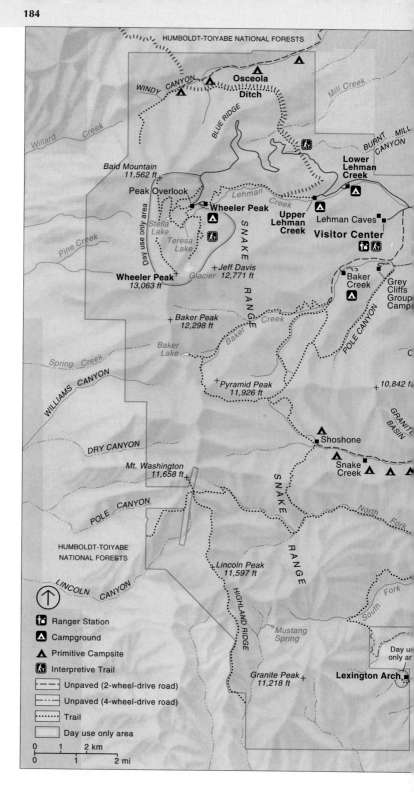

HUMBOLDT-TOIYABE NATIONAL FORESTS

Mill Creek

WINDY CANYON

Osceola Ditch

BLUE RIDGE

BURNT MILL CANYON

Willard Creek

Lower Lehman Creek

Bald Mountain 11,562 ft

Lehman Creek

Peak Overlook

Wheeler Peak

Upper Lehman Creek

Day use only area

Stella Lake

Lehman Caves

Visitor Center

Pine Creek

Teresa Lake

Wheeler Peak *13,063 ft*

+*Jeff Davis Glacier 12,771 ft*

SNAKE RANGE

Baker Creek

Baker Creek

Grey Cliffs Group Camp

+*Baker Peak 12,298 ft*

Baker Creek

POLE CANYON

Baker Lake

Spring Creek

WILLIAMS CANYON

+*Pyramid Peak 11,926 ft*

+*10,842 ft*

GRANITE BASIN

DRY CANYON

Shoshone

Mt. Washington 11,658 ft

Snake Creek

POLE CANYON

SNAKE RANGE

HUMBOLDT-TOIYABE NATIONAL FORESTS

North Fork

+*Lincoln Peak 11,597 ft*

LINCOLN CANYON

HIGHLAND RIDGE

South Fork

Day use only area

Mustang Spring

Ranger Station

Campground

Primitive Campsite

Interpretive Trail

+*Granite Peak 11,218 ft*

Lexington Arch

– – – Unpaved (2-wheel-drive road)

–·–·– Unpaved (4-wheel-drive road)

········· Trail

Day use only area

0   1   2 km

0   1   2 mi

To (93)
o Las Vegas
(6)(50)
To Salt Lake City

(487)

(488)
Baker

Lehman Creek

Baker Creek

(487)

CANYON

YOUNG CANYON

RSE HEAVEN

To (21)

Snake Creek

Big Wash

North Fork

Lexington Creek
To (21)

South Fork

HUMBOLDT-TOIYABE
NATIONAL FORESTS

Parry's primrose near alpine Stella Lake

Desert prickly pear cactus

Blue columbine on Baker Lake Trail

mahogany. These usually grow as
a shrub but here reach tree height.
Pull off at **Peak Overlook** for spectacular views of **Wheeler Peak** on the
right and **Jeff Davis Peak** on the left.
The north face of Wheeler drops
1,800 feet to a glacier below.
Snow often dusts the jagged walls
of gray quartzite.

The road ends at Wheeler Peak
Campground, where you have your
choice of several fine walks. One of the
most popular follows the 3-mile **Alpine**

Bristlecone pines worn smooth by centuries of wind, sand, and ice

New-growth bristlecones and needles

Climbing the northwest face of Mount Washington

Lakes Loop Trail past **Stella** and **Teresa Lakes.** This leads you to a dramatic alpine setting with a barren, sawtooth ridge rising above the smooth surface of the lake.

If time and stamina allow, follow the **Wheeler Summit Trail** to the ridge above the lakes for an overview of the park and sweeping views of Great Basin's seemingly endless succession of mountain ranges. The trail leaves the Alpine Lakes Loop Trail near Stella Lake and climbs another 3,000 feet to the summit. Once above tree line, watch for sturdy alpine flowers like primrose and phlox. And be prepared for harsh weather. A terse entry in the summit register reads, "Wind took no prisoners."

Just as spectacular is the 3-mile **Bristlecone/Glacier Trail.** This leaves from Teresa Lake and takes you to **Wheeler Cirque,** a glacier-hollowed valley enclosed by sheer cliffs. At the far end lies the glacier, the Great Basin's only permanent one and one of the southernmost in the country.

Before reaching the glacier be sure to take the **Bristlecone Forest Loop.** This self-guided nature trail passes ancient trees with twisted trunks carved and polished by wind-driven snow and ice. Nearby a tree called Prometheus lived for almost 5,000 years until it was cut down in 1964.

Even after most of its trunk and branches die, a bristlecone pine can continue to survive, sustained by very little moisture. The tree holds onto its needles for 20 to 30 years, assuring

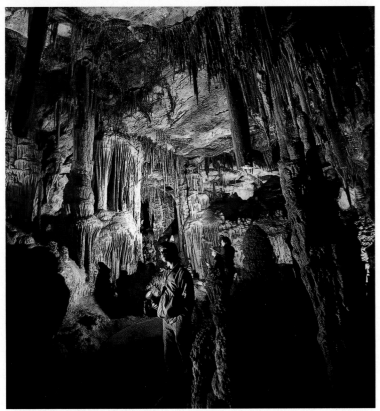

Stalactites and stalagmites in the Gothic Palace, Lehman Caves

stable photosynthesis regardless of environmental stress.

Lehman Caves

0.6 mile; 1.5 hours

Guided cave tours began in 1885 with Absalom Lehman, a miner turned rancher. Over the years dozens of legends have grown around his discovery of the cave. One claims he was racing along on horseback when he suddenly dropped through the entrance. He lassoed a tree and managed to hold on until rescued 4 days later. The hard part was keeping his legs wrapped around the horse to prevent it from falling.

Tour tickets must be purchased 1 day in advance (either stop by the visitor center or call 775-234-7331).You have a choice of three tours: 1.5 hours, 1 hour, or 0.5 hour (the latter visits only the Gothic Palace).

Meet your guide behind the visitor center near the cave entrance. The attraction of Lehman Caves lies in the beauty of its formations, well represented in the first room you visit, the **Gothic Palace.** The cave is so filled with columns, draperies, and stalactites that the first explorers used sledgehammers to break through them. Because of the cave's manageable scale, you get closeup views of bizarre helictites and delicate aragonite crystals.

The walkway takes you past fine examples of rare cave shields. These large disks grow from cracks in the ceiling where seeping water deposits minerals in flat, circular forms.

Continuing deeper, you reach two of the cave's most beautiful rooms. Rimstone pools and soda straws decorate the **Lake Room;** shields, massive columns, and bacon-rind draperies fill the **Grand Palace.**

A small variety of cave life makes its home here, including pack rats, cave crickets, and the rare pseudoscorpion—an arachnid with scorpionlike pinchers. Bats, however, stay away, finding the cave's vertical entrance too hard to negotiate.

Information & Activities

Headquarters
100 Great Basin National Park, Baker, NV 89311. Phone (775) 234-7331. www.nps.gov/grba

Seasons & Accessibility
Park open year-round. Snow may cover high-elevation trails until late June or July. Some park roads require four-wheel-drive vehicles. Call headquarters about current trail and road conditions.

Visitor & Information Centers
Visitor center and Lehman Caves, located on Nev. 488 at northeast end of park, open daily all year. Phone park headquarters number for visitor information.

Entrance Fees
None for park. Fee for cave tours.

Pets
Permitted on leashes except in visitor center, caves, backcountry, and on trails.

Facilities for Disabled
Visitor center and the first room in Lehman Caves are wheelchair accessible, as are some campsites.

Things to Do
Ranger-led activities: free nature walks and talks, exhibits, movie, campfire programs. Also available: cave tours, Wheeler Peak Scenic Drive, hiking, fishing (license required), climbing, and cross-country skiing.

Special Advisories
● Park's high elevation can cause altitude sickness. People who have heart or respiratory problems should take it slowly.
● Don't expect to find water sources along the trails; always carry drinking water when hiking.
● Watch out for rattlesnakes along hiking trails.
● Summer thunderstorms are common; check weather conditions with park before setting off on a hike.

Overnight Backpacking
Those heading out to the backcountry should stop at the park's visitor center and complete the free permit registration form. In addition to helping to ensure visitor safety, permits allow the park to monitor how its resources are being used.

Campgrounds
Four campgrounds, all with 14-day limit, all first come, first served. **Baker Creek** and **Upper Lehman Creek** open mid-May through October. **Wheeler Peak** open mid-June through September. **Lower Lehman Creek** open all year. Snowstorms may close campgrounds occasionally. No showers. Tent and RV sites; no hookups. Food services in the park. Potable water available year-round at visitor center, and in summer at RV sanitary station, picnic areas, and developed campgrounds.

Hotels, Motels & Inns
(unless otherwise noted, rates are for 2 persons in a double room, high season)
In Baker, NV 89311:
The Border Inn (on US 50) P.O. Box 30. (775) 234-7300. 28 units. $29-$39. AC, restaurant, RV park.
Silver Jack Motel (on Main St.) P.O. Box 166. (775) 234-7323. 9 units. $37-$60. AC.
In Ely, NV 89301:
Bristlecone Motel 700 Ave. I. (800) 497-7404 or (775) 289-8838. 31 units. $42-$44. AC.
Historic Hotel Nevada and Gaming Hall 501 Aultman St. (775) 289-6665. 58 units. $25-$85. AC, restaurant.
Jailhouse Motel and Casino 5th and High Sts. (800) 841-5430 or (775) 289-3033. 61 units. $57-$75. AC, rest.
Petrelli's Fireside Inn (2 miles north of Ely) SR 1, Box 2. (800) 732-0288 or (775) 289-3765. 14 units. $45. AC, restaurant.
Ramada Inn and Copper Queen Casino 805 Great Basin Blvd. (800) 851-9526 or (775) 289-4884. 65 units. $74-$90. AC, pool, restaurant.

For a complete list of accommodations contact the White Pine Chamber of Commerce. (775) 289-8877.

Excursions

Humboldt-Toiyabe National Forests

Elko, Nevada

This immense national forest is the largest in the continental United States. Contains glacier-carved Lamoille Canyon, historic mining towns, and Jarbridge Wilderness, in Nevada, one of the country's least used wilderness areas. About 6,300,000 acres. Hiking, boating, fishing, horseback riding, hunting, scenic drives, winter sports, water sports. 1,000 campsites, boat ramp, picnic areas, handicapped access. Open year-round; most campsites open late May through September. The forest's Snake Division surrounds Great Basin NP. (775) 355-5340.

Desert National Wildlife Range

Las Vegas, Nevada

Wildlife is the focus of this Mojave Desert refuge, just a long roll of the dice from Las Vegas. Bighorn sheep, mule deer, coyotes, and some 260 species of birds are found in the refuge, the largest in the lower 48. 1,600,000 acres. Primitive camping, hiking, hunting, scenic drives (high-clearance vehicle required). Open year-round. Interpretive kiosk at Corn Creek Field Station entrance, off US 95, about 250 miles from Great Basin NP. (702) 879-6110.

Spring Mountain National Recreation Area

Las Vegas, Nevada

Many people are surprised to find a forest so close to Las Vegas: The Spring Mountains rise to almost 12,000 feet from the harsh desert of southern Nevada. The cool mountain forests are home to a wilderness of ponderosa pine, sheer limestone cliffs, and assorted wildlife. About 316,000 acres. Camping, scenic drives, hiking, wildlife viewing. Picnic areas. Take US 95 to the Kyle Canyon turnoff (Nev. 157). About 250 miles from Great Basin NP. (702) 515-5400.

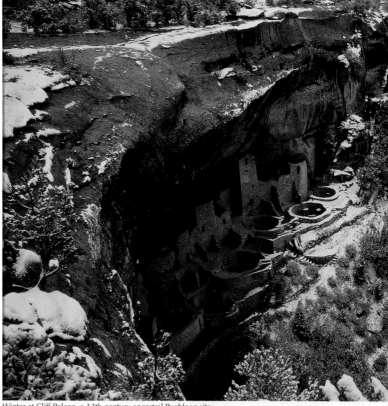

Winter at Cliff Palace, a 13th-century ancestral Puebloan site

Mesa Verde

Colorado

Established June 29, 1906

52,074 acres

At Mesa Verde, Spanish for "green table," ancient multistoried dwellings fill the cliff-rock alcoves that rise 2,000 feet above Montezuma Valley. Unique for their number and remarkable preservation, the cliff dwellings cluster in sandstone canyons that slice the mesa into narrow tablelands fingering southward. Here, and on the mesa top, archaeologists have located more than 600 cliff dwellings dating from about A.D. 550 to 1300.

The sites, from mesa-top pithouses and multistoried dwellings to cliffside villages, document the dramatic changes in the lives of a prehistoric people that archaeologists once dubbed the Anasazi. They are now more accurately called the ancestral Puebloans, and 24 Native American tribes in the Southwest today consider themselves descendants of these ancestral people. Some 40 pueblos and cliff dwellings are visible from park roads and overlooks; many of these are open to the public.

Beginning about A.D. 750, the ancestral Puebloans grouped their dwellings in mesa-top pueblos, or villages. About 1200 they moved down into recesses in the cliffs. Massive overhanging rock has so sheltered these later villages that they seem to stand outside of time, aloof to the present.

In 1888 two cowboys tracking stray cattle through snow stopped on the edge of a steep-walled canyon. Through the drifting flakes they could make out traces of walls and towers of a great cliff dwelling across the canyon. Novelist Willa Cather, a later visitor, described the scene: "The game hunted out, and soils depleted. Years of drought and poor crops may have been aggravated by village squabbles. By the end of the 13th century the ancestral Puebloans had left the plateau, never to return.

How to Get There

From Cortez, take US 160 east for 8 miles to the park entrance, then follow the winding park road 15 miles to Far View Visitor Center and 5.5 miles farther to park headquarters area, which includes the museum and main cliff dwellings. Trailers are not allowed past Morefield Village. Airports: Cortez and Durango.

When to Go

All-year park. Wetherill Mesa, Far View Visitor Center, Cliff Palace Loop, Balcony House, and many services are closed in winter. Wildflowers bloom from April through September. In winter, cross-country skiing is allowed on parts of Mesa Top Road when conditions permit.

How to Visit

On a 1-day visit, begin early and stop first at the **Far View Visitor Center,** open mid-April to mid-October, to purchase tickets. Then go to the **Chapin Mesa Museum** for an overview; and then visit nearby **Spruce Tree House.** From there take the **Cliff Palace Loop** of **Mesa Top Road.** In the afternoon, follow the other loop. Wear sturdy shoes and be prepared for some strenuous climbing if you plan to visit the cliff dwellings. Binoculars are useful for enhancing your views from across the canyon.

With extra time, visit less crowded **Wetherill Mesa.**

falling snowflakes sprinkling the piñons, gave it a special kind of solemnity. It was more like sculpture than anything else … preserved … like a fly in amber."

Climbing down a makeshift ladder to the deserted city, the excited cowboys explored the honeycombed network of rooms that they named Cliff Palace. Inside, they found stone tools and pottery and other artifacts. Later investigators learned that these rooms had been uninhabited for some seven centuries.

Why the Mesa Verde people eventually left their homes may never be known. Indeed, they lived in the cliffside dwellings for only about the last 75 to 100 years of their occupation of Mesa Verde. Early observers guessed warfare, and the evidence for this is still being debated. Archaeologists also think they may have been victims of their own success. Their productive dry farming allowed their populations to grow perhaps as high as 5,000. Gradually woodlands were cut, wild

---

Chapin Mesa Museum & Spruce Tree House

2 hours to a half day

Before descending to the sites, go through the **Chapin Mesa Museum,** located at the Spruce Tree House Trailhead and park headquarters area. Here you pick up self-guiding booklets to the major sites and view a 25-minute video.

Excellent dioramas bring to life the changing world of the Mesa Verde people. Also displayed are some of the Southwest's finest artifacts and Indian

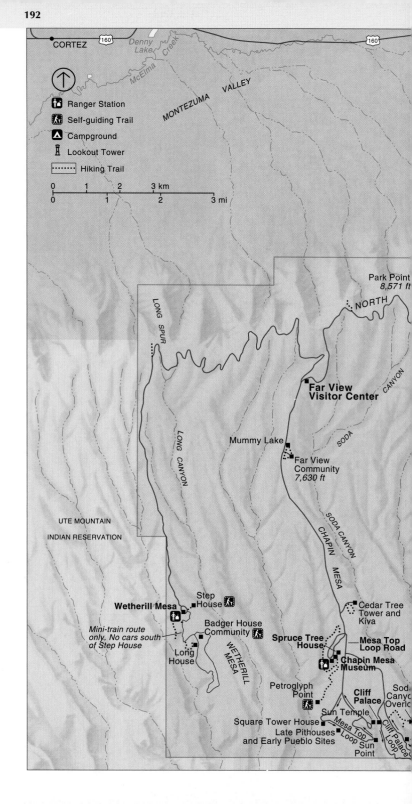

CORTEZ [160]

Denny Lake

Creek

McElma

↑

MONTEZUMA VALLEY

- 🏠 Ranger Station
- 🚶 Self-guiding Trail
- ⛺ Campground
- 🗼 Lookout Tower
- ·········· Hiking Trail

| 0 | 1 | 2 | 3 km |
| 0 | 1 | 2 | 3 mi |

[160]

Park Point
8,571 ft

NORTH

LONG SPUR

CANYON

Far View
Visitor Center

Mummy Lake

SODA

Far View
Community
7,630 ft

LONG CANYON

SODA CANYON

CHAPIN MESA

UTE MOUNTAIN

INDIAN RESERVATION

Wetherill Mesa

Step House

Cedar Tree
Tower and
Kiva

Mini-train route
only. No cars south
of Step House

Badger House
Community

Spruce Tree
House

Mesa Top
Loop Road

Chapin Mesa
Museum

Long
House

WETHERILL MESA

Petroglyph
Point

Cliff
Palace

Sod
Canyo
Overlc

Square Tower House

Sun Temple

Mesa Top

Late Pithouses
and Early Pueblo Sites

Loop

Sun
Point

Cliff
Palace
Loop

Narrow passageway in Balcony House

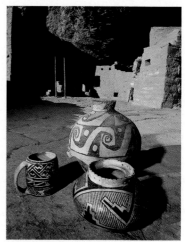

Pottery in Spruce Tree House

arts and crafts. Also view the collection of **Mesa Verde pottery.** Decorated with black geometric designs against a white background, the pots represent the highest artistic expression of the ancestral Puebloans.

The park naturally focuses on the dramatic cliff dwellings, but they represent only the final scene in a long story. The genius of the earlier culture was best expressed not in building but in weaving. Look for outstanding examples in the museum, including a long sash of braided dog hair still as strong and pliable as it was when worn 1,500 years ago.

During summer, pick up a self-guiding booklet to **Spruce Tree House** and walk the paved quarter-mile trail to the park's best preserved site. Here you will see the skillful building techniques and stonework of the ancestral Puebloans; 90 percent of the stonework is original. Rangers will be on duty to answer questions. (From mid-November to early March, when the park is less crowded, the rangers lead guided tours.) The trail crosses the canyon bottom, thick with Gambel oak, whose acorns were eaten by the Indians. The site got its name from a tall Douglas-fir that, it is said, early explorers climbed down to reach the site—they thought it was a spruce.

The cliff dwelling, built in an alcove more than 200 feet wide, housed 60 to 100 people. Three of its eight kivas—underground ceremonial rooms—have reconstructed roofs. At one of them, you may climb down the ladder

through the smoke hole into the dark chamber below.

Either now or later—if time and stamina allow—take the 2.8-mile **Petroglyph Point Trail,** a self-guided nature walk that branches off the Spruce Tree House Trail. Register and pick up a guidebook at the trailhead. The trail offers a good place to stretch your legs, familiarize yourself with plants and their prehistoric uses, and see one of the park's largest petroglyphs, a panel 12 feet across.

Mesa Top Loop Road

12 miles; a half day

Dotted with wayside interpretive exhibits, two 6-mile one-way loops wind through **Chapin Mesa's** fire-scarred pinyon-juniper woodland. If you purchased tickets, begin your tour by turning onto the **Cliff Palace Loop** and driving to the parking area at **Cliff Palace.** A short trail takes you to a striking view of the largest cliff dwelling in North America: The 150-room site once housed more than 100 people. A park ranger will meet you at the overlook and guide you down a quarter-mile trail to tour the dwelling.

The ancestral Puebloans built their dwellings in natural shelters formed by water percolating down through the sandstone. Where it reaches the denser shale layer, it seeps horizontally through the canyon wall, forming springs. These weaken the overlying rock, eroding the cliff face into eye-shaped alcoves.

Continue driving to the **Balcony House** parking area. This 40-room dwelling is one of the highlights of the park. But it is not for everyone. *Acrophobes and claustrophobes, beware!* Rangers guide adventurous groups up a 32-foot ladder to an easily defended ledge site and a panoramic view of **Soda Canyon.** To leave Balcony House, you must crawl through a tunnel on your hands and knees. Balcony House is closed in winter; you can view it then from a promontory at the end of the 0.75-mile **Soda Canyon Overlook Trail.**

Keep going along the road until the junction with the **Mesa Top Loop,** where you turn left. Stop at the first pull-off to pick up a guide booklet and continue on to the **Square Tower House** overlook. A 500-foot trail leads to a dramatic viewpoint above the park's tallest site, the four-story remnant of a more extensive, multitiered structure. The site itself is not open to the public.

Return to your car and continue a short distance to the **Late Pithouse and Early Pueblo Sites** pull-off. The squarish, sunken pithouses, earliest of Mesa Verde's permanent dwellings, were forerunners of the kivas. Farther along the trail are the excavated remains of three villages built on the same site between A.D. 900 and 1075. They show the evolution in architectural style, from post-and-adobe construction to stone masonry.

Drive to **Sun Point Overlook,** saving **Sun Point Pueblo** for your next trip. Here at the junction of **Fewkes Canyon** and **Cliff Canyon** you see a dozen cliff dwellings—among them, distant views of Cliff Palace to the northeast; **Sunset House** perched on a high rock ledge to the east; and **Mummy House,** directly across the canyon. The house was named for the naturally desiccated mummy of a child discovered there.

Continue past **Oak Tree House** and **Fire Temple** pull-offs to **Sun Temple.** Built by skilled masons—the stones were molded and their surfaces "dimpled"—this long, D-shaped structure with doorless chambers presents an enigma to archaeologists. Never inhabited, it may have been a ceremonial center; or perhaps it was used to record the annual movements of the sun, an attempt to counter the changeable weather. The canyon edge next to the parking area offers a superb view of Cliff Palace.

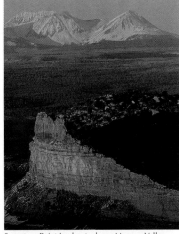

Sunset on Point Lookout, above Mancos Valley

Wetherill Mesa

13 miles; a half day or more

Accessible only in summer, the **Wetherill Mesa Road** starts on the west side of **Far View Visitor Center,** where you stop to purchase tickets for the 1.5-hour tour of Long House. The steep road takes you to sites opened to the public in 1972 after an extensive archaeological study. Under sponsorship of the National Geographic Society and National Park Service, several major cliff dwellings and mesa-top sites were excavated.

Drive to the kiosk area and park. From here take the half-mile, self-guided walk to **Step House,** named for its prehistoric stairway. The site is unusual, for pithouses have been uncovered next to a multistoried pueblo built in the same alcove.

Return to the kiosk area and take the mini-train to the head of **Long House Trail.** Rangers lead groups down the quarter-mile trail to the park's second largest cliff dwelling—150 rooms with 21 kivas, an unusually high number. Gustaf Nordenskiöld, a Swedish scientist, excavated portions of **Long House** and other sites in 1891, publishing the first scientific report on Mesa Verde.

You can extend your visit by taking the mini-train to the half-mile, self-guided trail that threads through the sites of **Badger House Community.** These excavated pithouses and pueblos show the contrast between life on the mesa top and that in the canyon alcoves below. The mini-train will return you to the kiosk area.

Information & Activities

Headquarters
Mesa Verde National Park, CO 81330.
Phone (970) 529-4465.
www.nps.gov/meve

Seasons & Accessibility
Park open year-round, but most visitor facilities and services available mid-May to mid-October only. Spruce Tree House open all year; Cliff Palace open early April to early November; Balcony House open mid-May to mid-October; Wetherill Mesa open summer only. In winter, snow or ice may close Mesa Top Road. For weather and road conditions, call (970) 529-4461 or (970) 529-4465.

Visitor & Information Centers
Far View Visitor Center at northwest section of park open daily mid-May to mid-October. **Chapin Mesa Museum** at southern end of park, located 21 miles from entrance, open daily year-round. Phone (970) 529-4465 for visitor information.

Entrance Fee
$10 per car per week. Additional tickets required for tours of Cliff Palace, Balcony House, and Long House; purchase for small fee at Far View Visitor Center.

Pets
Permitted on leashes. Not allowed in buildings, in sites, or on trails.

Facilities for Disabled
Visitor center, museum, half-mile trail at Wetherill Mesa, some campsites, and most rest rooms are wheelchair accessible. Site tours are not accessible, but most major cliff dwellings can be viewed from the mesa-top roads and overlooks. Free brochure.

Things to Do
Ranger-led activities: archaeological walks, tours of Balcony House (spring to fall), Spruce Tree House (fall to spring), and Long House (summer only); evening campfire programs. Also available, wayside exhibits, archaeological museum, self-guided tours; also, limited hiking (registration required for two trails), cross-country skiing, and snowshoeing.

Special Advisories
● Visits to the cliff dwellings are strenuous. Wear sturdy shoes and use caution, especially if you have heart or respiratory problems.
● Hold onto your children on cliff trails and canyon rims.

Overnight Backpacking
Not permitted in park.

Campgrounds
One campground, **Morefield,** with a 14-day limit. Open mid-April to mid-October. First come, first served. Fees $7-$14 per night. Showers within 1 mile of campground. Tent and RV sites; 14 hookups. **Morefield Group Campgrounds** available first come, first served. Food services in park (mid-April to mid-October).

Hotels, Motels, & Inns
(unless otherwise noted, rates are for 2 persons in a double room, high season)
INSIDE THE PARK:
Far View Lodge Mesa Verde Co., P.O. Box 277, Mancos, CO 81328. (800) 449-2288. 150 units. $101-$113. Restaurant. Open mid-April to mid-March.
OUTSIDE THE PARK:
In Cortez, CO 81321:
Anasazi Motor Inn 640 S. Broadway. (800) 972-6232 or (970) 565-3773. 85 units. $65-$71. AC, pool, restaurant.
Best Western Sands 1120 E. Main St. (800) 528-1234 or (970) 565-3761. 81 units. $89. AC, pool.
Best Western Turquoise Inn and Suites 535 E. Main St. (800) 547-3376 or (970) 565-3778. 77 units. $80-$129. AC, pool.
In Durango, CO 81301:
Strater Hotel 699 Main Ave. (800) 247-4431 or (970) 247-4431. 93 units. $139-$205. AC, restaurant.
In Mancos, CO 81328:
Mesa Verde Motel 191 Railroad Ave., P.O. Box 552. (800) 825-6372 or (970) 533-7741. 16 units. $59. AC.

For further suggestions contact the Cortez Chamber of Commerce. (970) 565-3414; or the Durango Chamber of Commerce. (800) 525-8855.

Excursions

San Juan National Forest
Durango, Colorado

The vegetation ranges from high alpine forest to sage-and-pinyon desert in this rugged San Juan Mountains area. Contains lakes, rivers, wilderness areas, and many archaeological sites. Two million acres. Hiking, boating, climbing, bicycling, fishing, horseback riding, llama trekking, hunting, winter sports, water sports. 36 campgrounds, boat ramps, limited handicapped access. Open all year; most campsites open May through November. Information at Durango on US 550, about 50 miles east of Mesa Verde NP. (970) 247-4874.

Aztec Ruins National Monument
Aztec, New Mexico

Misnamed by early Anglo settlers, this masonry-and-timber pueblo shows the influence of two ancestral Puebloan groups. It features the Southwest's only restored great kiva. 319 acres. Exhibits, picnic areas. Open all year. Off US 516, on Ruins Road, about 60 miles southeast of Mesa Verde NP. (505) 334-6174.

Hovenweep National Monument
Cortez, Colorado

Hovenweep—a Ute term meaning "deserted valley"—consists of six ancestral Puebloan sites: two in Utah and four in Colorado. They feature stone pueblos and square, circular, and D-shaped towers. Square Tower Group—located in Utah midway between Cortez and Blanding, Utah—is best preserved and most accessible. 785 acres. Open all year. Interpretive exhibits, hiking. 30 campsites (but not always available, so call ahead), picnic areas. Headquarters at Square Tower Group off Utah 262, about 55 miles from Mesa Verde NP. (970) 562-4282.

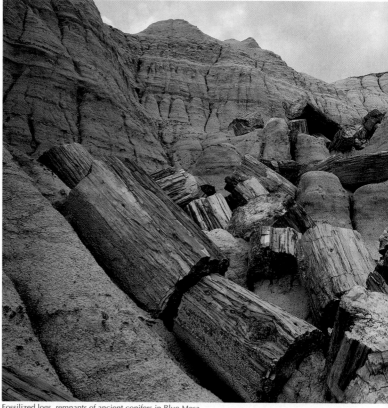

Fossilized logs, remnants of ancient conifers in Blue Mesa

Petrified Forest

Arizona

Established December 9, 1962

93,533 acres

A sun-swept corner of the Painted Desert draws more than 900,000 visitors each year. While most come to see one of the world's largest concentrations of brilliantly colored petrified wood, many leave having glimpsed something more. The 147 square miles of Petrified Forest open a window on an environment more than 200 million years old, one radically different from today's high desert.

Where you now see ravens soaring over a stark landscape, leathery-winged pterosaurs once glided over rivers teeming with armor-scaled fish and giant, spatula-headed amphibians. Nearby ran herds of some of the earliest dinosaurs. Scientists have identified several hundred species of fossil plants and animals in Petrified Forest.

The park consists of two main sections. Located in the south are the major concentrations of the famous petrified wood; in the north rise the colorful banded badlands of the Painted Desert. Giant fossilized logs, many of them fractured into cordwood-size segments, lie scattered throughout, like headstones bearing a deceased's likeness.

Much of the quartz rock that replaced the wood tissue 200 million years ago is tinted in rainbow hues. Many visitors cannot resist taking rocks, despite strict regulations and stiff fines against removing any material. To see if the petrified wood was actually disappearing at an alarming rate, resource managers established survey plots with a specific number of pieces of wood; some were completely barren in less than a week.

The problem is not new. Military survey parties passing through the region in 1851 filled their saddlebags with the petrified wood. As word of these remarkable deposits spread, fossil logs were hauled off by the wagonload for tabletops, lamps, and mantels. In the 1890s gem collectors began dynamiting logs searching for amethyst and quartz crystals. To prevent further destruction of its unique bounty, the area was designated a national monument in 1906 and a national park more than a half century later.

How to Get There

If you are traveling west on I-40, exit south into park. When leaving the south end of park, the road joins US 180. Follow US 180 for 19 miles to Holbrook and back to I-40. If you are traveling east on I-40, take the US 180 exit. The south entrance is 19 miles from Holbrook. After driving through park, leave via I-40. Airport: Flagstaff.

When to Go

All-year park. Summer's dramatic clouds and thunderstorms enhance the beauty of the landscape. Fall, with its milder weather, also attracts many visitors. Winter in the high desert can be cold with brief snowstorms, but moderate afternoon temperatures are not uncommon. The desert blooms colorfully in spring; winds can be high.

How to Visit

Many of the features at Petrified Forest are on a scale best appreciated by leaving the car. Plan enough time to walk among the fossil logs and **Painted Desert** badlands. For a half-day visit, follow the **park road** from the **Rainbow Forest Museum** to **Pintado Point.** If you can stay longer, include a walk to **Agate House,** take the trail into the **Blue Mesa** badlands, and consider a hike in the **Painted Desert Wilderness.**

The Park Road

28 miles; a half to full day

A scenic drive connecting the south and north entrances passes through high desert grasslands broken by unexpected escarpments and bare hills banded in pastels. Begin at the south entrance with a stop at the **Rainbow Forest Museum.** (Or, from the north, begin at the **Painted Desert Visitor Center** and reverse this tour.) Be sure to see the dioramas of the Triassic landscape and the displays of fossils and early dinosaurs.

The museum sits in the **Rainbow Forest,** one of four major concentrations of petrified logs called "forests." Behind it winds the half-mile **Giant Logs Trail** (closes 15 minutes before park); the largest fossil log is **Old Faithful** with a 9.5-foot diameter.

From the museum, a half-mile trail (closes 30 minutes before park) takes you to the trailhead for the 0.6-mile Long Logs loop and the 1-mile round-trip Agate House trail.

At **Long Logs,** you will see the largest concentration of petrified wood in the park, with logs up to 120 feet long—many crisscrossed in logjams. The majority of the park's petrified wood, including that found here, comes from tall conifers called *Araucarioxylon.* These ancient trees

CHINDE
MESA

+ Pilot Rock
6,234 ft

WILDERNESS AREA

P A I N T E D   D E S E R T

BLACK
FOREST

ONYX BRIDGE ■

To Gallup

Chinde Point ■
Kachina Point
Pintado Point ■
Painted Desert Inn
Tiponi Point

40

Lacey Point ■

Painted Desert
Visitor Center

No access to interstate

40

Burlington Northern Santa Fe Railroad

To Holbrook and
Grand Canyon NP

Santa Fe Railroad
Wayside Exhibit
Adamana ●

Puerco Pueblo

Newspaper Rock ■

The Tepees ■

Blue
Mesa

Black Knoll

Jasper
Forest ■

Agate
Bridge

PUERCO   RIDGE

Crystal
Forest

RIDGE

Rainbow
Forest
Museum

RAINBOW
FOREST

GIANT
LOGS

Long Logs

Agate House

PUERCO

To Holbrook and
Grand Canyon NP

180

Entrance Station

To St. Johns

Interpretive Trail

Trail

0   5 km

0   5 mi

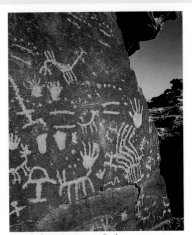
Petroglyphs on Newspaper Rock

grew more than 200 million years ago in distant highlands, where floods or perhaps mudflows uprooted them. Tumbled and abraded, the fallen trees washed into logjams and were quickly buried by silt and ash. Silica-laden water percolated through the wood, replacing organic tissue with multicolored quartz.

Next, if you have time, strike out on the paved trail to **Agate House.** During the 1930s crews restored one of the rooms in this eight-room dwelling built by ancestral Puebloans more than 800 years ago. The prehistoric structure was of wood and adobe; the reconstruction uses concrete to stabilize the walls.

Continue your drive north, bypassing three turnoffs—**Crystal Forest, Jasper Forest,** and **Agate Bridge,** unless you have plenty of time. Take the 3-mile spur road that climbs **Blue Mesa.** You loop through strange badlands layered in blue, purple, and cream colors that change with weather and time of day.

Along the way, you'll spot the trailhead for the **Blue Mesa Trail,** which winds along a 1-mile, 45-minute route through the badlands. The trail is paved and nearly level except for one very steep section. Even if you can't take the full hike, park your car and walk 100 feet to where the trail begins to descend. Here are good views of the intricately eroded mesa.

Return to the main road and drive north through **The Tepees,** bare, conical hills whose reddish hues are produced by iron and other minerals.

The trail to the **Newspaper Rock** petroglyphs has been closed, making them difficult to see from the overlook above. Skip this and continue driving a short distance to the **Puerco Pueblo,** one of the largest prehistoric sites in the park. Here you see the partially excavated remains of an ancestral Puebloan village abandoned about 1380 as well as many fine petroglyphs of animals and geometric designs pecked into the outcropping rock.

Scientists believe a chiseled circle here was used by the Indians as a solar calendar. The week preceding and following the advent of the summer solstice, the sun interacts with this petroglyph. Early in the morning on the day of the summer solstice, rangers guide observers to the place where a shaft of sunlight pierces and fills the very center of the ancient symbol.

The road crosses the intermittent **Puerco River,** which divides the park in two. No permanent streams flow in Petrified Forest, and fewer than nine inches of precipitation fall each year, half in summer thunderstorms.

After crossing I-40, the drive reaches the edge of a volcanic escarpment overlooking a particularly colorful section of the **Painted Desert.**

Pull off at **Lacey Point,** the first of eight overlooks. Here the bare Chinle slopes are tinted in the chalky shades of a Navajo rug. The colors are especially vivid when the sun shines on sediment still wet from a thunderstorm.

Continue on to the sweeping panoramic vista at **Pintado Point**—the highest along the Painted Desert rim. Below lies **Lithodendron Wash,** braiding through the red badlands of the **Black Forest.** In the distance stands the dark profile of **Pilot Rock,** at 6,234 feet the park's highest point.

For a longer hike, walk through the rugged beauty of the **Painted Desert Wilderness.** The trail begins at **Kachina Point** behind the old **Painted Desert Inn,** originally built as a roadside inn, now open daily as a historical site. Once in the flats below the rim, the trail disappears, requiring you to do your own route-finding. Look for the Black Forest, an area of dark fossilized wood, and **Onyx Bridge.** Finding the bridge can be an adventure since there are no landmarks to guide you.

The scenic drive ends at the **Painted Desert Visitor Center,** which is the park headquarters located at the north entrance.

Information & Activities

Headquarters
P.O. Box 2217, AZ 86028. Phone (928) 524-6228. www.nps.gov/pefo

Seasons & Accessibility
Open all year; extended hours May through August. Snow or icy roads may close park temporarily in winter.

Visitor & Information Centers
Painted Desert Visitor Center at north entrance, just off I-40, and **Rainbow Forest Museum** near south entrance, just off US 180. **Painted Desert Inn National Historic Landmark,** 2 miles from the north entrance, also has archaeological displays and historic information.

Entrance Fee
$10 per car, good for 7 days.

Pets & Horses
Pets permitted on leashes except in public buildings, wilderness areas, and on Giant Logs Trail. Horses permitted throughout park in groups of six or less when accompanied by riders, but grazing is prohibited. No water available.

Facilities for Disabled
Visitor centers, museum, and rest rooms are wheelchair accessible.

Things to Do
Free ranger-led, year-round activities: nature talks, wildlife viewing, and bird-watching. Also available, a film, interpretive exhibits, self-guided auto tours, hiking, horseback riding (no rentals in area).

Special Advisories
● Stay on trails to prevent damage to the fragile desert environment and personal injury from sharp edges of petrified logs.
● Take nothing from the park but memories, not even a tiny piece of petrified wood; pieces quickly add up to tons.
● Carry water when you hike; none is available outside developed areas.
● Do not approach any wildlife; as cute as they are, park animals may carry bubonic plague, Hantavirus, and rabies.

Overnight Backpacking
Allowed in the **Painted Desert Wilderness.** Permit required; available free at visitor center or museum up to one hour before park closing.

Campgrounds
None inside the park, but food service available.

Hotels, Motels, & Inns
(unless otherwise noted, rates are for 2 persons in a double room, high season)
In Holbrook, AZ 86025:
Best Inn 2211 E. Navajo Blvd. (800) 551-1923 or (928) 524-2654. 40 units. $41-$45. AC.
Best Western Adobe Inn 615 W. Hopi Dr. (928) 524-3948. 54 units. $50-$54. AC, pool.
Holbrook Comfort Inn 2602 E. Navajo Blvd. (800) 228-5150 or (928) 524-6131. 61 units. $70. AC, pool.

Contact the Holbrook Chamber of Commerce for additional accommodations: 100 E. Arizona St., Holbrook, AZ 86025. (928) 524-6558.

Excursions

El Morro
National Monument

Ramah, New Mexico

Here in 1605 Spaniard Juan de Oñate scratched his name at the base of a sandstone cliff. Others added inscriptions to the carvings of pre-Columbian Indians. Two ancestral Puebloan ruins sit on the cliff-top mesa. 1,279 acres. Hiking. 9 campsites (open May to mid-Oct.), picnic areas, handicapped access. Open year-round. On N. Mex. 53, off I-40, about 125 miles from Petrified Forest NP. (505) 783-4226.

El Malpais National
Monument and
National Conservation Area

Grants, New Mexico

El Malpais—"the badlands"—is located in the lava beds of western New Mexico. Featuring spatter cones, a 17-mile-long lava-tube system, and ice caves, the site also contains ancestral Puebloan ruins, a freestanding natural arch, and two wilderness areas. 376,000 acres. Primitive camping, hiking, bicycling, horseback riding, scenic drives. Open all year. Information center at N. Mex. 53 (23 miles south of Grants). About 140 miles east of Petrified Forest NP. (505) 783-4774.

Walnut Canyon
National Monument

Flagstaff, Arizona

More than 800 years ago, Indians now known as the Sinagua lived in caves in cliff dwellings here at the edge of Flagstaff. The Sinagua's name (Spanish for "without water") is a tribute to their remarkable ability to survive in a dry region. The cliff dwellings are accessible by trail. 3,541 acres. Visitor center, picnic areas. Open daily. Located off I-40, just east of Flagstaff. About 107 miles west of the I-40 exit at Petrified Forest NP. (928) 526-3367.

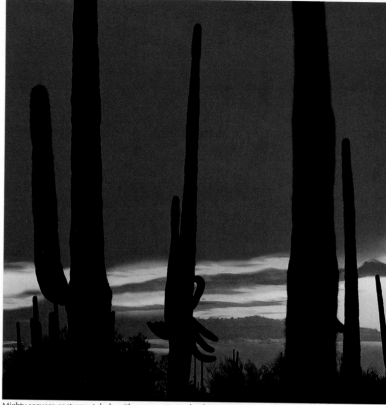

Mighty saguaro cactuses at dusk, with summer storm clouds

Saguaro

Arizona

Established October 14, 1994

91,445 acres

Symbol of the American Southwest and North America's largest cactus, the saguaro's imposing stature and uplifted arms give it a regal presence. Perhaps that's why this burly giant, whose only bits of exuberance are seasonal blossoms and figlike fruits at the tip of its limbs, has been dubbed the "desert monarch."

Carnegiea gigantea is the trademark of the Sonoran Desert, whose basins and ranges rumple 120,000 square miles of northwestern Mexico, southern Arizona, and southeastern California. Saguaro National Park is composed of two sections. The westerly Tucson Mountain District embraces about 24,000 acres of the hotter, drier, less-vegetated "low"

Sonoran ecosystem, which occurs below 3,000 feet. Thirty miles east, on the other side of Tucson's urban sprawl, is the 67,000-acre Rincon Mountain District, which occupies loftier ground and has a cooler, slightly wetter "high desert" environment. Most of it is inaccessible save by foot or on horseback. Here the terrain inclines from saguaro forests into nearly pristine woodlands of oak and pine. Hikers pressing on to higher elevations find Douglas-fir, ponderosa pine, and solitude.

The Sonoran Desert's extreme temperatures, perennial drought, frequent lightning, banshee winds, and voracious predators keep the saguaro forever at the limit of its endurance. Odds against survival rival a lottery: Though the cactus annually produces tens of thousands of pinhead-size seeds—some 40 mil-

How to Visit

On a 1-day visit, begin early and view the **Arizona-Sonora Desert Museum** before heading to **Saguaro West;** then pause at the **Red Hills Visitor Center** for an overview. Take the **Bajada Scenic Loop Drive,** stopping en route to walk the paved **Desert Discovery Nature Trail.** Return to Tucson, continuing east to Saguaro's **Rincon Mountain District.** Take the **Cactus Forest Drive** and walk the **Desert Ecology Trail.** For a scenic rest stop along the drive, visit **Mica View Picnic Area.**

Saguaro West: Tucson Mountain District

About 25 miles; a half day

The drive west through **Tucson Mountain County Park** takes you past the excellent, zoolike **Arizona-Sonora Desert Museum** (520-883-1380), whose 12 acres include every Sonoran Desert life zone and most of its animals and plants. It's worth a stop.

Continue on Kinney Road to the **Red Hills Visitor Center,** where an orientation slide show and desert life exhibits will enhance your understanding of what you'll encounter here and in Saguaro East. Walk the center's **Cactus Garden Trail,** a paved path through an unruly crowd of cactuses: hedgehog, barrel, fishhook, chainfruit cholla, and prickly pear.

Saguaros thrive in the coarse, absorbent soil of *bajadas*, long desert mountain slopes of eroded rock, gravel, sand, and clay, where a mature plant's shallow, wide-ranging roots can absorb up to 200 gallons from one rainstorm, enough to last a year. The 9-mile **Bajada Loop Drive** beginning at the visitor center explores one of these life zones. En route, about 1 mile west, look left for the **Desert Discovery Nature Trail,** a half-mile path across a bajada at the base of the Tucson Mountains.

Hook right onto **Hohokam Road.** (Part of the loop is one way; enter here to drive it all in one direction.) About 1.5 miles from the turnoff, **Valley View Overlook Trail** winds up about half a mile to panoramas of rugged, cactus-studded landscapes. Unpaved **Golden Gate Road** turns off about a mile farther on and passes a pleasant picnic area near the head of **Sendero Esperanza Trail,** a moderately

lion over a life that may last two centuries—few ever even sprout. Even fewer seedlings achieve the grandeur of towering 50 feet and weighing up to 16,000 pounds.

How to Get There

Saguaro West: From Tucson take Speedway Boulevard west to Gates Pass Road, turning right on Kinney Road. (Buses, RVs, and towed vehicles are not recommended on Gates Pass; instead take Ariz. 86 west from Tucson to Kinney.) Saguaro East: Take Broadway Boulevard east from central Tucson to Old Spanish Trail. Airport: Tucson.

When to Go

All-year park. From October through April, temperatures reach the upper 60s to mid-70s and can drop below freezing overnight. From May through September, highs routinely exceed 100°F. July through September is characterized by brief but fierce thunderstorms. Saguaros bloom nightly from late April into June.

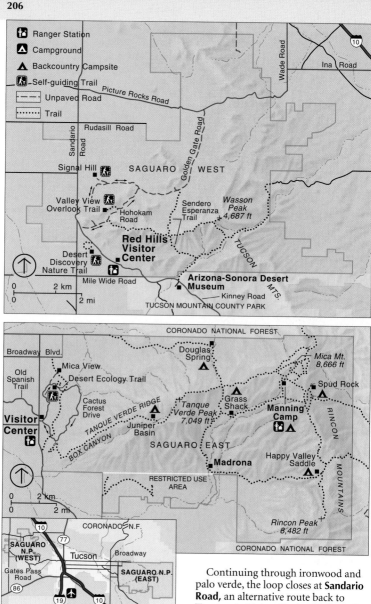

Legend (map symbols):
- 🏚 Ranger Station
- 🅰 Campground
- ▲ Backcountry Campsite
- 🅰 Self-guiding Trail
- --- Unpaved Road
- ···· Trail

SAGUARO WEST (map labels):
Picture Rocks Road
Wade Road
Ina Road
10
Sandario Road
Rudasill Road
Golden Gate Road
Signal Hill 🅰
SAGUARO WEST
Valley View Overlook Trail 🅰
Hohokam Road
Sendero Esperanza Trail
Wasson Peak +4,687 ft
Red Hills Visitor Center
Desert Discovery Nature Trail 🅰
Mile Wide Road
Arizona-Sonora Desert Museum
Kinney Road
TUCSON MOUNTAIN COUNTY PARK
TUCSON MTS.
0   2 km
0   2 mi

SAGUARO EAST (map labels):
CORONADO NATIONAL FOREST
Broadway Blvd.
Old Spanish Trail
Mica View
Desert Ecology Trail
Douglas Spring ▲
Mica Mt. 8,666 ft
Spud Rock ▲
Visitor Center
Cactus Forest Drive
TANQUE VERDE RIDGE
Tanque Verde Peak 7,049 ft
Grass Shack
Manning Camp 🏚▲
RINCON MOUNTAINS
BOX CANYON
Juniper Basin
SAGUARO EAST
Happy Valley Saddle ▲
Madrona ▲
RESTRICTED USE AREA
Rincon Peak + 8,482 ft
CORONADO NATIONAL FOREST
0   2 km
0   2 mi

CORONADO N.F.
10
77
SAGUARO N.P. (WEST)
Tucson
Broadway
Gates Pass Road
86
SAGUARO N.P. (EAST)
19
10

strenuous, popular half-day hike into the mountainous backcountry.

Backtrack on Golden Gate Road past Hohokam Road to **Signal Hill Picnic Area,** where rocks are etched with centuries-old Hohokam petroglyphs. Archaeologists believe the symbols, chipped through a brown patina of iron-manganese oxide called "desert varnish," signify territorial claims, clan migrations, personal accounts, visions, and pure artistic whimsy.

Continuing through ironwood and palo verde, the loop closes at **Sandario Road,** an alternative route back to Tucson via Picture Rocks, Wade, and Ina Roads to I-10.

Saguaro East: Rincon Mountain District

About 25 miles; a half day

Higher elevations here create Sonoran Desert environments different from Saguaro West's lowland desert zone. A steady, east-trending incline slants up into the roadless Rincon Mountain wilderness area, which is dotted with forests of oak, pine, and fir accessible only by foot or on horseback.

Make your first stop the **Saguaro East Visitor Center** at park headquarters. If you plan to hike into backcountry, this is the place to acquire trail guides, maps, and permits. If time is limited, pick up a guide to the **Cactus Forest Drive** and take the 8-mile loop, where many of the saguaros are more than 150 years old.

About 2 miles along the route, look left for a gravel road leading to scenic overlooks at **Mica View Picnic Area**, a pleasant place to stop. About a mile farther, the quarter-mile paved **Desert Ecology Trail** is designed to illustrate the crucial role of water in

Elf owl in its saguaro nest

desert ecosystems. What you are more likely to remember from this 20-minute amble, however, is the desert's perfect stillness.

Information & Activities

Headquarters
3693 S. Old Spanish Trail, Tucson, AZ 85730. For information call (520) 733-5158 (Saguaro West) or (520) 733-5153 (Saguaro East). www.nps.gov/sagu

Seasons
Park open year-round.

Visitor & Information Centers
Saguaro West Red Hills Visitor Center off Kinney Road. **Saguaro East Visitor Center** (park headquarters) on Old Spanish Trail. Open daily.

Entrance Fee
Saguaro West: None. Saguaro East: $6 per vehicle.

Pets
Not permitted on trails, in backcountry, or in public buildings; elsewhere allowed on leashes.

Facilities for Disabled
Visitor centers, nature trails, and roadside picnic areas wheelchair accessible.

Things to Do
Ranger-led hikes and night walks, scenic drives, trail walks, bird- and wildlife-watching, picnicking, bicycling, backcountry hiking. Horseback-ing riding is permitted on some trails.

Special Advisories
● Avoid open and low-lying areas during thunderstorms, when lightning and

flash floods pose a danger.
● Stay on trails. Abandoned mine shafts in Saguaro West make off-trail hiking and riding hazardous.
● Carry a flashlight at night to avoid encounters with rattlesnakes, scorpions, and Gila monsters.
● There is no water at picnic areas or along most trails. If hiking, carry at least one gallon of water per day.

Overnight Backpacking
Allowed only at designated backcountry sites. Use permits must be obtained at visitor centers in advance of trip.

Campgrounds
Four backcountry campsites in **Saguaro East,** accessible by trail. Campground in **Tucson Mountain County Park,** next to Saguaro West.

Hotels, Motels, & Inns
(Unless otherwise noted, rates for 2 persons, double room, high season) In Tucson, AZ:
Arizona Inn 2200 E. Elm St., 85711. (800) 933-1093 or (520) 325-1541. 86 units. $144-$224. AC, pool, rest. **Best Western** 1015 N. Stone Ave., 85705. (800) 528-1234. 79 units. $89-$139. AC, pool, rest. **Tucson East Hilton** 7600 E. Broadway, 85710. (800) 445-8667. 233 units. $145-$200. AC, pool, rest.

For more lodgings, contact Tucson Metropolitan Chamber of Commerce. (520) 792-1212.

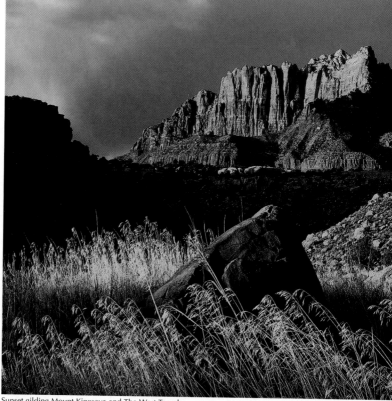

Sunset gilding Mount Kinesava and The West Temple

Zion

Utah

Established November 19, 1919

146,592 acres

Rising in Utah's high plateau country, the Virgin River carves its way to the desert below through a gorge so deep and narrow that sunlight rarely penetrates to the bottom. As the canyon widens, the river runs a gauntlet of great palisade walls rimmed with slick-rock peaks and hanging valleys.

The scale is immense—sheer cliffs dropping 3,000 feet, massive buttresses, deep alcoves. Nineteenth-century Mormon pioneers saw these sculptured rocks as the "natural temples of God." They called the canyon Little Zion after the celestial city.

A million years of flowing water has cut through the red and white beds of Navajo sandstone that form the sheer walls of Zion. The geologic heart of

the canyon began as a vast desert millions of years ago; almost incessant winds blew one dune on top of another until the sands reached a depth of more than 2,000 feet. You can still see the track of these ancient winds in the graceful crossbedded strata of Zion's mighty cliffs.

Unlike the Grand Canyon where you stand on the rim and look out, Zion Canyon is usually viewed from the bottom looking up. The vertical topography confines most of Zion's 2.5 million yearly visitors between canyon walls.

Streamside on the canyon floor grow thick stands of Fremont cottonwood, boxelder, willow, and, a short distance away, cactus and Utah juniper. Vegetation changes rapidly as the terrain rises almost a mile in elevation. The high plateaus support Douglas-fir and ponderosa pine.

hiking. Summer rains can bring spectacular clouds and numerous waterfalls. Rock colors are heightened by contrast with winter snows, green summer foliage, deep blue fall skies.

How to Visit

On a 1-day visit, take the **Zion-Mt. Carmel Highway** and the **Zion Canyon Scenic Drive** for the best overview of the park. For longer stays, begin with one of the classic walks in **Zion Canyon,** then take a road tour of the **Kolob Canyons** in late afternoon.

Zion-Mt. Carmel Highway & Zion Canyon Scenic Drive

18 miles; a half to full day

Within the park's 229 square miles lies a landscape of remote terraces and narrow gorges. A number of these canyons are so well hidden that early surveyors overlooked some that are 20 miles long. More than 100 miles of wilderness trails crisscross the backcountry, while 15 miles of paved trails encourage casual visits.

How to Get There

From Cedar City to the Kolob Canyons Entrance, take I-15 about 18 miles south. To Zion Canyon, take I-15 to Utah 17 then Utah 9 to the South Entrance (about 60 miles). From Kanab, take US 89 to Utah 9 (at Mt. Carmel junction) to the East Entrance. From Las Vegas and St. George, take I-15 and Utah 9 to the South Entrance. Airports: Las Vegas, Nevada, and St. George, Utah.

When to Go

Open all year, but main season is March through October. Mild spring and fall temperatures are ideal for

Zion-Mt. Carmel Highway (Utah 9) descends almost 2,000 feet from the high mesa country at the **East Entrance** to the **South Entrance** desert. Begin the drive on the east to see the park in the most dramatic possible way—from a

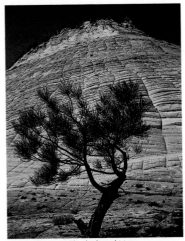

Pinyon pine near Checkerboard Mesa

To Cedar City and
Salt Lake City

15

Dirt roads are
impassable
when wet.
Closed in winter.

Horse Ranch Mt.
8,726 ft

Kolob
Canyons Road

*FINGER CANYONS
OF THE KOLOB*

**Kolob Canyons
Visitor Center**

South Fork

Lee
Pass

La Verkin
Creek Trail

KOLOB
PLATEAU

Kolob
Reservoir

OAK VALLEY

**Kolob
Canyons
Viewpoint**

*NAGUNT
MESA*

*BEARTRAP
CANYON*

HURRICANE CLIFFS

Kolob
Arch

*Timber Top
Mountain
8,055 ft*

*Langston
Mountain
7,408 ft*

UPPER KOLOB

La Verkin Creek

To
Zion Canyon

HOP VALLEY

Blue Springs
Reservoir

**Lava Point
7,890 ft**

West Rim Trail

*Firepit Knoll
7,265 ft*

SMITH MESA

LOWER KOLOB PLATEAU

*North Guardian
Angel
7,395 ft*

Left Fork

*Tabernacle
Dome
6,430 ft*

*South Guardian
Angel
7,140 ft*

Right Fork

*Double
Falls*

COUGAR MOUNTAIN

*HURRICANE
MESA*

*TOWERS
OF THE
VIRGIN*

To 15
and Kolob Canyons

Virgin

9

North Creek

*Crater Hill
5,192 ft*

*The West Temple
7,810 ft*

**Zion Canyon
Visitor Center
South Entrance**

Virgin

*Chinle
Trail*

9

Grafton
(ghost town)

Rockville

Dirt roads are
impassable
when wet.

To 59 and Pipe Spring NM

Ranger Station
Campground
Primitive Campsite
Self-guiding Trail
Unpaved Road
Trail

Volcano Knoll
6,735 ft

VIRGIN FLATS

Crystal Creek

Deep Creek

Kolob Creek

COGSWELL POINT

North Fork Virgin

ORSE PASTURE PLATEAU

North Fork Virgin

THE NARROWS

ORDERVILLE CANYON
Mountain of Mystery
6,565 ft
Temple of Sinawava

East Mesa Trail
Observation Point

Weeping Rock

Angels Landing

Grotto

The Great White Throne

East Entrance
5,700 ft
To Kanab and 89

COURT OF THE PATRIARCHS

ZION CANYON Scenic Drive

Canyon Overlook

Tunnel 9

Zion-Mt.Carmel Highway

Checkerboard Mesa
6,670 ft

Zion Museum
Tunnel

Springdale

The Watchman
6,545 ft

East Fork Virgin

PARUNUWEAP CANYON

tunnel on the wall of the canyon, 800 feet above the floor.

Shortly after passing through the East Entrance, stop at the **Checkerboard Mesa** pull-off. Here is a classic view of weathered sandstone beds crosshatched with vertical joints. Continue driving as the road winds along the normally dry creek bed. For the full impact of the approaching canyon, turn off at the **Canyon Overlook** parking area. If you are ready for a stop, this is a good place to stretch your legs along a 1-mile round-trip trail. You walk above the winding narrows of **Pine Creek** to an impressive view of **The West Temple** and the **Towers of the Virgin.**

The road disappears into the canyon wall at the narrow **Zion-Mt. Carmel Tunnel,** breaking into the blue sky again 1.1 miles farther. The tunnel was completed in 1930 at a cost of a half million dollars and the lives of two men. The road switchbacks down the side of **Pine Creek Canyon,** passing close to **The Great Arch,** which is 400 feet high. Geologists call it a blind arch because it is recessed into the cliff.

You next enter **Zion Canyon,** where Pine Creek meets the **North Fork Virgin River.** The canyon has an average width of half a mile, with walls 2,000 to 3,000 feet high. At Zion Canyon Visitor Center, catch a free shuttle for the 6.6-mile **Zion Canyon Scenic Drive** that follows the winding Virgin River. Get out at the **Court of the Patriarchs.** A short trail leads up the slope to a view of the **Three**

Isaac, one of the Three Patriarchs, in winter

Patriarchs, sheer faces carved by wind and water from Navajo sandstone.

Back on the shuttle, the road continues past the **Emerald Pools** area. This is the trailhead for a popular stroll on a paved walkway to natural rock basins fed by small streams. The lowest pool on the climbing path is a tiny oasis tucked into the side of the cliff and sheltered by bigtooth maple trees.

After a sojourn at the pools, the shuttle continues past **Zion Lodge** to the Grotto picnic area, a good place to take a break. Here is the trailhead for **Angels Landing** and **West Rim Trail.**

A short distance farther, the shuttle reaches **Weeping Rock.** Here, the trailhead of a self-guided nature walk (half-mile round-trip) leads behind a curtain of water showering from the ceiling of an alcove. Water percolates through the sandstone until it hits shale and then seeps through to the surface of Weeping Rock—1,000 to 4,000 years after falling as rain on the high plateau above. The strenuous **East Rim Trail** and a branch trail that climbs to **Hidden Canyon** start here.

Just past Weeping Rock, a stop offers superb views of **The Great White Throne** rising some 2,500 feet above the river. The scenic drive ends where the canyon narrows at the **Temple of Sinawava,** named for the coyote-spirit of the Paiute Indians.

Here and elsewhere in the park, keep watch for the tiny creatures of Sinawava's realm—canyon tree frogs, pocket gophers, eastern fence lizards. There are also more than 270 species of birds, including roadrunner, Gambel's quail, and the water-skimming American dipper.

Waterfall at Emerald Pools

Canyon treefrog

Indian paintbrush

Kolob Canyons Road

5.5 miles; 1 hour to a half day or more

One of the most spectacular and most accessible regions of the park is also one of the least visited. The **Hurricane Cliffs,** forming the western boundary of the park, screen the great towers of the Kolob from I-15. Follow the Kolob Canyons Road past the **Kolob Canyons Visitor Center** as it winds into **Taylor Creek Canyon.** Here you get a hint of what's to come when the jagged face of **Tucupit Point** appears.

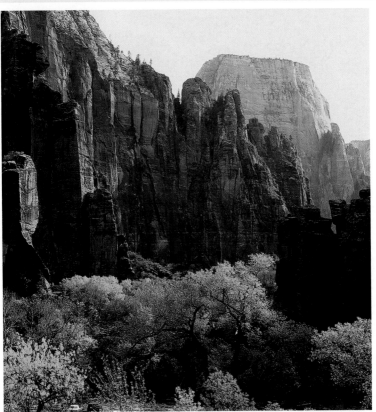

The Great White Throne from the Temple of Sinawava

The Narrows

Continue up the road, skirting the beautiful **South Fork** of **Taylor Creek.** Each vista becomes more striking as you cross **Lee Pass,** the trailhead for routes into the hidden canyons of **La Verkin Creek.** If time and stamina allow, you can backpack (usually done as an overnight; permit required for overnight trips) the 14-mile round-trip to **Kolob Arch,** one of the world's largest free-standing natural arches, 310 feet long.

Drive to the parking area at the end of the road for a dramatic view of the **Finger Canyons.** Sheer cliffs of pale red sandstone lift more than 2,000 feet into the blue sky. Narrow canyons work deep into the sides of **Timber Top Mountain,** connecting **Shuntavi Butte** with **Nagunt Mesa.**

Other Hikes

The full impact of Zion's great carved landscape is best experienced from a high vantage point above the river. The park's extensive trail system gives you a wide range of choices, from walks of half an hour to backpacking trips lasting for days.

The park's most popular trail is the **Riverside Walk,** an easy, 2-mile round-trip amble. This paved path can be

Virgin River Valley from Observation Point

Mountain lion

negotiated by strollers and assisted wheelchairs. Beginning where the Zion Canyon Scenic Drive ends at the Temple of Sinawava, the trail leads past hanging gardens of maidenhair fern and golden columbine and stands of shady cottonwood and ash. It ends where the North Fork rushes from a defile so narrow the only way to look is up. Flash floods here are a real danger; deeper in **The Narrows** the walls are 2,000 feet high but in places only 18 feet apart. In the 1960s, a sudden flood caught 26 hikers, drowning 5.

Perched midway between the river and the rim of the canyon, the high and open spire of rock called **Angels**

Landing provides one of Zion's best overall views. The strenuous trail climbs 2.5 miles, at times cutting into a knife-edge ridge that joins the landing to the western wall. Sheer 1,500-foot drops surround the promontory on three sides and allow excellent cross-canyon views of The Great White Throne and down the deep cut of Zion Canyon. *Not recommended for those with a fear of heights.*

The **Observation Point Trail**, 8 miles round-trip, is not recommended for acrophobes either. One of the best routes to reach the very top of the canyon, the strenuous trail passes through a beautiful narrows and winds into the slickrock country. As it swings back to the main canyon, the trail cuts into the very edge of the cliff and opens to dramatic views. After a thunderstorm, clouds steaming up from the white sandstone of the western wall look as if the rock itself is evaporating.

Once on top, the route crosses a sandy mesa through stands of pinyon pine and juniper to **Observation Point,** with fine views of the main canyon. Stand here and listen to what Frederick Dellenbaugh called "the whisper of the wind that comes and goes, breathing with the sound of centuries."

Information & Activities

Headquarters
State Rte. 9, Springdale, UT 84767.
Phone (435) 772-3256.
www.nps.gov/zion

Seasons & Accessibility
Park open year-round. Kolob Canyons
Road and main roads in Zion Canyon
are plowed in winter. Dirt roads are
impassable when wet. Lava Point
inaccessible in winter and early spring
due to snow. Call headquarters for
weather conditions.
   Shuttle service on Zion Canyon
Scenic Drive. Pick up free shuttle at
Springdale or the Zion Canyon Visitor
Center. Shuttle runs April through Oct.

Visitor & Information Centers
Zion Canyon Visitor Center, near the
South Entrance on Utah 9, and **Kolob
Canyons Visitor Center,** in the park's
northwest corner off I-15, are both
open daily year-round.

Entrance Fee
$20 per car per week, multiple entries.
Also, $10 charge for escorting oversize
vehicles through the mile-long tunnel
on East Entrance road.

Pets
Not permitted in backcountry, on
shuttles, in public buildings, or on
trails; elsewhere allowed on leashes.

Facilities for Disabled
Visitor centers, Zion Human History
Museum, shuttles, some rest rooms and
trails are wheelchair accessible. Handicapped sites available in campgrounds.

Things to Do
Free ranger-led activities: nature walks
and talks, evening programs, children's programs. Zion Human History
Museum. Also, hiking, horseback trail
rides—inquire at Zion Lodge or call
(435) 772-3810—climbing, bicycling
(bicyclists must transport their bikes
through the long tunnel—check at
entrance or visitor center), limited
cross-country skiing.

Special Advisories
● Summer temperatures in park can
exceed 105°F. Always carry bottled or
treated water when hiking—at least a
gallon a day per person in summer.

Overnight Backpacking
Permits required, $5; available at
visitor centers.

Campgrounds
Three campgrounds, 14-day limit.
Watchman open all year; **South** open
May through Sept.; **Lava Point** open
May through Oct., depending on
weather. Reservations for Watchman
through the National Park Reservation
Service (see p. 11). Others, first come,
first served. Fees $14 per night; $16 per
night for sites with hookups at Watch-
man. Showers nearby but outside park.
Tent and RV sites.

Hotels, Motels, & Inns
*(unless otherwise noted, rates are for 2
persons in a double room, high season)*
INSIDE THE PARK:
Zion Lodge (off Utah 9) Xanterra
Parks & Resorts, Cedar City, UT 84767.
(303) 297-2757. 81 rooms, with AC; 40
cabins. $107. Restaurant.
OUTSIDE THE PARK:
In Springdale, UT 84767:
Best Western Driftwood Lodge 1515
Zion Park Blvd., P.O. Box 98. (800)
528-1234 or (435) 772-3262. 42 units.
$82. AC, pool, hot tub. **Bumbleberry
Inn** 97 Bumbleberry Ln., P.O. Box 346.
(800) 828-1534 or (435) 772-3224. 47
units. $67-$77. AC, pool, rest. **Canyon
Ranch Motel** 668 Zion Park Blvd., P.O.
Box 175. (435) 772-3357. 22 units, 4
with kitchenettes. $68-$88. AC, pool.
Cliffrose Lodge & Gardens 281 Zion
Park Blvd., P.O. Box 510. (800) 243-
8824 or (435) 772-3234. 36 units.
$119-$145. AC, pool. **Flanigan's Inn**
428 Zion Park Blvd., P.O. Box 100.
(800) 765-7787 or (435) 772-3244. 35
units. $79. AC, pool, rest. **O'Toole's
Under the Eaves Guest House** 980
Zion Park Blvd. (435) 772-3457. 6
rooms, 4 private baths. $69-$125. AC.
In Kanab, UT 84741:
Parry Lodge 89 E. Center St. (800) 748-
4104 or (435) 644-2601. 89 units. $73.
AC, pool, rest. **Shilo Inn** 296 W. 100
North. (800) 222-2244 or (435) 644-
2562. 118 units. $55-$150. AC, pool.

*For additional accommodations near
Zion NP, call Kane County Travel. 78
S. 100 East, Kanab, UT 84741. (800)
733-5263 or (435) 644-5033.*

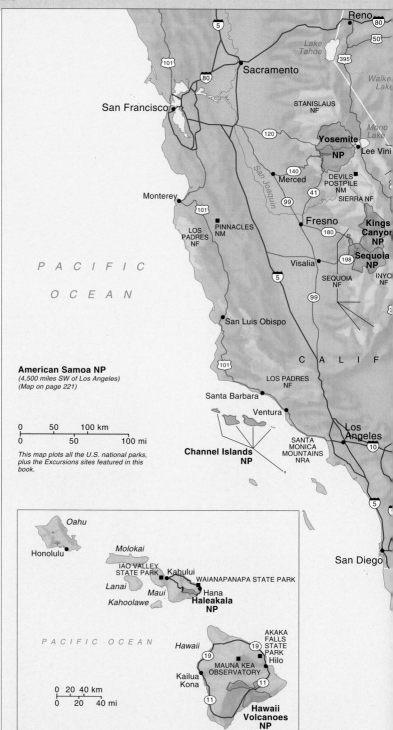

5

Reno

80

50

Lake
Tahoe

395

101

Walker
Lake

80

Sacramento

STANISLAUS
NF

120

Mono
Lake

Yosemite

San Francisco

NP

Lee Vini

140

Merced

DEVILS
POSTPILE
NM

SIERRA NF

41

99

Monterey

101

Fresno

Kings
Canyon
NP

P A C I F I C

LOS
PADRES
NF

PINNACLES
NM

180

198

Sequoia
NP

O C E A N

Visalia

SEQUOIA
NF

INYO
NF

99

American Samoa NP
(4,500 miles SW of Los Angeles)
(Map on page 221)

5

San Luis Obispo

C   A   L   I   F

| 0 | 50 | 100 km |

| 0 | 50 | 100 mi |

This map plots all the U.S. national parks, plus the Excursions sites featured in this book.

101

LOS PADRES
NF

Santa Barbara

Ventura

SANTA
MONICA
MOUNTAINS
NRA

**Channel Islands
NP**

Los
Angeles

10

5

San Diego

Oahu

Honolulu

Molokai

IAO VALLEY
STATE PARK

Kahului

WAIANAPANAPA STATE PARK

Lanai

Maui

Hana

Kahoolawe

**Haleakala
NP**

P A C I F I C   O C E A N

AKAKA
FALLS
STATE
PARK

Hawaii

19

19

Hilo

MAUNA KEA
OBSERVATORY

Kailua
Kona

11

| 0 | 20 | 40 km |

11

| 0 | 20 | 40 mi |

**Hawaii
Volcanoes
NP**

The Pacific Southwest

Visitors to the national parks of the Pacific Southwest can bask on a tropical isle or climb a snow-clad peak. They can watch the vegetation change from tropical to subalpine in a single Hawaii drive, observe plants and animals that make their home in only one place in the world, and see the Earth build itself.

The island parks, all of them on volcanoes except Channel Islands, are microcosms of evolution and laboratories of the effects of humans on the land. In Hawaii Volcanoes and Haleakala, preservation efforts seek to stem the damage done over centuries to the native plants, about 90 percent of which are endemic—found nowhere else. Some 2,300 miles southwest of Hawaii, American Samoa National Park shelters fragments of tropical rain forest and coral reef as well as an endangered 3,000-year-old human culture. Off the coast of California, the Channel Islands safeguard numerous threatened seals, sea lions, and seabirds. They also harbor some 70 endemic plants.

On the mainland, Sequoia & Kings Canyon and Yosemite National Parks provide haven for a multitude of plant and animal communities in what John Muir called "the range of light"—the Sierra Nevada. Chaparral and wild oats robe the foothills; cathedral-like groves of conifers embellish slopes; wildflowers overrun alpine meadows. Marmots and pikas scurry the glacier-carved heights, some of which soar 12,000 feet.

To the south, Joshua Tree National Park preserves the unique high Mojave Desert habitat of the giant branching yucca, while the 120-mile-long, erosion-sculptured basin that is Death Valley National Park—the continent's hottest spot—shelters more than 900 plant varieties, as well as bobcats and desert bighorn sheep.

Yosemite and Sequoia & Kings Canyon lie about 4 hours apart by car. From Sequoia, 6 road hours will get you to Death Valley, with 3.5 more to Joshua Tree. A drive from there to the Channel Islands takes 3 hours, plus a 90-minute boat ride. To reach Hawaii from California, count on at least a 5.5-hour flight, and to American Samoa, expect an 11-hour plane trip, see p. 221, plus a Honolulu layover.

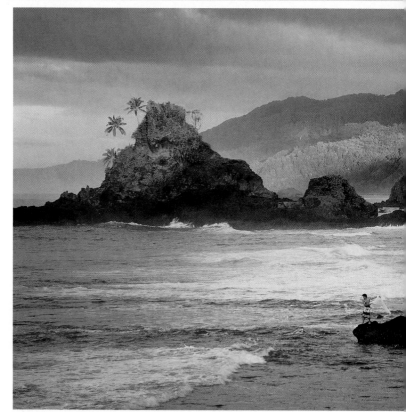

Fisherman casting his net off Tutuila's rocky coast

American Samoa

American Samoa	
Established 1993	
10,520 acres (7,970 land, 2,550 marine)	

For some 3,000 years, the people of Polynesia's oldest culture have been keenly attuned to their island environment, holding it to be precious and managing it communally. The name they gave their land reflects their attitude: Samoa means "sacred earth."

Located about 2,300 miles southwest of Hawaii, American Samoa, a U.S. territory, comprises five volcanic islands and two coral atolls. In 1988 Samoan chiefs agreed to lease a portion of their lands for a national park. In 1993 a 50-year lease was signed that enables the National Park Service to manage an area of rain forest, beach, and coral reef on three islands. Samoans help manage

the park, and their villages offer a few guest facilities (ask the park about its homestay program).

The park protects hundreds of plant species in five distinct rain forest communities: lowland, montane, coast, ridge, and cloud. It is the only such rain forest on American soil. Among the fauna visitors can see are tropical birds and the endangered flying fox—a fruit bat with the wingspan of an eagle.

On **Tutuila,** American Samoa's largest island, lofty volcanic ridges overlook the deep blue waters of **Pago Pago Harbor.** Except for a few villages, and the scenic drive that skirts the harbor and the dramatic southern coastline, there is little level land. Atop this crumbled terrain and plunging steeply toward the sea on the island's northern side lies the park area—about 2,500 acres of land and some 1,200 acres of ocean. Parkland

toward the rugged cliffs of the southern coast. Small, remote **Ofu Island**
includes what many call American
Samoa's loveliest beach. Its main
attraction is the 350-acre coral reef.

How to Get There

There are flights to Pago Pago from
Honolulu twice a week that take 5.5
hours. Time from California is about
14 hours, including a 3- or 4-hour Honolulu layover. From the airport, taxi or
rent a car to the Rainmaker Hotel, Pago
Airport Inn, Tessarea Vaitogi Inn, or
Motu-o-Fiafiaga Motel. You can reach
the park visitor center in Pago Pago by
bus or car, or by walking about 25 minutes. Accommodations are also available
on Ta'u, Ofu, and Olosega. To get to
Ta'u and Ofu requires about a half-hour
flight each from Pago Pago. Ofu's park
begins at the edge of the airport; parkland on Ta'u is about a half-hour walk
from the airport.

When to Go

Any time. The islands are 14° south
of the Equator, giving them a hot
and rainy climate year-round.
The heat and rain abate slightly from
June through September.

How to Visit

Contact the park headquarters
before you visit. For information,
write National Park of American
Samoa, Pago Pago, American Samoa
96799. Phone (011) (684) 633-7082.
www.nps.gov/npsa. Or drop in the new
visitor center, located at Pago Plaza at
the head of Pago Pago Harbor.

on **Ta'u,** the easternmost island,
encompasses about 5,400 acres—
including Lata Mountain, American
Samoa's highest peak—and 1,000
acres offshore. Unforgettable is the
panoramic view from the cloud forest

PACIFIC OCEAN

0   4 km
0   4 mi

National Park
Visitor Center
Pago Pago

North
Pioa Mt.
+ 1,718 ft

001

Aunuu

To Ofu and Tau,
60 miles

Matafao Peak +
2,142 ft

Tutuila

Pago Pago
International Airport

001

FAGATELE BAY
NATIONAL MARINE
SANCTUARY

Ofu
Olosega

PACIFIC
OCEAN

0   4 km
0   4 mi

Fitiuta

Tau Lata Mt. +
3,170 ft

Tau

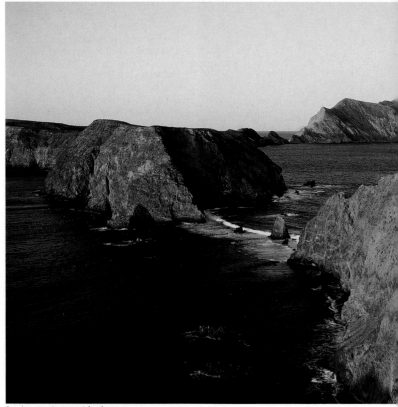

Sunrise over Anacapa Island

Channel Islands

California

Established March 5, 1980

249,354 acres

Strung along a stretch of California coast are five separate pieces of land surrounded by 1,252 square nautical miles of sea. Channel Islands National Park and Channel Islands National Marine Sanctuary protect these islands, the sea around them, and a dazzling array of wildlife.

Two of the islands in this unusual park, Anacapa and Santa Barbara, were earlier designated a national monument, a refuge for nesting seabirds, seals, sea lions, and other long-threatened marine animals. When those islands and three others were joined in a national park, the mission of refuge continued.

Today the park manages a long-term ecological research program that may

be the best in the park system. The marine sanctuary, also established in 1980, extends for 6 nautical miles around each island. Among the resources it protects is a giant kelp forest with nearly a thousand kinds of fish and marine plants. The park and sanctuary also guard the area from encroachment by another kind of island—the seagoing oil rigs of the Santa Barbara Channel.

About 70 different species of plants grow only on the Channel Islands, and some plants exist on but one of them. The islands shelter the only breeding colony of northern fur seals south of Alaska. To help native animals, park managers have gotten rid of such nonnative species as burros, rabbits, and house cats gone feral. Efforts to eradicate black rats—descendants of ancestors that jumped ship—are underway, though they have been less successful.

A permanent ranger resides on each island. Reservations are needed for camping. Fishing and diving are strictly regulated and airplanes are asked to keep their distance.

Chumash Indians lived on the Channel Islands until the early 19th century. They traveled from island to island in plank canoes caulked with tar from oil seeps. The tar from such seeps still appears on mainland beaches, reminding strollers of the reason for the oil rigs on the horizon.

How to Get There

Take US 101 to Ventura. Northbound, exit at Victoria Avenue; southbound, at Seaward Avenue. Follow park signs to the harbor and then to the visitor center on Spinnaker Drive. Get oriented here and then go to the nearby Island Packers office and inquire about boat and plane schedules to the islands. Airports: Camarillo, Oxnard, Santa Barbara, and Los Angeles International.

When to Go

All-year park. Boat schedules peak in spring and summer, but you should be able to book a trip in any month. Best whale-watching time: late December through March, and July and August.

How to Visit

Your exploration of this unique park depends on your time and resources. Even a short stop at the mainland visitor center will give you an understanding and appreciation of the park. Displays include a tide pool alive with creatures. For a 1-day visit, see the closest island, **Anacapa.** Take all necessities, especially food and water, and dress in layers for all types of weather. Trips to the other islands require substantial advance planning. (See **Information & Activities** p. 226.) The park cautions people from doing more than treading lightly on the islands, which are maintained for the well-being of the residents, both flora and fauna.

Anacapa Island

14 miles from Ventura; a full day

As the Island Packers boat plies through **Santa Barbara Channel,** flyingfish skip through the waves and pelicans skim over them. Oil rigs stand on dark stilts. Gray whales may glide by during winter trips. Seals appear and disappear in the channel waters year-round.

Approaching the landing cove, the boat passes Anacapa's **Arch Rock** and sails close enough to the rocky coast for you to see resident California sea lions. At the end of the 90-minute voyage (which can be rough), a dinghy transports you to the landing platform. Then you climb 154 steps up a metal-and-concrete stairway to the top of the cliff-girt island.

There you can walk the 1.5-mile nature trail on your own or fall in behind a ranger who dispenses island lore: That plain gray plant (giant coreopsis) is a tree sunflower; in late winter and spring it bursts into glorious gold. Those finely ground shells you are walking on are remnants of a Chumash midden. The Indians hunted on the island and used it as a stopover on trips to the mainland. The trail skirts the edge of a cliff 150 feet above the sea. Stand well

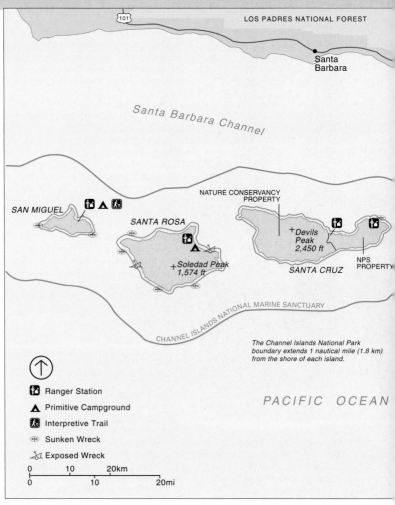

LOS PADRES NATIONAL FOREST

Santa Barbara

Santa Barbara Channel

NATURE CONSERVANCY PROPERTY

SAN MIGUEL

SANTA ROSA

+Devils Peak 2,450 ft

NPS PROPERTY

+Soledad Peak 1,574 ft

SANTA CRUZ

CHANNEL ISLANDS NATIONAL MARINE SANCTUARY

The Channel Islands National Park boundary extends 1 nautical mile (1.8 km) from the shore of each island.

PACIFIC OCEAN

🏢 Ranger Station

▲ Primitive Campground

🏞 Interpretive Trail

⊕ Sunken Wreck

⚓ Exposed Wreck

0   10   20km
0   10   20mi

back from the unstable cliff edges. You are ominously warned: *Don't risk your life for a view.*

A building that looks like a Spanish mission church is not what it seems. The structure protects two large water tanks. Vandals who in years past took potshots at the wooden tanks refrain from sniping at a "church." The few buildings date from days when the island lighthouse, now automated, had a crew. Your day ends with a descent to the boat, which picks up the passengers about 3 or 4 hours after arrival; the time depends on tide and sea conditions.

Anacapa consists of three islets. You visit only **East Anacapa.** Scuba divers, subject to strict conservation laws, plunge off **Middle Anacapa** to

see the kelp forests or the remains of the S.S. *Winfield Scott,* which sank here in 1853 with no loss of life. Divers can take only photographs. **West Anacapa** is closed to the public January through October to protect the largest nesting brown pelican population on the U.S. Pacific coast.

The Other Islands

If you decide to go to the other islands, your visits will be controlled by weather, regulations, and boat and plane schedules.

Santa Cruz (21 miles from Ventura; 60,000 acres) is the largest of the Channel Islands. The Nature Conservancy runs the western portion of the

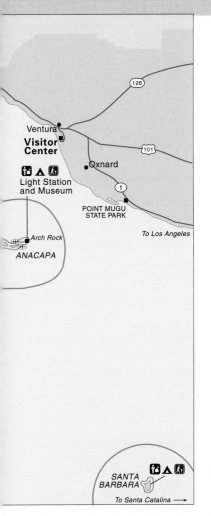

126

Ventura
**Visitor
Center**

101

🏕️ ▲ 🏠
Light Station
and Museum

●Oxnard

1

POINT MUGU
STATE PARK

To Los Angeles

Arch Rock

ANACAPA

SANTA
BARBARA   🏕️ ▲ 🏠

To Santa Catalina ⟶

island and strictly limits visitors. The park owns the east end. Among Santa Cruz's distinctive species are the island oak, the cat-size island fox, and the scrub jay.

Santa Rosa (45 miles from Ventura; 53,000 acres) has more than 160 archaeological sites; people may have lived there as long as 10,000 years ago. Ranchers raised sheep then cattle on the island's grasslands from the middle of the 19th century until 1997. A freshwater marsh sustains waterfowl. There are more than 195 bird species on the island.

San Miguel (55 miles from Ventura; 9,325 acres), the westernmost island, is also rich in archaeological sites. Five seal species gather here; as many as 35,000 haul out at times. A bizarre caliche "forest" spikes a plateau. Caliche—a kind of limey sand—encrusted vegetation that died and decayed, leaving only the hollow, calcified sand castings.

Once used as a bombing range and missile test site, the island is owned by the United States Navy and administered by the National Park Service, which limits visitors to the beach, ranch, and campground unless they are accompanied by one of the park's rangers.

Santa Barbara (52 miles from Ventura; 640 acres), once a sheep pasturage, has 5.5 miles of nature trails. In springtime, burrows on the island's steep hillsides house the world's largest known breeding population of the remarkable Xantus' murrelet. When a chick is only two days old, it makes a bold foray into

Caliche "forest" on San Miguel Island

night, tumbling down to the sea where it joins its waiting parents. Except for the nesting season, the murrelet will spend the remainder of its life on the ocean. In spring and summer, you can usually see pelicans and sea lions, but don't expect to come across the rock-dwelling island night lizard. It is shy, secretive, and protected; visitors are strictly forbidden to turn over any rock.

Protected elephant seal

Information & Activities

Headquarters
1901 Spinnaker Dr., Ventura, CA 93001. Phone (805) 658-5730. www.nps.gov/chis

Accessibility & Boat Information
Park open year-round. Access to islands subject to unpredictable weather conditions; the channel can be rough. Call headquarters for information.
To Anacapa, Santa Rosa, San Miguel, and Santa Barbara: Boat trips offered by Island Packers and Truth Aquatics, the park's authorized concessioners (see below). Visitors using private boats must obtain landing permits for Santa Rosa and San Miguel from the park. Air service available to Santa Rosa via Channel Island Aviation (see below).
To Santa Cruz: Island Packers and Truth Aquatics offer day trips to east end. For day trips to west end and permits for private boats, contact well in advance the Nature Conservancy, Santa Cruz Island Project Office, 2559 Puesta del Sol Rd., Santa Barbara, CA 93105 (located at Santa Barbara Museum of Natural History). (805) 898-1642.
Boats from Ventura: Contact headquarters or Island Packers, 1691 Spinnaker Dr., Ste. 105B, Ventura, CA 93001. (805) 642-1393 for information and reservations or www.islandpack ers.com. For weekend trips, reserve at least 3 to 5 days in advance.
Boats from Santa Barbara: Contact Truth Aquatics, 301 Cabrillo Blvd., Santa Barbara, CA 93101. (805) 962-1127. www.truthaquatics.com.
Plane information: Channel Island Aviation, 305 Durley Ave., Camarillo, CA 93010. (805) 987-1301.

Visitor & Information Centers
Visitor center on Spinnaker Drive in Ventura open daily year-round. Visitor

centers on East Anacapa and Santa Barbara also open year-round. Ranger station on San Miguel.

Entrance Fee
None. For boat fares to islands, inquire at headquarters, Island Packers, or Travel Aquatics (see above).

Pets
Not permitted in park headquarters or on islands.

Facilities for Disabled
Visitor center at Ventura, rest rooms, theater, exhibits, and observation tower accessible. Boats and islands are not.

Things to Do
Santa Barbara Channel: whale-watching late December through March and June through September.
Anacapa: free ranger-led walks and evening programs; also, wildlife watching, bird-watching, tide-pool walks, swimming and snorkeling, scuba and skin diving, fishing (license needed; certain areas closed). **Santa Barbara:** nature hikes, marine life observation, bird-watching, tide-pool walks. **Santa Rosa:** free ranger-led nature hike. **San Miguel:** free ranger-led hike to caliche "forest"; also, seal- and sea lion-watching, tide-pool walks. **Santa Cruz:** hikes, marine life observation, bird-watching.

Special Advisories
● When hiking on islands, stay on trails and away from cliffs.
● All birds, animals, tide pools, shells, rocks, and plants are protected; do not take anything but photos.
● Avoid Hantavirus pulmonary syndrome, a potentially fatal virus carried by the deer mouse, by staying away from

cabins and campsites where rodent droppings and burrows are evident.

Overnight Backpacking

All five islands have campgrounds; 14-day limit. Year-round. Reservations and permits required; contact the National Parks Reservation Service (see p. 11). $10 per night. Tent sites only. Cold shower on Santa Rosa. Drinking water at Scarpton on Santa Cruz. Group camping available. No food services.

Hotels, Motels, & Inns

(unless otherwise noted, rates for 2 persons, double room, high season) In Ventura, CA 93001:

Bella Maggiore Inn 67 S. California St. (800) 523-8479 or (805) 652-0277. 28 units. $75-$175. Rest. **Country Inn by the Sea** 298 S. Chestnut St. (800) 456-4000 or (805) 653-1434. 120 units. $99-$129. AC, pool. **Four Point Sheraton** 1050 Schooner Dr. (800) 229-5732 or (805) 658-1212. 150 units. $119-$169. Pool, rest. **Inn on the Beach** 1175 S. Seaward Ave. (805) 652-2000. 24 units. $100-$185. **La Mer European Bed & Breakfast** 411 Poli St. 93002. (805) 643-3600. 5 units. $115-$195.

For additional lodgings, contact Ventura Visitor & Convention Bureau. (805) 648-2075.

Excursions

Santa Monica Mountains National Recreation Area

Thousand Oaks, California

Here southern California's rare Mediterranean climate offers habitats ranging from chaparral to oak woodlands to rocky canyons to marshes and sandy beaches. Government and private efforts preserve the area's natural and cultural resources including Paramount Ranch (a working Hollywood set), spectacular Mulholland Drive, Zuma Beach, Cold Creek Canyon Preserve, and the Will Rogers State Historic Park. 150,000-acre boundary. Hiking, mountain biking, horseback riding. More than 100 campsites. Open all year, dawn to dusk (some areas 9 a.m. to sunset or by reservation). Information at NRA headquarters in Thousand Oaks, about 30 miles west of Los Angeles. (805) 370-2301.

Los Padres National Forest

Santa Barbara, California

This rugged forest preserves a vast area of central California coast and mountain ranges. Chaparral, high mountains, and desert ecosystems are all a short drive from Ventura. The Jacinto Reyes Scenic Byway (Calif. 33) threads through the park north of Ojai. 1,700,000 acres. Camping, backpacking, hiking. Picnic areas. Open year-round. Information at Ojai Ranger Station, approximately 30 miles from Channel Islands NP. (805) 646-4348.

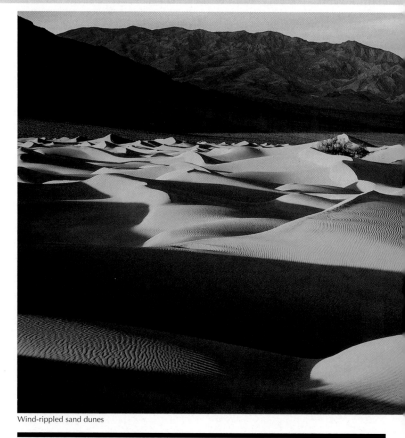

Wind-rippled sand dunes

Death Valley

California

Established October 31, 1994

About 3.4 million acres

Our largest national park south of Alaska, Death Valley is known for extremes: It is North America's driest and hottest spot (with fewer than 2 inches of rainfall annually and a record high of 134°F), and has the lowest elevation in the Western Hemisphere—282 feet below sea level. Even with its extremes, the park still receives 1.3 million visitors each year.

In 1849 emigrants bound for California's gold fields strayed into the 120-mile-long basin, enduring a two-month ordeal of "hunger and thirst and an awful silence." One of the last to leave looked down from a mountain at the narrow valley and said, "Good-bye, Death Valley."

The forbidding moniker belies the beauty in this vast graben, the geological term for a sunken fragment of the Earth's crust. Here are rocks sculptured by erosion, richly tinted mudstone hills and canyons, luminous sand dunes, lush oases, and a 200-square-mile salt pan surrounded by mountains, one of America's greatest vertical rises. In some years spring rains trigger wildflower blooms amid more than a thousand varieties of plants.

From 1883 to 1889, wagon teams hauled powdery white borax from mines since fallen to ruin, an enterprise that spread word of Death Valley's striking landscapes, deep solitude, and crystalline air.

As night falls, Death Valley's elusive population of bobcats, kit foxes, and rodents ventures out. Far above on steep mountain slopes, desert bighorn sheep forage among

Joshua trees, scrubby junipers, and pines, while hawks soar on thermals rising into vivid blue, usually cloudless skies.

How to Get There

No airlines, public transit services, or railroads serve the park. Most visitors arrive by automobile from Los Angeles, California, or Las Vegas, Nevada.

From L.A., the most scenic route crosses the eastern Mojave Desert via I-15 through Barstow. At Baker it turns north onto Calif. 127 to Shoshone, where Calif. 178 runs west and north along the valley floor to Furnace Creek.

From Las Vegas, take Nev. 160 west 42 miles to Old Spanish Trail (Tecopa Rd.), continuing through Tecopa to Calif. 127, turning north to Shoshone and picking up Calif. 178 to Furnace Creek. To include a visit to the early-20th-century Nevada gold-mining ghost town of Rhyolite, take US 95 to Beatty, picking up Nev. 374, which becomes Calif. 190 and leads west to the park.

When to Go

All-year park. Temperatures from November through February average between 25°F and 75°F. From May through September, average highs range between 100°F and 116°F; overnight lows may top 100°F.

How to Visit

Death Valley's remote location and size make an automobile essential. An overnight stay allows time for the valley's vivid sunrises and sunsets, and a visit to the **Death Valley Museum** and **Furnace Creek Visitor Center.** Plan also to visit the **Harmony Borax Works** near the Furnace Creek Campground, to walk the 1-mile **Golden Canyon Interpretive Trail,** and to drive to **Zabriskie Point** for fine views of the valley.

A second day permits exploration of the valley's northern reaches and **Scottys Castle,** the retreat of an early-20th-century millionaire, and nearby **Ubehebe Crater,** blasted out during the region's volcanic past. If you are a seasoned hiker, consider the strenuous all-day hike from **Wildrose Canyon** to sweeping views atop 11,049-foot **Telescope Peak,** Death Valley's highest point.

Entering from the East: Shoshone to Furnace Creek

130 miles (including side trips); 1 to 2 days

From the mining town of Shoshone, head west on Calif. 178 through the **Amargosa Range,** whose colorful dusky palette reflects the high mineral content in its sediments. Cresting 3,315-foot **Salsberry Pass,** you'll descend through the weathered **Black Mountains** to 1,290-foot **Jubilee Pass,** where wildflowers sometimes bloom in spring.

Approaching the ruins of gold-mining **Ashford Mill** and the **Death Valley Salt Pan**—the residue of a saline lake that existed over 20,000 years ago—you reach zero elevation. From here to Furnace Creek you travel *below* sea level, dipping to minus 282 feet at **Badwater** 27 miles north, the Western Hemisphere's lowest point. Park at Badwater, where sunrises ignite the Amargosa ridgeline. Continue north 4 miles to the turnoff onto a rough road to **Natural Bridge,** an arch spanning a

Kilns in Wildrose Canyon, a legacy of mining era

richly tinted conglomerate canyon. A quarter-mile trail to the bridge passes other striking formations.

About 1.5 miles north, look left for the half-mile spur road to **Devils Golf Course,** a meringue of rock salt pinnacles that forms as water evaporates up through the salty crust.

Another 5 miles north brings you to the 9-mile one-way **Artists Drive** loop road through the **Artists Palette,** a rumpled terrain of volcanic ash whose yellows, red-oranges, greens, and muted purples challenge plein-air painters. About 4 miles north, the moderate 1-mile-long **Golden Canyon Interpretive Trail** winds through a canyon that near sunset gleams as if dusted with gold.

Continue north to the Calif. 190 junction. If you want to rest or refuel, stop at the **Furnace Creek Visitor Center.** If not, turn right onto Calif. 190 for the short drive to **Zabriskie Point,** a popular sunrise viewing spot, where rain and wind have shaped rock into dramatic contours. The promontory commands a broad view of mudstone badlands. To explore them, continue on for a mile to **Twenty Mule Team Canyon,** which is threaded by a 3-mile gravel loop road.

Return to the highway, turn right, and continue to the 13-mile spur road to 5,475-foot **Dantes View.** The mile-high panorama plunges to Badwater and sweeps across the salt pan to the forbidding Panamint Range and 11,049-foot Telescope Peak.

If you have not yet visited Furnace Creek, backtrack 24 miles to the **Furnace Creek Visitor Center,** which

To Tonopah
and Reno
95

267

NEVADA
CALIFORNIA

Scottys
Castle

GRAPEVINE
CANYON

quite
ring

TITUS
CANYON

Rhyolite
(ghost
town)

Beatty

374

95

Amargosa

Lathrop
Wells

To
Las Vegas

DEATH

RANGE

AMARGOSA

Keane
Wonder Mine

373

SAND DUNES

190

MOSAIC CANYON

Stovepipe
Wells
Village

Salt Creek
Interpretive
Trail

Harmony Borax Works
Interpretive Trail

Devils Hole
Death Valley
National
Park

PANAMINT

Emigrant

Furnace Creek

Furnace Creek
Visitor Center
and Death Valley Museum

Sunset

Texas Spring

Furnace Creek Inn

Zabriskie Point

127

ASH
MEADOWS
NATIONAL
WILDLIFE
REFUGE

Golden Canyon
Interpretive Trail

TWENTY MULE TEAM CANYON

190

DEVILS GOLF COURSE

Lowest elevation in U.S.
−282 ft

Artists
Palette

190

Wildrose

Thorndike

Mahogany
Flat

WILDROSE
CANYON

Natural Bridge

Badwater

Dantes
View

Sea Level Elevation

RANGE

AMARGOSA

BLACK

MOUNTAINS

RANGE

Telescope Peak
11,049 ft

Panamint City
(ghost town)

VALLEY

VALLEY

Ballarat
(ghost town)

To
Las Vegas

Shoshone

178

Salsberry Pass
3,315

Ashford Mill
(ruins)

Jubilee Pass
1,290

127

178

Trona
Searles
Lake

To Baker

has exhibits and a bookstore. Check for ranger-guided walks and evening programs (Oct. through March) and visit the **Death Valley Museum.**

The springs at **Furnace Creek oasis** produce over a million gallons a day, watering oleanders, palms, and tamarisk trees, and the incongruously verdant fairways of the golf course at the **Furnace Creek Ranch.** Guests at the Furnace Creek Inn may explore the interior and gardens of this classic Spanish mission-style structure, constructed in 1927 of adobe and native stone.

Furnace Creek to Scottys Castle

90 miles (including excursions); a half day

One mile north of the Furnace Creek Visitor Center, leave your car and walk the quarter-mile paved **Harmony Borax Works Interpretive Trail** to the ruins of Death Valley's first successful borax mining venture. Original equipment includes a borax wagon with 6-foot-high rear wheels.

Continue north on Calif. 190 past the Beatty Cutoff to the 1-mile spur road to the **Salt Creek Interpretive Trail.** Spring-fed marshy pools here are home to Death Valley's unusual desert pupfish, descendant of creatures that flourished in the basin's ancient lake at least 12,000 years ago. Like the oasis at Scottys Castle, this is a prime bird-watching area, frequented by many of the 350 species found in Death Valley, including Canada geese, peregrine falcons, hawks, and eagles.

Nearby sand dunes ripple across 14 square miles. At sunrise and sunset the wind-sculptured waves of quartz-grain sand take on a luminous rosy glow. Accessible via paved road near Stovepipe Wells Village, these dunes have no established trails; park and walk where you please.

Back in the car, continue on for about 30 miles to **Grapevine Canyon** and **Scottys Castle,** a Mediterranean-style architectural gem dating from 1922. Once the retreat of a wealthy Chicago couple, the ranch is named for frequent house guest and "desert rat" Walter Scott. Daily on the hour, the Park Service conducts tours through the mansion, which holds original furnishings. In winter, be prepared to wait up to 2 hours for a tour. While waiting, consider a meal at the Castle's restaurant, a picnic outside, or an amble up **Windy Point Trail.**

Information & Activities

Headquarters
Visitor center, Calif. 190, P.O. Box 579, Death Valley, CA 92328. Phone (760) 786-3220. www.nps.gov/deva

Seasons & Accessibility
Open year-round.

Visitor & Information Centers
Furnace Creek Visitor Center in Furnace Creek, off Calif. 190.

Entrance Fee
$10 per vehicle, good for one week.

Pets
Must be leashed at all times. Not allowed on trails or in backcountry.

Facilities for Disabled
The visitor center; Scottys Castle; and Furnace Creek, Texas Spring, and Sunset Campgrounds are wheelchair accessible.

Things to Do
Free ranger- and naturalist-led activities available mid-October to mid-April: nature walks and talks, evening programs, children's programs. Also, hiking, nature trails, living history tours, bicycling, bird-watching, horseback riding.

Special Advisories
● Death Valley's heat can make any emergency situation life-threatening. For advice on hot weather travel, consult the *Death Valley Guide,* available at roadside kiosks, ranger stations, and the visitor center.
● Drink plenty of water; one gallon per person per day is recommended, two gallons if hiking. Emergency radiator water is available from barrels located along main park roads.
● Abandoned mineshafts and prospect holes pose dangers. *Never* enter an abandoned tunnel.

Salt crystals of Devils Golf Course

- Hat and sunglasses are essential.
- Desert rains, though brief, cause flash floods. Never ford washouts, even in a 4-wheel-drive vehicle.

Overnight Backpacking

Backcountry camping permitted in areas at least 2 miles from main roads and a quarter mile from water sources. Permit not required, but hikers should register at visitor center and inquire about which areas prohibit camping.

Campgrounds

Nine campgrounds, 30-day limit. **Furnace Creek, Mesquite Spring,** and **Wildrose** open year-round; **Texas Spring, Sunset,** and **Stovepipe Wells** open Oct. to April; **Emigrant, Thorndike,** and **Mahogany Flat** open April to Oct. Reservations taken only at Furnace Creek (call National Parks Reservation Service; see p. 11); all others first come, first served. Fees: $16 at Furnace Creek; $10 at Sunset, Stovepipe Wells,

Mesquite Spring; $12 at Texas Spring; free at Thorndike, Emigrant, Mahogany Flat, and Wildrose.

Hotels, Motels, & Inns

(unless otherwise noted, rates are for 2 persons in a double room, high season)
INSIDE THE PARK:
Furnace Creek Inn Furnace Creek off Calif. 190. (760) 786-2345. 66 units. $170-$335. Pool, restaurant.
Furnace Creek Ranch Furnace Creek off Calif. 190. P.O. Box 1, Death Valley 92328. (760) 786-2345. 225 units. $102-$165. Pool, 2 restaurants.
Stovepipe Wells Village Motel Stovepipe Wells Village, P.O. Box 559, Death Valley 92328. (760) 786-2387. 83 units. $70-$92. 14 RV hookups, $20. AC, pool, restaurant.

For additional lodgings, contact the Death Valley Chamber of Commerce, P.O. Box 157, Shoshone, CA 92384. (760) 852-4524.

Kaluu O Ka Oo cinder cone in the volcanic desert near Sliding Sands Trail

Haleakala

Maui, Hawaii

Established August 1, 1916

30,183 acres

Haleakala, a giant shield volcano, forms the eastern bulwark of the island of Maui. According to legend, it was here, in the awe-inspiring basin at the mountain's summit, that the demigod Maui snared the sun, releasing it only after it promised to move more slowly across the sky. Haleakala means "house of the sun"; the park encompasses the basin and portions of the volcano's flanks.

A United Nations International Biosphere Reserve, the park comprises starkly contrasting worlds of mountain and coast. The road to the summit of Haleakala rises from near sea level to 10,000 feet in 38 miles—possibly the steepest such gradient for autos in the world. Visitors ascend through several climate and vegetation zones, from humid subtropical lowlands to subalpine desert. Striking plants and animals such as the Haleakala silversword and the nene may be seen in this mountain section. The summit-area depression, misnamed Haleakala Crater, formed as erosion ate away the mountain, joining two valleys. This 19-square-mile wilderness area, 2,720 feet deep, is the park's major draw.

From east of the rim, the great rain forest valley of Kipahulu drops thousands of feet down to the coast. The upper Kipahulu Valley is a protected wilderness, home to a vast profusion of flora and fauna, including some of the world's rarest birds, plants, and invertebrates. Some insects evolved in the Kipahulu Valley and live nowhere else.

Visitors reach the lower valley of Kipahulu via a sliver of parkland on northwest entrance. Allow up to 2 hours.

For the 62-mile drive to Kipahulu, allow up to 3.5 hours. Take Hawaii 36 from Kahului around the northeastern side of the island to the town of Hana. The road to Hana, which becomes Hawaii 360, is famous for its narrow, tortuous course along 1,000-foot sea cliffs, into deep gorges. This drive affords many views of waterfalls and cascade pools, but few places to access them. Proceed past Hana on Hawaii 31 for about 9 miles. Just beyond the Pools of Oheo, signs will point to off-road parking.

When to Go

All-year park. Most rain comes in winter, although temperatures vary little month to month. To avoid crowds, visit the summit after 3 p.m.; sunsets can be as spectacular as the famous sunrises. At Kipahulu, avoid crowds by arriving early or camping overnight. Weather varies most at high elevations, and can change from very hot to rainy, cold, and windy in the same day. Temperatures can drop to freezing inside the wilderness area, although snow is rare. Coastal Kipahulu stays warm but receives considerable rain all year.

How to Visit

With an early start, it's possible to tour both the **Haleakala** summit and **Kipahulu** coastal regions of the park in 1 day, but you will spend much time in your car. To absorb more of the ambience of this unique sea-girt volcano, try to spend a day on the mountain, with a hike through the moonscape of the "crater," and a second day on the coast. Van and bus tours—some starting in predawn hours to take in a magical summit sunrise—can be arranged from most island hotels. Some companies will drive a group to the summit, then provide bicycles to ride down the mountain.

Consider taking a guided walk from **Hosmer Grove** into the Nature Conservancy's **Waikamoi Preserve**, home of living treasures including various species of honeycreepers, the premier family of native Hawaiian birds. Call ahead for the schedule.

Air tours of Maui and the park are available from Kahului, but regulations limit them to high altitude.

Maui's southeastern coast. Dominated by intense hues—azure sea, black rock, silver waterfalls, green forest and meadow—the coastal area was first farmed in early Polynesian times, more than 1,200 years ago. Mark Twain, who traveled to Hawaii in 1866, may well have had this part of Kipahulu in mind when he wrote: "For me its balmy airs are always blowing, its summer seas flashing in the sun; the pulsing of its surfbeat is in my ear; I can see its garlanded crags, its leaping cascades, its plumy palms drowsing by the shore."

How to Get There

Fly directly from the mainland, or from another Hawaiian island, to Kahului in central Maui. To reach the summit of Haleakala, follow, sequentially, Hawaii 36, 37, 377, and 378. The 38-mile route is well marked; last chance to buy food and gas is at Pukalani or Makawao. Continue on the switchback road through miles of lush mountain rangeland to the park's

WAIKAMOI PRESERVE

Hosmer Grove

To Kahului

378

Park Headquarters Visitor Center

Supply Trail

Halemauu Trailhead

KOOLAU GAP

Leleiwi Overlook

Holua Cabin

Kalahaku Overlook

Silversword Loop

+ Hanakauhi 8,907 ft

KALAPAW

Puu Kumu

Kawilinau

Halemauu Trail

WILDERNESS

Puu O Maui

Kaluu O Ka Oo

AREA

Puu Maile

Olipu

Haleakala Visitor Center

+ Magnetic Peak 10,008 ft

Sliding Sands (Keoneheehee) Trail

Kapalaoa Cabin

KAU

Puu Ulaula Summit 10,023 ft

+ Haupaakea 9,159 ft

Ranger Station

Campground

Primitive Campsite

Self-guiding Trail

Cinder Cone

Hiking Trail

0   1   2 km
0   1   2 mi

Hosmer Grove to Haleakala Summit

11 miles; at least a half day

A short distance above the park entrance lies **Hosmer Grove**, a cool, shady spot to picnic and camp. You may recognize some of the trees, which include Douglas-fir, California redwood, and eucalyptus. About 1910, forester Ralph Hosmer planted trees from all over the world to test their potential for watershed protection and timber here. A half-mile loop trail will refresh you after your drive. Guided nature walks are also available. Back on the road, you reach **Park Headquarters Visitor Center** about a mile above the Hosmer turnoff. At this 7,000-foot elevation, you will see vegetation native to Hawaii. In front

of headquarters, plantings of Haleakala geranium and silversword offer photo opportunities and biology lessons in adaptation and evolution. These two plants are endemic—found only on Haleakala volcano.

Leaving headquarters, drive up the mountain through subalpine heath of soft earthy hues. In spring, mamane, a dominant shrub, brightens these slopes with sprays of yellow blossoms. The small birds here are mainly native. With luck you may see some of the famous honeycreepers—brightly feathered birds that may be descendants of the first land birds to reach Hawaii. From their original ancestors, the honeycreepers have evolved at least 47 species, some adapted to only one island, some spread more widely. More than half of these species have become extinct. Driven from the

Nene, birds unique to Hawaii

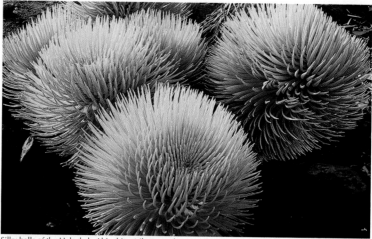
Silky balls of the Haleakala Ahinahina (silversword)

Iiwi, a tiny, rare honeycreeper

lowlands by habitat change and disease, others are making their last stand high on the mountain.

Summit hikers often start at the **Halemauu Trailhead,** 3 miles above the headquarters visitor center. This trail takes you through rolling country to the rim, then switchbacks as it steeply drops a thousand feet down the spectacular northwest wall of the wilderness area to **Holua Cabin** and the campground (4 miles from the trailhead). The wall is broken here by **Koolau Gap,** a wide, wet canyon that descends to the sea. In this corner, vegetation thrives on moisture carried by waves of clouds that slowly ebb and flow in the gap, and you will find the leathery amau fern and other unusual plants.

Motorists can get first views of the crater at **Leleiwi Overlook.** Drive approximately 2 more miles to the **Haleakala Visitor Center,** where rangers lead hikes partway into the center (call ahead for schedules).

An exhibit shelter crowns the highest point—**Puu Ulaula,** or "red hill"— where park naturalists give several interpretive talks daily.

At 10,023 feet, Puu Ulaula offers the ultimate view: Often you can see the giant volcanoes of the Big Island, as well as Maui's neighboring islands of **Lanai** and **Molokai** and sometimes, at night, far to the northwest, the lights of **Oahu.** Nearby, but outside the park, are the Haleakala Observatories, a cluster of buildings that are closed to the public.

The best way to experience the wilderness area is on a 2-day hike, spending the night at one of the three cabins or two campgrounds inside the crater. (Reserve well in advance for cabins—see **Information & Activities** p. 240.) One popular overnight trip involves hiking the **Sliding Sands Trail** to **Kapalaoa Cabin** (5.8 miles from the visitor center). This strenuous 7- to 10-hour hike loses and gains 3,000 feet on its descent and ascent through loose cinder. Many choose to exit via **Halemauu Trail,** an easier 8-mile hike from the cabin back to the road. You'll need to arrange a ride between the two trailheads.

Another challenging hike is to take the Sliding Sands Trail down to **Kaluu O Ka Oo,** the first big cinder cone; it is 5 miles round-trip.

Pools of Oheo

Kipahulu: Pools of Oheo

a full day

In this strip of parkland along the gorge of **Pipiwai Stream,** visitors hike through lush rain forest and past breathtaking ocean overlooks. Perhaps the area's greatest draw, however, is Hawaii's cultural past. Archaeological evidence shows that large numbers of Hawaiians once lived in Kipahulu, from precontact inhabitants (before 1778) to those who worked as cattle ranchers at the turn of the 20th century and in the sugar cane industry from 1880 to 1925. Trails reveal traces of the past: stone-walled gardens, pictographs, evidence of taro and sweet potato patches, and temple and shelter sites. Please respect this legacy by staying on trails and reporting to park rangers anyone seen damaging cultural resources.

Camping is permitted on the oceanfront meadows south of the stream at the **Kipahulu Campground.** Bring your own drinking water, or boil stream water or treat it with halozone. No permit is required, but there is a 3-night limit per month.

If you have 2 or 3 hours, take the **Pipiwai Trail,** one of the most memorable short hikes in the islands. This walk is easy for anyone in good health, but it is usually slippery with mud in spots; wear sturdy footgear. Don't hike if the river is swollen.

Begin about 200 yards south of the Oheo bridge, near the Kipahulu Visitor Center. Walk up through gently sloping pasture about half a mile to overlook the **Falls at Makahiku,** 184 feet high. After another half mile, the trail enters the woods and crosses two bridges near a lovely double falls. Continue about a mile more through lush forest, including a stand of dense, 50-foot-high bamboo, which on a breezy day clacks and creaks with a mysterious percussive music. Aromatic ginger and ti form the understory. Your destination looms above the forest as you get close: **Waimoku Falls,** more than 400 feet high, fills its jungle clearing with cool mists. Much of the year, mango, guava, and mountain apple provide refreshment.

Swimming is a pleasant pastime in this part of the park. Those who fancy a dip congregate around the big, cool pools and waterfalls below the highway bridge in **Oheo Gulch,** but less crowded spots await upstream. Some pools are deep, but beware of slippery or hidden rocks. Also, flash floods can follow heavy rains in the watershed above. There is no ocean access.

Information & Activities

Headquarters
P.O. Box 369, Makawao, Maui, HI 96768. Phone (808) 572-4400. www.nps.gov/hale

Seasons & Accessibility
All-year park. Call (808) 877-5111 for information on weather.

Visitor & Information Centers
Park Headquarters Visitor Center, 1 mile from park entrance, (808) 572-4400. **Haleakala Visitor Center,** near the summit, 11 miles from the park entrance, open daily all year. (808) 248-7375.

Entrance Fees
$10 per car per week, multiple entries; $20 for an annual pass.

Pets
Permitted on leashes in drive-in campgrounds only; not allowed on hiking trails.

Facilities for Disabled
All visitor centers, park headquarters, and some campsites are wheelchair accessible. A free brochure about visiting Maui is available from: Disability and Communication Access Board, 919 Ala Moana Blvd., Rm. 101, Honolulu, HI 96814. (808) 586-8121. www.hawaii.gov/health/dcab.

Things to Do
Free naturalist-led activities: nature walks and hikes, interpretive talks, cultural demonstrations. Also available, hiking, horseback riding, swimming in Pools of Oheo.

Special Advisory
• Wilderness area hikes are at high altitudes, with lower oxygen levels; take it easy. Be prepared for unpredictable weather that can change quickly from heat to cold and rain.

Overnight Backpacking
Tent camping allowed only at **Holua** and **Paliku** campsites; free permit required; issued first come, first served at park headquarters on the day of the hike; 2-night limit at each campground; limit of 3 nights total per month.

Three small, primitive cabins at **Holua, Kapalaoa,** and **Paliku** contain 12 bunks, minimum equipment; can be reached by trail only. Reservation requests must be received by mail before the first of the month, 3 months prior to desired stay; give alternate dates; assignments made by lottery; limited to 3 nights per month (2 consecutive nights in one cabin); $40 per night for 1 to 6 people; $80 per night for 7 to 12 people. Send request to headquarters. Call (808) 572-4400 for recorded information on cabins and campgrounds.

Campgrounds
Two drive-in campgrounds, both with 3-day limit. **Hosmer Grove** and **Kipahulu** open all year, first come, first served. No fees. No showers. Tent sites; no hookups.

Hotels, Motels, & Inns
(unless otherwise noted, rates are for 2 persons in a double room, high season)
In Hana, HI 96713:
Aloha Cottages 73 Keawa Pl., P.O. Box 205. (808) 248-8420. 5 small cottages, all with full kitchens, in residential areas of Hana. $65-$85.
Hana Kai Maui Resort Condominiums 1533 Uakea Rd., P.O. Box 38. (800) 346-2772 or (808) 248-7506. 16 units, kitchenettes. $125-$195.
Heavenly Hana Inn 4155 Hana Hwy., P.O. Box 790. (808) 248-8442. Three units. $185-$250.
Hotel Hana Maui P.O. Box 9. (800) 321-4262 or (808) 248-8211. 66 units. $295. 2 restaurants.
Josie's Hana Hideaway P.O. Box 265. (808) 248-7727. 12 cottages, all with full kitchens, in various areas of Hana. $85-$150.
In Kahului, HI 96732:
Maui Beach Hotel 170 Kaahumanu Ave.; contact Hawaii Reservation Center, 3 Waterfront Plaza, 500 Ala Moana Blvd., Ste. 555, Honolulu, HI 96826. (888) 649-3222 or (808) 877-0051. 164 units. $98-$450. AC, pool, restaurant.
Maui Seaside Hotel 100 W. Kaahumanu Ave. (800) 367-7000 or (808) 877-3311. 190 units, 10 with kitchenettes. $125. AC, pool, restaurant.
In Kula, HI 96790:
Kula Lodge Rte. 377, 15200 Haleakala Hwy. (800) 233-1535 or (808) 878-1535. 5 units. $110-$165. Restaurant.

Excursions

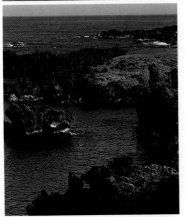

Waianapanapa State Park
Hana, Maui, Hawaii

Low volcanic cliffs and native hala (pandanus) forest line the coast in this remote, rugged park. Here, visitors can fish in the surf, explore a cave, observe an immense seabird colony, and hike the ancient coastal trail leading to Hana. 120 acres. Hiking, fishing, swimming. Campground (permits required), 12 cabins, picnic areas. Open year-round. Off Hawaii 360 (Hana Highway) about 80 miles from Haleakala NP. (808) 984-8109.

Iao Valley State Park
Wailuku, Maui, Hawaii

Velvety moss-covered cliffs surround the verdant Iao Valley and its center-piece, the Iao Needle, a 2,250-foot basalt spire sacred to the people of Maui. Swirling waters fashioned the spire from a natural altar in an ancient volcanic caldera. Six acres. Observation pavilion, botanic gardens. Open year-round. End of Iao Valley Road, off Hawaii 32, about 40 miles from Haleakala NP. (808) 984-8109.

Hawaiian ferns and ohia blossoms near Halemaumau crater, atop Kilauea

Hawaii Volcanoes

Hawaii

Established August 1, 1916

217,359 acres

Hawaii Volcanoes National Park, on the "Big Island" of Hawaii, offers the visitor a look at two of the world's most active volcanoes: Kilauea and Mauna Loa.

More than 4,000 feet high and still growing, Kilauea abuts the southeastern slope of the older and much larger Mauna Loa, or "long mountain." Mauna Loa towers some 13,677 feet above the sea: Measured from its base 18,000 feet below sea level, it exceeds Mount Everest in height. Mauna Loa's gently sloping bulk— some 19,000 cubic miles in volume— makes it the planet's most massive single mountain.

The park stretches from sea level to Mauna Loa's summit. Beyond the end of the road lies Mauna Loa's wilderness area, where backpackers encounter freezing nights and rough lava trails amid volcanic wonders: barren lava twisted into nightmarish shapes, cinder cones, gaping pits. Kilauea, however, provides easy access to a greater variety of scenery and cultural sites.

On the slopes of Kilauea, whose name means "spreading, much spewing," lush green rain forest borders stark, recent lava flows. This natural laboratory of ecological change displays all stages of forest regeneration— from early regrowth of lichens and ferns to dense forest. The rain forest on the windward side of Kilauea's summit gives way to the stark, windswept Kau Desert on the hot, dry southwestern slope. At the shore, waves create lines of jagged cliffs; periodic eruptions send fresh lava flows to meet the sea amid colossal clouds of steam.

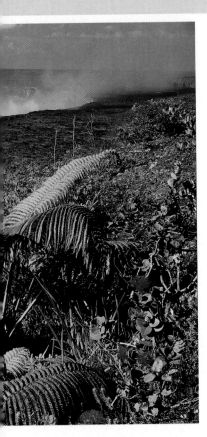

Geological dynamism forms the park's primary natural theme, followed closely by evolutionary biology. Thousands of unique species have evolved on the isolated Hawaiian islands. Cultural sites abound as well, reminders of the Polynesian pioneers who steered their great double-hulled canoes to Hawaii beginning some 1,500 years ago.

The United Nations has named the park both an international biosphere reserve and a World Heritage site. Many of the park's intriguing native plants and animals, however, are in peril, defenseless against alien species including weedy invasive plants and feral pigs.

How to Get There

Fly to the island of Hawaii, also called the Big Island. Airlines serve the Kona airport from the mainland and from other Hawaiian islands; only interisland flights land in Hilo. From Kona, head south around the island on Hawaii 11 past Kealakekua Bay, where Captain Cook met his death, and Ka

Lae, or South Point, southernmost land in the 50 states. You'll reach the Kilauea summit after a 95-mile drive on a good road.

From Hilo, Hawaii 11 rises 4,000 feet in 30 miles on your way past small towns, macadamia orchards, and rain forest, to reach the park at Kilauea's summit.

When to Go

All-year park. The weather is often driest in September and October. The climate ranges from warm and breezy on the coast, to cool and frequently wet at the summit of Kilauea, to nightly freezing with occasional snowstorms above about 10,000 feet on Mauna Loa. To avoid most tour bus crowds, plan to visit the major sights before 11 a.m. or after 3 p.m.

How to Visit

An intensive 1-day visit can encompass highlights of the **Kilauea** summit via **Crater Rim Drive** and the coastal region via **Chain of Craters Road.** Regular tours by bus and small van operate daily from many Hilo and Kona hotels. Those with a botanical or ornithological bent will enjoy exploring **Mauna Loa Road** (accessible from Hawaii 11), which takes you through upland forest to the **Mauna Loa trailhead** at 6,662 feet: At **Kipuka Puaulu,** be sure to take the 1-mile loop trail winding through 100-acre Kipuka (an island of vegetation surrounded by a more recent lava flow) containing one of Hawaii's richest concentrations of native plants and birdlife.

Puu Oo spewing molten lava

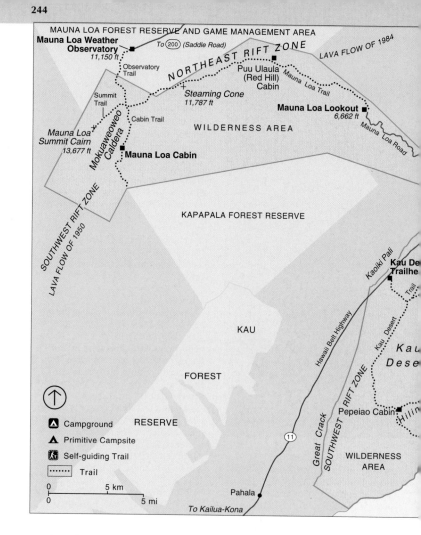

Map of Mauna Loa area, Kilauea, and surrounding regions. Labels include: Mauna Loa Forest Reserve and Game Management Area, Mauna Loa Weather Observatory 11,150 ft, To (200) (Saddle Road), Observatory Trail, Northeast Rift Zone, Lava Flow of 1984, Puu Ulaula (Red Hill) Cabin, Mauna Loa Trail, Summit Trail, Steaming Cone 11,787 ft, Mauna Loa Lookout 6,662 ft, Cabin Trail, Wilderness Area, Mauna Loa Summit Cairn 13,677 ft, Mokuaweoweo Caldera, Mauna Loa Cabin, Mauna Loa Road, Southwest Rift Zone, Lava Flow of 1950, Kapapala Forest Reserve, Kaoiki Pali, Kau Desert Trailhead, Trail, Hawaii Belt Highway, Kau, Kau Desert, Forest, Great Crack, Southwest Rift Zone, Pepeiao Cabin, Reserve, Campground, Primitive Campsite, Self-guiding Trail, Trail, 0 5 km, 0 5 mi, Pahala, Wilderness Area, Hilina, To Kailua-Kona, 11

Kilauea Summit: Crater Rim Drive

11-mile loop; about a half day

Since Kilauea's summit areas can be rainy and chilly at any time of the year, visitors should be prepared. Bring a windbreaker or jacket and wear long pants. Begin at the **Kilauea Visitor Center,** where you can get the latest information on park roads and safety precautions. Don't miss the stunning film of recent volcanic eruptions. The rustic **Volcano House** and the **Volcano Art Center Gallery** are just a short stroll away. Walk through the lobby of the Volcano House to the rear of the hotel for a first dramatic view across **Kilauea Caldera,** a 3-mile-wide, 400-foot-deep depression that marks the volcanic summit.

After leaving the visitor center, proceed clockwise on **Crater Rim Drive.** For a time, the road traverses rain forest featuring Hawaiian tree ferns that lend the roadsides a prehistoric look. Scenic turnouts begin with a huge crater, **Kilauea Iki** ("little Kilauea") just east of the main caldera. In 1959 Kilauea Iki erupted in a lava fountain 1,900 feet high, a record for Hawaiian volcanism.

Visit **Nahuku** (Thurston Lava Tube) by taking an easy 15-minute loop trail that starts in lush tropical rain forest. The lava tube formed when the surface of a lava stream cooled to a crust while the still molten interior lava flowed out.

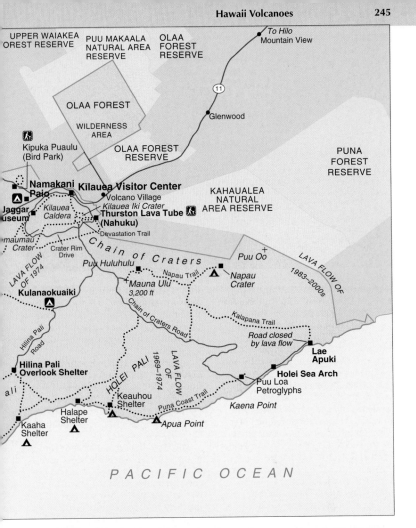

UPPER WAIAKEA FOREST RESERVE

PUU MAKAALA NATURAL AREA RESERVE

OLAA FOREST RESERVE

To Hilo
Mountain View

OLAA FOREST
WILDERNESS AREA

Glenwood

11

OLAA FOREST RESERVE

Kipuka Puaulu
(Bird Park)

PUNA FOREST RESERVE

Namakani Paio

Kilauea Visitor Center

KAHAUALEA NATURAL AREA RESERVE

Jaggar Museum

Kilauea Caldera

Volcano Village

Kilauea Iki Crater

Thurston Lava Tube (Nahuku)

maumau Crater

Crater Rim Drive

Devastation Trail

Chain of Craters

Puu Oo

LAVA FLOW OF 1983–2000s

LAVA FLOW OF 1974

Puu Huluhulu

Mauna Ulu
3,200 ft

Napau Trail

Napau Crater

Kulanaokuaiki

Chain of Craters Road

Kalapana Trail

Hilina Pali Road

HOLEI PALI

LAVA FLOW OF 1969–1974

Road closed by lava flow

Lae Apuki

Hilina Pali Overlook Shelter

Keauhou Shelter

Puna Coast Trail

Holei Sea Arch

Puu Loa Petroglyphs

Kaena Point

ali

Halape Shelter

Kaaha Shelter

Apua Point

PACIFIC OCEAN

The Nahuku (Thurston Lava Tube), a natural tunnel

Along the Devastation Trail

From the Nahuku parking area, trails lead down to the floor of **Kilauea Iki Crater** and along its rim. You can take a loop hike or walk back to Volcano House in 2 to 3 miles. Either way, you'll pass dramatic vistas of the Kilauea Caldera, vertical lava cliffs, and verdant rain forest.

Another option is to hike the popular 4-mile **Kilauea Iki Trail,** which winds around the rim and across the floor of a crater that last erupted in 1959. Taking about 2 hours to walk, the trail descends 400 feet, passing rain forest and steaming lava flows.

Now continuing back along Crater Rim Drive, look for koae kea, white-tailed tropicbirds. These ethereal-looking creatures nest on cliffside ledges, often soaring above **Kilauea Caldera.** With luck, you may spot a nene, an endemic Hawaiian bird probably descended from lost Canada geese that landed here. The state bird of Hawaii, the nene are a federally protected endangered species. Do not feed or approach any nene and take care to avoid hitting them when driving (you'll spot "nene crossing" road signs).

Devastation Trail is a short (half-mile) but unforgettable walk through the remains of a forest killed by falling cinder during the 1959 eruption. The forest is now beginning to recover.

As the road descends along the southwestern side of Kilauea Caldera, you will notice the landscape becoming more arid. In the rain shadow of the summit, the **Kau Desert** receives about half as much rain as the 100 inches which fall annually at the Kilauea Visitor Center. It also bears the brunt of trade winds blowing sulphuric volcanic fumes and natural acid rain—which stunt plants—down from above.

You reach the **Halemaumau Crater Overlook.** Walk the short path to look into the crater, a favorite abode of Pele, goddess of the volcano. Many native Hawaiians still revere her; throughout the year they privately chant and dance at the crater's edge.

The **Hawaiian Volcano Observatory** of the U.S. Geological Survey (closed to public), and the small, excellent **Jaggar Museum** of volcano lore and research are next on your route. Nearing the visitor center once more, you'll pass fumaroles, or steam vents. Some have produced the **Sulphur Banks** with crystalline deposits of pure sulphur. From here you can opt for a short hike back toward the visitor center. Alternatively, a 1- to 2-mile walk along the caldera rim provides fine views.

Chain of Craters Road

20 miles one way; about 3 hours

From the Kilauea Visitor Center follow Crater Rim Drive clockwise to the well-marked turnoff for Chain of Craters Road. For about 4 miles as you head toward the coast, your route follows the upper part of the active **East Rift Zone** of Kilauea volcano. Scenic turnouts and short walks bring you to the rims of several impressive craters. If you have time, hike the

Lava sizzling into ocean near the park

Ripples of hardened pahoehoe lava on Kilauea

Napau Trail up **Puu Huluhulu**
("shaggy hill") to the overlook at the
top, just over 1 mile. The overlook
provides splendid views of the East
Rift Zone and **Mauna Ulu,** the large,
steaming domelike hill directly to the
south. Look for steam from **Puu Oo,** a
major vent of Kilauea's ongoing eruption, far to the east.

Back on Chain of Craters Road,
you will drive over several miles of
pahoehoe lava flows produced when
Mauna Ulu formed in the 1970s.
At the turnouts, you stand on some
of the newest ground on Earth.
Pahoehoe (PA-hoy-hoy) lava flows at
more than 2,000°F. It begins fluid then
chills to a smooth, ropy surface. This
rock contrasts with aa (ah-ah)—
thicker, slow-moving lava that has
hardened into a chaotic jumble of
rough jagged cinders.

The climate becomes drier, and
patches of forest in various stages of
recovery appear, as you descend toward
the sea. Sulphur fumes sweep down
from active volcanic vents on the rift to

the east. Turnouts offer sweeping views
of lava flows and white-capped waves
pounding the black shoreline. About
21 miles off this coast, a huge undersea
volcano is building a future Hawaiian
island. Named Loihi, the volcano could
breach the ocean's surface in some
100,000 years.

A steep descent of about 800 feet
marks **Holei Pali,** a cliff formed by
vertical faulting; the huge coastal shelf
is breaking away from the uplands
and sinking into the sea, albeit slowly
on a human time scale. Reaching
the lowlands, look for the **Puu Loa
Petroglyphs** turnout; a modest hike
will bring you to fine examples of
ancient Hawaiian carvings, some
24,000 images and figures pecked
into the lava. Visitors are asked to
stay on the boardwalk to help preserve
these carvings.

Hawaiians lived on this dry, rocky
land for centuries. Your route along
the coast takes you past several of their
ancient settlements, though they are
difficult to discern.

The road ends abruptly at a 1995
lava flow. Since 1986, an almost
continuous flow of lava from Puu Oo
has buried several miles of the road,
as well as the Kamoamoa picnic site
and campground, and the Wahaula
Visitor Center. Park rangers mark a
path to a viewpoint close to current
flows. Lava flow viewing and access
are unpredictable; obey all off-limit
signs and heed the instructions of
any park rangers on duty here. Ask
at the visitor center for current lava
flow information.

Information & Activities

Headquarters
P.O. Box 52, Hawaii NP, HI 96718.
Phone (808) 985-6000.
www.nps.gov/havo

Seasons & Accessibility
Park open year-round. Chain of
Craters Road is closed by lava flow at
its eastern end. For eruption bulletins
call (808) 985-6000.

Visitor & Information Centers
Kilauea Visitor Center, located just
off Hawaii 11 on Crater Rim Drive,
a quarter mile from park entrance
gate, and the Thomas A. Jaggar
Museum on Crater Rim Drive, 3
miles from park entrance gate,
are both open all year.

Entrance Fee
$10 per car per week.

Pets
Not permitted on hiking trails or
in backcountry; elsewhere must
be leashed.

Facilities for Disabled
Kilauea Visitor Center, Jaggar Museum,
Volcano House Hotel, Volcano Art
Center Gallery all wheelchair accessi-
ble. Many paved trails and overlooks
along Crater Rim Drive and Chain of
Craters Road accessible with assistance.
Kulanaokuaiki Campground fully
wheelchair accessible. Free brochure
about visiting the Big Island from: Dis-
ability and Communication Access
Board, 919 Ala Moana Blvd., Rm. 101,
Honolulu, hi 96814. (808) 586-8121.
www.hawaii.gov/health/dcab

Things to Do
Free ranger-led activities: nature walks
and talks, slide shows, films, museum
exhibits on volcanism. Also, hiking,
art center, workshops, seminars.

Special Advisories
• Be prepared for intensive sunlight.
• Persons with heart or respiratory
problems must beware of noxious sulphur fumes.
• Stay on marked trails; vegetation
may conceal deep cracks.
• Coastline collapse can occur fast; do
not go beyond barriers.
• Strong winds and unpredictable surf
along the coast make swimming dangerous; it is prohibited in places.
• Do not enter any closed areas.

Overnight Backpacking
Registration at the visitor center is
required. No fee.

Campgrounds
Two campgrounds, Kulanaokuaiki and
Namakani Paio, all with a 7-day limit.
Open all year first come, first served.
No fees. No showers. Tent sites only.
Two patrol cabins on Mauna Loa Trail
and one at Kipuka Pepeiao may be
used free, first come, first served. Must
register at Kilauea Visitor Center. Food
services in park.

Hotels, Motels, & Inns
*(unless otherwise noted, rates are for 2
persons in a double room, high season)*
INSIDE THE PARK:
*The following are operated by the Vol-
cano House, P.O. Box 53, Hawaii Vol-
canoes NP, HI 96718. (808) 967-7321.*
Volcano House Crater Rim Dr. 42
rooms. $85-$185. Restaurant.
Namakani Paio Cabins (off Hawaii 11)
10 cabins with central bath. $40.
OUTSIDE THE PARK:
In Hilo, HI 96720:
Country Club Apartment Hotel 121
Banyan Dr. (808) 935-7171. 148 units,
24 with kitchenettes. $65-$125. AC, rest.
Dolphin Bay Hotel 333 Iliahi St. (808)
935-1466. 18 units with kitchenettes.
$69-$99.
Hawaii Naniloa Resorts 93 Banyan
Dr. (800) 367-5360 or (808) 969-3333.
325 units. $100-$140. AC, 2 pools,
2 restaurants.
In Kailua-Kona, HI 96740:
King Kamehameha Kona Beach Hotel
75-5660 Palani Rd. (800) 367-2111 or
(808) 329-2911. 456 units. $135-$200.
AC, pool, restaurant.
In Pahala, HI 96777:
Colony One at SeaMountain, Punaluu
(on Hawaii 11) P.O. Box 70. (800) 488-
8301 or (808) 928-8301. 28 condominiums. $95-$170. Pool, tennis, golf.

*For additional lodgings contact the
Chambers of Commerce of Hilo, 106
Kamehameha Ave., Ste. 208, Hilo, HI
96720, (808) 935-7178; and Kailua-
Kona, 75-5737 Kuakini Hwy., Kailua-
Kona, HI 96740, (808) 329-1758.*

Excursions

Mauna Kea Observatory
Hilo, Hawaii

Mauna Kea, the world's highest island mountain, is the world's premier astronomical site. Clear, dry skies and a 13,796-foot elevation provide ideal viewing conditions; ten countries have built state-of-the-art telescopes on the dormant volcano's summit. The visitor center at 9,300 feet has astronomical displays and evening stargazing from an 11-inch telescope. Saturday and Sunday tours to summit available for persons 16 and older who are not pregnant and have no heart or respiratory problems. Summit goers must provide their own vehicles equipped with four-wheel-drive. Seven-mile trail to summit from visitor center. Open year-round. Located off Hawaii 200 (Saddle Rd.), about 40 miles from Hilo. (808) 961-2180.

Akaka Falls State Park
Honomu, Hawaii

This park's ancient legend bears a decidedly modern ring: It says that the god Akaka, fleeing across the canyon after his wife returned home unexpectedly and discovered his infidelity, slipped and fell off 442-foot Akaka Falls. A self-guided paved path leads visitors through a lush jungle ablaze with colorful and fragrant blossoms to viewpoints over these falls and the 100-foot cascading Kahuna Falls. 65 acres. No facilities other than the hiking trails, rest rooms, scenic lookouts. Located at end of Akaka Falls Road, off Hawaii 220, about 15 miles north of Hilo. (808) 974-6200.

At sunset, Joshua trees etching the sky

Joshua Tree

California

Established October 31, 1994

794,000 acres

Two desert systems, the Mojave and the Colorado, abut within Joshua Tree, dividing California's southernmost national park into two arid ecosystems of profoundly contrasting appearance. The key to their differences is elevation. The Colorado, the western reach of the vast Sonoran Desert, thrives below 3,000 feet on the park's gently declining eastern flank, where temperatures are usually higher. Considered "low desert," compared to the loftier, wetter, and more vegetated Mojave "high desert," the Colorado seems sparse and forbidding. It begins at the park's midsection, sweeping east across empty basins stubbled with creosote bushes. Occasionally decorated by

"gardens" of flowering ocotillo and cholla cactus, it runs across arid Pinto Basin into a parched wilderness of broken rock in the Eagle and Coxcomb Mountains.

Many newcomers among the 1.3 million visitors who pass through each year are surprised by the abrupt transition between the Colorado and Mojave ecosystems. Above 3,000 feet, the Mojave section claims the park's western half, where giant branching yuccas thrive on sandy plains studded by massive granite monoliths and rock piles. These are among the most intriguing and photogenic geological phenomena found in California's many desert regions.

Joshua Tree's human history commenced sometime after the last ice age with the arrival of the Pinto people, hunter-gatherers who may have been part of the Southwest's earliest cul-

Palms Hwy.) to Twentynine Palms (about 140 miles total). The south entrance is located at Cottonwood Spring, approximately 25 miles east of Indio off I-10. Call (760) 367-5500 for recorded directions.

When to Go

All-year park. Temperatures are most comfortable in the spring and fall, with an average high and low of 85°F and 50°F. Winter brings cooler days, around 60°F, and freezing nights. Summers are hot, with midday temperatures frequently above 100°F, and ground temperatures reaching 180°F. The Mojave Desert zone on the park's western half is on average 11 degrees cooler than the Colorado. In winter, snow may blanket the Mojave's higher elevations.

Spring blooming periods vary according to winter precipitation and spring temperatures, usually beginning in February at lower elevations and peaking park-wide in March and April, although cactuses may bloom into June. (Check with park headquarters.) For up-to-date recorded wildflower information, call (760) 367-5500.

How to Visit

The park's premier attractions, forests of giant branching yuccas known as Joshua trees, massive rock formations, fan palm oases, and seasonal gardens of cholla and ocotillo, can be enjoyed on a leisurely half-day auto tour that includes both "high" and "low" desert zones—although most of your time will be spent in your car. Scenic paved roads lead to viewpoints, all campgrounds, and trailheads. Roadside interpretive exhibits have pull-outs and parking areas, and offer insights into the region's complex desert ecology, wildlife, and human history.

If you plan to explore the park by mountain bike, you would be wise to avoid the main paved roads, which are narrow and without shoulders. You'll find far greater solitude and safety cycling the park's backcountry dirt roads, many of which, like those in **Queen Valley,** date from the area's 19th-century homestead and gold-mining era. Be sure to acquire reliable information from headquarters about your route, however, as soft sand and occasional steep climbs can make for arduous pedaling.

tures. They lived in Pinto Basin, which though inhospitably arid today, had a wet climate and was crossed by a sluggish river some 5,000 to 7,000 years ago. Nomadic groups of Indians seasonally inhabited the region when harvests of pinyon nuts, mesquite beans, acorns, and cactus fruit offered sustenance. Bedrock mortars—holes ground into solid rock and used to pulverize seeds during food preparation—are scattered throughout the Wonderland of Rocks area south of the Indian Cove camping site.

A flurry of late 19th-century gold-mining ventures left ruins; some are accessible by hiking trails, or unmaintained roads suited only to four-wheel-drive vehicles and mountain bikes.

How to Get There

The west and north park entrances are at the towns of Joshua Tree and Twentynine Palms. From Los Angeles, take I-10 east to Calif. 62 (Twentynine

To Victorville and (15)
247) Joshua
Tree
Park
Blvd.
62
Entrance Station
Twentynine Palms
To A
To (4
Oasis Visitor Center
Indian Cove
Oasis of Mara
North Entrance Station

Black Rock
Canyon
West
Entrance
Station
Eureka
Peak
5,516 ft
Hidden Valley
Queen Mt.
+5,677 ft
Queen Valley
Park Blvd.
PINTO MOUNTAINS
Belle
White Tank
LITTLE SAN BERNARDINO MOUNTAINS
Keys View
5,185 ft
Sheep
Pass
Jumbo
Rocks
Arch Rock
Nature Trail
Pinto Mt.
+3,983 ft
Transition Zone
MOJAVE DESERT
Cholla Cactus
Garden
Ocotillo
Patch
PINTO BASIN

To
Los Angeles

San Andreas Fault
Sea Level
Indio
Pinto Basin Road

Ranger Station
Campground
Group Campsite
Interpretive Trail
Unpaved Road
4-wheel-drive Road
Hiking Trail

Cottonwood
Visitor
Center
COTTONWOOD
MOUNTAINS
10
EAG
Eagle
5,350
Bajada
Nature
Trail

For a half-day visit starting from the park's northern boundary, take the **Park Boulevard loop** either from the town of Joshua Tree through the West Entrance Station, or from Twentynine Pines, by way of the North Entrance Station. If the air is clear (ask at the entrance about haze conditions), take the 20-minute side trip to 5,185-foot-high **Keys View,** which overlooks a vast panorama of arid desert basin and range stretching south into Mexico. If you are starting from Joshua Tree, return to Park Boulevard and continue east over **Sheep Pass** to **Jumbo Rocks,** turning right (south) onto Pinto Basin Road for the drive down into long vistas in the Colorado Desert zone. Be sure to stroll the self-guided nature trails through the **Cholla Cactus Garden** and the **Ocotillo Patch.**

Backtrack to Twentynine Palms and the **Oasis Visitor Center,** which features a small cactus garden and superb desert ecology interpretive displays. It adjoins the historic **Oasis of Mara** (one of five spring-fed oases within the park's boundaries), where Indians once found water, shade, food, and game. If you are starting from Twentynine Palms and the Oasis Visitor Center, proceed south as far as the Ocotillo Patch, then backtrack to Park Boulevard and follow it westward to Joshua Tree.

Park Boulevard

64 miles (including side trips); a half to full day

A scenic drive connecting the north and west entrances skirts the sparse Colorado low desert ecosystem, then climbs into the Joshua tree forest and its surrounding plateau of mammoth rocks. Begin at the **Oasis Visitor Center** in Twentynine Palms. (Or, if entering from the south, begin at the **Cottonwood Visitor Center** and follow Pinto Basin Road north and east past the Ocotillo Patch and the Cholla Cactus Garden to the Oasis Visitor Center.) Both visitor centers provide insights into how plants and animals survive the region's withering heat and aridity, and how its unusual geology was formed, though the Oasis Visitor Center's interpretive displays are more extensive.

The Oasis Visitor Center adjoins the **Oasis of Mara,** a cluster of fan palms (the only palms native to the Southwest desert), Fremont cottonwood, arrow weed, and mesquite shrubs watered by a seeping spring. Take the half-mile path to this scruffy bit of green, which once sustained Indian encampments and later slaked the thirst of prospectors and homesteaders. A minute's stroll leads to a shady respite amid the chatter of birds. (Bird-when rocks are aglow in warm pinks and yellows. On weekends, ask at a visitor center about ranger-led campfire talks, walks, and tours, or check campground bulletin boards.

Continue south from Twentynine Palms on Park Boulevard to the North Entrance Station. The road climbs, skirting the **Pinto Mountains** that rise to the east. Where the pavement forks (after about 5 miles), bear left onto Pinto Basin Road. You'll soon enter **Wilson Canyon** and the transition zone, where the Mojave and Colorado Desert ecosystems join. The sweep of **Pinto Basin** trending east is in fact an ancient dry lakebed, and a typical Sonoran Desert landscape dominated by the pale creosote bush.

Stroll through the **Cholla Cactus Garden,** a picturesque cluster about 6.5 miles south of the fork and threaded by a short nature trail interestingly keyed to self-guided brochures provided there. Known as "jumping" cholla for the tendency of its spiny joints to break off and cling to hapless passersby, the crooked-arm cactus appears velvety but is actually covered by tiny, sharply piercing bristles.

Continue southeast about 2 miles to the **Ocotillo Patch,** where hundreds of the spindly Sonoran Desert plants seem to languish, their rigid gray spines wobbling skyward. After rains in March and April, their tips flame with dense bouquets of bloodred flowers, a lifesaver for hummingbirds migrating north from Mexico (and a highlight of the flowering calendar).

watchers may want to include a visit to **Cottonwood Springs,** an oasis sheltering many species and located about a mile from the Cottonwood Visitor Center at the south entrance.)

If your schedule allows a full day's visit, take time for short walks along nature trails that offer close-up looks at plant and animal life, or interesting terrain. (Park brochures describe trail highlights.) Consider starting early; sunlight playing across Joshua Tree's granite monoliths, peaks, and basins accentuates their contours and colors—especially at dawn and sunset—

Giant boulders at Jumbo Rocks campground

Backtrack northwest to the White Tank Campground and the **Arch Rock Nature Trail.** The easy 0.3-mile path to **Arch Rock** features interpretive information on how the surrounding geology and the natural arch were formed.

At the fork, turn left to rejoin Park Boulevard and enter the Mojave high desert. Westbound, you'll see mammoth granite formations rising from a sandy plateau. Some 800 million years in the making, worn by eons of weather into the contours of melting ice cream, the **Jumbo Rocks** are a product of this region's seismic restlessness—tectonic tumult evidenced by frequent small temblors that affect the flow of springs watering the park's oases.

Here visitors will likely see climbers scaling the monoliths, for Joshua Tree National Park contains one of America's most accessible, yet challenging, rock-climbing areas. Guidelines designed for safety and the protection of rock surfaces govern climbing within the park. Spectators gather in parking areas to watch the equipment-laden enthusiasts struggle hand-over-hand up seemingly impossible routes.

Keep an eye out for aptly named **Skull Rock,** which flanks the road as you continue west toward **Hidden Valley,** a scenic garden of huge piled-up boulders resembling animals, human faces, and abstract forms.

A popular picnic and camping area, this part of Joshua Tree is heavily populated by the park's trademark branching yucca. Named by early Mormon settlers who saw in its uplifted arms a symbol of the Biblical supplicant Joshua, *Yucca brevifolia* can reach 50 feet in height over a lifespan that may exceed 200 years. Some 25 bird species find protected nesting spots between its short, spiky leaves. The 1.25-mile **Hidden Valley Trail** follows a circuitous path through a stony maze to a "hidden" bowl where, according to local lore, rustlers once hid with their stolen cattle. The northern portion of this loop requires some boulder scrambling.

If you're not yet ready for a picnic, take the 6-mile scenic side trip up to **Keys View.** Just short of a mile high (5,185 feet), the mountaintop is the park's premier vantage point for motorists. Smog and natural haze from the Los Angeles Basin sometimes obscure the horizon; however, clear days afford a splendid southerly panorama of Coachella Valley farmlands, the Salton Sea, and Sonoran Desert mountains in Mexico. Across the valley looms 10,804-foot Mount Jacinto, towering above Palm Springs.

Park Boulevard continues northwest through the Joshua tree forest, descending to the West Entrance Station and the town of Joshua Tree.

Information & Activities

Headquarters
74485 National Park Dr., Twentynine Palms, CA 92277. Phone (760) 367-5500. www.nps.gov/jotr

Seasons & Accessibility
Open year-round.

Visitor & Information Centers
Park headquarters located at **Oasis Visitor Center,** off Calif. 62 near Twentynine Palms and the north entrance. **Cottonwood Visitor Center,** off I-10 at south entrance. Both visitor centers open daily.

Entrance Fee
$10 per vehicle, good for seven consecutive days; $25 for annual pass.

Pets
Permitted on leashes. Not allowed on trails or in backcountry (more than 100 yards from the road). Must be attended at all times.

Facilities for Disabled
The Oasis Visitor Center's interpretive displays, garden, and bookstore are all wheelchair accessible, as are the quarter- and half-mile loop trails to the adjoining Oasis of Mara. The Keys View wheelchair viewpoint is just below the summit. The Cap Rock Nature Trail (0.5-mile loop from parking area) and the Bajada Nature Trail (0.25-mile loop) are also accessible. No campsites are officially wheelchair accessible, however the Belle or White Tank camping areas have accessible rest rooms.

Chuckwalla lizard

Things to Do
Free ranger-led activities held weekends year-round, including tours to Keys Ranch homestead. Also, interpretive exhibits, self-guided cactus garden trails, auto touring, bicycling (on established roads only), hiking, rock climbing, horseback riding on approved trails, bird-watching. All-terrain vehicles and off-road motorized travel and bicycling prohibited.

Special Advisories
• Always carry water, even on short hikes. There are no potable water sources within the park. Potable water is available at the Oasis of Mara, at Black Rock and Cottonwood Campgrounds, and at the Indian Cove Ranger Station. Recommended: One gallon per person per day, two gallons if hiking.
• Campfires are not allowed in the backcountry. Collecting vegetation, living or dead, is prohibited, so bring your own firewood for campgrounds.
• Rock climbers should regard all fixed protection (bolting, for example) found in place as unsafe. Motorized drilling is prohibited within park boundaries.
• Bolting not allowed in designated wilderness areas without permit. Use extreme caution around old mine workings. Never enter abandoned tunnels or shafts.
• Hikers should carry a compass and a topographic map. Established trails can be obscured by washes and animal routes. Park landscapes have few prominent features, disorienting even experienced backcountry hikers.
• Avoid camping in washes, which are subject to flash flooding, even from distant mountain cloudbursts.
• Archaeological sites and remains may not be disturbed in any way. This includes rock art, habitation sites, and cultural remains such as pottery vessels and sherds, projectile points, stone tools, and beads.

• Climbing within 50 feet of Native American rock art is prohibited.

Overnight Backpacking
Registration required at one of 12 backcountry boards. Check with rangers at entrance stations about current conditions and rules governing backcountry camping. A permit is required for horses. Call (760) 367-5545.

Campgrounds
Nine campgrounds, all with 14-day limit from September through May, and a 30-day limit from June through August. Open all year on a first-come, first-served basis. Fees for individuals and groups up to six: None to $10. Group camping (site maximums vary from 20 to 70) available at **Cottonwood, Indian Cove,** and **Sheep Pass** by reservation only. Call the National Parks Reservation Service (see p. 11). Fees from $10 to $30. Horses permitted at **Black Rock.**

Hotels, Motels, & Inns
(unless otherwise noted, rates are for 2 persons in a double room, high season)
In Twentynine Palms, CA 92277:
Best Western Gardens Motel 71487 Twentynine Palms Hwy. (800) 528-1234 or (760) 367-9141. 84 units, 12 with kitchenettes. $85. AC, pool, spa.
Motel 6 72562 Twentynine Palms Hwy. (800) 466-8356 or (760) 367-2833. 124 units. $50. AC, pool.
In Indio, CA 92201:
Quality Inn 43-505 Monroe St. (760) 347-4044. 62 units. $69-$99. AC, pool, spa.
Royal Plaza Inn 82-347 Hwy. 111. (800) 228-9559 or (760) 347-0911. 99 units. $69-$110. AC, pool, restaurant.
In Yucca Valley, Calif. 92284:
Oasis of Eden Inn & Suites 56377 Twentynine Palms Hwy. (800) 606-6686 or (760) 365-6321. 40 units. $70-$199. AC, pool, spa.
Yucca Inn 7500 Camino del Cielo. (760) 365-3311. 75 units. $49-$60. AC, pool, spa.

For other lodgings contact Twentynine Palms Chamber of Commerce, 6455 Mesquite Ave., Unit A, Twentynine Palms, CA 92277. (760) 367-3445.

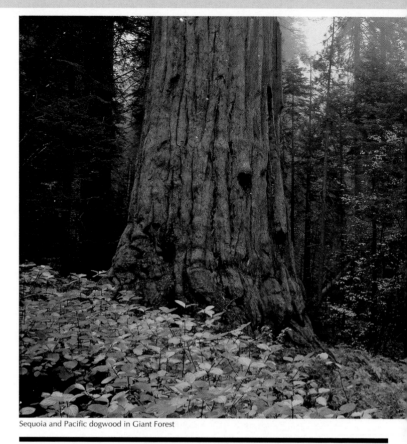

Sequoia and Pacific dogwood in Giant Forest

Sequoia & Kings Canyon

California

Sequoia established September 25, 1890; Kings Canyon established March 4, 1940

863,741 acres

Bigness—big trees and big canyons—inspired the separate founding of each of these parks. In 1943 Sequoia and Kings Canyon National Parks began to be jointly administered. The two contiguous parks form one superpark 66 miles long and 36 miles at its widest point.

Nearly every square mile of this vast park is wilderness. A backpacker here can hike to a spot that is farther from a road than any other place in the 48 contiguous states. But visitors can easily reach Sequoia's famed attraction, the Giant Forest of sequoias.

Relatively few visitors hike any of the parks' hundreds of miles of trails. Still, there are enough backpackers to worry officials, who protect the backcountry by regulating the number of people entering it.

Mount Whitney, at 14,494 feet the highest peak in the United States south of Alaska, rises at the border. Backpackers coming in from the east can get to Whitney in 1 or 2 days. From the park's western trailheads, backpackers reach it by a 70-mile, 8-day trek across the park's snow-swept, glacier-dotted heights.

Visitors are startled to learn that the smoke they sometimes see rises from "prescribed burning"—controlled fires deliberately set by park employees to help the sequoias by removing undergrowth. In the past, when the park fought all fires, brush and deadwood built up. This fueled fires that imperiled the sequoias, which resist flames at their bases but can die if fire attacks their crowns.

How to Get There

From Visalia (about 35 miles west), take Calif. 198 to Sequoia's Ash Mountain Entrance. From Fresno, take Calif. 180 to Kings Canyon's Big Stump Entrance. The only road entrance into the main part of Kings Canyon is a dead-end, summer-only extension of Calif. 180 into Cedar Grove. Airport: Fresno.

When to Go

Spring through fall is the best time for sequoia gazing. Generals Highway, which connects Sequoia and Kings Canyon, is open year-round except during heavy snows. From December to April, there is cross-country skiing and snowshoeing in the Giant Forest area and at Grant Grove.

How to Visit

The two immense parks challenge

anyone planning a 1-day visit. To appreciate the rugged splendor, you must hike a trail. No east-west road crosses either park. But a drive-in visitor, in a day, can see sequoias in **Giant Forest,** along the **Generals Highway,** and in **Grant Grove.** A quiet walk in a grove of sequoias will give you more than a drive to named trees, which are constantly surrounded by shutterbugs.

Stay long enough to explore both vast parks. Drive to Kings Canyon's beautiful valley, **Cedar Grove.** On another day visit **Crystal Cave** and climb **Moro Rock.** Hike in Sequoia's spectacular **Mineral King** area.

Giant Forest & Grant Grove

48 miles; a full day

From the **Ash Mountain Entrance,** on **Generals Highway,** drive 17 miles to **Giant Forest,** home of the **General Sherman Tree,** the world's largest tree. About 6 miles along the road from the Ash Mountain Entrance, stop to see the Indian exhibit at **Hospital Rock.** Indians lived here from prehistoric times until the 1870s, when the white man's diseases killed off the last of them. The Western Mono made flour from acorns—the most important staple food of California Indians. They crushed the acorns in small hollows gouged into streamside bedrock; you can see several such rock mortars at the exhibit.

The **Four Guardsmen,** a quartet of sequoias, stand as sentinels near the

Towering sequoia

Big Pine

To Bishop

168

395

INYO
NATIONAL
FOREST

Split Mt.
14,058 ft

Taboose Pass
11,400 ft
Bench Lake

Mt. Pinchot
13,495 ft

Rae Lakes

Independence

Charlotte Lake

395

INYO
NATIONAL
FOREST

To Lone
Pine

Tyndall Creek

To Lone
Pine

MOUNT
WHITNEY
14,494 ft

Crabtree   Mt. Muir
14,015 ft

Rock
Creek
Siberian Pass
10,950 ft

INYO
NATIONAL
FOREST

Kern Canyon

Kern

Pacific Crest Trail

entrance to Giant Forest. Trails radiate
from the star attraction, the General
Sherman Tree, about 2,100 years old,
274.9 feet tall, and 102.6 feet in circumference, with a volume of 52,500 cubic
feet. (In board feet, this is the equivalent of 119.3 miles of 1-by-12-inch
planks.) A 13-story building would fit
beneath its first large branch. The tree
was named by a pioneer cattleman
who had served in the Civil War under
Gen. William Tecumseh Sherman.

The easy 2-mile **Congress Trail** (the
name honors the institution that gave
legal protection to the sequoias) takes
1 to 2 hours and begins at the base of
the champion tree, where you can buy
a self-guiding pamphlet. At stops along
the way, you will see young sequoias
(a mere 140 or so years old); sequoias
scarred by fire but standing tall because
their bark, thick and lacking resin, protects them; and fallen sequoias, not
rotting because they contain tannin,
which helps them resist decay.

Return to Generals Highway and
begin the 30-mile drive to **Grant
Grove** in Kings Canyon by heading
northwest to Calif. 180. Turn east on
Calif. 180. On your right a road loops
in and out of Wilsonia, a private
community.

Just beyond the **Grant Grove Visitor
Center,** take the road on your left to
General Grant Tree Trail, a half-mile
loop leading to the **General Grant Tree**
(267.4 feet tall, 107.6 feet in circumference at ground). The name of the tree
recalls the original 1890 name of the
park, created to preserve General Grant
Grove. To counteract lumbering,
champions of the sequoias bought
more and more land to expand the
4-square-mile grove. To better understand the significance of the redwoods
and their ecological management
needs, visit the new **Giant Forest
Museum,** located in the 1928 building
designed by Gilbert Stanley Under-
wood (architect of the Ahwahnee).

On the trail are many giants saved
by the park, along with a reminder of
the years of casual havoc: **Centennial
Stump,** a sequoia cut down for exhibi-
tion at the 1875 Centennial in Philadel-
phia. Near the park entrance is **Big
Stump Trail** (1-mile loop), where
stumps, logs, downed trees, and a pile
of sawdust help you imagine the
sequoia logging of the past and where
regenerating trees grow into the giants
of the future.

Woods Creek near Rae Lakes

Drive back to the visitor center and head east on the steep, narrow, 2.5-mile road to **Panoramic Point** (no trailers or large vehicles allowed). From the parking lot, take the quarter-mile trail to the 7,520-foot ridge. Before you stretches the Sierra Nevada. A trailside diagram of the landscape names the mountains. You won't see Mount Whitney; the Great Western Divide blocks the view.

Cedar Grove

36 miles; a full day

Follow Calif. 180 for 30 miles north and east of Grant Grove, through Sequoia National Forest. The road winds into the canyon of the **South Fork Kings River.** Stop at **Junction View** to gaze down on a wild river flanked by sheer canyon walls glistening in the sun. The road dead-ends at **Cedar Grove,** a mile-deep valley. Scouring streams began the carving of the valley, which got its U-shape from subsequent glaciers that pushed into the canyon and widened the floor.

Incense-cedar, ponderosa pine, black oak, live oak, white fir, and sugar pine grow in the valley's flats. In the 1870s the area attracted stockmen as well as gold and silver prospectors. Even so, John Muir, who explored here in 1873, would still recognize this well-preserved high-country valley.

The **Cedar Grove Motor Nature Trail,** just beyond **Cedar Grove Village,** gives the drive-in visitor a tame tour on what had been a livestock trail. Better to park, get out, and walk, even for a short distance, to savor this beautiful hidden valley. The easy half-mile **River Trail** takes you from the South Fork Kings River to **Roaring River Falls.** Back at the parking lot you can return to your car or continue on for a hike along the curves of the river. Cross a suspension bridge and climb a slight rise for a view of the valley. Retrace your steps to the bridge and take the **Zumwalt Meadow Trail,** a 1-mile loop.

Crystal Cave

18 miles; a half day

The cave temperature is a constant 48°F, so bring a jacket. Tickets must be purchased at either the Lodgepole or Foothills Visitor Centers. Take the Generals Highway south from Lodgepole Visitor Center. Turn right down the rough, summer-only road (no trailers or large vehicles) to Crystal Cave. The twisting 9-mile trip consumes about 45 dusty minutes. From the parking lot you walk a paved, steep path along a canyon wall, down to the entrance. Don't expect multicolored lights or tales of goblins; the 1-hour tours, conducted from 11 a.m. to 4 p.m., introduce you to a cave that got its name from an unusual geological phenomenon. The cave is formed of marble—instead of limestone—that underground water slowly dissolved and then redeposited as dazzling stalactites, stalagmites, and columns.

Moro Rock

4.6 miles round-trip; a half day

Although you can drive to Moro Rock, a huge granite monolith, via the 2-mile **Moro Rock-Crescent Meadow Road** from Giant Forest Village, you get a better perception of its setting by hiking to it. Either way, try to be there at sunset when the view is spectacular. The 2-mile **Moro Rock Trail** begins near Giant Forest Museum and quickly leads you away from the throngs. About 1.3 miles along the trail, a short path veers off to **Hanging Rock,** a high granite stage for viewing Sierra Nevada scenery.

Return to the trail and continue to the base of Moro Rock. Here you start climbing a stone stairway of nearly 400 steps (and several welcome spots for resting). Your 300-foot ascent takes you to an elevation of 6,725 feet, about 4,000 feet above the canyon floor. From here you can look down on the tops of the sequoias you craned at from the ground. On clear days you can see the Coast Ranges, more than 100 miles west.

When you return from the summit, you can retrace your steps on the Moro Rock Trail or return to the Generals Highway via the 2.3-mile **Soldiers Trail,** named for the U.S. Cavalry troopers who patrolled the sequoias before the Park Service's rangers took over the task.

Mineral King

50 miles round-trip; at least a full day

Three miles north of the town of Three Rivers, near the Ash Mountain Entrance, is the sign for Mineral King, in 1978 Sequoia's last major addition. It was named in the 1870s by gold prospectors who gained little more than unfulfilled dreams from it. In the 1960s dreams of a ski resort also failed to come true because of public opposition.

Turn off Calif. 198 onto a narrow, twisting, 25-mile road. (One driver counted 29 turns in a single mile.) To avoid driving it twice in one grueling day, plan your schedule so that you'll be able to stay at least a night. But, if you must do it in a single day, start early. Mineral King is a hiker's paradise. And the road is the secret to the paradise's solitude. "The road is terrible," one grinning hiker said. "And we hope it stays that way."

During the summer, stop at the **Mineral King Ranger Station** and check to see whether a ranger-guided walk is scheduled that day. Or take a hike on your own. Get a map at the station, find a legal parking place, and select a trail. Remember that all trails here begin at altitudes of at least 7,500 feet and climb steeply. If you are not acclimated to the high elevations here, you may suffer altitude sickness.

A good hike for beginners just getting their legs in shape is **Eagle Lake Trail,** which starts at the Eagle-Mosquito Parking Area. This trail starts gently, then begins to get steep near **Spring Creek,** which sprouts from the mountainside. Every switchback treats visitors to an overlook with a stunning view. If you keep your eyes open, you may catch sight of marmots, which sometimes stand up and watch back, and tiny pikas, which whistle and scurry around. After a 2-mile climb, you reach the **Eagle Sink Holes,** where water disappears just as suddenly as the creek appeared. Here you can turn around and start down or continue up another 1.5 miles to **Eagle Lake,** a tarn.

Information & Activities

Headquarters
Ash Mountain, 47050 Generals Hwy.,
Three Rivers, CA 93271. Phone (559)
565-3341. www.nps.gov/seki

Seasons & Accessibility
Park open year-round. Roads to
Mineral King (Sequoia) and to
Cedar Grove (Kings Canyon) closed
winter; Generals Highway from
Lodgepole to Grant Grove may
close after heavy snowstorms;
also at night in winter. Call (559)
565-3341 for current weather and
road information.

Visitor & Information Centers
Sequoia: Lodgepole Visitor Center
and **Giant Forest Museum,** both in
the Giant Forest area; **Foothills Visitor
Center** in Ash Mountain, where Calif.
198 enters park; **Mineral King Ranger
Station** in south of park. Foothills open
daily all year; others open in winter,
reduced hours.
**Kings Canyon: Grant Grove Visitor
Center** open daily all year; **Cedar
Grove,** on Calif. 180, open daily in
summer. For visitor information call
(559) 565-3341.

Entrance Fees
$10 per vehicle per week, good for
multiple entries. $5 per person on bus,
foot, bicycle, motorcycle.

Facilities for Disabled
Visitor centers are wheelchair accessible, as are some trails in Grant Grove
and Giant Forest.

Things to Do
Free naturalist-led activities (many
offered in summer only): nature walks
and talks, night sky watches, children's
programs, evening programs, snowshoe walks. Also available, Crystal Cave
tours, nature center, fishing (license
needed), horseback trail rides, pack
trips, cross-country skiing.

Overnight Backpacking
Free permits required. Reservations
for specific trails and dates must
be made by mail. (Fee charged
for reservations.) A few permits
issued on departure day, first
come, first served. Information
(559) 565-3341.

Campgrounds
Sequoia: seven campgrounds, 14-day
limit mid-June to mid-September.
Lodgepole, Potwisha, and **South
Fork** open all year. Others open
spring to fall, depending on weather.
First come, first served, except
Lodgepole and **Dorst,** which require
reservations in advance through the
National Parks Reservation Service
(see p. 11) mid-May to mid-October.
Fees $6-$12 per night. Showers near
Lodgepole, closed in winter. RV sites
at Dorst, Lodgepole, and Potwisha; no
hookups. Food services available
in park.
Kings Canyon: seven campgrounds,
14-day summer limit. **Azalea** open
all year, others late April to mid-September. First come, first served. Fees
$14 per night. Showers nearby. Tent
and RV sites; no hookups. Reservations required for group campsites;
write Sunset/Canyon View Group
Sites, P.O. Box 926, Kings Canyon
National Park, CA 93633. Food services available in park.

Hotels, Motels, & Inns
*(unless otherwise noted, rates are for 2
persons in a double room, high season)*
INSIDE THE PARKS:
*For the following lodges in Sequoia,
call (888) 252-5757 :*
Bearpaw Meadow Camp Six group
tent cabins, central showers. $310,
includes meals. Mid-June to mid-Sept.
Wuksachi Village 102 units. $150-
$219. Restaurant, gift shop.
*For the following lodges in Kings
Canyon, call (559) 335-5500:*
Cedar Grove Lodge 21 units. $99. AC,
restaurant. May through October.
Grant Grove Lodge 24 lodge rooms,
$140; 8 bath cabins, $105; 27 rustic
cabins, $55-$60; 15 tent cabins, $45.
Restaurant.
Stoney Creek Lodge 11 units. $125.
Restaurant. Mid-May to mid-October.
OUTSIDE THE PARKS:
In Three Rivers, CA 93271:
Best Western Holiday Lodge 40105
Sierra Dr., P.O. Box 129. (559) 561-
4119. 54 units. $87. AC, pool.
Lazy J Ranch Motel 39625 Sierra Dr.
(800) 341-8000 or (559) 561-4449. 18
units, 7 with kitchenettes. $55. AC, pool.
The River Inn 45176 Sierra Dr. (559)
561-4367. 10 units. $59-$109. AC.

Excursions

Sequoia National Forest
Porterville, California

Thirty-eight groves of sequoias, including the largest tree in any national forest, are only part of the attractions. Four stretches of Wild and Scenic Rivers and six wilderness areas provide recreational challenges; part of the site has been declared a national monument. 1,123,100 acres. Hiking, boating, whitewater rafting, climbing, cycling, fishing, horseback riding, hunting, scenic drives, winter sports. 2,000-plus campsites, picnic areas, handicapped access. All year. Adjoins Sequoia and Kings Canyon NPs on south, west, north. (559) 784-1500.

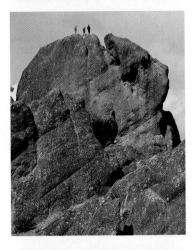

Pinnacles National Monument
Paicines, California

Rising abruptly from gentle hill country, the spires and crags of the Pinnacles formation are the remains of a volcanic mountain formed some 200 miles to the south. Pulled north and west by the San Andreas Rift, the Pinnacles are still in migration. Hiking trails, ranging from easy to extremely strenuous, take visitors from chaparral-covered slopes, through caves, to the high peaks. 24,154 acres. Climbing, picnic areas, handicapped access. Visitor center near east entrance off Calif. 25, about 130 miles west of Sequoia and Kings Canyon NPs. (831) 389-4485.

Inyo National Forest
Bishop, California

Inyo boasts Mount Whitney, at 14,494 feet the highest peak in the lower 48 states; the spectacular saline Mono Lake; and bristlecone pines, Earth's oldest living things. Also contains parts of seven wilderness areas, notably the John Muir and Ansel Adams areas. Two million acres. Hiking, boating, climbing, cycling, fishing, horseback riding, hunting, scenic drives, winter sports, water sports. 73 campgrounds, boat ramp, picnic areas. Open year-round; most campsites open May through October. Visitor center at Mammoth Lakes on Calif. 203. (760) 873-2400.

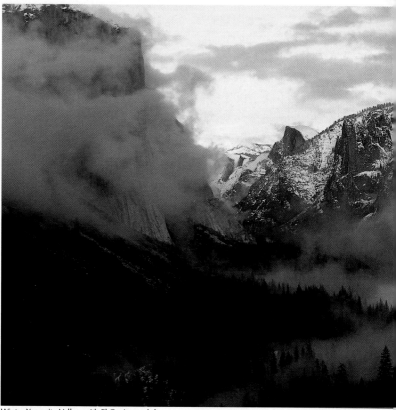

Wintry Yosemite Valley, with El Capitan at left

Yosemite

California

Established October 1, 1890

747,956 acres

In a high-country meadow two hikers crouch near the edge of a mirroring lake and watch a pika as it harvests blades of grass for a nest deep within a huge rock pile. When they resume walking, there is no other person in sight for as far as they can see. And on this sparkling summer's day, the view seems endless.

In the valley's crowded mall, families stroll by, eating ice cream, dodging bicycles. People pile in and out of buses. Shoppers hunt for souvenirs. Kids hang around a pizza place. Rock climbers, coils of rope slung over their shoulders, swap stories over beers on a patio. On this summer's day about 14,000 people are in Yosemite Village.

Both the solitude of the alpine ridge and the throngs of the valley are part of the experience when you visit Yosemite National Park. "No temple made with hands can compare with Yosemite," wrote naturalist John Muir, whose crusading led to the creation of the park. To this temple come 3.5 million visitors a year. And about 90 percent of them go to the valley, a mile-wide, 7-mile-long canyon cut by a river, then widened and deepened by glacial action. Walled by massive domes and soaring pinnacles, it covers about one percent of the park. In summer, the concentration of automobiles brings traffic jams and air pollution.

Beyond the valley, some 800 miles of marked trails offer hikers easy jaunts or grueling tests of endurance in the High Sierra wilderness. Even the casual visitor can explore this solitude without getting outfitted for a backpack expedition.

The park, roughly the size of Rhode Island, is a United Nations World Heritage site. Here, in five of the seven continental life zones, live the mule deer and chipmunks of the valley and the marmots and pikas of the heights; the brush rabbit and chaparral of the near desert; the dogwood and warblers of mid-elevation forests; the red fir and Jeffrey pine of mile-high forests; the dwarf willow and matted flowers of Yosemite's majestic mountains.

How to Get There

From Merced (about 70 miles away): Follow Calif. 140 to the Arch Rock Entrance. Also from the west: Take Calif. 120 to the Big Oak Flat Entrance.

From the south, via Fresno: Calif. 41 takes you to the South Entrance.

From the northeast, via Lee Vining: Follow Calif. 120 to the Tioga Pass Entrance (closed mid-November to late May, depending on weather).

Trains stop at Merced; check with Amtrak about connecting buses to Yosemite. Airports: Fresno and Merced.

When to Go

All-year park. Avoid holiday weekends. Expect filled campgrounds from June through August and some crowding in late spring and early fall. Be sure you have reserved accommodations before attempting an overnight visit. You will find skiing and other winter activities in the Badger Pass Ski Area from about Thanksgiving to mid-April.

How to Visit

When a visitor asked a Yosemite ranger what he would do if he had only a day to visit the park, the ranger answered, "I'd weep." If you must zip through this huge park in a day, begin with **Yosemite Valley.** But even a dawn-to-dusk, 1-day visit hardly allows enough time for more than a tour of the valley plus a look at one or two of the park's other major areas, such as the vistas from **Glacier Point** (in winter, road closed beyond the ski area) and the sequoias of the **Mariposa Grove.** As an alternative or on another day between late May and early November, take the High Sierra **Tioga Road** to explore the park's alpine country. Better still, stay long enough to get beyond the crowds and discover the sense of seclusion this great park can give you along one of its trails.

Yosemite Valley

12 miles; at least a half to full day

Don't add to the traffic congestion by driving the heavily used one-way valley roads. Park at one of the lots along the shuttle bus route and take the free bus, which loops through the east end of the valley. (See inset map on pp. 268-269.) You can also explore the valley on a rented bike or on foot. Or, buy a ticket for a 2-hour guided tram tour. (The open-air trams also venture out on moonlit nights and glide through the ghostly light that bathes the valley.)

If you're traveling by shuttle bus, get off at the **Valley Visitor Center** in **Yosemite Village,** where an award-winning film introduces Yosemite's history, grandeur, and geology. For an easy stroll in an oasis of quiet, look for **Cook's Meadow** just south of the visitor center. The trail begins at the west end of the mall; pick up a self-guiding

Yosemite Falls above meadows of cow parsnip

brochure. Deer and human sometimes encounter each other here. Keep your distance.

Walk around the nearby **Indian Village of Ahwahnee**, where exhibits and bark houses evoke the life of the valley's earlier dwellers. Visit the **Indian Cultural Exhibit** to see the baskets and other works of art produced by Yosemite area tribes.

At the bustling village shops you can find just about what you would find in any resort-town mall. But if you want to see the park, don't tarry here.

Get back on the bus and travel to the **Yosemite Falls** shuttle bus stop. The upper, middle, and lower falls form the highest waterfall in North America (2,425 feet) and the second highest in the world. A quarter-mile walk takes you to the base of **Lower Yosemite Fall.** If you have the stamina and another full day, take the strenuous 3.5-mile hike to **Upper Yosemite Fall,** where you will be rewarded with spectacular valley views away from the crowds. (Look for the trailhead behind the Camp 4 parking lot.)

Reboard the bus, and crane your neck for other scenic wonders. And get off when you want to absorb them; you will not have to wait long for another bus. On the 3,593-foot vertical wall of **El Capitan** you may spot the tiny figures of climbers. During their ascent, which may take days, they sleep in slings hanging from the cliff. After looping east you'll pass **Sentinel Rock** and then **Glacier Point,**

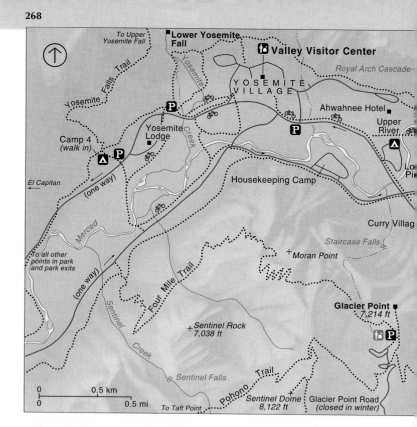

Map labels:
To Upper Yosemite Fall · Lower Yosemite Fall · Valley Visitor Center · Royal Arch Cascade · Yosemite Falls Trail · Yosemite Creek · YOSEMITE VILLAGE · Ahwahnee Hotel · Upper River · Camp 4 (walk in) · Yosemite Lodge · El Capitan · (one way) · Merced · Housekeeping Camp · Lo Pi · Curry Villag · To all other points in park and park exits · (one way) · Four Mile Trail · Staircase Falls · Moran Point · Sentinel Rock 7,038 ft · Sentinel Creek · Glacier Point 7,214 ft · Sentinel Falls · Pohono Trail · Sentinel Dome 8,122 ft · Glacier Point Road (closed in winter) · To Taft Point · 0 0.5 km · 0 0.5 mi

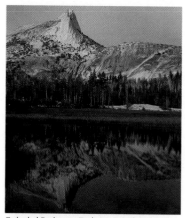

Cathedral Peak, near Tuolumne Meadows

Steller's jay

both giant granite blocks shaped by glaciers. (An arduous hike up **Four Mile Trail** takes you in 3 or 4 hours to Glacier Point's breathtaking vistas; for the trailhead, get off the bus at Yosemite Lodge and walk behind it to Southside Drive, then west a quarter mile to road marker V18.)

If you're still on the shuttle bus, alight at the stop near the **Happy Isles Nature Center.** After a walk around these two bridge-linked river islands, consider hiking the moderately strenuous 1.5-mile trail to the top of 317-foot **Vernal Fall.** From higher up this trail, you can also see **Nevada Fall** with its 594-foot cascade. Massive **Half Dome,** a cracked block of gray granite gnawed by a glacier, soars 4,733 feet above the valley floor, its sheer face dominating this part of the valley.

A gentle hike from the next shuttle bus stop takes you to lovely **Mirror Lake** a mile away; a 3-mile trail loops around it and above it. In spring and early summer, the lake's serene surface reflects stunning mountain scenery; during the sum-

Eroded granite atop Sentinel Dome

mer, most of its contents evaporate.

As the shuttle turns back toward Yosemite Village, you'll pass the **Royal Arches,** glacier-carved granite shells. You will see the full spectrum of Yosemite accommodations along the shuttle bus route: from tents, trailer hookups, and clusters of concrete shelters to comfortable lodges, cabins, and a luxury hotel—the Ahwahnee.

Glacier Point & Mariposa Grove

52 miles one way; a half to full day

Leave the valley by taking Calif. 41 (the Wawona Road) to the **Wawona Tunnel.** Park at the turnout at the tunnel's eastern end and walk over to the **Tunnel View Overlook** to see what has

Staghorn lichens on conifer

Wildflowers at Tuolumne Meadows

been called the most photographed vista on Earth. Spread before you is a granite panorama encompassing El Capitan, Half Dome, Sentinel Rock, **Cathedral Rocks,** and 620-foot **Bridalveil Fall,** in the late afternoon a scrim of shimmering rainbows. About 7 miles beyond the tunnel, turn left on the **Glacier Point Road** (in winter, closed beyond the ski area). The 16-mile road, flanked by fir-and-pine forests, ends in a parking lot. Walk about 300 yards to the first of several overlooks on Glacier Point, which thrusts 3,214 feet above the valley, providing an enormous stage for a scenic spectacular of lights and shadows. Mirror Lake lies below; Half Dome looms across; Vernal Fall and Nevada Fall hang like white tassels in the distance.

Return to the intersection of Calif. 41 and drive south 13 miles to **Wawona,** site of a hotel, golf course, and other facilities. Stop at the **Pioneer Yosemite History Center,** where, in summer, visitors enter restored buildings and chat about the past with costumed interpreters who portray such real people as a cavalry trooper, a 19th-century homesteader, and a mountaineer. From conversations with these players you learn Yosemite Valley's recent history, which, according to legend, began in 1851 when members of the Mariposa Battalion were tracking down Indians accused of raiding nearby trading posts. Foothill Miwok called Miwok living in the valley "*Yohemite,*" which means "some of them are killers." Thinking

that this was the Indians' name, the whites gave an approximation of it to the valley.

Word of the radiantly beautiful valley spread quickly, and the first tourists arrived in 1855. They were soon followed by homesteaders and hotelkeepers. Next came the nation's early conservationists, who campaigned to protect not only the valley but also a grove of giant sequoias.

Return to Calif. 41 and continue south. Near the **South Entrance** continue straight to Yosemite's other long-cherished feature, the **Mariposa Grove.** From early May to late October you can take a guided tram tour of the grove's giant sequoias ($11 adult, $5.50 child). Or, you can walk among them at any time of year.

On June 30, 1864, President Lincoln took time out from the Civil War to sign a bill granting both the valley and this grove to the State of California. Never before had a nation set aside land as a wilderness preserve. Yosemite became a national park in 1890, although not until 1906 did California formally give the original grants back to the federal government. More land was added in 1913, the year automobiles were again allowed in the park after a ban.

The best known of the grove's more than 200 giant sequoias is the **Grizzly Giant,** whose estimated age, 2,700 years, makes it one of the oldest living sequoias. A trail takes you past the **Fallen Monarch;** its shallow roots help explain why winds sometimes topple these giants. Another fallen star, the

Mule deer in Yosemite Valley

Wawona Tunnel Tree, recalls another era. The living sequoia, gutted in 1881 to make a drive-through tree for horse-drawn wagons, became a photogenic attraction for generations of automobile travelers. The tree toppled in 1969. The decision not to cut a hole in another tree symbolized the dawning of an ecologically enlightened age.

Tioga Road & Tuolumne Meadows

124 miles round-trip; at least a full day

Take the **Big Oak Flat Road,** a modern version of an old mining town road, west out of the valley for 9 miles to 6,200-foot **Crane Flat** (a local term for "meadow"). Turn right onto **Tioga Road,** which climbs into an alpine world of snowy peaks, crystal lakes, wind-tousled meadows, and relatively few people. The road (closed in winter) crosses the park. Even in July you may see snow alongside the road. Stop at the frequent turnouts for magnifi-

cent views and interpretive signs that explain the geology behind the splendor. Gauge your time and gasoline. Beyond Crane Flat, the nearest gas station on this winding, climbing mountain road is 1 mile east of the **Tuolumne Meadows Visitor Center,** 55 miles from **Yosemite Valley.**

At the visitor center await **Tuolumne Meadows,** which, millions of years ago, were under a sea of ice more than 2,000 feet deep. Wildflowers— among them Jeffrey shooting stars, Lewis paintbrushes, monkeyflowers, and marsh marigolds—carpet this High Sierra realm in spring and summer. Trails of varying difficulty branch out here and elsewhere along the road. Some trails link five commercially run High Sierra camps with showers and dining halls. (Reservations required. See **Information & Activities** p. 272.) The camps are spaced 8 to 10 miles apart.

The road climbs to 9,945-foot **Tioga Pass,** the highest automobile pass in California, at the park's eastern boundary. At a trailhead here you can take a half-day alpine hike that rewards you with glimpses of both beauty and history. The 2.5-mile trail climbs sharply from 9,945 feet to about 10,500, then descends to **Middle Gaylor Lake,** a gem set in a broad meadow prowled by marmots and Belding ground squirrels. The trail again winds upward, first to **Upper Gaylor Lake,** then to a surprise: the ruins of a stone cabin, rusting bits of machinery, and half-filled shafts—relics of a failed 19th-century silver mine.

Information & Activities

Headquarters
P.O. Box 577, Yosemite National Park, CA 95389. Phone (209) 372-0200. www.nps.gov/yose

Seasons & Accessibility
Park open year-round. Tioga (Calif. 120 east) and Glacier Point Roads closed by snow from about mid-November to late May. Call (209) 372-0200 for recorded conditions. In winter, call (209) 372-1000 for Badger Pass ski information.

Free shuttle buses operate in the valley year-round and at Wawona and Tuolumne Meadows in summer.

Visitor & Information Centers
Valley Visitor Center open all year. **Tuolumne Meadows Visitor Center** near Tioga Pass Entrance open summer only. Information also available at **Happy Isles Nature Center**, in valley, and at **Big Oak Flat Entrance** on Calif. 120 at western edge of park, both open spring through fall; and at **Wawona Information Station**, open summer through fall. For information call (209) 372-0200.

Entrance Fee
$20 per car per week.

Pets
Not permitted in buildings, backcountry, or trails.

Facilities for Disabled
Visitor centers, the nature and art centers, and some trails are wheelchair accessible. Free brochure.

Things to Do
Free naturalist-led activities: day and evening walks and talks, hikes, camera walks, children's and evening programs, living history; Indian cultural interpretation. Also, auto tape tours, bus and tram tours, films, plays, concerts, art and photography classes, museums, horseback riding—call (209) 372-8348—climbing, fishing, swimming, ice skating, downhill and cross-country skiing.

Overnight Backpacking
Free permit required; issued first come, first served; apply up to 24 hours in advance of trip to a park wilderness permit station. Advance reservations available by mail ($5 service fee); write wilderness office at park address. Call (209) 372-0200 for more information.

Campgrounds
Thirteen campgrounds; in summer, 7- day to 14-day limits; other times some have 30-day limit. Four open all year; others open mid-spring to mid-fall or summer only. Reservations through the National Parks Reservation Service (see p. 11) required year-round for all in the valley, except Camp 4, for **Hodg-don Meadow** spring through fall, and for **Crane Flat** and half of **Tuolumne Meadows** in summer. Fees $5-$18 per night. Most have RV sites, without hookups. Four group campgrounds; reserve through the National Parks Reservation Service.

Hotels, Motels, & Inns
(unless otherwise noted, rates are for 2 persons in a double room, high season)
INSIDE THE PARK:
Yosemite Concession Services Corp., 5410 E. Home Ave., Fresno, CA 93727, operates the following accommodations. Reservations: (559) 252-4848 or online at yosemitepark.com.
The Ahwahnee (Yosemite Valley) 123 units. $348. AC, pool, restaurant. **Curry Village** (Yosemite Valley) 18 rooms; 80 cabins; 427 tent-cabins. $40-$100. Pool, restaurant. **High Sierra Camps** 5 camps with tent-cabins. Accessible by hiking trail only. Guided trips available. $109 per person includes breakfast, dinner. Late June to Labor Day. Reserve by mail Sept. through Nov. **Tuolumne Meadows Lodge** (8,600 feet, at Tuolumne Meadows) 69 tent-cabins, central showers. $59. Restaurant. Open summer. **Wawona Hotel** (Calif. 41, 27 miles south of valley) (209) 375-6556. 104 rooms, 50 private baths. $101-$161. Pool, restaurant. Open all year. **White Wolf Lodge** (Tioga Rd.) 4 cabins, private baths; 24 tent-cabins, central bath. $55-$88. Restaurant. Open summer. **Yosemite Lodge** (Yosemite Valley) 245 rooms. $143. Pool, restaurant. **Redwoods In Yosemite** (Chilnualna Falls Rd.) P.O. Box 2085, Wawona Station, CA 95389. (209) 375-6666. 125 units with kitchens. $145-$570.

Excursions

Stanislaus National Forest
Sonora, California

This High Sierra forest offers an array of recreational activities—from white-water rafting on the Wild and Scenic Tuolumne River to trout fishing on timbered Alpine Lake. Contains parts of three wilderness areas. 898,322 acres. Hiking, boating, fishing, horseback riding, hunting, off-road-vehicle routes, scenic drives, winter sports, water sports. 1,143 campsites, boat ramp. Open all year; backcountry open June-Oct. (weather permitting). Most campsites open May-Oct. Adjoins Yosemite NP on north and east. Information at office at 19777 Greenley Rd. (off Calif. 108) in Sonora. (209) 532-3671.

Devils Postpile National Monument
Mammoth Lakes, California

Surrounded by the Inyo National Forest, this monument boasts a spectacular formation of basalt columns 60 feet high, which were born of the fire of volcanic eruptions and carved by the ice of overriding glaciers. At Rainbow Falls, water plunges 101 feet over a rhyodacite cliff. 798 acres. Hiking, fishing, shuttle bus. 21 campsites. Open mid-June to mid-October. Off Calif. 203 about 40 miles from Yosemite NP. Fee. (760) 934-2289. Access through Inyo NF, (760) 924-5500.

Sierra National Forest
Mariposa, California

Like the Stanislaus NF to the north, Sierra offers both rugged backcountry and developed recreational facilities. Contains parts of five wilderness areas, a stretch of white water on the Kings River, groves of giant sequoias, and the mountain-ringed Mammoth Pool Reservoir. 1,303,037 acres. Hiking, boating, bicycling, fishing, horseback riding, hunting, picnic areas, water sports, winter sports. 1,500 campsites, food services, boat ramp, handicapped access. Open all year; some backcountry areas closed in winter. Most campsites open May through Oct. Adjoins Yosemite NP. Office at 1600 Toll House Rd. in Clovis. (559) 297-0706.

Preceding pages: Aspens, Rocky Mountains

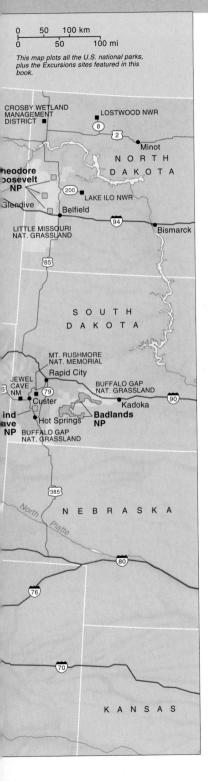

The Rocky Mountains

Craggy peaks capped by glimmering glaciers, fields run riot with wild-flowers, lakes as smooth and blue as a summer sky—these images from the Rocky Mountains epitomize for many just what a national park should look like. Not surprisingly, four of the Rockies' parks rank among the country's most visited.

Yet this region offers more than mountains, since the forces that created the peaks contoured neighboring land-scapes as well. The Black Hills of South Dakota uplifted along with the Rocky Mountains some 70 million years ago, cracking as they buckled upward. Enlarged by acidic groundwater, the cracks eventually produced the numer-ous underground passageways of Wind Cave. Streams flowing from the young Rockies also laid down the colorful mud that rivers would later carve into the buttes and gorges of the Dakota badlands, showcased in Badlands and Theodore Roosevelt National Parks.

The Rockies' parks and forests pre-serve the spirit of America's western frontier not only in their rugged scenery, but also in their historic ranches and ghost towns, and in their abundance of wildlife. Yellowstone and Waterton-Glacier—together with their surround-ing public lands—remain a stronghold of the grizzly bear. In some of the parks visitors can watch elk, bighorn sheep, mule deer, and remnants of the great bison herds that once thundered across the Great Plains.

Rockies parks provide case studies in how wilderness manages itself. In Yellowstone, for instance, the visitor can get excellent glimpses of natural recovery in the wake of forest fires. Less encouraging are the real estate development and plans for industry on the fringes of some parks. Such activities can shrink the habitats of wide-roaming animals, endangering their future.

The Rocky Mountain region invites the visitor to experience peaks along the Continental Divide, plus geysers, prairies, caverns, badlands, sand dunes—and lots of driving. Count on a drive of 520 miles from Rocky Mountain National Park to Grand Teton and nearly 400 miles from Yellowstone to Waterton-Glacier.

Badlands, feared by early pioneers, dwarfing a car headed west through the North Unit

Badlands

South Dakota

Established November 10, 1978

244,300 acres

They call it The Wall. It extends for a hundred miles through the dry plains of South Dakota—a huge natural barrier ridging the landscape, sculptured into fantastic pinnacles and tortuous gullies by the forces of water. Those who pass through the upper prairie a few miles north might not even know it exists. Those who traverse the lower prairie to the south, however, can't miss it; it rises above them like a city skyline in ruins, petrified.

The Badlands Wall, much of which is preserved within the boundaries of Badlands National Park, may not conform to everyone's idea of beauty, but nobody can deny its theatricality. It's been compared to an enormous stage set—colorful, dramatic, and not

quite real. Water, the main player on this stage, has been carving away at the cliffs for the past half million years or so, and it carves away an entire inch or more in some places each year. But there have been other players, too. Beasts with names like titanothere and archaeotherium once roamed here; their fossilized bones can be found by the hundreds. And today the Badlands Wall serves as a backdrop for bison, pronghorn, and bighorn sheep, as well as the million human visitors who pass through the park every year.

A national monument since 1939, Badlands acquired the South Unit in 1976, adding yet another dimension to the drama. This large stretch of land belongs to the Oglala, and one of their most sacred places is now preserved within it. It was here, on Stronghold Table, that the final Ghost

Make sure to take advantage of the informative nature trails. For those with a second day and a pioneering spirit, a trip to the park's undeveloped **South Unit** can be rewarding; don't fail to check with rangers about road conditions before going.

North Unit: Badlands Loop

32 or 89 miles; a half day or full day

Enter the park at the **Northeast Entrance** on S. Dak. 240 and stop at the **Big Badlands Overlook** for your first, but by no means best, view of **The Wall** from above. Before you are the characteristic tiered cliffs of the badlands, dropping precipitously to the lower prairie, where the **White River** meanders between a fringe of cottonwood trees.

Stop next at the **Windows Overlook,** which serves as the trailhead for three short nature trails—each of which is highlighted by exhibits and/or wayfinding markers. While these trails may sound like the components of an architectural tour, they are actually brief forays into the Badlands Wall. The **Door Trail** (0.75-mile round-trip, boardwalk) passes through a narrow opening in The Wall into a jumble of barren, eroded hills reminiscent of the lunar surface. The **Window Trail** (quarter-mile round-trip, paved) leads to a natural window overlooking a deeply cut canyon. And the **Notch Trail** (1.5 miles round-trip, very rough) leads up a ladder and along the side of a gully to a break in The Wall, where you can look out over prairie and badlands, the White River, and the Pine Ridge Reservation on the plain down below.

Back in the car, a short drive brings you to the head of the **Cliff Shelf Nature Trail** (trail guide available at trailhead). This half-mile, steep loop takes you through a fascinating microenvironment in the badlands. Many years ago, a giant block of stone fell from the surrounding cliffs, creating this relatively flat shelf. The impact of the fall compacted the stone, making it less porous and allowing water to collect here. The resulting vegetation makes this place a delightful oasis in the otherwise barren wall. You can see mule deer browsing at dawn or dusk, and

Dance took place in 1890, just a few weeks before more than 150 Lakota were massacred at Wounded Knee, 25 miles south.

How to Get There

The park is about 3 miles south of I-90 at S. Dak. 240, 75 miles east of Rapid City and 27 miles west of Kadoka. Airport: Rapid City Regional.

When to Go

All-year park. Summer is the most popular season, though daytime temperatures may top 100°F. Spring and fall are usually pleasant, with moderate temperatures and fewer crowds. Winters can be bitter cold, but snow accumulations are rarely a problem in this arid climate.

How to Visit

The 30-mile **Badlands Loop** provides a rich eyeful of classic badlands for a 1-day **North Unit** visit (a shorter loop can be devised as described below).

↑

🚻 Ranger Station

🔺 Campground

🚶 Self-guiding Trail

- - - Unpaved Road

-·-·- Primitive Road (passable only when dry)

········· Trail

0   5   10 km
0   5   10 mi

To Rapid City

Rapid Creek

QUINN TABLE

Beaver Creek

44

Bear Creek

590

🔺 Sage Creek

Scenic

NORTH UNIT

44

To Hermosa

BUFFALO GAP NATIONAL GRASSLAND

Cheyenne

589

SHEEP MOUNTAIN TABLE

To Buffalo Gap

40

Red Shirt

RED SHIRT TABLE

BLINDMAN TABLE

Battle Creek

Cedar Creek

41

PLENTY STAR TABLE

SOUTH UNIT

STRONGHOLD TABLE

GALIGO TABLE

PINE RIDGE INDIAN RESERVATION

27

Cottonwood Creek

White River Visitor Center

White River

CUNY TABLE

2

2

33 27

To Wounded Knee

flamboyant magpies careening across the sky anytime.

Stop next at the **Ben Reifel Visitor Center,** where a video and various exhibits provide a good introduction to the park's history and geology. From this point, the road descends to the lower prairie for a brief stretch and then begins a gradual, stunning climb back up the Badlands Wall. The **Fossil Exhibit Trail** takes you on a quarter-mile paved walk through an area dense with fossils. Copies of some are displayed at trailside under clear plastic domes.

The road then continues level for 15 miles, punctuated by a dozen or so pullouts; each offers a slightly different perspective on the knife-sharp ridges, twisted canyons, and multicolored hills

that characterize this broken terrain. Particularly spectacular among these are the **Yellow Mounds** and **Pinnacles Overlooks.**

If you're short of time, exit the park at this point and rejoin the interstate at the town of Wall. Otherwise make a left turn onto Sage Creek Rim Road and continue along the **Sage Creek Wilderness.** This is excellent wildlife country; bison and pronghorn are numerous, and the road passes a town of those always entertaining prairie dogs. Longer hikes into the wilderness area start at the primitive campground about a mile off the road near the park's western boundary.

Beyond the campground turnoff, the road leaves the park. To complete the

Bison grazing on open prairie

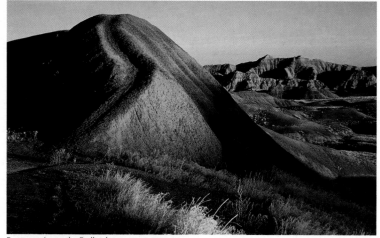

Frosty sunrise on the Badlands

Male pronghorn, Badlands denizen

loop, continue along unpaved County Road 590 and make a left (south) onto S. Dak. 44. If you're heading toward Rapid City, turn right; this stretch takes you through beautiful **Cheyenne River Valley** prairie and gives you views of the Black Hills. The highway goes through Scenic, the turnoff for the **South Unit,** if you want to continue directly there.

South Unit Drive

about 54 miles; at least a half day

The South Unit is almost entirely undeveloped, so exploring it by car will involve backtracking, driving on rough dirt roads, and generally putting a lot of wear and tear on your vehicle. For your safety, be sure to check with a ranger before setting out.

Begin at the town of **Scenic,** with its automobile graveyard and shanty-like saloon, and head south on County Road 589 for 4 miles. The turnoff for **Sheep Mountain Table** is marked.

Follow the road across the flats and up a seemingly impregnable cliff to a grass-topped table dotted with yuccas. If you go on to the juniper grove at the road's end, you can stand on a finger of high land and be almost surrounded by a stunning assortment of rock spires and pinnacles—perhaps the park's best view.

Return to the paved road and continue south for 16 miles until you arrive at the **White River Visitor Center** (open only in summer). It offers exhibits on Indian culture and a videotape on the Oglala. Here you can also get detailed directions to the many other sites worth visiting in the South Unit.

A visit to the **Stronghold Table** will either be a disappointment or the emotional culmination of your visit, depending on your perspective and imagination. Getting there involves driving some extremely rutted tracks through lonely grasslands, where you will probably get lost (bring along a topographical map). It also involves opening and closing many gates. The reward for this effort? An unspectacular view, but the chance to stand in the place where, in December 1890, a group of Sioux danced the Ghost Dance for the last time. In this impassioned ritual, converts fell into hypnotic trances, "died," and envisioned the paradise soon to come, sweeping the white man from the land and repopulating it with bison, elk, and pronghorn. If you go there, keep in mind that for Indians this is a sacred place.

Information & Activities

Headquarters
Interior, SD 57750. Phone (605) 433-5361. www.nps.gov/badl

Seasons & Accessibility
Park open year-round. Snowstorms may block roads temporarily in winter. Call park headquarters to check on current road and weather conditions and accessibility to the undeveloped South Unit.

Visitor & Information Centers
Ben Reifel Visitor Center, in the North Unit, open daily all year.
White River Visitor Center, in the South Unit, open only in summer.

Entrance Fee
$10 per car; $20 annual.

Pets
Permitted on leashes except in Sage Creek Wilderness and on trails.

Facilities for Disabled
Visitor centers and some trails are wheelchair accessible. Free brochure available.

Things to Do
Free naturalist-led activities during summer: nature walks and hikes, evening programs, night walks, fossil demonstrations. Also available, interpretive exhibits and audiovisual programs, hiking, wildlife watching.

Special Advisories
• Prairie rattlesnakes and cactuses live here: Watch where you step when walking.
• Bison are unpredictable and can be dangerous: Keep your distance.
• Be prepared for sudden changes in weather and severe thunderstorms in summer. Check weather conditions by contacting headquarters or a visitor center before you hike.

Overnight Backpacking
No permit required; ask a ranger for advisories.

Campgrounds
Two campgrounds, both with a 14-day limit. **Cedar Pass** and **Sage Creek** rarely fill up and are open all year, first come, first served. (Heavy snows may close them in winter.) Cedar Pass is $10 in summer, with water; $8 in winter, without water; Sage Creek is free year-round, without water. No showers. Tent and RV sites; no hookups.
Cedar Pass Group Campground, reservations accepted Memorial Day to Labor Day; campsites $2 per person, $20 minimum; contact park headquarters. Food service in park.

Hotels, Motels, & Inns
(unless otherwise noted, rates are for 2 persons in a double room, high season)
INSIDE THE PARK:
Cedar Pass Lodge (on S. Dak. 240 near visitor center) P.O. Box 5, Interior, SD 57750. (605) 433-5460. 24 cabins. $53. AC, restaurant. Open mid-April through October.
OUTSIDE THE PARK:
In Interior, SD 57750:
Badlands Inn (half mile from park entrance) P.O. Box 5. (605) 433-5401. 24 units. $60. AC, pool. Open mid-May to Labor Day.
In Wall, SD 57790:
Best Western Plains Motel (1 block off I-90) 712 Glenn St., P.O. Box 393. (800) 528-1234 or (605) 279-2145. 74 units. $75-$95. AC, pool. Open March through November.
Hitching Post Motel Tenth Ave., P.O. Box 76. (888) 279-2233 or (605) 279-2133. 30 units. $35-$110. AC, pool. Open May through October.
Kings Inn Motel 608 Main St. (800) 782-2613 or (605) 279-2178. 26 units. $60. AC.
Knights Inn South Blvd., P.O. Box 424. (800) 782-9402 or (605) 279-2127. 47 units. $56. AC, pool.
Walls Econolodge 804 Glenn St., P.O. Box 426. (800) 341-8000 or (605) 279-2121. 49 units. $100. AC, pool. Open May through October.

For additional accommodations contact the Wall Chamber of Commerce, P.O. Box 527, Wall, SD 57790. (605) 279-2665.

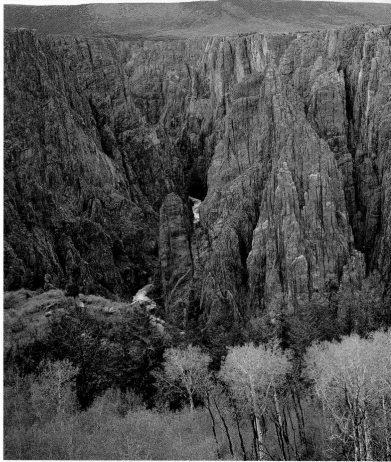

Aspens above the Gunnison River, along the Oak Flat Trail

Black Canyon of the Gunnison

Colorado

Established October 21, 1999

30,385 acres

Sheer walls of dark gray stone rise more than 2,600 feet above the swift and turbulent Gunnison River to create one of the most dramatic canyons in the country. Deeper than it is wide in some places, this great slit in the Earth is so narrow that sunlight penetrates to the bottom only at midday. The park protects the deepest, most thrilling 14 miles of the gorge, about 75 miles upstream of the Gunnison's junction with the Colorado River.

Imagine chiseling two parallel walls of hard gneiss and schist running the length of Manhattan and standing higher than two Empire State Buildings stacked atop one another, with water as your only tool. At the inconceivable rate of one inch per century, it would take all of human history just to cut through five feet of rock. What you see from the rim is the product of two million years of patient work.

The metamorphic rocks exposed at the bottom of the canyon are nearly two billion years old, dating from the Precambrian or oldest era of the Earth. Here and there swirling pink veins of igneous pegmatite shoot

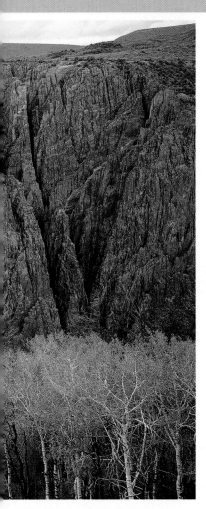

further tamed the Gunnison, but the canyon and its section of river remain wild.

Rim drives and hikes offer plenty of opportunities for peering into the magnificent canyon and marveling at its cliffs and towers of stone. Ravens, golden eagles, and peregrine falcons soar the great gulf of air out in front. On top grows a thick forest of Gambel oak and serviceberry, which provide cover for mule deer and black bear, while farther down the canyon Douglas-firs thrive in the shade, and cottonwoods and box elders find footholds along the river.

How to Get There

The South Rim is located 15 miles northeast of Montrose, via US 50 and Colo. 347. The North Rim is 80 miles by car from the South Rim, via US 50W and Colo. 92. Turn south off Colo. 92 onto the 15-mile North Rim Road, the first half of which is paved. Airports: Montrose and Gunnison.

When to Go

Summer is the most popular time to visit. But be prepared to perspire if you hike at midday on exposed trails, and bring lots of water. Crisp days in late spring and early fall make for excellent walks. Winter affords opportunities for backcountry camp-

through the walls, livening up the canyon's somber appearance.

Indians and white explorers generally avoided the formidable canyon up through the 19th century. In 1900, five men attempted to run the river in wooden boats to survey it as a possible source of irrigation for the Uncompahgre Valley. After a month, with their boats in splinters and their supplies gone, they gave up. But the next year two men ran it in nine days on rubber air mattresses. A water diversion tunnel was soon in the works; the four-year project, completed in 1909, resulted in a 6-mile-long tunnel through rock, clay, and sand. The labor was so grueling and dangerous that the average period of employment was only two weeks. Today, three dams upstream have

Gnarled juniper trunk

ing, cross-country skiing, and snow-shoeing. With the rim at 8,000 feet above sea level, winter can set in as early as November and last until April. Snow closes vehicle access to the North Rim; the South Rim road stays open as far as the second overlook year-round.

How to Visit

You can spend most of a day driving the 7-mile (one-way) **South Rim,** exploring its 5 or so miles of trails. Reserve the afternoon, or a second day, for a walk down to the canyon floor. If you have more time, visit the **North Rim** and its 5-mile (unpaved) drive.

South Rim

Rim Drive, 7 miles one way; 2 to 3 hours

With a dozen scenic overlooks and several short trails, this dramatic drive offers plenty of topside angles on the canyon and river. The first overlook, **Tomichi Point,** allows access to the **Rim Rock Trail,** which runs north-south for about a mile between the campground and the visitor center. This trail gives you fine views of the vertiginous walls of the eastern part of the canyon and the glinting ribbon of water sluicing down its middle. You walk through a scrubby forest of Gambel oak and sagebrush, studded with pinyon pine and juniper. The latter has dark purple berries and a cedary look and smell. Breathe in the refreshing air; look for tracks of elk, bobcat, mountain lion, and other rim dwellers; and listen for the scold of Steller's jays.

Make a 2-mile loop by following the **Uplands Trail** across the road. Continue up through scrub oak forest before walking past the visitor center and rejoining the Rim Rock Trail. At the **visitor center,** exhibits on the park's geology, history, flora, and fauna will help get you started.

Just outside the visitor center you can take the invigorating **Oak Flat Trail,** which makes a loop of about 2 miles and gets you a little way below the rim. Head west, then turn right at the River Access sign and dip into a grove of aspens. At the next junction, turn left and wind through a thicket of scrub oak to an outcrop with a good view. Circle back through a forest of aspen and Douglas-fir.

One of the shortest ways to the

Ranger Station
Campground
- - - Unpaved Road
.... Hiking Trail

0   1   2 km
0   1   2 mi

canyon floor is the **Gunnison Route,** off the Oak Flat Trail. It's a mere mile to the river, but it's a tough one—even for those in good shape, the walk down takes at least an hour. Since most of the canyon is a designated wilderness, hikers end up following drainage gullies, which plunge 1,800 vertical feet over scree slopes littered with big rocks. To avoid ankle injuries in some places, crouch and slide; a mounted 80-foot-long chain helps out on one stretch, but the rest is a wild free-for-all. At the bottom, rest and massage your legs, staring up at the spectacular stonework all around. The walk back up—at times a hand-over-hand pull—is harder than the downhill.

Back on the road, continue driving northwest. The aptly named **Pulpit Rock** offers a terrific long view of the river knifing its way through the canyon. A walk out to **Chasm View** takes you to within about 1,100 feet of the North Rim, on the opposite side of the canyon. At this point, the canyon's 1,800-foot depth exceeds its width, and it looks extremely narrow. But the narrowness is a result of the river's precipitous angle and its high volume. You're left with a sense of something newly created, which in geological terms is true.

The road now bends southwest. Several pull-offs provide views of the magnificent **Painted Wall,** a 2,250-foot sheer cliff decorated with stripes and flourishes of pink and white crystalline pegmatite, an extrusion of magma that seeped into cracks and hardened. Take the **Cedar Point Nature Trail,** an easy 0.6-mile out-and-back, to views of the

wall, the river, and islands of stone rising from the canyon depths.

Drive on to **High Point,** the end of the road and, at 8,289 feet, the highest point on the rim. From here it is a dizzying 2,689-foot drop to the river. You can take a 1.5-mile round-trip walk out to **Warner Point** for exquisite canyon views to the north. Turning to the south you can see the verdant farmlands of the Uncompahgre Valley irrigated by water diverted from the canyon's own Gunnison River. Beyond rise the San Juan Mountains. The trail meanders among pinyon pine, juniper, mountain mahogany, and white-flowering serviceberry. Other plants scattered about include Fendler bush, mule's ear, lupine, and scarlet gilia, the latter bearing lovely tubular flowers.

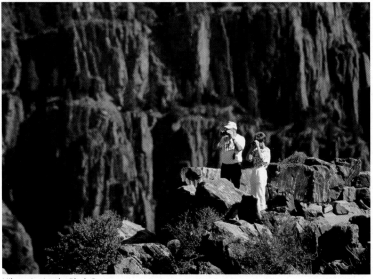

Hikers viewing the Black Canyon

North Rim

*Rim Drive (unpaved) 5 miles
one way; 2 to 3 hours*

While it is only 1,100 feet from one side of the canyon to the other, you must endure an 80-mile drive to reach the North Rim from the South Rim—the last several miles of it unpaved along North Rim Road. You can also reach the North Rim from the east side—a 90-mile drive on US 50 and Colo. 92 thru the Curecanti National Recreation Area. On the North Rim, you'll find yourself in a remote and awesome wilderness where the canyon walls plunge nearly vertically.

Whichever way you come, leave Colo. 92 at North Rim Road and follow it to the end. Turn right and drive to the ranger station, where one of the finest hikes in the park begins. The **North Vista Trail** wanders in and out of scrub forest along the rim for 1.5 miles. Detour at **Exclamation Point** for a jaw-dropping look into the canyon's depths. Turn back around, or continue 2 more miles to trail's end on Green Mountain. This difficult section climbs from 7,702 feet to 8,563 feet. Here stirring panoramas take in Grand Mesa and the Uncompahgre Plateau to the west, the West Elk Mountains to the north, and, in the south, the San Juans.

Once back at the ranger station, drive about a mile south and get out for the short **Chasm View Nature Trail,** which meanders through a pinyon-juniper forest and comes out at two stunning overlooks. White-throated swifts and violet-green swallows dart from cliffside nests. The southern 4 miles of the drive zigzag along the canyon's rim. At **Balanced Rock View** and **Kneeling Camel View,** near the end of the drive, steep unmarked trails wind down side canyons to the river.

Practical Information

Headquarters
102 Elk Creek, Gunnison, CO 81230. Phone (970) 641-2337. www.nps.gov/blca

Seasons & Accessibility
South Rim open daily, limited access in winter; North Rim Road and Ranger Station closed in winter. Contact park for current information.

Visitor & Information Centers
Visitor center open daily except holidays in winter. **North Rim Ranger Station** open in summer only.

Entrance Fees
$7 per vehicle per week; yearly fee $15.

Pets
Pets allowed in park on leash; not allowed on trails or in backcountry.

Facilities for Disabled

South Rim: visitor center, comfort stations, 2 camping sites; and Tomichi Point, Chasm View, and Sunset View overlooks. **North Rim:** Balanced Rock overlook accessible.

Things to do

Free naturalist-led activities. Exhibits, scenic drives, hiking, fishing, kayaking, rock climbing, winter activities. Contact park headquarters for a list of concessioners.

Special Advisory

● Permits required for all inner canyon routes; available at visitor center and North Rim Ranger Station.

Overnight Backpacking

Backcountry permits required. Wood fires prohibited; use camp stoves only.

Campgrounds

South Rim: 102 sites; **North Rim:** 13 sites. Auto campgrounds $10 per night. All sites first come, first served, usually available. Vault toilets, limited water, no hookups.

For accommodations contact the Montrose Visitors & Convention Bureau. (800) 873-0244 or (970) 240-1414; and the Gunnison County Chamber of Commerce. (970) 641-1501.

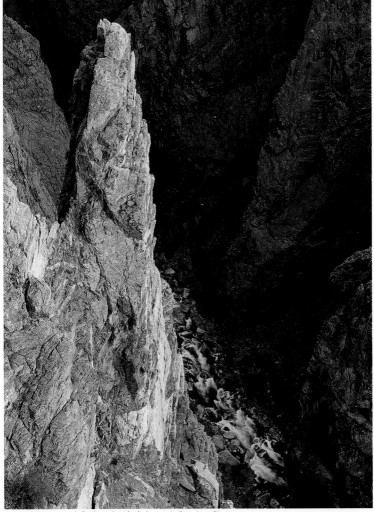

Precambrian-era rock flanking the Black Canyon's Gunnison River

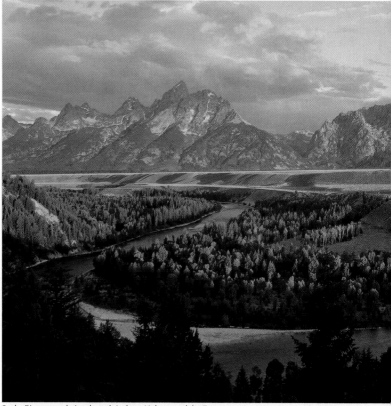

Snake River meandering through Jackson Hole toward the Tetons

Grand Teton

Wyoming

Established February 26, 1929

309,994 acres

The peaks of the Teton Range, regal and imposing as they stand nearly 7,000 feet above the valley floor, make one of the boldest geologic statements in the Rockies. Unencumbered by foothills, they rise through steep coniferous forest into alpine meadows strewn with wildflowers, past blue and white glaciers to naked granite pinnacles. The Grand, Middle, and South Tetons form the heart of the range. But their neighbors, especially Mount Owen, Teewinot Mountain, and Mount Moran, are no less spectacular.

A string of jewel-like lakes, fed by mountain streams, are set tightly against the steep foot of the mountains. Beyond them extends the broad valley called Jackson Hole, covered with sagebrush and punctuated by occasional forested buttes and groves of aspen trees—excellent habitats for pronghorn, deer, elk, and other animals. The Snake River, having begun its journey in southern Yellowstone National Park near the Teton Wilderness, winds leisurely past the Tetons on its way to Idaho. The braided sections of the river create wetlands that support moose, elk, deer, beavers, trumpeter swans, sandhill cranes, Canada geese, and all sorts of ducks.

The Tetons are normal fault-block mountains. About 13 million years ago, two blocks of Earth's crust began to shift along a fault line, one tilting down while the other lifted up. So far, movement has measured some 30,000 vertical feet, most of it from the subsidence of Jackson Hole.

Before Europeans arrived, the Teton

visitors see moose, elk, deer, and all kinds of birds.

How to Get There

From Jackson, take US 26/89/191 north past the National Elk Refuge; entrance station and Moose Visitor Center are at Moose. From Dubois, follow US 26/287 to Moran Junction and turn west to the Moran Entrance Station. From Yellowstone NP's South Entrance, the John D. Rockefeller, Jr., Memorial Parkway leads directly into the park.

The Jackson Hole Airport is inside the park—a concern for environmentalists.

When to Go

Any time of year is a joy in the Tetons. Most people visit during July and August, when it's sunny and warm, after the snow has melted in the high country. In September and October, the days are pleasant, nights are brisk, the park is less crowded, and the animals are still active. You have a better chance of seeing elk than in summer.

Winter, although spectacular, can be very demanding; snowshoeing and cross-country skiing are popular. The main park road, US 26/89/191, remains open all year, but snow closes Teton Park Road (the "inner road") north of Cottonwood Creek from November through April. The Moose-Wilson Road is also closed. At Teton Village, just south of the park, you'll find excellent downhill skiing.

area was an important plant-gathering and hunting ground for Indians of various tribes. In the early 1800s, mountain men spent time here; it was they who called this flat valley ringed by mountains Jackson's Hole after the trapper Davey Jackson. (In recent times the name has lost its apostrophe s.) The first settlers were ranchers and farmers. Some of their buildings are historic sites today, although ranching is still practiced in the vicinity. When the park was established, it included only the mountains and the glacial lakes at their feet. Portions of the valley were added in 1950.

Today the park's 485 square miles encompass both the Teton Range and much of Jackson Hole. Park roads, all in the valley, offer an ever changing panorama of the Tetons. Most visitors never go far from the road. But the Tetons are also popular with hikers; backcountry trails climb high into the mountains—and behind them. Easy trails in the valley lead around lakes and beside wetlands where

Arrowleaf balsam root, early summer

WINEGAR HOLE
WILDERNESS AREA

JOHN D. ROCKEFELLER, JR.
MEMORIAL PARKWAY

To Yellowstone N.P.
and West Thumb

Flagg Ranch

Survey Peak
9,277 ft

Lizard Creek

89
191
287

Moose
Mountain
10,054 ft

MOOSE BASIN

COLTER CANYON

JACKSON
LAKE

Ranger Peak
11,355 ft

CARIBOU-TARGHEE
NATIONAL
FOREST

Eagles Rest Peak
11,258 ft

Rolling Thunder
Mountain
10,908 ft

Colter Bay
Visitor Center

Jackson Lak
Lodge

Raynolds Peak
10,910 ft

Elk
Island

Jackso
Lake Da

JEDEDIAH SMITH
WILDERNESS AREA

Mount Moran
12,605 ft

Falling Ice
Glacier

Signal Mountain Lodge

TETON RANGE

Leigh
Lake

Teton Park Road

Mount
Woodring
11,590 ft

Grand Targhee
Resort Ski Area

Lake
Solitude

String
Lake

Inspiration
Point

Teton Canyon

CASCADE CANYON

North
Jenny Lake
Junction

Hidden Falls

Jenny
Lake

Mount Owen 12,928 ft

Teewinot Mt.
12,325 ft

South
Jenny Lake

Grand Teton 13,770 ft

Teton
Glacier

Middle Teton 12,804 ft

Amphitheater
Lake

Lupine Meadows
Trailhead

South Teton
12,514 ft

Nez Perce Peak
11,901 ft

Cottonwood
Creek

26

Snake

89
191

ANTELOPE FLATS

Taggart
Lake

Teto
Scienc
Schoo

Teton Crest Trail

DEATH CANYON

Mount Hunt
10,783 ft

Death
Canyon
Trailhead

Menors Ferry
Historic Area

Taggart Lake
Trailhead

JACKSON

CARIBOU-TARGHEE
NATIONAL
FOREST

Phelps
Lake

Moose Visitor Cente

HOLE

Moose
Junction

Kelly

Aerial
Tramway

Moose-Wilson Road (closed in winter)

Jackson
Hole
Airport

Gros Ventre

Jackson Hole
Ski Area

Teton
Village

Rendezvous Peak
10,927 ft

Fish Creek

Snake

JACKSON

Gros Ventre

NATIONAL
ELK REFUGE

BRIDGER-
TETON
NATIONAL
FOREST

Jackson National
Fish Hatchery

To Jackson

Ranger Station

Campground

Self-guiding Nature Trail

Unpaved Road

Hiking Trail

0   5 km
0   5 mi

BRIDGER-TETON
NATIONAL FOREST

Pacific Creek

TETON
WILDERNESS
AREA

Two Ocean
Lake

Emma
Matilda
Lake

Jackson Lake
Junction

OXBOW BEND

Moran
Entrance Station

Signal
Mountain
7,593 ft

Moran
Junction

To
Dubois

26   287

Hatchet

Snake

26

89

191

Cunningham Cabin
Historic Site

BRIDGER-TETON

NATIONAL FOREST

Atherton
Creek

Lower
Slide
Lake

Red Hills

Crystal
Creek

Gros Ventre

GROS VENTRE

WILDERNESS AREA

How to Visit

On a 1-day visit take the **Teton Park Road** from **Moose Junction** to **Jenny Lake** for excellent views of the **Tetons** and short walks or longer hikes. On the second day, go farther north to **Signal Mountain** and **Jackson Lake.** For a longer stay, consider floating the **Snake River,** hiking, canoeing, climbing, or attending a ranger-guided activity.

Teton Park Road & Jenny Lake Loop

17 miles; at least a half day

From **Moose Junction,** cross the **Snake River** to the **Moose Visitor Center,** which includes a small exhibit area. The first right turn after the entrance station leads to **Menor-Noble Historic District,** a pioneer homestead. Save that for another day; there are mountains ahead. The **Teton Park Road** climbs up from the river onto a sage-covered flat with the whole Teton panorama in view. You will see the mountains clearly throughout this drive from various changing angles; each viewpoint reveals striking perspectives different from the last.

If you look toward the mountains at Taggart Parking Area, you can see the results of a 1985 forest fire. An easy trail offers a closeup view of forest regeneration—an especially interesting and encouraging sight if you plan to visit Yellowstone, where fires burned extensively in the summer of 1988. Stop at Teton Glacier Turnout for a close-in view of the three Tetons. The Grand Teton, at 13,770 feet, is the highest point in the range. A major route used by climbers follows the left-hand, southern skyline; just as it appears, there is no easy way to the top.

Cottonwood Creek Turnout

Looking over a field of wildflowers into Targhee National Forest

Looking to the left of the Grand, you see the **Middle** and **South Tetons.** The sharp pinnacle jutting up over the shoulder of the South Teton (actually in front of it), is the peak called **Nez Perce.** To the right of the Grand are the sharp peak of **Mount Owen** and, in the foreground, the craggy battlements of **Teewinot Mountain.**

Notice the steep, glacier-carved gulch coming straight down from the Grand Teton. At the head of the gulch, beneath the mountain's near-vertical northeast face, lies **Teton Glacier.** During an ancient ice age, glaciers covered Jackson Hole to a depth of 3,000 feet and carved the canyons in the Teton Range. The glaciers that exist now only at high elevations established themselves more recently.

If you can take your eyes off the mountains, scan the sage flats on both sides of the road for pronghorn, elk, deer, and coyotes, especially in the fall. Across Jackson Hole to the southeast is the **Gros Ventre Range,** where herds of elk and mule deer roam the deeply forested gorges and bighorn sheep the highest peaks.

Heading north, the **Lupine Meadows** spur road leads to a major trailhead. From here you can take a very rewarding but strenuous hike, which climbs 3,000 feet to **Amphitheater Lake** near timberline. Lupine Meadows itself is a good place to look for wildlife in the evening.

Back on the main road, the **South Jenny Lake** area is next, but unless you're planning to hike around the lake, or to take the boat across to **Cascade Canyon** at this point in your tour, you should drive past it for now.

Four miles ahead is the junction for **Jenny Lake Scenic Drive,** where a narrow 1-mile loop road provides the best approach to the area, which many consider to be the scenic heart of the Tetons. The road angles back to the southwest, offering stunning views of the central peaks. Stop at **Cathedral Group Turnout** to take it all in. The north face of the Grand is visible from here, flanked by Teewinot on the left and Owen on the right. North of them, in order, are precipitous **Cascade Canyon** (one of the park's best hikes), **Mount Saint John, Mount Woodring,** and then the massive, flat-topped **Mount Moran.** Moran's **Falling Ice Glacier** is prominent. Notice also the obvious line of black rock rising above the glacier. Called the **Black Dike,** it was caused when molten rock intruded into a crack in the older metamorphic rock called gneiss, before the Tetons rose. The dike, now exposed by erosion of the gneiss, actually stands out from

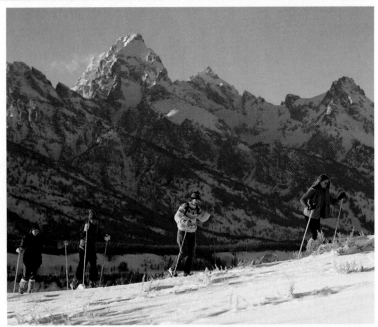

The Grand, highest peak in the Tetons, towering over skiers on Blacktail Butte

the mountain face near the summit. Similar dikes are on the Middle Teton (not visible from here) and Grand Teton.

Just ahead, a short road forks off the scenic drive and leads to tiny **String Lake.** An easy trail leaves from the end of the road to follow the shoreline through open forest to sparkling **Leigh Lake,** named after a 19th-century mountain man, Richard "Beaver Dick" Leigh, who, it was said, could "trap beaver where there warn't any." The lake has superb views of soaring Mount Moran, and, in summer, the water is sometimes warm enough for swimming.

Continuing on, the scenic drive reaches **Jenny Lake** and becomes one way. For understandable reasons, this place is highly popular; the road in summer is crowded with vehicles. Even so, if you desire solitude amid the grandeur, you can generally find it. Leave your car in a parking area and walk down to the shore. Instantly you are isolated from the world of automobiles. If you have more time, catch the boat that usually leaves three times an hour from the southeast end of the lake. Near the parking area you will find the **Jenny Lake Visitor Center,** rest rooms, ranger station, a store, and a campground for tents only.

Hidden Falls

The passenger boat crosses Jenny Lake to join **Cascade Canyon Trail.** It is a half-mile walk to **Hidden Falls,** one of the park's beauties. A half-mile farther, aptly named **Inspiration Point** overlooks the lake. If you still have the energy, the trail is not steep after Inspiration Point, and the views keep getting better. You might consider walking back to the visitor center along the south shore; the easy trail is nearly 3 miles long.

Jackson Lake

about 30 miles; at least a half day

Start at North Jenny Lake Junction on the Teton Park Road. Drive north 2.5 miles through sage land and lodgepole pine to the **Mount Moran Turnout.** Mount Moran, at 12,605 feet, is more than a thousand feet lower than the Grand Teton, but you wouldn't know that looking up. On its summit a patch of sandstone corresponds to a sandstone layer an estimated 24,000 feet below where you stand; 13 million years of movement on the Teton fault has separated the layers by some 30,000 feet.

North of Mount Moran, **Bivouac Peak, Rolling Thunder Mountain,** and **Eagles Rest Peak** dominate the most remote section of the park, cut off from roads and easy trail access by **Jackson Lake,** just ahead. The natural lake was enlarged by a dam built before the park was established.

Before you get to the lake, take the right-hand turn to **Signal Mountain.** The road, on which trailers and RVs are not allowed, winds to the summit of a low mountain which, because it stands alone in Jackson Hole, provides a panoramic view of the region. There's no better place than here to appreciate the unusual geology of the Teton area: the abrupt meeting of valley floor and the Teton Range; the meandering course of the Snake River through deposits of gravel and clay brought down by Ice Age glaciers; and the ranges to the east. From Signal Mountain, it is easy to see why the early trappers thought of mountain-ringed valleys like this one as holes.

Back on the Teton Park Road, you pass Signal Mountain Campground and cross the Snake River over the rebuilt dam. A mile farther, the road joins US 89/191/287. If you're headed north toward Yellowstone, it's worthwhile to turn right and take a short side trip (about a mile) to **Oxbow Bend,** for a classic view of the Tetons dominated by Mount Moran. Wildlife frequents this area.

Going north once again, stop at **Willow Flats Overlook.** The willows are a likely place to see moose. Failing that, watch the meadows below the bridge just to the north as you cross **Christian Creek.**

Day breaking over Mount Moran and Oxbow Bend

Bull moose in rut

Climbing Blacktail Butte, just east of Moose

A few minutes north, **Colter Bay Visitor Center** has an excellent **Indian Arts Museum.** Consider stretching your legs on the easy 3-mile **Colter Bay Nature Trail;** self-guiding booklets can be had at the trailhead or at the visitor center.

North of **Colter Bay,** the main road stays close to the lake. Just before Lizard Creek Campground, you catch one last glimpse of the Tetons and Jackson Lake, before entering dense lodgepole forest. Ten miles farther, along the John D. Rockefeller, Jr., Memorial Parkway, is the South Entrance to Yellowstone.

Other Hikes & Activities

The park has more than 200 miles of maintained trails; many lead up canyons separating the major peaks. All the trails have something to offer, but they vary in difficulty, and some are more scenic than others. Keep in mind that most trails begin at about 6,800 feet, so shortness of breath can come quickly.

Cascade Canyon is most popular. Begin at Jenny Lake and either walk along the lakeshore or take the boat across to Hidden Falls and Inspiration Point. It is a long hike to **Lake Soli-** tude—7 miles if you take the boat, 9.5 miles if you walk the lakeshore— but it's worthwhile to go at least part-way up the canyon.

From Lupine Meadows parking area, the **Amphitheater Lake Trail** climbs to 9,700 feet and rewards those who make the strenuous 9-mile round-trip with a breathtaking view of Jackson Hole. The lake nestles beneath craggy peaks; allow 8 hours minimum.

Death Canyon Trailhead, off the Moose-Wilson Road, leads up to a nice view of **Phelps Lake;** from there, the trail climbs to join the **Teton Crest Trail,** a magnificent backcountry route that traverses the range and ends at **Paintbrush Canyon** near String Lake, a trip of about 40 miles and 3 days (backcountry permit required).

Consider taking a raft trip on the **Snake River** for fine Teton views and a chance to see beavers, otters, moose, eagles, ospreys, and waterfowl. Ask about outfitters at a visitor center or check the park newspaper, *Teewinot.*

You can also sign up for a mountain climbing lesson; rent a canoe and paddle on a lake; or take a summer course taught by the **Teton Science School.** The school offers 1- to 5-day seminars on ecology and the region's natural history for ages 8 and up.

Information & Activities

Headquarters
Post Office Drawer 170, Moose, WY 83012. Phone (307) 739-3300. www.nps.gov/grte

Seasons & Accessibility
Main road into park (US 26/89/191) open year-round. Snow closes side roads closed from about November to May. Call headquarters number for winter road conditions.

Visitor & Information Centers
Moose Visitor Center, at park's south end, open daily all year. **Colter Bay Visitor Center,** on Jackson Lake, open mid-May through September. **Jenny Lake Visitor Center** open June through Labor Day. Call (307) 739-3399.

Entrance Fee
$20 per car, good for one week at both Grand Teton and Yellowstone. $40 annual for both parks.

Pets
Permitted on leashes except on trails, at ranger-led activities, in backcountry and visitor centers; not permitted on boats on the Snake River or on lakes other than Jackson Lake.

Facilities for Disabled
Visitor centers, Indian Arts Museum, some rest rooms, some ranger-led activities are accessible. Also, some trails and Menor-Noble historic district.

Things to Do
Free ranger-led activities: wildlife walks and talks, day and twilight hikes, bicycle tours, slide talks, illustrated campfire programs, children's programs, skill development programs, tepee demonstration, wildlife watches, snowshoe walks. Also, boat cruise, natural history seminars, wayside exhibits, boating (permit required), river rafting, climbing, bicycling, horseback riding (stables in park), fishing and ice fishing (license required), snowshoeing, cross-country skiing, dogsledding, snowmobiling. Ask park for list of concessioners offering variety of rental and guide services.

Overnight Backpacking
Permits required. Free, they can be obtained at visitor centers and Jenny Lake Ranger Station. One-third of permits can be reserved for a nonrefundable $15 fee; the rest are first come, first served. Mail requests between January and mid-May to Permits Office, in care of park.

Campgrounds
Five campgrounds, **Jenny Lake** has 7-day limit, others 14-day limit. Generally late May to Oct., except **Lizard Creek,** mid-June to early Sept. All first come, first served. $12 per night. Showers at **Colter Bay.** Tent sites only at Jenny Lake; all others have tent and trailer sites, no hookups. Two group campgrounds; reservations suggested; contact park headquarters. RV sites only at **Colter Bay RV Park,** $22 per night. Reservations required; contact Grand Teton Lodge Co., Box 250, Moran, WY 83013. (307) 543-2855. Food and gas services in park.

Hotels, Motels, & Inns
(unless otherwise noted, rates for 2 persons, double room, high season)
INSIDE THE PARK:
The following 3 lodges and cabins are operated by Grand Teton Lodge Co., P.O. Box 250, Moran, WY 83013. (800) 628-9988 or (307) 543-2811.
Colter Bay Village and Marina 208 cabins. $68-$125. Restaurant. Mid-May to Oct. **Jackson Lake Lodge** (1 mile north of Jackson Lake Jct.) 385 units. $120-$210. Restaurant, pool. Mid-May to mid-Oct. **Jenny Lake Lodge** 37 cabins. $340-$590, includes 2 meals. Restaurant. Late May to early Oct.
Also, **Lost Creek Ranch** (8 miles north of Moose) P.O. Box 95, Moose, WY 83012. (307) 733-3435. 13 cabins. $5,395-$12,860 per week, all inclusive. June through Nov. **Signal Mountain Lodge** P.O. Box 50, Moran, WY 83013. (800) 672-6012 or (307) 543-2831. 79 units. Cabins $95-$140; rooms $115-$185. Two restaurants. Mid-May to mid-Oct. **Triangle X Ranch** Moose, WY 83012. (307) 733-2183. 22 cabins. $1,145-$1,610 per person, per week, all inclusive. End of May through Oct.

Contact the Jackson Hole Chamber of Commerce for a full list of accommodations: P.O. Box 550, Jackson Hole, WY 83001. (307) 733-3316. Open year-round.

Excursions

National Elk Refuge

Jackson, Wyoming

In winter, visitors can ride a horse-drawn sleigh into the protected winter range of a 7,000- to 8,000-head herd of elk. The refuge offers supplemental feeding to the animals, many of which migrate south from Yellowstone. 24,700 acres. Fishing (Aug. through Oct.), scenic drives, visitor center. Open year-round, dawn to dusk. Adjoins Grand Teton NP on south. (307) 733-9212.

Bridger-Teton National Forest

Jackson, Wyoming

This immense forest encompasses wildlife-rich Jackson Hole; the glaciers and lakes of the Wind River Range; and Two Ocean Creek along the Continental Divide. Contains three wilderness areas. 3.4 million acres. Hiking, boating, fishing, horseback riding, hunting, water sports, winter sports. 30 campgrounds, boat ramp. Open all year; campgrounds open spring to fall. Adjoins Grand Teton NP on east. (307) 739-5500.

Targhee National Forest

St. Anthony, Idaho

Here, on the Tetons' western flank, lies a forest of lodgepole pine and fir with many rivers, streams, and lakes. Contains two wilderness areas. 1,810,000 acres, part in Wyoming. Hiking, boating, fishing, horseback riding, hunting, picnic areas, winter sports, water sports. 32 campgrounds, boat ramp. Open all year; campsites open late May through September. Adjoins Grand Teton and Yellowstone NPs. (208) 624-3151.

Fossil Butte National Monument

Kemmerer, Wyoming

Fifty million years ago, this semiarid niche was the site of Fossil Lake, a rich depository of the Eocene. Features exquisitely preserved freshwater fishes. 8,198 acres. Hiking, picnic area, scenic drive. Visitor center open all year; site usually closed by snow Nov. through early May. Off US 30, 180 miles south of Grand Teton NP. (307) 877-4455.

Sand dunes at sunset, with Sangre de Cristo Mountains in the background

Great Sand Dunes

Colorado

Authorized November 22, 2000

107,000 acres

Visitors to the Great Sand Dunes experience an undeniable sense of wonder, just as happens in so many of our most spectacular national parks. In contrast to the sudden shock of walking to the rim of the Grand Canyon, though, or topping a rise to view Crater Lake, the emotions evoked by this otherworldly landscape arrive in slow motion.

The dunes appear in the distance as you approach, but at first seem dwarfed by their backdrop, the 13,000-foot peaks of the Sangre de Cristo Mountains. Not until you're nearly at their border does their vast scale become apparent: dunes up to 750 feet tall, extending for mile after mile—an ocean of sand hills of breathtaking magnitude. That's just how the explorer Zebulon Pike described them piling them up against the foothills. The resulting dunes are the tallest in North America, covering more than 30 square miles. Adults hike across them and marvel at their beauty; children run and slide down their steep faces, enjoying a playground of fairy-tale proportion.

Winds that often top 40 miles an hour continually reshape the crests of the tall dunes, and smaller dunes may "migrate" several feet in a week. The dunes show a remarkable permanence of form, though, which geologists attribute to their unusual moisture content. The San Luis Valley receives only about ten inches of rain a year, but that amount, plus snowmelt and underground water, helps keep the Great Sand Dunes great.

The need to protect the water that protects the dunes has led to a number of changes at Great Sand Dunes. Through a cooperative effort among government agencies and private conservation groups, Great Sand Dunes National Monument and surrounding lands are in the process of being designated a national park and preserve. This new entity will comprise the national monument, lands west of the monument known as the Baca Ranch, and mountains east of the monument previously managed by the U.S. Forest Service. This latter realm was established as a preserve in 2000 to safeguard the small streams flowing into the area. Official designation of the national park is awaiting final land purchases, scheduled to occur by 2005.

All this means that visitors have access to a great diversity of habitats, beginning in the desert dunes, continuing up to the pinyon pines, cottonwoods, and aspens of the foothills, and arriving even higher at the spruce-fir forests and tundra of the summits of the Sangre de Cristos, with seven peaks over 14,000 feet. The region's geology and biology make it a fascinating place, unique among our national parks. It's well worth the drive across south Colorado, even if all you do is gaze in awe at this extraordinary and lovely terrain.

How to Get There

From the east or north, take US 160 west from Walsenburg 59 miles to Colo. 150 and drive north 16 miles. From the south or west, take US 285 to Alamosa and drive 14 miles east to Colo. 150, continuing north to the

in 1807: "Their appearance was exactly that of a sea in a storm (except as to color), not the least sign of vegetation existing thereon."

The dunes sprawl across part of southern Colorado's San Luis Valley, a broad, arid plain between the San Juan Mountains on the west and the Sangre de Cristos on the east. The Rio Grande flows through the valley, and in millennia of meandering has spread a deep layer of sand—eroded from the rock of the surrounding mountains—across its ancient floodplain. Strong prevailing southwesterly winds carry the tiny grains toward the Sangre de Cristos,

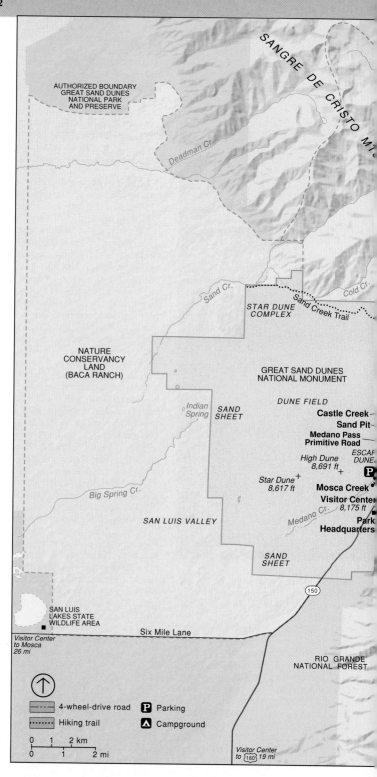

SANGRE DE CRISTO MTS

AUTHORIZED BOUNDARY
GREAT SAND DUNES
NATIONAL PARK
AND PRESERVE

Deadman Cr.

Cold Cr.

Sand Cr.

Sand Creek Trail

STAR DUNE
COMPLEX

NATURE
CONSERVANCY
LAND
(BACA RANCH)

GREAT SAND DUNES
NATIONAL MONUMENT

DUNE FIELD

Indian
Spring

SAND
SHEET

Castle Creek
Sand Pit
Medano Pass
Primitive Road

ESCAP
DUNE

High Dune
8,691 ft

P

Star Dune
8,617 ft

Mosca Creek

Visitor Center
8,175 ft

Big Spring Cr.

Medano Cr.

Park
Headquarters

SAN LUIS VALLEY

SAND
SHEET

150

SAN LUIS
LAKES STATE
WILDLIFE AREA

Six Mile Lane

RIO GRANDE
NATIONAL FOREST

Visitor Center
to Mosca
26 mi

4-wheel-drive road   P Parking

Hiking trail   ▲ Campground

0   1   2 km
0   1   2 mi

Visitor Center
to 160 19 mi

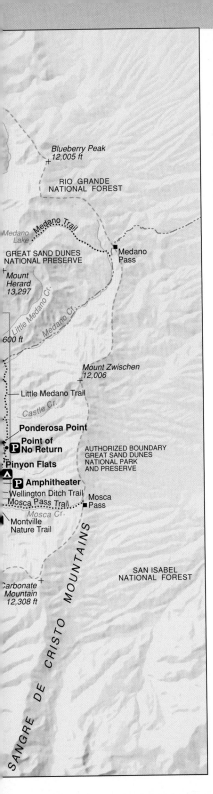

Blueberry Peak
12,005 ft

RIO GRANDE
NATIONAL FOREST

Medano Trail

Medano
Lake

GREAT SAND DUNES
NATIONAL PRESERVE

Medano
Pass

Mount
Herard
13,297

Little Medano Cr.

Medano Cr.

600 ft

Mount Zwischen
12,006

Little Medano Trail

Castle Cr.

Ponderosa Point

Point of
No Return

AUTHORIZED BOUNDARY
GREAT SAND DUNES
NATIONAL PARK
AND PRESERVE

Pinyon Flats

Amphitheater

Wellington Ditch Trail

Mosca Pass Trail

Mosca
Pass

Mosca Cr.

Montville
Nature Trail

SAN ISABEL
NATIONAL FOREST

Carbonate
Mountain
12,308 ft

SANGRE DE CRISTO MOUNTAINS

Mule deer herd near Great Sand Dunes

monument and preserve. Airport: Colorado Springs.

When to Go

All-year park. Moderate temperatures make spring and fall best. The sand dunes can get very hot in summer, although they can be traversed comfortably early and late in the day; summer is also the park's most crowded season. Winter snow curtails trips into the high mountains, though the dunes can still be visited.

How To Visit

Stop at the **visitor center** (temporarily located next to the Dunes parking area) for a quick lesson in the Great Sand Dunes environment, and to learn the schedule of ranger-led walks and programs (summer only). From there, walk out into the dunes, going as far and climbing as high as time and energy permit; the **High Dune** is a popular, moderately strenuous destination.

Kids and adults alike enjoy splashing along **Medano Creek,** which meanders along the base of the dunes (when there is enough water from the spring snowmelt). The **Montville Nature Trail** and the **Mosca Pass Trail** offer additional options for exploration, from short walks to mountain hikes.

If you have a high-clearance four-wheel-drive vehicle, and are very careful, you can drive the **Medano Pass Primitive Road,** which leads 11 miles up into the Sangre de Cristo Mountains in the national preserve, exploring different habitats along the way, from foothills to coniferous forest at the 9,950-foot pass. A park concessioner offers tours of the northern part of the national monument along this road; ask a ranger for details.

The Dunes & Medano Creek

Short hikes; a half day

A 15-minute video at the **visitor center** offers a good introduction to the geology and history of the park. Rangers in summer present programs here, as well as at other sites and trails. Depending on when you visit, guided events might include nature walks, children's activities, or programs on wildlife, plants, hiking, geology, or the archaeology of the dunes.

Begin your exploration at the **Dunes** parking lot. The imposing dunes, like buff-brown miniatures of the surrounding Sangre de Cristo crests, rise invitingly to the west. But first take time to discover **Medano Creek**. This small stream flows along the edge of the dunes; the moisture it carries is a vital part of the dune-system environment. Kids may want to build sand castles, or just enjoy a shoes-off walk along the squishy stream bed. The wet sand is a good place to look for the tracks of coyotes, kangaroo rats, mule deer, or bobcats.

Medano Creek usually flows only in spring, carrying snowmelt down from the mountain tops. When it contains adequate water, watch for a phenomenon called "surge flow," which occurs when a small, temporary dam of sand upstream collapses, sending down a wave of water that can be up to a foot high.

Next, hike out into the dunes, where you'll quickly learn that walking in the soft sand is more strenuous than you might think. Take your time, and angle up the ridgelines of the dunes, rather

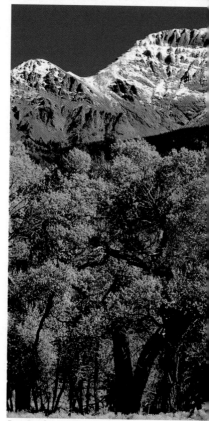

Baca Ranch

than climbing straight up. While it might seem like fun to go barefoot, remember that in summer the sand surface can reach blistering temperatures. Wear protective shoes, as well as a hat, and apply sunscreen. Carry plenty of water if you plan on walking far. One thing you don't need to be concerned about is poisonous animals: There are no snakes or scorpions in the dunes.

You can strike out in any direction, but be sure to keep track of your location. While most people can easily orient themselves by noting the ever present peaks of the Sangre de Cristos, a compass or GPS unit isn't a bad idea for extended hikes. Many people make the 1-mile (one-way) trip to the aptly named **High Dune**, which towers 650 feet above the floor of the San Luis Valley. You'll find a great panorama at the top, taking in mountains, dunes, and valley. Another mile to the west rises the **Star Dune**, with an equally fine view. "Star" dunes are so named because they have three

Bee plant on edge of the dunes

or more "arms," rather than the single axis of most dunes.

Photography in the dunes is best early and late in the day, when the low angle of the sun creates shadows that accentuate their contours and crests.

A night walk into the dunes can be a little eerie, but thrilling in its sense of solitude and peace. When the moon is out, the dimly lit landscape seems even more haunting.

East of the Dunes

A full day or more

Though the dunes are fascinating and beautiful, there is a certain uniformness about them, and very few plants and animals make their homes there. The same is certainly not true for the foothills and high peaks of the Sangre de Cristo range, a large part of which is now encompassed in **Great Sand Dunes National Preserve.** (The preserve is administered similarly to the adjoining monument, although hunting is allowed.) Here, you can hike or, with the proper vehicle, drive from the scrubby habitat of junipers and pinyon pines, along creeks lined with aspens and cottonwoods, up into forests of ponderosa pine and, even higher, spruce and fir. Alpine tundra tops the tallest summits above tree line, where only grasses, compact shrubs, low wildflowers, and other ground-hugging plants can survive.

East of the main road, just north of the visitor center, you'll find a parking area for three varied trails. The easy, half-mile **Montville Nature Trail** loops into the foothills, where you might spot mule deer, a least chipmunk, a desert cottontail, or a coyote. Black-billed magpies, long-tailed and conspicuous, have learned to beg for food (don't feed them or other wildlife), and friendly mountain chickadees flit from tree to tree. The **Wellington Ditch Trail** splits off the Montville trail partway around the loop, following an old irrigation ditch 1 mile north to the NPS campground.

Also beginning at the Montville trailhead, the **Mosca Pass Trail** follows an old toll road up Mosca Creek, a tributary of Medano, across the national monument boundary and into the preserve. You'll walk past cottonwoods and aspens, ascending into a forest of Engelmann spruce and subalpine fir, reaching 9,730-foot Mosca Pass after 3.5 miles; the elevation gain is just under 1,500 feet. For a moderate amount of effort, you'll get a fine overview of the way habitats change with altitude in the Rockies.

Visitors with a four-wheel-drive vehicle can take the **Medano Pass Primitive Road,** which follows the national monument's eastern border before heading into the national preserve, climbing to reach 9,950-foot Medano Pass 11 miles from the road entrance. This trip offers a nonstrenuous way to explore the high Sangre de Cristos, although certain hazards must be taken into account. The road traverses soft sand for several miles and is not recommended for smaller SUVs lacking wide tires and high ground clearance. Even large vehicles may need to lower tire pressure to make it through the sand without bogging down. (Air to reinflate tires is available near the monument amphitheater.) The road crosses creeks several times, which can be problematic during spring high water, and it's closed in winter.

For those without the proper vehicle, a concessioner is authorized by the NPS to operate tours along the Medano Pass Primitive Road from May through September. The narrated, 2-hour trips do not climb into the preserve, but remain in the national monument, offering a look at areas unseen by most visitors.

Like the Mosca Pass Trail, the Medano Pass road provides a natural-history lesson along with excellent scenery. Ascending from the foothills into lush montane forest is, in effect, like traveling from the southwestern desert to Canada. Ecologists call the different habitats encountered along mountain slopes "life zones"—each an altitudinal band boasting its own related set of plants and animals. Pinyon jays and mule deer, for instance, dwell among the arid-looking habitat of scattered junipers and pinyon pines, while gray jays and bighorn sheep live high on the mountain slopes.

One of the preserve's most popular hikes begins along the Medano Pass road, a half-mile west of the pass. The **Medano Lake Trail** climbs 1,900 feet in 4 miles to reach the lake, strikingly situated in a cirque under 13,350-foot Mount Herard. The trail passes through aspen groves that turn brilliant yellow in fall. The last mile of the trail is rugged, and to have a view westward over the sand dunes you must expend a little more effort, climbing the ridge above the lake. Your reward is a visit to an alpine world of flowery meadows, dense spruce-fir woodland, and wind-stunted trees at timberline, where elk bugle in fall and Clark's nutcrackers give their raucous calls. Listen for the sharp squeaks of pikas, mammals that live among rockpiles, looking like small rabbits without the long ears.

People enjoying Medano Creek

Information & Activities

Headquarters
11500 Hwy. 150, Mosca, CO 81146.
(719) 378-2312.
www.nps.gov/grsa

Seasons & Accessibility
The park is open year-round. Sand
temperatures can spike to 140°F during
the summer.

Visitor & Information Centers
The current visitor center on Colo. 150
is being renovated. A temporary visitor
center has been erected at the Dunes
parking lot to provide information
assistance, bookstore, and theater location. (719) 378-2312 ext. 220.

Entrance Fee
$3 per person per week; $10 annual
pass.

Pets
Permitted on leashes. Be aware that
mountain lions, coyotes, and foxes
hunt within the park. Horses are not
allowed in the dunes area.

Facilities for Disabled
Access to the dunes is difficult for
persons with traditional wheeled
chairs. Check with the visitor center
about borrowing a "sand wheel chair."
Accessible camping sites are available
at Pinyon campground as well as at
the Sawmill Canyon Backcountry
Campsite along Medano Pass Primitive
Road. Check with park staff for other
needs questions.

Things to Do
Dunes hiking, photography, wildlife
viewing, snowshoeing, nature walks,
climbing, cross-country skiing, bird-
watching, biking on trails away from
the dunes. Summer events include
sandcastle competitions and kite flying. Four-wheel-drive tours: contact
Great Sand Dunes Oasis campground,
(719) 378-2222.

Overnight Backpacking
Free backcountry permits required for
overnight camping. Primitive camping
permitted without fires. Backcountry
camping is allowed with horses and
pack animals in most of the monument and preserve. Groups are limited
to six people and animals within the

monument borders and ten in the preserve. Check with park officials on specific limitations.

Campgrounds
Pinyon Flats Campground, with 88
campsites, open year-round on a first-
come, first-served basis. $10 per night.
   Outside the monument, **San Luis
Lakes State Park** (13 miles on Six Mile
Ln.) has 51 campsites with views of the
Sangre de Cristo Mountains and the
Great Sand Dunes. (719) 378-2020.
$10 per night.
   Also see **Great Sand Dunes Lodge
and Campground,** below.

Special Advisories
● Shoes are necessary for walking
on the dunes as sand can burn
bare feet.
● Carry plenty of water—more
than you normally would—for hikes
of any length.
● Wear sunscreen and protective
head covering.

Hotels, Motels, & Inns
*(unless otherwise noted, rates for 2
persons, double room, high season)*
OUTSIDE THE PARK:
**Great Sand Dunes Lodge and Camp-
ground** 7900 Hwy. 150, N. Mosca, CO
81146. (719) 378-2900 (lodge). 10
rooms $79-$99. Pool, restaurant. (719)
378-2222 (campground reservations
for RV, cabin, and tepees). 130 tent
sites. $10 first come, first serve and 20
RV ($15). Also available, two camping
cabins and two tepees.

*For other local accommodations,
contact the park; the Alamosa Chamber of Commerce, (719) 589-3681 for
information on locations near the
monument entrance; or the Westcliffe
Chamber of Commerce, (719) 783-
9163 for information on the lodging
near the preserve entrance.*

Tundra along Trail Ridge Road, with Longs Peak in the distance

Rocky Mountain

Colorado

Established January 26, 1915

265,769 acres

Nowhere else in the United States can a visitor see so much alpine country with such ease. A mere 2-hour drive from Denver, Trail Ridge Road takes visitors into the heart of Rocky Mountain National Park, traversing a ridge above 11,000 feet for 10 miles. Along the way, tiny tundra flowers and other wild blooms contrast with sweeping vistas of towering summits; 78 of them exceed 12,000 feet. Alpine lakes reflect the grandeur.

The summits form at least the third generation of mountains to rise in this region. The first probably protruded as islands above a shallow sea more than 135 million years ago, when dinosaurs reigned. Another range grew out of a later sea some 75 million years

ago. Over the eons these summits eroded to rolling hills, which rose once again, although unevenly: Some portions sank along fault lines, helping create the striking texture of the current scenery.

Rock as old as that at the bottom of the Grand Canyon—nearly two billion years—caps the Rockies' summits. Within the last million years, glaciers, grinding boulders beneath them, carved deep canyons. Erosion later scoured the more jagged summits into their present profiles.

Rocky Mountain, though only about an eighth the size of Yellowstone, accommodates nearly as many visitors—3.3 million or more a year. In 1917 a superintendent promoted the park by hiring a young woman to live off the land, clad in a leopardskin; visitation soared. But today overcrowding worries park officials to visit: Elk move to lower elevations, and you can hear their mating bugles. The tundra turns crimson early in the month; aspens turn golden later. In the winter there is skiing and snow-shoeing.

How to Visit

On a 1-day blitz, drive **Trail Ridge Road** as far as **Farview Curve** for the classic overview of the park's mountains, valleys, and tundra, then double back and take **Bear Lake Road** to see a collection of scenic lakes (which can get very congested in summer). If you wish, make a loop of the first leg by driving one-way, unpaved **Old Fall River Road** west, then Trail Ridge Road east. Old Fall River Road gives you an intimate look at a wooded mountainside, but it's usually closed by snow until early July.

With more time, drive all the way to **Grand Lake** on the west side the first day, then take your trip to **Bear Lake** the second day. Spend extra time on the excellent nature trails and day hikes.

If you go in summer and plan to backpack and hike, be sure not to be caught above timberline between about 12 and 4 p.m., when lightning storms are frequent.

Trail Ridge Road to Grand Lake, via Farview Curve

50 miles; at least a full day

Trail Ridge Road roughly follows a 10,000-year-old trail; prehistoric people once hunted where you'll drive. The road climbs to a land like the vast arctic expanses of Siberia, Alaska, and northern Canada. Take warm clothing and sunscreen. From Estes Park, enter the park on US 36 and stop by the visitor center to pick up information—including a useful booklet ($1) about Trail Ridge Road—and a weather report. (If coming from the west on US 34, stop at the visitor center near Grand Lake and reverse this tour.) Continue straight on US 36 after the entrance station. The road ascends **Deer Mountain** through open ponderosa woodland.

At **Deer Ridge Junction,** either bear left onto Trail Ridge Road or, if it's summer, detour to the right, circling

and conservationists, who cite distressed animals, trodden plants, and eroded trails. Condominium development is crowding the park's borders also, shrinking the habitats of elk and other wildlife and threatening to turn the park into an island of nature.

How to Get There

Take I-25 north from Denver (about 65 miles away) or south from Cheyenne, Wyoming (about 90 miles away), then US 34 west at Loveland. From the west, pick up US 34 at Granby. Airports: Denver and Cheyenne, Wyoming.

When to Go

If possible, avoid mid-June to mid-August, when the park receives about half its yearly visitors. Trail Ridge Road stays open from roughly late May to mid-October; trails thaw out by around July 4. In May, sub-alpine wildflowers bloom; in early July, the tundra flowers. September, the sunniest month, is a prime time

0 1 2 3 km
0 1 2 3 mi

ROUTT NF

COLORADO
STATE FOREST

ROOSEVELT
NATIONAL
FOREST

Corral Creek
NPS/USFS

Long Draw
Reservoir

Mummy
Pass
11,440 ft

Thunder Mountain
12,070 ft

Flatiron
Mountain
12,335 ft

Hagues Pea
13,560

LITTLE
YELLOWSTONE
Mount Richthofen
12,940 ft

Fairchild Mountain
13,502 ft

Ypsilon Mountain
13,514 ft

Site of
Lulu City

Fall River Pass
11,796 ft

Alpine Visitor Center

Milner Pass
10,758 ft

Highest point
on road
12,183 ft

Old Fall River Road
One way

Endovalley

Mount Cumulus
12,725 ft

34

Trail   Ridge

Rock Cut

Chasm
Falls

HORSESH

Colorado River
Trailhead

Farview Curve

Road

Forest Canyon

34

Mount Nimbus
12,706 ft

Jackstraw Mountain
11,704 ft

Timber Creek

Never Summer
Ranch

Mount Ida
12,880 ft

Stones Peak
12,922 ft

Bowen/Baker
Trailhead

North Fork
Colorado River

Cu
Lak

ARAPAHO
NATIONAL
FOREST

Coyote Valley

BIG
MEADOWS

Flattop
Mountain
12,324 ft

Be
Lak

Ranger
Station

Snowdrift Peak
12,274 ft

Hallett Peak
12,713 ft

Glacier Gorge
Junction
Trailhead

Campground

Green Mountain
Trailhead

Self-guiding Trail

34

The
Loc

Unpaved
Road

Hiking Trail

Grand Lake
Entrance

Alva B. Adams Tunnel
(water diversion structure)

Taylor Peak
13,153 ft

Continental
Divide

Kawuneeche
Visitor Center

Ptarmigan Mountain
12,324 ft

Lake
Nanita

Chiefs Hea
13,579

Grand Lake

West Portal

Andrews Peak
12,565 ft

Mount Alice
13,310 ft

Shadow Mountain
10,155 ft

Adams
Falls

Lake Verna

Mount Craig
12,007 ft

Shadow Mountain

4

34

Green Ridge

Mount Bryant
11,034 ft

PARADISE
PARK

41

Mount Adams
12,121 ft

Copeland
Mountain
13,176 ft

Cutthroat Bay

Stillwater

ARAPAHO
NATIONAL RECREATION
AREA

Ogalalla Peak
13,138 ft

To
Granby

Lake Granby

ARAPAHO NATIONAL FOREST

Indian paintbrush and death camas

through **Horseshoe Park** and past **Sheep Lakes** to look for bighorn sheep, which sometimes visit the natural mineral lick there. (In fall, take time to see Horseshoe Park at dawn or dusk to view elk; bugling mating calls start soon after sunset.) If you made the detour, either continue on Old Fall River Road to Fall River Pass (see next tour), or return to Deer Ridge Junction and turn west onto US 34, Trail Ridge Road.

Continue along Trail Ridge Road, which soon enters the subalpine zone, dominated by forests of Engelmann spruce and subalpine fir. Stop again on the right just past **Many Parks Curve,** and walk back to the overlook. The "parks" in the Rockies are mountain meadows: When the glaciers of the last ice age melted, they often left lakes, dammed in by debris the glaciers had pushed along their edges. The lakes eventually silted up and drained, becoming flat meadows. In another 5.8 miles, the road crosses timberline, where subzero winter temperatures and 100-mph winds blast trees into twisted shrubs. Higher still, the road enters tundra. Don't miss the 5-minute stroll to the overlooks of **Forest Canyon,** a glacier-carved, U-shaped valley 2,500 feet below. *Do stay on the trail*—damaged tundra plants take decades to recover.

Back in your car, drive on 2 miles, crossing smooth mountaintops that are part of a plain formed when an ancestral mountain range eroded. The plain was uplifted largely intact and remained above the ice age glaciers. Stop at **Rock Cut** (12,110 feet) and hike the 1-mile round-trip, paved nature trail. High altitude can cause dizziness and nausea, *so walk slowly and don't overdo.* (If you feel ill, you'll most likely recover as soon as the road descends.) The trail leads from a

Bighorn sheep on a winter slope near Fall River

parking lot to the **Toll Memorial Mountain Index,** a peak-finder atop a rock pile. The 360-degree views of mountain, tundra, and weird rocks are splendid.

About 4 miles farther along the road, exhibits on alpine life—and a chance to quench your thirst—await you at the **Alpine Visitor Center** and the Trail Ridge store and snack shop at Fall River Pass.

To continue the tour, exit the visitor center parking lot and turn right. Trail Ridge Road crosses the Continental divide after about 4 miles, at **Milner Pass,** named for the surveyor of a never-built railway route through the Rockies. Water flowing east of the Divide will eventually find its way to the Atlantic, and water wending west will flow to the Pacific. The overlook at **Farview Curve,** about 2 miles farther, provides a riveting view of the **Never Summer Mountains** and glacier-carved **Kawuneeche Valley.** Through this valley winds the infant **Colorado River,** whose headwaters lie just 5 miles north. About halfway up on the western part of the Never Summer range, you can see a horizontal scar. It is the 14-mile-long **Grand Ditch,** built between 1890 and 1932 to divert water from the wetter western side of the Continental Divide to the drier Great Plains to the east.

If short of time, turn back now. Otherwise continue the 14 miles remaining on Trail Ridge Road, descending to the beaver ponds, willows, and conifer forests of the valley floor. You might spot moose, reintro-duced in 1978 after settlers eliminated them in this area. Hunters also killed off wolves, grizzly bears, and bison in the region.

In the late 19th century, smatterings of silver and gold lured miners by the hundreds to the valley. Resulting boomtowns vanished as quickly as they arose when mining claims proved unprofitable. From the **Colorado River Trailhead,** about 4 miles past Farview Curve, an easy 1.8-mile hike brings you to the decaying 1870s cabins of miner Joe Shipler. About 2.5 miles farther up the trail lies the site of **Lulu City,** once a bustling mining camp. Whether or not you hike, pick up an engaging leaflet on the human and natural history of this area at the visitor center.

Stop again 2 miles down the road to stroll the easy half-mile through the rippling grasses, and over the Colorado River, to **Never Summer Ranch,** a dude ranch dating from the 1920s. By that time it had become clear that the real gold was in tourists' pockets. Return to your car; the road exits the park near Grand Lake.

Old Fall River Road to Fall River Pass

9.4 miles; a scant half day

Old Fall River Road provides an unpaved, leisurely (15 mph) drive through conifer forest and tundra. It is also a self-guided auto tour, with flyers for sale at the visitor center, about 4 miles from the **Fall River Entrance**

Sunrise over Sprague Lake

Station (no RVs or vehicles over 25 feet long). En route you'll see traces of ancient glaciers and of recent rockslides and avalanches.

You can enter the park at the entrance station on US 34 or begin the tour off US 34 shortly before Sheep Lakes. (See **Trail Ridge Road** pp. 309-312 for information on Sheep Lakes and Horseshoe Park.) Turn onto the **Endovalley** road. The huge assembly of boulders the road crosses is a reminder of the 1982 Lawn Lake flood. A dam, built prior to the creation of the park, burst one July morning, releasing a flood that turned the **Roaring River** into a tree-ripping torrent and deposited boulders, mud, and debris as far as the main street of Estes Park.

Pull over at the alluvial fan trailhead and take a few minutes to stroll the short paved pathway over the debris—up to 44 feet thick—and observe how nature recovers: Young aspens and conifers and dozens of species of willows and grasses are claiming the area, as are a wide variety of birds and other animals. Walk back to your car along the trail, not the road.

As you drive on, note the scars on the aspens: Elk and other animals gnaw the bark, which then becomes infected with the black fungus you see; given

enough damage, the aspens eventually die. Some observers cite the extent of aspen damage within the park as evidence that elk have reached or exceeded their population limit here. At Endovalley, continue on to the one-way Old Fall River Road with your self-guiding leaflet. Join Trail Ridge Road at Fall River Pass.

Bear Lake Road

10 miles; at least a half day

Popular especially for its trails, wildflowers, and fall foliage, Bear Lake Road starts off US 36 just past the **Beaver Meadows Entrance Station.** Make your first stop the **Moraine Park Museum,** near the homestead of pioneer and resort owner Abner Sprague. Buy a pamphlet for the nature trail, an easy stroll that starts in front of the building. Along the trail, be sure to smell the ponderosa pine bark; its vanilla scent is luscious.

Note that the road between **Sprague Lake** and **Bear Lake** is closed until 2004 for rebuilding. You will be required to take a shuttle to Bear Lake (operating May through October). However, even when construction is complete, the shuttle will be a welcome alternative, especially in sum-

Beaver damming a river to make a pond and home

mer, when the park is crowded. The bus comes frequently; its schedule is in the park newspaper.

The road tunnels through stands of lodgepole pine and aspen—dazzling in fall. At **Sprague Lake** awaits one of the park's wheelchair-accessible trails; as you stroll along, the forest things out a bit to offer distant views of Flattop and Hallett.

At **Bear Lake,** buy a pamphlet and stroll the half-mile **Bear Lake Nature Walk,** enjoying this dramatic, often photographed scenery while you learn about forest ecology. The park's most popular hike climbs a mile from Bear to **Dream Lake,** over which tower the distinctive profiles of **Hallett Peak** and **Flattop Mountain.**

For a somewhat less crowded walk to another spectacular lake, start from the **Glacier Gorge Junction Trailhead,** about three-quarters of a mile back down the road. The **Loch Trail** passes **Alberta Falls** in half a mile, and reaches the rocky shoreline of **The Loch** in a moderately steep 2.7 miles.

Other Hikes

The park's excellent 355-mile trail system presents you with endless possibilities, just a few of which are listed below. See a ranger for details and ideas on less crowded walks.

Sprague Lake: Located off Bear Lake Road, Sprague Lake is a fishing pond created by Abner Sprague. Here's an easy, half-mile self-guided nature walk,

a loop dominated by views of Continental Divide peaks.

Wild Basin: This corner of the park—14 miles south of Estes Park off Colo. 7—offers fine day hikes, including those to **Calypso Cascades** (1.8 miles) and **Ouzel Falls** (2.7 miles) through spruce-fir and mixed conifer forests along **North Saint Vrain Creek** and its tributaries. Pick up a nature booklet to learn how the forest has been making a comeback since a major fire in 1978.

Longs Peak, Chasm Lake: More than 800 people were counted climbing Longs on a summer's day. The predawn climb (8 miles one way) to the park's tallest peak requires planning—check with a ranger, especially about lightning. Some consider the challenging trail to Chasm Lake (4.2 miles one way) the park's most beautiful and rewarding hike. Both hikes begin at **Longs Peak Ranger Station,** 1 mile off Colo. 7, 10 miles south of Estes Park. Note that parking is limited.

Cub Lake: The less traveled **Cub Lake Trail** (an easy 4.6-mile round-trip) is known for birding and wildflowers, including the yellow water lilies afloat on Cub Lake in summer. The trail begins from a spur road off Bear Lake Road at **Moraine Park.**

Green Mountain Trail to **Big Meadows:** This easy trail (3.6 miles round-trip) passes spruce-aspen woods, lodgepole forest, marshland, beaver ponds, and meadow. It starts from Trail Ridge Road, about 3 miles north of the Grand Lake Entrance.

Information & Activities

Headquarters
1000 Hwy. 36, Estes Park, CO 80517. Phone (970) 586-1206. www.nps.gov/romo

Seasons & Accessibility
Park open year-round. Trail Ridge Road closes mid-October to late May, depending on snow. Old Fall River Road closes October to early July. In summer, free shuttle bus service on Bear Lake Road. (Note: Construction will close Bear Lake Road to cars between Sprague Lake and Bear Lake until 2004; shuttle buses will be operating.)

Visitor & Information Centers
Beaver Meadows Visitor Center, on US 36 at east entrance to park, and **Kawuneeche Visitor Center,** on US 34, all year. **Alpine Visitor Center,** June to mid-Oct. (weather permitting). **Fall River Visitor Center,** on US 34 west of Estes. Park at Fall River entrance, May through Oct. **Moraine Park Museum and Visitor Center,** May to mid-Oct. Call (970) 586-1206 for information.

Entrance Fee
$15 per car; $30 annual.

Pets
Not permitted on trails or in back-country. Must be on leashes at all times in parking lots and campgrounds.

Facilities for Disabled
Visitor centers and museum are wheel-chair accessible, as are amphitheaters in campgrounds, but not all rest rooms. Also accessible, the Lily Lake, Bear Lake, and Sprague Lake nature walks. Handicamp, at Sprague Lake, accommodates wheelchair backcountry campers—call (970) 586-1242.

Things to Do
Free naturalist-led activities: nature and history walks, hikes, campfire talks, slide shows, arts programs, snowshoe walks. Also, hiking, horseback trail rides (stables in Grand Lake; phone 303-627-3514), bicycling, fishing, ice fishing, rock climbing, mountain climbing, cross-country skiing, snowshoeing, limited snowmobiling.

Overnight Backpacking
Permits required, obtainable by mail or in person from headquarters or the Kawuneeche Visitor Center. Call (970) 586-1242. Fees charged for backcountry permits in summer.

Campgrounds
Five campgrounds. **Longs Peak,** 3-day limit; others, 7-day limit June through September. Additional days permitted other times of year. **Glacier Basin** and **Moraine Park** open June through September; reservations required late May to mid-September. Reserve through the National Parks Reservation Service (see p. 11). Other campgrounds open all year—first come, first served. $18 per night in summer; $12 per night in winter, when water is not available. No showers. RV sites at all except Longs Peak; no hookups. Reservations required at Glacier Basin Group Campground; contact National Parks Reservation Service. Cafeteria in Trail Ridge store (summer only).

Hotels, Motels, & Inns
(unless otherwise noted, rates are for 2 persons in a double room, high season)
In Estes Park, CO 80517:
Aspen Lodge Ranch Resort 6120 Hwy. 7, Longs Peak Rte. (800) 332-6867 or (970) 586-8133. 56 units. $450 per person, all inclusive. 3-day minimum. April through November. Pool. **Romantic RiverSong Bed & Breakfast Inn** P.O. Box 1910. (970) 586-4666. 10 units. $150-$295, includes breakfast. **The Stanley Hotel** 333 Wonderview Ave. (800) 976-1377 or (970) 586-3371. 140 units. $159-$299. Pool, restaurant. **Winding River Ranch** 5770 Hwy. 7. (970) 586-4212. 28 units. $1,000 per person per week, includes meals. Pool. June through August. *In Grand Lake, CO 80447:* **Bighorn Lodge** 613 Grand Ave. (800) 341-8000 or (970) 627-8101. 20 units. $90. **Driftwood Lodge** 12255 Hwy. 34. (970) 627-3654. 17 units, 9 with kitchenettes. $75-$95. Pool. **Western Riviera Motel** 419 Garfield. (970) 627-3580. 15 rooms, 4 cabins, 2-bedroom condo, 3-bedroom house with dock. $75-$250.

For additional accommodations, contact the Chambers of Commerce of Estes Park, (800) 443-7837; and Grand Lake, (970) 627-3372.

Excursions

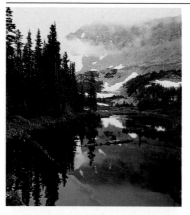

Roosevelt National Forest
Fort Collins, Colorado

This high mountain forest in the Front Range offers craggy peaks with canyons and passes and clear alpine lakes. Contains five wilderness areas. 788,333 acres. Hiking, boating, fishing, horseback riding, hunting, scenic drives, water sports, winter sports. More than 800 campsites, boat ramp, picnic areas. Four campgrounds open all year; others May through Sept. Backcountry accessible July through Oct. Adjoins Rocky Mountain NP on east. Information at Fort Collins off I-25, 45 miles from Rocky Mountain NP. (970) 498-2770.

Routt National Forest
Steamboat Springs, Colorado

Routt's three sections encompass high grasslands, forests, and jagged peaks along the Continental Divide. Alpine lakes brim with trout. Also contains waterfalls and parts of three wilderness areas. 1,124,774 acres. Hiking, boating, fishing, horseback riding, hunting, winter sports, water sports. 450 campsites, boat ramp, picnic areas, handicapped access. Open all year; most campsites open May through October. Information at Steamboat Springs, off US 40, about 75 miles from Rocky Mountain NP. (970) 879-1870.

Arapaho National Wildlife Refuge
Walden, Colorado

Set in a glacial basin ringed by mountains, Arapaho offers carefully maintained irrigated meadows that provide essential nesting habitat for waterfowl such as gadwall, lesser scaup, mallard, and wigeon. Black-crowned night herons breed along the Illinois River and sage grouse winter in upland hills. Features 6-mile-long self-guided auto tour (sometimes closed in winter due to snow). 24,804 acres. Fishing, hunting, scenic drives, nature trails. Open year-round, dawn to dusk. Headquarters on Colo. 125 south of Walden, about 60 miles from Rocky Mountain NP. (970) 723-8202.

Arapaho National Forest
Fort Collins, Colorado

The nation's highest paved highway traverses the steep mountains of this ski-country forest. Five wilderness areas feature stands of virgin timber, alpine lakes, and streams. 1,025,077 acres. Hiking, boating, climbing, bicycling, fishing, horseback riding, hunting, scenic drives, winter sports, water sports. 633 campsites, boat ramp, picnic areas. Open year-round, most campsites open June through September. Visitor center at Idaho Springs on I-70, about 50 miles south of Rocky Mountain NP. (970) 498-2770.

Florissant Fossil Beds National Monument
Florissant, Colorado

Some 35 million years ago a nearby volcanic field erupted, trapping wildlife in the ash that fell on ancient Lake Florissant. More than 1,000 species of fossil insects, 140 plants, and numerous fish, bird, and small mammal species have been excavated from the Florissant shales—making this one of the world's most comprehensive fossil sites. 5,998 acres. Hiking, horseback riding, cross-country skiing. Picnic areas, handicapped access. Open all year, dawn to dusk. Visitor center on Teller County Road 1, off US 24, about 150 miles south of Rocky Mountain NP. (719) 748-3253.

Dinosaur National Monument
Dinosaur, Colorado

Apatosaurus, Diplodocus, Stegosaurus—these Jurassic period giants once roamed here. Now their bones lie exposed in a fossil-filled cliff in the Dinosaur Quarry building. Each summer excavators add to the specimens. White-water rafting on Green and Yampa Rivers and Fremont pictographs and petroglyphs are also featured. 210,278 acres, part in Utah. Hiking, swimming, boating, fishing. 125 campsites, picnic areas, handicapped access. Open all year; most campsites open May through October. Dinosaur Quarry on Utah 149, off US 40, about 220 miles west of Rocky Mountain NP. (435) 789-2115.

Trail riders from the Peaceful Valley Ranch crossing the Little Missouri River

Theodore Roosevelt

North Dakota

Established November 10, 1978

70,447 acres

Theodore Roosevelt is unique among the scenic parks in that it preserves not only an extraordinary landscape but also the memory of an extraordinary man. It honors the president who probably did more for the National Park System than anyone before or since.

Theodore Roosevelt, who would later establish five national parks and help found the U.S. Forest Service, first came to Dakota Territory as a young man in 1883 to "bag a buffalo." He tried cattle ranching with no luck, but returned many times over the next 13 years, developing into a confirmed conservationist. It was the rugged badlands that taught him a healthy respect for nature while toughening him phys-

ically and mentally. "I would not have been President," he would later say, "had it not been for my experience in North Dakota."

The history of the North Dakota badlands, however, goes back long before Roosevelt—65 million years, to be exact. It was then that streams flowing from the newly arisen Rockies began depositing sediments here that would later be carved by the Little Missouri River and its tributaries. The results of this ongoing process of deposition and erosion are spectacular: wildly corrugated cliffs; steep, convoluted gullies; and dome-shaped hills, their layers of rock and sediment forming multicolored horizontal stripes that run for miles.

This austere landscape is home to a surprisingly dense population of wildlife. Bison, pronghorn, elk, white-tailed and mule deer, wild horses, and bighorn sheep inhabit the three units of the park, as do numerous smaller mammals, amphibians, and reptiles. After a rainy spring, a wealth of wildflowers colors the river bottomlands and prairie flats. And perhaps best of all is the shortage of one particular mammal—human beings. This relatively isolated park is hardly ever crowded, so you can experience the gorgeous loneliness of the badlands much the way Roosevelt did more than a hundred years ago.

How to Get There

South Unit: From Bismarck, 130 miles east, take I-94 west across the prairie to the entrance near Medora. From points south, take US 85 north to Belfield, then I-94 west 17 miles to Medora.

North Unit: US 85 north from Belfield will bring you to the North Unit entrance.

Airports: Bismarck and, from the west, Billings, Montana (280 miles).

When to Go

Although this is an all-year park, portions of the park road may close in winter, and services are quite limited from October to May. Summer is the most popular time to visit; the days are very long.

Late spring and early autumn are best for wildflower enthusiasts.

How to Visit

If you have only 1 day, take the **Scenic Loop Drive** in the **South Unit**, allowing yourself time for nature trails and longer hikes. A second day can be devoted to the **Scenic Drive** in the **North Unit**, 70 miles away. A visit to the undeveloped site of Roosevelt's **Elkhorn Ranch** or an overnight horse-packing trip from the **Peaceful Valley Ranch** in the South Unit can fill out a longer stay.

South Unit: Scenic Loop Drive

36 miles; a half to full day

Start at the **visitor center** near Medora, where you can visit the relocated **Maltese Cross Cabin.** The rustic headquarters of Roosevelt's first ranch, it contains period furnishings, ranching equipment, and some of Roosevelt's personal belongings. Then follow the road up the side of the eroded cliff to the **Medora Overlook.** Here you get a good view of the rough little town that epitomized the Wild West back in Roosevelt's day.

Cabin from Roosevelt's Maltese Cross Ranch

To Watford City

85

Prairie
• Dog
Town
Cannonball
Concretions
out

Slump
Block
Pullout

**North Unit
Visitor Center**

Longhorn
Pullout

CCC
Campground,
Forest Service

85

LITTLE MISSOURI
NATIONAL GRASSLAND

To Belfield

| 0 | 1 | 2 km |
| 0 | 1 | 2 mi |

LITTLE MISSOURI
NATIONAL
GRASSLAND

🏠 Ranger Station

🔺 Campground

△ Campground (private)

🚶 Self-guiding Trail

┈┈ Unpaved Road

⋯⋯ Trail

Prairie Dog
Town

Buck Hill
2,855 ft
Coal Vein Trail

Talkington
Trail

Prairie
Dog
Town

**Painted
Canyon
Visitor
Center**

To Belfield
and
Bismarck

Continue on, making sure to stop at the roadside prairie dog town (they bark warnings to each other as you approach). A little farther along is the **Skyline Vista.** Here you are on a high plateau, looking over the broken badlands. Actually, you are not so much "up" as the badlands are "down." The plateau is just a remnant of the original prairie before erosion took its toll, scooping out the bewildering landscape below.

The road descends again to the **River Woodland Overlook.** Beyond the row of cottonwood trees on the left lies an agent of the visual feast around you— the **Little Missouri River.** Notice how, in this arid environment, the vegetation is rigidly stratified according to the availability of water. There are tall cottonwoods near the river, and dark green junipers on the relatively moist northern hillsides and in places where water-bearing layers are exposed. On the dry southern slopes, where the sun quickly evaporates rainwater, little grows except grasses.

Turn right at the T to begin the **Scenic Loop Drive.** When you reach **Scoria Point,** you are deep into classic badlands territory. The bricklike material around you, which provides the brightest color in the badlands palette, was formed when a layer of black coal ignited. It baked the gray clay above, turning it into the reddish material known locally (but inaccurately) as scoria.

Along the next 6 miles of road, you will encounter two self-guided nature trails that are well worth

Calf from the South Unit's herd of 400 bison

Horse and rider exploring Theodore Roosevelt's vast beauty

taking. The **Ridgeline Nature Trail,** while only 0.6 mile long, involves some strenuous climbing; a pamphlet at the trailhead introduces the complex interaction of wind, fire, water, and vegetation in this harsh environment. The **Coal Vein Trail,** at the end of the short unpaved road branching off at mile 15.6 (there's a sign), is a full mile but less difficult; look for the manifold effects of a lignite bed that burned here from 1951 until early 1977. Between these two trails, pull off at the **North Dakota Badlands Overlook** for an exceptional view of the surroundings.

One-and-a-half miles past the turnoff for Coal Vein is the short road to **Buck Hill.** Take the 100-yard path to the summit for a 360-degree panorama of the eastern end of the park and beyond. Those oil wells on the horizon remind you that, although the badlands stretch for hundreds of miles, the park does not.

Return to the main road and turn right. The backstretch of the loop, running from Buck Hill to **Wind Canyon,** offers several possibilities for longer hikes. The **Talkington Trail** can be followed to the east or to the west, but even better is the **Jones Creek Trail** at mile 21. This trail follows a deeply eroded creek bed for about 3.5 miles, bisecting the loop road and offering good opportunities to see wildlife (including prairie rattlesnakes, *so be careful*). Since this trail is not a loop, you'll want to turn back at the halfway point or arrange to be picked up at the other end.

Back in the car, continue to the **Wind Canyon Trail.** This short but steep path offers a double treat: Not only do you get a magnificent vista of a long oxbow curve in the Little Missouri River, you also get a glimpse of how wind plays a part in shaping this unique landscape. The prevailing winds pick up sand from the riverbed and elsewhere and blow it into the northwest-facing canyon to your left, sandblasting the rock into smooth, bizarre shapes.

Back on the road, you pass another prairie dog town and then the **Peaceful Valley Ranch** on your right. These historic buildings have had a number of incarnations over the years, from working cattle ranch to park headquarters. These days the ranch is a private saddle horse concession, so you can stop for a ride (May to September) before rejoining the entrance road back to the visitor center.

North Unit: Scenic Drive

30 miles round-trip; a half to full day

Many people regard the North Unit as the more attractive of the two major portions of the park. Certainly the canyons seem steeper here, the river bottomlands lusher, and the blue, black, red, and beige stripes on every butte more pronounced. Located about 52 miles north of I-94, the North Unit is also more isolated, and consequently less visited. According to one ranger, there are times off-season when visitors can be almost alone in the North Unit.

Starting at the visitor center, take the **Scenic Drive** west into the park. Stop at the **Longhorn Pullout** to catch a glimpse of the park's demonstration herd of longhorn steers, kept here to commemorate the historic Long-X Trail, the major conduit for longhorns traveling from Texas to the Long-X Ranch just north of the park. If you hike the 11-mile **Buckhorn Trail Loop,** you'll travel along a part of this Old West "highway."

Stop at the **Slump Block Pullout** to see badlands erosion in action. The small hill to your right was once part of the higher cliff beyond— until unstable underlying sediments caused this piece to slump away. Try matching the diagonal layers of the slump block to the horizontal layers on the cliff to see how the block once fit in.

Pull off at the **Cannonball Concretions Pullout** to see how weathering agents have eroded out sandstone spheres formed by groundwater minerals cementing. Opposite the pullout, look for the **Little Mo Nature Trail.** This easy half-mile loop takes you through typical river woodlands, and a guide leaflet (available at the trailhead) allows you to identify many native plants the Plains Indians used for medicine, food, and raw materials. Watch for beavers and white-tailed deer.

Returning to the car, follow the road to the **Caprock Coulee Pullout,** where you can pick up the nature trail of the same name. Take this easy trail 0.75 mile up a dry canyon (a "coulee") to a grove of pedestal rocks ("caprocks"). The harder caprocks protect the sediments below while the surrounding sediments erode away, leaving the mushroom-shaped formations around you. At the end of the nature trail, you can either turn back or make a 5-mile loop by continuing to the **Upper Caprock Coulee Trail,** a choice which involves some steeper climbing but lots of opportunities to view wildlife.

Beyond the Caprock parking lot, the road climbs steeply to the level of the original prairie. At the top, the **River Bend Overlook** offers an absolutely stunning vista of the deep Little Missouri Valley and the extensive badlands on either side. The **Bentonitic Clay Overlook** a little farther on offers a less dramatic but perhaps more

Caprock formation

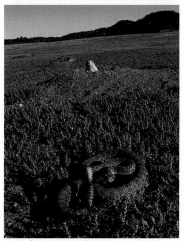

Prairie dog eyeing a rattler

instructive view. The blue-colored bentonite layer visible for miles is composed of an extremely absorbent volcanic ash that flows when wet. The plasticity of this layer accounts for much of the dynamism of the badlands landscape.

The road now traces the edge of a grassy plateau. This is prime bison territory; you may even have to wait while a herd crosses the road in front of you. At the **Man and Grass Pullout** you can get some idea of the extensive grasslands that made this part of Dakota worth the trip up the Long-X Trail. Finally, the road ends—spectacularly—at the **Oxbow Overlook.** After enjoying the visual banquet of badlands, return along the same road to the visitor center.

Information & Activities

Headquarters
P.O. Box 7, Medora, ND 58645. Phone (701) 623-4466. www.nps.gov/thro

Seasons & Accessibility
Park open all year, but access may be limited in winter due to snow. The South Unit road from Medora Visitor Center through Wind Canyon to the north boundary is kept plowed, but not the Scenic Loop Drive. The North Unit road is plowed from the entrance to the Caprock Coulee Trailhead. Call headquarters for weather and road information.

Visitor & Information Centers
Medora Visitor Center and the **Maltese Cross Cabin,** at the entrance to the South Unit, open daily all year. **Painted Canyon Visitor Center,** in the southeastern part of the South Unit off I-94, open from April to mid-November. **North Unit Visitor Center,** open daily April through September, and weekends in winter. Call headquarters for visitor information.

Entrance Fee
$5 per person, maximum of $10 per vehicle per week; $20 annually.

Pets & Horses
Pets are permitted on leashes except on trails and in buildings. Horses are prohibited in campgrounds, picnic areas, and on self-guided trails.

Facilities for Disabled
Visitor centers, rest rooms, campground sites, and some trails are wheelchair accessible.

Things to Do
Free naturalist-led activities: nature walks and talks, tours of Roosevelt's Maltese Cross Cabin (mid-June to mid-September), evening campfire programs. Also available, hiking, horseback riding (contact the Peaceful Valley Ranch in South Unit, 701-623-4568), interpretive exhibits, auto tours, limited canoeing and float trips, fishing (license required), and cross-country skiing.

Special Advisories
● View bison from a distance; they are known to attack if provoked.
● Rattlesnakes and black widow spiders often live in prairie dog burrows; be alert for them when hiking.
● Do not feed the prairie dogs; they bite and may carry disease.
● Be prepared for extremes of temperatures and sudden violent thunderstorms.

Overnight Backpacking
Permits required. They are free and can be obtained at visitor centers.

Campgrounds
Two campgrounds, both with 14-day limit. **Cottonwood** and **Juniper** open all year, first come, first served. Fees $10 per night. No showers. Tent and RV sites; no hookups. Three group campgrounds, **Cottonwood, Juniper,** and **Roundup** (horses); reservations required; contact park headquarters.

Hotels, Motels, & Inns
(unless otherwise noted, rates are for 2 persons in a double room, high season)
OUTSIDE THE PARK:
In Dickinson, ND 58601:
Comfort Inn 493 Elk Dr. (800) 228-5150 or (701) 264-7300. 115 units. $75. AC, pool.
Oasis Motel 1000 W. Villerd St. (701) 225-6703. 35 units, 6 with kitchenettes. $49-$54. AC, pool.
Travelodge 532 15th St. W. (800) 422-0949 or (701) 227-1853. 149 units. $69. AC, pool, restaurant.
In Medora, ND 58645:
Badlands Motel 501 Pacific Ave. (800) 633-6721 or (701) 623-4444. 116 units. $85. AC, pool. Open May to Oct.
Medora Motel 1 Main St. (mailing address: 400 E. River Rd. S.) (800) 633-6721 or (701) 623-4444. 208 units. $64. AC, pool. Open June to Labor Day.
Rough Riders Hotel 301 3rd Ave. (800) 633-6721 or (701) 623-4444. 10 units. $85. AC, restaurant. Open June to Labor Day.
In Watford City, ND 58854:
Roosevelt Inn 600 2nd Ave. S.W., P.O. Box 1003. (800) 887-9170 or (701) 842-3686. 42 units. $45. AC, pool, hot tub.

Excursions

Little Missouri National Grassland

Dickinson & Watford City, North Dakota

Bighorn sheep, elk, pronghorn, eagles, hawks, and grouse live in the prairie and badlands around Theodore Roosevelt NP. 1.1 million acres. Hiking, horseback riding, hunting. 5 campgrounds. Open all year; campgrounds late May to Labor Day. Information in Dickinson, off I-94. (701) 225-5151 or (701) 250-4443.

Lake Ilo National Wildlife Refuge

Dunn Center, North Dakota

Waterfowl nest in the grasslands surrounding 1,240-acre Lake Ilo, offering recreation not found on all refuges. 3,903 acres. Boating, fishing, picnic areas, nature trail, archaeological exhibits, scenic drives. Open year-round. Located on N. Dak. 200, about 50 miles east of Theodore Roosevelt NP's North Unit. (701) 548-8110.

Lostwood National Wildlife Refuge

Kenmare, North Dakota

Ducks, marsh birds, grouse, hawks, Baird's sparrows, and Sprague's pipits inhabit this stretch of prairie dotted with shallow glacial lakes, attracting bird-watchers from near and far. 26,900 acres. Hiking, hunting, scenic drives. Open May through September, dawn to dusk. Located off N. Dak. 8, about 135 miles northeast of Theodore Roosevelt NP's North Unit. (701) 848-2722.

Crosby Wetland Management District

Crosby, North Dakota

This prairie region comprises 92 waterfowl areas as well as Lake Zahl NWR. Features whooping cranes in migration, grouse on spring dancing grounds. 85,819 acres. Hunting. Permission required to use privately owned easement areas. Open all year. Lake Zahl NWR is off US 85, north of Theodore Roosevelt NP's North Unit. (701) 965-6488.

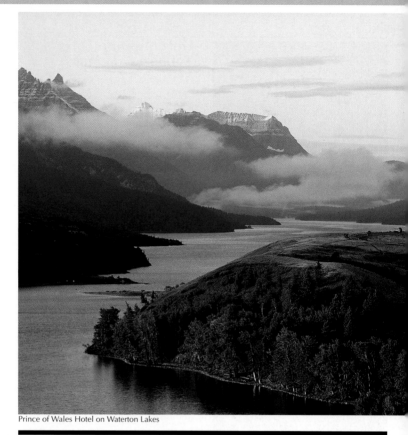

Prince of Wales Hotel on Waterton Lakes

Waterton-Glacier

Alberta, Canada, and Montana

Established June 18, 1932

Waterton Lakes, 73,800 acres;

Glacier, 1,013,572 acres

Waterton-Glacier International Peace Park World Heritage site contains 2,000 square miles of what naturalist John Muir called "the best care-killing scenery on the continent." Many-hued summits—whittled by ancient glaciers into walls and horns—rise abruptly from gently rolling plains. Some 650 lakes, dozens of glaciers, and innumerable waterfalls glisten in forested valleys. A scenic highway crosses the park, making much of its beauty accessible to the casual visitor. More than 700 miles of trails await hikers and horseback riders.

In 1932 Canada and the United States declared Waterton Lakes National Park (founded in 1895)

and neighboring Glacier National Park (founded in 1910) the world's first International Peace Park. While administered separately, the park's two sections cooperate in wildlife management, scientific research, and some visitor services.

The tremendous range of topography in Waterton-Glacier supports a rich variety of plants and wildlife. More than 1,800 plant species provide food and haven for 63 native species of mammals and more than 270 species of birds. In the 1980s the gray wolf settled into Glacier for the first time since the 1950s.

But now strip-mining and oil, gas, housing, and logging projects proposed or underway near the park's borders threaten the habitats of both water and land animals, including elk, bighorn sheep, and the threatened grizzly. Park officials and conservation groups are working with the U.S. Forest Service, the Canadian government, the Blackfeet Indian Reservation, and private companies to try to protect critical habitats.

Sheltered valleys and bountiful food have lured people here for nearly 10,000 years. Ancient cultures tracked bison across the plains, fished the lakes, and traversed the mountain passes. The Blackfeet controlled this land during the 18th and much of the 19th centuries.

How to Get There

Approach West Glacier (from Kalispell, Montana, about 35 miles) and East Glacier Park from US 2. US 89 leads to Many Glacier and St. Mary in the east; US 89 and Mont. 17 (Chief Mountain International Hwy.) form the shortest connection between Glacier and Waterton Lakes. Coming from Canada, follow Alberta 2, 5, or 6. Amtrak trains from Chicago and Seattle stop year-round just outside the park at West Glacier (Belton), Essex, Browning, and East Glacier Park; by prior arrangement, buses take travelers into the park. Nearest airports: Kalispell and Great Falls, Montana; and Lethbridge, Alberta.

When to Go

Summer. All of Going-to-the-Sun Road open about mid-June to mid-October; Chief Mountain International Highway, mid-May to late September. Trails at lower elevations usually clear of snow by mid-June; higher trails can remain snowed-in until mid-July. Cross-country skiing popular late December to April in many areas of the park.

How to Visit

Spend your first day on and around **Going-to-the-Sun Road,** considered by many one of the world's most spectacular highways. On a second day, travel the **Chief Mountain International Highway** north to Waterton Lakes, enjoying the contrast of peak and prairie. Drive Waterton's **Akamina Parkway** and **Red Rock Canyon Parkway.** Stay at least another day to visit Glacier's **Many Glacier.** For a longer visit, drive to **Two Medicine** for a boat ride and walk to an exquisite lake, then continue on to the **Walton Goat Lick Overlook,** both also in Glacier. If you have the stamina and overnight reservations, hike or ride horseback to one of the two remaining chalets built in Glacier early in the 20th century by the Great Northern Railway.

Going-to-the-Sun Road

50 miles; a full day

Note: Vehicles longer than 21 feet and wider than 8 feet prohibited on this road.

Begin early at **Apgar** on Glacier's west side. At the visitor center pick up details about trails and, since this is grizzly and black bear country, cautionary advice on avoiding encounters. Take time to admire **Lake McDonald** from the vantage point a little farther down the road. The park's largest lake, McDonald is 10 miles long and 472 feet deep; a glacier more than 2,000 feet thick gouged out its basin. Kootenai Indians, who performed lakeshore ceremonies, called the waters Sacred Dancing Lake.

Continue driving the Apgar loop and turn left at Going-to-the-Sun

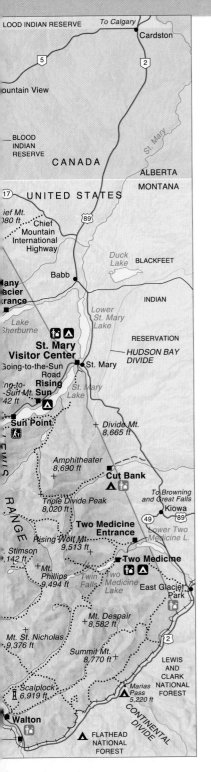

LOOD INDIAN RESERVE
To Calgary
Cardston

ountain View

BLOOD
INDIAN
RESERVE
CANADA
ALBERTA
MONTANA

UNITED STATES

ief Mt.
80 ft
Chief
Mountain
International
Highway

Duck
Lake   BLACKFEET

Babb

INDIAN

Lower
St. Mary
Lake

Lake
Sherburne

RESERVATION
HUDSON BAY
DIVIDE

St. Mary
Visitor Center
Going-to-the-Sun
Road   St. Mary

Rising
ng-to-
-Sun Mt. Sun
42 ft

St. Mary
Lake

Sun Point

Divide Mt.
8,665 ft

Amphitheater
8,690 ft

Cut Bank

Triple Divide Peak
8,020 ft

To Browning
and Great Falls
Kiowa

Two Medicine
Entrance
Rising Wolf Mt.
9,513 ft

Lower Two
Medicine L.

Stimson
142 ft

Mt.
Phillips
9,494 ft

Twin
Falls

Two
Medicine
Lake

Two Medicine

East Glacier
Park

Mt. Despair
8,582 ft

Mt. St. Nicholas
9,376 ft

Summit Mt.
8,770 ft

LEWIS
AND
CLARK
NATIONAL
FOREST

Scalplock
6,919 ft

Marias
Pass
5,220 ft

Walton

CONTINENTAL
DIVIDE

FLATHEAD
NATIONAL
FOREST

LEWIS RANGE

Road. Then pull over at **McDonald Falls,** on your left after about 10 miles. Stroll down to the viewpoint and note the layered rock. Waterton-Glacier's mountains are built mainly of sedimentary rock formed from mud and sand at the bottom of a sea that existed here for nearly a billion years. Over the eons, pressures in the Earth uplifted, thrusted, and folded the seabed into mountains. The rock exposed at McDonald Falls is among the oldest in the park.

Pull over near the campground at **Avalanche Creek** and start the self-guided **Trail of the Cedars** from the right side of the road. This wheelchair-accessible trail is on a boardwalk. The easy, quite popular, 0.75-mile nature stroll acquaints you with the cedar-hemlock forest through which you've been driving. Along the trail, Avalanche Creek tumbles through contoured walls of surprisingly red stone, formed during a period when the sea here retreated. In contact with oxygen, iron-bearing minerals in the mud formed the bright red mineral hematite that colors the rock. Extend your walk, if you wish, by taking the **Avalanche Lake Trail** from near the gorge up to glacier-fed **Avalanche Lake.** The gently climbing trail, about 4 miles round-trip, offers fine views of creek, lake, and waterfalls.

Return to your car. Directly ahead, in about 2 miles, you'll see the **Garden Wall,** part of the Continental Divide. West of the divide, waters flow to the Pacific; east of it, to the Arctic or Atlantic. Two glaciers ground down

Going-to-the-Sun Road in autumn

Massive Grinnell Glacier

opposite sides of a ridge to form the knife-edged Garden Wall. At the **Bird Woman Falls** viewpoint (some 10 miles from the campground at Avalanche Creek), an exhibit illustrates how glaciers also carved this spectacular U-shaped valley. Glacier National Park takes its name from the huge rivers of ice that sculptured the landscape during ice ages of the last two million years.

At **Logan Pass,** atop the Continental Divide, the peaks crowd around as if nearly close enough to touch. Park and walk up the hill past the visitor center to take the **Hidden Lake Nature Trail.** Be sure to buy or borrow a self-guiding pamphlet at the trailhead. The 3-mile round-trip begins on the boardwalk and offers vast displays of wildflowers framed by dramatic peaks. A breathtaking vista of **Hidden Lake** awaits you at the end. Watch for mountain goats grazing, marmots sunning, and golden eagles scanning for rodents. *Always stay on the trail:* Alpine plants, growing for short seasons in thin soil, are extremely fragile.

Return to your car and turn right onto the main road. Soon you'll be approaching **Going-to-the-Sun Mountain**—at 9,642 feet, the highest in this area of the park. The name comes, depending on which story you believe,

from a Blackfeet legend or an early explorer. The legend says that Napi, the creator, came to help the Blackfeet, then climbed this mountain to return to the sun.

Pull over again to view **Jackson Glacier,** one of the few glaciers visible from the road, about 4.5 miles after Logan Pass. The turnoff for **Sun Point** leads to picnic tables, fine vistas of **St. Mary Lake,** and a nature trail that introduces the ecology of the drier eastern portion of the park. Stop at the **Wild Goose Island Overlook,** another 1.5 miles down the road, and again at the display about **Triple Divide Peak,** less than 3 miles beyond. The road now crosses grasslands punctuated by groves of aspen and conifers. Going-to-the-Sun Road ends at **Divide Creek,** the border of the Blackfeet Indian Reservation.

Chief Mountain International Highway to Waterton Lakes

75 miles; at least a full day

Chief Mountain International Highway begins north of Babb off US 89. **Chief Mountain** (9,080 feet) dominates the horizon to your left, a soli-

Rainbows on Swiftcurrent Lake

Mountain goat and kid

tary peak that commands awe. Black-feet seeking spiritual guidance still tie a traditional offering of colored cloth to trees at its base.

Chief Mountain also represents the easternmost extension of the Lewis Overthrust, a major geological feature. About 8.5 miles after the U.S.-Canada customs station, an exhibit explains the overthrust. Pull over again in 1.5 miles for a superb view of **Waterton Valley** and a display that identifies the summits.

Follow the signs for Waterton Lakes National Park. The park's main information center will be on your right, about 4 miles beyond the park entrance, just before Waterton Park townsite. On your left stands the **Prince of Wales Hotel,** which commands a first-rate view of **Upper Waterton Lake** from its lobby. For a loftier panorama, climb the steep but gratifying **Bears Hump Trail,** 2 miles round-trip. The path starts from the information center.

At road's end awaits **Waterton Park** townsite, a village of about a hundred year-round residents. It blossoms in summer with eateries and gift shops. Wildlife is often on-hand: Bighorn sheep and deer may be hiding in the shadows; you'll less likely spot the rare mountain lion or bear. On the

lakeshore, near the end of the road, a pavilion reviews the park's history.

Back in your car, turn onto **Akamina Parkway,** which traces **Cameron Valley** 10 miles to **Cameron Lake.** At the lake, which lies in a large glacier-carved basin, rent a boat, fish for trout, or stroll the 2-mile round-trip **Cameron Lakeshore Trail** through the forest of Englemann spruce and subalpine fir. *Do not continue past the end of the trail*—grizzlies are often sighted there.

Back in your car, return to Alberta 5; turn left, then left again onto 10-mile-long **Red Rock Canyon Parkway.** The prairie here brims with flowers in May, June, and early July. Indians hunted bison along **Blakiston Creek,** driving them over the cliff to your left. In about 3 miles, near Crandell Mountain Campground, stop at the exhibit on ancient Indian life. Drive on to the road's end at **Red Rock Canyon,** where archaeologists found a camp dating from 8,400 years ago. Don't miss the half-mile **Red Rock Canyon Loop Trail.**

Many Glacier & Swiftcurrent Valley

13 miles from Babb; at least a half day

Many Glacier, named for the glaciers on surrounding mountains, is a hiker's Eden and a good place to see bighorn sheep and other wildlife. A dam a few miles outside the park created **Lake Sherburne,** on your left as you enter the park. The lake submerged much of Altyn, a boomtown built during the mining frenzy that started and fizzled out here at the turn of the 20th century.

Just beyond the lake, to your left, is the **Many Glacier Hotel.** The Great Northern Railway built this hotel in 1915 to help promote tourism along its tracks. The company also built more than a dozen backcountry tent camps and chalets in Waterton-Glacier. Early tourists rode horses between the railway stations, hotels, and chalets. Park at the hotel and, for an easy walk and fine introduction to the area's plants, animals, peaks, and glaciers, take the **Swiftcurrent Nature Trail.** This 2.6-mile loop around the lake starts at the shore south of the hotel. The trail traverses both 400-year-old spruce-fir forest and 60-year-old lodgepole pine forest, planted in the aftermath of a great fire in 1936.

For an easy 2.5-mile stroll through old-growth forest, go on the **Swiftcurrent and Josephine Lakes** boat tour and hike. With more time and plenty of stamina, join a naturalist-led hike (11 miles round-trip) to the edge of **Grinnell Glacier,** one of the largest in the park. Check departure times in the park newspaper.

Other Sights & Trails

Before hiking, be sure to stop by a visitor center or ranger station to pick up maps and schedules—and check for trail closings due to bears.

Drive to **Two Medicine,** inside the park's southeastern border off Mont. 49, and take the boat across **Two Medicine Lake.** Then walk past **Twin Falls** through huckleberry meadows to **Upper Two Medicine,** which is surrounded by brightly colored cliffs (4.4 miles round-trip). Back in your car, head south on Mont. 49 and west on US 2 to the **Walton Goat Lick Overlook.** A natural salt lick attracts mountain goats from miles around,

usually in spring and early summer.

From Logan Pass, the **Highline Trail** offers splendid panoramic views on the way to **Granite Park Chalet** (7.6 miles one way), one of the Great Northern's two remaining chalets. Part of the trail is cut into the cliff face, so it is not for the fainthearted. The other chalet, **Sperry,** was recently restored. Sperry can be reached by horseback or hiking from **Jackson Glacier Overlook** or Lake McDonald.

From Many Glacier, **Iceberg Lake Trail** leads you among wide panoramas to an iceberg-studded turquoise lake, a 10-mile round-trip. **Cracker Lake Trail,** 12.3 miles round-trip, parallels boulder-strewn **Canyon Creek** partway to this glacier-fed lake. Nearby lie remains of **Cracker Mine.**

From Waterton Park townsite, **Rowe Meadow** (a moderately strenuous, 6.5-mile round-trip) offers a rainbow of wildflowers in early summer. Climb another seven-tenths of a mile to **Upper Rowe Lake** through an alpine larch forest. The **International Peace Park Hike,** held on Saturday mornings, leads 8.4 miles from Waterton Park to **Goat Haunt** in the United States. Return by boat.

The Grizzly

Blackfeet Indians called it Real Bear, this huge, intelligent, unpredictable animal we call the grizzly. An adult male may weigh 400 to 600 pounds, twice as much as a black bear, yet it can sprint up to 35 mph.

Tens of thousands of grizzlies roamed western North America in 1850; by 1975, the guns of settlers, hunters, and livestock owners, coupled with loss of habitat, had driven the bears close to extinction in the lower 48 states. While some 50,000 grizzlies may remain in Alaska and Canada, fewer than a thousand now inhabit the rest of the United States, perhaps 300 of them in Waterton-Glacier and nearby wilderness lands.

Though mythologized as a ruthless predator, the grizzly eats mostly grass, berries, and roots. It will also consume insects and rodents and even larger animals if easy prey. Unless accustomed to human scent and food, most grizzlies will move on when they hear a human coming.

Grizzly

In Glacier it's said that 90 percent of grizzly management is people management. And people management has changed greatly since 1967, when two Glacier campers were killed by grizzlies accustomed to eating garbage. (Before then at least one park lodge fed bears garbage to entertain visitors.) Today rangers carefully instruct visitors on sharing the wilderness with bears.

Information & Activities

Headquarters
Waterton: Waterton Park, Alberta, T0K 2M0, Canada. (403) 859-2224. **Glacier:** West Glacier, MT 59936. (406) 888-7800. www.nps.gov/glac

Seasons & Accessibility
Parks open year-round; winter snows limit access and services.

Visitor & Information Centers
Waterton: Waterton Information Centre in Waterton Park. (403) 859-5133. Usually open mid-May through September; call ahead.
Glacier: Apgar Visitor Center, inside West Entrance, open daily late April through October, weekends in winter. (406) 888-7800. **Logan Pass Visitor Center,** open mid-June to mid-October. **St. Mary Visitor Center** at East Entrance open late May to mid-October.

Entrance Fees
Waterton: Canadian $5 per person. **Glacier:** $10 per car valid for 7 days; $20 annual.

Facilities for Disabled
Waterton: International Peace Park Pavilion, Heritage Centre, Cameron Lake exhibit building wheelchair accessible. Also, several camping facilities, Lake Linnet Trail, drive through the Bison Paddock, and most rest rooms. **Glacier:** Most visitor center facilities accessible; also, Trail of the Cedars, Running Eagle Falls Trail, Oberlin Bend Trail, and Apgar Bike Path.

Things to Do
Waterton: Free naturalist-led activities: walks and hikes, slide shows, campfire programs. Also, swimming, fishing (license needed), boating, launch tours, nature courses, horseback rides, golf, fishing, cross-country skiing. **Glacier:** Free naturalist-led activities: walks and hikes, slide talks, campfire programs. Also, hiking, horseback rides, boating, fishing (no license required), bicycling, launch tours, nature courses, cross-country skiing.

Overnight Backpacking
Permits required. Call in advance about reservations and fees. Waterton backcountry: (403) 859-5133; Glacier backcountry: (406) 888-7857.

Backcountry Chalets
Granite Park Chalet (800) 521-7238, $72; and **Sperry Chalet** (406) 387-5654, $50 per room plus $100 per person, offer lodgings and food services.

Campgrounds
Waterton: Three campgrounds, 14-day limit. Open mid-May to early Sept. (**Townsite** open to mid-Oct.). First come, first served. Fees Can. $12-$24 per night. Tent and RV sites; hookups at Townsite. Must reserve at **Belly River Group Campgrounds;** contact park. Food services available in park. **Glacier:** 13 campgrounds, limit 7 days July through August, otherwise 14 days. **Apgar** and **St. Mary** open all year, others late spring to mid-fall. Reservations for Fish Creek and St. Mary through the National Parks Reservation Service (see p. 11). Others, first come, first served. Fees $12-$17 per night. Tent and RV sites; no hookups. **Apgar Group Campground** first come, first served. Food in park.

Hotels, Motels, & Inns
(unless otherwise noted, rates are for 2 persons in a double room, high season)
INSIDE WATERTON, Alberta T0K 2M0: **Aspen Village Inn** P.O. Box 100. (403) 859-2255. 50 units. Can. $129. Open mid-May to mid-Oct. **Bayshore Inn** 111 Waterton Ave. Summer (403) 859-2211; winter (403) 238-4847. 70 units. Can. $139. Rest. April to Oct. **Crandell Mt. Lodge** 1 Waterton Park. (403) 859-2288. 17 units, 8 with kitchenettes. Can. $129-$149. March to Oct. **Prince of Wales Hotel** (in Waterton Townsite) Reservations: Glacier Park, Inc., P.O. Box 2025, 774 Railroad St., Columbia Falls, MT 59912. (406) 756-2444. 86 units. Can. $259-$799. Rest. Mid-May to late Sept. INSIDE GLACIER:
The following are open from June to mid-Sept. Contact Glacier Park, Inc., P.O. Box 2025, 774 Railroad St., Columbia Falls, MT 59912. (406) 756-2444. **Glacier Park Lodge** 161 units. $135-$500. Pool, restaurant. **Lake McDonald Lodge** 100 units. $92-$142. Restaurant. **Many Glacier Hotel** 216 units. $111-$219. Rest. **Rising Sun Motor Inn** 72 units. Rooms $90-$98. Rest. **Swiftcurrent Motor Inn** 88 units. Cabins $43-$73; rooms $88. **The Village Inn** 36 units. $100-$165.

Excursions

Flathead National Forest
Kalispell, Montana

Recreation opportunities abound here amid mountains, lakes, Wild and Scenic Rivers, and more than 2,000 miles of trails. Contains parts of three wilderness areas, notably the Bob Marshall. 2,346,000 acres. Hiking, boating, climbing, fishing, horseback riding, hunting, scenic drives, winter sports, water sports. 400 campsites, boat ramp, picnic areas. Open all year; campsites open June to mid-September. Visitor center off US 2 at Hungry Horse Dam, about 7 miles from Waterton-Glacier NP. (406) 758-5200.

Lewis & Clark National Forest
Great Falls, Montana

This forest has two sections separated by plains: The Rockies section boasts steep terrain with parts of two wilderness areas; the Jefferson section contains gentler peaks and rolling hills with broad plateaus. Large bighorn herd. 1,812,156 acres. Hiking, boating, climbing, fishing, horseback riding, hunting, winter sports, water sports. 24 campsites, 5 winter cabins (reservations required), boat ramp, handicapped access. Open all year; campsites open late spring to fall. Adjoins Waterton-Glacier NP on south. Information: 1101 15th St. N., Great Falls. (406) 791-7700.

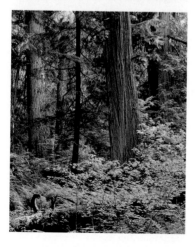

Kootenai National Forest
Libby, Montana

With a climate closer to that of the Pacific coast than to the rest of Montana, Kootenai features virgin stands of western red cedar. Lake Koocanusa, 90 miles long, and many other streams and reservoirs offer abundant recreation. Contains Cabinet Mountains Wilderness. 2,250,000 acres, part in Idaho. Hiking, boating, climbing, bicycling, fishing, hunting, scenic drives, winter sports. 703 campsites, picnic areas. Open all year; most campsites open late spring to fall. Information at Libby on US 2, about 120 miles from Waterton-Glacier NP. (406) 293-6211.

Pine Butte Swamp Preserve

Choteau, Montana

Pine Butte, a 500-foot promontory, overlooks this Nature Conservancy refuge dedicated to maintaining the essential habitat of the grizzly. Also contains many other wildlife species, including lynx, mountain lion, sandhill crane, golden eagle, mink, and bighorn sheep. Features the Egg Mountain duckbill dinosaur nesting site; daily paleontological tours during summer. Permission required to explore. 18,000 acres, along the Teton River. Hiking. The Pine Butte Guest Ranch offers horseback riding, natural history tours (open May through October). Preserve open all year. Off US 89, about 60 miles southeast of Waterton-Glacier NP. (406) 466-5526.

Benton Lake National Wildlife Refuge

Black Eagle, Montana

More than 200 species of birds find food, protection, and carefully maintained nesting areas on this prairie marsh in the midst of wheat fields and grasslands. Northern pintail, gadwall, white-faced ibis, and Canada goose are among the species that nest in the ancient glacial lakebed that holds the marsh. 12,383 acres. Hunting, birdwatching, self-guided auto tour. Open when accessible (snow drifts often cover road Nov. to March), dawn to dusk. Headquarters off US 87, 100 miles from Waterton-Glacier NP. (406) 727-7400.

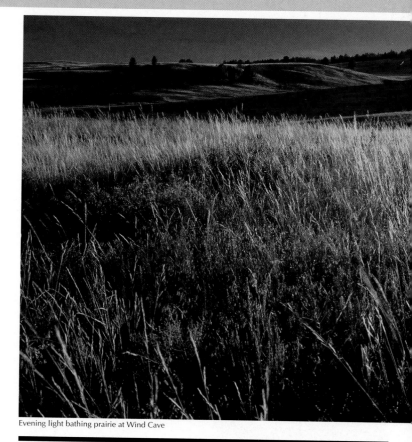

Evening light bathing prairie at Wind Cave

Wind Cave

South Dakota

Established January 9, 1903

28,295 acres

Too many visitors leave Wind Cave National Park knowing only half of its charms. Ironically, the half they know is the half that's not visible from the surface.

Above the spectacular underground labyrinth for which the park is named lies an unusual ecosystem, one that marks the boundary between the mixed-grass prairie of the western Great Plains and the ponderosa pine forests of the Black Hills. Thus, the park plays host to plant and animal species from several distinct geographical areas—prairie falcons and meadowlarks from the grasslands coexist here with nuthatches and wild turkeys from the forests.

Wildlife should be a major draw here. Because of the park's small size and relatively large bison population, the chances of seeing bison—the so-called American buffalo—are probably better at this park than at almost any other; indeed it's often difficult to avoid the great beasts. Pronghorn, mule deer, and prairie dogs are present in large numbers—and highly visible since 75 percent of the park is open grassland. Elk live in the forest fringes; you probably won't see many of them, but if you have the good luck to come in the autumn you'll hear their eerie bugling.

Below ground lies Wind Cave, where more than 104 miles of explored passages make it one of the world's longest caves. Because the cave is relatively dry, it contains few of the stalactites and stalagmites you see in other caves. But it has many unusual mineral formations, including perhaps the world's best collection of boxwork, a calcite formation resembling irregular honeycombs. The most distinctive feature of the cave may be the strong winds that alternately rush in and out of its mouth, equalizing air pressure between the passages inside and the atmosphere outside.

How to Get There

For the scenic route from Rapid City (74 miles away), take US 16 to US 16A south, detouring for a glimpse of Mount Rushmore, to S. Dak. 87 south. This route—not open to RVs and trailers—takes you along the Needles Highway and through Custer State Park to Wind Cave's north entrance. The faster route is to follow S. Dak. 79 south from Rapid City to Hot Springs and then turn north onto US 385 to the south entrance. From the west, take US 16 east to Custer and US 385 south from there. Airport: Rapid City Regional.

When to Go

All-year park. Although the cave and visitor center are open every day except Thanksgiving and Christmas and New Year's Days, the park offers far fewer cave tours off-season (late September to May). Late spring to midsummer are best for wildflowers. Saturdays and Sundays in summer are the days least likely to be crowded. The campground is rarely, if ever, full.

How to Visit

A good plan of action for a single-day visit would be to spend the morning in **Wind Cave** on one of the shorter introductory tours and the afternoon exploring the park's prairies and forests on the **Scenic Drive.** A second day would be the time for one of the longer **Candlelight** or **Caving Tours.**

People with physical limitations will want to stick to the shorter, less strenuous tours, although even the shortest involves climbing up and down about 150 steps. (If claustrophobia is a problem for you, you might think twice about entering the cave at all.) Wear good walking shoes, and, since the cave temperature is a constant 53°F, take a jacket even on hot summer days. Reservations for tours are recommended. You must be 8 years old for the Candlelight Tour and 16 years old for the Wild Caving Tour.

Wind Cave: Guided Tours

1 hour to a half day

All tours begin at the visitor center, where several exhibits provide important background information. A video explains the connection between the park's subsurface world and the aboveground prairie. The same forces that lifted the nearby Black Hills created cracks in the limestone layers beneath the present-day park. Water seeped into these cracks and, over millions of years, gradually dissolved the rock, creating the maze of passages and tunnels we see today.

Most first-timers will choose to take either the **Natural Entrance Tour,** which lasts about an hour and 15 minutes, or the **Fairgrounds Tour,** which is 15 minutes longer. These tours introduce you to the under-

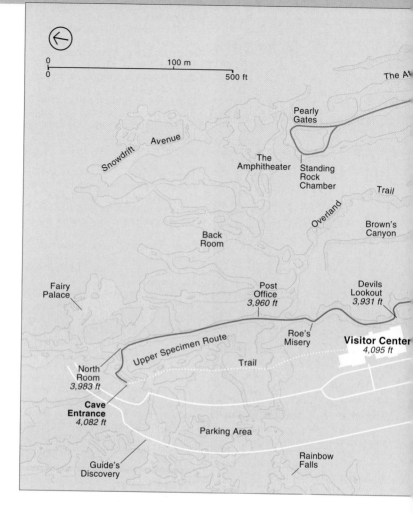

The map contains the following labels:

0 / 100 m

0 / 500 ft

The A

Pearly Gates

Avenue

Snowdrift

The Amphitheater

Standing Rock Chamber

Trail

Overland

Brown's Canyon

Back Room

Fairy Palace

Post Office 3,960 ft

Devils Lookout 3,931 ft

Roe's Misery

Visitor Center 4,095 ft

Upper Specimen Route

Trail

North Room 3,983 ft

Cave Entrance 4,082 ft

Parking Area

Guide's Discovery

Rainbow Falls

ground world, stressing basic information about caves and cave formations; they take you through such colorfully named places as the **Post Office** (named for the extensive boxwork on the walls), the **Devil's Lookout,** and the **Blue Grotto.**

The **Garden of Eden Tour** is a loop around from the elevator to the **Garden of Eden** lasting one hour; it is recommended for people with time or physical limitations.

If you are a history buff, by all means take the **Candlelight Tour** (summer only). Conducted by the light of candle lanterns, this 2-hour tour harkens back to the 1890s, when Wind Cave was owned by the Wonderful Wind Cave Improvement Company and tours were measured by the number of candles needed to complete them. The tour goes past the **Blue Grotto** to the **Pearly Gates** and beyond; it stresses the cave's ambience and exploration. The tour involves some stooping and stairclimbing.

For those in good physical condition with a keen interest in caves, the park offers a 4-hour **Wild Caving Tour,** designed to simulate a cave exploration trip. Rangers lead participants into the ghostly far reaches of the cave. You crawl through narrow openings, squeeze into tight passages, and make a glorious mess of yourself (take a change of clothes). The guide's commentary focuses on recreational caving and its impact on cave ecology.

To Mount Rushmore NM
87
CUSTER STATE PARK
5
6
385
WIND CAVE NATIONAL PARK
BLACK
HILLS
NATIONAL
FOREST
Elk Mountain Campground
■ **Visitor Center**
5
101
385
79
0   5 km
0   5 mi
● Hot Springs

Fairgrounds
3,967 ft

Bachelor's Quarters

Three-way Stair

Blue Grotto
3,835 ft

Chert Room

Elks Room
3,911 ft

Temple Room

Elevator Building
4,055 ft

Crossroads
3,885 ft

Garden of Eden

Methodist Church

Assembly Room
3,863 ft

Trail

Rome

Parking Area

🔺 Campground

🗼 Lookout Tower

Natural Entrance Tour

Fairgrounds Tour

Candlelight Tour

Caving Tour

Garden of Eden Tour

Unpaved Road

Muddle Room

Omnibus Hall

The cave's famous boxwork, a calcite formation

Scenic Drive

13 miles; at least a half day

Begin on US 385 at the southern boundary of the park, about 11 miles north of Hot Springs. At the **Bison Pullout** you get the first of many excellent views of the prairie, much as it existed before the plows of the white man drastically changed it. You may see bison and pronghorn grazing side by side on the grassy hillsides. The **Mineral Lick Pullout** a little farther on overlooks a site where bison lick salt from the soil.

From the visitor center, drive out to the campground for the self-guided **Elk Mountain Nature Trail.** This easy 1-mile hike takes you through a transitional prairie-and-pine-forest environment, where you'll see the grasses and trees encroaching on each other's domain. An accompanying trail guide points out some of the plant life around you, including prickly pear cactus and yucca.

Back on the road, continue to the junction with S. Dak. 87 and turn right, stopping at the **Prairie Dog Pullout** just after the turn. This is a good place to observe these once abundant rodents, who survive the predation of many natural enemies by their system of scanning territory and warning their fellows of eminent danger. Your approach will probably set off a cacophony of barks. If you stay in the car, you'll have more to watch; cars don't spook the prairie dogs but people do. At dawn or dusk, watch the outskirts of the prairie dog town for patrolling coyotes.

The road now climbs from the prairie into the higher ponderosa pine forests that cover much of the Black Hills. Stop at the **Ancient Foundations Pullout** to learn about the granite core of the Black Hills. Other pullouts show how various kinds of plants and animals coexist in this dynamic prairie-forest border area.

Turn right at the **Rankin Ridge Pullout** and follow the half-mile road to the trailhead. The Rankin Ridge Trail, a 1-mile loop, climbs up among the pines to a fire tower. In summer, you can climb the tower for a great view.

Back in the car, return to the main road and continue to the north entrance of the park to complete the tour. Those with maneuverable vehicles may wish to make a loop by turning right on unpaved Park Road 5. This road connects with Park Road 6 and then County Road 101; it takes you through pronghorn and bison territory. Turn right on County Road 101 to return to US 385 south of the park.

Information & Activities

Headquarters
Hot Springs, SD 57747. Phone (605) 745-4600. www.nps.gov/wica

Seasons & Accessibility
Open year-round.

Visitor & Information Centers
Visitor center located 11 miles from Hot Springs on US 385; both it and the cave open all year. A variety of tours offered daily Memorial Day to Labor Day.

Entrance Fees
None. Fees for cave tours: $6 to $20 adults; $3 children ages 6 to 16.

Facilities for Disabled
The visitor center and a cave tour are wheelchair accessible.

Things to Do
Naturalist-led activities: a variety of cave tours, nature walks, campfire talks. Also, interpretive exhibits, scenic drive, nature trails, hiking, bicycling, wildlife watching.

Overnight Backpacking
Permits required; free at visitor center.

Campgrounds
One campground; 14-day limit. Fees $10 per night mid-May to mid-September; $5 per night April to mid-May and mid-September to late October, with reduced services. Closed remainder of year. First come, first served. Tent and RV sites; no hookups or showers.

Hotels, Motels, & Inns
(unless otherwise noted, rates are for 2 persons in a double room, high season)
In Custer, SD 57730:
Bavarian Inn Motel P.O. Box 152. (800) 657-4312 or (605) 673-2802. 64 units, 1 condo. $96. AC, pool, rest.
Dakota Cowboy Inn 208 W. Mt. Rushmore Rd. (800) 279-5079 or (605) 673-4659. 48 units. $94. AC, pool, restaurant. Open May to early October.
In Hot Springs, SD 57747:
Best Western Inn by the River 602 W. River St. (888) 605-4292 or (605) 745-4292. 31 units. $104. AC, pool.
Historic Braun Hotel 902 N. River St. (605) 745-3187. 11 units. $85. AC, rest.

Also, write or phone adjacent Custer State Park for information about its lodges: HC 83 Box 70, Custer, SD 57730. Phone (800) 710-2267 or (605) 255-4515.

Excursions

Buffalo Gap National Grassland
Wall, South Dakota

These mixed grasslands and badlands dotted with prairie dog towns offer superb rock hunting. 591,727 acres. Hiking, fishing, horseback riding, hunting, mountain biking, camping. Open year-round. National Grassland Visitor Center at Wall, off I-90, about 75 miles from Wind Cave NP. Surrounds Badlands NP. (605) 279-2125.

Mount Rushmore National Memorial
Keystone, South Dakota

Colossal visages of Washington, Jefferson, Theodore Roosevelt, and Lincoln gaze out over the Black Hills NF. From June through September the sculptor's studio is open; a year-round evening program ends in the dramatic lighting of the memorial. 1,240 acres. Food services, handicapped access. Located on S. Dak. 244, about 25 miles north of Wind Cave NP. (605) 574-2523.

Jewel Cave National Monument
Custer, South Dakota

Sparkling crystals of calcite are the "jewels" of this 107-mile-long cave. 12,776 acres. Spelunking, hiking, picnic areas, visitor center. Open all year (cave tours year-round). In Black Hills National Forest on US 16, about 35 miles northwest of Wind Cave NP. (605) 673-2288.

Devils Tower National Monument
Devils Tower, Wyoming

Theodore Roosevelt established the first national monument in 1906 to preserve this 865-foot column of hardened magma—now a mecca for technical rock climbers. 1,347 acres. Hiking. 35 campsites, picnic areas, handicapped access. Open all year, roads plowed in winter; full facility open mid-April through November. Campground closed Nov. to mid-April. On Wyo. 110, off Wyo. 24, about 130 miles from Wind Cave NP. (307) 467-5283.

Summer morning along the Yellowstone River at Lower Falls

Yellowstone

Wyoming, Idaho, and Montana

Established March 1, 1872

2,221,766 acres

Yellowstone is a geological smoking gun that reminds us of how violent the Earth can be. One event overshadows all others: Some 600,000 years ago, an area many miles square at what is now the center of the park suddenly exploded. In minutes the landscape was devastated. Fast-moving ash flows covered thousands of square miles. At the center there remained only a smoldering caldera, a collapsed crater 28 by 47 miles. At least two other cataclysmic events preceded this one. Boiling hot springs, fumaroles, and geysers serve as reminders that another could occur.

Yellowstone, however, is much more than hot ground and gushing steam. Located astride the Continental Divide, most of the park occupies a high plateau surrounded by mountains and drained by several rivers. Park boundaries enclose craggy peaks, alpine lakes, deep canyons, and vast forests. In 1872, Yellowstone became the world's first national park, the result of great foresight on the part of many people about our eventual need for the solace and beauty of wild places.

In early years, what made Yellowstone stand out was the extravaganza of geysers and hot springs. The wild landscape and the bison, elk, and bears were nice but, after all, America was still a pioneer country filled with scenic beauty and animals.

As the West was settled, however, Yellowstone's importance as a wildlife sanctuary grew. The list of park animals is a compendium of Rocky Mountain fauna: elk, bison, mule resource projects. Cooperative management between the park and the seven forests that make up the greater Yellowstone ecosystem is essential if wildlife and thermal features are to survive.

How to Get There

There are five entrances: from the west, West Yellowstone (Montana); from the north and northeast, Gardiner and Cooke City (Montana); from the east, on US 14/16/20 from Cody (Wyoming); and from the south, at Flagg Ranch (Wyoming), which is north of Grand Teton National Park and Jackson (64 miles away). Airports: West Yellowstone (summer only), Bozeman, and Billings in Montana; Cody and Jackson in Wyoming.

When to Go

More than half of the 3 million annual visitors come in July and August. In September and early October, the weather is good, the visitors few, and the wildlife abundant. In May and June, you can see newborn animals, but the weather may be cold, wet, and even snowy. Between about November through April most park roads are closed to vehicles.

deer, bighorn sheep, grizzly bear, black bear, moose, pronghorn, coyote, mountain lion, beaver, trumpeter swan, eagle, osprey, white pelican, and more.

During the summer of 1988, fire touched many sections of the park, in some areas dramatically changing the appearance of the landscape. Yet not one major feature was destroyed. The geysers, waterfalls, and herds of wildlife are still here. Many places show no impact at all, while those that are regenerating benefit both vegetation and animal life. Side by side, burned areas and nonburned areas provide an intriguing study in the causes and effects of fire in wild places. Yellowstone has witnessed bigger natural events than this and may well again.

Of far greater concern to environmentalists than the fires are the impact of increasing numbers of visitors, the threatened grizzly bear population, and, on nearby lands, the planned development of natural

Bull moose wading in the Yellowstone River

Ranger Station
Campground
Interpretive Trail
-·-·- Unpaved Road
········· Hiking Trail

0   5   10 km
0   5   10 mi

CUSTER
NATIONAL
FOREST

GALLATIN
NATIONAL
FOREST

Cooke
City   212
Silver Gate
Northeast Entrance

MONTANA
WYOMING

Baronnette Peak
10,404 ft

Abiathar
Peak
10,928 ft

To Red Lodge

Forces of
the Northern Range

Slough Creek

Tower-
Roosevelt

Pebble Creek

Road

The Thunderer
10,554 ft

Cache Mountain
9,596 ft

SHOSHONE
NATIONAL
FOREST

Prospect
Peak
9,525 ft

Tower Fall

Mt. Norris
9,936 ft

SPECIMEN RIDGE

Mt. Washburn
10,243 ft

MIRROR PLATEAU

Observation
Peak
9,397 ft

Inspiration
Point

Lamar

Approximate Caldera Boundary

Parker Peak
10,203 ft

Saddle Mountain
10,670 ft

Canyon
Village
Visitor
Center

Artist Point

Lower Falls
Upper Falls

Pollux Peak
11,067 ft

HAYDEN
VALLEY

Yellowstone

Pelican Cone
9,643 ft

Castor Peak
10,854 ft

Mud Volcano

LeHardys Rapids

Fishing Bridge
Visitor Center

PELICAN VALLEY

RANGE

Pyramid Peak
10,497 ft

SHOSHONE
NATIONAL
FOREST

Bridge Bay

Lake Village

Gull Point

Cody Peak
10,267 ft

East
Entrance

14

Grand Loop
Road

Yellowstone
Lake

Avalanche Peak
10,566 ft

16

20

To Cody

West
Thumb

West Thumb
Geyser Basin

Grant Village
Visitor Center

Top Notch Peak
10,238 ft

Sylvan Pass
8,530 ft

Reservation Peak
10,629 ft

Mt. Doane
10,656 ft

Mt. Stevenson
10,352 ft

Mt. Langford
10,774 ft

ABSAROKA

Mt. Schurz
11,139 ft

CONTINENTAL

DIVIDE

THE PROMONTORY

RED
MOUNTAINS

Heart
Lake

Eagle Peak
11,358 ft

Mt. Sheridan
10,308 ft

Yellowstone

Turret Mountain
10,995 ft

Snake

TWO OCEAN PLATEAU

THE TRIDENT

Mt. Hancock
10,214 ft

Thorofare

BRIDGER-TETON   NATIONAL   FOREST

Old Faithful blasting off at sunset

During the winter season, mid-December to mid-March, Yellowstone becomes a fantasy of steam and ice; facilities are limited but sufficient. Only the road between the North and Northeast Entrances stays open to cars, but snowmobiling is permitted on unplowed roads. Heated snow coaches offer tours and give cross-country skiers access to about 50 miles of groomed trails.

How to Visit

The 142-mile **Grand Loop Road** forms a figure eight, with connecting spurs to the five entrances. In early years, visitors took a week going around the loop—still a good idea. On any visit, start with the geyser basins and **Mammoth Hot Springs** to see wildlife and thermal features *(caution: both can be hazardous if approached too closely)*. On the second day, travel to the **Grand Canyon of the Yellowstone, Hayden Valley,** and **Yellowstone Lake.**

On a longer stay, visit the **Northern Range,** or consider a boating or fishing trip on Yellowstone Lake; a backcountry excursion on foot or horse; or any of the numerous easy nature trails throughout the park.

Your best chance of seeing wildlife is in early morning or evening.

The Geyser Basins: Old Faithful to Mammoth Hot Springs

51 miles; a full day

Begin by leaving your car in the parking lot at **Old Faithful.** Check at the visitor center for predicted eruption times of the major geysers. While there, pick up an **Upper Geyser Basin** map (also available from area dispensers). Wait on benches near the visitor center for the eruption of Old Faithful (named and celebrated for its steadiness rather than a predictable schedule of eruptions) or walk the path that circles it. Almost any point along the path offers a good view of the eruption, so don't worry if you're not at the benches when it happens. You can see from here that Old Faithful is not alone. The mile-long Upper

Morning Glory Pool, named for the flower

Mud pot near the Grand Canyon

Fumaroles in Norris Geyser Basin

Geyser Basin contains the world's greatest concentration of hot springs and geysers.

Try to allow a minimum of two hours to see more of it. This must be done on foot, but trails are easy and diversions many. The best choice is to start from the back side of Old Faithful, on the trail that crosses the **Firehole River** to **Geyser Hill,** and follow the map (or your nose; you can't get lost here). You can cross the river at several points and return on the other side, making the walk as long or short as you like. You'll pass dozens of colorful boiling springs and delicate formations of geyserite, a silicate mineral deposited by hot water. Chances are good to see one or more geysers erupt at short range. Keep an eye out for elk and bison. **Morning Glory Pool,** named for its resemblance to the flower, marks the far end of the basin.

Back in your car, drive north. **Black Sand Basin** is worth a quick stop, but bypass **Biscuit Basin.** The road follows the Firehole River several miles to **Midway Geyser Basin,** where a 20-minute stroll on the boardwalk takes you past the enormous crater of **Excelsior Geyser.** It erupted for two days in 1985. A huge boiling vat, it produces about 4,000 gallons of

Minerva Terrace at Mammoth Hot Springs

scalding water each minute. The boardwalk continues across the delicate terraces of **Grand Prismatic Spring,** 370 feet wide, the largest and most beautiful hot spring in the park. The bright colors are caused by algae and bacteria, different types of which thrive in different water temperatures.

Two miles farther, turn right on the one-way **Firehole Lake Drive** to **Great Fountain Geyser.** Check the prediction board for the estimated time of eruption. Great Fountain goes off every 11 hours or so. If you have the time, wait. This eruption is one of the best. A bit farther along is **White Dome Geyser.** Its cone may be massive, but its eruption is a thin spray. Perhaps centuries ago it had more power. Yellowstone is always changing.

Rejoin the main road at **Fountain Paint Pot,** a cauldron of hot reddish-pinkish mud, blooping and spitting—always entertaining. Any hot spring could become a mud pot with the right balance of acidity, moisture, and clay; however, a constant flow of water keeps most springs clear.

For the next few miles, rest your eyes on meadows and forest. Look for bison on **Fountain Flat;** also for purple-colored western fringed

gentian, the park flower. **Fountain Flat Drive** is closed to vehicles 1 mile from the main road. But it's open to visitors walking to **Goose Lake,** a peaceful picnic site. The Firehole River, warmed by hot water from springs and geysers along its course, flows through the meadows and along the main road before dropping into a canyon with nice waterfalls; to see them, turn left on **Firehole Canyon Drive** just before **Madison Junction.**

At Madison Junction, a left turn follows the Madison River to the West Entrance, but stay on the road to Norris. In this area, the fires of 1988 burned extensively. Their effects—the jagged sweeps of charred lodgepole pine forest—will be visible for a long time. However, millions of new lodgepole pines have since grown back (the fires' heat released seedlings from cones on the forest floor). And, because the fires moved erratically, the burned areas are not far from unburned areas, another source of seeds for regrowth.

The road climbs beside the **Gibbon River** to **Gibbon Falls** and continues through the **Gibbon Canyon** and large meadows, where elk are commonly seen, to Norris.

Norris Geyser Basin contains the hottest ground in the park, as well as

Bison grazing near Firehole River

Male elk during fall mating season

Storm Creek fire, near Northeast Entrance, 1988

Rust-colored cones that release seeds after fire

the world's tallest geyser, **Steamboat.** The geyser's eruptions are infrequent and unpredictable; it may stay quiet for years at a time. Steamboat last erupted on April 26, 2002, the second time since October 2, 1991. Contrast its sleepy behavior with that of **Echinus,** which goes off about every 40 to 80 minutes, an easy show to witness.

Highlights of the drive north include the steamy fumaroles of **Roaring Mountain** that snore rather than roar and **Obsidian Cliff,** an outcrop containing black volcanic glass that was valued for arrowpoints by Indians throughout the area. The road crosses **Gardners Hole,** with nice views of the **Gallatin Range** to the west, and drops toward Mammoth through **Golden Gate,** cliffs gilded with the bright yellow lichen that grows on them.

At **Mammoth Hot Springs** you can drive or walk around the dozens of colorful steaming terraces. They are made of travertine—calcium carbonate—which the hot water brings to the surface from beds of limestone. The formations look quite different from the silica-based geyserite deposits seen elsewhere in the park. The park's headquarters and largest visitor center are at Mammoth. The **North Entrance** is located 5 miles down the **Gardner River Canyon.**

Landing a cutthroat trout on Slough Creek

Yellowstone Lake & River: Canyon to West Thumb

37 miles; at least a half day

From the **Canyon Village Visitor Center,** follow the one-way **Canyon Rim Drive** to lookout points for great views of the canyon and the **Yellowstone River'**s 308-foot **Lower Falls,** nearly twice as high as Niagara. The bright yellow, orange, and red of the canyon walls are caused by heat and chemical action on gray or brown rhyolite rock.

Walk the rim trail from **Inspiration Point** to **Grandview Point** for the best look at the canyon's natural grandeur. Also consider the paved but strenuous **Brink of the Lower Falls Trail,** which descends several hundred feet through steep forest. Standing beside the green river where it suddenly drops into space is one of the most exciting experiences in the park.

Continue south on the main road. The **Upper Falls** are, at 109 feet high, almost as impressive as the Lower Falls and easier to reach. A short trail leads to **Upper Falls View.** Half a mile far-

ther south, a side road crosses the river to **Artist Point,** the best overall view of the canyon.

Upriver, the Yellowstone flows gently through the sage-covered hills of **Hayden Valley.** Go slowly and stop often in the roadside parking areas; this is prime wildlife country. American white pelicans and trumpeter swans share the river with Canada geese, gulls, and ducks. Bison are visible most of the year. *Keep your distance.* Use binoculars to check meadows across the river for grizzlies digging for roots or rodents. Grizzlies are often seen in the open; black bears, their smaller, shier relations, rarely. But be careful not to surprise one; both are dangerous.

Well-named **Mud Volcano** and **Black Dragon's Caldron** are not pretty to look at, but they are impressive. Springs in this area have been known to hurl football-sized blobs of mud tens of feet. From here to the lake, the **Yellowstone River** provides excellent catch-and-release fishing for cutthroat trout. At **Le Hardy Rapids** in June you can watch cutthroat jumping on their way to spawning grounds (no fishing).

Look for trout also at **Fishing Bridge** (no fishing allowed) where the river flows out of the lake. Two miles farther east is **Pelican Valley,** a lush lakeside meadow where you might find moose or white pelicans.

Return to the loop road, following the shore of **Yellowstone Lake** most of the next 21 miles. This is the largest lake in North America above 7,000

Petrified Forest on Specimen Ridge

feet. The **Absaroka Range,** visible across the blue waters, was named for the Absaroka, or Crow Indians. The volcanic peaks define the park's eastern boundary.

Bison frequent the meadows near **Bridge Bay,** while moose favor ponds along the **Gull Point Road. Gull Point** is a good picnic site.

West Thumb, almost a separate lake, is a water-filled caldera created by an eruption about 150,000 years ago, a smaller version of the great Yellowstone caldera. A boardwalk leads around the **West Thumb Geyser Basin,** a modest group of thermal features made charming by its location beside the lake.

Northern Range

Between Mammoth Hot Springs and Cooke City, Yellowstone is warmer and drier than the interior. Called the Northern Range for its importance as wintering ground for large animals, this area is characterized by sagebrush and grassy valleys. Open all year, the road from Mammoth stays high above the Yellowstone River, crosses it near **Tower-Roosevelt,** and follows the **Lamar River** and **Soda Butte Creek**

to the **Northeast Entrance,** a magnificent little-used gateway. A few miles past Tower, **Specimen Ridge** contains the world's largest fossil forest. More than a hundred plant species, including redwoods, are found in 27 layers of volcanic ash from repeated eruptions 50 million years ago.

Hiking, Fishing, & Boating

More than a thousand miles of trails lead to wilderness valleys, mountaintops, lakes, and thermal basins. Take horses and a guide for a week-long trip, or go on foot for an hour or two. Even a short walk can put you in a wilderness setting beyond roads and crowds. Ask for recommended hikes at any visitor center.

Yellowstone offers fine trout fishing, especially for the fly-fisherman. A permit is required ($10 for 10 days; $20 for the season), available at visitor centers and ranger stations. Regulations are complicated, so read them carefully. Guide services are available at fishing shops in surrounding communities.

Motorboating is permitted on most of **Yellowstone Lake** and **Lewis Lake;** passenger boats operate from **Bridge Bay Marina** for sight-seeing and fishing. Other lakes are limited to hand-propelled craft. Rivers and streams are closed to all boating to avoid disturbing wildlife; an exception is the channel between Lewis and **Shoshone Lakes,** where paddlers are permitted.

Information & Activities

Headquarters
P.O. Box 168, WY 82190.
Phone (307) 344-7381.
www.nps.gov/yell

Seasons & Accessibility
Park open year-round. Road from
North Entrance to Northeast Entrance
open all year; most other park roads
closed to cars November through
April. Call headquarters for latest
weather and road conditions.

Visitor & Information Centers
**Mammoth Hot Springs/Albright
Visitor Center** open daily all year.
Old Faithful Visitor Center open May
through October and mid-December
to mid-March, depending on weather.
Canyon Village Visitor Center, near
center of park, and **Fishing Bridge and
Grant Village Visitor Centers,** on Yellowstone Lake, open May through September (reduced hours in Sept.).

Entrance Fees
$20 per vehicle, good for one week
at both Yellowstone and Grand Teton.
$40 annual.

Facilities for Disabled
Visitor centers; exhibits; Madison
Canyon; Bridge Bay; Grant, Lewis
Lake, and Fishing Bridge Campgrounds; most rest rooms; amphitheaters; and numerous ranger-led
activities and walks are wheelchair
accessible. Free brochure available.

Things to Do
Free naturalist-led activities: nature walks, camera walks, evening
programs. Also available, hiking,
boating, fishing (permit required),
horseback riding (stables at Roosevelt,
Canyon, and Mammoth), bicycling,
stagecoach rides, courses in natural
history and photography, art exhibits,
children's activities, bus and boat
tours, snow-coach tours, cross-country skiing, ice-skating, snowshoeing,
and snowmobiling.

Overnight Backpacking
Permits required. They are free and
available at visitor centers and ranger
stations; apply in person not more
than 48 hours in advance of use.
Advance reservations $15.

Campgrounds
Twelve campgrounds, all with 14-day
limit (except Fishing Bridge RV Park)
from May through October; other
times 30-day limit. **Mammoth** open
all year, others open late spring to
mid-fall. Reservations accepted for
**Fishing Bridge RV Park, Madison,
Grant Village, Canyon Village,** and
Bridge Bay; contact Xanterra Parks &
Resorts, P.O. Box 165, Yellowstone NP,
WY 82190. (307) 344-7311. All others
first come, first served. Fees $10-$15
per night; Fishing Bridge RV Park $29.
Pay showers near several campgrounds. Both tent and RV sites
at most campgrounds; at Fishing
Bridge RV Park hard-sided units only.
Hookups at Fishing Bridge RV Park
only. For group campgrounds, reserve
through Xanterra Parks & Resorts.
Food services in park.

Hotels, Motels, & Inns
*(unless otherwise noted, rates are for 2
persons in a double room, high season)*
INSIDE THE PARK:
*The following are operated by Xan-
terra Parks & Resorts, Yellowstone NP,
P.O. BOX 165, WY 82190. For reserva-
tions call (307) 344-7311.*
Canyon Lodge 527 cabins, 81 rooms.
$62-$136. Restaurant.
Grant Village 300 units. $98-$111.
Restaurant. Open May through Sept.
Lake Lodge & Cabins 186 units. $55-
$118. Restaurant. Open June to mid-
Sept.
Lake Yellowstone Hotel & Cabins 194
rooms, 102 cabins. $88-$415. Restau-
rant. Open mid-May through Sept.
**Mammoth Hot Springs Hotel & Cab-
ins** 97 rooms, 116 cabins. $57-$299.
Rest. Open May to Oct. and late Dec.
to early March.
Old Faithful Inn 327 units. $72-$369.
Rest. Open early May to late Oct.
Old Faithful Lodge & Cabins 97 units.
$42-$69. Open mid-May to late Sept.
Old Faithful Snow Lodge & Cabins
100 rooms, 34 cabins. $69-$140.
Restaurant. Open mid-May to early
Nov. and mid-Dec. to mid-March.
Roosevelt Lodge & Cabins 80 cabins.
$48-$95. Restaurant. Open mid-June
to late Aug.

*See also Grand Teton NP listings,
p. 298.*

Excursions

Shoshone National Forest
Cody, Wyoming

Theodore Roosevelt dubbed this forest's Wapiti Valley the "most scenic 52 miles in the United States." Wapiti (elk) find a year-round home here in the lee of the Absaroka and Beartooth Ranges, as do bighorn sheep, grizzlies, moose, and deer. Contains parts or all of five wilderness areas. 2,433,000 acres. Hiking, boating, fishing, horseback riding, hunting, winter sports. 374 campsites, food services, boat ramp, picnic areas. Some parts open year-round; campsites open June through September. Adjoins Yellowstone NP on the east. (307) 527-6241.

Red Rock Lakes National Wildlife Refuge
Lakeview, Montana

In this Centennial Valley refuge, trumpeter swans and nesting sandhill cranes find shelter among grasslands, lakes, and marshes. Large mammals include moose, mule deer, pronghorn, and coyotes. 45,000 acres. 10 campsites, hiking, canoeing, fishing, hunting, scenic drives. Open all year, though snow closes roads in winter. Off US 20/191, about 45 miles from Yellowstone NP. (406) 276-3536.

Bighorn Canyon National Recreation Area
Fort Smith, Montana

Water-based recreation is the focus of this 71-mile-long reservoir impounded from the Bighorn River by the Yellowtail Dam. Fossils exposed in steep canyon walls, wildlife from four life zones, and historic and archaeological sites also featured. Surrounded by Crow Indian Reservation. 120,284 acres, part in Wyoming. Hiking, boating, bicycling, fishing (and ice fishing), hunting, scenic drives, water sports. 125 campsites, boat ramps, picnic areas, handicapped access. Visitor center at Lovell on US 14A, about 100 miles east of Yellowstone NP. (307) 548-2251.

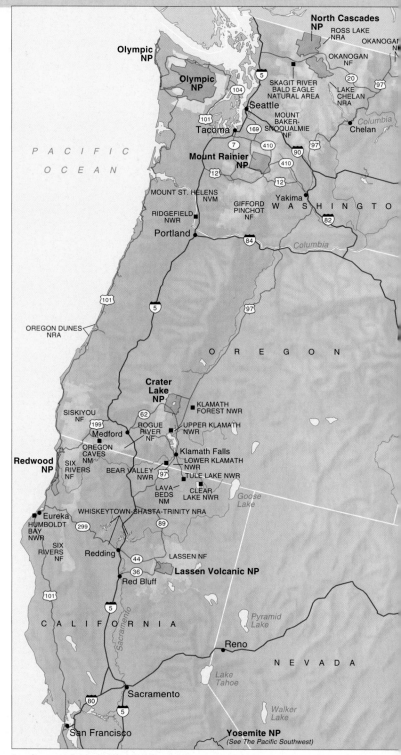

North Cascades
NP

ROSS LAKE
NRA

OKANOGAN
NF

OKANOGAN
NF

LAKE
CHELAN
NRA

Olympic
NP

Olympic
NP

SKAGIT RIVER
BALD EAGLE
NATURAL AREA

Seattle

MOUNT
BAKER-
SNOQUALMIE
NF

Columbia

Chelan

Tacoma

Mount Rainier
NP

MOUNT ST. HELENS
NVM

GIFFORD
PINCHOT
NF

Yakima

W A S H I N G T O

RIDGEFIELD
NWR

Portland

Columbia

P A C I F I C

O C E A N

OREGON DUNES
NRA

O R E G O N

Crater
Lake
NP

KLAMATH
FOREST NWR

SISKIYOU
NF

ROGUE
RIVER
NF

Medford

UPPER KLAMATH
NWR

OREGON
CAVES
NM

Klamath Falls

Redwood
NP

SIX
RIVERS
NF

BEAR VALLEY
NWR

LOWER KLAMATH
NWR

TULE LAKE NWR

LAVA-
BEDS
NM

CLEAR
LAKE NWR

Goose
Lake

WHISKEYTOWN-SHASTA-TRINITY NRA

Eureka

HUMBOLDT
BAY
NWR

SIX
RIVERS
NF

Redding

LASSEN NF

Lassen Volcanic NP

Red Bluff

C A L I F O R N I A

Sacramento

Pyramid
Lake

Reno

N E V A D A

Lake
Tahoe

Sacramento

San Francisco

Walker
Lake

Yosemite NP
(See The Pacific Southwest)

Preceding pages: Sea stacks, Olympic Peninsula

0 50 100 km
0 50 100 mi

This map plots all the U.S. national parks, plus the Excursions sites featured in this book.

CANADA

20

Waterton-Glacier NP
(See The Rocky Mountains)

2

Spokane

2

90

MONTANA

Snake

IDAHO

Boise

84

Snake

86

84

80

15

Salt Lake City

UTAH

Great Basin NP
(See The Colorado Plateau)

15

The Pacific Northwest

In the late 19th and early 20th centuries, East Coast loggers pushed west, downing mile after mile of the continent's primeval forests. Today, almost all of the large ancient forests left in the lower 48 states grow in the Pacific Northwest, most of them in national forests and parks.

Visitors to Mount Rainier, Olympic, and North Cascades can hike cathedral-like glades of Douglas-fir, western red cedar, and other conifers. The redwoods in the park named for them include trees in their second millennium, some of the tallest on Earth. In Olympic, temperate rain forests soar near some of the nation's wildest coastline; in the United States, only there and at Mount Rainier do such forests still exist. All these ancient forests knit together the lives of hundreds of species of plants, animals, and microbes in a web we don't fully understand. Yet the web is increasingly threatened as trees in private, state, and national forests are cut down.

The Northwest is also known for its volcanoes, many of which, including Mount Rainier and Mount St. Helens, lie in the Pacific Ring of Fire, the great belt of crustal instability responsible for three-quarters of the world's active volcanoes. Visitors to Lassen Volcanic can see evidence of the planet's violence in broken mountains and boiling mud pots. At Crater Lake, they can imagine the titanic forces that collapsed a mountaintop, turning it into a lake 6 miles wide and the deepest in the nation. They can marvel at the majesty of cloud-swathed Mount Rainier, which grew on a foundation of lava flows from extinct volcanoes, and now shoulders breathtaking wildflowers and more glaciers than any other U.S. peak south of Alaska.

Each of the region's northernmost national parks is less than half a day's drive from Seattle. This group merits at least a week of touring, more if you want to visit other natural areas nearby. The more southern peaks can each be seen in a day, but allow plenty of time for travel between them. Beautiful but winding Calif. 299 that connects the Lassen Volcanic and Redwood areas can wash out in spring, so check conditions if that's when you plan to go.

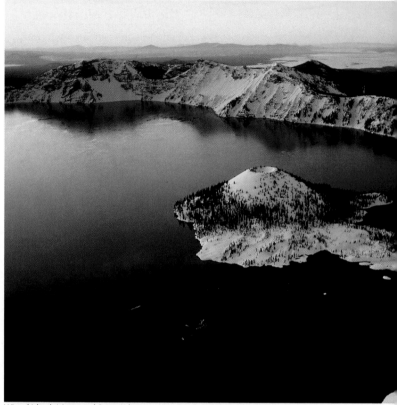

Wizard Island rising out of Crater Lake

Crater Lake

Oregon

Established May 22, 1902

183,224 acres

Few forget their first glimpse of Crater Lake on a clear summer's day—21 square miles of water so intensely blue it looks like ink, ringed by cliffs towering up to 2,000 feet above its surface. The mountain bluebird, Indian legend says, was gray before dipping into Crater Lake's waters.

The tranquil Gem of the Cascades is set in a dormant volcano called Mount Mazama, one in the chain of volcanoes that includes Mount St. Helens. Mount Mazama's biggest eruption occurred about 5700 B.C. The explosion catapulted volcanic ash miles into the sky and expelled so much pumice and ash that soon Mount Mazama's summit collapsed, creating a huge, smoldering caldera.

Over the centuries, rain and snowmelt accumulated in this caldera, forming a lake more than 1,900 feet deep, the deepest lake in the United States. Wildflowers, along with hemlock, fir, and pine, recolonized the lava-covered surroundings. Black bears and bobcats, deer and marmots, eagles and hawks returned.

Scientists have yet to understand completely Crater Lake's ecology. In 1988 and 1989, using a manned submarine, they discovered evidence that proves hydrothermal venting exists on the lake's bottom and may play a role in the lake's character.

Crater Lake forms a superb setting for day hikes. Thanks to some of the cleanest air in the nation, you can see more than 100 miles from points along many of the park's 140 miles of trails. Forests of mountain hemlock and Shasta red fir predominate near the caldera rim. At the rim twisted white-bark pine testify to the harshness of the long winter, during which, on average, 44 feet of snow fall. Ponderosa pine, the park's largest tree, and lodgepole pine are common farther down from the rim.

How to Get There

Enter the park from the west (Medford, about 75 miles away) or the south (Klamath Falls, about 55 miles away) on Oreg. 62, or from the north on Oreg. 138. Airports: Medford and Klamath Falls.

When to Go

The lake best displays its dazzling color in summer. Oreg. 62 and the access road leading to Rim Village remain open during daylight in winter, and cross-country skiing is becoming increasingly popular. The drive around the lake usually closes in October because of snow; in some years, the drive may not reopen completely until mid-July.

How to Visit

Spend at least a half day touring the 33-mile **Rim Drive,** enjoying its many overlooks and several hiking trails. On a second day, consider a hike down to the shore for the hour-and-45-minute, narrated **boat tour of the lake.** The boat stops at **Wizard Island;** if time and weather permit, climb to the top of it and catch a later boat back.

Rim Drive & Godfrey Glen Trail

33 to 38 miles; a half to full day

Rim Drive circles Crater Lake, providing more than 25 scenic overlooks and some good picnic areas. (Trailers and other oversize vehicles not recommended on east Rim Drive.) Begin your tour by parking in **Rim Village** and strolling to the **Sinnott Memorial Overlook,** a prime vantage point directly over the lake. Crater Lake's vivid color is a sign of purity and depth. The lake contains few minerals and impurities. Its only fish—rainbow trout and kokanee salmon—were introduced. As sunlight penetrates the deep, pure lake, water molecules absorb the colors of the spectrum except for blue, which is scattered back to the surface. Scientists have found green algae growing at a record 725 feet below the surface, indicating that sunlight may penetrate deeper here than in any other body of water in the world.

To begin your lake tour, set your car's odometer at zero (or note the setting) as you leave Rim Village parking lot. Head west or clockwise around the lake, and be careful: The road is narrow and has sharp curves. Watch out for bikers and pedestrians. Turn right at 0.1 mile for Rim Drive. The first stop (mile 1.3) brings you near **Discovery Point,** where, on June 12, 1853, a group of prospectors searching for a gold mine happened upon the lake, which they named Deep Blue Lake. Indians, believing the lake sacred, had told no outsiders about it. **Hillman Peak,** to the far left on the rim, is named for one of the prospectors. The peak is a 70,000-year-old volcano—one of the compact cluster of overlapping volcanic cones that formed Mount Mazama. It was cleaved in half when the summit collapsed. At 1,978 feet

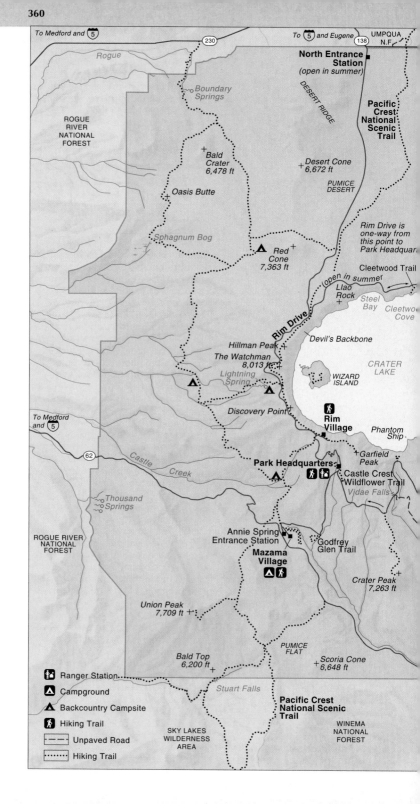

To Medford and (5)

230

To (5) and Eugene

138

UMPQUA
N.F.

**North Entrance
Station**
(open in summer)

Rogue

**Pacific
Crest
National
Scenic
Trail**

DESERT RIDGE

Boundary
Springs

ROGUE
RIVER
NATIONAL
FOREST

Bald
Crater
6,478 ft

Desert Cone
6,672 ft

PUMICE
DESERT

Oasis Butte

*Rim Drive is
one-way from
this point to
Park Headquar...*

Sphagnum Bog

Red
Cone
7,363 ft

Cleetwood Trail

(open in summer)

Llao
Rock

Steel
Bay

Cleetwo...
Cove

Rim Drive

Hillman Peak

Devil's Backbone

The Watchman
8,013 ft

CRATER
LAKE

Lightning
Spring

WIZARD
ISLAND

Discovery Point

**Rim
Village**

To Medford
and (5)

*Phantom
Ship*

62

Castle

Creek

Garfield
Peak

Park Headquarters

Castle Crest
Wildflower Trail

Vidae Falls

Thousand
Springs

ROGUE RIVER
NATIONAL
FOREST

Annie Spring
Entrance Station

Godfrey
Glen Trail

**Mazama
Village**

Union Peak
7,709 ft

Crater Peak
7,263 ft

PUMICE
FLAT

Bald Top
6,200 ft

Scoria Cone
6,648 ft

	Ranger Station
	Campground
	Backcountry Campsite
	Hiking Trail
– ⋅ –	Unpaved Road
⋯	Hiking Trail

Stuart Falls

**Pacific Crest
National Scenic
Trail**

SKY LAKES
WILDERNESS
AREA

WINEMA
NATIONAL
FOREST

Rabbitbrush at Cleetwood Cove

above the water, it forms the highest point on the rim.

The overlook at mile 4 offers a good view of **Wizard Island,** named for its resemblance to a sorcerer's hat. Rising 767 feet above the surface of the lake, Wizard Island is a classic cinder cone—built of red-hot cinders ejected from the caldera floor sometime after Mount Mazama collapsed. An Indian legend portrays the island as the head of Llao, Chief of the Below World. Skell, Chief of the Above World, killed and dismembered Llao in the final, literally earth-shattering battle waged on the mountain top. Time and weather permitting, you'll enjoy superb views in every direction if you take the moderately steep, 0.8-mile trail that leads from here to the fire tower on **The Watchman** (8,013 feet) south of the overlook.

Back in your car, turn away from the lake at the **Mount Thielsen Overview** on the left. A plaque identifies the major landmarks of the countryside. When the road forks at North Junction (mile 6.1), bear right to remain on Rim Drive. (Straight, the road leads to the **North Entrance.**)

Steel Bay (mile 8.8) commemorates William Gladstone Steel, who dedicated his fortune and career to making Crater Lake a national park. Steel became fascinated by the lake when he read about it in a newspaper used to wrap his school lunch. Seventeen years of lobbying, culminating in a personal appeal to President Theodore Roosevelt, succeeded in making it the country's sixth national park in 1902. The tireless Steel stocked the lake with fish and led the efforts to build Rim Drive and the Crater Lake Lodge.

Six miles farther on, pull off the road at **Skell Head** for another

The Pinnacles, southeast of Kerr Notch

and ash 250 feet thick. The fluted pinnacles on the walls of the gorges began as the same material, but hot gases seeped up from within the Earth and hardened these areas. They defied erosion as the creeks formed canyons.

Boat Tour & Hikes

The mile-long **Cleetwood Trail,** whose trailhead is found at mile 10.7 at the visitor center, leads steeply down to the water and the landing for the boat tour (fee). The hike back up is strenuous (and there's no other way), so only attempt the trail if you are in good physical condition, and take it slowly. Wear sturdy shoes and bring water, a snack, and a jacket.

The boat tour shows you the lake from a different perspective. You will see waterfalls and geological features invisible from the rim, and a ranger-guide offers a detailed account of the lake and its environs. The tour leaves every hour between 10 a.m.and 4 p.m. (July to mid-September).

If you have timed it right, you can get off the boat for the 2 p.m. Wizard Island tour (weather permitting; check schedule for next boat to pick you up). The relatively steep **Wizard Island Summit Trail** (0.9 mile one way) begins at the island's dock and winds through mountain hemlock, Shasta red fir, and wildflowers to the crater at the top. Awaiting you are superb views of bleached, contorted whitebark pines against the blue water, as well as a wonderful panorama of the inside of the 90-foot-deep caldera.

Another good park hike is on the **Annie Creek Canyon Trail,** a 1.7-mile self-guided loop that winds through beds of wildflowers to the bottom of a deep, stream-cut canyon and back. It begins behind the amphitheater at the Mazama Campground.

The **Mount Scott Trail,** considered by many to be the most spectacular in the park, starts from the left side of Rim Drive just after mile 17, 14 miles east of park headquarters. It ascends 2.5 miles to the park's highest point, offering panoramic views of the lake, as well as over the east side of the park and Klamath Basin. On this trail you might see falcons, hawks, and eagles, particularly in spring and fall.

excellent view of the entire lake. **Mount Scott,** highest point in the park, looms ahead as you drive on toward Cloudcap; it may have been the oldest of Mount Mazama's volcanic cones. Bear right (mile 17.4) for the short spur road to **Cloudcap,** Rim Drive's highest overlook (7,960 feet). **Phantom Ship,** an island to the southwest, consists of 400,000-year-old lava flows from the extinct Phantom cone. Dwarfed by the surrounding cliffs, it nevertheless stands 160 feet above the water.

Circle back to Rim Drive and turn right. For a closer look at Phantom Ship, which in some lights seems to vanish and reappear, stop at **Kerr Notch** (mile 23.2), one of the U-shaped valleys carved by a glacier before Mount Mazama exploded. A road here leads to **The Pinnacles,** spires of hardened volcanic ash. Just after Kerr Notch, bear right to stay on Rim Drive.

At mile 31.2 you can stretch your legs on the **Castle Crest Wildflower Trail.** This fragrant half-mile loop begins in a forest of mountain hemlock and red fir, then enters a meadow run riot with flowers, many of them identified by plaques. Watch your step—the wet rocks can be slippery.

From here you can either proceed back to Rim Village or, if time permits, turn left toward Oreg. 62 and, after 2.3 miles, park on the left for a final stroll on the **Godfrey Glen Trail,** an easy, 1-mile-loop accessible nature trail. The path leads through forest that developed on a flow of pumice

Information & Activities

Headquarters
P.O. Box 7, Crater Lake, OR 97604.
Phone (541) 594-3000.
www.nps.gov/crla

Seasons & Accessibility
South and West Entrances open
year-round. North Entrance open
mid-June to mid-October, snow permitting. East side of Rim Drive, from
Cleetwood Cove to park headquarters,
may remain closed by snow until
mid-July. Call (541) 594-3000 for
weather information.

Visitor & Information Centers
Rim Village Visitor Center, on rim
overlooking the lake, 7 miles off
Oreg. 62, open daily from early June
to end of September. Closed rest of
year. **Steel Center,** located at park
headquarters, open daily all year.

Entrance Fee
$10 per car per week; $20 annual.

Pets
Pets must be leashed at all times and
are not permitted on the trails.

Facilities for Disabled
Most viewpoints are accessible to
wheelchairs, as are the visitor centers,
Mazama Campground, the cafeteria
and gift shop at Rim Village, the Crater Lake Lodge, and the 1-mile Godfrey Glen Trail.

Things to Do
Free naturalist-led activities: nature
walks, children's programs, campfire
programs. Fees for the ranger-narrated
boat tours. Also available, hiking, bicycling, fishing (license required), snowshoeing, and cross-country skiing.

Special Advisory
● Hiking inside the caldera rim permitted only on the Cleetwood Trail.
Volcanic rock and soil are unstable
and dangerous to climb on.

Overnight Backpacking
Permits required. They are free and can
be obtained at the Steel Information
Center, the Rim Village Visitor Center,
and on the Pacific Crest Trail where it
enters the park.

Campgrounds
Two campgrounds, both with 14-day
limit. **Lost Creek** open mid-July to late
September. **Mazama** open late-June
to mid-October. Both first come, first
served. Fees $10-$15 per night. Showers at Mazama Village. Both tent and
RV sites at Mazama; no hookups. Tent
sites only at Lost Creek. Food services
at Rim Village.

Hotels, Motels, & Inns
*(unless otherwise noted, rates are for 2
persons in a double room, high season)*
INSIDE THE PARK:
Rim Village/Crater Lake Lodge
1211 Ave. C, White City, OR 97503.
(541) 830-8700. 71 units. $117-$190.
Restaurant. Open late May to mid-Oct.
Mazama Village Motor Inn (541) 830-
8700. 40 units. $100. Open early June
to mid-Oct.
OUTSIDE THE PARK:
In Chiloquin, OR 97624:
Melita's Motel 39500 Hwy. 97. (541)
783-2401. 14 units. $33-$42. 20 RV
hookups. $16. AC, restaurant.
Sportsman Motel 27627 Hwy. 97 N.
(541) 783-2867. 9 units, 6 with
kitchenettes. $42.
Spring Creek Ranch Motel 47600 Hwy.
97 N. (541) 783-2775. 10 units,
7 with kitchenettes. $42-$55.
Rapid River Bend Motel 33551 Hwy.
97 N. (541) 783-2271. 10 units. $47-
$52. Restaurant.
In Diamond Lake, OR 97731:
Diamond Lake Resort 350 Resort Dr.
(541) 793-3333. 92 units, 42 with
kitchenettes. Rooms $75; cabins $139-
$195; studios $88.
In Prospect, OR 97536:
Union Creek Resort 56484 Hwy. 62.
(541) 560-3565. 14 cabins, 8 with
kitchenettes; 9 rooms with shared
baths. Cabins $55-$135; rooms $40-
$50. Restaurant.

*Ask the park for a complete list
of accommodations within a
1-hour drive.*

Excursions

Rogue River National Forest
Medford, Oregon

Sugar pines and Douglas-firs here cloak the slopes of the western Cascades where the Rogue River emerges from underground lava tubes. Forest contains parts of three wilderness areas, numerous lakes, and a stretch of the Pacific Crest Trail. 628,750 acres, part in California. Hiking, boating, fishing, horseback riding, hunting, scenic drives, winter sports, water sports. 400 campsites, food services, boat ramp, picnic areas. Open all year; most campsites open May through September. In two sections; one adjoins Crater Lake NP on west and south, with entrance at Prospect on Oreg. 62. Lower section reached by following I-5 south of Ashland, about 85 miles from Crater Lake NP. (541) 858-2200.

Oregon Caves National Monument
Cave Junction, Oregon

Guided tours take visitors through the "Marble Halls of Oregon," chambers and corridors formed by groundwater dissolving marble bedrock. 480 acres. Hiking. 22 rooms, food services, picnic areas. Open mid-March through November. East on Oreg. 46 from Cave Junction, about 150 miles from Crater Lake NP. (541) 592-2100.

Siskiyou National Forest
Grants Pass, Oregon

This coniferous forest boasts five wilderness areas, notably the Kalmiopsis, named for a flowering plant unique to the area. A section of the Wild and Scenic Rogue River offers white-water boating, fishing, and hiking along the river's National Scenic Trail. 1,163,986 acres, part in California. Hiking, boating, fishing, horseback riding, hunting, scenic drives, water sports. More than 300 campsites, boat ramp, picnic areas. Open year-round; most campsites open May through September. Headquarters at Grants Pass on I-5, about 100 miles southwest of Crater Lake NP. (541) 471-6500.

Oregon Dunes National Recreation Area
Reedsport, Oregon

Forty-seven miles of towering dunes—some as high as 400 feet—stretch along the Pacific coast, inviting visitors to explore. Half of area open to off-road vehicles. The 426 wildlife species include black bear, black-tailed deer, and tundra swan. 32,000 acres. 13 hiking trails, boating, fishing, horseback riding, swimming. 13 campgrounds, picnic areas, handicapped access. Open all year. Headquarters at Reedsport on US 101, about 200 miles west of Crater Lake NP. (541) 271-3611.

Lava Beds National Monument
Tulelake, California

Myriad lava-tube caves and cinder cones mark this rugged terrain where prehistoric Indians left glyphs on the soft rock. Excellent spring and fall bird-watching. 46,560 acres. Hiking. 41 campsites, picnic areas. Open year-round. Headquarters 30 miles south of Tulelake (26 miles off Calif. 139), about 120 miles south of Crater Lake NP. (530) 667-2282.

Klamath Basin National Wildlife Refuges
Tulelake, California

These six refuges protect diverse habitats—marsh, open water, meadows, croplands, coniferous forest, sagebrush and juniper uplands, rocky slopes—and numerous waterfowl. The basin also provides a home for the largest wintering bald eagle population in the lower 48 states. Bicycling, hiking, boating, fishing, hunting. Open all year, dawn to dusk, except Bear Valley (closed Nov. through April to protect eagles) and Clear Lake (closed spring and summer). In Oregon: Klamath Forest, 16,376 acres; Upper Klamath, 14,886 acres; Bear Valley, 4,120 acres; Lower Klamath, 51,713 acres (part in Calif.). In California: Tule Lake, 38,908 acres; Clear Lake, 33,440 acres. Visitor center near Tulelake, off Calif. 139, about 100 miles from Crater Lake NP. (530) 667-2231.

Lassen Peak looming over the remains of Mount Tehama

Lassen Volcanic

California

Established August 9, 1916

106,372 acres

On June 14, 1914, three men climbed Lassen Peak to see why a seemingly dormant volcano had started rumbling 16 days before. Now, peering into a newborn crater, they felt the ground tremble. As they turned and ran down the steep slope, the mountain erupted. Rocks hurtled through the ash-filled air. One struck a man, knocking him out. Ashes rained down on the men. They seemed doomed. But the eruption stopped as suddenly as it had begun, and the three men survived.

From 1914 to early 1915, Lassen spewed steam and ashes in more than 150 eruptions. Finally, on May 19, 1915, the mountaintop exploded. Lava crashed through the 1914 crater. A 20-foot-high wall of mud, ash, and melted snow roared down the mountain, snapping tree trunks. Three days later, a huge mass of ashes and gases shot out of the volcano, devastating a swath a mile wide and 3 miles long. Above the havoc a cloud of volcanic steam and ash rose 30,000 feet.

Since then, except for a small eruption in 1921, Lassen Peak has been quiet. But it is still a volcano, the centerpiece of a vast panorama, where volcanism displays its spectaculars—wrecked mountains, devastated land, bubbling cauldrons of mud. Until Mount St. Helens blew in 1980, Lassen's eruption was the most recent volcanic explosion in the lower 48 states. Ecologists now study Lassen's landscape to see what the future may bring to the terrain around St. Helens.

Manzanita Lake Entrances, encompasses the major volcanic features. Explore **Bumpass Hell** and other sites along the way. If you can stay longer, climb **Cinder Cone,** an outstanding example of the results of volcanism, and, if you have the stamina for a more demanding trek, try **Lassen Peak.**

Park Road & Bumpass Hell Trail

30 miles; a half to full day

If you start at the Southwest Entrance, your first stop on this twisting, climbing road will be the **Sulphur Works.** At a roadside exhibit you walk through sulphur fumes and see hissing fumaroles, sputtering mud, and gurgling clay tinted in pastels by minerals. Here was the heart of ancestral Mount Tehama. The peaks around you once formed part of Tehama's rim, created by lava oozing from the inner Earth 600,000 to 200,000 years ago. Layer by layer, the lava built a mountain 11,500 feet high and 11 miles across.

Tehama gave birth to small volcanoes that emerged on its flanks. Repeated eruptions weakened the structure of the volcano, which collapsed, leaving behind a bowl-like caldera. Glaciers later scoured the caldera, wiping out the last remains of Tehama. **Lassen Peak,** born at least 27,000 years ago, was one of Tehama's offspring.

At **Bumpass Hell,** the road's next

How to Get There

From Redding (about 45 miles away), take Calif. 44 east then Calif. 89 south to Manzanita Lake Entrance; from Red Bluff, follow Calif. 36 east to Mineral, turn north on Calif. 89 to Southwest Entrance. The three other entrances—at Warner Valley, Butte Lake, and Juniper Lake— are reached via unpaved roads. Airports: Redding and Chico; Reno, Nevada.

When to Go

The volcanic areas are best visited in summer and fall. Heavy snows close most of the main road in winter. But small sections at the southern and northern ends remain open for snowshoe hikes and cross-country skiing.

How to Visit

On a 1-day visit, drive the **main park road,** linking Calif. 89. The road, snaking across the western side of the park between the Southwest and

Thermal steam at Bumpass Hell

Ranger Station
Campground
Self-guiding Trail
Unpaved Road
Hiking Trail

To 299
Badger Mountain
6,973 ft
Par
BADG
FLA
LASSEN NATIONAL FOREST
Crags
Lost Creek
Group Camp
89
44
89
To
Redding
CHAOS
JUMBLES
Reflection
Lake
Raker
Peak
7,483 ft
Entrance
Station
Crags Lake
Hot Rock
Main Park Road
Manzanita
Lake
Manzanita Lake
(closed in winter)
CHAOS CRAGS
DEVASTATED AREA
Emigrant Pass
LASSEN
NATIONAL
FOREST
Manzanita Creek
Crescent Crater
8,645 ft
Summit
Lake
North
WILDERNESS   AREA
Summit Lake
7,000 ft
Summit
Lake South
89
Loomis Peak
8,658 ft
Lassen Peak
10,457 ft
Shadow
Lake
NORTH FORK BAILEY CREEK
BLUE LAKE CANYON
Eagle Peak
9,222 ft
Lake
Helen
Bumpass
Hell
Bumpass Mountain
8,753 ft
READING PEAK
8,701 ft
Main Park Road
(closed in winter)
Mount Diller
9,087 ft
Bumpass
Hell
Kings Cr
Falls
Brokeoff
Mountain
9,235 ft
Sulphur
Works
Mill Creek
Falls
Devils Kitchen
6,020 ft
Lassen
Chalet
Drake
Lake
Southwest Information Station
Entrance Station
89
LASSEN NATIONAL FOREST
Ridge
Lake
To Mineral

major stop, note a large balanced rock at the edge of the parking lot; it's a glacial erratic—a polished, glacier-borne boulder. Nearby begins the **Bumpass Hell Trail,** a fairly easy 3-mile hike that takes about 3 hours. Go on it if you have time. The place is named after K.V. Bumpass, a local guide and promoter who, in the 1860s, plunged a leg through the thin crust covering a seething mud pot. Though badly burned, he wisecracked about his easy descent into hell.

As you walk along, you'll note (and smell) sulphurous vapors drifting over parts of the trail, which leads down to a railed boardwalk that winds past boiling mud pots, rumbling fumaroles, and hissing hot springs. At the springs' steamy pools look for floating golden flakes. They are crystals of iron pyrite—fool's gold—carried along in the superheated steam.

Resume driving on the road, which curves around Lassen Peak. Continue

To 44

Prospect Peak
8,338 ft

Butte Lake

Butte
Lake

Sunrise Peak
7,139 ft

Cinder Cone
6,907 ft

National Scenic Trail

PAINTED DUNES

FANTASTIC LAVA BEDS

WILDERNESS AREA

Cluster
Lakes

Widow
Lake

Ash Butte
7,577 ft

Fairfield Peak
7,272 ft

Rainbow
Lake

Snag
Lake

Lower Twin
Lake

Mount Hoffman
7,883 ft

Mountain
5 ft

Upper Twin
Lake

Swan Lake

Red Cinder Cone
8,008 ft

Echo
Lake

CAMERON
MEADOW

CARIBOU WILDERNESS

Crater Butte
7,267 ft

Pacific Crest National Scenic Trail

Grassy Creek

Inspiration Point

Horseshoe
Lake

Kings Creek

Horseshoe
Lake

Crystal Cliffs
7,548 ft

Pilot Mountain
7,175 ft

Crystal Lake

Juniper
Lake

Juniper Lake
(no water)

akesbad
est
nch

Warner Valley

Saddle Mountain
7,638 ft

Boiling
prings
Lake

Hot Springs Creek

Mount Harkness
8,048 ft

Terminal
Geyser

KELLY MOUNTAIN

fford Mountain
408 ft

6,919 ft

Willow Lake

To Chester

0   1   2 km
0   1   2 mi

---

to the **Devastated Area,** wrecked
by the massive May 1915 eruption.
Amid the scarred and fallen trees
you will notice the signs of renewal:
Young trees and stubborn grasses are
growing in a slow, natural comeback
unaided by human hand. The road
offers many turnoffs for viewing the
crags and canyons that are Lassen's
volcanic heritage.

You'll pass churned-up landscape
dubbed **Chaos Crags** and **Chaos Jumbles;** if space along the road permits,
stop and walk around it. Here, about
300 years ago, a nearby volcanic dome
suddenly collapsed, perhaps because
of an earth tremor. Millions of tons
of rock, riding a cushion of trapped
air, sped across 2 miles of flat land.
The horizontal avalanche smashed
into a mountain and veered into a
creek, damming it and forming
Manzanita Lake.

Just beyond, the road ends its
course through the park and enters
Lassen National Forest.

Cinder Cone Nature Trail
31-mile drive, 5-mile hike; a full day

Leave the park via the Manzanita Lake Entrance. Head north on Calif. 44 toward the Butte Lake Entrance. From Calif. 44 take the marked dirt road 6 miles to the Butte Lake Campground, where the trail begins. **Cinder Cone,** a nearly symmetrical, 755-foot-high mound of lava surrounded by multicolored cinders, stands black and solitary above a pine forest. Why all the cinders? This type of cone volcano ejects light lava that shatters in the air and falls back as cinders, which pile up around the volcanic vent. Don't expect to hurry on the trail, a round-trip of about 5 miles. Walking on loose cinders is like walking through sand, your feet sinking with every step. At the top (6,907 feet), you will see the craters of recent eruptions; the last was in the mid-1600s.

Lassen Peak Trail
5 miles round-trip; a half to full day

The Lassen Peak Trail is a steep, arduous climb. The zigzagging trail begins at 8,463 feet, near the park road, and takes you to the 10,457-foot summit. The going can get tough for people used to breathing at sea level. Before you try the climb, be sure you are acclimatized to the park's high elevations. Carry water, wear a hat, and bring a jacket. Turn back if a storm threatens; the peak is a lightning attractor. Lassen has scant vegetation. "A desert standing on end," a parched climber called it. But you can almost always spot a ground squirrel. And sometimes thousands of tortoiseshell butterflies suddenly flit by, their shadows cascading along the grayish volcanic rocks. At the summit, you can see the hardened vestige of the 1915 lava flow. And visible on a clear day, 75 miles away, is Mount Shasta.

Information & Activities

Headquarters
P.O. Box 100, Mineral, CA 96063.
Phone (530) 595-4444.
www.nps.gov/lavo

Seasons & Accessibility
Park and both its entrances open year-round. The main park road can be closed by snow from late October to late June. For road conditions in the park, phone (530) 595-4444.

Visitor & Information Centers
Both the visitor center on Calif. 89 at **Manzanita Lake** and the **Southwest Information Station** are open daily from mid-June to Labor Day. Contact the park headquarters for current information.

Entrance Fees
$10 per car; good for 7 days. Those entering on foot or by bicycle pay $5 for 7 days.

Facilities for Disabled
Park headquarters, Loomis Museum, some rest rooms, the Devastated Area Nature Trail, and some picnic areas are wheelchair accessible. Free brochures available.

Things to Do
Among the free ranger-led activities are nature walks and hikes, talks, nature and history demonstrations, children's programs, evening programs (including stargazing in summer), and snowshoe walks. Other activities include hiking, swimming, fishing, boating (no motors), and cross-country skiing.

Overnight Backpacking
Permits required. They are free and can be obtained at headquarters, visitor centers, and ranger stations. No wood fires permitted.

Campgrounds
Eight campgrounds, **Summit Lake-North** and **Summit Lake-South** have a 7-day limit; all others have a 14-day limit. Open late May through September, weather permitting. First come, first served. Fees $10-$14 per night. Showers are available at **Manzanita Lake.** Roads to Warner Valley and Juniper Lake not recommended for RVs. Three group campgrounds; reservations required; contact headquarters. Food services in park.

Hotels, Motels, & Inns
(unless otherwise noted, rates are for 2 persons in a double room, high season)
INSIDE THE PARK:
Drakesbad Guest Ranch (47 miles southeast of headquarters) Chester, CA 96020. Call (530) 529-1512 and leave a message; or call long-distance operator and ask for Drakesbad #2 in the 530 area code. 6 lodge rooms, 4 cabins. $242. 6 bungalows. $278. All meals included. Pool. Open June to early October.
OUTSIDE THE PARK:
In Mineral, CA 96063:
Lassen Mineral Lodge (on Calif. 36, 8 miles from park gate) P.O. Box 160. (530) 595-4422. 20 units, 2 with kitchenettes. $75. Restaurant.
In Redding, CA 96002:
Best Western Hilltop Inn 2300 Hilltop Dr. (800) 336-4880 or (530) 221-6100. 114 units. $99. AC, pool, restaurant.
Comfort Inn 2059 Hilltop Dr. (800) 228-5150 or (530) 221-6530. 90 units. $74-$86. AC, pool.
Red Lion Hotel 1830 Hilltop Dr. (800) 547-8010 or (530) 221-8700. 192 units. $94-$114. AC, pool, restaurant.
Vagabond Inn 536 E. Cypress Ave. (800) 522-1555 or (530) 223-1600. 71 units. $80-$85. AC, pool, restaurant.

For more information on area accommodations, contact the park or the Redding Chamber of Commerce, 747 Auditorium Dr., Redding, CA 96001. (530) 225-4433.

Excursions

Lassen National Forest
Susanville, California

Volcanic features dot this mountain forest surrounding Lassen Volcanic National Park. Also contains many lakes and streams. 1.5 million acres. Hiking, boating, fishing, horseback riding, hunting, winter sports, water sports. More than 40 campgrounds, boat ramp, picnic areas, handicapped access. Open year-round; most campsites open from mid-May to mid-October. Information at Chester on Calif. 36, about 40 miles from Lassen Volcanic NP. (530) 258-2141.

Whiskeytown-Shasta-Trinity National Recreation Area
Whiskeytown, California

Here in Gold Rush country, three impounded lakes provide unlimited opportunities for recreation on, in, and around water. Backcountry hiking and recreational gold panning also featured. 254,388 acres. Hiking, boating, fishing, horseback riding, mountain biking, hunting, picnic areas, scenic drives, water sports. 1,156 campsites, cabins, boat ramp, food services, handicapped access. Open year-round. Whiskeytown headquarters on Calif. 299, off I-5, about 60 miles west of Lassen Volcanic NP. (530) 242-3400. For Shasta and Trinity units call (530) 244-2978.

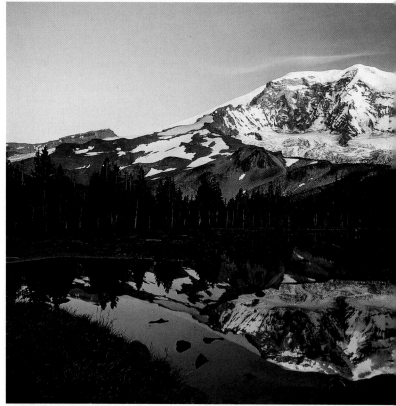

Mount Rainier, known to Indians as Tahoma—"the great mountain"

Mount Rainier

Washington

Established March 2, 1899

235,625 acres

One of the world's most massive volcanoes, Mount Rainier can dominate the skyline for 100 miles before you reach the park named after it. At nearly 3 miles in height, Mount Rainier is the tallest peak in the Cascade Range; it dwarfs 6,000-foot surrounding summits, appearing to float alone among the clouds.

Mount Rainier may be the centerpiece of the park, but it is hardly the only attraction. Here, less than 3 hours' drive from Seattle, you can stroll through seemingly endless fields of wildflowers, listen to a glacier flow, wander among trees nearly a thousand years old. The park's convenient location, however, also leads to weekend traffic jams, both summer and winter, and guarantees you company on popular trails.

Mount Rainier is the offspring of fire and ice. Still active, it was probably born more than a half million years ago, on a base of lava spewed out by previous volcanoes. Lava and ash surged out of the young volcano's vent thousands of times, filling the neighboring canyons and building up a summit cone, layer by layer, to a height of some 16,000 feet.

Even while Mount Rainier was growing, glaciers carved valleys on and around the mountain. The 25 major glaciers here form the largest collection of permanent ice on a single U.S. peak south of Alaska.

Mount Rainier's summit deteriorated over time, but eruptions in the last 2,000 years rebuilt it to its current height of 14,410 feet. The mountain last erupted about a century ago.

How to Visit (Summer)

If you have only a day, drive from the **Nisqually Entrance** in the southwest to the flowered fields of **Paradise,** then on to **Sunrise,** the highest point accessible by car, open early July to early October. If you have 2 days, take the same route but do it more leisurely: Plan to explore as far as Paradise the first day, then tour **Stevens Canyon Road** and the route to Sunrise the next; arrive before 10 a.m. to catch the early light and wend your way back.

For a longer stay, drive out and reenter the less known northwest corner at **Carbon River** for a look at a rain forest and a hike to a dark, shiny glacier. Because Mount Rainier creates its own clouds and can hide for days or weeks at a time, come prepared to focus on delights close at hand: waterfalls, woods, and wildflowers.

Nisqually to Paradise

18 miles; a half to full day

The pilgrimage to Paradise has been a classic for nearly a century. The first miles of your tour wind through a forest of giant Douglas-fir, western red cedar, and western hemlock. As you cross **Kautz Creek,** about 3 miles from the Nisqually Entrance, look for flood debris and dead trees amid the recovering forest. In 1947 the **Kautz Glacier** disgorged a flash flood of meltwater. The flood raged down the creek valley, carrying volcanic debris, trees, and boulders, and burying the road under 28 feet of mud. Similar, though mostly smaller, mudflows occur at least every few years at Mount Rainier.

Park at **Longmire Museum,** 6 miles from the entrance. Pioneer James Longmire discovered mineral springs here in 1883 and built Mount Rainier's first hotel; his ads for miraculous water cures helped generate early tourism and a constituency for the creation of the park. Take time for the easy half-mile **Trail of the Shadows** that starts on the opposite side of the main road. While in Longmire, also visit the **Wilderness Information Center,** closed between October and late April, for trail and weather information and backcountry permits.

Back in your car, continue east for about 6.5 miles, then take the spur road to the right to **Ricksecker Point.**

How to Get There

From Seattle (95 miles) or Tacoma (70 miles) to the Nisqually Entrance (open year-round), take I-5 to Wash. 7, then follow Wash. 706. From Yakima, take Wash. 12 west to Wash. 123 or Wash. 410, and enter from the park's east side (Stevens Canyon or White River Entrances closed in winter). For the northwest entrances (Carbon River and Mowich Lake), take Wash. 410 to Wash. 169 to Wash. 165, then follow the signs. Carbon River Road is subject to flooding in all seasons and may close at any time. Contact the park. Airports: Seattle and Portland, Oregon.

When to Go

All seasons. Wildflowers are at their best in July and August. High trails may remain snow covered until mid-July. Cross-country skiing and snowshoeing are popular in winter. Summer and winter, to miss the crowds, time your visit to midweek.

Road subject to flooding, may close at anytime.   MOUNT BAKER-SNOQUALMIE NATIONAL FOREST

Carbon

To 165

Carbon River Entrance

Florence Peak 5,508 ft

Gove Peak+ 5,310 ft

RUST RIDGE

ALKI CREST

Tolmie Peak 5,939 ft

MOUNTAIN MEADOWS

165

Ipsut Creek

Tirzah Peak +5,208 ft

Pigeon Peak+

Chenuis Creek

YELLOWSTONE CLIFFS

Natural Bridge

Castle Peak +6,110 ft

MOTHER MOUNTAIN

Ipsut Creek

NORTHERN CRAGS

CRESCENT MOUNTAIN

ECHO CLIFFS

Mowich Lake

Mowich Lake

+Mt. Pleasant 6,454 ft

SEATTLE PARK

GOAT ISLAND ROCKS

Skyscraper Mountain 7,078 ft+

White

West Fork

EAGLE CLIFF

SPRAY PARK

Carbon Glacier

Mineral Mountain +6,500 ft

BERKELE PARK

BURROU

Giant Falls

South Mowich

PTARMIGAN RIDGE

North Mowich Glacier

+Observation Rock 8,364 ft

Winthrop Glacier

GLACIER BASIN

Wonderland Trail

SUNSET PARK

Puyallup Glacier

Steamboat Prow 9,702 ft

WILLIS WALL

Emmo Glac

Camp Schurma

SUNSET AMPHITHEATER

+Liberty Cap 14,122 ft

MOUNT RAINIER

Little Tahom. Peak +11,138

KLAPATCHE RIDGE

ST. ANDREWS PARK

Tokaloo Rock +7,684 ft

Tahoma Glacier

Columbia Crest + 14,410 ft

Gibraltar Rock + 12,660 ft

Ingraham Glacier

Camp Muir 10,188 ft

Kautz Glacier

Nisqually Glacier

Cowlitz Glacier

GLACIER ISLAND

EMERALD RIDGE

Gobblers Knob 5,485 ft

Tahoma Vista

Lake George

Mt. Ararat 6,010 ft

HENRY'S HUNTING GROUND

Iron Mt. +6,283 ft

Pyramid Peak +6,937 ft

VANTRUMP PARK

Panorama Poi

Henry M. Jackson Memorial Visitor Center

Paradise

STEVE

GLACIER VIEW WILDERNESS

MOUNT WOW

Tahoma

Satulick Mt.+ 5,577 ft

Pyramid Creek

Cougar Rock

Narada Falls

Reflection Lakes

Bench Lake

Kautz Creek

Paradise

TATOOSH RANGE

Pinnacle Peak +6,562 ft

Road closed in winter.

706

Nisqually Entrance

+Tumtum Peak 4,678 ft

Sunshine Point

Nisqually

Unicorn Peak 6,917 ft+

Longmire Museum

Ⅰ Lookout Tower

Unpaved Road

Hiking Trail

Ranger Station

Campground

Interpretive Trail

GIFF

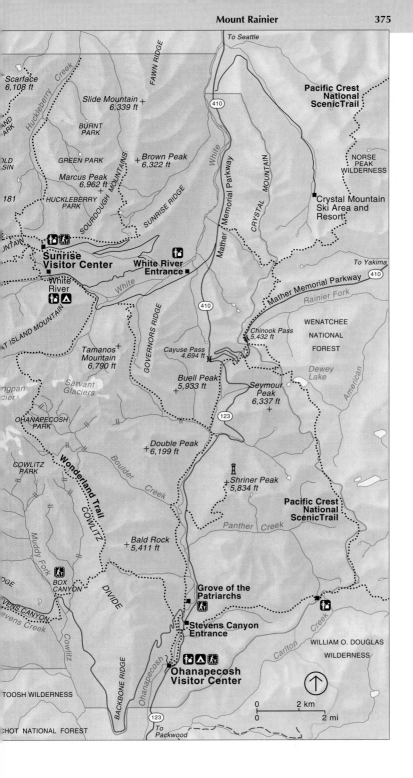

To Seattle

Scarface
6,108 ft

Slide Mountain +
6,339 ft

Pacific Crest National Scenic Trail

FAWN RIDGE

BURNT PARK

410

GREEN PARK

Brown Peak +
6,322 ft

NORSE PEAK WILDERNESS

Marcus Peak
6,962 ft +

181

HUCKLEBERRY PARK

SOURDOUGH MOUNTAINS

SUNRISE RIDGE

CRYSTAL MOUNTAIN

Crystal Mountain Ski Area and Resort

UNTAIN

Sunrise Visitor Center

White River Entrance

White River

To Yakima

Mather Memorial Parkway

410

White

Mather Memorial Parkway

Rainier Fork

410

T ISLAND MOUNTAIN

GOVERNORS RIDGE

Chinook Pass
5,432 ft

WENATCHEE

Tamanos +
Mountain
6,790 ft

Cayuse Pass
4,694 ft

NATIONAL

FOREST

Sarvant Glaciers

Buell Peak +
5,933 ft

Seymour Peak
6,337 ft +

Dewey Lake

ngpan
cier

OHANAPECOSH PARK

123

American

COWLITZ PARK

Wonderland Trail

COWLITZ

Boulder Creek

Double Peak +
6,199 ft

Shriner Peak +
5,834 ft

Pacific Crest National Scenic Trail

Muddy Fork

Bald Rock +
5,411 ft

Panther Creek

DIVIDE

BOX CANYON

Grove of the Patriarchs

GE

VENS CANYON

evens Creek

Cowlitz

Stevens Canyon Entrance

Carlton Creek

WILLIAM O. DOUGLAS

BACKBONE RIDGE

Ohanapecosh

Ohanapecosh Visitor Center

WILDERNESS

TOOSH WILDERNESS

123

CHOT NATIONAL FOREST

To Packwood

0   2 km

0   2 mi

Paradise Valley and visitor center

To the south loom the sawtoothed peaks of the **Tatoosh Range,** dramatic remains of lava flows that predated Mount Rainier by some 25 to 35 million years. Glaciers that developed and receded during the last million years carved the sharp pinnacles and the steep-sided mountainside hollows called cirques. Below meanders the **Nisqually River,** which originates at the snout of the **Nisqually Glacier,** which faces you on Mount Rainier. This glacier is about 4 miles long and flows downhill a foot every summer's day.

Rejoin the highway. Another 1.5 miles brings you to the **Narada Falls** pullover. The shimmering, 168-foot plunge of the **Paradise River** is well worth the steep but short walk down to the viewing area below the bridge. Climb back up to your car and proceed; in less than 3 miles you'll reach the most popular part of the park.

"It looks just like paradise!" exclaimed Martha Longmire in 1885 on first sighting the rolling hills swathed in wildflowers and framed by Mount Rainier's white dome. An average of 140 inches of precipitation falls here each year; as many as 40 species of flowers bloom on the thin, volcanic soil during July and August. Park near the **Henry M. Jackson Memorial Visitor Center,** or the **Paradise Inn,** built in 1917.

Begin your exploration of Paradise meadows on the **Nisqually Vista Trail** (1.2 miles), especially if time is short. This easy, self-guided nature walk

Narada Falls in summer

starts at the staircase to the west of the visitor center. Its booklet acquaints you with the geology and meadow life of Mount Rainier.

Make sure you stay on the path, no matter how tempting a meadow stroll. Trampling by just a few people can kill these fragile plants. Park staffers are still at work replanting old trails and other damaged areas. Only recently have the meadows recovered from the Camp of the Clouds, a tent city in operation here from 1898 to 1915. Not only people damage meadows, though. Elk, introduced in the first part of the century and now numbering some 2,000 inside the park, trample and graze the meadows. Researchers are seeking a solution to the problem.

If you're up to tackling some steep

hills, try the 5-mile **Skyline Trail.** Start from the staircase west of the visitor center. The trail will take you to **Panorama Point** for some spectacular views.

Paradise to Sunrise

50 miles; a half to full day

Leaving Paradise, turn left at the sign for **Sunrise** and Yakima. You'll soon pass the glacier-carved **Reflection Lakes** on your left; on a calm day, the reflection looks as solid as the mountain. Continue a mile past the lakes' pullover and park on the right for a 2.5-mile, hilly, round-trip walk to **Snow** and **Bench Lakes,** gems surrounded by the steep headwalls of the Tatoosh Range.

Drive on and stop after about 3 miles at an overlook of **Stevens Canyon.** Huge glaciers grating through this river gorge deepened and widened it into a classic U-shaped valley. Tributaries of **Stevens Creek** spill from the canyon's rim as waterfalls. Drive on another 3 miles, to **Box Canyon** (just past the picnic area). Park and cross the street for the nearly level half-mile **Canyon Stroll** and you'll see a 100-foot-deep gorge whose straight walls were carved by the **Muddy Fork** of the **Cowlitz River.**

Continue another 9.5 miles, then park to walk the **Grove of the Patriarchs** nature trail. This easy 1.3-mile loop leads to an island in the **Ohanapecosh River** dominated by grand Douglas-fir, western red cedar, and western hemlock, many of them 500 to 1,000 years old. After rejoining the road, turn left on Wash. 123 for Sunrise. If time allows, take a short detour south on Wash. 123 to visit the **Ohanapecosh Visitor Center.**

At **Cayuse Pass,** continue north on Wash. 410, then make a sharp left toward the **White River Entrance.** The road ends at Sunrise. Spire-shaped subalpine fir and whitebark pine grow here. Near tree line, harsh temperatures and winds stunt the trees into twisted shrubs called krummholz, or elfin timber; trees only inches in diameter may be 250 years old. Fragile wildflowers bloom among grass and sedge in terrain inhospitable to trees.

At the visitor center, ask about snow conditions on the higher trails. If time is short, take the self-guided

Grove of the Patriarchs

Marmot eating Indian paintbrush

Northern saw-whet owl

Camping on 4-mile-long Nisqually Glacier

Sourdough Ridge Nature Trail for 1.5 miles, then the **Emmons Vista Trail** for half a mile. The Sourdough Ridge trail, which starts with a climb, introduces plants and animals of the subalpine region. The former flourish in this fertile but fragile volcanic soil. The Emmons Vista Trail offers an easy way to view **Emmons Glacier,** Mount Rainier's largest, covering more than 4 square miles.

If you have more time and energy, and the snow has melted (snow on the slopes can be dangerous if you're not equipped with an ice ax and trained to use it), take the **Burroughs Mountain Trail** (5 miles to **First Burroughs,** or 7 miles to **Second Burroughs**). Begin as you did for the nature trail, but turn left about half way up the hill and follow the signs. The trail soon enters tundra. Compact little plants sport exquisite lilliputian blossoms and leaves that are a dull gray from the tiny hairs that protect them against drying winds. *It is most important that you stay on the trail:* If trod on, these delicate plants can take decades to heal. At Second Burroughs it feels as if you could almost touch Mount Rainier's imposing peak. Return to your car by way of the **Sunrise Rim Trail.**

The Northwest Corner: Carbon River

5 miles inside park boundary; a half day

Note: The Carbon River is subject to flooding. Call the park's visitor center for status before attempting this drive.

To visit a rare inland temperate rain forest and peer at a glacier, take the **Carbon River Road** (it forks left off Wash. 165 about 6 miles past Wilkeson). Unpaved inside the park, the road may be passable for ordinary cars. Stop at the entrance to take the self-guided **Carbon River Rain Forest Trail,** a half-mile loop among colossal Sitka spruce, Douglas-fir, and western red cedar. If the road is passable, drive to the parking lot at Ipsut Creek Campground. If you're up to a 7-mile round-trip hike with a short, moderately steep climb, take the **Carbon Glacier Trail.** Bear right at first fork, left at second, then cross the swinging bridge over the river and continue on to the glistening glacier. *Don't get close:* Boulders continually tumble off the glacier's snout.

Mountain Wildflowers

Giant red paintbrush and daisies along Tatoosh Range

Glacier lilies

Pink mountain heather

Fireweed

Western pasqueflowers

Phlox

Shooting star

Information & Activities

Headquarters
Tahoma Woods, Star Route, Ashford, WA 98304. Phone (360) 569-2211. www.nps.gov/mora

Seasons & Accessibility
Park open year-round. Many roads closed by snow from late November through May or June. Call (360) 569-2211 for recorded weather, road, and trail information, or in the Nisqually area tune in to 1610 AM.

Visitor & Information Centers
Longmire Wilderness Information Center open daily mid-May through September. **Longmire Museum** open daily. **Henry M. Jackson Memorial Visitor Center,** at Paradise, open daily from early May to mid-October, weekends the rest of the year. **Ohanapecosh Visitor Center,** at park's southeast entrance, open daily Memorial Day to mid-October. **Sunrise Visitor Center** open daily, July to early October.

Entrance Fee
$10 per car per week; $20 annual.

Pets
Permitted leashed on roads. Pets not allowed on trails or in the backcountry.

Facilities for Disabled
Most public buildings and some rest rooms are wheelchair accessible. Portions of some trails may be accessible (assistance may be needed). Inquire at park for details.

Things to Do
Free naturalist-led activities: nature and history walks, hikes, campfire and children's programs, talks, films, slide shows. Also available, hiking, mountain climbing, fishing (license not needed), cross-country skiing, snowshoeing.

Special Advisories
• Mount Rainier is an active volcano. While eruptions are usually preceded by an increase in earthquake activity, other hazards, such as mudflows, glacial outburst floods, or rockfalls can occur without warning.
• Watch out for falling rocks, debris, and avalanches. Look up!
• Some areas may be subject to flash floods, especially in late summer and fall. Inquire about current conditions before hiking.
• Stop by a visitor center for additional safety information.

Overnight Backpacking
Permit required; available from visitor centers, ranger stations, and wilderness centers, where you can also get help with your trip planning. Contact the Wilderness Information Center in care of park headquarters, or call (360) 569-2211. Make reservations through the National Parks Reservation Service (see p. 11).

Campgrounds
Five campgrounds, all with 14-day limit. **Sunshine Point** open all year. Others open late spring to early fall. Fees $10-$14 per night. Showers available in the visitor center at Paradise. Both tent and RV sites; no hookups. Advance reservations required at **Cougar Rock** and **Ohanapecosh** from late June to Labor Day. Call National Parks Reservation Service (see p. 11). All others, first come, first served. Food services in park.

Hotels, Motels, & Inns
(unless otherwise noted, rates are for 2 persons in a double room, high season) INSIDE THE PARK:
The following are operated by Mt. Rainier Guest Services, P.O. Box 108, Ashford, WA 98304. (360) 569-2275.
National Park Inn (at 2,700-foot level of Mount Rainier) 25 units, 18 with private baths. $78-$110. Restaurant.
Paradise Inn (at 5,400-foot level of Mount Rainier) 118 units, 86 with private baths. $77-$115. Restaurant. Open late May to early October.

For more information on area accommodations, contact the park's Guest Services (see above) or refer to the website.

Excursions

Gifford Pinchot National Forest

Vancouver, Washington

Dense coniferous forest encompassing Mount St. Helens National Volcanic Monument offers superb views of the volcano. Contains glaciers and seven wilderness areas. 1.3 million acres. Hiking, boating, climbing, fishing, horseback riding, hunting, winter sports, water sports. 35 campgrounds, 3 group campgrounds, picnic areas, handicapped access. Open all year; most campsites open June through October. Adjoins Mount Rainier NP on the south. Information at Packwood on Wash. 12, about 10 miles from the park. (360) 494-0600.

Mount St. Helens National Volcanic Monument

Amboy, Washington

This monument owes its existence to the day in May 1980 when Mount St. Helens erupted, laying waste to the surrounding forest. Visitors witness the rebirth of a forest through interpretive programs and tours. 110,000 acres. Hiking, bicycling, climbing (reservations required), fishing, hunting, scenic drives, winter sports. Picnic areas, handicapped access. Open year-round, but winter snows close many roads. Within Gifford Pinchot NF. Five visitor centers east of Castle Rock on Wash. 504. Many viewpoints and trails accessed from the north via Wash. 12 at Randle and from the south via Wash. 503 at Woodland. (360) 274-2100.

Ridgefield National Wildlife Refuge

Ridgefield, Washington

Established to protect the winter habitat of the dusky Canada goose, this site on the floodplain of the Columbia River provides a winter haven for many waterfowl species. It also serves as a year-round home for great blue herons and a resting spot for migrating sandhill cranes. 5,150 acres. Hiking, boating, hunting, scenic drives. Open all year, dawn to dusk (winter best time). Off I-5, about 90 miles from Mount Rainier NP. (360) 887-4106.

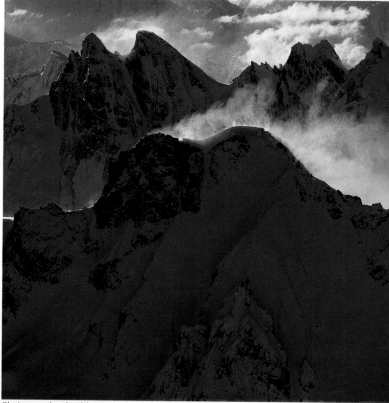

Glacier-carved peaks of the North Cascades

North Cascades

Washington

Established October 2, 1968

684,000 acres, includes two recreation areas

With glacier-clad peaks rising almost vertically from thickly forested valleys, the North Cascades are often called the American Alps. The national park forms two units, North and South, of the North Cascades National Park Service Complex. The two other units—Ross Lake National Recreation Area and Lake Chelan National Recreation Area—contain most visitor facilities and permit private land ownership and commercial activity.

The park complex preserves virgin forests, fragile subalpine meadows, and hundreds of glaciers. Mule deer and black-tailed deer graze the high meadows, where black bears gorge on berries and hoary marmots sun-

bathe. Mountain goats clamber on rock faces. Mountain lions and bobcats, seldom seen, help keep other wildlife populations in balance.

The wildness and ruggedness of the park especially lure hikers, backpackers, and mountaineers. "A more difficult route to travel never fell to man's lot," complained trapper Alexander Ross, who came here in 1814. But today the main road (through Ross Lake NRA) and easy access into the park—on some of its 360 miles of trails—also allow more casual visitors to experience the peaceful forests and the drama of the mountains.

The region forms part of the Cascade Range, named for its innumerable waterfalls. The range extends from British Columbia to northern California. A geological theory proposes that the mountains

How to Get There

From Seattle (about 115 miles from the park), take I-5 to Wash. 20, also called the North Cascades Highway. From the east, get on Wash. 20 south of Mazama. To reach Stehekin Valley, either hike over Cascade Pass from the Cascade River Road or take a 1-hour, high-speed catamaran or chartered floatplane from Chelan, at the southern tip of Lake Chelan. Chelan is on US 97. Airports: Seattle and Bellingham.

When to Go

Summer gives the best access, though snow can block high trails into July. The North Cascades Highway, from Ross Dam to beyond Washington Pass, closes in winter. Stehekin, a year-round community, offers winter cross-country skiing.

How to Visit

On a day trip, take the **North Cascades Highway** through the **Ross Lake National Recreation Area** for an overview of the recreation area's lakes and dams, the park's mountains, and the glacier-fed **Skagit River.** If you have 2 days, drive up the unpaved **Cascade River Road** and picnic and hike among the park's peaks and alpine meadows. On a longer stay, drive south to **Chelan,** and take the ferry or fly to **Stehekin** to overnight in a serene, isolated community or in the backcountry.

North Cascades Highway: Marblemount to Washington Pass

60 miles; a half to full day

The ease of driving the North Cascades Highway belies the terrain's ruggedness, although names supplied by explorers and climbers attest to it: Mount Terror, Mount Despair, Damnation Peak, Mount Fury, Mount Challenger. This transmountain road was completed only in 1972.

Enter the **Ross Lake National Recreation Area** after crossing **Bacon Creek,** 6.5 miles beyond the Wilderness Information Center at Marblemount. Parallel to the road, the **Skagit River** appears emerald in summer—evidence of the park's many glaciers. As they move, glaciers grind bedrock into a fine "flour." Water carrying a

began as a micro-continent several hundred miles out in the Pacific Ocean. Over the eons a series of islands floated on their plate toward North America. About a hundred million years ago, the plate smashed into the North American continent, folding and crumpling into a mountain range as it lodged against the landmass. Those mountains eroded; the Cascades you see today rose only five or six million years ago.

The western part of the park differs markedly from the east. Moisture blows in from Puget Sound and the Strait of Juan de Fuca. It hits the western slopes and rises, condensing to rain and snow. Western red cedar, hemlock, and Douglas-fir luxuriate on slopes that receive 110 inches of precipitation a year. When the winds reach the east, they are mostly wrung dry: Only 35 inches of precipitation fall in Stehekin at the head of Lake Chelan. Arid-dwelling sagebrush and ponderosa pine grow in the peaks' rain shadow.

BRITISH COLUMBIA
WASHINGTON

To Hope, 6

MT. BAKER-SNOQUALMIE
NATIONAL FOREST

To Glacier
542

Copper Mt.
7,142 ft

Mt. Redoubt
8,957 ft

Redoubt
Glacier

**Mount Baker
Ski Area**

**Heather
Meadows
Visitor Center**

Whatcom Pass
5,218 ft

Little

Beaver

Little Beaver Trail

Creek

Arctic

Creek

+Mt. Shuksan
9,131 ft

Whatcom Peak
7,575 ft

PICKET RANGE

Mt. Challenger
+8,248 ft

Big

Beaver

Mt. Prophet
+7,579 ft

ROSS L
NATIO
RECREA
ARE

NORTH UNIT

+Mt. Fury
8,291 ft

Big Beaver Trail

Creek

+Mt. Blum
7,680 ft

Mt. Terror
8,151 ft

+Elephant Butte
7,379 ft

Ross Lake
Resort

Baker
Lake

+Mt. Despair
7,293 ft

Mt. Triumph
7,271 ft

Gorge Creek
Falls

Diablo

Diablo
Lake

Ruby M
7,408

+Bacon Peak
7,067 ft

Goodell Creek

NEWHALEM

Colonial Cree

**North
Cascades
Visitor Center**

Neve
Glacier

Skagit

To Sedro-Wooley

**Wilderness
Information
Center**

ORANGE CLIFFS

Lookout Mt.
5,592 ft

+Snowfield Peak
8,346 ft

Thunder Creek
Trail

Klawatti
Glacier

20

**Rockport
State
Park**

McAllister
Glacier

Cascade River Road

Eldorado Peak+
8,672 ft

+Inspiration
Glacier

Marblemount

Boston Peak
8,894 ft

Boston
Glacier

Johannesburg Mt
+8,200 ft

Mineral Park

Cascade
Pass Trail

Stehek

Sauk

MT. BAKER-SNOQUALMIE
NATIONAL FOREST

Cottonwood

Flat Creek

530

Mt. Formidable
8,324 ft

+Sentinel Peak
8,261 ft

GLACIER PEAK WILDERNESS

Ranger Station

Campground

Interpretive Trail

Unpaved Road

Trail

Sulattle

Dome Peak
8,595 ft

**Pacific Crest
National Scenic Trail**

0   5 km

0   5 mi

high concentration of glacial flour reflects the green part of the light spectrum. In winter bald eagles feast on salmon running the Skagit.

At **Goodell Creek Bridge** (milepost 119), look left to catch a rare glimpse of the high, sawtoothed peaks of the **Picket Range.** Discover the natural and human history of these mountains along trails or at the **North Cascade Visitor Center.** The visitor center features slide and film programs about the North Cascade Wilderness. Nearby is an accessible viewpoint trail.

Farther east on Wash. 20, turn right onto Main Street at **Newhalem,** a town of Seattle City Light (milepost 121). The company's dams—Gorge, Diablo, and Ross—generate about a quarter of Seattle's peak-time electricity. The dams created **Diablo, Ross, and Gorge Lakes.** To haul men and materials for construction, the company built a railway from Rockport to Diablo in the 1920s.

Drive on to **Diablo,** another City Light settlement, by turning left at milepost 126. Near here in 1901, pioneer Lucinda Davis and her three children cleared land and put up a roadhouse to feed and house the miners who still trudged the mountains in the wake of two abortive gold rushes. The Davis family built the first hydroelectric project on the Skagit— a waterwheel that generated enough electricity to light three light bulbs. A replica of the waterwheel stands next to the modern Diablo powerhouse; the **Davis Museum** preserves mementoes of the era.

Call the Seattle City Light information center to see if there is room on City Light's 2.5-hour tour of Diablo Lake. If you are without a boat, this is the only way to actually get on the water. (Or board a City Light ferry traveling between **Diablo** and **Ross.** This enjoyable 1-hour round-trip begins across Diablo Dam Road, near the parking for the Ross Lake Resort.)

Drive back to the highway and, if you are looking for an invigorating climb, turn right after about 4 miles at Colonial Creek Campground. Behind the amphitheater the **Thunder Woods Nature Trail** begins. This moderately steep 1-mile loop rises among giant, fragrant cedar trees, some of them more than three centuries old. The red cedar—characterized by ropy,

Backpacker walking by black-tailed deer, with Johannesburg Mountain beyond

cinnamon-colored bark and fern-like foliage—provided Indians with wood for canoes and houses and fiber for mats, clothing, and baskets. To extend your walk, continue along the 19-mile **Thunder Creek Trail** for a while; the views are good and the hiking relatively easy at first. (Eventually it ascends 6,100 feet.)

When you're back in the car, don't miss the **Diablo Lake Overlook** (1,600 feet), milepost 132. Amid the splendid scenery are exhibits that honor Senator Henry M. Jackson, who helped create the park and to whom Congress dedicated it in 1987. The highest mountain visible here is **Colonial Peak** (7,771 feet) to the southwest; note the glacial cirque, or bowl-shaped depression, carved out of its side. North is **Sourdough Mountain,** site of a fire lookout.

Near milepost 134 you'll find an informative 0.3-mile boardwalk nature trail, the **Happy Creek Forest Walk.** A few miles farther on, the highway leaves the park complex and enters the **Okanogan National Forest** (milepost 139). For a superb overview of Cascade peaks, follow the road about 20 miles to **Washington Pass Overlook** (5,477 feet), the highest point on the North Cascades Highway. Exit to the left at milepost 162, and walk to the overlook. Directly to the south is massive **Liberty Bell Mountain** (7,720 feet), south of that the **Early Winter Spires** (7,807 feet). With binoculars you might spot climbers and mountain goats on the solid granite faces.

Cascade River Road

45 miles round-trip; a half day

The Cascade River Road, the only road to enter the park proper from the west, passes through national forest for most of its length. The road starts in front of the Log House Inn in Marblemount. Before departing, pick up maps and check road conditions at Marblemount's **Wilderness Information Center.** The road becomes progressively narrower, steeper, and bumpier, though high-clearance cars can travel it in an hour without difficulty (trailers should not attempt the last few miles). The drive ends at a parking lot and picnic area (3,660 feet) between the glacier-studded summits of **Johannesburg Mountain** (8,200 feet) to the west and **Boston Peak** (8,894 feet) to the east.

Hikers will enjoy the 3.75-mile trail to **Cascade Pass** (5,384 feet). The Skagit and Chelan Indians used the pass to and from **Lake Chelan** for hunting and trading. The trail leaves the lowland forest to enter woods of silver fir, mountain hemlock, and Alaska yellow cedar, then flower-strewn subalpine meadows. Stay on the path; previous visitors have damaged the fragile meadow flora.

Park employees grow native plants in a greenhouse in Marblemount, then backpack or airlift them in for planting in summer to revegetate the pass. The greenhouse (near the Wilderness Information Center in Marblemount) is open for visits.

Lake Chelan, a year-round resort

Stehekin Valley

An overnight or 2

Stehekin has been a tourist hide-away since hotels first opened here at the turn of the 20th century and miners spread tales of magical scenery. On the northern shores of glacier-carved Lake Chelan and inaccessible by road, Stehekin is a community of hardy contemporary home-steaders, complete with a one-room schoolhouse in use from 1921 to 1988. The valley offers many lodging alternatives as well as backcountry camping without backpacking: Simply fill out a backcountry permit after you get there, take a shuttle bus to any of 12 backcountry camps, and stake your claim.

Even if you don't plan to camp, head for the **Golden West Visitor Center** when you arrive at Stehekin Landing to pick up hiking maps and schedules of tours and buses. Be sure to ask about trail conditions; high trails—and the last stretch of the shuttle bus route—can be closed by snow or flood damage.

After lunch, tour the **Buckner Homestead.** Home of the Buckner family from 1911 to 1970, it offers a look at the challenges of frontier life.

Next morning follow the nature trails near the landing. The informative 0.75-mile **Imus Creek Nature Trail** starts near the visitor center, and the **McKellar Cabin Historical Trail** begins just past the post office. Or catch the early shuttle bus upvalley. The buses currently run 20 winding miles on the old mine-to-market road. Ask ranger for latest bus schedule; reservations may be required. The scenic round-trip to the terminus at Glory Mountain takes 4 hours and can be wearing. If you have the time, it may be better to get off at a trail-head, hike, and catch the later bus back. Another good bet is the **Horse-shoe Basin Trail** (off the **Cascade Pass Trail**), a moderately steep 5.75-mile trail that passes more than 15 water-falls among spectacular glacial and mountain views.

For an easier hike try the **Agnes Gorge Trail,** 5 miles round-trip and level. Get off the bus at **High Bridge** near the intersection with the Pacific Crest Trail and walk across the bridge, past the sign for **Agnes Creek,** to the trailhead for **Agnes Gorge.** The trail provides excellent views of the 210-foot gorge and **Agnes Mountain** (8,115 feet). Be sure to keep a bus schedule with you at all times to avoid being stranded.

Information & Activities

Headquarters
810 State Rte. 20, Sedro Woolley, WA 98284. Phone (360) 856-5700. www.nps.gov/noca

Seasons & Accessibility
Park open year-round, but snow prevents access to much of it from mid-October to April.

Visitor & Information Centers
North Cascades Visitor Center (near Newhalem) open daily mid-April to mid-Nov., weekends only rest of year. Call (206) 386-4495. **Information center** on Wash. 20 (North Cascades Hwy.), in Sedro Woolley, open daily late May to mid-Oct., weekdays rest of year. **Wilderness Information Center** in Marblemount (just west of park boundary off North Cascades Hwy.) open daily summer only.
Lake Chelan NRA: Golden West Visitor Center (Stehekin), access by ferry, floatplane, or foot, open mid-May to mid-Oct. Ranger station open weekdays all year. call (509) 682-2549.

Entrance Fee
No entrance fee, but $5 for one-day vehicle pass to park at some trailheads. $30 for annual Northwest Forest pass.

Pets
Prohibited in national park except in front country and on Pacific Crest Trail, if leashed. Permitted on leashes in NRAs.

Facilities for Disabled
Information facilities and numerous short trails near North Cascades Highway are wheelchair accessible.

Things to Do
Free naturalist-led activities: **Ross Lake NRA:** guided nature walks, evening campfire programs. **Lake Chelan NRA:** nature and Buckner Orchard walks, evening programs.

Also available, hiking, boating, fishing, hunting (NRAs only, in season), horseback riding, rafting on upper Skagit, cross-country skiing. In summer, Seattle City Light sponsors tours of Diablo Lake and Ross Lake. Reserve at least a month in advance through Seattle City Light's Skagit Tour Desk, 500 Newhalem St., Rockport, WA 98283. Phone (206) 684-3030.

Overnight Backpacking
Permits required; available free at Wilderness Information Center in Marblemount and Golden West Visitor Center.

Campgrounds
Ross Lake NRA: Three campgrounds, 14-day limit. **Colonial Creek** open mid-spring to mid-fall. **Newhalem Creek** open mid-May to early Oct. **Goodell Creek** open all year. All first come, first served. Fees: None to $12 per night. No showers. Tent and RV sites; no hookups. Goodell Creek and Newhalem Creek Group Campground, reservations required; contact the park (206) 386-4495.
Lake Chelan NRA: Three campgrounds, **Harlequin, Bullion,** and **Purple Point,** 14-day limit. Open mid-spring to mid-fall. First come, first served. No fees. Showers are located near Purple Point. Tent sites only. Reservations required at **Harlequin Group Campground** (see above); contact the park (see above). Limited food service is available in Lake Chelan NRA.

Hotels, Motels, & Inns
(unless otherwise noted, rates are for 2 persons in a double room, high season)
In Ross Lake NRA:
Ross Lake Resort (Access by boat or foot) 503 Diablo St., Rockport, WA 98283. (206) 386-4437. 15 units floating on lake, kitchens. $75-$175. Open mid-June to late Oct.
In Lake Chelan NRA:
North Cascades Stehekin Lodge P.O. Box 457, Chelan, WA 98816. (509) 682-4494. 28 units. $104. Rest. **Silver Bay Inn** P.O. Box 85, Stehekin, WA 98852. (509) 682-2212. 4 cabins, 3 kitchenettes, $145-$295. **Stehekin Valley Ranch** P.O. Box 36, Stehekin, WA 98852. (509) 682-4677. 12 tent cabins some with showers. $65-$85 per person, meals. Open June through Sept.
In Concrete, WA 98237:
Cascade Mountain Inn 40418 Pioneer Ln., Birdsview. (360) 826-4333. 6 units. $120, includes breakfast.

For information on accommodations in Chelan, contact the Chamber of Commerce, P.O. Box 216, Chelan, WA 98816. (800) 424-3526 or (509) 682-3503.

Excursions

Mt. Baker-Snoqualmie National Forest

Mountlake Terrace, Washington

The Cascades' evergreen-covered western slopes feature active and dormant volcanoes, glaciers, lakes, streams, and waterfalls. Eight wilderness areas. Long winter sports season. Over 1.7 million acres. Hiking, boating, swimming, climbing, fishing, horseback riding, hunting, scenic drives, winter sports. More than 700 campsites, boat ramp, picnic areas. Open all year; campsites open May through Sept. Roads often impassable in winter. Adjoins North Cascades NP on west; also borders Mount Rainier NP. (425) 775-9702.

Skagit River Bald Eagle Natural Area

Rockport, Washington

This refuge, partially controlled by the Nature Conservancy, is the favored wintering ground of several hundred bald eagles that feed on chum salmon carcasses along the upper Skagit River. Population peaks in mid-Jan. 10,000 acres. No visitor facilities. Marked viewing vistas with handicapped access located off Wash. 20 about 10 miles from North Cascades NP. (425) 775-1311.

Okanogan National Forest

Okanogan, Washington

In a remote, rugged mountain area, this national forest features high peaks, mountain lakes, meadows, evergreens, and open woodlands. Contains the Pasayten and Lake Chelan-Sawtooth Wildernesses. 1,706,000 acres. Hiking, boating, climbing, fishing, horseback riding, hunting, scenic drives, winter sports. 39 campgrounds, boat ramp, picnic areas. Open year-round; most campsites open May through October. Adjoins North Cascades NP on east. (509) 826-3275.

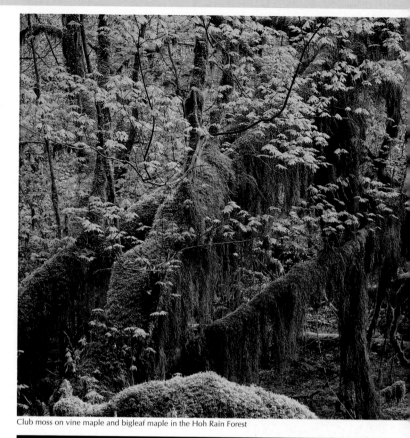

Club moss on vine maple and bigleaf maple in the Hoh Rain Forest

Olympic

Washington

Established June 29, 1938

922,000 acres

Encompassing 1,441 square miles of the Olympic Peninsula, Olympic National Park invites visitors to explore three distinct ecosystems: subalpine forest and wildflower meadow; temperate forest; and the rugged Pacific shore. Because of the park's relatively unspoiled condition and outstanding scenery, the United Nations has declared Olympic both an international biosphere reserve and a World Heritage site.

Inside the park, the Olympic mountain range is nearly circular, contoured by 13 rivers that radiate out like the spokes of a wheel. No road traverses the park, but a dozen spur roads lead into it from US 101, making it easily accessible from outside the park.

Residents of the Olympic Peninsula refer to it as a gift from the sea, and its features were indeed shaped by water and ice. The rock of the Olympics developed under the ocean—marine fossils are embedded in the mountain summits. Another component, basalt, originated from undersea lava vents. About 30 million years ago, the plate carrying the Pacific Ocean floor collided with the plate supporting the North American continent. As the heavy oceanic plate slid beneath the lighter continental plate, the upper layers of seabed jammed against the coastline, crumpling into what would become the Olympic Mountains. Glaciers and streams sculptured the mountains into their current profiles.

Glaciers nearly 1-mile thick also gouged out Puget Sound and Hood Canal to the east, and the Strait of Juan

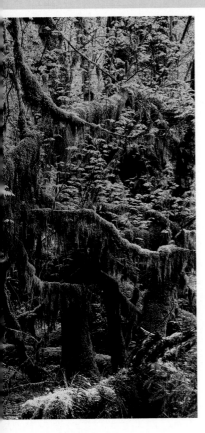

How to Get There

Approach the park from US 101, which skirts three sides of the Olympic Peninsula. The main visitor center and entrance are in Port Angeles. From Seattle, take the Washington State Ferry to Bainbridge Island, then drive north to Wash. 104 to join US 101 west to Port Angeles, a drive of about 60 miles. Airports: Port Angeles, Seattle, Sequim, and Olympia.

When to Go

All-year park. Summer is the "dry" season, but be prepared for cool temperatures, fog, and rain at any time. Hurricane Ridge opens for skiing on winter weekends and holidays, weather permitting.

How to Visit

Plan to spend at least 2 days. On the first day, stroll subalpine meadows at **Hurricane Ridge** while admiring the peaks and glaciers in the distance. Savor the **Lake Crescent** area and, if you're feeling energetic, wind up with a dip at **Sol Duc Hot Springs.** On the second day, drive to the **Hoh Rain Forest** and sample its nature trails before heading west for the Pacific Ocean beaches and tide pools. If you have more time, consider a trip to **Ozette** along the coast, or visit less known **Quinault.**

de Fuca to the north, isolating the peninsula from the mainland.

Ice Age isolation led to the 15 animals and 8 plants that evolved nowhere else on Earth, including the Olympic mountain milkvetch, Olympic marmot, Olympic Mazama pocket gopher, and Olympic mud minnow.

There are also the 11 mammals common in the nearby Cascades and Rockies that either died out in the Olympics or never found their way into the peninsula. The missing include the grizzly bear, lynx, and mountain sheep. Mountain goats, introduced in the 1920s, have so damaged alpine meadows in Olympic that in 1988 the park staff began efforts to manage the population.

Moist winds from the Pacific condense in the cool air of the Olympics and drop rain or snow, bestowing on the mountains' western slopes the wettest climate in the lower 48 states. Mount Olympus, which crowns the park at 7,965 feet, receives 200 inches of precipitation a year.

Port Angeles to Hurricane Ridge, Lake Crescent, & Sol Duc

76 miles; a very full day

Plan to spend the night in the area to get an early start. At the **Olympic National Park Visitor Center** in Port Angeles, inquire about the weather on Hurricane Ridge and pick up a tide table for the next day. On a clear day, the ridge offers spectacular views of the **Olympic Mountains** and northward as far as the Strait of Juan de Fuca and Canada's Vancouver Island. The 17-mile drive to Hurricane Ridge—so named for the force of its winter

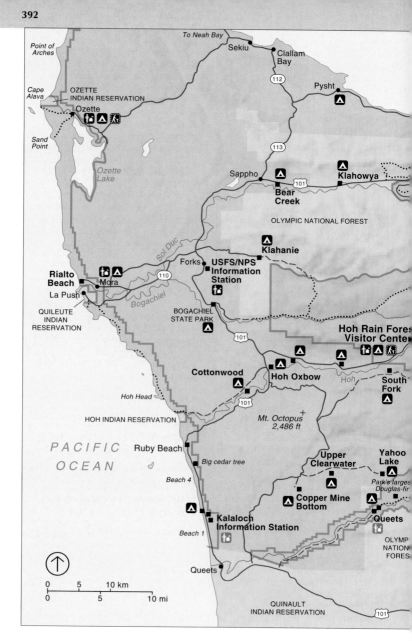

winds—takes you from lowland forest to tree line, nearly a mile above sea level, and reveals some of the remarkable geology of the peninsula.

After the tunnels, 9 miles in, stop at a pullover and look at the rock faces above the road. The bubbles of rock, called pillow basalt, are a clue that these mountains began under the ocean; when hot lava oozes into seawater, its surface cools and hardens quickly, often forming the globules you see here.

Drive on toward **Hurricane Ridge Visitor Center.** Plaques identify the peaks and glaciers of the inner Olympics. **Mount Olympus** carries 7 of Olympic's 60 major glaciers. Its **Blue Glacier** can receive up to 100 feet of snow a year and flows downhill as much as 5 inches a day.

You will probably see black-tailed

Unpaved Road
Trail
Ranger Station
Ranger Station (summer only)
Campground
Self-guiding Trail

Strait of Juan de Fuca

DUNGENESS NATIONAL
WILDLIFE REFUGE

re River
Salt Creek
Joyce

Dungeness
Recreation Area

yramid Mt.
3,000 ft

Port Angeles

Olympic National Park
Visitor Center

holm

Lake
Sutherland

Sequim

Storm King
Information Station

Heart O' the Hills

Lake Crescent

Altaire · Elwha

Mt. Storm King
4,500 ft

L. Mills

Blue Mountain
6,007 ft

Eagle
Sol Duc
Hot Springs Resort

Observation
Point

Hurricane Ridge
Visitor Center

Deer Park

OLYMPIC
NATIONAL
FOREST

SEVEN LAKES
BASIN

Mt. Carrie
6,995 ft

Obstruction
Peak
6,450 ft

O L Y M P I C

Elkhorn

Olympus

Lost Peak
6,515 ft

Glacier Meadows
Blue
Glacier

Mt. Deception
7,788 ft

Mt. Olympus
7,965 ft

Mt. Queets
6,480 ft

Hatana Falls

M O U N T A I N S

Dosewallips

Low Divide

Mt. Anderson
7,321 ft

To
101

Kimta Peak
5,399 ft

World's largest
western hemlock

Anderson Pass

Queets

Enchanted Valley

TSHLETSHY RIDGE

Mt. Lena
5,995 ft

To 101

World's largest
Alaska-cedar

North
Fork

Mt. Olson
5,289 ft

Lena Creek

Graves Creek

Flapjack Lakes

Lilliwaup
Creek

ly
ek

Quinault Rain Forest

Staircase

Big Creek

OLYMPIC NATIONAL FOREST

Quinault Lake

Camp
Harms

Lake
Cushman

Quinault USFS

deer here, and possibly Olympic marmots that whistle when approached. Most of the trees are subalpine fir. Their distinctive steeple shape helps shed snow. Near tree line, a 3-foot-tall tree may be 100 years old; summer wildflowers thrive where no tree can take hold.

Fine picnic sites lie toward the end of the road, about a mile beyond Hurricane Ridge. Try the **Hurricane Hill Trail,** starting where the road ends, for 3 miles (round-trip) of wildflowers and stunning mountain views. Layers of sedimentary rock along the trail stand folded and tilted on end from the continental collision.

If you prefer to continue driving— some of it is tricky—take the 8-mile, unpaved road to **Obstruction Peak** from the east end of the Hurricane Ridge parking lot for the park's best

Fog-filled Elwha Valley at sunset, from Hurricane Ridge

Glacier-carved Lake Crescent

windshield view of Mount Olympus and some of Olympic's most diverse wildflower displays. The road generally opens by July 4. **Grand Valley Trail** (3.5 miles one way) starts at the parking lot at road's end. Take at least a stroll on it for grand ridgetop views. Then double back to Port Angeles and pick up US 101 west.

The highway passes **Lake Sutherland** before tracing the southern shore of **Lake Crescent.** Carved by a glacier, the two lakes began as one, but a great landslide created the dam that now divides them. Indian legend says that Mount Storm King, angered at the fighting between the Quileute and Clallam Indians, threw down a boulder, killing the combatants and splitting the lake in two. Lake Crescent, 600 feet deep, is known for its azure waters and trout.

Turn off at the **Storm King Information Station** to walk the **Marymere Falls Trail,** a 1.75-mile round-trip through lowland forest to a graceful, 90-foot waterfall. Fifty cents buys a booklet that identifies the trees—mostly Douglas-fir and western hemlock, with a few western red cedar. Back in the car, time permitting, turn left 1.5 miles west of Fairholm to take the 14-mile road to **Sol Duc.** Indians, who named the springs Sol Duc, or "sparkling water," probably used the hot springs for medicinal treatments. Travelers have soothed tired muscles in pools here since a resort was first established in 1912. In case you want to stroll before you soak, the **Sol Duc Falls Trail,** starting at the end of the road, leads through three-quarters of a mile of dense forest to a waterfall.

Marymere Falls

Hoh Rain Forest to the Pacific Beaches

45 miles; a full day

The Hoh Rain Forest is located 2.5 hours from Port Angeles. To see it and the coast, continue skirting the park as you drive west and south on US 101. Check the schedule of guided tide-pool walks in your park newspaper and then decide whether to go first to the rain forest or to the beaches.

For the rain forest, take the **Hoh Road** inland 19 miles to the visitor center. You'll pass large recently reforested areas on private, state, and national forest lands, once entirely clear-cut. Logging is prohibited in the park, yet environmentalists cite evidence of damage done to park wildlife—some of whose living area extends outside the park—by shrinking habitat.

Two nature trails start behind the visitor center and are well worth taking: the **Hall of Mosses Trail** (0.75 mile) and the **Spruce Nature Trail** (1.25 miles). This is an enchanted land. Sitka spruce, western hemlock, and western red cedar, measuring up to 25 feet in circumference, tower 300 feet in the air. Club moss and licorice ferns drape the conifers and bigleaf maples, suffusing the air with green. Seedlings, unable to compete on the crowded forest floor, sprout luxuriantly on fallen trees, called nurse logs. Aged giants, lined up in colonnades, stand on huge roots called stilts where their nurse log rotted away. You may see Roosevelt elk—members of the largest herd in the nation—or hear their eerie bugle.

The Spruce Nature Trail shows how the forest develops. Where the **Hoh River** has shifted course in the last few decades, the first trees to move in needed full sunlight to grow—red alder, willow, and Douglas-fir. Later, shade-tolerant spruce and hemlock will succeed these pioneers to dominate the forest. As you stroll, note how the downed trees provide nutrients for the emerging seedlings.

After your forest sojourn, rejoin US 101 south, stopping at Ruby Beach. Walk the trail down to the sand—and keep track of where you came out of the woods. It might be hard to find the trail again, and the tough, oval-leaved shrubs off the trail are virtually impenetrable.

Olympic preserves over 60 miles of coastal wilderness: To the north, the beaches tend to have more pebbles and rocks; to the south, the beaches are broader and sandier. Rock outcroppings called sea stacks, isolated from the shoreline by erosion, have caused many a shipwreck.

The driftwood you might have to climb over once grew where you just were: upriver in the forest. Toppled by a winter storm or undercut by a flooding creek, trees tumbled

Frost-clad ferns and grape leaves

downstream to the sea. *Beware: Picturesque at low tide, drift logs can suddenly roll with lethal force at high tide.*

You may see harbor seals, the most common marine mammal on this coast, swimming or lounging on the rocks. In the spring and fall, California gray whales dive and spout near land on their migration between Alaska and Baja California. Gulls and crows drop clams from 50 feet in the air to crack them open on the rocks. Bald eagles soar from their forest perches to nab fish.

Continue south on US 101 and turn left at the sign for the big cedar tree, one of the world's largest. Standing at the end of a short spur road, the tree looks like something conjured up from the land of Oz. Monstrous in scale, its girth exceeds 66 feet.

US 101 from here to the park's southwest border is dotted with overlooks and short access trails to the beaches. If it's low tide—and you missed the guided tide-pool walk—try the trail at **Beach 4,** just north of milepost 160. A short, steep hike brings you to the shoreline and the rocky tide pools. Alternately battered by waves and dried out by the sun, tide pools nevertheless teem with life. An area 1 foot square may support 4,000 individual creatures belonging to more than 20 species. Look closely to spot gooseneck and acorn barnacles, periwinkle snails, and rocks with holes drilled by piddock clams. Brightly

colored sea stars, or starfish, prowl the rocky pools, preying on the mussels and other mollusks. Green sea anemones stun their tiny prey with stinging cells on their tentacles. Purple sea urchins dine on bits of kelp and other algae.

To view a third mood of Olympic beach, park near **Beach 1,** a stroller's delight, at milepost 155. Follow the sign to the **Spruce Burl Trail** for a brief detour before descending to the sand. Near the ocean, Sitka spruce commonly develop large, nobby growths that may be triggered by a virus, a bacterium, or some substance carried in the ocean spray.

For a remote and peaceful visit to the rain forest, drive south to **Quinault** (32 miles from Kalaloch) and take the North Shore spur road. Walk the half-mile **Maple Glades Nature Trail** from near the **North Shore Quinault Ranger Station** or the 2.2-mile round-trip **Irely Lake Trail,** which begins a quarter mile before the North Fork Campground. Look for beaver dams, herons, and ospreys, which often nest at the lake.

Ozette

Remote Ozette, a town near the northernmost realm of the park, offers a good departure point for supreme coastal hiking. To get there, take US 101 to Sappho, then head north to Wash. 112; follow this into Sekiu. From here, head southwest to the town.

For a level 9.3-mile loop, take the triangular route shaped by the **Ozette Lake-Cape Alava-Sand Point Trail.** The jaunt begins at the ranger station on the north end of **Ozette Lake** (where you must register), off Hoko-Ozette Road. The 3-mile trail goes southwest to Sand Point, tunneling through coastal forest, taking you over marshes and bogs on wooden walkways. You emerge at the Pacific at **Sand Point.** Here head north along the rocky beach to **Capa Alava,** the westernmost point of the contiguous United States. Along the way, you are treated to stunning seacoast scenery, tide pools filled with sea critters, and rock etchings left by Indians who lived by whaling and fishing. Watch for rhinoceros auklets, tufted puffins, oyster catchers, and perhaps even a black bear.

Information & Activities

Headquarters
600 E. Park Ave., Port Angeles, WA
98362. Phone (360) 565-3000.
www.nps.gov/olym

Seasons & Accessibility
Park open year-round. Some roads
closed in winter. For weather and road
information, call (360) 565-3131.

Visitor & Information Centers
In Port Angeles, the **Olympic National
Park Visitor Center,** 3002 Mt. Angeles
Road; call (360) 565-3132. The **Hoh
Rain Forest Visitor Center** off US 101
at western edge of park, (360) 374-
6925. Both open daily all year. **Hurricane Ridge Visitor Center** also open
all year, weather permitting.

In summer, information stations
open at **Storm King** on Lake Crescent,
Kalaloch, and other locations.

For park information, tune in to 530
AM in the Port Angeles and Lake Crescent areas.

Entrance Fee
$10 per vehicle for 7-day pass May
to September. Some areas charge an
entrance fee in winter.

Pets
Allowed on leashes except on trails and
in backcountry.

Facilities for Disabled
Visitor centers and some campsites
are accessible to wheelchairs. Also
accessible are Hurricane Ridge's paved
trails; a short loop trail into the Hoh
Rain Forest; the Madison Falls Trail in
the Elwha Valley, and the Moments in
Time Trail at Lake Crescent.

Things to Do
Free naturalist-led activities: meadow,
forest, beach, and tide-pool walks;
campfire programs. Also available,
hiking, boating, fishing (no license
needed), climbing, swimming, windsurfing, waterskiing, river rafting, cross-
country and alpine skiing, snowshoeing.

Special Advisory
● Be careful when hiking along the
coast; rocks and logs can be slippery
and unstable. Be aware of incoming
tides (current tables posted at trailheads). Surf logs can kill.

Overnight Backpacking
Call ahead for reservations. Permits
required; obtain at Wilderness Information Center (directly behind
Olympic National Park Visitor Center,
360-565-3131), visitor centers, ranger
stations, or trailheads.

Campgrounds
Fifteen campgrounds, all with a 14-day
limit. **Deer Park, Dosewallips, North
Fork,** and **Queets** campgrounds do not
allow RVs. All first come, first served.
Fees: None to $12 per night. No show-
ers. Three group campgrounds; reservations required; contact headquarters.
Food services in park.

Hotels, Motels, & Inns
*(unless otherwise noted, rates are for 2
persons in a double room, high season)*
INSIDE THE PARK:
Kalaloch Lodge (on US 101, 36 miles
south of Forks) 157151 Hwy. 101,
Forks, WA 98331. (360) 962-2271. 20
rooms; 44 cabins, 38 with kitchenettes.
Rooms $135-$244; cabins $170-$258.
Restaurant.
Lake Crescent Lodge (on US 101) 416
Lake Crescent Rd., Port Angeles, WA
98363. (360) 928-3211. 52 units, 47 with
private bath. $71-$157. Restaurant.
Open late April through Oct.
Log Cabin Resort (on Lake Crescent)
3183 E. Beach Rd., Port Angeles, WA
98363. (360) 928-3325 or (360) 928-
3245. 28 units, 3 with kitchenettes. $55-
$129. 10 tent sites. $15. 23 RV hookups.
$30. Restaurant. Open April through
Sept.
Sol Duc Hot Springs Resort (12 miles
off US 101) P.O. Box 2169, Port Angeles,
WA 98362. (360) 327-3583. 32 cabins, 6
kitchens. $110-$130. Pool, restaurant.
Open mid-May through Sept.

*For other lodgings, contact the
Chambers of Commerce in Port
Angeles, 121 E. Railroad, 98362.
(360) 452-2363; and Forks, P.O.
Box 1249, 98331. (800) 443-6757
or (360) 374-2531.*

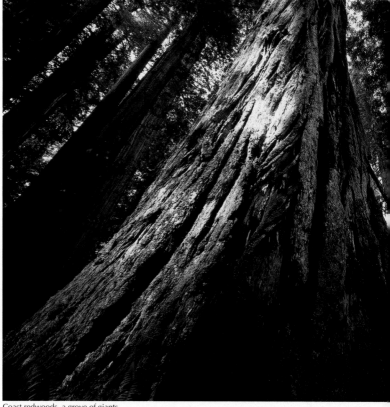

Coast redwoods, a grove of giants

Redwood

California

Established October 2, 1968

108,400 acres including 3 state parks

Sometimes, when the morning fog caresses the great trees, you can imagine the past flowing through the long, misty shadows ... Vast redwood forests flourishing across a lush and humid North America ... After the final ice age, a last stand here in the sustaining climate along the Pacific coast ... Tree after tree falling to the loggers. Then, in a windswept moment, the past vanishes and you stand beside other visitors, gazing up at the Earth's tallest living things. That is the essence of Redwood National and State Parks.

The park, near the northern limit of the coast redwood's narrow range, preserves the remnants of a forest that once covered two million acres and, at the turn of the 20th century, was badly threatened by logging. The state of California and the Save-the-Redwoods League came to the rescue by acquiring hundreds of groves and protecting them within 26 state parks. Three redwood state parks—Jedediah Smith, Del Norte Coast, and Prairie Creek—were encompassed by the national park when it was created in 1968.

Logging on surrounding private land, however, threatened the parks' protected redwoods. Soil and sediments from the logged-over tracts washed into the rivers and creeks, settling to the bottom downstream. Silt deposits can smother redwoods—for the giants are amazingly vulnerable. And the waterlogged soil weakens the trees' resistance to wind. Their roots are shallow, often only 10 feet deep.

From the south, take US 101 to the information center near Orick, about 40 miles north of Eureka. From the north, enter through Crescent City, also an information center site. From the east, take US 199, another redwood-flanked highway, to Hiouchi. Airports: Arcata and Crescent City.

When to Go

All-year park. Summer draws highway-clogging crowds, so think about a visit in spring or fall. In both seasons, bird migrations enhance the redwood groves. Rhododendrons burst forth in spring; deciduous trees add color in fall. Rains, welcome to the redwoods but not to visitors, drench the park in winter.

How to Visit

US 101, with its many redwood sentinels, gives you a windshield-framed panorama of the trees. But to appreciate the redwoods, you must walk among them. If you have only a day to visit this 50-mile-long park, stop and see the **Lady Bird Johnson Grove** and **Big Tree.** Hike or just stretch your legs (depending on your time) along the **Coastal Trail** and savor the Pacific prospect of the park. For a longer stay, visit the **Tall Trees Grove,** drive **Howland Hill Road,** and end your visit with a splash in a kayak on the **Klamath River** or a jouncy drive to **Fern Canyon** and **Gold Bluffs Beach.** If you are driving an RV or towing a trailer, some stretches of road may be closed to you; check at information centers.

In 1978 Congress added 48,000 acres to the national park's 58,000 acres, including about 36,000 that had been logged. The raw, clear-cut land, a park official wrote, had "the look of an active war zone." Today, in an epic earthmoving project—a redwood renaissance—crews are beginning to reclaim vast stretches of logged-over lands. Hillsides, carved away for logging roads, are being restored. Most of the 400 miles of roads are being erased. It will take at least 50 years for the scars of logging to disappear and another 250 or so years for the replanted redwood seedlings to grow to modest size.

The renaissance has added a new dimension to the traditional rite of staring up at redwoods. Today's visitor can look at hillsides shorn of giants and know that generations from now the trees will grow there again.

How to Get There

Tree-lined US 101, the Redwood Highway, runs the length of the park.

Lady Bird Johnson Grove & Big Tree

13 miles; 2 hours

Just before Orick, stop at the **Redwood Information Center** (once the site of a redwood-slicing lumber mill) to see the exhibits, and then continue north on US 101 to the Bald Hills Road sign. Turn right and drive 2 miles to **Lady Bird Johnson Grove,** a jewel that gives you an understanding of the entire park treasure. On the grove's mile-long trail you feel the cool, moist air that redwoods need. You see a hollowed-out tree that still lives. Such redwoods—"goose-pen" trees—once sheltered settlers' fowl and livestock. You smell and touch

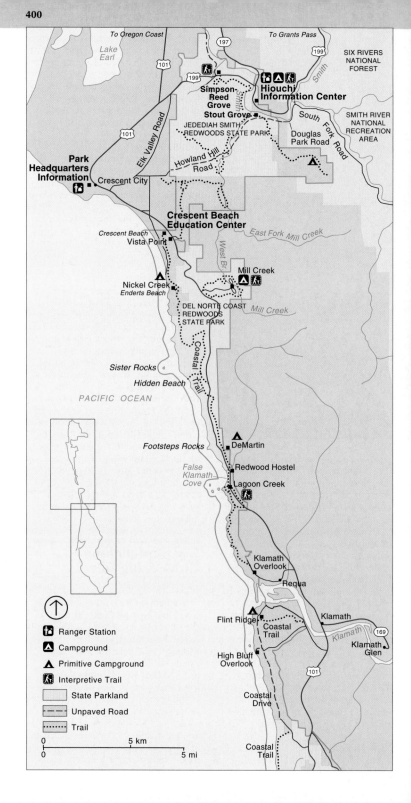

To Oregon Coast
To Grants Pass

Lake Earl

SIX RIVERS NATIONAL FOREST

197

199

101

Simpson-Reed Grove
Stout Grove

Hiouchi Information Center

JEDEDIAH SMITH REDWOODS STATE PARK

Smith

South Fork

SMITH RIVER NATIONAL RECREATION AREA

Douglas Park Road

Howland Hill Road

Elk Valley Road

Park Headquarters Information

Crescent City

Crescent Beach Education Center

East Fork Mill Creek

Crescent Beach
Vista Point

West Br.

Mill Creek

Nickel Creek
Enderts Beach

DEL NORTE COAST REDWOODS STATE PARK

Mill Creek

Sister Rocks

Hidden Beach

Coastal Trail

PACIFIC OCEAN

Footsteps Rocks

DeMartin

Redwood Hostel

False Klamath Cove

Lagoon Creek

Klamath Overlook

Requa

Flint Ridge

Coastal Trail

Klamath

169

Klamath Glen

High Bluff Overlook

101

Coastal Drive

Coastal Trail

Ranger Station
Campground
Primitive Campground
Interpretive Trail
State Parkland
Unpaved Road
Trail

0   5 km
0   5 mi

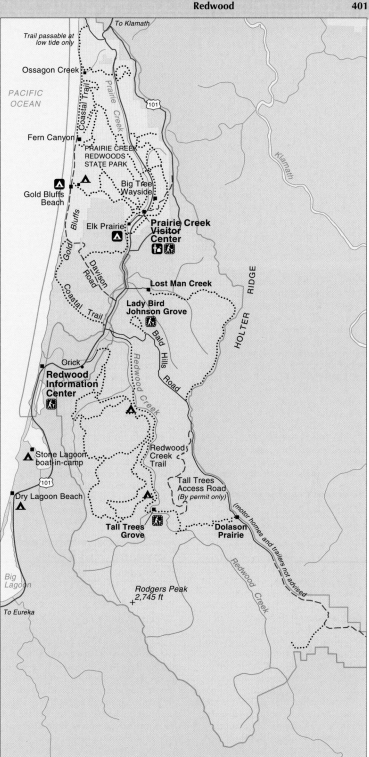

To Klamath

Trail passable at low tide only

Ossagon Creek

PACIFIC OCEAN

101

Fern Canyon

PRAIRIE CREEK REDWOODS STATE PARK

Prairie Creek

Big Tree Wayside

Gold Bluffs Beach

Elk Prairie

Prairie Creek Visitor Center

Coastal Trail

Davison Road

Gold Bluffs

Lost Man Creek

Lady Bird Johnson Grove

HOLTER RIDGE

Bald Hills Road

Coastal Trail

Orick

Redwood Information Center

Redwood Creek

Stone Lagoon boat-in-camp

Redwood Creek Trail

Tall Trees Access Road (By permit only)

101

Dry Lagoon Beach

Tall Trees Grove

Dolason Prairie

(motor homes and trailers not advised)

Redwood Creek

Big Lagoon

Rodgers Peak 2,745 ft

To Eureka

Klamath

Lady Bird Johnson Grove

the many plants that share the red-woods' domain. Most of all, you feel the peace; visitors speak quietly in this pillared place.

Return to US 101 and continue north about 4 miles. Near the entrance to **Prairie Creek Redwoods State Park,** pull into the turnout to watch the free-roaming Roosevelt elk that live in the park. A mile ahead on the right is a wayside sign for **Big Tree.** A short trail from the parking lot leads to the aptly named tree. It's 304 feet tall, 21.6 feet in diameter, 66 feet in circumference, and about 1,500 years old. Here the experience is singular: you and one great tree.

Coastal Trail

4 miles one way; at least 2 hours

From Orick, drive north 20 miles on US 101, passing Klamath, and turn left onto Requa Road. Park and picnic at **Klamath Overlook,** a high hill. On a clear day you can see 65 miles down the bluff-guarded coast. **The Hidden Beach Section** of the Coastal Trail begins here, heads west, and then veers north along the wild, driftwood-decorated shore. Yurok Indians walked these shores, as did Jedediah Smith, the first white man to reach California's northern coast by land.

The trail, often bowered by branches of spruce and alder, sometimes seals you from the sight—though not the sounds—of the ocean. But there are many spots where you can sit and gaze out to sea. In spring and fall you may

see migrating gray whales. Almost any time you will see gulls, cormorants, and ospreys.

A short side path leads down to **Hidden Beach.** Even on a day when the park is crowded yours may be the only footprints on the sand. Look at the ocean but don't swim: The undertow is dangerous all along the park's coast. The beach walk ends at a wall of gnarled black rocks. Follow your footprints back to the path and return to the trail, which heads north along the wild shore, then veers inland.

The north trailhead is at **Lagoon Creek,** where fresh water and forest meet ocean and high bluff. If you don't want to trudge the 4 miles back, have someone drive up to meet you at the parking lot.

Tall Trees Grove

2.6 miles; a half day

Obtain a permit to drive your vehicle to the Tall Trees Grove parking area, off Bald Hills Road. (Permits can be obtained at any of the information centers.) From the parking area, the trail is a very steep 2.6-mile round-trip. The hike down to the grove, replete with ferns and rhodo-dendrons, takes at least 30 minutes. Plan on another 30 to 45 minutes in the grove among the giant coast red-woods. The star is the **Nugget Tree,** which was measured at 365.5 feet in 1995. This is one of the world's tallest known trees. It's estimated to be between 900 and 1,500 years old.

Howland Hill Road

8 miles; about 2 hours

Just south of Crescent City, take Elk Valley Road northeast. Keep a sharp watch on your right for the turnoff to Howland Hill Road, once a miners' supply road partially red-wood-planked for oxcarts and horse-drawn wagons. The 6-mile road winds between redwoods that loom much closer than the ones along the high-ways. Mostly unpaved and often one lane, motor homes and trailers are not recommended. Stop at **Stout Grove,** where you can see one of many pre-serves set aside, this one donated by the wife of a logging company owner.

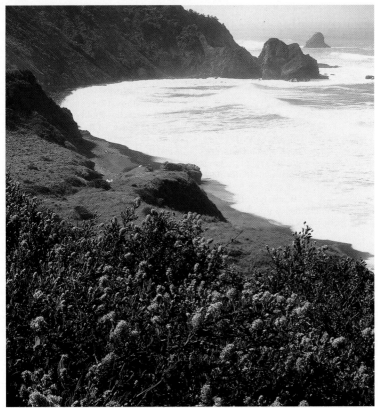

Blueblossom, Enderts Beach

Take time to enjoy the 1-mile trail among the redwoods. (In summer you can also reach the grove from the **Hiouchi Information Center** via a footbridge across the crystal-clear **Smith River.**)

Continue past the grove to Douglas Park Road, which ends at South Fork Road. Turn left to US 199 and drive west about 2.5 miles to the Hiouchi Information Center. Park here and sign up for an interpretive walk with a ranger. Or, continue west on US 199 to **Simpson-Reed Grove,** where you'll find a short pleasant self-guided trail.

Gold Bluffs Beach & Fern Canyon

20 miles; a half day

From the Redwood Information Center, head north for 4.5 miles to Davison Road, on your left. Elk are often spotted along the first few hundred yards on this road. The rough dirt road bounces you for about 4 miles down to **Gold Bluffs,** named for the gold found here. The road continues for 4 miles along the beach, ending near **Fern Canyon,** where a 0.75-mile loop trail climbs to a prairie—site of a vanished mining camp. Back down the canyon, walk through elk-roamed grass to a beautiful, desolate beach sprinkled with driftwood and often shrouded in fog.

Return the way you came, pausing to admire the fern-covered, 30-foot-high walls. The more adventurous can make a longer hike by climbing to **Prairie Creek** and walking along its banks before heading back toward the ocean. Return to the parking area at Fern Canyon via the windswept southern stretch of the **Coastal Trail.** Be on the lookout for a variety of birds, including pelicans, terns, gulls, and wading birds. In the fall or spring scan the horizon for the telltale spouts of migrating gray whales, en route to or from their winter retreat in Baja California.

Information & Activities

Headquarters
1111 2nd St., Crescent City, CA 95531. Phone (707) 464-6101. www.nps.gov/redw

Seasons & Accessibility
Open year-round.

Visitor & Information Centers
Crescent City Park Headquarters Information Center, at north end of park, open daily all year. **Redwood Information Center,** at south end of park near Orick, also open all year. **Hiouchi Information Center,** at north end of park, open spring through summer.

Entrance Fee
No admission fee. $2 day-use fee for Jedediah Smith, Del Norte Coast, and Prairie Creek State Parks.

Pets
Permitted on leashes except on trails and in backcountry.

Facilities for Disabled
Information centers, Crescent Beach, Lagoon Creek picnic area, Klamath Overlook, and some trails are accessible to wheelchairs.

Things to Do
Free naturalist-led activities: tide-pool and seashore walks, evening programs. Also available, hiking, canoeing, guided kayak trips, horseback riding, freshwater and ocean fishing (need license), swimming (inland only), whale watching.

Special Advisories
● Be aware that ticks may transmit Lyme disease.
● Ocean swimming is not advised due to extremely cold water and treacherous undertow.

Overnight Backpacking
Permit required; can be obtained free at trailheads and at the National Park Information Centers and State Park Visitor Centers. The National Park lands offer three backcountry campsites—**DeMartin, Flint Ridge,** and **Nickel Creek;** 14-day limit. Open all year, first come, first served. No fees. Tent sites only. No showers.
Butler Creek campsite in Prairie Creek State Park is available to bikers and hikers only (for a fee). Reserve at Prairie Creek Visitor Center.

Campgrounds
There are four state-run campgrounds inside the park—**Gold Bluffs Beach, Jedediah Smith, Mill Creek,** and **Elk Prairie;** 15-day limit. Mill Creek open April to October; others open all year; Gold Bluffs Beach may close in bad weather. Showers available nearby. Tent and rv sites; no hookups; large RVs not recommended and trailers prohibited at Gold Bluffs Beach. Fees $12 per night. Reservations recommended from mid-May through August and available at www.reserveamerica .com. The reservations number for these state-run campgrounds is (800) 444-7275. No food services inside park.

Hotels, Motels, & Inns
(unless otherwise noted, rates are for 2 persons in a double room, high season)
In Crescent City, CA 95531:
Best Value Inn 440 Hwy. 101 N. (707) 464-4141. 61 units. $62.
Curly Redwood Lodge 701 Hwy. 101 S. (707) 464-2137. 36 units. $60-$70.
Econo Lodge Crescent City 725 Hwy. 101 N. (800) 228-5151 or (707) 464-6106. 52 units. $59-$80.
Royal Inn Motel 102 L St. (800) 752-9610 or (707) 464-4113. 35 units. $35-$55.
In Eureka, CA 95501:
Eureka Inn 518 7th St. (800) 862-4906 or (707) 442-6441. 176 units. $109. Pool, 2 restaurants.
Hotel Carter 301 L St. (800) 404-1390 or (707) 444-8062. 31 units. $105-$497, includes continental breakfast. Restaurant.
In Klamath, CA 95548:
Historic Requa Inn 451 Requa Rd. (866) 800-8777 or (707) 482-8205. 10 units. $69-$115, includes breakfast. Restaurant.
Motel Trees 15495 Hwy. 101. (800) 848-2982 or (707) 482-1425. 23 units. $55. Restaurant.

Excursions

Humboldt Bay National Wildlife Refuge
Loleta, California

The islands and wetlands of Humboldt Bay provide critical habitat for the brant, a small, stocky sea goose. From late winter to early spring, thousands of brant use the refuge as a staging area en route to northern nesting grounds. Other waterfowl and peregrine falcons are also present. 3,500 acres. Excellent bird-watching from the Hookton Slough Trail and Salmon Creek. Off US 101, about 40 miles south of Redwood NP. (707) 733-5406

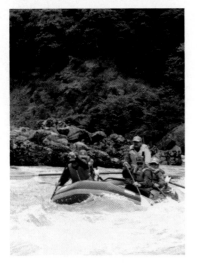

Six Rivers National Forest
Eureka, California

Six major rivers cross this mountain forest of pine, fir, spruce, and cedar, providing nearly 10 percent of the state's runoff. Recreational opportunities include white-water rafting, kayaking, and excellent steelhead and salmon fishing. Contains parts of four wilderness areas. 957,590 acres. Hiking, boating, fishing, horseback riding, hunting, scenic drives, winter sports, water sports. 355 campsites, boat ramp, picnic areas, handicapped access. Open all year, though most off-highway routes close in winter. Campsites open May through November, weather permitting. Information at Gasquet on US 199, about 15 miles from Redwood NP. (707) 457-3131.

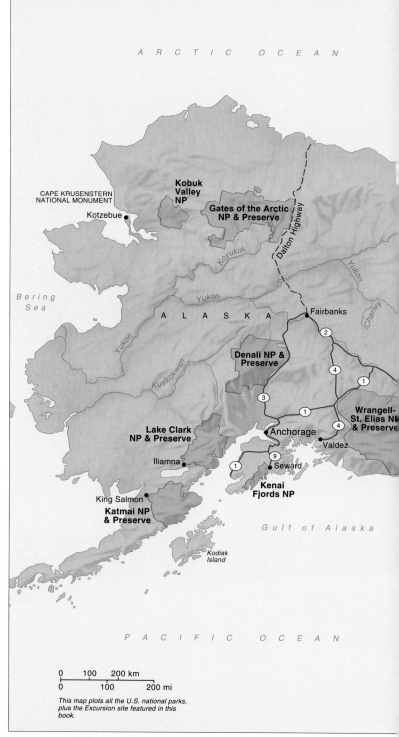

A R C T I C   O C E A N

CAPE KRUSENSTERN
NATIONAL MONUMENT

**Kobuk
Valley
NP**

Kotzebue

**Gates of the Arctic
NP & Preserve**

Koyukuk

Dalton Highway

Yukon

*B e r i n g
S e a*

Yukon

A L A S K A

Fairbanks

Charley

2

**Denali NP &
Preserve**

4

1

Kuskokwim

3

1

**Wrangell-
St. Elias NP
& Preserve**

**Lake Clark
NP & Preserve**

4

Anchorage

Valdez

Iliamna

1

9

Seward

**Kenai
Fjords NP**

King Salmon

**Katmai NP
& Preserve**

Gulf of Alaska

*Kodiak
Island*

P A C I F I C   O C E A N

0   100   200 km

0   100   200 mi

*This map plots all the U.S. national parks,
plus the Excursion site featured in this
book.*

Preceding pages: Lake Clark, Alaska

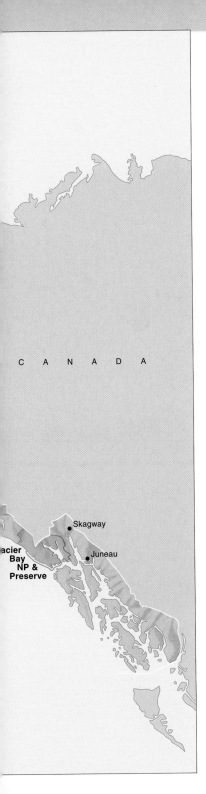

C A N A D A

Skagway

acier
Bay
NP &
Preserve

Juneau

Alaska

In 1867 Secretary of State William Seward bought Alaska from Russia for two cents an acre—and the public labeled the vast empty land Seward's Folly. Today, more than 13 billion barrels of oil have gushed through the Prudhoe Bay pipeline, and Alaska's wilderness and wildlife attract visitors by the thousands.

Eight national parks protect 41.5 million acres of these natural treasures. Katmai and Lake Clark lie along the Pacific Ring of Fire—a region of active volcanoes, earthquakes, giant brown bears, and salmon. Whales, sea lions, and flocks of seabirds seek out the cold, food-laden waters of Glacier Bay and Kenai Fjords. Wrangell-St. Elias is a jumble of mountains and glaciers so rugged that many remain unnamed and untrodden by humans. Above the Arctic Circle, Gates of the Arctic and Kobuk Valley protect the tundra and migrant herds of caribou. By comparison, Denali seems civilized with its nearby railroad and hotels; yet here the wildlife is so abundant and visible, the park is called a "subarctic Serengeti."

Alaska parks include national preserves that allow hunting, vast wilderness areas that prohibit buildings and roads, and native-owned lands still used for subsistence in a tradition thousands of years old.

In 1989 the *Exxon Valdez* ran aground in Prince William Sound, spilling nearly 11 million gallons of oil. The slick spread into the Gulf of Alaska and onto the beaches of Katmai and Kenai Fjords. It killed more than 3,500 sea otters and 350,000 seabirds, as well as unknown numbers of scavenging mammals. The visible oil slick is gone, but the damage to the area's ecological balance may well last forever.

Most of Alaska's national parks are accessible only by plane or boat, but you can drive to Denali and Wrangell-St. Elias and to the edges of Kenai Fjords and Gates of the Arctic. The loop connecting Anchorage to Denali to Fairbanks to Wrangell-St. Elias, with a side trip to Kenai Fjords, is 1,100 miles. It's a 600-mile round-trip from Fairbanks to Gates of the Arctic on the unpaved Dalton Highway. Alaska parks are rugged, yet fragile; tread lightly.

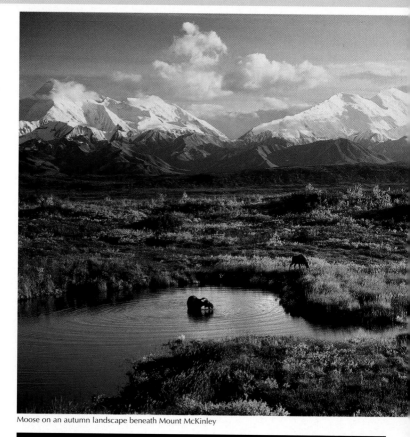

Moose on an autumn landscape beneath Mount McKinley

Denali

Alaska

Established February 26, 1917

6,028,924 acres

On any summer day in Denali, Alaska's most popular national park, hundreds of people see sights that will stay with them the rest of their lives. Perhaps a golden eagle will soar off the cliffs at Polychrome Pass, or 20 Dall's sheep will rest on a green shoulder of Primrose Ridge, or a grizzly will ramble over the tundra at Sable Pass. Maybe a caribou will pause on a ridgetop, silhouetted by the warm light of day's end, or a loon will call across Wonder Lake, or clouds will part to reveal the great massif of Mount McKinley, 20,320 feet high, the roof of North America. The drama is always there. To see it, all you need to do is travel the 85-mile park road. The farther you go, the

more you'll see, for the subarctic landscape will open up as big as the sky and the animals will move through it with wild, ancient poetry.

Other North American parks have their wildlife, but none has animals so visible or diverse as Denali. And other parks have their mountains, but none with a stature so stunning, a summit so towering as McKinley.

Denali's visitors have increased 1,000 percent in 30 years. How to accommodate that many people without eroding the park's wilderness? A bus system has been designed that permits maximum wildlife viewing while holding down traffic. Campgrounds have been kept modest and unobtrusive. And the wilderness area has been divided into management units with strict visitation ceilings to prevent overcrowding and damage to the flora and fauna. Unless you plan ahead by using the rich tones of red, orange, and yellow. In winter, visitors can take the road 3 miles to park headquarters and cross-country ski, snowshoe, or dogsled from there.

May and early June are the best times to climb Mount McKinley; after June, avalanches and crevasses threaten. Most mountaineers fly by ski-plane from Talkeetna and land at 7,200 feet on the Kahiltna Glacier to begin a climb that will take 15 to 30 days.

How to Visit

The more time the better, but plan on at least 2 days. The park is currently undergoing significant changes to allow for the increase in visitors; check ahead for road and trail changes.

If you have a camping permit, you can drive your car on the **park road** as far as the **Savage River Check Station** at mile 14. For everyone else, shuttle buses and tour buses operate on the road by day and into evening, late May to mid-September; schedules vary.

The 85-mile shuttle bus trip along the park road to **Wonder Lake** takes 11 hours round-trip, including many stops to watch wildlife; other buses go part way. Take a jacket, binoculars, and a lunch (available near the **Visitor Center** or outside the park; no food along the way). In the park, consider getting off the bus for a hike; buses will stop almost anywhere. To get on another bus, just wave one down. In busy times, you may have to wait a while for one with space.

Park campgrounds and buses are usually full, so plan on the possibility of staying a night or two in a hotel or nearby private campground if you must wait for a campsite or bus ticket.

Mount McKinley is often covered with clouds; you may be more likely to get a clear view of it early or late in the long day.

parks easy-to-use reservation system, you may have to wait a day or two to get your preferred campsite or bus reservation.

How to Get There

From Anchorage, take Alas. 1 (Glenn Hwy.) 35 miles north to Alas. 3 (George Parks Hwy.). Go north 205 miles. From Fairbanks, take Alas. 3 west and south 120 miles. In summer, the Alaska Railroad runs between Anchorage and Fairbanks and stops daily at the Denali railroad station. In winter, the train runs on weekends only. Air service available in summer to the nearby airstrips from Anchorage, Fairbanks, and Talkeetna.

When to Go

In summer, there are up to 21 hours of daylight. The park road is open from late May to mid-September. June is usually less crowded than July and August. In late August or early September, the tundra turns

Park Road by Bus

85 miles one way; 11 hours round-trip

Your bus journey begins at the **Visitor Center** (at mile 0.7), surrounded by the spruce forest, or taiga. Within minutes you'll see the railroad station used by the Alaska Railroad, and you'll pass park headquarters, where sled dogs are kept for winter patrols and summer demonstrations.

Soon the road begins climbing

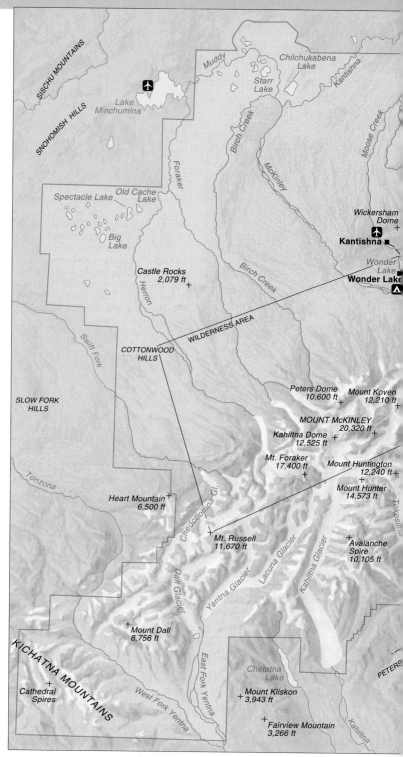

SISCHU MOUNTAINS

SNOHOMISH HILLS

Lake
Minchumina

Muddy

Chilchukabena
Lake

Starr
Lake

Kantishna

Birch Creek

Moose Creek

Foraker

McKinley

Spectacle Lake

Old Cache
Lake

Big
Lake

Wickersham
Dome

Kantishna ■

Herron

Castle Rocks
2,079 ft

Birch Creek

Wonder
Lake

Wonder Lake

Swift Fork

WILDERNESS AREA

COTTONWOOD
HILLS

SLOW FORK
HILLS

Peters Dome
10,600 ft

Mount Koven
12,210 ft

MOUNT McKINLEY
20,320 ft

Kahiltna Dome
12,525 ft

Tonzona

Mt. Foraker
17,400 ft

Mount Huntington
12,240 ft

Mount Hunter
14,573 ft

Heart Mountain
6,500 ft

Chedollothna Gl.

Mt. Russell
11,670 ft

Avalanche
Spire
10,105 ft

Tokositna

Dall Glacier

Yentna Glacier

Lacuna Glacier

Kahiltna Glacier

KICHATNA MOUNTAINS

Mount Dall
8,756 ft

Cathedral
Spires

East Fork Yentna

Chelatna
Lake

PETERS

West Fork Yentna

Mount Kliskon
3,943 ft

Fairview Mountain
3,266 ft

Kahiltna

To Fairbanks

Nenana

Chitsia Mtn. +
3,862 ft

Toklat

Teklanika

KANTISHNA HILLS

Healy
✈

3

Mount Healy +
5,716 ft
McKinley Park

Visitor Center
🚹 △ ✈

Yahert Fork

🚹 △ PRIMROSE RIDGE
Sanctuary River

Savage River

Riley Creek
△

Kankone Peak
+

Private vehicles restricted beyond this point

Only open to campers with permits

Teklanika River
△

Igloo Mountain +
4,800 ft

Igloo Creek
🚹 △

Fang Mountain
6,736 ft +

Polychrome Mountain
5,790 ft

Sable Pass

Cathedral Mountain
4,905 ft
+

Toklat
🚹

Polychrome Overlook

Stony Hill
+

Thorofare Pass
Highway Pass

Stony Dome
4,700 ft

Foggy Pass

✈

Denali Highway

△

Eielson Visitor Center

Mount Pendleton
7,840 ft +

Cantwell

8

(closed in winter)

To Paxson

Scott Peak
8,838 ft +

Muldrow Glacier

Summit
✈

Mount Brooks
11,940 ft
+

Mt. Mather
12,123 ft
+

+ Mount Deception
11,768 ft

Mt. Silverthrone
13,220 ft
+

Eldridge Glacier

Ruth Amphitheater

Mount Dickey
9,545 ft
+

Chulitna Pass

The Great Gorge

DEVILS CANYON

Susitna

Ruth Glacier

DENALI STATE PARK

The Alaska Railroad

Petersville

3

Petersville Road

🚹 ✈
Talkeetna

To Anchorage   To Alaska Highway 3

↑

🚹 Ranger Station

△ Campground

✈ Airstrip

- - - - Unpaved Road

-·-·- Primitive Road

Park/Preserve

0   10   20 km
0   10   20 mi

Backpackers above tree line

out of the taiga and into the treeless expanse of the tundra. Magnificent vistas open up; on clear days **Mount McKinley** can be seen 70 miles to the southwest. As the bus crosses the **Savage River Bridge** (mile 14.8), note how the gentle, glacier-sculptured topography to the south meets the rugged river-cut canyon to the north; this spot marks the farthest advance of a glacier that flowed north out of the **Alaska Range** and across the valley thousands of years ago.

The road winds along **Primrose Ridge** before dropping into a marshy flat where spruce trees lean haphazardly in all directions. This "drunken forest" forms as permafrost thaws and the land slumps gradually downhill, tilting the trees. Watch for moose here and in other spruce forests, especially in areas with willow, their favorite browse.

Just beyond Teklanika River Campground (mile 29) is the **Teklanika River Bridge.** Like other rivers in Denali, the Teklanika is braided by channels. Its Athabaskan name means "middle water." The road passes Igloo Creek Campground and cuts between **Igloo** and **Cathedral Mountains,** favorite haunts of Dall's sheep, the world's only species of wild white sheep. Watch for them on the upper slopes.

If you want to see grizzly bears, a good place is just up the road at **Sable Pass** (3,895 feet). The grizzlies feed primarily on roots, berries, and other plant materials, and occasionally on arctic ground squirrels,

moose calves, injured or infirm caribou, and carrion. To protect the bears' habitat, the Sable Pass area is closed to foot traffic, except on the road.

About 5 miles farther, the road climbs a steep slope to **Polychrome Pass** and a spectacular view of the Alaska Range to the south. Below see the **Plains of Murie,** where fast running water has created alluvial terraces. At mile 53.1 the **Toklat River** has special significance, for it was here (5 miles north of where the bridge crosses the river today) that the naturalist Charles Sheldon built a cabin and wintered in 1907-08. The area so inspired him that he moved back East and spent 9 years lobbying for legislation to create Alaska's first national park. Originally called Mount McKinley, the park in 1980 was renamed Denali—an Athabaskan name for the mountain meaning "the high one."

The road reaches its highest elevation at **Highway Pass** (3,980 feet) before descending to cross **Stony Creek** and climbing again to the **Stony Hill Overlook,** where, weather permitting, Mount McKinley looms into view 40 miles away. Watch for caribou as they funnel through the Stony Hill area. Although the total Denali herd numbers about 2,700, the caribou usually move in small groups. They can appear almost any time of day anywhere in the lowlands between the park road and the Alaska Range.

Eielson Visitor Center (mile 66) is a scenic rest stop 33 miles from Mount McKinley. Arctic ground squirrels scamper about, begging for handouts

Tussock of grass near Wonder Lake

they don't need and shouldn't have. Wildflowers splash the tundra with reds and yellows, and sometimes you'll see a grizzly on a distant ridge or on the road.

Continuing west, the road cuts along a steep cliff, then enters more gentle terrain as it comes within a mile of the dark, gravel-covered snout of the **Muldrow Glacier** to the south. Beginning just below the summit of Mount McKinley, the Muldrow flows 35 miles through a granite gorge and across the tundra to its terminus. Twice in the last hundred years (and for reasons not fully understood) the Muldrow has surged forward, most recently in the winter of 1956-57, when it advanced 5 miles.

The road passes several ponds where chances improve for sighting beaver, moose, and waterfowl, and finally arrives at Wonder Lake Campground. Here the shuttle bus will turn around for the 5.5-hour trip back, after allowing you time to stroll and take pictures. Twenty-seven miles to the south looms Mount McKinley, its north face— the **Wickersham Wall**—rising more than 14,000 feet in a single precipice, one of the greatest mountain walls in the world. And just north of the campground lies **Wonder Lake,** 2.6 miles long, 280 feet deep, and home to lake trout, burbot, and moose that occasionally wade in belly-deep to feed on aquatic vegetation near the shore. Loons, grebes, and mergansers also visit the lake.

Hikes

In a park larger than New Hampshire, the hiking opportunities are endless, but the only maintained trails are in the front country, beginning at the Visitor Center, where maps are available, and at the railroad station, near the park entrance.

The **Horseshoe Lake Trail** winds gently through a handsome forest of aspen and spruce 1.25 miles to **Horseshoe Lake,** an old oxbow of the **Nenana River.** It takes about 1 hour round-trip. Branching off this trail just past the stream-crossing is a more strenuous one, the **Mount Healy Overlook Trail.** Climbing 1,700 feet in less than 3 miles (one way), it breaks above timberline and arrives at the overlook among wildflowers, rock outcrops, arctic ground squirrels, and pikas. And, if the weather is clear, Mount McKinley is visible more than 80 miles to the southwest. A new accessible quarter-mile trail begins at the Savage Cabin Campground and leads to **Savage Cabin,** where demonstrations are held in summer.

For those seeking a moderate hike, the 3-mile **Triple Lakes Trail** is a good choice with its excellent views of **Mount Fellows, Pyramid Mountain,** and other peaks in the Alaska Range.

In the backcountry, hiking is a matter of taking whatever route you wish—down a drainage, up a ridge, across a valley. The object is to spread out and tread lightly, leaving no evidence of your visit.

Popular backcountry hiking areas (without trails) include Primrose Ridge, Mount Wright, Igloo Mountain, Cathedral Mountain, Calico Creek, Tattler Creek, the Polychrome Cliffs Loop, Stony Dome and Stony Hill, the Stony Creek Loop, the Sunrise Glacier Loop, Sunset Glacier, Eielson Visitor Center Ridge, and around Wonder Lake. Some of these hikes take an hour or more, some take several days.

Since a backcountry management unit might be closed or full, those wishing to camp are required to check at the Visitor Center before choosing an overnight hike. Some areas may be restricted in order to protect critical wildlife habitats, and animal activity may temporarily close backcountry sections.

Float Trips

If you enjoy rafting through a mix of calm water and white water, don't miss a trip down the **Nenana River,** along the George Parks Highway and the park's eastern border. Several companies offer guided trips lasting from 2 hours to 4 days. From McKinley Village, about 6 miles south of the park entrance, a 2-hour float takes you to the McKinley Chalet Resort, just outside the entrance. The next 2 hours, to Healy, offer a whitewater experience. Allow an hour or two for travel and instruction.

Rafting along the Nenana River

Animals of Denali

Grizzly stretching in the sunshine

Dall's sheep

Willow ptarmigan

Caribou

Information & Activities

Headquarters
P.O. Box 9, Denali, AK 99755. Phone (907) 683-2294. www.nps.gov/dena

Seasons & Accessibility
Park open year-round. Park road open, weather permitting, Memorial Day to mid-September. Car travel to Savage River, 14 miles into the park, restricted to persons with camping permits. During snow season, park road is not plowed beyond headquarters (mile 3.1), which limits access to skiers, snowshoers, and dogsledders.

Visitor & Information Centers
Visitor Center, at east border of park, open daily late April to late September. **Eielson Visitor Center** open early June to mid-September. **Talkeetna Ranger Station** open daily mid-April to Labor Day; Monday through Friday rest of year. Off-season information available at headquarters, open daily all year.

Entrance Fees
$5 fee per person per week; $10 per family; $20 annual.

Shuttle Bus Transportation
From the Visitor Center, buses operate regularly from 5:00 a.m. to 3:00 p.m. between late May and mid-September. Reserve in person. Fees range from $2 to $33, depending on destination. To make reservations, call (800) 622-7275 or (907) 272-7275. Trips not narrated, but buses stop for wildlife watching. Also, twice daily campers bus. Also, Tundra Wilderness tour ($74) and Natural History tour ($40). (800) 276-7234 or (907) 276-7234 for required reservations.

Facilities for Disabled
Most buildings accessible to wheelchairs, as are some tour and shuttle buses. Please advise staff of need when making reservations.

Things to Do
Free ranger-led activities: nature walks and hikes, children's programs, sled-dog demonstrations, talks, slide shows, and films. Also, narrated bus tours, hiking, limited fishing, mountain climbing, rafting, horseback riding, cross-country skiing, dogsledding.

Overnight Backpacking
Backcountry divided into units with limits (2-12) on the number of campers. Permits required; available free at Visitor Center, first come, first served. Must carry bear-proof containers. Backpacker shuttle fee $18.50.

Campgrounds
Five campgrounds (294 sites), 14-day limit from mid-May to mid-Sept.; other times, 30-day limit. **Riley Creek** open all year. Others open late spring to early fall. In summer, reservations strongly recommended (800) 622-7275 or (907) 272-7275. Fees $6-$16 per night. RV sites except at **Sanctuary** and **Wonder Lake;** no hookups. Buses transport campers to Sanctuary, **Igloo Creek,** Wonder Lake, and farther. Must reserve for **Savage River Group Campground;** contact headquarters.

Hotels, Motels, & Inns
(unless otherwise noted, rates are for 2 persons in a double room, high season)
INSIDE THE PARK:
Camp Denali and **North Face Lodge** P.O. Box 67, Denali NP, AK 99775. (907) 683-2290. Camp Denali: 17 cabins, central showers. North Face Lodge: 15 rooms. $365 per person, all inclusive. Early June to mid-Sept.
Denali Backcountry Lodge Denali NP, AK 99775 (800) 841-0692. 30 units. $340 per person per night, all inclusive. June to Sept.
OUTSIDE THE PARK:
Denali Cabins (8 miles south of entrance) P.O. Box 229, Denali NP, AK 99755. (907) 683-2643. 42 cabins. $159. Restaurant. Mid-May to mid-Sept.
Denali Princess Lodge (half mile from entrance) P.O. Box 110, Denali NP, AK 99755. (907) 683-2282. 352 units. $179-$249. Restaurant. Mid-May to mid-Sept.
McKinley Chalet Resort (1 mile from entrance) (907) 276-7234. 352 units. $213. Pool, restaurant. Mid-May to mid-Sept.
McKinley Village Lodge (6 miles from entrance) (907) 276-7234. 150 units. $203. Restaurant. Late May to early September.

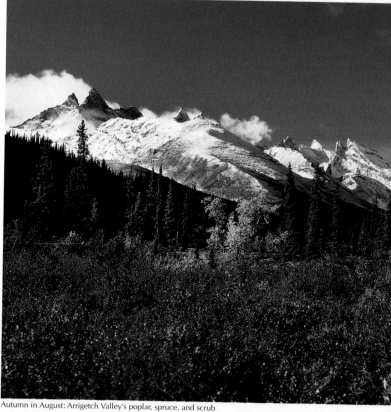

Autumn in August: Arrigetch Valley's poplar, spruce, and scrub

Gates of the Arctic

Alaska

Established December 2, 1980

8,500,000 acres

"The view from the top gave us an excellent idea of the jagged country toward which we were heading. The main Brooks Range divide was entirely covered with snow. Close at hand, only about ten miles to the north, was a precipitous pair of mountains, one on each side of the North Fork. I bestowed the name Gates of the Arctic on them."

It was the early 1930s, and Robert Marshall had found his wilderness home, an unpeopled, uncluttered source of inspiration that would make him one of America's greatest conservationists. Gates of the Arctic was the ultimate North American wilderness. Congress created the park to keep it that way.

Climb practically any ridge in the heart of the park and you'll see a dozen glacial cirques side by side; serrated mountains that scythe the sky; and storms that snap out of dark, brooding clouds. Six National Wild and Scenic Rivers—Alatna, John, Kobuk, Noatak, North Fork Koyukuk, and Tinayguk—tumble out of high alpine valleys into forested lowlands. The park lies entirely above the Arctic Circle, straddling the Brooks Range, one of the world's northernmost mountain chains.

With Kobuk Valley National Park and Noatak National Preserve, Gates of the Arctic protects much of the habitat of the western arctic caribou. Grizzlies, wolves, wolverines, and foxes also roam over the severe land in search of food. Ptarmigan nibble on willow, and gyrfalcons dive for ptarmigan. Shafts of cinnabar sunlight pour through the mountains at 2 a.m. in June, setting the wild land ablaze. "No sight or sound or smell or feeling even remotely hinted of men or their creations," wrote Marshall. "It seemed as if time had dropped away a million years and we were back in a primordial world."

How to Get There

Bush pilots say that where the road ends, the real Alaska begins. And so it is in Gates of the Arctic. You can fly or walk in; most people fly. From Fairbanks (about 250 miles away), scheduled flights serve Anaktuvuk Pass, an Eskimo village within the park borders; Bettles/Evansville; and Ambler, to the west. From those points or from Fairbanks, you can air taxi into the park. Allow time for bad weather and delayed flights. From Anaktuvuk Pass, you can also hike into the park along the John River.

Or, you can drive up from Fairbanks on the unpaved Dalton Highway (a pipeline haul road that's also open to the public) and hike to the park from Wiseman or other points. But it's a long, hard walk into the interior.

When to Go

Summer. It is short, but days are very long and for a while temperatures may be relatively mild. Weather is highly unpredictable. Expect snow or rain in any month. August can be very wet, with freezing temperatures by mid-month. Mosquitoes and gnats are bad in late June and July. Fall colors peak in mid-August at high elevations, late August to early September at low elevations.

How to Visit

Give yourself time to savor the subtle beauty of this vast wilderness. A combination river-hiking trip offers the best of both. Air taxis are equipped to land on lakes and gravel bars for drop-offs and pickups.

Plan carefully and bring everything you need; there are no visitor facilities in the park. This spare, harsh land is so fragile that a hiker's step can kill lichens that take 150 years to reach full growth. Certain areas were badly damaged by the increase in visitors after Gates of the Arctic became a park.

Write or call park headquarters in Fairbanks before planning a trip. There are no trails in the park, but you can ask for suggestions about areas to visit, along with names of air taxis, guides, and outfitters who operate in the park.

Black granite peaks of the Arrigetch

River Trips

Rivers are the main travel routes through Gates of the Arctic. Alaskan natives and caribou have followed them for centuries. Near some are lakes on which aircraft can land. Camping is good on the gravel bars, but be aware that summer rainstorms can quickly raise water levels. Most rivers are at their highest in May and June. Hiking is difficult but rewarding, especially in alpine areas. The following six rivers are only a sampling of what the park has to offer:

Alatna River is ideal for a first wilderness float trip. It takes 4 to 7 days, running gently down from the treeless Arctic Divide through beautiful tundra to the forested **Koyukuk River** lowlands. There are put-ins at **Takahula**

Castle Mt.
3,409 ft+
WILDERNESS
AREA

Chandler

Anaktuvuk

Itkillik

Itkillik
Lake

Shainin
Lake

Nanushuk

Chandler
Lake

BROOKS **RANGE**

**Anaktuvuk
Pass**

John

Summit
Lake

ENDICOTT MOUNTAINS

Koyukuk

+ Mount Doonerak
7,457 ft

Hunt Fork John

Frigid Crags
5,501 ft + ■ **Gates of the Arctic**
+ **Boreal Mountain**
6,654 ft

Dalton Highway
(Haul Road)

Hunt Fork
Lake

WILDERNESS
AREA

OUNTAINS

Tinayguk

North Fork

North Fork

Koyukuk

Wild
Lake

Middle Fork Koyukuk

•Wiseman

John

•**Coldfoot**

akuk
ke

Wild

Bettles/
Evansville

South Fork Koyukuk

Ice Road
(winter use only)

Dalton Highway
(Haul Road)

•Prospect Creek

Ranger Station

Airport

Unpaved Road

Park/Preserve

KANUTI
NATIONAL WILDLIFE
REFUGE

0 10 20 30 40 km

0 10 20 30 40 mi

To Allakaket

To Fairbanks

Lake, **Circle Lake,** or at a series of
unnamed lakes farther upstream.
Most boaters take-out at the village
of Allakaket (75 and 85 miles from
Takahula and Circle Lakes, respectively), where the Alatna meets the
Koyukuk River.

John River is a mere stream at its
headwater at Anaktuvuk Pass (the
permanent settlement of the inland
Nunamiut Eskimo), but it gains power

Tundra swan, a bird of summer

North Fork Koyukuk near the Gates of the Arctic

Purple saxifrage

and momentum as it flows south through the alpine heart of the park. **Hunt Fork Lake** is the best put-in; water levels above this point are usually too low. The John drops into lowland forest and joins the Koyukuk River just downstream of Bettles, a journey of a hundred miles.

Kobuk River begins at **Walker Lake** (a good put-in) and runs south and west through the mountains, canyons, foothills, and lowlands of Gates of the Arctic. Kobuk village, 140 river miles from Walker Lake, is a popular take-out. Or you can continue downriver to Ambler and on through Kobuk Valley National Park to Kiana.

North Fork Koyukuk begins at **Summit Lake** and cuts between **Boreal Mountain** and **Frigid Crags**— the **Gates of the Arctic**—then flows past **Redstar Creek Lakes** (a good put-in) and continues south a hundred miles to Bettles.

Comprising one of the largest wilderness river basins in North America, the **Noatak** flows west 450 miles from Gates of the Arctic through Noatak National Preserve into the Chukchi Sea. The trip from a put-in at **Lake Matcharak** to Noatak village is 350 miles. The river, a major thoroughfare in a trackless realm, demands minimal boating skills but maximal planning. Give yourself a month for the trip.

The seldom visited **Tinayguk** flows through a broad glacier-cut valley before joining the Koyukuk below Boreal Mountain and Frigid Crags. Put in after landing on a gravel bar along the Tinayguk 35 miles north of where it joins the Koyukuk. (Consult local maps and outfitters for the exact location.) Float down to the Koyukuk, then continue on for another 80 miles to Bettles.

Information & Activities

Headquarters
201 1st Ave., Doyon Bldg., Fairbanks, AK 99701. Phone (907) 456-0281. For visitor information, write Gates of the Arctic NP, P.O. Box 26030, Bettles, AK 99726. www.nps.gov/gaar

Seasons & Accessibility
Park open year-round. Access by air or foot; there are no roads to the park (except Dalton Highway, an unpaved pipeline haul road that's parallel to park's east boundary). There are no roads in the park. Contact park headquarters before planning a visit.

Visitor & Information Centers
There are no visitor centers or facilities of any kind within the park. The only ranger stations are located in Bettles and Anaktuvuk Pass. An interagency visitor center is staffed in Coldfoot during the summer.

Gas & Supplies
Bring supplies with you (Fairbanks has a full selection); few available in communities of Bettles and Anaktuvuk Pass, which are not accessible by road. Gas stations on the Dalton Highway at milepost 56 (just north of the Yukon River) and at Coldfoot, milepost 173.6.

Pets
Only pack dogs allowed.

Facilities for Disabled
Bettles and Anaktuvuk Pass Ranger Stations and Coldfoot Visitor Center.

Things to Do
Hiking (no established trails), backpacking, canoeing, kayaking and rafting, fishing (license required), hunting (in preserve only, with license), rock-and mountain climbing, wildlife watching. In winter: cross-country skiing, snowshoeing, dogmushing, skiing. Ask park for list of licensed guides and outfitters (www.nps.gov/gaar/com mops.htm.)

Special Advisories
● All visitors should be well skilled in the outdoors; firearms may be carried for protection.
● Grizzly bears are unpredictable and dangerous. Visit ranger station in Bettles or Coldfoot for advice on preventing an encounter.
● Eskimos and other Native Alaskans use the park for subsistence fishing and hunting; respect them and their property.
● From mid-June through July, be prepared for plenty of mosquitoes and gnats; bring insect repellent, a head net, and an insect-proof tent.
● Swift currents and freezing water can make river crossings particularly hazardous.

Overnight Backpacking
No permit required, but get up-to-date bear information from ranger station. An orientation is available at ranger stations. Food, stoves, and all equipment must be carried. Camp on gravel bars to avoid damaging fragile tundra. Bear barrels recommended; purchase or rent beforehand.

Campgrounds
None; backcountry camping only.

Hotels, Motels, & Inns
(unless otherwise noted, rates are for 2 persons in a double room, high season)
INSIDE THE PARK:
Alatna Lodge (on headwaters of the Alatna River) Alatna Guide Service, P.O. Box 80424, Fairbanks, AK 99708. (907) 479-6354. 1 cabin, 6 beds. $4,150 per person for 3 days, including airfare from Fairbanks and activities. Open July to early Sept.
Nahtuk Wilderness Cabins (on Alatna River near Arrigetch Peaks) P.O. Box 80424, Fairbanks, AK 99708. (907) 479-6354. 1 cabin, 4 beds. $2,950 per person for 3 nights, including airfare. Open mid-June to early Sept.
OUTSIDE THE PARK:
Slate Creek Inn Mile 175, Dalton Hwy., Coldfoot, AK 99701. (907) 678-5201. 52 units. $145. Restaurant. Mid-May to mid-Sept.
Coldfoot Services Motel Mile 175, Dalton Hwy., Coldfoot, AK 99701. (907) 678-5201. 50 units. $125. Restaurant. Open year-round.
Iniakuk Lake Wilderness Lodge (on Iniakuk Lake) P.O. Box 80424, Fairbanks, AK 99708. (907) 479-6354. 6 rooms, central bath. $3,225 per person for 3 nights, including airfare. Mid-June to mid-Sept.

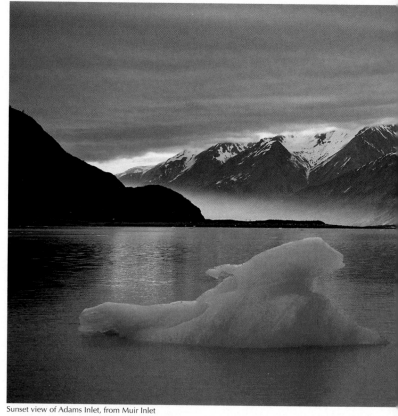

Sunset view of Adams Inlet, from Muir Inlet

Glacier Bay

Alaska

Established December 2, 1980

3,280,198 acres

When Capt. George Vancouver sailed the Alaska coast in 1794, Glacier Bay did not exist. It lay beneath a sheet of glacial ice several miles wide and thousands of feet thick. Since then, in one of the fastest glacial retreats on record, the ice has shrunk back 65 miles to unveil new land and a new bay, now returning to life after a long winter's sleep.

Scientists call Glacier Bay a living laboratory for the grand processes of glacial retreat, plant succession, and animal dynamics. It is an open book on the last ice age. At the southern end of the bay, where the ice departed 200 years ago, a spruce-hemlock rain forest has taken root. Farther north, in areas more recently deglaciated, the land becomes rugged and thinly vegetated.

The bay branches into two major arms, the west arm and Muir Inlet, which themselves branch into smaller inlets. There, on slopes deglaciated 50 to 100 years ago, alder and willow grow, while mosses, mountain avens, and dwarf fireweed pioneer areas exposed within the last two or three decades.

The new vegetation creates habitats for wolves, moose, mountain goats, black bears, brown bears, ptarmigan, and other wildlife, and the sea supports a food chain that includes salmon, bald eagles, harbor seals, harbor porpoises, humpback whales, and killer whales—all in an environment less than 200 years old.

Roughly 13 tidewater glaciers still flow into the park. In part because of variations in snow accumulations, most glaciers in the eastern and southwestern areas of the bay are receding, while several on its west side are advancing. The glaciers calve icebergs that hit the water with a sound like cannon shot. "White thunder," the Tlingit Indians called it, the awesome voice of glacial ice. An iceberg's color often reveals its makeup; dense bergs are blue, while those filled with trapped air bubbles are white.

How to Get There

By boat or plane only. From Juneau, take a scheduled flight 53 miles to Gustavus. Catch the bus to Glacier Bay Lodge and Bartlett Cove Campground, 10 miles away at the park's southern end. Charter flights also service Gustavus from Juneau, Skagway, Haines, and Hoonah. The Glacier Bay Cruiseline ferry departs Monday, Wednesday, Friday, and Sunday from Juneau to Gustavus then Bartlett Cove. Private boats can enter the bay with permits (required June to August) obtained by phone, by mail from headquarters

at Bartlett Cove, or online (www.nps .gov/glba).

When to Go

Late May to mid-September. Summer days are long and temperatures cool. May and June have the most sunshine, but the upper inlets can be thick with icebergs then and the tidewater glaciers less approachable. September is often rainy and windy.

How to Visit

Glacier Bay is a marine highway. Most visitors experience the park from the deck of a cruise ship, or a tour boat, or from the waterline of a sea kayak. Many of the large cruise ships that travel southeastern Alaska's Inside Passage go into Glacier Bay. Other tours offer accommodations at **Glacier Bay Lodge** (the park's center of activity) and a 1-day or overnight boat trip to the glaciers and back. Campers and kayakers can take the boat and be dropped off at one of three sites up the bay, either to be picked up at a later date or to paddle back to Bartlett Cove.

The Lower Bay

The lower bay reaches from **Bartlett Cove** north to **Tlingit Point,** where it separates into its two arms and continues north. Bartlett Cove has the only three maintained trails in the park. Beginning at the **Glacier Bay Lodge,** the **Forest Loop Trail** is a 1-mile, 1-hour round-trip through the young spruce-hemlock rain forest. A boardwalk covers the first part of the trail out to **Blackwater Pond.** For a half-day trip (and more rugged walking), the **Bartlett River Trail** begins at the roadside, a half mile from the lodge, and winds another 1.5 miles through the rain forest to the **Bartlett River,** ending in a quiet meadow. It's not unusual to see red squirrels, blue grouse, and black bears along either of these trails. Finally, the new **Beach Trail** runs 6 miles from the lodge area to park headquarters along the beachline. It is especially popular among walkers and cyclists.

If you want to kayak, the **Beardslee Islands** just north of Bartlett Cove offer a maze of shorelines and waterways—a quiet counterpoint to the buses and boats coming and going at Bartlett Cove.

Reaching across the lower bay, **Sitakaday Narrows** is a shoal that

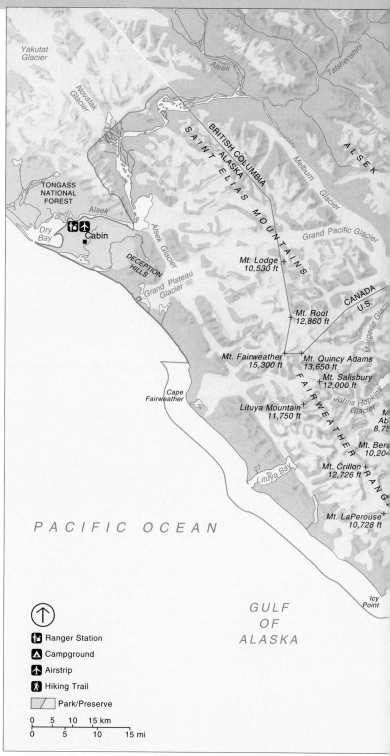

Yakutat Glacier

Novatak Glacier

Alsek

Tatshenshini

BRITISH COLUMBIA
ALASKA

S A I N T   E L I A S   M O U N T A I N S

ALSEK

Melburn Glacier

TONGASS NATIONAL FOREST

Alsek

Dry Bay

Cabin

DECEPTION HILLS

Alsek Glacier

Grand Plateau Glacier

Grand Pacific Glacier

Mt. Lodge
10,530 ft

CANADA
U.S.

Mt. Root
12,860 ft

Margerie Glacier

Mt. Fairweather
15,300 ft

Mt. Quincy Adams
13,650 ft

Mt. Salisbury
12,000 ft

F A I R W E A T H E R

Cape Fairweather

Johns Hopkins Glacier

Lituya Mountain
11,750 ft

M
Ab
8,75

Mt. Ber
10,20

Mt. Crillon
12,726 ft

R A N G E

Lituya Bay

PACIFIC OCEAN

Mt. LaPerouse
10,728 ft

Icy Point

GULF
OF
ALASKA

↑

👤 Ranger Station
△ Campground
✈ Airstrip
🚶 Hiking Trail
▨ Park/Preserve

0   5   10   15 km
0   5   10   15 mi

Steller's sea lions

creates strong and dangerous whirl-pools and currents as the tides (rising and falling an average of 15 feet in 6 hours) rush over it. Check the tide before venturing into the Narrows. Watch for phalaropes, gulls, terns, and other birds feeding here as the swirling water flushes small fish to the surface. To the north, the **Marble Islands** rise abruptly out of the middle of the bay. The islands, deglaciated about 1835, today support breeding colonies of gulls, cormorants, puffins, and murres (and are off-limits to visitors during the summer). Watch for Steller's sea lions on **South Marble Island.**

The West Arm

The bay's west arm contains the park's highest mountains and most active tidewater glaciers. Clear days afford stunning views of the **Fair-weather Range,** crowned by **Mount Fairweather** at 15,300 feet; cloudy days lend a moody, rich blue cast to the tidewater faces of the **Margerie, Grand Pacific, Lamplugh,** and **Reid Glaciers.**

In the wildest inlet, **Johns Hopkins,** seven glaciers tumble down moun-tains, whose surrounding peaks reach 8,000 feet. While glaciers are in retreat on the bay's east and south-west sides, here on the west side several of the glaciers are advancing. Each June thousands of harbor seals give birth to their pups on icebergs in Johns Hopkins Inlet (to protect the seals, the inlet is closed from May through June).

Blue Mouse Cove and the north-west corner of **Reid Inlet** are the best anchorages. Good camping sites can be found almost anywhere (except in Johns Hopkins Inlet where the terrain is generally too steep). Hiking is a matter of going where the spirit and

the topography take you. Brown bears are common. This is their home, and you are the visitor. *Be careful.*

Muir Inlet

Reaching 25 miles into the north-east corner of the park, **Muir Inlet** is a mecca for kayakers. Tour boats, cruise ships, and fishing boats seldom come in here (and the waters north of McBride Glacier are closed to motor boats from June to mid-July). The camping is good, and so is the hiking, if you avoid thickets of alder.

Adams Inlet branches east off lower Muir Inlet and is a favorite among kayakers; motorboats are not allowed in the inlet from May to mid-September. You can time your entry and exit by the strong tides that flow in and out through the narrow open-ing. To the north, **Sealers Island** was once a breeding site for arctic terns and black oystercatchers.

Nearby is **Goose Cove,** an anchor-age in Muir Inlet. In contrast to the tidewater glaciers that are advancing in the west arm, most in Muir Inlet continue to retreat. The **McBride** and **Riggs Glaciers** separated from the retreating **Muir Glacier** in 1941 and 1960 respectively; since then, all three have retreated long distances.

A journey up **White Thunder Ridge** or **McConnell Ridge** rewards hikers with spectacular views of upper Muir Inlet. Both hikes are strenuous. Be prepared to struggle through alder— it takes a lot of time and energy. Each hike takes a full day and climbs about 1,500 feet. Also rewarding is a hike along **Wolf Creek** (beginning at the south end of White Thunder Ridge), where running water has exposed the remains of a forest buried by a glacier 4,000 to 7,000 years ago.

Information & Activities

Headquarters
P.O. Box 140, Gustavus, AK 99826.
Phone (907) 697-2230.
www.nps.gov/glba

Seasons & Accessibility
Park open year-round, but late May to mid-September is visitor season; transportation and facilities limited rest of year. Call the park before going in the off-season.

There are no roads to the park; access by airplane, boat, or ferry only. Glacier Bay Cruiseline (800-451-5952) offers ferry service between Auke Bay (north of Juneau) and Bartlett Cove. Visitors with private boats need a permit from June through August; phone (907) 697-2627.

Visitor & Information Centers
Information centers on the dock at **Bartlett Cove** and at **Glacier Bay Lodge.** Call (907) 697-2627 for visitor information.

Entrance Fee
None.

Pets
Permitted on leashes on Bartlett Cove roads only. Prohibited in backcountry; boaters must keep pets aboard vessels.

Facilities for Disabled
Glacier Bay Lodge is accessible to wheelchairs. One trail, with a stretch of boardwalk, is also accessible.

Things to Do
Free ranger-led activities (from Glacier Bay Lodge): nature walks, films, slide presentations, and evening programs. Also available, kayaking, fishing (license required), scheduled boat tours, glacier viewing, whale-watching and bird-watching, crabbing (license required), hiking, berry picking, mountain and glacier climbing (for the experienced only), aerial sight-seeing, cross-country skiing.

For information and reservations for ranger-guided boat tours from Bartlett Cove, contact Glacier Bay Lodge, Inc., P.O. Box 199, Gustavus, AK 99826. (800) 451-5952 or (907) 697-2225. Ask the park for a list of other concessioners offering a variety of rental and guide services.
www.nps.gov/glba/visit/services.htm

Special Advisories
● Do not get too close to icebergs when boating, and do not climb on the glaciers without a guide or plenty of experience.
● Load up on insect repellent.
● Be aware of bears. Obtain safety guidelines from information centers or rangers.

Overnight Backpacking
Permit required. Backcountry users must receive orientation from rangers before setting out. Use of Park Service food storage canisters required.

Campgrounds
One campground only; **Bartlett Cove** has 14-day limit. Open all year; first come, first served. No fees. Showers at lodge (within a mile) available only seasonally. Warming hut provided. Tent sites only. **Bartlett Cove Group Campground;** open all year; first come, first served.

Hotels, Motels, & Inns
(unless otherwise noted, rates are for 2 persons in a double room, high season)
INSIDE THE PARK:
Glacier Bay Lodge P.O. Box 199, Gustavus, AK 99826. (800) 451-5952 or (907) 697-2225. 55 units. $179. Packages that include airfare available. Restaurant. Open mid-May to early September.
OUTSIDE THE PARK:
In Gustavus, AK 99826
Glacier Bay Country Inn P.O. Box 5. (800) 628-0912 or (907) 697-2288. 10 units. $390, includes all meals. Open mid-May to mid-Sept.
Gustavus Inn P.O. Box 60. (907) 697-2254. 13 units, 11 with private baths. $150 per person, includes all meals and some activities. Open May to mid-Sept.
Salmon River Cabins P.O. Box 13. (907) 697-2245. 10 rustic cabins with kitchenettes, 4 private baths. $75. Open mid-May through Sept.

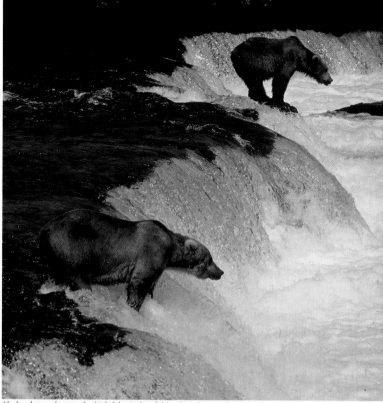

Alaskan brown bears—the frightful grizzly—fishing for salmon at Brooks Falls

Katmai

Alaska

Established December 2, 1980

4,090,000 acres

Volcanoes and bears—powerful, unpredictable, and awe inspiring—embody the wild heart of Katmai. Within the borders of the national park and preserve are 15 volcanoes, some of them still steaming, and North America's largest population of protected brown bears—about 1,500 of them. You can hike, kayak, and canoe here. You can fish waist-deep in rivers as clear as glass. And you can watch the best fish catcher of all, the great Alaskan brown bear, sometimes diving completely under the water for its prey, sometimes catching fish in midair. At the end of the day you can relax in a rustic yet sumptuous lodge on the shore of a sapphire lake and recount the day's enchantments.

In 1912 a volcano here erupted with a force ten times that of Mount St. Helens in 1980. Suddenly Katmai, a place hardly anyone had heard of, was on front pages around the world. Ash filled the air, global temperatures cooled, acid rain burned clothing off lines in Vancouver, British Columbia, and on Kodiak Island, just across Shelikof Strait from Katmai, day became night.

Leading a 1916 expedition sponsored by the National Geographic Society, botanist Robert Griggs ascended Katmai Pass from Shelikof Strait. "The whole valley as far as the eye could reach was full of hundreds, no thousands—literally, tens of thousands—of smokes curling up from its fissured floor," he wrote. The smokes were fumaroles steaming 500 to 1,000 feet into the air. Griggs, who named the Valley of Ten Thousand ins, and Brooks Camp Campground open. Bear watching, an increasingly popular pastime, is best in July when the sockeye salmon spawn (bear watching suffers a brief lull in June and again in August). Fishing and hiking are good throughout summer, but come prepared for rain. Heavy snow-pack may remain in the upper elevations into July. Summer daytime temperatures range from the mid-50s to mid-60s; the average low is 44°F.

How to Visit

If your time is short, get to **Brooks Camp.** People, fish, bears, boats, and planes concentrate here. Compared to the rest of the park, it's crowded. But the lodge and campground are comfortable (reservations required) and the bear viewing unforgettable. You'll find good hiking and fishing.

If at all possible, take the bus or van tour 23 miles out from Brooks Camp to the **Valley of Ten Thousand Smokes.** Return the same day or hike into the valley and camp. You can extend your stay by boating or flying to the many other lakes, streams, rivers, and lodges in the park. Pick your area, make a safe plan, and go.

Brooks Camp & Valley of Ten Thousand Smokes

Some very pleasant hikes begin near Brooks Camp. The trail you'll first want to take goes to the bear-viewing platform. The half-mile boardwalk starts between Brooks Camp and **Brooks Lake** and winds gently through the forest to **Brooks Falls,** ending at the viewing platform. Wooden steps ascend a balcony overlooking the fascinating spectacle of jumping fish and feeding bears. Averaging a thousand pounds and measuring up to ten feet long, these Alaskan brown bears are the largest land carnivores on the continent of North America.

The hike up **Dumpling Mountain** is a good day trip. The trail begins at the campground and climbs to an 800-foot overlook in 1.5 miles. From there you can continue another 2 miles over alpine tundra to the summit, elevation 2,440 feet. Both the overlook and summit afford tremendous views of **Naknek Lake** and the surrounding mountains.

Smokes, spearheaded the campaign to include Katmai in the National Park System.

The smokes are gone from the valley. But steam vents still appear elsewhere in the park.

How to Get There

From Anchorage, scheduled jets fly the 290 miles to King Salmon, park headquarters; from there, June to mid-September, daily floatplanes fly the last 33 miles to Brooks Camp, site of a summer visitor center and the center of activity. Air charters can be arranged into other areas. You can drive the 9 miles from King Salmon to Lake Camp, at the western end of the park on the Naknek River, then go by boat to Brooks Camp, the Bay of Islands, and other areas of Naknek Lake.

When to Go

June to early September. Only then, with transportation available between Brooks Camp and the Valley of Ten Thousand Smokes, are the lodges, cab-

Iliamna Lake

Kukaklek Lake

Alagnak

Battle Lake Cabins■

ALAGNAK WILD RIVER

Nonvianuk Camp■

Nonvianuk Lake

Kulik Lod

Enchanted Lake Lodge■

Oakley Peak +
4,625 ft

American Creek

+ Sugarloaf Mountain
2,085 ft

Lake Coville

Grosvenor Lake Lodge

Lake Grosvenor

To King Salmon
Park Headquarters
and Visitor Center
⌐■ **Lake Camp**

Portage Trail

Naknek Lake

North Arm

Bay of Islands

Naknek

Dumpling Mountain +
2,440 ft

Brooks Camp■

Mount La Gorce
+ 3,183 ft

Brooks Falls ■

Iliuk Arm

Brooks Lake

Visitor Center

Mount Kelez +
3,250 ft

Ukak

Baked Mountain
3,695 ft ■

Granite Peak
+ 1,683 ft

Yori Pass)(

Three Forks Overlook

VALLEY OF TEN THOUSAND SMOKES

+Mount Gr
7,600 ft

Novarupta
4,860 ft +

Knife Cre
Glacier

C
L

Red Mountain
+ 1,721 ft

Angle   Creek

Katmai Pass)(

Mount Megeik
7,250 ft +

Gertrude Peak
1,141 ft

Takayato

+
Mount Martin
6,050 ft

Creek

K
E
J
U
L
I
K

M
T
S.

Katmai

BECHAROF NATIONAL
WILDLIFE REFUGE

Katma
Bay

Becharof
Lake

Kejulik

Kashvik
Bay

Cape
Kubugak

Alinchak
Bay

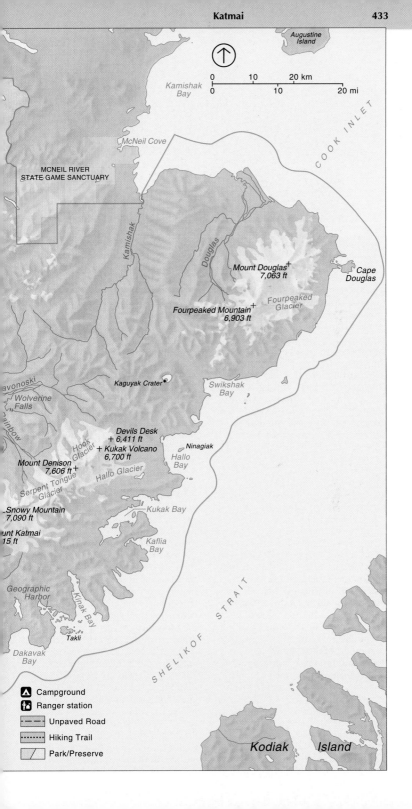

Augustine
Island

Kamishak
Bay

0   10   20 km
0   10   20 mi

COOK INLET

McNeil Cove

MCNEIL RIVER
STATE GAME SANCTUARY

Douglas

Kamishak

Mount Douglas⁺
7,063 ft

Cape
Douglas

Fourpeaked
Glacier

Fourpeaked Mountain⁺
6,903 ft

avonoski

Wolverine
Falls

Kaguyak Crater

Swikshak
Bay

ainbow

Hook
Glacier

Devils Desk
+ 6,411 ft
+ Kukak Volcano
6,700 ft

Ninagiak

Hallo
Bay

Mount Denison
7,606 ft

Hallo Glacier

Serpent Tongue
Glacier

Kukak Bay

Snowy Mountain
7,090 ft

Kaflia
Bay

unt Katmai
15 ft

Geographic
Harbor

Kinak Bay

SHELIKOF STRAIT

Takli

Dakavak
Bay

Kodiak   Island

△ Campground
🧍 Ranger station
– – – Unpaved Road
· · · · · Hiking Trail
▱ Park/Preserve

Mount Katolinat bordering the Valley of Ten Thousand Smokes

The most popular and spectacular hiking in the park is in the **Valley of Ten Thousand Smokes.** There's no other landscape like it in the world. Daily tours connect Brooks Camp with the **Three Forks Overlook** and a cabin at the north end of the valley, where you can camp or picnic. A short trail descends 200 feet to where the **Ukak River** roars through a bedrock canyon crowned by cliffs of volcanic ash.

To hike into the valley, take the trail that begins a half mile back from the end of the road and plan to camp overnight. The trail crosses **Windy Creek,** passes the north end of the **Buttress Range,** crosses the **River Lethe,** and finally climbs a thousand feet to the Baked Mountain Cabin, a shelter available for overnights. The challenging 12-mile trip takes a full day; drinking water is scarce. The river crossing can be extremely dangerous; be sure to be briefed at the visitor center before you hike.

Due south 5.5 miles from the cabin is **Katmai Pass,** where Robert Griggs first beheld the valley in 1916. Strong winds often funnel through here.

A fascinating side trip between **Baked Mountain** and Katmai Pass is to **Novarupta,** a 200-foot-high dome of volcanic rock that was the extrusion plug of the great eruption. Scientists believe most of the 1912 lava and ash spewed out through a fissure here, drawing magma from nearby **Mount Katmai** and causing its summit to collapse into a caldera.

To reach the caldera (a strenuous 1- to 2-day trip), head east from Novarupta or Baked Mountain to the stagnant, ash-covered **Knife Creek Glaciers,** then climb 3,800 feet up ash and ice to the caldera rim, where, if you peer over the edge, you'll see what Robert Griggs saw: "a wonderful lake, of a weird vitriolic robin's-egg blue."

Water & Air Trips

Boaters, kayakers, and canoeists find no shortage of places to explore in Katmai. Guides and equipment are available for hire through Brooks Lodge or one of the other, smaller lodges catering mostly to fishermen. An especially popular and picturesque spot is the **Bay of Islands** in the **North Arm** of Naknek Lake, 22 miles from Brooks Camp.

For serious paddlers looking for the truly wild side of Katmai, the **Savonoski Loop** is an 85-mile round-trip from Brooks Camp that takes 4 to 8 days, depending on the weather. You paddle through the Bay of Islands, portage to **Lake Grosvenor,** and float the **Grosvenor** and **Savonoski Rivers** into the **Iliuk Arm** of Naknek Lake for the return to Brooks Camp. Follow the shorelines, for the wind can suddenly transform lakes from tranquil to tempestuous. If you'd like to take a river trip, inquire about the **Alagnak River,** a designated Wild and Scenic River, and the **Ukak River,** which, with class V rapids, is for the very experienced only.

Like Alaska's other national parks, Katmai is spectacular from the air. Flight-seeing trips can be arranged in **King Salmon** or Brooks Camp. The grand tour might swing over the Valley of Ten Thousand Smokes, through Katmai Pass, up the coast from **Katmai Bay** to **Swikshak Bay,** over **Kaguyak Crater,** and down the Savonoski River back to Brooks Camp. Take plenty of film and a calm stomach.

Information & Activities

Headquarters
P.O. Box 7, King Salmon, AK 99613.
Phone (907) 246-3305.
www.nps.gov/katm

Seasons & Accessibility
Park open year-round, but scheduled flights from Anchorage to King Salmon (with connecting seaplane flights into the park) available June to mid-September only. Reserve well in advance. Accessible by private or charter plane all year; the park has a list of licensed air charter companies.

Visitor & Information Centers
Brooks Camp Visitor Center and the concessions are open from June to mid-September. All visitors to Brooks Camp are required to attend the 15-minute orientation on bear etiquette. For visitor information contact park or Katmailand, Inc., the park's main concessioner, at 4125 Aircraft Dr., Anchorage, AK 99502; or call (800) 544-0551 or (907) 243-5448. **King Salmon Visitor Center** is open year-round.

Entrance Fee
None, but $10 per person fee for day users of Brooks Camp. Call National Parks Reservation Service (see p. 11) for advanced permits. Limited day-use permits and advanced reservations are required.

Facilities for Disabled
Brooks Lodge is accessible, but with assistance.

Things to Do
Free ranger-led activities: daily interpretive programs, evening programs, nature walks. Also, bus trips to the Valley of Ten Thousand Smokes, bear watching, hiking, kayaking, canoeing, boating, mountain climbing, aerial sight-seeing, fishing (license required; available in park), float trips.

Katmailand, Inc., has guides, boating, and fishing equipment available at Brooks Lodge. Reserve ahead. Ask the park for a list of other outfitters and guides within its borders.

Special Advisories
● Alaskan brown bears, or grizzlies, are unpredictable and dangerous; stay far away from them unless at the bear-viewing platforms.
● Be very careful when crossing glacial streams.

Overnight Backpacking
Camping allowed anywhere in park without reservations, except at Brooks Camp (see below). Backcountry permits required, but are free and unlimited. Information pamphlet available. Bear-resistant food canisters, required for overnight stays, available free at visitor center.

Campgrounds
One backcountry campground, **Brooks Camp** (with 7-day limit in July and September). Open June to mid-September; reservations required. Call the National Parks Reservation Service (see p. 11) for reservations. Campground fee $8 per night for groups up to six people. Showers at Brooks Lodge. Tent sites only. Three-sided shelters for cooking. Limited food services in park.

Hotels, Motels, & Inns
INSIDE THE PARK:
Katmailand, Inc., offers multiday package tours from Anchorage that can include airfare; lodging at Brooks Lodge, Grosvenor Lake Lodge, or Kulik Lodge; meals; guides; fishing tackle; rafts; licenses; and boats or planes to fishing spots. For information, write Katmailand, Inc., 4125 Aircraft Dr., Anchorage, AK 99502; or call (800) 544-0551 or (907) 243-5448.
Brooks Lodge 16 cabins. Packages starting from $348 per person. Open June to mid-September.
Grosvenor Lake Lodge 3 cabins. Packages starting from $1,900 per person. Open June to late September.
Kulik Lodge 12 cabins. Packages starting from $2,025 per person. Open mid-June to late September.

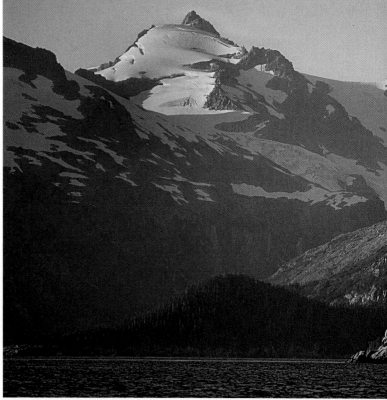

Granite Passage at the tip of Harris Peninsula

Kenai Fjords

Alaska

Established December 2, 1980

607,000 acres

Distill the essence of coastal Alaska into one place—wild, dynamic, and scenic, rich with the signatures of glaciers, light with the marks of people, unforgiving in stormy seas, unforgettable in warm sunshine—and you have Kenai Fjords, the smallest national park in Alaska. Here the south-central part of the state tumbles into the Gulf of Alaska; here the land challenges the sea with talonlike peninsulas and rocky headlands, while the sea itself reaches inland with long fjords and hundreds of quiet bays and coves.

Crowning the park is the Harding Icefield, almost 700 square miles of ice up to a mile thick. It feeds over 30 glaciers flowing out of the mountains, 6 of them to tidewater. The Harding Icefield is a vestige of the massive ice sheet that covered much of Alaska in the Pleistocene era.

The ancient ice gouged out Kenai's fjords, creating habitats for throngs of sea animals. About 20 species of seabirds nest along the rocky coastline; most of the birds are clown-faced puffins. Bald eagles swoop along the towering cliffs, and peregrine falcons hunt over the outer islands. Seabirds, by the tens of thousands, migrate or congregate here.

Approximately 23 species of mammals, including harbor seals, northern sea lions, and sea otters, live here. Moose, black bears, wolverines, lynx, and marten roam narrow bands of forest between the coast and icefield. And just above them, on the treeless slopes, climb surefooted mountain goats.

How to Get There

Seward is the gateway to Kenai Fjords. To get to Seward, take the Seward Highway (Alas. 9) south from Anchorage. The 130-mile drive is spectacular. Buses and small commuter planes also connect Anchorage and Seward, and the Alaska Marine Highway (ferry) links Seward with Homer, Seldovia, Kodiak, Valdez, and Cordova.

You can also charter a flight from Seward or Homer directly to the park. In summer, the Alaska Railroad serves Seward from Anchorage (with connections to Fairbanks and Whittier).

When to Go

Usually summer. The days lengthen, the seas calm down. The road to Exit Glacier generally opens in May and closes with the first snowfall, usually in October. Many winter visitors ski the road into Exit Glacier, or snowmobile in. Flight-seeing trips can be arranged in Seward any time of the year, subject to weather.

How to Visit

The most popular and accessible area in the park is **Exit Glacier,** 13 miles northwest of Seward. You can drive to it or take a tour bus. Trails offer half-hour hikes to the glacier and a half-day hike to the **Harding Icefield.**

Otherwise, hiking is a matter of exploring wilderness shores and ridges accessible only by boat and plane. From mid-May to late September, daily tour boats from Seward offer round-trip half-day and full-day excursions to the fjords and outlying islands. Charter boats take kayakers and campers to any fjord they wish (most often **Aialik Bay**) and pick them up the same day or days later. Kayaking, fishing, and backpacking guides are available. Ask the park for a list.

From Seward or Homer you can book a breathtaking 1-hour flight over the Harding Icefield and Kenai coast. For extended adventures, skiplanes drop off and pick up skiers on the icefield, and floatplanes do the same for kayakers in the fjords, weather permitting.

Exit Glacier & Harding Icefield

Exit Glacier is one of many rivers of ice that flow off the Harding Icefield. From Seward, follow the highway north to mile 3.7, where a paved road leads 9 miles to a parking lot. There are three trails: The **Main Trail**

Climber on Bear Glacier

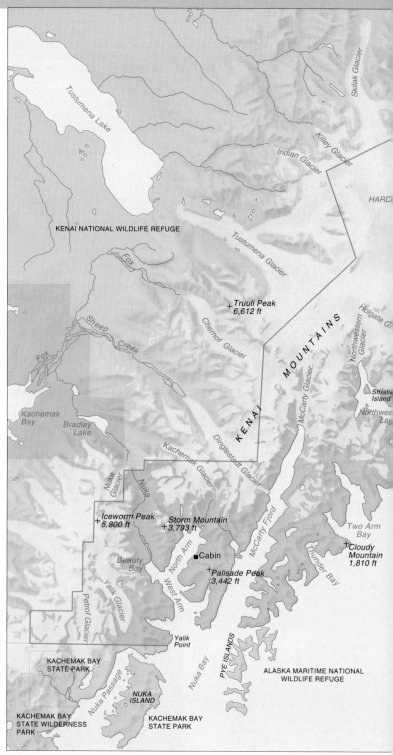

Tustumena Lake

Skilak Glacier

Killey Glacier

Indian Glacier

HARD

KENAI NATIONAL WILDLIFE REFUGE

Fox

Tustumena Glacier

+ Truuli Peak
6,612 ft

Sheep

Creek

Chernof Glacier

M O U N T A I N S

Holgate G.

Northwestern Glacier

Fox

Kachemak
Bay

Bradley
Lake

K E N A I

Striatic
Island

Northwes
Lag

Kachemak Glacier

Dinglestadt Glacier

McCarty Glacier

Nuka Glacier

Nuka

+ Iceworm Peak
5,800 ft

Storm Mountain
+ 3,793 ft

■ Cabin

McCarty Fjord

Two Arm
Bay

+ Cloudy
Mountain
1,810 ft

Beauty
Bay

North Arm

+ Palisade Peak
3,442 ft

Thunder Bay

Yalik Glacier

West Arm

Petrof Glacier

Yalik
Point

KACHEMAK BAY
STATE PARK

Nuka Passage

Nuka Bay

PYE ISLANDS

ALASKA MARITIME NATIONAL
WILDLIFE REFUGE

NUKA
ISLAND

KACHEMAK BAY
STATE WILDERNESS
PARK

KACHEMAK BAY
STATE PARK

Resurrection
River Trail
To Anchorage
Cabin
CHUGACH
NATIONAL
FOREST
Harding
Icefield
Trail
Lost Lake
Trail
9
Lowell Glacier
Exit Glacier
Cabin
Exit Glacier Road
Seward
Phoenix Peak
5,155 ft
Visitor
Center
IELD
Resurrection Bay
Bear Glacier
CAINES HEAD
STATE
RECREATION AREA
alik Glacier
Fox
Island
Callisto
Head
Bulldog
Cove
Cabin
AIALIK PENINSULA
Cabin
Rugged
Island
Holgate Arm
Aialik Bay
RIS PENINSULA
Aialik Cape
Granite
ALASKA
MARITIME NATIONAL
WILDLIFE REFUGE
Aligo
Point
Granite
Cape
CHISWELL ISLANDS
Gulf of Alaska

↑

🏠 Ranger Station

- - - Unpaved Road

······ Hiking Trail

0   5   10 km

0   5   10 mi

is paved for a third of a mile to a viewing area. The trail then separates into two loops. The lower loop continues to the outwash plain for a close view of the glacier terminus; the upper loop climbs a third of a mile for a view of deep crevasses and towering seracs along the glacier's flank.

A half-mile **nature trail** begins at the glacier and winds over old moraines and through cottonwood, alder, and willow before following **Exit Creek** to connect with the Main Trail. The **Harding Icefield Trail** branches off the Main Trail and climbs 3,000 feet in 3.5 miles, ending on the icefield. The upper section of the trail is usually snow covered; the lower portion is slippery and muddy after rain. Ask a ranger about current conditions and sign in at the trail register. On the slopes you may see mountain goats and black bears.

The Fjords

Daily tour boats travel down **Resurrection Bay,** pass picturesque **Caines Head** and **Callisto Head,** then round rugged **Aialik Cape** and enter **Aialik Bay,** the most visited fjord in the park. The **Holgate** and **Aialik Glaciers** flow into this fjord. Tour boats usually visit the Holgate, then return to Seward via the **Chiswell Islands** (part of the Alaska Maritime NWR), an excellent place to see sea lions hauled out on rocks and nesting seabirds.

Endless exploring awaits boaters and hikers on the shores of Kenai Fjords. If you are without a guide, be sure to inquire at the visitor center about weather, landing sites, tides, and hazards. The farther down the coast to the southwest, the fewer the people. Narrow **Granite Passage** is an exciting entrance into **Harris Bay.** From 1910 to 1960, **Northwestern Glacier** retreated 9.5 miles and opened up **Northwestern Lagoon** at the head of Harris Bay. The lagoon should be entered on calm water (preferably in a kayak) and at high tide only. Once you are inside and on the shore, you will find excellent hiking, especially to **Northeastern, Southwestern,** and **Sunlight Glaciers.**

Down the coast, **Thunder Bay** is a welcome anchorage during inclement weather. A narrow waterway cuts between the mainland and the **Pye Islands.** From here, **McCarty Fjord** slices 23 miles into the coast, its steep walls rising more than 4,000 feet overhead on either side of **McCarty Glacier.** The **West** and **North Arms** of **Nuka Bay** offer a variety of terrain and wildlife. Watch for the craggy profile of **Palisade Peak,** a 900-foot waterfall, historic gold mine sites, and for black bears, moose, and river otters near the **Nuka River,** for shorebirds along the mud flats at **Shelter Cove,** and for black-sand beaches around **Yalik Point,** at the park's southern end. Few people come here; travel to Nuka Bay and you might have it all to yourself.

Horned puffins

Red fox

Northern sea lions

Humpback whale in Aialik Bay

Information & Activities

Headquarters
P.O. Box 1727, Seward, AK 99664.
Phone (907) 224-3175.
www.nps.gov/kefj

Seasons & Accessibility
Park open year-round, but, from
about mid-October to May, snow may
close the road to Exit Glacier. Access
then is by ski, snowmobile, dog team,
or snowshoe only. Call headquarters
for information about weather and
road conditions.

Visitor & Information Centers
Visitor center in Seward, on Alas. 9
just outside the eastern border of the
park, open daily from Memorial Day
to Labor Day; weekdays only rest
of the year. **Ranger Station** at Exit
Glacier open intermittently in summer only. Phone headquarters number for visitor information.

Entrance Fee
$5 per vehicle, per day; $15 annually.

Pets
Permitted leashed on the Exit Glacier
Road and in parking areas. Prohibited
on all trails.

Facilities for Disabled
Exit Glacier is the most accessible area.
From the Ranger Station, wheelchairs
can maneuver the glacier trail for the
first third of a mile, to an interpretive
shelter offering exhibits and views of
the glacier. Visitor center is also wheelchair accessible.

Things to Do
Free ranger-led activities: In summer
(from the Ranger Station at Exit Glacier), walks to the glacier's base, and
all-day hikes to the icefield. Also available, advanced mountain climbing,
sailing, fishing (license required),
wildlife watching, cross-country skiing, dogsledding, snowshoeing.
    Authorized commercial guides
offer camping, fishing, kayaking,
flight-seeing, and boat trips for
exploring the fjords and watching
seabirds, whales, porpoises, and other
wildlife. Write or call park headquarters for a list of companies that do
business in the park.

Special Advisories
● If planning a backcountry trip without a guide, first check conditions with
park staff.
● Hypothermia is a danger on the icefield, even in summer.
● Do not venture out in a boat unless
well experienced in rough water.

Overnight Backpacking
Permits, free at the visitor center, are
required; registration requested for
Harding Icefield.

Campgrounds
One walk-in campground at **Exit
Glacier.** Four cabins in the fjords available May through September for
overnight use by permit. Access by boat
or plane only. In winter, a public-use
cabin is available at Exit Glacier. Write
or phone the visitor center.

Hotels, Motels & Inns
*(unless otherwise noted, rates are for 2
persons in a double room, high season)
In Seward, AK 99664:*
Breeze Inn 1306 Seward Hwy., P.O.
Box 2147. (907) 224-5237. 86 units,
1 with a kitchenette. $119-$170.
Restaurant.
Hotel Seward (on 5th Ave.) P.O.
Box 670. (907) 224-2378. 38 units.
$125-$224. AC.
Marina Motel (on Alas. 9) P.O. Box
1134. (907) 224-5518. 18 units, 1 with
a kitchenette. $105-$130.
Murphy's Motel 911 4th Ave., P.O.
Box 736. (907) 224-8090. 24 units.
$99-$140.
Van Gilder Hotel 308 Adams St.,
P.O. Box 609. (800) 204-6835, (907)
224-3525, or (907) 224-3079. 24 units,
20 with private baths. $135. Suites
$185.

Great Kobuk Sand Dunes, encroaching on a spruce forest

Kobuk Valley

Alaska

Established December 2, 1980

1,750,000 acres

"Now we were alone between fringes of spruce by a clear stream where tundra went up the sides of mountains," wrote John McPhee in *Coming into the Country*. The Kobuk Valley, said McPhee, "was, in all likelihood, the most isolated wilderness I would ever see." Located entirely above the Arctic Circle, Kobuk Valley has fewer tourist visits than any other national park. Float a river here in late August and the only other humans you're likely to encounter are Inupiat hunting the caribou that migrate through each year.

Twelve thousand years ago, when continental glaciers covered much of North America and a land bridge connected Alaska and Asia, Kobuk Valley was an ice-free refuge with grassy tundra similar to that found in Siberia today. Bison, mastodons, and mammoths roamed the valley, along with the humans who hunted them. Since then, the climate has shifted, and sea level has risen to flood the land bridge; many of the early mammals have disappeared. But today's shrubby flora harbors relics of the preglacial steppe, and in the cold, hard ground lie the legacies of ancient animals and peoples.

Here in Kobuk Valley the boreal forest reaches its northern limit, and the North American and Asiatic flyways cross. Pockets of tundra blend into birch and spruce, dwarfed by blasts of freezing air. And along the Kobuk River stretch 25 square miles of active sand dunes, where summer temperatures can climb to 100°F.

How to Get There

Commercial planes fly daily from Anchorage to Kotzebue, where the park's information center is located. Connecting flights serve the villages of Kiana and Ambler, both of which are situated along the Kobuk River, on the park's western and eastern sides respectively. From these two villages you can charter a boat or plane into the park.

A boat or plane can also be chartered from the village of Kotzebue.

When to Go

Summer. Days are long (from about June 6 to July 3 the sun doesn't set at all), and temperatures in many places can reach into the 80s or more. Ice breaks up on the Kobuk River in May and begins to form again by mid-October. Ranger station at Onion Portage is staffed periodically from June to September. Middle to late June is best for wildflowers. August can bring rain and September snow. In late August, the aspens begin to turn yellow and the tundra red, and the caribou migration begins.

How to Visit

Take a combination river-hiking trip that alternates between days out on the open water with days exploring the surrounding land. That way you can paddle to different landing points, leave your gear in the canoe, and hike unencumbered. Bring everything you need; no visitor facilities exist within the park. The **Kobuk River,** wide and placid, is a pleasant river to travel by canoe, kayak, or motorboat. Most people put in at Ambler and take out at Kiana, both outside the park. You can charter a boat in Kiana. You can also float or paddle the **Salmon,** a Wild and Scenic River, but it has rougher water and is harder to reach. Hiking in most places is excellent, but the park maintains no trails or river crossings. So be sure to plan your trip carefully.

While in the park, be respectful of Inuit lands, most of which are along the Kobuk River.

Caribou migrating across the Kobuk River

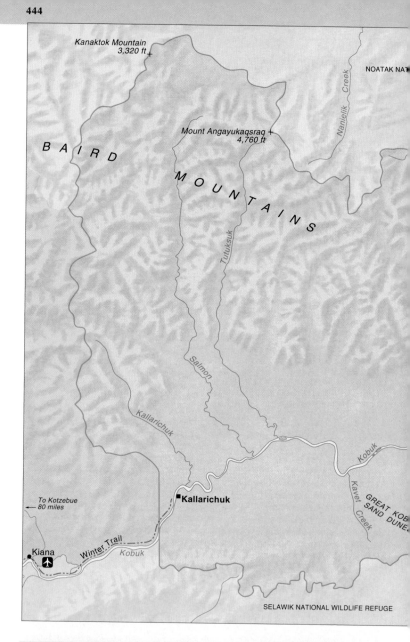

Kanaktok Mountain
3,320 ft

Mount Angayukaqsraq
4,760 ft

B A I R D

M O U N T A I N S

Nanielik Creek

NOATAK NAT

Tutuksuk

Salmon

Kallarichuk

■ **Kallarichuk**

Kobuk

Kavet Creek

GREAT KOB
SAND DUNE

To Kotzebue
← 80 miles

Kiana

Winter Trail

Kobuk

SELAWIK NATIONAL WILDLIFE REFUGE

Cranberries, club moss, and sphagnum in the tundra

Brown bear and cubs

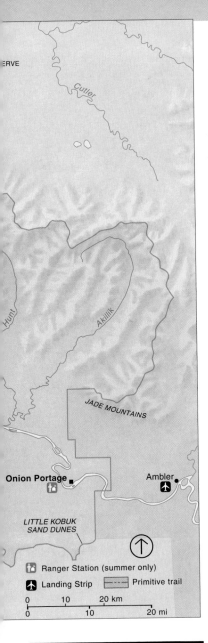

Ranger Station (summer only)

Landing Strip *Primitive trail*

| 0 | 10 | 20 km |
| 0 | 10 | 20 mi |

Kobuk River

Beginning in the central Brooks Range, the Kobuk River flows west 200 miles, winds slowly through the park for 50 miles, dropping only 2 to 3 inches per mile, and then continues west to drain into **Hotham Inlet,** off **Kotzebue Sound.** At times its placid aspect makes it seem more like a lake than a river, with a current that's hardly detectable.

Although steep bluffs sometimes rise above the riverbanks, hiking opportunities from the Kobuk are limitless. Both shores have forest, lakes, and tundra; the south shore has sand dunes also. Hike high ground to avoid swamps. In late August and early September you can sit on a bluff and watch caribou in striking autumn pelage as they swim across the river. Huge antlers and white ruffs mark the bulls.

A river trip through the park from Ambler to Kiana, with plenty of time for hiking, takes about a week. Or, if you want a more ambitious trip (requiring 2 to 3 weeks, depending on weather and river conditions), begin at **Walker Lake,** in Gates of the Arctic National Park (see p. 418), and paddle or motor all the way to Kiana.

On either trip you'll pass **Onion Portage,** a river bend, where for thousands of years migrating caribou have crossed the Kobuk. Here, in 1961, archaeologist J. Louis Giddings dug into the earth and could hardly believe his eyes. He had discovered what a Smithsonian Institution ethnologist would later call "the most important archaeological site ever found in the Arctic." Giddings' 2-acre plot yielded 30 artifact-bearing layers, reflecting seven stages of flintworking technology, the oldest dating back at least 10,000 years.

Today, the archaeological site is inactive and largely overgrown. But in late summer and fall, Inuit hunt caribou

Easily stowed inflatable craft for river runners

Great Kobuk Sand Dunes

here as they've done for millennia. During the summer, a backcountry ranger is sometimes stationed at Giddings' old cabin. Hiking is good at Onion Portage. The name comes from the wild chives that grow here.

Great Kobuk Sand Dunes

Farther downstream sprawl the Great Kobuk Sand Dunes, a 25-square-mile mini-Sahara. Visitors arrive by the river and leave their boats on shore for the short hike to the adventure of scaling the dunes. An Ice Age relic, the dunes formed from the windblown outwash of melting glaciers. A special combination of topography and eastern and northern winds keeps the dunes moving and inhospitable to vegetation. Some dunes measure a hundred feet high. Older, thinly vegetated dunes surround this ever changing landscape located 35 miles above the Arctic Circle.

Information & Activities

Headquarters
P.O. Box 1029, Kotzebue, AK 99752.
Phone (907) 442-3890.
www.nps.gov/kova

Seasons & Accessibility
Open year-round but access—by boat
or charter aircraft from Kotzebue—
generally June through September.
(The Kobuk River usually thaws by
June 1 and freezes by mid-October.)
There are no roads to or in the park.
Be prepared for severe arctic weather
at any time. Contact park headquarters before visiting. If you plan to
charter in by air, ask the park for a
list of licensed companies.

Information Centers
Located 80 miles from the park,
the **Kotzebue Headquarters and
Information Center** is open daily
in summer and Monday through
Friday rest of year.

Entrance Fee
None.

Pets
Strongly discouraged.

Facilities for Disabled
Kotzebue information center accessible
to wheelchairs; otherwise none.

Things to Do
Films at Kotzebue information center.
The park organizes no activities, but
rafting, kayaking, canoeing, hiking,
sportfishing (license required), and
aerial sight-seeing are available.
Commercial outfitters offer a variety
of private guide services for floating,
fishing, trekking trips. Call or write
headquarters for a list of those licensed
to work in the park.

Special Advisories
● Take a guide along unless you are
well experienced in the wilderness.
● Mosquitoes and gnats can be brutal;
bring plenty of repellent, a head net,
and an insect-proof tent.
● Inuit own much of the land
along the river and engage in subsistence hunting and fishing. Respect
them and their property.

Overnight Backpacking
No permit required, but call park for
current information on weather, river
conditions, bears, and resident subsistence activities before venturing out.

Campgrounds
None; backcountry camping only.

Hotel
*(unless otherwise noted, rates are for 2
persons in a double room, high season)
In Kotzebue, AK 99752:*
Nullagvik Hotel 308 Front St., P.O. Box
336. (907) 442-3331. 73 units. $149.
Restaurant.

Excursion

Cape Krusenstern National Monument

Kotzebue, Alaska

For more than 6,000 years, Eskimos
have forged a living on this stretch of
gravel projecting into the Chukchi Sea;
its 114 beach ridges, rich in artifacts,
reveal their archaeological benchmarks.
Today, the cape's large land and sea
mammals are still crucial to local subsistence. 560,000 acres. Primitive camping,
boating, fishing. Open year-round.
Access by charter boat or plane from
Kotzebue. (907) 442-3890.

Turquoise Lake, tinted by glacial silt

Lake Clark

Alaska

Established December 2, 1980

4,045,000 acres

"Think of all the splendors that bespeak Alaska," conservationist John Kauffmann has written. "Glaciers, volcanoes, alpine spires, wild rivers, lakes with grayling on the rise. Picture coasts feathered with countless seabirds. Imagine dense forests and far-sweeping tundra, herds of caribou, great roving bears. Now concentrate all these and more into less than one percent of the state—and behold the Lake Clark region, Alaska's epitome."

Diversity is Lake Clark's hallmark. The Turquoise-Telaquana Plateau has tundra similar to Alaska's North Slope, while the coast has forests similar to the southeast panhandle. Black bears and Dall's sheep reach their southern limits here, and Sitka spruce, Alaska's state tree, reaches its northern limit. Three rivers— the Mulchatna, Chilikadrotna, and Tlikakila—have been officially designated Wild and Scenic.

The Chigmit Mountains, spine of the park, are as rugged as mountains get. They lie on the edge of the North American plate where the oceanic plate slides under it, and their jumbled contours reflect centuries of geological violence. Two volcanoes here, Iliamna and Redoubt, are still active and vent gases regularly. Redoubt erupted in 1966, spewing clouds of ash 40,000 feet into the air—and it erupted dramatically again in late 1989 and early 1990. The area averages one to two earthquakes per year that register at least a 5 on the Richter scale.

Archaeological finds show that humans, most recently Dena'ina Indians,

When to Go

Summer. Wildflowers are best in late June. Autumn colors peak in early September at upper elevations, in mid-September lower down. June through August, daytime temperatures usually hover in the 50s and low 60s in the eastern part of the park and are somewhat higher in the western part and the interior.

How to Visit

Most visitors fly into the interior lake region of the park. Air taxis can make drop-offs and pickups at prearranged places. The smaller lakes offer excellent kayaking, and several rivers give kayakers and rafters great white-water experiences. Hiking is good around the lakes and from lake to lake. Fishing is usually first class. Write to park headquarters in Anchorage for information about guide services and lodges. Remember to make your reservations early. If you don't plan to be completely self-sufficient, be sure to make thorough arrangements before going.

On the Lakes & Rivers

Fishing is superb on the lakes and rivers of this fly-in park. Rainbow trout, arctic grayling, northern pike, and five kinds of salmon—king, chum, coho, humpback, and sockeye—lure anglers, many of whom take off from Port Alsworth, site of the park's field headquarters.

As in many Alaska parks, a kayak in Lake Clark is an invitation to freedom. You can explore large areas, carry a lot of gear, and take intermittent hikes as the mood strikes you. Keep in mind that sudden winds can stir up large waves in a matter of minutes. Good lakes for paddling are **Telaquana, Turquoise, Twin, Lake Clark, Kontrashibuna,** and **Tazimina.**

Another way to see the country is to let a river take you through it. Your options are long trips (averaging three to four days) on the Wild and Scenic **Mulchatna, Chilikadrotna,** and **Tlikakila,** or short trips (averaging one to two days) on the **Tanalian** and the **Tazimina.** Hire a guide or check with rangers on water conditions, places to put in and take out, and what to look out for along the way.

have lived in the area for centuries. The abundant salmon and game made their settled existence possible.

How to Get There

Take a plane into the heart of the park, or travel by boat or plane to the coast. Bush pilots in Anchorage say, "Lake Clark is just out the back-door"—a 1-hour flight. From Anchorage you can charter a plane to Port Alsworth, a small community on the southeast shore of Lake Clark. The flight through Lake Clark Pass takes you over immense blue glaciers, winding rivers, and snowcapped mountains. Planes also land on the coast for salmon fishing.

Another alternative is to take a scheduled flight from Anchorage to Iliamna, 30 miles outside the park, and an air taxi from there into the park. Air taxis fly in from Homer and Kenai, too. To reach the park by boat, you must travel down Cook Inlet from Anchorage or across the inlet from the Kenai Peninsula.

Ranger Station

Hiking Trail

Park/Preserve

Native Corporations Lands

0   10   20 km

0   10   20 mi

Snowcap
Mountain

Stony

Merrill

Merr
Pass

T
Te

Stony

Two
Lakes

Necons

Whitefish
Lake

Telaquana

Telaquana
Lake

Neacola

ALA

Telaquana
Pass

Mulchatna

Telaquana Mountain
+8,020 ft

BONANZA HILLS

Turquoise
Lake

Twin
Lakes

Chilikadrotna

Snipe
Lake

Tlikakila

Fishtrap
Lake

Portage
Lake

Caribou
Lakes

Kijik

Lachbuna
Lake

Portage
Creek

RANGE

CHIGM

Kijik
Lake

Lake Clark

Currant   Creek

Koksetna

Port
Alsworth

Kontrashibuna
Lake

Tanalian
River

NATIVE
CORPORATIONS
LANDS
Do not trespass

Tazimina

ALEUTIAN

Sixmile
Lake

Nondalton

Pickerel
Lakes

West Glacier
Creek

Roadhouse
Mountain

Newhalen

Pile

Clearwater
Creek

To Newhalen and Iliamna

Autumn rainbow over Stony River

Hiking

In a park with no trail system and only one maintained hiking trail, route selection is critical. So is being prepared: wind and rain gear for swift changes in the weather and repellent for mosquitoes. If you intend to hike without a guide, consult with a park ranger before starting out and take a good map with you. Some general rules for hikers are: Stay as long as possible on dry tundra where footing is good, avoid heavy brush, and choose your river crossings carefully. Hiking is generally best above 2,000 feet in the interior (where the dry tundra begins), or along the coast on the numerous gravel river bars. Below tree line the vegetation can be thick and nearly impenetrable, especially the alder.

The 2.5-mile **Tanalian Falls Trail** is the only developed trail in the park. Beginning in Port Alsworth, this easy hike takes you through a forest of black spruce and birch, past bogs and ponds, up along the tumbling Tanalian River, to Kontrashibuna Lake, and on to the falls, a half mile beyond. Watch for moose in the ponds, arctic grayling in the river, Dall's sheep on Tanalian Mountain, and bears everywhere.

Another hike from Port Alsworth is the strenuous 3,600-foot climb up **Tanalian Mountain.** You can begin the climb off the Tanalian Falls Trail, or by hiking the shore of Lake Clark and heading up a ridge where the

Tanalian Mountain rising from Lake Clark shores

Alpine bearberry and lichens

Arctic ground squirrel nibbling a fireweed flower

walking is easier, a round-trip of about 7 miles.

North of Lake Clark, several lakes offer excellent hiking. You can take an air taxi to one and hike to another, or stay at one lake—a world in itself—and go on day hikes along the shore and up the ridges. If a lake-to-lake trek appeals to you, try the 16 miles from **Telaquana Lake** south to **Turquoise Lake,** or from Turquoise Lake 13 miles south to **Twin Lakes.**

From Twin Lakes you can hike 17 miles to **Portage Lake,** a beautiful tarn in an alpine valley, and from there 11 miles to **Lachbuna Lake,** over a ridge and down the **Portage Creek** drainage to Lake Clark.

For a longer, wilder, and more demanding hike through truly spectacular country, try taking the 50-mile trek from **Telaquana Lake** east over **Telaquana Pass,** along the **Neacola River** to **Kenibuna Lake.** From there, continue your hike to the huge rock spire called **The Tusk.**

Information & Activities

Headquarters
4230 University Dr. #311, Anchorage, AK 99508. (907) 271-3751. www.nps.gov/lacl

Seasons & Accessibility
Park open and accessible by small aircraft from Anchorage, Kenai, Homer, and Iliamna year-round. There are no roads to or in the park.

Weather changes rapidly. Call Port Alsworth at (907) 781-2218 for up-to-date conditions.

Visitor & Information Centers
Field headquarters and a visitor center are located in **Port Alsworth,** on the south shore of Lake Clark (1 Park Pl., Port Alsworth, AK 99653). Call Anchorage headquarters at (907) 271-3751, or Port Alsworth field headquarters at (907) 781-2218 for visitor information.

Gas & Supplies
Bring everything you will need.

Entrance Fee
None.

Pets
Park recommends that you leave your pets at home because they can attract bears.

Facilities for Disabled
All park buildings and lodges are accessible.

Things to Do
Minimal interpretive programs (June through September). Also, hiking, backpacking, climbing, rafting, kayaking, fishing (license required), boating, bird-watching and wildlife watching, aerial sight-seeing, hunting (in preserve).

Call or write headquarters for a list of concessioners offering a variety of guide services in the park, or visit the website at www.nps.gov/lacl/visiting_the_park.htm

Special Advisories
• You must possess good wilderness skills if you intend to hike, camp, or fish without a guide.
• Do not trespass onto or in any way disturb the property of local residents.

• Be sure to bring insect repellent. A head net and insect-proof tent are also desirable.

Overnight Backpacking
No permit required, but campers are encouraged to contact field station before setting out. (907) 781-2218.

Campgrounds
None. Backcountry camping only. No showers or other visitor amenities except in lodges. Rest rooms at the field headquarters at Port Alsworth.

Hotels, Motels, & Inns
INSIDE THE PARK:
Alaska's Wilderness Lodge (on southern shore of Lake Clark) P.O. Box 90748, Anchorage, AK 99519. (907) 781-2223. 7 cabins. $5,950 per person, per week. 7-day sportfishing packages available. All inclusive as well as airfare. Open mid-June to early October.
OUTSIDE THE PARK:
Newhalen Lodge (On Six Mile Lake near Nondalton). (907) 294-2233 (lodge) or (907) 522-3355 (all year). 9 rooms. Sportfishing packages. $5,800 per person, per week all inclusive. Open June to October.

Contact park headquarters for additional lodgings in and near the park.

Flowing Kennicott Glacier, with Mount Blackburn at left

Wrangell-St. Elias

Alaska

Established December 2, 1980

13,188,000 acres

Even in a state famous for its size, Wrangell-St. Elias stands out. It is by far the largest national park in the United States—almost six times the size of Yellowstone. You fly over it and see mountains beyond mountains, glaciers after glaciers, rivers upon rivers. You float a river and watch the moods and mountains change by the minute. As you walk the tundra slopes, you find Dall's sheep and mountain goats grazing.

Four major mountain ranges converge here: the volcanic Wrangells, the Alaska, the Chugach, and the St. Elias—tallest coastal mountains in the world. Together they contain 9 of the 16 highest peaks in the United States, 4 of them above 16,000 feet. There are more than 150 glaciers; one, the

Malaspina, is larger than Rhode Island. In 1980 Wrangell-St. Elias and adjoining Kluane National Park Reserve in Canada, along with Glacier Bay NP and Tatshenshini in British Columbia, were designated a United Nations World Heritage site.

Vast and rugged as it is, the park is not a fortress. Two roads lead into small communities, remnants of the gold- and copper-mining towns that thrived in the early days of this century. Today not mining but the nearly limitless hiking, rafting, kayaking, and climbing opportunities beckon.

How to Get There

Drive or charter a plane. By car from Anchorage, take Alas. 1 (Glenn Hwy.) 189 miles northeast to Glennallen. Continue northeast 74 miles along the Copper River and the park's western boundary to Slana, where an unpaved

When to Go

Summer. Lodges and guide services operate in the park from about mid-May to the end of September. June is best for wildflowers; July has the warmest days; berries ripen in August. Be prepared for cloudy skies, but September can be beautiful with clear skies, autumn colors, no mosquitoes, and a dusting of new snow on the mountain peaks. March and April offer excellent cross-country skiing for those of stout heart and strong will.

How to Visit

Take one of the two unpaved roads into the park. The **McCarthy Road** is maintained and usually passable in summer, though a four-wheel drive may be required. Stop at park headquarters in Copper Center for latest road conditions. The **Slana-Nabesna Road** is also maintained. Both roads bring you to trailheads for many hikes into the backcountry.

Or, charter a plane into a remote part of the park and hike or run a river. Several commercial companies offer guided rafting or kayaking trips on the rivers and in the spectacular coastal bays. You can get a full listing of them from the park.

McCarthy Road to Kennecott

61 miles one way; a half day

From the town of Chitina and the confluence of the **Chitina** and **Copper Rivers,** the road follows the abandoned Copper River and Northwest Railroad bed. At mile 17 the road crosses the **Kuskulana River Bridge.** It spans 525 feet, crossing 238 feet above the river. Another abandoned railroad trestle spans the **Gilahina River** at mile 28.5. At the end of the road is a parking lot and the **Kennicott River.** To reach the old mining town of **McCarthy** on the other side of the river you walk across a footbridge. Today a tiny community of hardy individualists, McCarthy had a population near 2,000 in mining days.

From McCarthy, a dirt road climbs 500 feet in 5 miles to the former town and millsite of **Kennecott.** You can take a taxi or rent a bike in McCarthy if you prefer not to walk. Kennecott was once the site of the

road branches into the park for 42 miles, ending at the town of Nabesna.

Or, head toward the town of McCarthy by taking Alas. 4 (Richardson Hwy.) from Glennallen 32 miles southeast to the Edgerton cutoff (Alas. 10), then turning left and continuing 33 miles to Chitina. There the pavement ends and a road follows an old railroad bed about 60 miles into the park. These same roads can be reached from Fairbanks via Delta Junction, and from Haines, Skagway, and Whitehorse (along the Alaska-Canada Hwy. in the Yukon) via Haines Junction and Tok. Buses run regularly in summer from Anchorage to Valdez with stops in Glennallen.

Air charters into the park operate out of Anchorage, Fairbanks, Yakutat, Cordova, Glennallen, Gulkana, Tok, Chitina, McCarthy, Nabesna, and Northway. Commercial jets service Yakutat and Cordova year-round. In summer, the Alaska State Ferry serves Valdez from Whittier and Seward (reachable by car from Anchorage).

To Delta Junction
and Fairbanks

Slana

To Tok

MENTASTA MOUNTAINS

Chistochina

Nabesna Road

4

1

Tanada
Lake

Gulkana

Gakona

NUTZOTIN

Nabesna

Nabesna

Mt. Allen
9,480 ft

Glenallen

Mt. Drum
12,010 ft

Mt. Sanford
16,237 ft

Copper Glacier

Cooper Pass

1

Park Headquarters

Copper Center

Mt. Wrangell
14,163 ft

NABESNA GLACIER

Chisana

WRANGELL

10

Tonsina

Nugget Creek
Trail

Dixie Pass

Kuskulana

Mt. Blackburn
16,390 ft

Regal Mountain
13,845 ft

MOUNTAINS

Kennicott Glacier

Root Glacier

Chitina

Copper

Chitina

Gilahina

Kennicott

Kennicott

McCarthy

4

To Valdez

Nizina

Chitina

Tana

Bremner

CHUGACH

MOUNTAINS

Miles Glacier

Mt. Tom White
11,210 ft

Mt. Hawkins
10,295 ft

BAGLEY ICEFIELD

To Cordova

10

Copper
River
Delta

CHUGACH
NATIONAL
FOREST

Bering

Mt. Steller
10,617 ft

BERING GLACIER

ROBINSON MOUNTAIN

Katella

Bering

Cape Suckling

GULF OF ALASKA

Kayak
Island

Ranger Station

Unpaved Road

Hiking Trail

Park/Preserve

0   10   20 km
0   10   20 mi

TETLIN NATIONAL
WILDLIFE REFUGE

D A W S O N

R A N G E

Wellesley
Lake

White

Beaver Creek

Y
U
K
O
N

T
E
R
R
I
T
O
R
Y

A
L
A
S
K
A

Kluane

Alaska   Highway

Wiki Peak
7,655 ft

Solo Mountain
5,875 ft

White

KLUANE
GAME
SANCTUARY

Doniek

Mt. Natazhat
13,435 ft

Mt. Bona
16,421 ft

Kluane Lake

Destruction Bay

Duke

MOUNTAINS

U
N
I
T
E
D

S
T
A
T
E
S

C
A
N
A
D
A

Mt. Wood
15,885 ft

To Haines Junction

Chitina Glacier

Mt. Lucania
17,147 ft

Logan   Glacier

KLUANE
NATIONAL PARK

S
A
I
N
T

E
L
I
A
S

M
O
U
N
T
A
I
N
S

King Peak
16,971 ft

Mt. Logan
19,850 ft

Columbus Glacier

SEWARD GLACIER

Mt. St. Elias
18,008 ft

Mt. Vancouver
15,700 ft

Haydon Peak
11,945 ft

Hubbard Glacier

Mt. Cook
13,760 ft

YUKON
TERR.
B.C.

Russell

Fiord

ahtse Glacier

vot Glacier

Icy Bay

MALASPINA GLACIER

Yakutat Bay

TONGASS
NATIONAL FOREST

Kennecott Mine, silent since 1938

world's richest copper mine. From 1906 to 1938, when the mine closed, it yielded 591,000 tons of copper and 900,000 ounces of silver. Today, the silent 13-story mill and other Kennecott buildings are still dressed in mineral oxide red with white trim. Currently being renovated, they form one of Alaska's most photogenic collections of historic structures and are, since 1978, on the National Register of Historic Places.

After exploring Kennecott, you can hike the trail north of town for spectacular views of the Kennicott and Root Glaciers and Mount Blackburn.

Nabesna Road
42 miles one way; a half day

Since parts of this road into the **Wrangell Mountains** are subject to washouts, be sure to check conditions with the Park Service before you set out. Beginning in **Slana,** the road passes homesteads and fishing camps on privately owned land and then climbs over the watershed divide (mile 25) between the **Copper River,** which drains into the Gulf of Alaska, and the **Nabesna River,** which drains into the Tanana River, the Yukon River, and finally the Bering Sea. There are excellent views of **Mount Sanford** and the **Copper Glacier** to the southwest. The final 4 miles, from **Devil's Mountain Lodge** to **Nabesna,** are the most rugged.

Other Hikes & Water Trips

At mile 13.5 on the McCarthy Road, the Nugget Creek-Kotsina Road branches northeast 2.5 miles to the **Nugget Creek Trail.** Sixteen miles later and a thousand feet higher, the trail arrives at a public-use cabin beneath Mount Blackburn, where you can picnic and camp. A dozen good day hikes can be taken from here. Watch for Dall's sheep. A little more than a mile past the Nugget Creek trailhead begins the **Dixie Pass Trail.** Climbing 3,600 feet in 10 miles, it's a strenuous hike, but worth it if the weather is clear.

Off the Nabesna Road, **Trail Creek** at mile 30 and **Lost Creek** at mile 30.8 offer good hiking routes. There are no defined trails; simply follow the creek beds northward as far as you like. Though the hiking is not generally difficult, you will run into rocky patches and may have to hop or wade the creeks. But you will be rewarded with excellent views of the upper Copper River basin. Talk to a ranger and fill out a backcountry itinerary before any overnight stays.

Commercial outfitters offer rafting trips down the **Nabesna, Kennicott, Copper, Chitina,** and **Nizina Rivers.** Short trips last 3 hours, extended ones two weeks; there are all classes of water. It's an adventuresome way to see Wrangell-St. Elias. Contact the park for a full listing of the outfitters that operate there.

Information & Activities

Headquarters
P.O. Box 439, Copper Center, AK 99573. Phone (907) 822-5234. www.nps.gov/wrst

Seasons & Accessibility
Park open year-round, but best time is mid-May through September. Snow limits winter access.

Call headquarters for road conditions before attempting to drive to the park.

Visitor & Information Centers
Park headquarters at mile 106.8 on Old Richardson Highway at western edge of park. Open daily Memorial Day through Labor Day, weekdays the rest of year. Information also available at **Yakutat, Slana,** and **Chitina Ranger Stations,** all outside park boundaries. Chitina closed October through May. Call headquarters for information.

Entrance Fee
None.

Pets
Permitted on leashes except in public buildings; permitted off leashes in the backcountry.

Facilities for Disabled
None.

Things to Do
No park-organized activities, but the following are available: hiking, horseback riding (rentals in McCarthy), pack trips, river running, kayaking, jet-boat rentals, lake fishing, mountain climbing, air tours, cross-country skiing. Ask park for list of companies that offer guide and outfitting services, or visit the park website at www.nps.gov/wrst/wrstcommer cialservices.htm.

Special Advisories
● This is a wilderness park; hikers and backpackers must be wholly self-sufficient; do not attempt the backcountry without a guide unless you're experienced and equipped.
● Choose your river crossings carefully; many rivers are impassable.
● Be respectful of native camps, fish-nets, and other private property.
● Mosquitoes can be brutal in June, July, and August; bring repellent, a head net, and an insect-proof tent.

Overnight Backpacking
Permit not required, but best to register before going into backcountry.

Campgrounds & Cabins
Two private campgrounds within park: **Silver Lake Campground** (milepost 9.3 on McCarthy Road) offers camping and limited services. **Tram Station Campground** and **Glacier View Campground** at end of McCarthy Road. Camping also available at several roadside pull-outs along Nabesna Road. First come, first served. No fee. The park also maintains 12 public-use cabins. Fees $15 per night. Contact headquarters for information.

Hotels, Motels, & Inns
(unless otherwise noted, rates are for 2 persons in a double room, high season)
INSIDE THE PARK:
Kennicott Glacier Lodge (in Kennecott) P.O. Box 103940, Anchorage, AK 99510. (800) 582-5128 or (907) 258-2350. 25 rooms, shared baths. $179 per person, includes meals.
OUTSIDE THE PARK:
Copper Center Lodge (mile 101.5 on Old Richardson Hwy.) Drawer J, Copper Center, AK 99573. (907) 822-3245. 21 rooms, 11 with private baths. $99-$109. Restaurant.
Gakona Lodge (on Alas. 1, north of Glennallen) P.O. Box 285, Gakona, AK 99586. (907) 822-3482. 1 cabin, private bath $100; 8 rooms, shared baths $80. Open May through September. Restaurant.

Contact headquarters for additional accommodations in and near the park.

Acknowledgments

We are indebted to the many individuals and the federal, state, and private agencies that helped prepare this guide, especially to the National Park Service and the superintendents and chiefs of interpretation and their staffs at each park. Our thanks go also to the National Parks and Conservation Association for its cooperation and to Frances Kennedy, who offered wise counsel.

Illustrations Credits

Abbreviations for terms appearing below: (t)–top; (b)-bottom; (l)-left; (r)-right; (c)-center; BPS-Biological Photo Service; NGS-National Geographic Society Image Collection; PR-Photo Researchers, Inc.

Cover, George H.H. Huey; 2-3, Gary Moon/Getty Images; 6-7, Pat O'Hara; 8, Frank S. Balthis; 9, Tom Bean.

The East

12-13, Richard A. Cooke III; 18-19, Adam Jones/Getty Images; 19, John Netherton; 20, Sonja Bullaty; 23, John Netherton; 24, Glenn Van Nimwegen; 25 (t), Alan Nyiri; (b), Clyde Smith; 27 (t), Bill Silliker, Jr.; (c), John Netherton; (b), Jeff Lepore/PR; 28-29, Stephen Frink/WaterHouse; 29, Robert Holland; 31 (t), James Valentine; (b), Brian Skerry, NGS; 32, Bruce Mounier; 33 (t), (cr), (bl) & (br), Stephen Frink/WaterHouse; (cl), Charles V. Angelo/PR; 35 (t), James Valentine; (tc), C.C. Lockwood; (bc), Caulion Singletary; (b), Chris Johns, NGS; 36-39 (all), Tom Jones; 40, Melissa Farlow, NGS; 41, Diane Seskes; 42-43, Matt Bradley; 43, Stephen Frink/WaterHouse; 45, Matt Bradley; 46-47, James P. Blair; 50 (t), Stephen J. Krasemann/Peter Arnold, Inc.; (c), James A. Kern; (b), Ron Sanford; 51, David Hiser/Network Aspen; 52 (t), Otis Imboden; (b), Bianca Lavies; 53 (t), Glenn Van Nimwegen; (b), Fred Hirschmann; 55 (t), James Valentine; (c), Farrell Grehan; (b), Glenn Van Nimwegen; 56-57, John Netherton; 59, James P. Blair; 60, Dennis Flaherty; 61 (both), Tim Black; 62 (t), Raymond Gehman; (bl), Tim Black; (br), John Netherton; 64 (t) & (c), Larry Ulrich; (b), Dick Durrance II; 65 (t), Bill Deane; (c), Pat O'Hara; (b), James Valentine; 66-67, Declan Haun; 67, Matt Bradley; 69, Declan Haun; 71, (t), (bc) & (b), Matt Bradley; (tc), Stephen J. Krasemann; 72-73, Daniel J. Cox; 73 & 75, John & Ann Mahan; 76, Jim Brandenburg; 78 (t) & (b), John & Ann Mahan; (c), Tom Bean; 79 (t), John & Ann Mahan; (c), Carl R. Sams II; (b), Rod Planck/PR; 80-83 (photos), Chip Clark; 82-85 (artwork), Richard Schlecht; 84, Laurence Parent; 85, Chip Clark; 87 (t), Dan Dry; (b), David Muench; 88-89, Jeff Gnass; 92, David Muench; 93 (both), Stephen J. Krasemann; 95 (t) & (c), Carr Clifton; (b), Jeff Lepore/PR; 96-97, M. Dillon/CORBIS; 99, Farrell Grehan/CORBIS; 100-101, Jodi Cobb, NGS; 101, George Grall, NGS; 103, Stephen Frink/WaterHouse; 104-105, John & Ann Mahan; 105, Erwin & Peggy Bauer; 107, Jeff Gnass; 108 (t), Erwin & Peggy Bauer; (b), R. Stottlemyer, Michigan Technological University/BPS; 109, Richard Olsenius; 111 (t), John & Ann Mahan; (c), Jim Zipp/PR; (b), David Hiser.

The Southwest

112-113, David Muench; 116-117, Tom Bean; 117 & 120, Matt Bradley; 121 (t), Jim Steinberg/PR; (b), Larry Ulrich; 122, George F. Mobley; 123 (t), Larry Ulrich; (b),Tom Bean; 124 (t), Bruce Dale; (b), Stephen J. Krasemann; 125, David Muench; 126-127, Danny Lehman; 128-129, Tibor Toth; 130, David S. Boyer; 131 (both), Stephen J. Krasemann; 133 (t) & (b), Wendy Shattil/Bob Rozinski; (c), Lewis Kemper; 134-135 & 138, Matt Bradley.

The Colorado Plateau

140-141, W.M. Edwards; 144-145, Tom Bean; 147, George H.H. Huey; 149 (t), Farrell Grehan; (b), Larry Ulrich; 150-151, Larry Ulrich; 152, Fred Hirschmann; 153, Grant Haist; 155 (t), Fred Hirschmann; (c), Larry Ulrich; (b), Pat O'Hara; 156-157, George F. Mobley; 157, David Muench; 159, Becky & Gary Vestal; 160 (t), W.M. Edwards; (b), Becky & Gary Vestal; 161 (t), Pat O'Hara; (b), David Hiser/Network Aspen; 162, Becky & Gary Vestal; 164 (t), Tom Till; (c), Farrell Grehan; (b), Donna Ikenberry/Earth Scenes; 165 (t), Larry Ulrich; (b), David Hiser/Network Aspen; 166-167, Gordon Anderson; 167, Larry Ulrich; 169 (t), Charlie Borland; (b), Galen Rowell/Mountain Light; 170 (t), Kerrick James; (b), Joel Grimes; 172-173, Larry Ulrich; 175, Ron Sanford; 176, W. Perry Conway/CORBIS; 177, Jack Dykinga; 178, George H.H. Huey; 179, Ned Seidler; 181 (t) & (b), Jeff Gnass; (c), Larry Ulrich; 182-183, Jeff Gnass; 183, David Muench; 185 (all), Larry Ulrich; 186 (all), Richard Olsenius; 187, Phil Schofield/Aperture; 189 (t), Jack Olson; (c), Gary Brettnacher; (b), Jan Nachlinger; 190-191, David Muench; 194 (l), Dewitt Jones; (r), Richard A. Cooke III; 195, William Belknap; 197 (t), Larry Ulrich; (c) & (b), Tom Till; 198-199, Tom Algire; 201, Larry Ulrich; 203 (t) & (c), Fred Hirschmann; (b), George H.H. Huey; 204-205 & 207, George H.H. Huey; 208-209, Tom Algire; 209, James Randklev; 211, Fred Hirschmann; 212 (t), John Telford; (c), Fred Hirschmann; (b), George F. Mobley; 213 (t), Larry Ulrich; (b), David Muench; 214 (t), Pat O'Hara; (b), Jeff Lepore/PR.

The Pacific Southwest

216-217, Galen Rowell/Mountain Light; 220-221, Thomas Nebbia; 222-223, Jeff Gnass; 225, James P. Blair; 226, Nicholas DeVore III; 227 (t), Caroline Sheen; (b), David Muench; 28-229, Carr Clifton; 230, Marc Muench; 233, David Muench; 234-235, B.F. Molnia, Terraphotographics/BPS; 237, Stephen J. Krasemann; 238 (t), David Muench; (b), Robert J. Western; 239, David Muench; 241 (t), Jeff Gnass; (b), Steve Raymer; 242-243, David Muench; 243, James A. Sugar; 245, David Muench; 246, Darodents/Pacific Stock; 247 (t), Scott Rutherford; (b), Jeff Gnass; 249 (t), Roger Ressmeyer; (b), Jeff Gnass; 250-251, Harald Sund; 253 & 255, Peter Essick; 256-257, Larry Ulrich; 257, Angelo Lomeo; 260, David Muench; 263 (t) & (b), Pat O'Hara; (c), Richard Frear, National Park Service; 264-265, Dewitt Jones; 267, David Muench; 268 (t), Pat O'Hara; (b), Jim Brandenburg; 269, Gordon Wiltsie/Bruce Coleman, Inc. 270, Farrell Grehan; 270-271, Glenn Van Nimwegen; 271, Steve Raymer; 273 (t), Pat O'Hara; (c), Lewis Kemper; (b), Larry Ulrich.

Index

One of the world's largest nonprofit scientific
and educational organizations, the National
Geographic Society was founded in 1888
"for the increase and diffusion of geographic
knowledge." Fulfilling this mission,
the Society educates and inspires millions
every day through its magazines, books,
television programs, videos, maps and atlases,
research grants, the National Geographic Bee,
teacher workshops, and innovative classroom
materials. The Society is supported through
membership dues, charitable gifts, and income
from the sale of its educational products.
This support is vital to National Geographic's
mission to increase global understanding and
promote conservation of our planet through
exploration, research, and education.

For more information, please call 1-800-NGS
LINE (647-5463) or write to the following
address:

National Geographic Society
1145 17th Street N.W.
Washington, D.C. 20036-4688 U.S.A.

Visit the Society's Web site at
www.nationalgeographic.com.

Composition for this book by the National Geographic
Society Book Division. Printed and bound by R.R.
Donnelley & Sons, Willard, Ohio. Color separations
by Quad Graphics, Alexandria, Virginia. Cover printed
by Miken Companies, Inc. Cheektowaga, New York.